# THE CAMBRIDGE COMPANION TO
## EUROPEAN NOVELISTS

A lively and comprehensive account of the whole tradition of European fiction for students and teachers of comparative literature, this volume covers twenty-five of the most significant and influential novelists in Europe from Cervantes to Kundera. Each essay examines an author's use of and contributions to the genre and also engages with an important aspect of the form, such as its relation to romance, or one of its sub-genres, such as the *Bildungsroman*. Larger theoretical questions are introduced through specific readings of exemplary novels. Taking a broad historical and geographic view, the essays keep in mind the role the novel itself has played in the development of European national identities and in cultural history over the last four centuries. While conveying essential introductory information for new readers, these authoritative essays reflect up-to-date scholarship and also review, and sometimes challenge, conventional accounts.

D0217115

# THE CAMBRIDGE
## COMPANION TO
# EUROPEAN NOVELISTS

EDITED BY
MICHAEL BELL

CAMBRIDGE
UNIVERSITY PRESS

CAMBRIDGE UNIVERSITY PRESS
Cambridge, New York, Melbourne, Madrid, Cape Town,
Singapore, São Paulo, Delhi, Mexico City

Cambridge University Press
The Edinburgh Building, Cambridge CB2 8RU, UK

Published in the United States of America by Cambridge University Press, New York

www.cambridge.org
Information on this title: www.cambridge.org/9780521735698

© Cambridge University Press 2012

First published 2012

Printed in the United Kingdom at the University Press, Cambridge

*A catalogue record for this publication is available from the British Library*

*Library of Congress Cataloging-in-Publication Data*

The Cambridge companion to European novelists / edited by Michael Bell.
p. cm.
ISBN 978-0-521-51504-7 (Hardback) – ISBN 978-0-521-73569-8 (Paperback)
1. European fiction–History and criticism. I. Bell, Michael, 1941–
PN3491.C33 2012
809.3–dc23
2011043662

ISBN 978-0-521-51504-7 Hardback
ISBN 978-0-521-73569-8 Paperback

# CONTENTS

*Notes on contributors*                                          *page* viii

*Note on references*                                                    xiii

Introduction: The novel in Europe 1600–1900                                 1
MICHAEL BELL

1  Miguel de Cervantes (1547–1616): *Don Quixote*: romance and picaresque   17
EDWIN WILLIAMSON

2  Daniel Defoe (1660–1731): Journalism, myth and verisimilitude            36
CYNTHIA WALL

3  Samuel Richardson (1689–1761): The epistolary novel                      54
THOMAS KEYMER

4  Henry Fielding (1707–1754): The comic epic in prose                      72
THOMAS LOCKWOOD

5  Jean-Jacques Rousseau (1712–1778): The novel of sensibility              89
TIMOTHY O'HAGAN

6  Laurence Sterne (1713–1768): The fiction of sentiment                    107
MICHAEL BELL

7  Johann Wolfgang von Goethe (1749–1832): The German
   *Bildungsroman*                                                          124
MARTIN SWALES

8  Walter Scott (1771–1832): The historical novel                           140
SUSAN MANNING

CONTENTS

9   Stendhal (1783–1842): Romantic irony                                159
    ANN JEFFERSON

10  Mary Shelley (1797–1851): The Gothic novel                          176
    DAVID PUNTER

11  Honoré de Balzac (1799–1850): 'Realism' and authority               192
    MICHAEL TILBY

12  Charles Dickens (1812–1870): Englishman and European                209
    JOHN BOWEN

13  George Eliot (1819–1880): Reality and sympathy                      227
    JOHN RIGNALL

14  Gustave Flaubert (1821–1880): Realism and aestheticism              244
    TIMOTHY UNWIN

15  Fyodor Dostoevsky (1821–1881): 'Fantastic realism'                  259
    SARAH J. YOUNG

16  Leo Tolstoy (1828–1910): Art and truth                              277
    DONNA TUSSING ORWIN

17  Émile Zola (1840–1902): Naturalism                                  294
    BRIAN NELSON

18  Henry James (1843–1916): Henry James's Europe                       310
    ANGUS WRENN

19  Marcel Proust (1871–1922): A modernist novel of time                327
    MARION SCHMID

20  Thomas Mann (1875–1955): Modernism and ideas                        343
    RITCHIE ROBERTSON

21  James Joyce (1882–1941): Modernism and language                     361
    CHRISTOPHER BUTLER

22  Virginia Woolf (1882–1941): Re-forming the novel                    378
    LAURA MARCUS

vi

CONTENTS

23  Samuel Beckett (1906–1989): Language, narrative, authority          394
    LESLIE HILL

24  Milan Kundera (1929–): The idea of the novel          410
    RAJENDRA A. CHITNIS

    Conclusion: The European novel after 1900          428
    MICHAEL BELL

    *Further reading*          444
    *Index*          448

# CONTRIBUTORS

MICHAEL BELL is Professor Emeritus of English and Comparative Literature at the University of Warwick and Associate Fellow of the Centre for Research in Philosophy, Literature and the Arts. His publications include *Primitivism* (1972); *The Sentiment of Reality: Truth of Feeling in the European Novel* (1983); *D. H. Lawrence: Language and Being* (1992); *Gabriel García Márquez: Solitude and Solidarity* (1993); *Literature, Modernism and Myth* (1997); *Sentimentalism, Ethics and the Culture of Feeling* (2000); and *Open Secrets: Literature, Education and Authority from J.-J. Rousseau to J. M. Coetzee* (2007).

JOHN BOWEN is Professor of Nineteenth-Century Literature at the University of York, a faculty member of the University of California Dickens Project and a former president of the Dickens Society. His publications include *Other Dickens: Pickwick to Chuzzlewit* (2000); the Penguin edition of *Barnaby Rudge* (2003); and, co-edited with Robert L. Patten, *Palgrave Advances in Charles Dickens Studies* (2005).

CHRISTOPHER BUTLER is former Professor of English Language and Literature at the University of Oxford and Student Emeritus of Christ Church. His books include Very Short Introductions to Modernism (2010) and to Postmodernism (2002); *Pleasure and the Arts* (2004); and *Early Modernism: Literature, Music and Painting in Europe 1900–1916* (1994).

RAJENDRA A. CHITNIS is a senior lecturer in Czech and Russian Studies at the University of Bristol. He is the author of *Literature in Post-Communist Russia and Eastern Europe: The Russian, Czech and Slovak Fiction of Changes, 1988–1998* (2005); *Vladislav Vančura: The Heart of the Czech Avantgarde* (2007); and articles on post-war Czech and Slovak novelists. He is currently writing a book on Czech ruralist-nationalist literature between the wars.

LESLIE HILL is Professor of French Studies at the University of Warwick, and the author of *Beckett's Fiction: In Different Words* (1990, republished 2009); *Marguerite Duras: Apocalyptic Desires* (1993); *Blanchot: Extreme Contemporary* (1997); *Bataille, Klossowski, Blanchot: Writing at the Limit* (2001); *The Cambridge*

*Introduction to Jacques Derrida* (2007); and *Radical Indecision: Barthes, Blanchot, Derrida and the Future of Criticism* (2010).

ANN JEFFERSON is Fellow and Tutor in French at New College, Oxford, and a fellow of the British Academy. Her publications include *Reading Realism in Stendhal* (1988); and *Stendhal: La Chartreuse de Parme* (2003). Her most recent book is *Biography and the Question of Literature in France* (2007).

THOMAS KEYMER is Chancellor Jackman Professor of English at the University of Toronto and General Editor of the *Review of English Studies*. His books include *Sterne, the Moderns and the Novel* (2002); with Peter Sabor, *Pamela in the Marketplace: Literary Controversy and Print Culture in Eighteenth-Century Britain and Ireland* (2005); and recent editions of works by Daniel Defoe, Henry Fielding and Samuel Johnson.

THOMAS LOCKWOOD is Professor and former Chair of Department of English at the University of Washington, Seattle. He has published widely on Fielding and other eighteenth-century subjects and is the editor of the drama volumes of the Oxford 'Wesleyan' edition of the works of Fielding: *Plays*, vol. I (2004), vol. II (2007) and vol. III (2011).

SUSAN MANNING is Grierson Professor of English Literature and Director of the Institute of Advanced Studies in the Humanities at the University of Edinburgh. She works on the Scottish Enlightenment and Scottish–American literary relations as in *The Puritan Provincial Vision* (1990) and *Fragments of Union* (2001). Her edited texts include Henry Mackenzie, *Julia de Roubigné* (1999); Walter Scott, *Quentin Durward* (1992); Washington Irving, *The Sketch-Book of Geoffrey Crayon, Gent* (1996); Hector St-John de Crèvecoeur, *Letters from an American Farmer* (1997); and Nathaniel Hawthorne, *The Marble Faun* (2002). She is one of the editors of the *Edinburgh History of Scottish Literature*, 3 vols. (2006) and has co-edited the first *Transatlantic Literary Studies Reader* (2007). She is currently completing a book on transatlantic character.

LAURA MARCUS is Goldsmiths' Professor of English Literature and Fellow of New College, Oxford. She has published widely on modernist literature, including the work of Virginia Woolf. Her books include *Virginia Woolf: Writers and their Work* (1997, 2004); *The Cambridge History of Twentieth-Century English Literature*, co-edited with Peter Nicholls (2005); and *The Tenth Muse: Writing about Cinema in the Modernist Period* (2007), which was awarded the James Russell Lowell Prize 2008 by the MLA.

BRIAN NELSON is Professor Emeritus of French Studies and Translation Studies at Monash University, Melbourne. He is the editor of the *Australian Journal of French Studies* and the author or editor of twelve books including *The Cambridge*

*Companion to Zola* (2007). He has also edited and translated *The Ladies' Paradise* (*Au Bonheur des Dames*); *Pot Luck* (*Pot-Bouille*); *The Kill* (*La Curée*); *The Belly of Paris* (*Le Ventre de Paris*); and *The Fortunes of the Rougons* (*La Fortune des Rougon*) for Oxford World Classics.

TIMOTHY O'HAGAN is Emeritus Professor of Philosophy at the University of East Anglia. He is the author of *Rousseau* (2003) in the Arguments of the Philosophers series, editor of *Jean-Jacques Rousseau and the Sources of the Self* (1997), and of *Jean-Jacques Rousseau* (2007) in the International Library of Essays in the History of Social and Political Thought.

DONNA TUSSING ORWIN teaches Russian Literature at the University of Toronto. She is President of the North American Tolstoy Society, and the author of books and articles on Leo Tolstoy, including *Tolstoy's Art and Thought, 1847–1880* (1993) and *Consequences of Consciousness: Turgenev, Dostoevsky and Tolstoy* (2007). She is the editor of *The Cambridge Companion to Tolstoy* (2002) and *Anniversary Essays on Tolstoy* (2010).

DAVID PUNTER is Professor of English at the University of Bristol and has published extensively on literature of all the post-medieval periods. His book-length publications include *The Literature of Terror* (1980, rev. 2 vol. edition 1996); *The Romantic Unconscious* (1989); *Postcolonial Imaginings* (2000); *Writing the Passions* (2000); *Modernity* (2007); and *Rapture: Literature, Addiction, Secrecy* (2009).

JOHN RIGNALL is Emeritus Reader in English and Comparative Literary Studies at the University of Warwick. He is the author of *Realist Fiction and Strolling Spectator* (1992); co-editor of the *George Eliot Review*; and the editor of *George Eliot and Europe* (1997); the Everyman paperback edition of *Daniel Deronda* (1999); and the *Oxford Reader's Companion to George Eliot* (2000). His monograph, *George Eliot, European Novelist*, is forthcoming.

RITCHIE ROBERTSON is Taylor Professor of German at Oxford University and a Fellow of the Queen's College. His books include *Kafka: Judaism, Politics and Literature* (1985); *The 'Jewish Question' in German Literature 1749–1939: Emancipation and Its Discontents* (1999); *The Cambridge Companion to Thomas Mann*, ed. (2002); *Kafka: A Very Short Introduction* (2004); *Mock-Epic Poetry from Pope to Heine* (2009).

MARION SCHMID is Reader in French at the University of Edinburgh. She is author of *Chantal Akerman* (2010); *Proust dans la décadence* (2008); *Proust at the Movies*, co-authored with Martine Beignet (2005); and *Processes of Literary Creation: Flaubert and Proust* (1998). She is co-editor (with Nigel Harkness) of *Au seuil de la modernité: Proust, Literature and the Arts. Essays in Honour of*

*Richard Bales* (2011) and (with Paul Gifford) of *La Création en acte: devenir de la critique génétique* (2007).

MARTIN SWALES was educated at the Universities of Cambridge and Birmingham, and has taught at the Universities of Birmingham and Toronto, King's College London and University College London, where he is Emeritus Professor of German. His principal publications include monographs on Goethe, Adalbert Stifter, Arthur Schnitzler, Thomas Mann, the German *Novelle*, the German *Bildungsroman* and German realism.

MICHAEL TILBY is Fellow in French at Selwyn College, Cambridge. He has written extensively on nineteenth-century French literature, above all on Honoré de Balzac's *Comédie humaine* and its literary and historical context. He is the editor of the volume on Balzac in the Modern Literatures in Perspective series (1995) and is currently working towards a study of the evolution of the Balzacian novel in terms of language and fictional form.

TIMOTHY UNWIN is Emeritus Professor at the University of Bristol, where he was formerly Ashley Watkins Professor of French. His books include *Art et infini: l'œuvre de jeunesse de Gustave Flaubert* (1991); *Textes réfléchissants: réalisme et réflexivité au dix-neuvième siècle* (2000); and *Jules Verne: Journeys in Writing* (2005). He edited *The Cambridge Companion to the French Novel: 1800 to the Present* (1997) and *The Cambridge Companion to Flaubert* (2004). He is currently working on a critical edition of Jules Verne's *Une ville flottante*.

CYNTHIA WALL is Professor of English at the University of Virginia. She is the author of *The Prose of Things: Transformations of Description in the Eighteenth Century* (2006, Honourable Mention for James Russell Lowell Prize) and *The Literary and Cultural Spaces of Restoration London* (1998). She has edited works of Daniel Defoe, Alexander Pope and John Bunyan.

EDWIN WILLIAMSON is the King Alfonso XIII Professor of Spanish Studies in the University of Oxford and a Fellow of Exeter College. His publications reflect his interest in Latin America as well as early-modern Spain, and they include *The Half-Way House of Fiction: 'Don Quixote' and Arthurian Romance* (1984); *The Penguin History of Latin America* (updated edition 2009); and *Borges: A Life* (2004), which has been translated into several languages. He is the editor of the forthcoming *Cambridge Companion to Borges*, and is currently working on a critical study of the evolution of Jorge Luis Borges's literary ideas.

ANGUS WRENN teaches comparative literature at the London School of Economics. His main research interests are Henry James, Ford Madox Ford and George Bernard Shaw. His publications include *Henry James and the Second Empire* (2009); and 'Eager Disciple and Reluctant Master' in *The Reception of Henry*

*James in Europe*, ed. Annick Duperray (2006). He is co-author with Olga Soboleva of a book on George Bernard Shaw and Russia (forthcoming).

SARAH J. YOUNG is Lecturer in Russian at the School of Slavonic and East European Studies, University College London. After completing her doctoral thesis on Fyodor Dostoevsky at the University of Nottingham, she was awarded a Leverhulme early career fellowship and then a post at the University of Toronto. She is the author of *Dostoevsky's 'The Idiot' and the Ethical Foundations of Narrative* and editor of *Dostoevsky on the Threshold of Other Worlds*.

# NOTE ON REFERENCES

For convenient use by readers with different editions, quotations from primary texts will usually be identified by reference to chapter rather than page. Where specific editions are cited, this will be explained in the note on editions at the end of the chapter, or in an endnote.

MICHAEL BELL

# Introduction: The novel in Europe 1600–1900

A history of European novelists from Miguel de Cervantes to Milan Kundera could be told in many ways, all of them partial.[1] While the present volume is not a continuous history, the introductory and concluding essays, along with the Index, offer coordinates for linking the chosen writers' contributions not just to the novel, but to the idea of the novel, in Europe as it acquired a growing consciousness of itself as a distinctive artistic genre and as providing the most complete, complex and intimate form of self-inspection for modern social man.

This is a question of truth claims as much as subject-matter, and the nature of its own truth-telling has been a constant preoccupation of the form. The novel grew partly from non-literary genres, such as letters, memoirs and histories, with which it has maintained an ambiguous relation. Even while progressively defining itself as artistically distinct, the novel has repeatedly stolen the clothes of these non-literary forms. It has continued to invoke other sources of authority, whether scientific, historical or philosophical, even as it has affirmed its own special value as fiction. Honoré de Balzac's declaration in the opening chapter of *Le Père Goriot*, 'All is true', expresses this ambition in a bold, but elusive, formula. Hence, the problematic, if unavoidable, term 'realism' denotes not a single mode of representation so much as a complex, shifting ambition to give fiction a weight of historical or sociological insight. An inevitable starting-point for the truth-telling ambitions of the form is the fraught relation of 'realism' to 'romance'.

### Realism versus romance?

As the new genre of the novel became self-conscious over the course particularly of the eighteenth century, it continued to be defined most notably in relation to romance; a term with multiple aspects which variously had an impact on the novel. In one interpretation, Cervantes, the father of the modern novel, had laughed away the chivalric romance to found what Henry Fielding called a 'new province' of writing from which the 'marvellous' was banished (*Tom Jones*, bk II, ch. 1; bk VIII, ch. 1). Yet, as Edwin Williamson shows (20), Cervantes appreciated romance and, in J. L. Borges's view, Don Quixote's mad illusions were a way of continuing to enjoy its spell in 'a secret, nostalgic farewell'.[2]

In this latter reading, Cervantes rather inaugurated the radical ambiguity of the new genre; an ambiguity encapsulated in the contrast of the English word 'novel' with the French and German *roman* and *Roman*. Is the novel opposed to romance, or a cunning means of preserving it? As Ian Watt noted long ago, if the new genre adopted the protocols of 'realism of presentation', Fielding's rejection of the marvellous, that did not necessarily guarantee 'realism of assessment'.[3] Hence Fielding's distrust both of Samuel Richardson's Pamela and of his *Pamela*. For what he saw as the heroine's seductive manipulation of her would-be seducer Mr B was equally a feature of Richardson's narrative mode: its emotionally fraught 'writing to the moment' (Keymer, 57) was a way of entrancing the reader's feelings. And Fielding was right in so far as romance, in the sense of emotional wish-fulfilment, became a popular staple of the genre, but the great novelists would use it as a point of contrast and departure as Richardson was to do in the tragic drama of *Clarissa* (1748) and Fielding himself in the emotional ordeal of *Amelia* (1751). In this sense of the word, Jane Austen created the most artful combination of the emotional power of romance with sharp assessment and unillusioned worldliness.

But as well as this ground bass of popular wish-fulfilment in the new genre, the word romance also refers to a deeper emotional formation in the European tradition. When Jean-Jacques Rousseau added to his *Julie* (1761) the last-minute subtitle *the New Eloisa*, he linked the contemporary vogue of sensibility, the period's upward evaluation of feeling, to a suggestive precedent. The tragic figures of Héloïse and Abelard had a mythic power partly because their story enacted the underlying structure of medieval romance. Medieval romance was the literary embodiment of an enormous, but enigmatic, cultural shift: the spiritualisation of sexual love in a way that had no precedent in classical antiquity. The high value now placed on romantic love was such that it transcended the values of this world. Its prototypical object, the lord's lady, is unobtainable within the moral requirements of worldly existence: romantic passion is illusory and destructive. This development has attracted speculative explanations of which two now venerable classics illuminate the subsequent history of the novel in Europe.

C. S. Lewis's *The Allegory of Love* (1936) traced a distinctively English and Christian tradition through Geoffrey Chaucer, Edmund Spenser, William

Shakespeare and John Milton whereby romantic love is reconciled with, indeed irradiates, the marriage relation. By contrast, the francophone Denis de Rougement's *Love in the Western World* (*L'Amour et l'occident* 1938) saw romantic love as a destructive illusion for which Richard Wagner's *Tristan and Isolde* indicates the continuing power. Rougement concludes with a highly rational argument in favour of marriage as the necessary form of social order and continuity for which romance must be sacrificed. René Girard's *Deceit, Desire and the Novel*, whose dual thrust is more sharply indicated in its original title *Mensonge romantique et vérité romanesque* (1961), similarly sets the illusion of romance against the sober, social truth of the novel. Taken together, these books invite the reflection that man is a mythopoeic animal, and most crucially so when least aware of it. For they each express deep structures of feeling, indeed assumptions about feeling itself, which run through their respective traditions of the novel. Whereas the line of major English novelists, from Fielding, through Austen, George Eliot and Charles Dickens, tends to focus on the education of the heart whereby it finds its proper fulfilment in social assimilation, the French novel, from Mme de Lafayette, through Rousseau, Choderlos de Laclos, Stendhal, Gustave Flaubert and Marcel Proust to Jean-Paul Sartre, harbours an abiding distrust of romantic feeling even when it is still acknowledged as the supreme good. The dual recognition, that romantic passion is both illusory and yet the highest value in human life, provides the emotional structure of 'romantic irony', most notably in Stendhal, and its internal tension underlies the philosophical clarity and formal command that characterise the French novel.

Besides the ambiguous persistence of its emotional structures, romance survived at the level of form. The supposed banishing of the 'marvellous' was always something of a feint: it affirmed an important principle but one which took its meaning from a partly rhetorical opposition. Fielding was concerned to remove magical and supernatural causalities which were incompatible with the Enlightened modes of understanding to which the novel aspired. His pre-eminently social intelligence, however, was not best adapted for exploring the inner lives of individuals, and for this purpose the novel continued to draw on the power of romance but now only as that was transposed and internalised; as Cervantes had begun to do in the episode of the Cave of Montesinos (Williamson, 29). The popularity of the Arabian Nights, and the rise of Gothic fiction in the eighteenth century, both represent a contrast with the ambitions of the realist novel, yet these supposedly contrasting worlds were constantly porous to each other. Throughout its history, the novel has needed the romance both to define itself against, and as an emotional experience to be assimilated. For example, in Anne Radcliffe's Gothic tale, *The Mysteries of Udolpho* (1794), the young heroine's sensibility is excited and distressed by mysterious events which are finally given a rational explanation. The heroine is a proxy for the reader's licensed indulgence in the thrill. But in so far as the Gothic thrill requires an individual sensibility as its medium, it is from the outset an expression of the character's inner state. And if the character is unaware of projecting an internal condition as Gothic thrill, that only increases its dramatic potential as a notation of the unconscious. By the mid nineteenth century, Charlotte and Emily Brontë had internalised the Gothic motifs as psychological symbolism. Likewise, Balzac and Dickens, while impelled by motives of social and moral critique, and honouring the protocols of formal realism, drew on metaphorical and poetic powers.

In Chapter 23 of *Dombey and Son* (1848), for example, Dickens enforces the potentially destructive effect on Florence Dombey of her effective abandonment by her father after the death of her brother, Paul, by repeating for several pages that she was threatened by no evil, supernatural powers. Precisely by these denials he builds a vivid sense of the emotional danger and desolation to which the child is subjected: 'There were not two dragon sentries keeping ward before the gate of this abode, as in magic legend are usually found on duty over the wronged innocence imprisoned.' Dickens's sentence encapsulates in miniature how the power of the marvellous is invoked within its supposed erasure. At the same time, a literalistically inclined reader might wonder if Florence was really left in this expensive townhouse without a retinue of servants, and there were other novelists, such as William Makepeace Thackeray and Anthony Trollope, who disapproved of what they saw as the Dickensian tendency to moral melodrama. In this respect, Chapter 42 of *Vanity Fair* (1848) provides an instructive comparison with the Florence Dombey episode as Thackeray uses the literal features of the domestic setting to express the desolate life of Jane Osborne living alone with her father after the death of the spoiled son, George. Where Dickens overrides literal considerations for a psychological insight, Thackeray derives his emotional power from the felt reality of the external world. The creative tension, then, between realism and romance occurs across different traditions of the novel as well as internally to particular works. But if 'realism' and 'romance' represent in some degree the orders of external and internal truth, two other polar genres likewise live on within the novel, constantly reframing the meaningfulness of its experience. These are epic and drama, two genres which variously affect the sense of time.

## Epic and drama, history and temporality

Behind romance lies the older form of the epic which provided in the eighteenth century a classically educated perspective on contemporary society and illuminated the new genre of the novel by placing it within a larger sweep of cultural evolution. Hence, Fielding, a man of the law as well as the theatre, in his Preface to *Joseph Andrews* (1742) called it a 'comic epic-poem in prose' and, although his masterpiece *Tom Jones* (1749) had a dramatic tautness of structure, and many other theatrical features, it developed above all the summative sweep of the epic as the embodiment of its moral generality. In 1774, however, just before Johann Wolfgang von Goethe's *The Sorrows of the Young Werther*, Friedrich von Blanckenburg argued, in his *Essay on the Novel*, that the novel stands to modern society as the epic stood to the ancient heroic community. He contrasted these genres particularly over the question of the individual. In the ancient world, in which the success, indeed the survival, of the community depended on heroic values, the individual was ultimately subordinate to the social whole. By contrast, in the post-Cartesian, post-Rousseauan world dominated by commercial enterprise, and historically formed by Christianity, the individual was becoming a more intrinsic, if not a supreme, value. And one might add that the individual was not just an enhanced centre of value but an ontological claim. Rousseau broke with his former friend Denis Diderot partly over this question: whereas Diderot saw man as an essentially social being, Rousseau believed there was something in the individual which was irreducible to social explanation. Goethe's Werther is Rousseau's individual as man of feeling so that, when defending a young man who has committed a crime of passion, he feels his own identity to be at stake in resisting the socially principled arguments of his friend Albert, and especially so when these have the institutional support of a magistrate.

Moreover, the rising importance of the individual is reflected in the form itself. The novel gradually internalises the world by transposing it into the stuff of consciousness until it is assimilated into the modernist 'stream of consciousness'. This aspect of the novel's history begins with the picaresque, the episodic narrative form which was popular throughout Europe in the seventeenth and eighteenth centuries, and which shared the structural looseness of the romance. The picaresque, derived from the Spanish *picaro*, adopted the viewpoint of the low-life outsider who lives off, and finds entertainment in exploiting, the vulnerability of his fellow beings (Williamson, 18–19). Yet although the *picaro* provides both social satire and entertainment, and can be the basis of a wide social purview, he usually has little inner life, so that the episodic narrative can continue indefinitely until it comes to some arbitrary conclusion such as death or a rich marriage. *Tom Jones*, however, was an artful adaptation of the picaresque. The action appears to spill over the countryside with a constant succession of chance encounters on the way, but the narrative threads prove to have secret connections and the entire action has an unconscious symmetry: six books set in the Allworthy country seat, six on the road and six in London, with the philosophical tale of the 'Man of the Hill', a counter-image of the whole book, placed at its exact centre. And so the final socialisation of Tom, the concluding addition of 'prudence' to his 'lively parts', is enacted in the narrative dynamic rather than in his consciousness; a method which aptly endorses Fielding's essentially social view of man.

Writing some decades later, Goethe had a greater commitment to the notion of the individual, although he was taken aback that readers identified with Werther, reading his story as a romantic tragedy rather than as a novelistic critique of the Rousseauan man of feeling. Yet Goethe's 'sympathetic' narration from Werther's viewpoint was crucial to an internal critique of the sentimentalist individualism he represented. Perhaps to escape this dilemma, Goethe adopted for his next novel, *Wilhelm Meister's Apprenticeship* (1796), Fielding's overt irony and picaresque expansion. But Wilhelm is an artistically inclined intellectual with cultural curiosity and ambitions, so that, in his case, the apparently random process of the narrative is drawn together not just by narrative manipulation but by the development of his self-understanding, which is itself connected to his deeper understanding of his chosen art of theatre.

It might be noted here that Rousseau's commitment to the value of the individual was based on a pre-modern conception of it as preceding society. Society, in his view, derived from the willing collaboration of pre-existing individuals. The German Enlightenment, by contrast, was forming the more modern recognition that the very category of the individual is a late and fragile development from an initial collective, or primordial herd. In that light, it is not surprising that social understanding through the individual should also be a late development in the history of fiction. Goethe's internalising of the picaresque as individual development, and his experience of contemporary social developments through the eyes and mind of the individual, were perhaps among the features that led Friedrich Schlegel to rank *Wilhelm Meister's Apprenticeship* with the French Revolution and J. G. Fichte's philosophy as one of three crucial events of the period.[4] Only in the mind and feelings of a suitable individual could the extensive social purview of the novel be given experiential depth and *gravitas*. Yet Schlegel appreciated above all the peculiar artistic self-consciousness of the novel which Goethe had adapted partly from Fielding.

*Wilhelm Meister's Apprenticeship* was the defining instance of the *Bildungsroman*, a term which has acquired in the anglophone academy the loose meaning of any novel in which a young person matures through socialisation. The usage is broad enough to cover most European fiction and

Goethe's achievement was indeed significant for this wider tradition. But the German term refers more specifically to the attempted acquisition of an Enlightenment conception of rounded humanistic culture derived from such thinkers as Johann Gottfried Herder, Wilhelm von Humboldt and Friedrich Schiller as well as Goethe himself. The works in this tradition often foreground their own fictive status, partly because they are philosophical reflections on the educational process, but also to emphasise its fragility. Indeed, Goethe, who most strikingly embodied the ideal of humanistic *Bildung*, actually rejected it in the sequel novel *Wilhelm Meister's Years of Travel* (1829). The German *Bildungsroman*, which was to suffer seemingly terminal critique in the twentieth century, had harboured from the outset a radical self-irony. It is a familiar theme that the German tradition, which had most overtly theorised a commitment to an ideal of humane culture, produced the moral catastrophe of Nazism. But the theme is even more poignant for the fragility which its great thinkers had always recognised within this ideal.

Since Goethe was writing just after the French Revolution, and was always highly conscious of the historical transitions through which he lived, it is especially fitting that his theme of a young man committed to the social importance of theatre should be narrated in the form of a novel. Throughout the eighteenth century, and still for Goethe and Schiller, theatre would seem to be the primary imaginative form in which society sought to view or express itself. Moreover, the social culture was itself highly theatrical, with ordering principles expressed in rigid dress codes and ceremonial, while personal identity was largely, and properly, conceived in terms of social position and function. But this order is disintegrating in Goethe's novel and the new post-revolutionary world was indeed to shift to more internal or intrinsic conceptions of personal value, for which the form of the novel, at once more private and more broadly historical, became the primary vehicle. Thomas Keneally's *The Playmaker* (1987), set in 1789, ingeniously embeds a theatrical production in a 'novel' assembled from historical sources and catches the moment when the novel begins to take over as the central form of social self-reflection.

The contrast between narrative and drama is discussed in Book v, Chapter 7 of Goethe's novel: the characteristic power of drama is said to be concentration, bringing matters to a crisis, whereas narrative, commonly called 'epic' in the German tradition, is extensive and reflective so that it requires a central character who delays the action. This raises a large question about how experience is conditioned by time; a question which was to become central to the novel both at the micro level of personal temporality and the macro level of history. The polar possibilities in this regard are strikingly exemplified in Fyodor Dostoevsky and Leo Tolstoy. Dostoevsky typically concentrates the impact of several life stories into moments of crisis, whereas Tolstoy diffuses the intensity of a moment into a lifetime. In *The Possessed* (1871) by Dostoevsky, Lisa Tushin says she has given her 'whole life for one hour' with Nicholas Stavrogin and is 'content' (pt III, ch. 3), while in Tolstoy's *Anna Karenina* (1876), it is said of Kitty Shtcherbatsky, when Vronsky, newly entranced by Anna, fails to respond to her loving look, that she felt 'an agony of shame' that lasted 'long afterwards – for several years afterwards' (pt I, ch. 23). This indicates an intense hurt, but also its eventual passing. What, then, is the true 'meaning' of an experience: its intensity at the time, or its assimilated impact when virtually forgotten? Although there is no answer to this question, it animates all extended fiction. And the same applies to the macro level of history, for Goethe's historical sense also anticipated another imminent shift in the novel.

Alongside the Enlightenment commitment to the universality of reason, there was growing awareness of the historical relativity of human cultures. The pressures for social change, which were both aroused and disappointed by the French Revolution, were only one element in a deepening historical consciousness. Another was to be the nineteenth century's dawning aware-ness of the age of the earth, and the consequent evolution of the human. G. W. F. Hegel, in many estimates the greatest philosopher of the nineteenth century, saw not just that human experience is historical, but that the very modes of human understanding are themselves subject to historical devel-opment. Indeed, his masterwork on the intellectual evolution of man, *The Phenomenology of Mind* (1807), invokes the form of a *Bildungsroman*. At a more popular level, Walter Scott picked up the Gothic fascination with an exotically conceived past and spawned two genres which continue to this day. One was the costume drama, a staple of popular narrative. The other was the historical novel.

In his first novel, *Waverley* (1814), Scott, another man of the law, revisited the 1745 Jacobite rebellion which had been a significant threat to social order in Fielding's *Tom Jones*. By a kind of historical compression, Edinburgh, one of the most advanced centres of Enlightenment thought, was adjacent to the pre-modern world of the Scottish Highlands and, in the anxiously oppressive period in Britain following the French Revolution, Scott was able both to indulge and to distance the dangerous fascination of the clans. As Susan Manning recounts, Scott's incorporation of historical consciousness transformed the novel. It was not just that so many of the major novelists of the nineteenth century wrote a historical novel set in the past, but that their perception of the present was radically historicised in all their fiction. Of course, what history meant was a matter of interpretation, whether conscious or not: it may be an oppressive weight; a Burkean resource and guide; a blindly careering juggernaut; a tissue of romantic illusions; a tale of progress, or of decline. Most human beings have some implicit conception of history, even if it is never brought explicitly to consciousness, and the novel provides a rich field for testing a range of such models. Following Blanckenburg, we may say that if historical scholarship is modernity's *replacement* of the epic, historical fiction is its *equivalent*.

Cervantes had reflected on fiction and history with his device of the Arab historian, Cide Hamete Benengeli, in *Don Quixote*, but this was when history was still thought of as a source of moral examples, like Shakespeare's history plays, so that there was a proper overlap of truth claims between history and fiction. But, as the modern discipline of history developed truth claims defined precisely by their contrast with fiction, so the novel was increasingly obliged, as with the romance, to negotiate its relation with a necessary other. For one can no more remove all the history from the novel than all the narrative interpretation from history. Hence, while the novel's power derives largely from its combination of fictional and historical insight, the internal tension of its truth claims was variously resolved or suppressed through the eras of nineteenth-century historicism, early twentieth-century modernism and late twentieth-century postmodernism.

Meanwhile, just as history was developing its distinctive truth claims, so too was fiction. The conscious artifice and poetry already noted in Goethe and Dickens are part of a larger shift in the novel between the eighteenth and nineteenth centuries: it becomes more conscious of its integrity as an imaginative genre.

In the early eighteenth century, Daniel Defoe's fictional memoirs had an air of reality so compelling as to be illusionistic. This arose largely from the pragmatic and acquisitive outlook of his narrators: the world was typically seen through eyes concerned with survival, utility or gain. When Robinson Crusoe ends the list of items washed up after his shipwreck with two shoes that 'were not fellows' the persuasive detail of his observation includes their uselessness. For quite different reasons, the mid-century literature of sentiment, as in Richardson and Rousseau, also cultivated a literalistic illusion of reality. This was to arouse the feelings of the reader. For the optimistic Enlightenment myth of moral sentiment, a belief that the moral life could be based on the feelings, encouraged intensity, immediacy and identification in the reader's emotional response. Moreover, it was thought that consciously fictive objects might diminish, or even invalidate, such a response as Rousseau insisted in his *Letter to D'Alembert on the Theatre* (1757). Hence, the literalistic psychology of moral sentiment encouraged a literalistic conception of fictional response.

Fielding, of course, reacted against this by baring the artifice of fiction, and Laurence Sterne was later to sophisticate the sentimental response with narrative games. But Sterne was still playing essentially within a literalistic conception, and the true influence of Fielding took a while to be felt creatively. For the late eighteenth-century recognition of the aesthetic, most notably in Schiller's *On the Aesthetic Education of Man* (1795), was a slow process partly generated by the need to overcome the literalism of the period. It was in the new century, therefore, that the novel developed a more robust confidence in its own moral authority as fiction. Yet even as this happened, the novel also sought confirmation in another form of authority, natural science. Once again, there is an ambiguity of truth claims.

## The novel and science

If the novel is a romantic genre, in an indissoluble marriage with history, its great love affair, lasting through most of the nineteenth century, was with science. There had always been a quasi-scientific dimension to the novel in so far as it sought to conduct experiments on human nature. Rousseau introduced into *Émile*, a treatise on education, the imaginary figure of Émile so as to base his argument on a 'real' instance with a demonstrative and generalisable value. If Rousseau uses fiction here while eliding the categories of fiction and educational treatise, his contemporaries used their fiction in a related spirit. Richardson's Lovelace attempts to seduce Clarissa for philosophical as much as erotic motives. When he finally drugs and rapes her, this is at one level an acknowledgement of his failure to conquer her will, yet it still makes sense as part of his desire to show the purely material being of woman. Most notably, Valmont, in Laclos' *Dangerous Liaisons* (*Les Liaisons dangereuses*, 1782), shows his demonstrative motive by writing in advance how the women he seduces will behave. At the same time, what those examples also have in common is a framework of religious belief, and the tradition of Protestant self-examination was a powerful current in eighteenth-century fiction, while, in the anglophone world, Bunyan's *The Pilgrim's Progress* (1678) and Jeremy Taylor's *Holy Living* (1650) and *Holy Dying* (1651) were widely read by the same reading public. It was only over the course of the nineteenth century, then, that natural science rose in prestige to became the paradigmatic form of truth statement, and novelists began widely to invoke its authority.

Balzac, for example, is credited with introducing the scientific term 'milieu' into general usage in his attempt to register the effects of socio-economic environment on the individual. This did not mean, however, that religion ceased to be a significant motive as well. It is rather that the novel is an imaginative arena in which the mutual jostling of science and religion in the period is staged. In Balzac these various currents flow without finding, or perhaps seeking, resolution: just as he mixes scientism and melodrama, so his religious impulse finds expression in forms resistant to traditional institutionalisation. Eliot was the other way round: having abandoned religious faith, she treasured the cultural institutions, including religion, in which humanity had traditionally developed its spiritual and moral understanding. And her invocation of science had a similar indirection. *Middlemarch* (1872) has a network of scientific analogies revealing the laws operating beneath the phenomenal surface; a mode of insight that, in Chapter 15, she contrasts with Fielding's omniscient transparency. Yet the nostalgic reference to Fielding also denotes continuity, since her purpose is equally one of generalisable moral wisdom, and she invoked science rather as a metaphor for the law-like consequentiality in human behaviour. After all, to speak of the 'laws' of nature is always a metaphorical leap from the normative to the descriptive and Eliot merely reverses the metaphorical direction. So, as in Balzac's Bianchon, the doctor is a model of humane science.

But natural science also expressed the century's growing sense of the indifference of the universe to man. The objective standpoint of science, as well as bracketing larger human purposes and values, could be an image of man's existential situation. Flaubert's stance of narrative impersonality carries this philosophical charge even while the progressive ambitions of science as a social institution are derided. Charles Bovary's botched operation on the hapless Hippolyte is under the influence of Homais, the repository, both sinister and ludicrous, of progressive Enlightenment cliché. Yet Flaubert's imagination also hungered for a humane infinity, and his narrative indifference is ultimately a rhetorical stance which takes its meaning from this. Emma's romantic longing, for all its naive vulgarity, is also the archetype of the human emotional condition. Once again, the mutuality of romance and realism gives point to each.

By the later decades of the century, which also saw the rise of the practices known in English, rather oxymoronically, as the social sciences, the ambition to promote through the novel an understanding of social processes was intensified in the form of naturalism. Émile Zola's *The Experimental Novel* (1880) was the most direct expression of this ambition. Zola proposed a version of what Rousseau had sought to do with *Émile*; an imagined complex of human material is to be used, not just to illustrate, but to discover, social and psychological principles. In truth, as Brian Nelson indicates in his essay, Zola's fiction was much richer than this unlikely, or merely self-fulfilling, theory might produce. In so far as it was manifest in his fiction, it was rather a vehicle for his concentrated, informed social indignation and his curiosity about human potentiality.

Nonetheless, the theoretical armature of naturalism focused two related concerns. One was that as the individual was increasingly understood to be a function of impersonal forces, both biological and social, the very category of the individual, with its traditional moral autonomy, became more and more illusory. The other was a sense that the social whole was no longer amenable, if it ever had been, to a holistic human understanding. This is vividly expressed in the attitude to Dickens of the naturalistically inclined George Gissing (1857–1903). Gissing admired Dickens's achievement but saw that his poetic summations of society were no longer adequate to the complexity of contemporary social experience and, once you realise this, you realise they never were, although Dickens's genius and social belief had carried conviction, and still do. The newly felt complexity was perhaps less of substance than of viewpoint. Part of the contrast between Dickens and Thackeray was that each saw society as a whole but from different standpoints: Thackeray, who was of the Bulwer Lytton 'silver fork' school, a popular genre depicting upper-class Georgian and Regency society, saw it from the standpoint of gentility whereas Dickens, of whom it was said that he could not 'do' gentlemen, saw it from below. But by Gissing's time the relativity of viewpoint (such as that of women and the articulate working class) had become pressingly self-conscious.

It became clear, therefore, that while the novel had sought a prestigious authority in science, their love affair would be destructive if it continued. In the great novels of the mid century, social purview was given wholeness and *gravitas* in the experience of the individual, but 'science' increasingly undermined the notion of the autonomous individual, while giving only a narrow and external purchase on the complexity of the social whole. The predicament of fiction at the end of the nineteenth century was to be taken up by the modernist generation, and will be discussed in the Conclusion, but it can be noted here that what in English came to be called science was still known in the eighteenth century as natural philosophy. In so far as philosophy is a broader and more fundamental category than science, it links the early period of the novel's development to its modernist flowerings and its subsequent twentieth-century varieties.

## The novel and philosophy

The novel's relation to philosophy, as to history, is one of mutual dependence and rivalry. Thinkers from Gianbattista Vico to Martin Heidegger have argued that poetry is the primordial activity of man as a world-creating being. In the evolution of culture, poetry precedes analytic thought and therefore philosophy and science too. Moreover, for these thinkers, this is not a remote fact about the evolutionary past but a continuing truth of human being in the world. The human world is an unconscious poem, unconscious because the formative and evaluative investment in its creation now seems merely part of the world itself. In one aspect, the novel re-enacts this same process. The novelist creates a world, and although the literary process is self-conscious, the underlying philosophical assumptions may not be. The novel will then be seen as merely representing, or describing, the world. At the same time, within this subliminally 'poetic' background, the novel has a foreground activity central to its modernity. For the fact that the novel is written in analytic as well as poetic prose accords with its function of testing rival models of the world, society and the self.

The novel has, indeed, been an important means of testing beliefs and ideas. For this purpose it needs both a porous sensitivity to philosophy and a distinctive difference. As D. H. Lawrence put it:

> Plato's Dialogues ... are queer little novels ... it was the greatest pity in the world, when philosophy and fiction got split. They used to be one, right from the days of myth. Then they went and parted, like a nagging married couple, with Aristotle and Thomas Aquinas and that beastly Kant. So the novel went sloppy, and philosophy went abstract dry. The two should come together again in the novel.[5]

Lawrence sees the *Dialogues*, not as expository vehicles for a pre-existing doctrine, but as passionate exchanges with much left unresolved, while his marriage image conveys a necessary complementarity founded on difference. Above all, perhaps, the relationship is not a matter of fiction illustrating ideas, but of ideas embodied in the novel. For philosophical thought runs through the European novel as its skeletal structure: and if you can see the bones the novel is probably dead. In other words, the novel is most truly philosophical when least overtly so, when it trusts its own distinctiveness as a form of thought.

In this respect, the eighteenth-century philosophical tale is multiply illuminating. The best-known examples, such as Jonathon Swift's *Gulliver's Travels* (1726), Voltaire's *Candide* (1759) and Samuel Johnson's *Rasselas* (1759), give the Cervantean theme a common Enlightenment thrust by exposing abstract and systematic theory to hard experience. These works are rather two-dimensional: they too readily oppose 'ideas' to 'experience', and their picaresque progress can after all represent only an idea of experience. Yet, as in Fielding, what readers truly respond to is a narrative personality in which a wide hinterland of experience is almost tangibly invoked. Moreover, the wider import of the genre is to focus an impulse that runs through most great fiction. The experimental spirit in the period is still philosophical rather than scientific: *Clarissa*, *Tom Jones*, *Julie*, Sterne's *Tristram Shandy*, Diderot's *Jacques le fataliste* (1780, 1796) and Laclos' *Dangerous Liaisons* are all philosophical reflections on the nature of man and the structures of experience. And as philosophical concerns enter the suffusive medium of extended narrative fiction, the putative contrast of 'idea' and 'experience' begins to shimmer.

This is perhaps the greatest lesson of the novel. Although an idea is a necessary trans-personal and trans-historical abstraction, important ideas are usually the focus of passionately held beliefs shaped by experience, while experience is never neutral, it is itself always constructed by our ideas. Moreover, ideas are always understood, or more importantly lived, by individuals in specific historical circumstances. The 'same' idea may have a completely different meaning as enacted in different lives, although it is often supposed that an idea or belief must entail a given behaviour. Indeed, the capacity to distinguish speculative ideas from action, to avoid confusing ideas with experience, is important for both individuals and political societies. Dostoevsky and Tolstoy, writing in a culture in which the most advanced modern ideas of the liberal elite were kept in frustrated isolation from the regressive political order, understood the multifaceted dangers and ironies of ideas when infused with human passions and infecting whole societies. The modern version of the Cervantean illusion is not to see windmills as giants but to see everything through ideological eyes. Nor is there any simple recovery from this condition. The novel is rather an education in living in philosophical uncertainty without necessarily falling into moral disorientation or metaphysical homelessness.

At the same time, of course, it takes one to know one, and even the greatest novelists, including Dostoevsky and Tolstoy, were themselves subject to the power of ideas. These authors, for example, shared a belief in the unique spiritual power of the Russian people, the Russian 'soul', in a world of rootless Enlightenment. Indeed, if the story of the European novel is the invention of the modern individual, it is also that of the individual writ large in the form of the nation, for all the novelists in this volume can be seen, not just as reflecting, but as creating these national characters. The essays on Defoe, Fielding, Sterne, Mary Shelley, Dickens and Eliot show the formation of English self-conceptions ranging from happily insular eccentricity to lamentable provinciality. The French novel, by contrast, even as it criticises its home culture, tends to perceive it as the universal and representative case. Even when the eighteenth-century *philosophes* cited British constitutional liberties against the absolutism of the contemporary

French monarchy, their viewpoint was still rationalist. The German lands, like the Italian and Spanish, had a common culture before they had a single nation, and German cultural identity grew in conscious opposition to both British empiricism and French rationalism. It is sometimes charged with idealistic indifference to the everyday and the political, but its privileging of the apparent privacy of the aesthetic is underwritten by the great tradition of German philosophical thought over the same centuries. For, in that tradition, the aesthetic constantly recurred as the fundamental category in human understanding of the self and the world.

The British, French and German traditions provided models for other national cultures, as for example Benito Perez Galdos's *Episodios nacionales* (1873–9, 1898–1905), a series of novels intended to record and analyse Spain as Balzac had done with France. One of his best-known novels, *Doña Perfecta* (1876), focuses on the repressive, and self-suppressive, nature of the socio-religious culture, a theme that has its most striking impact in *La regenta* of Leopoldo Alas, or 'Clarin' (1884). Behind all these is Scott, who was important to all situations of conscious national formation including the Italian. Alessandro Manzoni's *I promessi sposi* (1827, rev. 1842) was the product of such a moment, although its author struggled with successive versions and eventually decided that the historical novel was an impossible, or illegitimate, genre.[6] Indeed, Scott's confident narrative purview was dependent on a distanced historical perspective from a settled constitutional vantage point and, after his immense prestige in the first half of the century, he went into eclipse as a serious novelist until at least the latter half of the twentieth century.

In short, if the nation state was an important preoccupation of the nineteenth century, its mythic formation can be seen in the novel. For myth is not just the putative origins of a people, but a whole complex of largely unconscious assumptions experienced as a common identity. So too, the larger imaginary of Europe can be felt in the early and later history of the novel. The year 1609, between the two parts of *Don Quixote*, saw a major expulsion of the Spanish Moors, and in Part II Sancho meets his old neighbour, Ricote, the Moor, disguised as a Christian pilgrim. Unable to bear the pain of exile, he has risked revisiting his homeland. The scholar Americo Castro once argued that Alonso Quijano, the immediate creator of Don Quixote, and Cervantes himself, were new Christians, or converted Jews (*conversos*).[7] Whether or not this is true, it would be highly appropriate if this foundational modern identity crisis should come from a *converso*. In the succeeding centuries, Europe defined itself partly by its opposition to the Islamic world, represented most challengingly by the Ottoman Empire. Meanwhile, the Jews found refuge around Europe, but under recurrent threat and constant exclusion. In 1813, Count Potocki published in Paris *Manuscript Found at Zaragossa*. A Polish author writes in French of a Dutch hero on a military quest in Spain where he is almost endlessly sidetracked by digressive Cervantean sub-narratives involving Jewish and Islamic characters who negotiate their differences humanely in the act of telling their stories. It is an inclusive tapestry in the spirit of Cervantes. But Primo Levi, who was descended from Spanish Jews settled in Piedmont, records how, in the Nazi concentration camps, with their overwhelmingly Jewish inmates, those who had given up, and were reduced to a subhuman condition of apathy before their deaths, were referred to as *Müsselmänner*, or Muslims.[8] The single word brutally figures the gradations of exclusion.

By the beginning of the twenty-first century, the nation state, once a seemingly natural and desirable form, has come increasingly under question and especially so in Europe as the continent explores new modes of federation and new relations with Islam. The parallel story of the novel, and its negotiation of history and myth, is continued in the Conclusion.

## Notes

1 For the earlier Greek and Roman novel, see *The Cambridge Companion to the Greek and Roman Novel*, ed. Tim Whitmarsh (Cambridge University Press, 2008).
2 J. L. Borges, *Labyrinths*, trans. Donald A. Yates and James E. Irby (London: Penguin, 1970), p. 229.
3 Ian Watt, *The Rise of the Novel: Studies in Defoe, Richardson and Fielding* (London: Chatto and Windus, 1957), pp. 32–4, 288.
4 Kathleen M. Wheeler, ed., *German Aesthetic and Literary Criticism: The Romantic Ironists and Goethe* (Cambridge University Press, 1984), p. 48.
5 D. H. Lawrence, *Study of Thomas Hardy and Other Essays*, ed. Bruce Steele (Cambridge University Press, 1985), p. 154.
6 Alessandro Manzoni, *On the Historical Novel*, trans. Sandra Bermann (Lincoln, NE: University of Nebraska Press, 1984).
7 Americo Castro, *Cervantes y los casticismos españolas* (Madrid: Allianza, 1974).
8 Primo Levi, *If This Is a Man and The Truce*, trans. Stuart Woolf (London: Abacus, 1987), p. 94.

# I

EDWIN WILLIAMSON

# Miguel de Cervantes (1547–1616): *Don Quixote*: romance and picaresque

*Don Quixote* met with immediate success. Within a short time of the publication of Part I in 1605, the book became hugely popular in the Spanish-speaking world. Already in 1607, the figures of Quixote and Sancho had appeared in street pageants in Peru, as they may well have done in Spain itself, though our first record of this is a pageant at a public fiesta held in Salamanca in 1610. The Bodleian Library at Oxford received a copy in 1605, and a couple of years later, the English writer John Fletcher based a story on one of the tales interpolated in the novel. Another interpolated tale inspired a play, *Cardenio*, now lost, which Fletcher may have written in collaboration with William Shakespeare. The first English translation of the *Quixote* appeared in 1612, the French in 1614; that is to say, even before Cervantes had published Part II in 1615. The book's influence has scarcely diminished since. In a poll conducted in 2002 by the Norwegian Nobel Institute, 100 leading writers from 54 countries voted *Don Quixote* 'the best work of fiction ever written'.[1]

According to Harold Bloom, 'This great book contains within itself all the novels that have followed in its sublime wake. Like Shakespeare, Cervantes is inescapable for all writers who have come after him. Dickens and Flaubert, Joyce and Proust reflect the narrative procedures of Cervantes, and their glories of characterisation mingle strains of Shakespeare and Cervantes.'[2] Still, how could a Spanish writer have created a work that has had the power to influence world literature for some 400 years? In order to attempt an answer to this question, one should consider not just Cervantes's inventive genius but also the context in which the book was written and the nature of the enterprise itself.

The Spain of Cervantes's birth was experiencing the most prodigious expansion of power and territory that Europe had ever known. In the course of the sixteenth century, an entire 'New World' was discovered and settled by Spanish explorers and conquerors. During the reign of Charles V, the Low Countries, much of Italy and parts of modern

Germany and France came under the Spanish Crown. When Philip II succeeded to the throne of Portugal in 1580, he added its possessions in Brazil, Africa, India and the Far East to his already vast realms. This imperial expansion was driven and sustained by an outpouring of creative energy which led to the revitalisation of religion, art, literature, drama, philosophy and science, as Spain first absorbed foreign influences – from Renaissance Italy in particular – and then produced great works of its own. At this time of cultural ferment, the dominant mode of fiction was what we now call 'romance'. Several varieties of romance were in vogue – sentimental romances based on courtly love, pastoral romances portraying shepherds and shepherdesses debating their amorous predicaments, Byzantine and Moorish romances which alternated the trials of love with exciting adventure stories set in exotic places. But the most popular type by far was the romance of chivalry, which is perhaps not surprising given that Spaniards were engaged in war and adventure across the globe. Certainly, many of the conquerors of America were devotees of these books. There is a famous passage in a chronicle of the conquest of Mexico where the marvels of the Aztec capital are compared to the wonders described in the books of chivalry, and indeed California was named after the kingdom of a warrior queen who appeared in a well-known Spanish romance.

Yet if Cervantes knew Spain at the zenith of its imperial power, he would also witness the beginnings of a gradual decline from its position of unchallenged global supremacy. Already under Charles V, the silver of the New World was being spent on wars against the Turks and the old rival, France, and under Philip II, on additional conflicts with rising Protestant powers like England and the Dutch Republic. The steady depletion of its resources in defence of the ideal of a Christendom united under the spiritual authority of Rome, would lead to Spain's being affected earlier and more deeply than other countries by the economic depression that would ravage Europe for much of the seventeenth century. Taxes were constantly being raised to pay for the endless wars abroad, inflation raged and famines became frequent. A great mass of unemployed men, women and children roamed from town to town in search of a living. In these volatile conditions, social status was increasingly felt to be precarious and fluid – down-at-heel gentry strove to keep up appearances, while the newly rich often purchased titles of nobility in order to be admitted to the ranks of the well born.

In the early seventeenth century, a new genre of fiction, nowadays called picaresque, began to reflect the unstable social and economic realities of contemporary Spain. The prototype of the genre was established by a short narrative called *Lazarillo de Tormes*, published by an anonymous author in 1554, but picaresque fiction did not take off until the publication in 1599 of Mateo Alemán's *Guzmán de Alfarache*, which became a best-seller and soon produced large numbers of imitators in the same decade that *Don Quixote* Part I appeared. The Spanish picaresque novel purports to be the autobiography of an eponymous protagonist whose basic motivation is survival in a cruel world, for the *pícaro* is illegitimate, poor, malicious and cunning, and he desperately strives to claw his way up from the lower depths to attain to a position of honour or, failing that, one of relative material comfort. Picaresque fiction thus represents the antithesis of chivalric romance, for if the hero of romance embodies the values of the nobility in a manner which is idealising and exemplary, the picaresque anti-hero challenges those values by portraying honour as a mere convenience and by forcing the reader to judge whether society is not, in fact, a jungle riddled with fraud and hypocrisy. Cervantes was himself drawn to the genre and was certainly familiar with the sordid milieux portrayed in these stories from his own experience of travelling the byways of southern Spain, but he appears not to have tried his hand at the picaresque until after he had embarked on the first part of the *Quixote*, when he started to experiment with the new fiction in several of the *Novelas ejemplares* which he would later publish as a collection in 1613.

The pattern of hope followed by disillusion that seemed to characterise the history of imperial Spain at the turn of the sixteenth century was to become the sad reality of Cervantes's own life. The son of a modest barber-surgeon, little is known for certain about his early years other than that he lived in a number of different cities with his debt-ridden family. In 1569 or thereabouts, he went to Italy and soon afterwards joined the army, seeing action in several campaigns. His moment of glory came at the great sea battle of Lepanto against the Turks in which he lost the use of his left hand, a wound of which he would boast as a mark of heroism for the rest of his life. In 1575, he was captured at sea by Muslim pirates and kept as a slave in Algiers for five years, during which time he organised and led several escape attempts by Spanish captives until he was finally ransomed in 1580. After returning to Spain, he failed to be granted the kind of well-paid position he hoped to receive in recognition of his heroic service to the Crown, and he would struggle financially in poorly rewarded itinerant jobs, even finding himself in prison on at least two occasions. The immense success of *Don Quixote* Part I brought no relief from hardship and insufficient recognition, but he would continue to publish novels and plays until his death in 1616, just over a year after the publication of *Don Quixote* Part II.

## Chivalric romance

Although Cervantes stated that his sole aim in *Don Quixote* was to demolish 'the ill-founded fabric of these books of chivalry' (Prologue, 16),[3] the romances of chivalry were not in themselves ridiculous. Their origins lay in the work of the twelfth-century French poet Chrétien de Troyes, who combined Celtic myths about King Arthur with the ideas of courtly love which reached the courts of northern France from Provence. Chrétien's verse romances each relate the adventures of a young knight striving to achieve *courtoisie*, a balance of martial prowess and the love of a beautiful and virtuous lady. This quest structure would remain the standard pattern of the chivalric romance right up to Cervantes's day, but the books Cervantes was parodying were not these early French narratives; they belonged to a sub-genre known as the *libro de caballerías*, which became hugely popular in Spain in the sixteenth century after the publication in 1508 of *Amadís de Gaula* by Garci Rodríguez de Montalvo. *Amadís de Gaula* was actually a very good work of fiction in its own right and became widely admired throughout Europe, but it was to spawn countless sequels and imitations by different writers of quite varying talent, and in the course of the sixteenth century the *libro de caballerías* would become ever more extravagant, aesthetically incoherent and worthy of ridicule.

The chief target of Cervantes's parody was the *libros de caballerías*'s absurd claim to be 'true histories'. The Spanish authors employed a number of standard devices to pretend that their books were historical chronicles – they invariably claimed to be editing manuscripts found by chance in some remote place; these had been written in a foreign tongue and translated into Spanish; and, to cap it all, the incredible adventures were said to have been witnessed by a sage historian who was attributed magical powers at times, no doubt to explain how he had managed to be at the scene of each and every one of the hero's exploits, however far flung, fantastical or implausible these might have been. In the hands of Cervantes, these pseudo-historical trappings are transformed into a wonderfully ludic mediation of the text of *Don Quixote* to the reader. The first eight chapters of Part 1 are said to be a historical account of the knight's adventures written by a 'first author' and based on several unknown or unnamed Spanish sources. This version has been edited by a 'second author' who turns out to be Cervantes himself, but at the point in Chapter 8 when Don Quixote and an opponent are poised to strike each other with their swords, the narrative suddenly runs out and we are informed that the rest of the text has been lost. Cervantes expresses his disappointment at this loss but then goes on to relate in Chapter 9 how he happened upon some Arabic notebooks in a street market in Toledo and had them translated by a Spanish Moor, only to find that they offered a different account of the history of Don Quixote's adventures written by a 'chronicler' called Cide Hamete Benengeli. Now Cervantes had already mocked the preternatural omniscience of the Spanish chivalric 'chroniclers' – every knight errant had 'one or two sages, made to measure for him, who not only recorded his exploits but also depicted his least thoughts and most trivial actions, however hidden from the public gaze they were' (1.9.73–4) – but Cide Hamete Benengeli was an Arab, 'and since it's a well-known feature of Arabs that they're all liars', the reliability of his account was very much open to doubt, and so this problem required that Cervantes himself take on the role of editor and occasional commentator of such a dubious, translated version. In the *Quixote*, therefore, we find that the all-knowing historian of the books of chivalry has degenerated into the shifty, infidel chronicler, Cide Hamete, an unreliable narrator if ever there was one, and Cervantes himself has become a metafictional character in his own book. All of these devices, of course, turn the act of storytelling into an ironic performance, a self-conscious game which shows that the adventures of Don Quixote have nothing to do with history but are entirely, and gloriously, fictional.

Cervantes was certainly not the first writer to parody chivalric romance: the Italian, Ludovico Ariosto, for one, had already done so in *Orlando Furioso*, a famous burlesque masterpiece that Cervantes alludes to repeatedly in his own book. What made the critical difference was the Spaniard's brilliant idea of making his hero mad, for the ideal world of chivalric romance, which had so captivated the European imagination since the twelfth century, was condensed at a stroke into a reality existing nowhere other than inside the mad knight's head. Thus was born one of the most fertile and enduring themes of modern fiction – the clash of illusion and reality.

But the story of Don Quixote is also the story of how Cervantes gradually discovered the potentialities of the knight's madness. To begin with, the madness forced Cervantes to break with the conventions of chivalric romance. In Chapter 21, for instance, Don Quixote outlines a vision of his future career for the benefit of Sancho Panza (1.21.171–3), explaining that 'one must wander about the world on probation as it were, in search of adventures, so that ... one gains such fame and renown that when one goes to some great monarch's court one is known as a knight by one's deeds'. The king's daughter will fall in love with the knight, and eventually, after helping the king to win a great war against a rival, and further glorious victories, the knight will marry the princess, and will himself succeed to the throne after the king's death, and marry his squire to the daughter of a duke. 'Do not doubt it, Sancho ... because in the way and by the steps I have related knights errant rise and always have risen to be kings and emperors.' This account is a fair summary of the action of a *libro de caballerías*, and we can see how it preserves the quest structure of Chrétien de Troyes's romances, but since the knight is now a madman, the quest for glory becomes an absurd fantasy, so Cervantes will have to invent new ways of developing his narrative beyond the traditional generic pattern of chivalric romance. Writing thus became an adventure for Cervantes, for it is clear that *Don Quixote* was not conceived whole, it took shape gradually and passed through different phases, moods and transformations as its author explored the creative possibilities opened up for him by the crazy obsession that had taken hold of his would-be hero.

At first sight, the knight's madness would appear to leave little room for character development. Alonso Quijano, a fifty-year-old gentleman of La Mancha, loses his sanity because he believes the fraudulent claim that the *libros de caballerías* are 'true histories'. So long as he believes this absurdity he will be mad, but there is a further level to his madness: 'By now quite insane, he conceived the strangest notion that ever took shape in a mad-man's head, considering it desirable and necessary, both for the increase of his honour and for the common good, to become a knight errant, and to travel the world with his armour and his arms and his horse in search of adventures' (I.1.27). This secondary belief introduces a dynamic element into the basic delusion – it drives the old gentleman to reinvent himself as Don Quixote de La Mancha and set out to restore the world of chivalry. Although the madman will never waver in his primary belief that the romances of chivalry are literally true, his secondary belief in his chivalric destiny is indeed capable of changing over time, and it was this potential for self-doubt that allowed Cervantes to take Don Quixote far beyond the limits of the buffoon he might otherwise have remained, and create in due course one of the greatest characters in world literature.

## *Don Quixote*, Part 1, 1605

'When Don Quixote went out into the world,' Milan Kundera observed, 'that world turned into a mystery before his eyes. That is the legacy of the first European novel to the entire subsequent history of the genre.'[4] Yet if the world becomes a mystery for Don Quixote it is because he sees that the reality around him does not correspond to the world portrayed in the books he takes to be 'true histories'. The knight can no longer simply follow the code of chivalry, as did his predecessors in the romances: he must interpret everyday phenomena in a world where the ravages of time and evil are so far advanced that appearances belie their presumed chivalric character. Don Quixote's madness therefore amounts to a kind of creative misreading of everyday situations caused by his desire to make them fit his chivalric obsession. His assertions about the world cannot, however, be validated by empirical methods because he cannot trust the evidence of his senses to identify the true nature of reality, so he tests phenomena by engaging them in a chivalric manner (which usually means armed combat), and if the response accords with the books of chivalry then the truth of the assertion will have been objectively demonstrated in his view. When in doubt, Don Quixote goes by the books of chivalry; the whole of his epistemology is founded on the authority of literary reminiscence.

In the first five chapters, Don Quixote undertakes a number of adventures on his own, but the mad knight's onslaughts on the everyday world would soon have become tedious had Cervantes not found the means to vary this basic narrative formula. At this stage, however, Cervantes was uncertain of the qualities of his burlesque hero – at times the knight appears to be living in a world of his own, at others he tries to explain his crazy actions to other people, but sometimes he shows an extraordinary ingenuity which suggests an underlying intelligence, and this trait will be developed into the 'mad–sane paradox' – the knight will discourse with lucidity and coherence on all matters except chivalry. The most far-reaching transformation would come about with the invention of Sancho Panza in Chapter 7, for once the ignorant rustic appears on the scene, Don Quixote will be forced to engage in a sustained dialogue with another character. In this way, the enterprise of chivalric restoration turns into a mad epistemological argument over the true nature of reality, and the more the knight is forced to argue with the crudely empirical Sancho, all the more ingenious will his justifications of failure become, to the point where he appears to concede a certain relativism in other people's perceptions of reality. In Chapter 25, for example, they encounter a barber wearing a brass basin on his head to shield it from the rain. Don Quixote declares the basin to be the enchanted helmet of the Moorish King Mambrino, which the knight Rinaldo captured in Ariosto's *Orlando Furioso*. But when Sancho insists that it is a barber's basin, his master replies: 'We are always attended by a crew of enchanters who keep transforming everything and changing it into whatever they like, according to whether they have a mind to help or destroy us; and so what looks to you like a barber's basin looks to me like Mambrino's helmet, and will look like something else to another person' (1.25.209).

Sancho Panza takes up service with Don Quixote because he wants to rise in the world and gain some material reward. A feudal relationship is established in Chapter 7 when the knight promises Sancho an island to govern and some noble title in exchange for the servant's loyalty and obedience. Even so, Sancho's relation to Don Quixote is intrinsically subversive, in the sense that his point of view must inevitably be at odds with the madman's, and this disparity of perspectives will be comically reinforced and enriched by disparities of language, manners, values, attitudes and temperament between the two men. The dialectic between knight and squire will evolve into a Bakhtinian contest of discourses that threatens to level differences of status and value, but in Part I, Sancho will never openly challenge his master's authority, and the central relationship, as a result, will remain at the level of comic play, a series of amusing exchanges between an endearing madman and a country bumpkin.

Cervantes, in fact, would complain about having to devote so much attention to Don Quixote and Sancho, a restriction he found to be 'intolerable drudgery', so he decided to extend the narrative by interpolating a number of extraneous stories (II.44.776). This sort of interpolation was a conventional way of introducing variety into a long narrative and there were innumerable precedents in the Renaissance epic, in the pastoral romances and in the books of chivalry. There are no fewer than seven interpolated stories in Part I: some are pastoral tales, one is a Moorish adventure, several others tell of star-crossed lovers, but all of them feature characters who are involved in plots that deal with questions of love and honour. In short, these tales are all romances in some degree or other, and this shows the peculiar difficulty Cervantes had to face with his interpolations, for how does one insert romantic tales into a frame narrative which is itself a parody of the idealising tendencies inherent in all kinds of romance? Cervantes's solution was to insert these tales into the main narrative in ways that would test the reader's capacity to lend them credence. He thus found the means, as it were, of having his cake and eating it – the tales work in their own right, but the manner in which they are woven into the frame narrative serves to remind the reader of the interplay between fact and fiction which is the basic concern of the *Quixote* itself.

Cervantes, moreover, invented a highly original way of orchestrating these tales within the overall movement of Part I. He increased the tempo of his interpolations by progressively assembling the various characters in a roadside inn thanks to a series of amazing coincidences, and it is here, at the same inn which the mad knight takes to be a castle, that one plot is resolved after another until suddenly in Chapter 44 the whole precarious edifice of romance that Cervantes has built up with his sequence of interpolated tales gives way to chaotic farce, when, by yet another strange coincidence, the barber whose basin Don Quixote took as a trophy of battle in Chapter 20, turns up at the inn and claims it back, together with his packsaddle. Don Quixote now assumes that wicked enchanters have put him under a spell, and so he asks the other characters to judge these objects, 'since your understanding will be free, and you will be able to judge of the affairs of this castle as they really and truly are, and not as they appear to me'. The madman thereby involves all the other characters in a trial to determine the nature of reality, and the outcome is a surprise, even for the reader – the sane characters secretly agree to declare that the barber's basin really is Mambrino's helmet and the donkey's packsaddle a horse's caparison. This outrageous verdict leads to a violent melee which is followed by yet another bout of fisticuffs in the next chapter.

This episode shows how deception plays a critical role in sustaining Don Quixote's illusions, and it also points to another important function of Sancho Panza in the development of the narrative, for the madman needs his servant to deceive him if he is to persevere in his absurd mission to restore the world of chivalry. In fact, it is the knight who unwittingly forces Sancho to tell a lie when in Chapter 25 he orders the squire to deliver a letter to the lady Dulcinea in her village. Sancho never actually visits El Toboso, but in Chapter 31 he returns to Don Quixote in the Sierra Morena and invents a story about an interview he has had with Dulcinea, assuring the knight that his lady has accepted his love service. This news is the best evidence Don Quixote has had so far that his mission to restore the world of chivalry is succeeding, and it would explain why he is so optimistic for the rest of Part I, to the point where he is even capable of putting a positive gloss on his being trussed up in a cage and conveyed back home by the priest and barber of his village.

*Don Quixote* Part I is a marvellous Baroque composition of ever more ingenious variations on the contrast between illusion and reality, verisimilitude and the marvellous, story and history, but already Cervantes's unfolding of the madness has led to several innovations that can be identified with hindsight as major features of modern fiction. The narrative observes a basic realist aesthetic, but the dialectic between illusion and reality also generates an interplay of perspectives among the characters which at times gives an impression of relativism. The two protagonists evolve into multifaceted characters whose relationship tends to dissolve the rigid hierarchies of aesthetic and social decorum. At a metafictional level, Cervantes has hit upon the device of the unreliable narrator, and together with other self-referential tricks, he turns the process of storytelling into an ironic game between author and reader which continually provokes the issue of fiction's relation to the world. Cervantes's attack on the 'authority and influence of the books of chivalry' led him to question the notion of literary authority itself. In the Prologue to Part I, he makes great play of his reluctance to publish the book without the support of quotations from the Ancients, the Bible or the Church Fathers, fearing that without them it would not gain the respect of the reading public. He then recounts how a friend chided him for his timidity, telling him there was no need 'to go begging maxims from philosophers, counsels from Holy Scripture, fables from poets, clauses from rhetoricians or miracles from saints'; instead, he should write to the best of his ability, 'setting out your ideas without complicating or obscuring them' (Prologue, 11).

Cervantes is suggesting that a literary work must live or die according to its merits. He is, in fact, prepared to abdicate his authority, inviting the reader to consider himself the sovereign judge of the book's worth: 'And you have a soul in your body, and a will as free as anyone's, and you are in your own house, where you are lord, as the sovereign is master of his taxes.' But Cervantes continues his teasing address thus: 'and you know the old saying: under cover of my cloak I can kill the king'.[5] The traditional hierarchy of author and reader is replaced here by a kind of ironic encounter between equals, for the self-effacing author may have ostensibly renounced his authority, but he still retains the power to surprise the 'king-like' reader and overturn his expectations.

Cervantes again inverts the conventional hierarchy of literary authority in the Prologue to the *Novelas ejemplares* of 1613, presenting himself as 'blank and faceless' before his reader, but also likening relations between them to a playful contest, an ironic game, specifically a 'game of billiards'. In these novellas, moreover, Cervantes tried out various blends of genre, style and form. We find him experimenting with the new picaresque fiction, and even combining romance and picaresque elements in novels like *La gitanilla* or *La ilustre fregona*. In the latter, for instance, he turned the picaresque format on its head: instead of having a rogue trying to rise in society by acquiring honour, he portrayed two young gentlemen who leave home and pretend to be *pícaros* in order to enjoy a 'free life' among the lower orders. The notion of honour as a birthright becomes an open question as Cervantes interrogates the relationship between status and virtue, and, by extension, the notion of social hierarchy itself.

## Don Quixote, Part II (1615)

If some of Cervantes's experiments in his *Novelas ejemplares* implied criticism of the established order, this is also the case in the second Part of *Don Quixote*. In Part I, Don Quixote's adventures took place on the open road, in coaching inns, or in wild places like the Sierra Morena, but the sequel offers the reader a wider panorama of Spanish society – the mad knight is invited to people's houses, attends a wedding, stays at the castle of a duke and duchess, comes across a gang of Catalan bandits, and visits the city of Barcelona, all of which provide occasion for social observation and critique.

The metafictional innovations of Part I become more subtle and complex in Part II. The unreliable chronicler, Cide Hamete Benengeli, intervenes more often in the narrative and in a variety of ways, commenting on the plausibility of certain incidents, questioning Don Quixote's declarations, and even voicing criticism of Part I itself. Another brilliant invention is the metaleptic relationship Cervantes establishes between the two Parts of the novel – Don Quixote and Sancho become aware of themselves as literary characters when they hear of the publication of a book about their adventures, and they also fall prey to the machinations of certain characters who have read the 1605 *Quixote*, so that Part I will begin to shape in Part II the destinies of the protagonists themselves. A further link is made through Master Pedro, one of the galley slaves whom Don Quixote had 'liberated' in Part I, Chapter 22, but who is now revealed to be a picaresque rogue who turns up disguised as a travelling mountebank and puts on a puppet show which is itself a parody of chivalric romance, and which reproduces in farcical mode the metafictional relations between author, narrator, characters and spectators that characterise Cervantes's novel as a whole (II.26.663–70).

Still, the parody of chivalric romance as such yields to a new focus of interest after it undergoes a critical change near the beginning of Part II. The essential elements of this change have already been foreshadowed in Part I. Towards the end of the first Part, the Canon of Toledo is 'moved by pity' for the mad knight as he marvels at Don Quixote's lucidity in all matters other than chivalry (1.49.451). In the earlier Part, too, Sancho found himself having to deceive his master from time to time, if only to get out of a tight spot. These two elements will cohere in Chapter 10 of Part II to produce an almost tragic pathos when the knight is cruelly deceived by Sancho and thenceforward becomes the helpless victim of his own madness, without ceasing to be a figure of fun. It is this transformative paradox that will generate the enduring mythic power of Cervantes's novel.

The narrative action is set in motion when Don Quixote decides to pay his respects to the 'princess' Dulcinea at her 'palace' in El Toboso. Cervantes is, in fact, taking up a thread he had left hanging as far back as Chapter 31 of the first Part, when the knight postponed his visit to El Toboso, even though Sancho had claimed that Dulcinea had accepted his declaration of love for her. The mad knight's decision to visit his ladylove will produce a crisis because Dulcinea does not, of course, exist and Sancho's claim to have had an audience with her was a total fabrication. Once again, therefore, the squire will be forced to deceive his master but, unlike in Part I, he is no longer in fear of Don Quixote and, in Part II Chapter 10, he pulls off an amazingly daring trick, claiming that three peasant girls who happen to be riding by on donkeys are none other than the lady Dulcinea and her maidservants. When Don Quixote says he can see only the three ugly girls, Sancho replies that an evil enchanter must have cast a spell on the lady, and he proceeds to describe Dulcinea's beauty with great relish. The knight curses the wicked enchanter who 'has placed clouds and cataracts over my eyes', and he laments his blindness: 'And to think I could not see any of that, Sancho! . . . I say it again, and I shall say it a thousand times: I am the most unfortunate of men' (II.10.551).

The episode of the 'enchantment' of Dulcinea possesses some of the qualities of a tragic crisis: after the knight discovers that his lady has been transformed into an uncouth country wench, the crazy optimism of Part I will be replaced by deepening misery as he searches ever more anxiously in Part II for signs that it is he who has been chosen to restore the world of chivalry. Yet, even though he is plagued by doubts about his destiny, he will never question his primary belief that the books of chivalry are literally true. The knight, in short, becomes the victim of his madness, which now takes on the characteristics of an undeserved misfortune. The novel, even so, cannot become fully tragic because the hero's madness remains inherently absurd; what we get in Part II, therefore, is pathos mingled with parody as we laugh at the mad knight's antics yet pity his strange helplessness.

The episode of Dulcinea's enchantment also marks the beginning of a shift of power from master to servant in the course of Part II. In this episode, for instance, the roles of the protagonists are reversed – Sancho claims to see everyday reality in chivalric terms whereas Don Quixote appears to have lost the gift of chivalric insight which had impelled him to adventure throughout Part I. As Don Quixote yields to melancholy and self-doubt, Sancho will lose his fear of his master and apply his new-found power to pursue his own interest and rise in the world, so that in Part II the ideals of chivalric romance will gradually succumb to the self-interest and bad faith characteristic of the picaresque anti-hero.

The crisis over Dulcinea changes the emphasis from the parody of chivalric romance as such, to the development of character. The protagonists are more firmly locked into their relationship, for Don Quixote's overriding concern will be to disenchant his lady, whereas Sancho will do his best to avoid being found out, while at the same time trying to advance the career of his master so that he might eventually gain the promised island. At the same time, this greater emphasis on character begins to uncover new areas of literary interest, such as the emotions and inner life of the main characters. Nowhere is this more evident than in the amazing episode when Don Quixote descends into the Cave of Montesinos (Chapters 22 and 23).

Caves have long been represented in literary tradition as magical places which afford access to some supernatural dimension; they are associated, too, with the mythical theme of the descent into the underworld, and when Don Quixote is lowered into the Cave of Montesinos he becomes an Orphic figure seeking to release his chimerical Eurydice from the Hades into which Sancho's lie had cast her. Indeed, the episode provides an insight into the knight's distress at his alienation from the world of chivalry. A modern reader might even see in it a representation of Quixote's unconscious mind (Freud was a great admirer of Cervantes's work), for the knight's account of what he saw inside the cave appears to be a dream which comically mixes elements of romance with instances of crude realism, suggesting both delusions of grandeur and fears of inadequacy. Don Quixote describes how he fell into a deep sleep inside the cave and then awoke to encounter Montesinos and other famous personages from the Spanish romance tradition, all of them having been enchanted by Merlin. He also claims to have seen Dulcinea herself in her enchanted state as an ugly peasant, and to have been approached by one of her maidservants, who asked to pawn a petticoat for six *reales* because the lady Dulcinea was 'in great need' (II.23.646). Don Quixote, alas, has only four *reales* to offer his lady but he promises never to rest until he is able to disenchant her. Montesinos then assures him that he will one day disenchant Dulcinea, as well as all the other characters in the cave, and this prophecy boosts the knight's morale and enables him to recover a degree of self-belief.

Sancho, however, is not convinced that his master's experience was not, in fact, a dream or a fantasy, so the knight will on various occasions attempt to verify his account in order to refute Sancho's persistent scepticism about it. Time and again, he will look for signs that Providence will favour him, but he is never given an unequivocal sign. When an adventure on a boat in the River Ebro ends in failure yet again, he is utterly despondent: 'May God send a remedy; for everything in this world is trickery, stage machinery, every part of it working against every other part. I have done all I can' (II.29.687).

This low point in Don Quixote's fortunes is followed by an apparent upturn when he and Sancho are given an astonishing reception at the palace of a genuine duke and duchess. Hailed as 'the crème de la crème of knight errantry', Don Quixote is delighted at being 'treated in the same way as he'd read that such knights used to be treated in centuries past' (II.31.693). The truth, of course, is that the duke and duchess have read Part 1 and wish to have some sport at the expense of the knight and his amusing squire by exploiting the madman's obsession with chivalry.

Of the various tricks the duke and duchess play on the unsuspecting duo, the most destructive is the one in which a servant disguised as Merlin declares that Dulcinea will be released from her spell if Sancho whips himself 3,300 times on his backside. It is a totally absurd remedy, of course, but it makes the madman critically dependent on his servant for the one thing that matters most to him – the disenchantment of his lady. Another of the duke's jokes is to award Sancho the governorship of the island of Barataria. This promotion feeds Sancho's will to power, and, to everyone's surprise, the peasant proves a wise and capable governor. As far as Don Quixote is concerned, however, the duke's gift to Sancho fatally weakens his authority, given that it was the promise of an island that had formed the basis of his feudal relationship with his squire. What should have been a high point in his career as a knight errant appears to have come to nothing much after all, and he attributes this failure to the fact that wicked enchanters have put a spell on his lady Dulcinea. In Chapter 60, Don Quixote becomes so frustrated with Sancho's reluctance to apply Merlin's remedy that he tries to whip the squire himself. Sancho reacts by wrestling his master to the ground and placing his knee on his chest to hold him down. The knight is horrified by this effrontery: '"What, you traitor? You defy your own natural lord? You raise your hand against the man who feeds you?"' But Sancho remains defiant: '"I depose no king, I impose no king", responded Sancho, "but I'll help myself, for I'm my own lord".'[6] Amazingly, Don Quixote yields to Sancho and promises never to lay hands on him again.

Don Quixote's defeat by Sancho represents the climax of the squire's rise to power in Part II – here at last the peasant achieves complete dominance over his mad master, who must thenceforth accept his impotence to determine his own destiny. As the knight sinks ever deeper into gloom, Cervantes will not flinch from drawing out the awful consequences of his defeat. In Chapter 69, Quixote falls to his knees before the entire ducal court and begs Sancho yet again to press on with the disenchantment of Dulcinea. Sancho still refuses to humour the wretched madman in his desperate plight, and in Chapter 71, we witness the final triumph of picaresque values over those of chivalric romance when Don Quixote offers to pay Sancho to whip himself, and the squire is all too willing to negotiate a price. Don Quixote is abject in his gratitude, so abject indeed that he suggests that not only he, but Dulcinea too, will serve Sancho for the rest of their days. Yet, heartless even now, Sancho goes off into a wood and, rather than whip himself, as he had promised his master, he whips trees instead.

Cervantes was not unaware of the wider political dimension of the situation he contrived to bring about towards the end of Part II. Sancho's assertion: 'I'll help myself, for I'm my own lord', is a deliberate rejection of the traditional basis of authority and status, and his readiness to put a price on the disenchantment of Dulcinea converts the feudal bond between master and servant into a mere cash nexus. The disintegration of this central relationship portends the emergence of a world that Cervantes himself must have imagined with disquiet, if not with dread: a world in which the God-given hierarchy and the bonds of honour and deference that sustain it – the world reflected in chivalric romance – might be replaced by self-interest and individual freedom, the values of the picaresque anti-hero. Cervantes may well have started out with the purely literary aim of discrediting the *libros de caballerías*, but, by a series of logical steps arising from the interaction of master and servant, he was led to undermine the principle of hierarchy that was a cornerstone of the ideology of his day.

## Authorship and authority

What we have in this late phase of the *Quixote* is, indeed, a general crisis of authority. We have seen how the mad knight's authority as Sancho's 'natural lord' is challenged and violently rejected by the squire's picaresque ambition. But, analogously, and at about the same time, Cervantes's own literary authority was assailed by a rival author. Towards the middle of 1614, when he had not yet finished Part II, another sequel to *Don Quixote* Part I was published by a writer using the *nom de plume* Alonso Fernández de Avellaneda. Cervantes's anger at being usurped as the creator of the mad knight is unmistakable, and for the rest of his own Part II he would make disparaging references to his rival. But his response went beyond mere insult – he invented a number of ingenious devices to discredit Avellaneda. For instance, at an inn on the way to Zaragoza, Don Quixote overhears two gentlemen talking about a Second Part in which the knight renounces his love for Dulcinea. The 'true' Don Quixote declares that to be an impossibility, and then decides to prove his autonomy from Avellaneda's version by changing his plan to visit Zaragoza – where Avellaneda's 'false' knight had gone – and visit Barcelona instead. On their way back from Barcelona, Quixote and Sancho will come across Don Álvaro Tarfe, a character from Avellaneda's novel, who will acknowledge the 'authenticity' of Cervantes's Don Quixote, even signing a legal document to that effect.

These literary tricks, one might say, are worthy of a modernist or even a postmodernist, but they are not merely playful in Cervantes's case, for in a marketplace where intellectual property was not protected by copyright, he had to find the means to discredit the rival who threatened to rob him of his most successful creation. And, in this extremity, all he had to show for himself was his creative genius, which he could scarcely bring himself to trust the reader to recognise. The carefree, self-confident author of Part I now turned into a jealous proprietor, furiously trying to prevent a usurper from stealing his ideas. In this respect, Cervantes's changing authorial role can be seen in his use of Cide Hamete Benengeli, who had started out as a breezy parody of the chronicler-magician of the chivalric romances but who is latterly converted into a mouthpiece for a defensive Cervantes, desperate to win the reader's approval for his own Don Quixote. So much so, that at the very end of the novel, Cervantes has Cide Hamete declare:

> For me alone was Don Quixote born, and I for him; it was for him to act, for me to write; we two are as one, in spite of that false writer from Tordesillas who has had and may even again have the effrontery to write with such a coarse and clumsy ostrich quill about my valiant knight's deeds, because this is not a burden for his shoulders or a subject for his torpid wit. (II.74.981)

Avellaneda's plagiarism forced Cervantes to come to terms with the risks and complexities of modern authorship. In the Prologue to Part I Cervantes had renounced whatever *auctoritas* he might have laid claim to, so when faced with the challenge of Avellaneda's sequel he could not appeal to higher authorities to endorse the value of his work; and lacking any institutional or doctrinal entitlement to legitimise his claim to Don Quixote, he had instead to rely on the judgement of his readers in order to repel Avellaneda's attack on his self-made authority as the inventor of Don Quixote and Sancho Panza.

In these fluid and treacherous conditions of authorial freedom, what reveals the essential difference between the two writers is the fact that Cervantes understood the value of his invention whereas Avellaneda did not. Avellaneda has Don Quixote forsake his love for Dulcinea, and then ends the knight's career in a madhouse. But Cervantes knew that Dulcinea was the embodiment of the knight's lunatic quest to rise above the common order of reality and achieve the overmastering glory described in the books. In his version, the knight remains mad until the very last chapter, when he falls ill and is then cured of his folly before dying, but what stands out ever more poignantly until that final scene is Don Quixote's integrity – his unwavering belief in the authority of the books of chivalry. This is precisely the belief that makes him mad, but it is also what makes him cleave to Dulcinea with a strange, transcendent zeal. Thus, even in defeat the 'real' Don Quixote will refuse to abjure his lady. Cast down to the ground by the Knight of the White Moon and with a lance pointed at his breast, he will insist: 'Dulcinea is the most beautiful woman in the world, and I am the most unfortunate knight in it, and it would not be right for my weakness to obscure that truth. Drive your lance home, sir knight, and take away my life, since you have taken away my honour' (II.64.928). The image of the fallen knight uttering these words from within his shuttered helmet captures the blind futility of his passion for this figment of his madness. Here, in its purest form, is the paradox that has proved so fascinating to the modern imagination: Don Quixote's heroism lies in his loyalty to ideas which render him a fool. And so, the general comic atmosphere of the book is finally distilled into a timeless tragic moment in which the hero is condemned to make a fool of himself with no hope even of knowing why.

Cervantes's masterpiece represents a transition from romance to the novel. The authors of medieval and Renaissance romances were essentially didactic in so far as they sought to interpret experience according to an authoritative and universal tradition. Cervantes, however, broke with that tradition and, thanks to his inspired handling of Don Quixote's madness, he arrived at a new manner of storytelling we have come to call 'the novel'. As Henry James famously observed, 'a novel is in its broader definition a personal, a direct impression of life' whose 'intensity' and 'value' depend on the 'freedom to feel and say'.[7] Modern writers are free to create fiction on their own terms, free to express their sense of the world in the loose, open genre of the novel. According to Henry James, 'there is no limit' to 'possible experiments, efforts, discoveries, successes',[8] but in that unpredictable struggle to give form to their fictions, novelists are following, however distantly, in the footsteps of Cervantes, the writer who first risked that lonely adventure.

## Note on editions/translations

For the complete works, see *Obras completas de Miguel de Cervantes Saavedra*, ed. R. Schevill and A. Bonilla (Madrid: Gráficas Reunidas, 1914–41). The most complete critical edition of *Don Quixote* is *Don Quijote de la Mancha*, ed. Francisco Rico, 2 vols. (Barcelona: Galaxia Gutenberg, Centro para la Edición de los Clásicos Españoles, 2005). For the *Novelas ejemplares* see *Novelas ejemplares*, ed. Jorge García López (Barcelona: Crítica, 2003).

Reliable modern translations of *Don Quixote* include John Rutherford (Harmondsworth; Penguin, 2000) and Edith Grossman (New York: Ecco/HarperCollins, 2003). For the *Novelas ejemplares* see *Exemplary Stories*, trans. Lesley Lipson (Oxford University Press, 1998) and *Cervantes: The Complete Exemplary Novels*, ed. Barry Ife and Jonathan Thacker (Oxford: Aris and Phillips, 2011).

## Notes

1 BBC News, 7 May 2002.
2 'Introduction', in Miguel de Cervantes, *Don Quixote*, trans. Edith Grossman (New York: Ecco/HarperCollins, 2003), p. xxii.
3 Unless otherwise indicated, all quotations are from Miguel de Cervantes, *Don Quixote*, trans. John Rutherford (Harmondsworth: Penguin, 2000). I include them in parenthesis in my text, referring to Parts I or II, followed by the chapter and page numbers, e.g. (II.20.154).
4 'Afterword', in Milan Kundera, *The Book of Laughter and Forgetting* (Harmondsworth: Penguin, 1983), p. 237.
5 Cervantes, *Don Quixote*, trans. Edith Grossman, p. 3.
6 Cervantes, *Don Quixote*, trans. Edith Grossman, p. 851.
7 'The Art of Fiction', in Henry James, *The House of Fiction: Essays on the Novel*, ed. Leon Edel (London: Hart-Davis, 1957), p. 29.
8 *Ibid.*

## Further reading

Ardila, J. A. G., ed., *The Cervantean Heritage: Reception and Influence of Cervantes in Britain* (London: Legenda, 2009)

Bloom, Harold, ed., *Miguel de Cervantes*, Modern Critical Views (Philadelphia: Chelsea House, 2005)

Borges, J. L., 'Partial Magic in the *Quixote*' in *Labyrinths: Selected Stories and Other Writings* (Harmondsworth: Penguin, 1970), pp. 228–31.

Cascardi, A. J., ed., *The Cambridge Companion to Cervantes* (Cambridge University Press, 2002)

Cervantes, Miguel de, *Exemplary Stories*, trans. L. Lipson (Oxford University Press, 1998)

Close, A. J., *The Romantic Approach to Don Quixote* (Cambridge University Press, 1978)

Cruz, A. J. and C. B. Johnson, eds., *Cervantes and His Postmodern Constituencies, Hispanic Issues*, 17 (New York: Garland, 1999)

Dunn, P. N., *Spanish Picaresque Fiction: A New Literary History* (Ithaca, NY: Cornell University Press, 1993)

El Saffar, Ruth, ed., *Critical Essays on Cervantes* (Boston: G. K. Hall, 1986)

Fernández-Morera, D. and M. Hanke, eds., *Cervantes in the English-Speaking World* (Kassel: Reichenberger, 2005)

González Echevarría, Roberto, ed., *Cervantes' Don Quixote: A Casebook* (Oxford University Press, 2005)

Haley, G., 'The Narrator in *Don Quijote*: Maese Pedro's Puppet Show', *Modern Language Notes*, 80 (1965), 146–65

Nelson Jr, L., ed., *Cervantes: A Collection of Critical Essays* (Englewood Cliffs, NJ: Prentice-Hall, 1969)

Paulson, Ronald, *Don Quixote in England: The Aesthetics of Laughter* (Baltimore: The Johns Hopkins University Press, 1998)

Riley, E. C., *Cervantes's Theory of the Novel* (Oxford: Clarendon Press, 1962)
*Don Quixote* (London: Allen and Unwin, 1986)

Robert, M., *The Old and the New: From Quixote to Kafka*, trans. C. Cosman (Berkeley: University of California Press, 1977)

Welsh, A., *Reflections on the Hero as Quixote* (Princeton University Press, 1981)

Williamson, Edwin, 'Challenging the Hierarchies: The Interplay of Romance and the Picaresque in *La ilustre fregona*', *Bulletin of Spanish Studies*, 81 (2004), 655–74

*The Half-Way House of Fiction: 'Don Quixote' and Arthurian Romance* (Oxford: Clarendon Press, 1984)

'The Power-Struggle between Don Quixote and Sancho: Four Crises in the Development of the Narrative', *Bulletin of Spanish Studies*, 84 (2007), 837–58

ed., *Cervantes and the Modernists: The Question of Influence* (London: Tamesis, 1994)

# 2

CYNTHIA WALL

# Daniel Defoe (1660–1731): Journalism, myth and verisimilitude

> I discover'd a Locker with Drawers in it, in one of which I found two or three Razors, and one Pair of large Sizzers, with some ten or a Dozen of good Knives and Forks; in another I found about Thirty six Pounds value in Money, some *European* Coin, some *Brasil*, some Pieces of Eight, Some Gold, some Silver.
>
> I smil'd to my self at the Sight of this Money, O Drug! Said I aloud, what art thou good for ... However, upon Second Thoughts, I took it away, ... wrapping all this in a Piece of Canvas.[1]

Daniel Defoe was responsible for one of the world's greatest myths: Robinson Crusoe, shipwrecked on a desert island for twenty-eight years. Published in 1719, *The Life, and Strange Surprizing Adventures of Robinson Crusoe* had gone through 196 English editions by the end of the nineteenth century, along with multiple translations into French, German, Dutch, Italian, Swedish, Hebrew, Armenian, Danish, Turkish, Hungarian, Bengali, Polish, Arabic, Estonian, Maltese, Coptic, Welsh, Persian and even Ancient Greek.[2] Then there were the imitations, abridgements and adaptations – what in Germany and France was called the *Robinsonade*. August Kippenberg has referred to 'Defoes allbekanntes Werk', which has exerted 'as extraordinary an influence on world literature as any book'.[3] Yet this larger-than-life, transcontinental myth (in European coin) was created from the smallest, most ordinary bits of life, from the details pebbling about our shoes – scissors, knives and forks, a piece of canvas. Before he began his novelistic career, Defoe had been a journalist, merchant, economist and spy, and from these ongoing and intersecting careers he developed both a sweeping and a local sense of history, an attention to 'human-interest' stories, an impressive knowledge of geography and a taste for the realistic tiny detail.

Defoe was born in London in 1660 into a family of tallow chandlers. As a Dissenter from the Church of England, he was educated outside the traditional schools, learning astronomy, geography and modern languages instead of the usual Latin and Greek. He married Mary Tuffley in 1684, who had a dowry of £3,700 (about £320,000 or $500,000 today); they had seven children. Defoe was imprisoned several times for bankruptcy, going through that dowry to set up various businesses – a pantile factory, a hosiery, a civet-cat perfumery. As a merchant and later a spy for the (effectively) first prime minister Robert Harley, Defoe travelled widely throughout England, Scotland and Europe. During his first prison term he wrote *An Essay Upon Projects* (published 1697) – his first of many how-to books, outlining projects for toll roads, a national bank, an academy for women, new kinds of hospitals and life and health insurance. He published satirical poems (such as *The True-Born Englishman* in 1701, defending the Dutch-born William III and suggesting that in fact there was no such thing as a true-born Englishman – the country was a mongrel nation) and political pamphlets (posing as 'Andrew Moreton,' he was instrumental in forging the union between England and Scotland in 1707 that created Great Britain). For much of his life he contributed to or edited various newspapers. He wrote conduct books for family life (*The Family Instructor* in 1715 and *Conjugal Lewdness* in 1727) and a charming manual for beginning tradesmen (*The Complete English Tradesman*, 1725), all of which feature realistic characters, colloquial dialogue and vivid settings. Throw in some travel narratives (*A Tour thro' the whole Island of Great Britain*, 1724–6), a history of pirates (1724), *The Political History of the Devil* (1726), *An Essay on the History and Reality of Apparitions* (1727), *A Plan of the English Commerce* (1730), not to mention hundreds of other attributed works, and we have a sense of an astonishing range of interest and knowledge. As Paula Backscheider recognises: 'Somehow the world seemed small to him; he easily grasped continents, distances, products, and the state of their commercial advancement. Space and time presented no obstacles.'[4]

Defoe's novels are concentrated in a small period, beginning in 1719 (when Defoe was fifty-nine) with the publication of *Robinson Crusoe* – immediately popular, going through four editions before its first sequel, *Farther Adventures of Robinson Crusoe*, appeared later in the year. Then came *Memoirs of a Cavalier, Captain Singleton* and the *Serious Reflections ... of Robinson Crusoe* (1720), *The Fortunes and Misfortunes of the Famous Moll Flanders, A Journal of the Plague Year* and *Colonel Jack* (1722), and *The Fortunate Mistress* (or *Roxana*), 1724. All his novels, to some extent, reflect his experience as journalist, merchant, traveller, spy: they feature global travel, play with the intersections of fact and fiction, relish the grainy texture of everyday life, create a verisimilitude of time and space (criteria for the 'realist' novel, according to Ian Watt), inhabit different psychological interiors and reproduce the circular, circuitous patterns of human thought and behaviour. And the legacy of Defoe as a novelist is profound. He has come to be seen not just as the rather surprising parent of one of the world's great myths, but also as a prolific, self-conscious and powerful parent of a dominant literary form and a national literary identity.

### Journalism and national identity: *The Storm* and the *Review*

In late 1703, a devastating storm blasted through southern England, with hurricane-level winds of 120 m.p.h., destroying thousands of trees, piling up ships in the English Channel, tearing roofs off houses and buildings (including Westminster Abbey) and killing somewhere between 8000 and 15,000 people.[5] It was the first weather event to be reported on a national scale, with broadsides issued detailing damages. Defoe prepared his own full-length account, published in July 1704: *The Storm: Or, a Collection of the most Remarkable Casualties and Disasters Which happen'd in the Late Dreadful Tempest, Both by Sea and Land* (1704).[6] In this work, he begins to balance the 'proper Duty of an Historian' with the 'great many Stories, which may in their own nature seem incredible', that a historian must tell (*Storm*, Preface). Although Defoe scholars may debate the term 'journalist' as applied to Defoe, modern journalists recognise in the author of *The Storm* and the *Review* the creator of 'a journalistic style that lasted' in his 'excellent, clear, uncluttered, reporterly English full of relatively short sentences of plain description'.[7] Newspapers of a sort had been around in England since the *London Gazette* was established by the government as an official news organ in 1666; the lapse in 1695 of the pre-censoring 1662 Licensing Act set off an 'anarchic' proliferation of print that included wildly new forms of news and opinion reporting.[8] As his first major prose work, *The Storm* sets up a template for Defoe's writerly style and thematic interests: brief clear prose, a nose for narrative, an interest in ordinary people and ordinary circumstances, an often metatextual connection with the reader through direct or implicit address, and an interest in comparing and connecting distant and local, past and present.

*The Storm* gathers together all viewpoints, from the global to the bird's eye to the eyewitness. 'We feel nothing here of the Hurricanes of *Barbadoes*, the North-Wests of *New England* and *Virginia*, the terrible Gusts of the *Levant*, or the frequent Tempests of the *North Cape*', he begins (*Storm*, 39). But then he brings us blinking into the morning: 'Indeed the City was a strange Spectacle, the Morning after the Storm, as soon as the People could put their Heads out of Doors: though I believe, every Body expected the Destruction was bad enough; yet I question very much, if any Body believed the Hundredth Part of what they saw' (*Storm*, 57). And then he looks into houses, inns, taverns, churches, shops:

> A Carpenter in *White-Cross-street* was kill'd ... by a Stack of Chimneys of the *Swan* Tavern; which fell into his House: it was reported, That his Wife earnestly desir'd him not to go to Bed; and had prevailed upon him to sit up till near two a Clock, but then finding himself very heavy, he would go to Bed against all his Wife's Intreaties; after which ... [he] was kill'd in his Bed: and his Wife, who would not go to Bed, escap'd. (*Storm*, 59)

To get the point of view of the countryside, Defoe advertised in the *London Gazette* (13–16 December 1703) and interpolated the responses verbatim:

> *From* Kingstone-upon-Thames, *the following Letter is very particular, and the truth of it may be depended upon.*
> SIR,
> I Have inform'd my self of the following matters; here was blown down a Stack of Chimneys of Mrs. *Copper*, Widow, which fell on the Bed, on which she lay; but she being just got up, and gone down, she received no harm on her Body: ... Here was a new Brick Malt-House of one Mr. *Francis Best* blown down, had not been built above two Years, blown off at the second Floor; besides many Barns, and out Houses; ... and Multitudes of Trees, in particular. 11 Elms of one Mr. *John Bowles*, Shooe-maker: ... One *Walter Kent*, Esq; had about 20 Rod of new Brick-wall of his Garden blown down: ... Also Mr. *Blitha*, Merchant, had all his Walling blown down, and other extraordinary Losses. These are the most considerable Damages done here,
> *Your humble Servant,*<br>C. Castleman. (*Storm*, 129)

This one letter offers a cross-section of an entire village, widows, children, tradesmen, gentlemen; and in its particularity of detail and unembarrassed repetition, is a real-life slice of what Defoe would rather magically turn into realistic fiction. Defoe combines vignettes with documents, numbers with narratives. For the historian, the journalist, the novelist – the narrative should be true(ish), and the narrative must be interesting.

On 19 February 1704, after the Great Storm but before *The Storm*, Defoe issued the first of a long-running political periodical, the *Weekly Review of the Affairs of France* (later *A Review of the State of the British Nation*). Its purpose is to set 'the Affairs of *Europe* in a Clear Light, and to prevent the various uncertain Accounts, and the Partial Reflections of our Street-Scriblers'.[9] With the *Review*, Defoe begins a more-or-less lifelong agenda to create and define a national identity, through historical and geographic comparisons, idealised projections and sheer badgering.

The *Review* begins when England is at war with the French, and the first issue is designed to correct the national prejudice against them as an ultimately defensive measure: 'OUR Ancient *English* Histories have always spoken of the *French* with a great deal of Contempt, and the *English* Nation have been apt enough to have very mean Thoughts of them from Tradition, as an Effeminate Nation' (*Review* 1.7, 19 February 1704). Well, they're not, he argues. The British must recognise French strength, but the British must also control French strength. In a sense, Defoe defines not just Britain, but a political Europe in a 'ballance of Power' that is 'a Keeping all the Powers of *Europe* in such a Posture, so leagued and so separated, so jointed and so disjointed, as that no one or no united Interest may be able to subject the rest' (*Review* 6.26, 19 April 1709).

The English character in particular for Defoe is defined against its neighbours' – and not always to the good. He notes that 'of all the Nations now at War, *England* has the fewest of her Nobility and Gentry in the Feild [*sic*], I mean compared to the great Number of Gentlemen we have in this Nation'; the reason is a national contempt for learning and a national preference for staying at home. In the same passage, the Scots, on the other hand, teach their children the arts and sciences before they train them militarily:

> And let no Man wonder, why the *Scots* Nobility and Gentry obtain so much Reputation abroad, at the same time that we endeavour to put so much Contempt upon them at home. The Reason is plain – they have the true liberal Education of a Gentleman, they are bred to Letters first, and then to Arms; the first teaches them to behave, inspires them with generous Principles, and true Notions of Honour ... – And why have we so many People misbehave in the World, Especially at Sea? The Case is plain, they are bred *Boors*, empty and swinish Sots and Fops, and they are not capable of having a right Sence of Honour in the World. (*Review* 5.407, 20 November 1708)

In the same passage, the effects of English contempt for an education that teaches about other countries, other cultures, other languages, other arts and other sciences, is having 'the worst Name among the Nations of *Europe* for Behaviour to Strangers', and Defoe recounts a particularly horrifying example of a Spanish captain who,

> having been shipwreck'd somewhere on the Coast of *England*, the People, instead of saving him and his Ship, came off and robb'd him, tore the Ship almost to pieces, and left him and his Men to swim a-shoar for their Lives, while they plunder'd the Cargoe – Upon which he and his whole Crew had sworn never to help an *English* Man in whatever Distress he should find them, whether at Sea or on Shoar. (*Review* 6.223, 11 August 1709)

Defoe argues for global reciprocity on the kinder side: 'if you will be clothed and fed when you may be found naked and starv'd abroad ... begin at home and show yourselves a Nation of Pity and Compassion to miserable Strangers, that others may show your distress'd Friends the same Beneficence' (*Review* 6.223). The European balance of power should also reflect a balance of humanity.

## Myth and verisimilitude: *A Journal of the Plague Year*

IT was about the Beginning of *September* 1664, that I, among the Rest of my Neighbours, heard in ordinary Discourse, that the Plague was return'd again in *Holland*; for it had been very violent there, and particularly at *Amsterdam* and *Roterdam*, in the Year 1663, whither *they* say, it was brought, some said from *Italy*, others from the *Levant* among some Goods, which were brought home by their Turkey Fleet; others said it was brought from *Candia*; others from *Cyprus*. It matter'd not, from whence it come; but all agreed, it was come into *Holland* again.

This opening paragraph of Defoe's fictional treatment of the Great Plague in London of 1665 (meant to waken the Londoners of 1722 to another imminent threat) encapsulates his novelistic magic: nothing, not even narrative, moves in a straight line, but wanders and buffets and reaches and returns. Human behaviour is shaped as much by what '*they* say' as by what *is*; facts need to be sorted from fictions, but often as not facts are grounded on fictions, and fiction, in the early eighteenth century, was only slowly coming to be seen as a possible representation of fact.

The status and legitimacy – not to mention the identity – of the novel was quite murky in the late seventeenth and early eighteenth centuries. For much of the eighteenth century, most fiction pretended to be based on historical fact, vociferous on its own authenticity in its title pages and prefatory remarks: Eliza Haywood published 'Secret Histories' in the 1720s; Richardson's *Pamela* (1740) is a series of transcribed letters which has 'its Foundation in TRUTH and NATURE'; Fielding's parody of *Pamela*, *Shamela* (1741) is based on 'exact Copies of authentick Papers delivered to the Editor'; *Tom Jones* (1749) is a *History*, Fanny Hill writes her *Memoirs* (1759); and Defoe's novels feature histories, lives and memorandums. Decades of Puritan investment in truth and reality militated against anything that smacked of misleading pretence. John Bunyan 'apologized' for his *Pilgrim's Progress* by pointing out that Jesus used parables to convey truths; religious allegory was allowed to tell a story; and anything else fictional worked hard to cover itself with fact. As J. Paul Hunter has noted:

Had there not been stories *pretending* to tell actual tales – and following distinctions that assumed an absolute difference between fact and fiction – there could not have been the novel as we have come to know it. And had not audiences not bought into – literally – publications that honored the distinction but bridged it anyway, there could not have been cultural space for something between fiction and fact.[10]

Defoe's *A Journal of the Plague Year* (1722) is just such an exercise in the blending of history and fiction, and the sorting of myth from truth. Its subtitle declares itself the 'OBSERVATIONS OR MEMORIALS, OF THE MOST REMARKABLE OCCURRENCES, AS WELL PUBLICK AS PRIVATE, WHICH HAPPENED IN LONDON DURING THE LAST GREAT VISITATION IN 1665, Written by a Citizen who continued all the while in *London*'.[11] The narrator is a saddler, H. F. (scholars speculate that Defoe got much of his anecdotal information from his uncle, Henry Foe), who decides to stay with his business and spends the plague year circling the streets, public spaces and burial pits in horrified fascination. He is a relentless empiricist, trying to anchor the amorphous horrors to some sort of graspable reality, combating myth and superstition with theory and numbers. He notes that the 'Apprehensions of the People, were ... strangely encreas'd by the Error of the Times; in which, I think, the People from what Principle I cannot imagine, were more addicted to Prophesies, and Astrological Conjurations, Dreams, and old Wives Tales, than ever they were before or since' (*Journal*, 22). Fear was as contagious as the disease and conjured up its own unreliable realities:

> In this narrow Passage stands a Man looking thro' between the Palisadoe's into the Burying Place ... and affirming, that he saw a Ghost walking upon such a Grave Stone there; he describ'd the Shape, the Posture, and the Movement of it so exactly, that it was the greatest Matter of Amazement to him in the World, that every Body did not see it as well as he. On a sudden he would cry, *There it is: Now it comes this Way*: Then, *'Tis turn'd back*; till at length he persuaded the People into so firm a Belief of it, that one fancied he saw it, and another fancied he saw it. (*Journal*, 25)

Quacks preyed on the superstitious: 'if but a grave Fellow in a Velvet Jacket, a Band, and a black Cloak, which was the Habit those Quack Conjurers generally went in, was but seen in the Streets, the People would follow them, in Crowds ... the midling People, and the working labouring Poor ... threw away their money in a most distracted Manner upon those Whymsies' (*Journal*, 28–9). Rumours were another swirling threat, terrifying people away from common-sense or at any rate institutional efforts at containment and control:

> We had at this Time a great many frightful Stories told us of Nurses and Watchmen, who looked after the dying People, *that is to say*, hir'd Nurses, who attended infected People, using them barbarously, starving them, smothering them, or by other wicked Means, hastening their End, *that is to*

*say*, murthering of them: And watchmen being set to guard Houses that were shut up, when there has been but one person left, and perhaps, that one lying sick that they have broke in and murthered that Body, and immediately thrown them out into the Dead-Cart! (*Journal*, 80–1)

The panicked people would lie about their condition, conceal the tokens of the plague, escape from their quarantined house, and spread the contagion of fear as well as of plague farther and faster.

H. F. counteracts this miasma of misunderstanding, misinformation and mistrust with documents and numbers and common sense. He undermines the stories of cruelty and murder on the part of the official nurses and watchers with a few suspicious distinguishing marks:

(1.) That wherever it was that we heard it, they always placed the Scene at the farther End of the Town ... In the next Place, of what Part soever you heard the Story, the Particulars were always the same, especially that of laying a wet double Clout on a dying Man's Face, and that of smothering a young Gentle-woman; so that it was apparent, at least to my Judgment, that there was more of tale than of Truth in those Things. (*Journal*, 83)

Urban myth, in fact. The Bills of Mortality – the aseptic numbers of burials in the parishes – also punctuate the text with hard-edged reality and regularity. In the beginning (of text and plague) they mark a rise in deaths, but not a rise in plague:

| From *Dec.* 27th to *Jan.* 3. | St. *Giles's* ----- 16 |
| | St. *Andrew's* -----17 ... |
| *Jan.* 30. to *Feb.* 7. | St. *Giles's* ----- 21 |
| | St. *Andrew's* -----23 |
| *Feb.* 7. to ---- 14. | St. *Giles's* ----- 24 |
| | whereof one of the Plague. (*Journal*, 5) |

By September, the total number of deaths throughout London had risen exponentially:

| From *August* the 22nd to the 29th | 7496 |
| To the 7th of *September* ---------- | 8252 |
| To the 12th ----- ----- ----- ----- | 7690 |
| To the 19th ----- ----- ----- ----- | 8297 |
| To the 26th ----- ----- ---------- | 6460 |
| | 38195 (*Journal*, 172) |

And yet, all the factual material does little to settle the fears of the public – or the unease of the reader. In fact, in Defoe's narrative hands, the cooling antidotes of arithmetic and printed orders push insistently against the horror and by their efforts – or failure – swell its suspense. 'Whereof one of the Plague', is a tiny detail at the beginning of what, in the reader's hands, is clearly a long narrative, a thick book of horrors – there is More to Come. 'One' already stands as a lone, foreboding, *misleading* figure hiding others. And indeed, the swollen numbers of September are themselves devious: 'This was a prodigious Number of itself, but if I should add the Reasons which I have to believe that this Account was deficient, and how deficient it was, you would with me, make no Scruple to believe that there died above ten Thousand a Week for all those Weeks, one Week with another' (*Journal*, 172). The numbers, meant by H.F. to moor his readers, are used by Defoe to unmoor us.

Verisimilitude, authenticity, realism – these are not simply provided by Defoe in the platter of numbers and documents, but also in the journalistic telling and the cumulative fiction. It is that attention to and evocation of the details of ordinary life that prompted one early nineteenth-century critic to declare that the *Journal* 'is the most lively Picture of Truth which ever proceeded from imagination: ... we cannot take it up, after a hundredth perusal, without yielding, before we have traversed twenty pages, to a full conviction that we are conversing with one who passed through and survived the horrors which he describes'.[12] The Picture of Truth emerges from the constellation of detail, sometimes compressed into a small moment that reverberates beyond its telling:

> Passing thro' *Token-House-Yard* in *Lothbury*, of a sudden a Casement violently opened just over my Head, and a Woman gave three frightful Skreetches, and then cry'd, *Oh! Death, Death, Death!* in a most inimitable Tone, and which struck me with Horror and a Chilness, in my very Blood. There was no Body to be seen in the whole Street, neither did any other Window open; for People had no Curiosity now in any Case; nor could any Body help one another; so I went on to pass into *Bell-Alley.* (*Journal*, 79)

The disembodied cry that stops the walker in his tracks, the resumption of motion when nothing is to be done, nothing more to be seen or heard, and the bookending of the isolated moment by the street signs of Token House Yard (the physical signs of the plague on the body included the small hard round blisters called 'tokens') and Bell Alley (what does that token betoken – for whom does that bell toll?), is an echoing example of how Defoe, like the man looking through the railings into Bishopsgate churchyard, makes us see (or hear) ghosts. By the height of the plague, the landscape itself is haunted: 'the great Streets within the City, such as *Leaden-hall-Street, Bishopgate-Street, Cornhill*, and even the *Exchange* it self, had Grass growing in them'

(*Journal*, 98), and 'whole Streets seem'd to be desolated and not to be shut up only, but to be emptied of their Inhabitants; Doors were left open, Windows stood shattering with the Wind in empty Houses, for want of People to shut them' (*Journal*, 164).

Defoe's earlier self-training in the journalistic attention to detail, individual stories, the process of documentation, the specificity of time and place, the wider contexts and implications of events, would be folded into all his novels, creating worlds of verisimilitude that in some cases would carry afterlives of myth. As the opening paragraph of the *Journal* shows, the stuff of life is marked by *this* date and *that* place, filled with what 'they say', and shaped by forces without and within.

## Europe in Defoe: *Roxana*

Defoe's travels as merchant, spy and journalist early familiarised him with the rest of Britain and much of Europe, and his lifelong interest in geography, maps, piracy and trade routes extended his intellectual, historical and imaginative reach around the world. All his novels feature some sort of European or transnational context: Robinson Crusoe comes from a German family (Kreutznaer), and after his island stay he retravels Europe. Both Moll Flanders and Colonel Jack are transported to and make their fortunes in Virginia; Jack wanders on to pursue various military and amorous adventures in France. *Memoirs of a Cavalier* (1720) is set during the reign of Gustavus Adolphus of Sweden, and the Cavalier from Shropshire fights battles in Vienna and Magdeburgh. *Captain Singleton* (1722) more or less reconvenes Europe on the high seas, as Portuguese, English, French, Dutch and Spanish ships meet, trade with and capture each other in the imperial enterprise. *A Journal of the Plague Year*, as we have seen, opens with an eye on the European reports of recurrence. And Defoe's last novel, *The Fortunate Mistress*, better known as *Roxana* (1724), features a naturalised French woman who lives variously in Paris, London, Germany, Italy and Holland.

The 'editor' announces in the Preface the usual Defovian truth claims: '*this* Story *differs from most of the Modern Performances of this Kind, tho' some of them have met with a very good Reception in the World*: ... Namely, *That the Foundation of This is laid in Truth* of Fact; *and so the Work is not a Story, but a History*'.[13] The story begins historically, as the narrator, eventually known as 'Roxana' for her famous exotic Turkish dance in London, recounts: 'I was born, *as my Friends told me*, at the City of POICTIERS, in the Province, or County of POICTOU, in *France*, from whence I was brought to *England* by my Parents, who fled for their Religion about the Year 1683, when the Protestants were Banish'd from *France* by the Cruelty of their Persecutors' (*Roxana*, 1). A good portion of the novel becomes travel narrative, as Roxana and her most illustrious conquest spend several years traversing Europe, during which she acquires, not just money and men, but dare I say a certain *je ne sais quoi* about handling that money and those men through her detailed, comparative observations.

When her second 'husband' (her first, the 'Brewer', ran away and hasn't been heard of since), the Jeweller, has to go to France for two months, Roxana decides to go with him, and narrates the journey along a realistically detailed space-time continuum: 'Things being thus concerted, we went away to *France*, arriv'd safe at *Calais*, and by easie Journeys, came in eight Days more to *Paris*, where we lodg'd in the House of an *English* Merchant of his Acquaintance, and was very courteously entertain'd' (*Roxana*, 50). Business goes well: 'I began to think we should take up our constant Residence there, which I was not very averse to it, being my Native Country, and I spoke the Language perfectly well; so we took a good House in *Paris*, and liv'd very well there' (*Roxana*, 51). But international affairs cut things short: a bill from Amsterdam needs cashing, and the Jeweller is robbed and killed on his way to Versailles to see the Prince of —. Said Prince sets eyes on *la Belle veuve de Poictou*, as she is soon known, and very soon after that they begin a nice little tryst, *à la française*, complete with 'Champaign' (*Roxana*, 62).

Roxana is quite happy to join the prince soon after in his travels to Italy. She points out that 'the History of our Journey, and Stay abroad ... would almost fill up a Volume of itself' (*Roxana*, 99), and she nearly *does* give us a little volume, from the evening spent in 'chearful Consultations about the Manner of our Travelling; the Equipage and Figure he shou'd go in; and in what Manner I shou'd go' (*Roxana*, 99), to negotiating the Alps on a horse litter carried by mules, to their arrival in Venice.

> We were near two year upon this *Grand Tour*, as it may be call'd, during most of which, I resided at *Rome* or at *Venice*, having only been twice at *Florence*, and once at *Naples*: I made some very diverting and useful Observations in all these Places; and particularly, of the conduct of the Ladies; for I had Opportunity to converse very much among them. (*Roxana*, 102)

Roxana is one of the few fictional (or for that matter, actual) females to go on the Grand Tour – the experiential finishing school for young English gentlemen who were sent to learn the languages, culture and customs of other countries, so that they were *not* 'bred *Boors*, empty and swinish Sots and Fops ... not capable of having a right Sence of Honour in the World' (*Review*, 5.407). Roxana learns Turkish from her female slave (as well as Turkish ways of dressing, dancing and singing, which would make her name and fame in London later on). She immerses herself in her new country, and fantasises about permanence: '[I] lov'd the Language, I read all the *Italian Books* I cou'd come at. I began to be so in Love with *Italy*, especially with *Naples* and *Venice*, that I cou'd have been very well satisfied to have sent for *Amy*, and have taken up my Residence there for Life' (*Roxana*, 102–3). Rome she does not like for its 'Swarms of Ecclesiasticks of all Kinds' and 'the scoundrell-Rabbles of the Common People ... [who] have an Air or sharping and couzening, quarrelling and scolding, upon their general Behaviour' (*Roxana*, 103). She repeats she has 'no-Mind to write the History of [her] Travels' – at least, 'not now' (*Roxana*, 103), but two pages later she is still narrating their return from Venice to Turin via Milan, back over the Alps, meeting the coaches between Chambéry and Lyon, and concludes: 'and so, by easie Journeys, we arriv'd safely at *Paris*, having been absent about two Years, wanting about eleven Days, as above' (*Roxana*, 105).

This liaison with the prince and their European travel narrative occupies a good quarter of the novel; the last quarter is dominated by Roxana's courtship and eventual marriage with the Dutch merchant (whom she originally met in Paris), and ends in The Hague, where, as in many parts of the world, money could buy titles. (England is not mentioned, but of course that venerable practice would have been quite visible to English readers as a subtextual bump.) And here, indeed, the merchant buys Roxana her title and her general *raison d'être*: 'I was now in the height of my Glory and Prosperity, and I was call'd the *Countess de* -----; for I had obtain'd that unlook'd for, which I secretly aim'd at, and was really the main Reason of my coming Abroad' (*Roxana*, 261–2). Most critical emphasis fastens here on the darker questions tormenting Roxana: did her maid Amy kill her stalker daughter Susan? Is Roxana's penitence any more or less convincing than Moll's? What tragedy descended on her after this, to which she alludes darkly in her final sentences? But for the purposes of this volume, Roxana carries interest as an international figure, every moment of whose life is shaped by European contexts: born in France, raised in England, courtesaned in Paris, named and renowned for her Turkish dance in London, married to a Dutchman, completing her fortunes and covering her tracks in Holland. Roxana is a woman of the world.

## Defoe in Europe: *Robinson Crusoe*

And Robinson Crusoe is *the* man of the world, both within the text and because of it. He was born, he says, in 1632 to the Bremen family Kreutznaer, 'but by the usual Corruption of Words in *England*, we are now called, nay we call our selves, and write our Name *Crusoe*' (*Crusoe*, 3). Before the shipwreck flung him on the island off Oroonoko, Crusoe defined himself by European contexts and travels. His older brother was killed near Dunkirk by the Spanish, and young Robinson wanted nothing more than to leave England in a ship for other lands. He becomes a trader off the coast of Guinea in Africa; his ship is captured by a Turkish rover and taken into the Moroccan port of Sallee, where he is made a slave; when he and fellow slave Xury escape in their master's boat, Crusoe hunts the African waters for a European ship: 'I knew that all the Ships from *Europe*, which sail'd either to the Coast of *Guiney*, or to *Brasil*, or to the *East-Indies*, made this *Cape* or those *Islands* ... I must meet with some Ship, or must perish' (*Crusoe*, 29). A Portuguese ship finally finds them:

> They ask'd me what I was, in *Portuguese*, and in *Spanish*, and in *French*, but I understood none of them; but at last a *Scots* Sailor who was on board, call'd to me, and I answer'd him, and told him I was an *Englishman*, that I had made my escape out of Slavery from the *Moors* at *Sallee*; then they bad me come on board, and very kindly took me in, and all my Goods. (*Crusoe*, 32–3)

Eventually, he becomes a planter in Brazil and makes his fortune.

The time after his twenty-eight years on the island is also trans-European, trans-global. He and Friday rescue the Spanish prisoners from the cannibals and set up a colony with the rest of the Spanish crew; he returns to England, then voyages back to Brazil and Lisbon to re-collect the massed pieces of his fortune. He then travels with Friday through Spain and France during 'the severest Winter all over *Europe* that had been known in the Memory of Man' (*Crusoe*, 290), where Friday 'teaches' a bear to 'dance' in the tree, then kills it. They fight off a pack of wolves; arrive in Toulouse; travel on to Paris, Calais, Dover; back again to Brazil; back again to the island, now run by the Spaniards; and back once more to Brazil. (In the sequel to *Robinson Crusoe*, the *Farther Adventures*, Crusoe explores east to Madagascar, the Persian Gulf, the Indian Ocean, then overland across China and Tartary to Archangel.) The island, then, floats textually as well as literally in a sea bounded by the sites of travel, a long empty stillness at the centre of frenetic travel.

The middle of the book, the years on the island, are of course the mythic part, the instant image conjured by the name 'Robinson Crusoe'. Critics have attributed numerous reasons for the myth. Jean-Jacques Rousseau summarised: 'Robinson Crusoe on his island, alone, deprived of the help of his fellows and of all artificial aids, yet providing for his own support, for his own safety and even achieving a sort of well-being – this is a matter of interest for any age.'[14] Coleridge found Defoe's artful simplicity, in the epigraph that opens this essay ('O Drug! Said I aloud, what art thou good for ... However, upon Second

Thoughts, I took it away'), to be 'worthy of Shakespeare; ... the simple semi-colon after it, the instant passing on without the least pause of reflex consciousness is more exquisite and masterlike than the touch itself'.[15] David Blewett argues that the English image of Crusoe was consistently of an 'ordinary man in an extraordinary situation' (whether he was the romantic solitary, the practical manager or the apostle of Victorian progress), while French illustration produced 'a tradition of Crusoe as a superman, the powerful figure dominating both his physical environment and Friday'. Blewett also marks how the nature of the myth can change over time or across countries, from 'the depiction of an idealized, sometimes even idyllic, life of successful problem-solving' to a more sinister, satirical reading of Crusoe's emotional and imperial landscapes.[16] Karl Marx found in Crusoe's labours on the island and his relations with 'the objects that form this wealth of his own creation ... all that is essential to the determination of value'.[17] Martin Green insists that *Robinson Crusoe* is simply the most important of the adventure tales that articulated 'the expansive imperialist thrust of the white race, the nations of Europe, which started around 1600 and which has not ended yet', citing the forty German *Robinsonaden* that appeared between 1722 and 1769, and the many English adaptations for boys in the nineteenth century. He also paraphrases James Joyce, who argued that 'Crusoe's personal dourness and apathy are just what make him a convincing hero of British imperialism'.[18]

Whatever the source or nature of the myth, the status of Crusoe *as* myth is unquestioned. As Philip Gove notes, '*Robinson Crusoe* was hardly allowed to dry before it was imitated ... [Throughout Europe] writers of fiction ... soon tried to deflect some of its popularity toward their own writing.'[19] As Pat Rogers notes, 'Signs of this influence appear in the very titles, from *Der französische Robinson* (and so with every other nationality) in the 1720s to La Bédollière's *Dernier Robinson* (1860) and Montgomery Gibb's *Six Hundred Robinson Crusoes* (1877).'[20] Green tracks yet another path of influence through the adventure tale more generally (with a few exceptions – several early German versions centered on sturdy women castaways, for example): *Émile* (1762), *Robinson der Jüngere* (1779), *Der Schwizerische Robinson* (1812), *Masterman Ready* (1841), *The Crater* (1847), *The Coral Island* (1858), *L'Île mystérieuse* (1874), *Treasure Island* (1883), *Peter Pan* (1904), *Le Solitaire du Pacifique* (1922), *Lord of the Flies* (1954), *Vendredi, ou Les limbes du Pacifique* (1967).[21] None of Defoe's other works came anywhere close to such a legacy of influence.[22]

And yet *Robinson Crusoe*, for all its global positioning, is largely a small tale, constrained in a small space and preoccupied with small things – raisins, the baking of bread, the dilemmas of an umbrella and in Virginia

Woolf's words, 'a large earthenware pot'.[23] And it's a myth that's hardly *sui generis*. Like all of Defoe's other works of fiction, this one is founded on fact. In 1713, Richard Steele published an account of the castaway Alexander Selkirk in *The Englishman* (no. 26, Tuesday 1 December to Thursday 3 December 1713). His island was populated by goats, cats and rats; he tamed the goats and cats; the cats ate the rats. He learned to love turtle flesh. He decorated his dwelling and called it his Bower. He made clothes of goatskin and learned to live the contemplative life for four years and four months. But *Robinson Crusoe* also has fictional antecedents. Desert islands and dramatic shipwrecks are very old themes in French prose fiction, for example. As Geoffrey Atkinson points out, the sentimental novel *Les Amours de Clidamant et de Marilinde* (1603) features a desert island episode, the satirical *L'Île des hermaphrodites* (1605) a shipwreck. 'Accounts of such adventures in the "true voyage" literature of the first half of the 17th century in France are numerous' and '*Robinson Crusoe* was considered by one French critic in 1719 to be a novel in the style of *Jacques Sadeur* (1676) and of the *Histoire des Sévarambes* (1677–1679).'[24] A number of writers have traced its origins in the picaresque and the spiritual autobiography.[25] The context of *Robinson Crusoe* was European as well as English; its influence, in turn, was global. And it may well be that the greatness of the myth lies in part in the loving smallness of its detail – because, as Virginia Woolf asks as she shuts the book, 'is there any reason why the perspective that a plain earthenware pot exacts should not satisfy us as completely, once we grasp it, as man himself in all his sublimity standing against a background of broken mountains and tumbling oceans with stars flaming in the sky?'[26]

## Note on editions

The standard scholarly edition is *The Novels of Daniel Defoe*, 10 vols., (London: Pickering and Chatto, 2007) under the general editorship of P. N. Furbank and W. R. Owens. Good paperback editions, with introductions and notes, are available from Norton, Oxford World's Classics and Penguin.

### Notes

1 Daniel Defoe, *The Life, and Strange Surprizing Adventures of Robinson Crusoe, of York, Mariner* (1719), ed. J. Donald Crowley (Oxford University Press, 1981), p. 57.
2 See Pat Rogers, ed., *Defoe: The Critical Heritage* (London/Boston: Routledge & Kegan Paul, 1972), pp. 23–4.

3 August Kippenberg, *Robinson in Deutschland 1731–43* (Hanover, 1892). Quoted in Rogers, ed., *Critical Heritage*, p. 23.

4 Paula R. Backscheider, 'Defoe: The Man in the Works', in *The Cambridge Companion to Daniel Defoe*, ed. John Richetti (Cambridge University Press, 2008), pp. 5–24 (19).

5 For a meteorologist's account of the Great Storm, see Ian Currie, editor of the *BBC Weather Eye Magazine*, 'The great tempest of 26 November 1703', at: www.bbc.co.uk/weather/features/understanding/1703_storm.shtml

6 Daniel Defoe, *The Storm* (1704), ed. Richard Hamblyn (London: Penguin, 2005). Subsequent page references to this edition are given in parenthesis in the text.

7 Andrew Marr (former BBC political editor), *My Trade: A Short History of British Journalism* (London: Macmillan, 2004), p. 8. See also Katherine E. Ellison, *Fatal News: Reading and Information Overload in Early Eighteenth-Century Literature* (London: Routledge, 2006); Jenny McKay, 'Defoe's *The Storm* as a Model for Contemporary Reporting', in *The Journalistic Imagination: Literary Journalists from Defoe to Capote and Carter*, ed. Richard Kemble and Sharon Wheeler (Abingdon/New York: Routledge, 2007), pp. 15–28; Doug Underwood, *Journalism and the Novel: Truth and Fiction, 1700–2000* (Cambridge University Press, 2008).

8 Paula McDowell, 'Mediating Media Past and Present: Toward a Genealogy of "Print Culture" and "Oral Tradition"', in *This Is Enlightenment*, ed. Clifford Siskin and William B. Warner (University of Chicago Press, 2010), p. 234. See also McKay, 'Defoe's *The Storm*', p. 18.

9 Daniel Defoe, *Defoe's Review*, 22 vols., ed. Arthur Wellesley Secord (New York: Facsimile Text Society, Columbia University Press, 1938), vol. i, p. 1. Subsequent page references are given in parenthesis in the text.

10 J. Paul Hunter, 'Protesting Fiction, Constructing History', in *The Historical Imagination in Early Modern Britain: History, Rhetoric, and Fiction, 1500–1800*, ed. Donald R. Kelley and David Harris Sacks (Cambridge, MA: Woodrow Wilson Center Press and Cambridge University Press, 1997), pp. 312–13.

11 Daniel Defoe, *A Journal of the Plague Year* (1722), ed. Cynthia Wall (London: Penguin, 2003). Subsequent page references are given in parenthesis in the text.

12 From the *British Critic and Quarterly Theological Review*, 7 (January 1830); quoted in Rogers, ed., *The Critical Heritage*, p. 114.

13 Daniel Defoe, *Roxana, or The Fortunate Mistress* (1724), ed. Jane Jack (Oxford/New York: Oxford University Press, 1964, 1981), p. 1. Subsequent page references are given in parenthesis in the text.

14 Jean-Jacques Rousseau, *Émile, ou de l'éducation* (1762), quoted in Rogers, *Critical Heritage*, p. 52.

15 Samuel Taylor Coleridge, marginalia (c.1830) on a copy of the 1812 edition of *Robinson Crusoe*; quoted in Rogers, ed., *Critical Heritage*, p. 82.

16 David Blewett, *The Illustrations of Robinson Crusoe 1719–1920* (Gerrards Cross: Colin Smythe, 1995), pp. 126, 116; see also p. 37.

17 Karl Marx, *Das Kapital* (1867), quoted in Rogers, ed., Critical Heritage, p. 166.

18 Martin Green, *The Robinson Crusoe Story* (University Park, PA/London: The Pennsylvania University Press, 1990), pp. 2, 29. See also Srinivas Aravamudan, 'Defoe, Commerce and Empire', in *The Cambridge Companion to Daniel Defoe*, ed. John Richetti (Cambridge University Press, 2008), pp. 45–63 (45–7).

19 Philip B. Gove, *The Imaginary Voyage in Prose Fiction: A History of Its Criticism and a Guide for Its Study, With an Annotated Checklist of 215 Imaginary Voyages from 1700 to 1800* (1941; New York: Octagon Books, 1975), p. 122.

20 Rogers, *Critical Heritage*, p. 23.

21 Green, *The Robinson Crusoe Story*, p. 6.

22 Although *Roxana* was early translated into German (*Die Glückliche Maitresse* and *Die Schöne Maitresse* in 1735–6), Rogers notes that it wasn't until 1780–1830 that Defoe obtained gradual acceptance as a major author, first from reviews in the *Gentleman's Magazine* and the *Monthly Review*, from the critics Beattie, Blair, Coleridge, Lamb and Scott, from a few French critics in the early nineteenth century and from the biographies by George Chalmers (1775) and Walter Wilson (1830) (see Rogers, ed., *Critical Heritage*, pp. 14–16, 24–5, 62, 95ff.).

23 Virginia Woolf, 'Robinson Crusoe', *The Common Reader, Second Series*, ed. Andrew McNeillie (1932; London: The Hogarth Press, 1986), pp. 54, 57.

24 Geoffroy Atkinson, 'A French Desert Island Novel of 1708', *PMLA*, 36.4 (December 1921), 509–10.

25 See, for example, Virgil Nemoianu, 'Picaresque Retreat: From Xenophon's "Anabasis" to Defoe's "Singleton"', *Comparative Literature Studies*, 23.2 (Summer 1986), 91–102; Howard Mancing, 'The Picaresque Novel: A Protean Form', *College Literature*, 6.3, *The Picaresque Tradition* (Fall 1979), 182–204; J. Paul Hunter, *The Reluctant Pilgrim: Defoe's Emblematic Method and the Quest for Form in 'Robinson Crusoe'* (Baltimore: Johns Hopkins University Press, 1966); G. A. Starr, *Defoe and Spiritual Autobiography* (Princeton University Press, 1965).

26 Woolf, 'Robinson Crusoe', p. 58.

## Further reading

Aravamudan, Srinivas, 'Defoe, Commerce and Empire', in *The Cambridge Companion to Daniel Defoe*, ed. John Richetti (Cambridge University Press, 2008), pp. 45–63

Backscheider, Paula R., *Daniel Defoe: His Life* (Baltimore: Johns Hopkins University Press, 1989)

Downie, J. A., 'Defoe, Imperialism, and the Travel Books Reconsidered', *The Yearbook of English Studies*, 13 (1983), 66–83

'Periodicals, the Book Trade and the "Bourgeois Public Sphere"', *Media History*, 14.3 (2008), 262–74

Gove, Philip B., *The Imaginary Voyage in Prose Fiction: A History of Its Criticism and a Guide for Its Study, With an Annotated Checklist of 215 Imaginary Voyages from 1700 to 1800* (1941; New York: Octagon Books, 1975)

Hunter, J. Paul, *Before Novels: The Cultural Contexts of Eighteenth-Century English Fiction* (New York/London: Norton, 1990)

*The Reluctant Pilgrim: Defoe's Emblematic Method and the Quest for Form in 'Robinson Crusoe'* (Baltimore: Johns Hopkins University Press, 1966)

McDowell, Paula, 'Defoe and the Contagion of the Oral: Modeling Media Shift in *A Journal of the Plague Year*', *PMLA*, 121.1 (2006), 87–106

McKay, Jenny, 'Defoe's *The Storm* as a Model for Contemporary Reporting', in *The Journalistic Imagination: Literary Journalists from Defoe to Capote and Carter*, ed. Richard Kemble and Sharon Wheeler (Abingdon/New York: Routledge, 2007), pp. 15–28

Mann, William-Edward, *Robinson Crusoé en France: étude sur l'influence de Cette Oeuvre dans la Littérature Française. Thèse pour le Doctorat d'Université de Paris* (Paris: Typographie A. Davy, 1916)

Mayer, Robert, *History and the Early English Novel: Matters of Fact from Bacon to Defoe* (Cambridge University Press, 1997)

Novak, Maximilian E., 'Defoe's Political and Religious Journalism', in *The Cambridge Companion to Daniel Defoe*, ed. John Richetti (Cambridge University Press, 2008), pp. 25–44

  *Realism, Myth and History in Defoe's Fiction* (Lincoln, NE: University of Nebraska Press, 1983)

Payne, W. L., *The Best of Defoe's Review: An Anthology* (New York: Columbia University Press, 1951)

*Realism, Reality, and the Novel: A Symposium on the Novel*, in *Novel: A Forum on Fiction*, 2.3 (Spring 1969), 197–211

Richetti, John, *The Life of Daniel Defoe* (Malden, MA: Blackwell, 2005)

Rogers, Pat, 'Defoe's *Tour* and the Identity of Britain', in *The Cambridge Companion to Daniel Defoe*, ed. John Richetti (Cambridge University Press, 2008), pp. 102–20

Seidel, Michael, *Robinson Crusoe: Island Myths and the Novel* (Boston: Twayne, 1991)

Spaas, Lieve and Brian Stimpson, eds., *Robinson Crusoe: Myths and Metamorphoses* (Basingstoke: Macmillan; New York: St Martin's Press, 1996)

Stach, Reinhard, *Robinson und Robinsonaden in der deutschsprachigen Literatur: eine Bibliographie* (Würzburg: Könighausen & Neumann, 1991)

Starr, G. A., *Defoe and Spiritual Autobiography* (Princeton University Press, 1965)

Sutherland, J., *The Restoration Newspaper and Its Development* (Cambridge University Press, 1986)

Ulrich, Hermann, *Robinson und Robinsonaden: Bibliographie, Geschichte, Kritik* (Weimar: E. Felber, 1898)

Watt, Ian, *The Rise of the Novel: Studies in Defoe, Richardson and Fielding* (London: Chatto and Windus, 1957)

West, Richard, *The Life and Strange Adventures of Daniel Defoe* (London: Harper Collins, 1997)

# 3

THOMAS KEYMER

# Samuel Richardson (1689–1761):
# The epistolary novel

Samuel Richardson had a simple story to tell about the invention of the epistolary novel, a genre that embodies its narrative in fictional letters. By the age of fifty he had established himself in business as one of the leading master printers in London, and was also known in the trade for his ability to write good copy; he had composed numerous prefaces, dedications and 'other little Things of the Pamphlet-kind',[1] he later told his Dutch translator, only some of which can now be traced. It was doubtless with this reputation in mind that Richardson had been urged for years by two influential publishers to produce a letter-writing manual for which they sensed a market opening, aimed at a predominantly rural readership and offering template letters for practical implementation in everyday life. Richardson was slow to accept the commission, but on starting work in 1739 he became absorbed by the imaginative and moral potential of the project, and began developing scenarios that involved fictionalised ethical dilemmas as well as epistolary solutions. One such scenario grew under his hands, about a maidservant importuned by her predatory master, and within a mere two months that winter he drafted a full-length novel from scratch while the manual limped slowly behind: 'And hence sprung Pamela', he briskly recalled (*Selected Letters*, 232). *Pamela, or Virtue Rewarded* was published to immediate acclaim in November 1740, almost a year to the day after composition began; *Letters Written to and for Particular Friends, On the Most Important Occasions*, appeared early the next year, and then – as its miraculous offspring became an international craze – disappeared again.

For Richardson, there could be no question of any more extended or diffusive story than this about the origins of *Pamela*, and by implication about the epistolary novel as it was practised by countless imitators in the decades that followed. For the remainder of his career, he was reluctant to acknowledge that *Pamela* and its successors *Clarissa* (1747–8) and *Sir Charles Grandison* (1753–4) had anything much to do with any existing tradition of fiction, or even that it was right to call them novels at all. These were histories, presented – albeit by increasingly transparent convention – as edited collections of documents from real life, and when Richardson began putting his name on their title pages, as he did from the sixth edition of *Pamela* onwards, he did so in his capacity as printer, not as author. Part of his motive was plainly to distance himself from the more or less disreputable varieties of amatory fiction and escapist romance that were normally indicated at the time by the term 'novel'. His one surviving mention of Aphra Behn, Delarivier Manley and Eliza Haywood (in a letter of 1750 to the pioneering feminist Sarah Chapone) invokes them as figures of scandal, and the same three writers are the implied targets of a 1739 preface that has been plausibly attributed to Richardson, deploring the 'Disreputation' brought on the genre by novelists who 'make it their Study to corrupt the Minds of others'.[2] In this context, *Pamela* was not so much novel as anti-novel, a book in which a radically alternative approach to prose fiction was pioneered. This was a work intended to reform a whole genre, explained Richardson to the poet and critic Aaron Hill, conveniently forgetting that Hill had been at the heart of the coterie from which Haywood's fiction emanated in the 1720s. *Pamela* would introduce 'a new species of writing ... different from the pomp and parade of romance-writing, and dismissing the improbable and marvellous, with which novels generally abound, might tend to promote the cause of religion and virtue' (*Selected Letters*, 41).

The intermingled motive here was authorial vainglory, a desire to be thought a novelist in the root sense of 'innovator' (still the primary meaning in Johnson's *Dictionary* of 1755): a writer indebted to no previous discourse or tradition for the fruits of his original genius. It is in this role that Richardson was canonised near the end of his life by that seminal treatise for the Romantic age, Edward Young's *Conjectures on Original Composition* (1759), and by then he had been promoting himself for years as the founder of a genre or 'species'. When one of the foremost literary pundits of the day, William Warburton, contributed a Preface to *Clarissa* explaining the work as modelled on recent French fiction, Richardson remonstrated with Warburton and dropped the Preface from later editions. 'I am not acquainted in the least either with the French Language or Writers', he insisted, and 'it was Chance and not Skill or Learning, that made me fall into this way of Scribbling' (*Selected Letters*, 86). The modesty of the disavowal is superficial; what matters here, unmistakably, is not Richardson's lack of skill or learning but the absolute originality of his woodnotes wild.

Yet this is not how books get written, even the most groundbreaking books. One does not have to invoke a post-structuralist notion of infinite intertextuality to question Richardson's story of how *Pamela* came into being, and with it a new species of writing. The work may indeed have 'sprung' in a local sense from imaginative processes triggered by the letter-manual project, with all the connotations of organic growth, gushing creativity or elastic projection suggested by Richardson's verb. But could it really have done so without significant precursors operating at some level or another in the mind of a man who was, after all, one of the most astute and seasoned book-trade professionals of the time? As Robert Adams Day put it years ago with reference to another mythology of singular origin, and with audible sarcasm: 'Were *Pamela* and *Clarissa* literary Minervas, sprung full-grown from the head of Richardson?'[3] In his pioneering survey *Told in Letters*, Day went on to demonstrate that the epistolary novel was no such immaculate conception, and significant evidence has accumulated since then to connect Richardson with its prior development.

Where Day's study focused on English fiction of the Restoration and early eighteenth century, recent accounts of the novel in letters present it as a broad-based European – and now global – tradition that can be traced to antiquity. The celebrated epistolary laments of Ovid's *Heroides* involved a finely discriminated range of female voices and models of subjectivity in crisis, and these poems were an enormous influence on seventeenth- and eighteenth-century verse epistles as well as epistolary fiction. In the second or third century BCE, the prose epistolographer Alciphron produced a four-book collection of letters in different plebeian voices, narrating fictional predicaments with rudimentary plot development; embedded letters are an important component of romances by Heliodorus and Achilles Tatius from roughly the same era. In *Chion of Heraclea*, a skilfully plotted tyrannicide narrative of unknown authorship, the hero's education and adventures are reported entirely in letters sent to his father and other recipients. None of these Greek sources had the currency of Ovid during and after the Renaissance, but they were supplemented in Latin by the celebrated twelfth-century correspondence of Abelard and Heloïse, the later impact of which can be seen in novelising appropriations such as John Hughes's *Letters of Abelard and Heloise* (1713) and in the titles of major French novels: not only Jean-Jacques Rousseau's *Julie, ou La Nouvelle Héloïse* (1761) but also Rétif de la Bretonne's *Le Nouvel Abeilard* (1778). The plaintive tones of the historical Heloïse and Ovid's mythological lovers coalesce most obviously in *Lettres portugaises* (1669), an intense, ornate novel of abandonment by Gabriel Joseph de Lavergne, comte de Guilleragues, which on translation into English set in motion a native tradition that includes Behn's three-part *Love-Letters between a Nobleman and His Sister* (1684–7), the anonymous *Lindamira* (1702) and Mary Davys's *Familiar Letters betwixt a Gentleman and a Lady* (1725). To these we may add several Haywood novels, from *Love in Excess* (1719–20) onwards, in which interpolated letters play a crucial role as expressions of passion and vehicles of plot. Haywood also uses letters dramatically, as the visible medium in which her characters seduce, deceive, and intrigue against one another. Thus Lysander's letters in *The British Recluse* (1722) are read first by the heroine Cleomira as tokens of emotional sincerity, and then with hindsight as just the reverse, as 'Witnesses of your well-dissembled Tenderness'.[4]

For Richardson's contemporaries, the novelist most obviously called to mind by *Pamela* and *Clarissa* was Pierre Carlet de Chamblain de Marivaux, author of *La Vie de Marianne*, a work written and published in eleven epistolary parts between 1731 and 1742. This is the novel Warburton had in mind in his Preface to *Clarissa*, and he made that point explicit when recycling the Preface elsewhere (in perfect revenge) as a compliment to Richardson's greatest rival: now the foremost novelists in the world, Warburton declares, are 'Mr. De Marivaux in France, and Mr. FIELDING in England'.[5] This same connection with *La Vie de Marianne* had already been made by a German reviewer of *Pamela* on grounds of both plot and form, and it lies at the heart of one of the most intelligent early commentaries on *Clarissa*, by the Swiss physiologist and poet Albrecht von Haller. Originally published in the *Bibliothèque raisonnée*, an Amsterdam-based organ of Enlightenment thought, and translated into English in the wide-circulation *Gentleman's Magazine*, Haller's essay compares Richardson with Marivaux on several grounds, but always to Richardson's advantage.

The key breakthrough was the technique that Richardson was to call 'writing to the moment', in which narrative is produced in step with the action (rather than, as in Marivaux, in distant retrospect). Richardson talks in his preface to *Grandison* about narrative 'written, as it were, to the *Moment*, while the Heart is agitated by Hopes and Fears, on Events undecided' and he elaborates on 'this way of writing, to the moment', in a letter to Lady Bradshaigh.[6] For Haller, the resulting impression of immediacy and spontaneity made possible an intimacy of representation in *Clarissa* that Marivaux had failed to achieve. This sense that in Richardson's hands the epistolary form could open up new kinds of psychological inwardness is best conveyed by Haller's original wording. Where the English version praises the representation in *Clarissa* of 'private and domestic occurrences' and 'the minutiae of *Virtue*', the French text specifies access to inner experience: 'l'intérieur de la vie'; 'l'intérieur de ses occupations'.[7]

Much the same point about interiority was being made about *Pamela* even before publication – 'one may judge of, nay, almost see, the inmost Recesses of her Mind', proclaimed the *Weekly Miscellany* for 11 October 1740 – and this idea was to become a commonplace of eighteenth-century criticism. It finds its most alarming articulation in the Marquis de Sade, who contrasted 'the mannered style of Marivaux' with 'the profound study of man's heart – Nature's veritable labyrinth' in Richardson, a writer Sade praised as unafraid to represent man 'not only as he is ... but as he is capable of being when subjected to the modifying influences of vice and the full impact of passion'.[8]

Responding in public to Haller's review, Richardson made no effort to dispute a comparison that worked so much to his advantage, and since three English versions of *La Vie de Marianne* had already preceded *Clarissa* (the best of them is Mary Collyer's free translation of 1742, *The Virtuous Orphan*), there was no point continuing to protest his ignorance of French. It is with the much earlier *Lettres portugaises*, however, that the relevance to his work of translated fiction is most intriguing. Though still sometimes attributed to Mariana Alcoforado, a real-life Portuguese nun who rose to become abbess of Beja, this compelling work almost certainly originates in the fine-tuned neoclassical French of Guilleragues, and in its original form has something of the resonance of Racinian tragedy, with its concentrated, relentless vocabulary of passion. That said, it is in the English translation of 1678, as *Five Love-Letters from a Nun to a Cavalier*, that the work comes most fully to life. Here the *précieux* refinement of the original text meets the coffee-house demotic of its English translator, the pugnacious Tory journalist Sir Roger L'Estrange, and the nun's outpourings gain a volatile new energy in the mix. No comment survives from Richardson about this remarkable English version of *Lettres portugaises*, but it may be significant that he selected another L'Estrange translation as the base text for his own 1739 edition of *Aesop's Fables*, published a few days after he began writing *Pamela*. Here he defends his preference for the by now politically discredited L'Estrange on stylistic grounds, citing 'the Benefit which the *English* Tongue has received from his masterly Hand' and 'that fine Humour, apposite Language, accurate and lively Manner, which will always render Sir *Roger* delightful'.[9]

*Lettres portugaises* is modelled in obvious ways on the traditions of Heloïse and Ovid, and consists simply of five letters addressed by the cloistered writer – cloistered first within the walls of her convent, but also by the loneliness of romantic fixation and the prison house of artificial language – to the unresponding lover who has left her. Beyond this, almost nothing happens, except that the cavalier each time fails to reply, and the stranded nun addresses him again, creating an almost Beckettian effect of immobility that was only partly destroyed when an enterprising hack came out with *Five Love-Letters Written by a Cavalier, In Answer* (1683). Nothing happens outwardly, to be more exact. Yet for just this reason the text unfolds as a single-minded narrative of inwardness: a study of consciousness as it fluctuates in the isolation of obsession and ongoing private crisis. For although formally addressing the lover who has abandoned her, and who reaffirms this abandonment between each letter by his unbroken silence, the nun is really writing to herself alone, as she comes to acknowledge. Her cloistered condition is one in which she has 'only my single self to encounter', and by the close of the fourth letter she realises that ''Tis not so much for your sake that I write, as my own'.[10] Struggling with her own subjectivity and the effort to fix it in language, her letters function not to narrate an action, there being no action to narrate; rather, they constitute, in her state of tragic solipsism, the narrative action in themselves. They simultaneously advance and communicate the process of self-expression and debate she comes to call 'this Trial to get the Mastery of my Passion' (*Five Love-Letters*, 52) – a process that, rather than taking simple linear form, circles endlessly back and forth, without determinate outcome. In the second letter, language fails to catch the extremity of the nun's condition, with implications of self-alienation that seem heightened by her insistent reflexive verbs: 'There is so great a difference betwixt the Love I write, and That which I feel, that if you measure the One by the Other, I have undone my self' (*Five Love-Letters*, 41). By the end of the fifth letter the most she can say, with a plangent effect of straining for measure, is that she is 'not yet out of hope of a more peaceable Condition, which I will either Compass, or take some other Course with my self' (*Five Love-Letters*, 57).

The ardent voice of the Portuguese nun continues to echo in Haywood, who goes further than L'Estrange – with his teasing observation that '*a Woman may be Flesh and Blood, in a Cloyster, as well as in a Palace*' (*Five Love-Letters*, 38) – in connecting the psychological voyeurism of *Lettres portuguaises* with the libertine tradition of cloistral pornography: a tradition most famously represented in English by *Venus in the Cloister, or The Nun in Her Smock* (1683), an obscene satire from the French of Jean Barrin. In Haywood's novels, which frequently turn on confinement or intrigue within, and abduction or elopement beyond, the cells and grills of convents, the nunnery is a space of desire and transgression, laden with erotic charge. The charge is typically intensified by Haywood's strategic use of included letters, which parallel the alluring secrecy behind the convent grate with entrancing glimpses of inward female passion. As already begins to happen in Behn's epistolary fiction of the 1680s, the psychological intimacy of the Portuguese mode becomes intimately and illicitly sexual.

It was this heady blend of erotic signals in Haywood that elicited Richardson's moral censure, but we now know that it also occupied his professional attention, and that what he deplored he also printed. Few of his business records survive, but it has been established on the evidence of unique printers' ornaments that Richardson handled five of Haywood's steamiest novels, including *Love in Excess*, for the 1732 edition of her collected works (which seems to have been divided between three printing houses).[11] More than that, he used these ornaments, or instructed his compositor to use them, to render visual and accentuate the fervid atmosphere of the text. Where other early editions of Haywood, including the non-Richardson volumes of 1732, are sparingly ornamented with conventional devices such as cornucopias or classical busts, the Richardson volumes throb with glowing hearts, cupid's arrows and all the iconography of erotic rapture. Bibliographical evidence stops short of proving that he actually read *Love in Excess* as he supervised its production, but his rueful general admission that he could 'seldom read but as a Printer, having so much of that' (*Selected Letters*, 59) makes clear his normal practice, and the likelihood is confirmed by frequent traces of Haywoodian eroticism in his own fiction. Readers may or may not have picked up *Pamela*'s teasing replays of particular Haywood motifs, such as the 'plain and rural Dress' in which the heroine of *Fantomina* (1725) disguises herself to rekindle her lover's ardour, echoed when Mr B alleges Pamela's 'Country Habit' to be a similar ruse (*Secret Histories*, III.271; *Pamela*, 55–7). But the novel as a whole – which Ian Watt once neatly characterised as offering 'the combined attractions of a sermon and a striptease' – was widely denounced in its day as disguised pornography. It was even rumoured that Richardson was behind the most eye-catching denunciation, an anonymous pamphlet entitled *Pamela Censured* (1741), as a surreptitious marketing gambit.[12] Later, in *Clarissa*, the most controversial passages were those in which Lovelace, the heroine's rakish suitor and eventual rapist, dwells on her physicality in terms straight from the pheromone-charged lexicon of *Love in Excess*. 'She was even fainting as I clasped her in my supporting arms. What a precious moment that!', Lovelace reports in a characteristic moment of anticipatory innuendo: 'How near, how sweetly near, the throbbing partners!'[13]

In the standard theoretical account of epistolary narrative and its formal properties, Janet Altman pays little attention to included letters or semi-epistolary fiction in the Behn-Haywood vein, and represents even Richardson as failing to exploit the full potential of letter narration. Altman postulates here a set of distinct national traditions associating English texts with empiricism and realism, French texts with rhetorical performance, and she comments that typically in eighteenth-century novels 'the German letter writer is a diarist, the English correspondent a witness, and the French *épistolier* a verbal duellist'. Underlying this scheme is a taxonomy inherited from the structuralist narratology of François Jost, in which letter narration is either 'static' (reporting the action to addressees remote from it) or 'kinetic' (embodying the action in letters between protagonists that function as agents of plot); these types then divide into three subcategories ('monologue', 'dialogue', 'polylogue') according to the number and direction of the correspondences involved. In this generally useful scheme, an unspoken but evident hierarchy is implied, in which 'static' monologues such as *Pamela*, or for that matter Goethe's *Werther* (1774), stand below the 'kinetic' *Lettres portugaises*, while multi-voiced novels such as *Clarissa* and its raucous comic counterpart, Tobias Smollett's *Humphry Clinker* (1771), never quite match the dramatic, dynamic epistolarity of *Les Liaisons dangereuses* (1782), the masterpiece of the French tradition by Choderlos de Laclos. As Altman sums up her case in national terms, 'whereas the German and English traditions tend to opt for the static method of narration (confidential letters), using language to present a seemingly unmediated transcription of internal and external reality, the French tradition of letter writing prefers the kinetic method (dramatic letters), in which the letter is used as a weapon and as a mask'.[14]

On the face of it, *Pamela* looks to illustrate this pattern to perfection. As a sequence of letters addressed by the heroine to her appalled parents, modulating at times into the privacy of a personal journal, the narrative presents itself as confessional, a transparent window through which inner life and outward action are fully disclosed. Not only written to the moment, it is also written from the heart: as the heroine protests near the novel's midpoint, 'I know I wrote my Heart; and that is not deceitful' (*Pamela*, 230). It is for this cardiographic quality that Richardson's narrators are sometimes said to pave the way for stream of consciousness novels in the twentieth century – a point that may or may not be acknowledged by the given name of Virginia Woolf's Mrs Dalloway. Yet there is a good case to be made for *Pamela* as a novel in which writing and reading, the act of narration and the reception of it, assume an importance that has no real equivalent in stream of consciousness, in which mental processes emerge on the page without effort of intelligence or will by the character concerned. In Richardson the letters that constitute the narrative turn out to be profoundly instrumental, and even as Pamela repeats her view of them as receptacles of intimate, spontaneous truth – 'the naked Sentiments of my Heart ... deliver'd to those, whose Indulgence I was sure of; and for whose Sight, only, they were written' (455) – other voices at the margin of her text are more in tune with Altman's alternative model of mask or weapon.

To be sure, Richardson's novel does not replicate the rhetorical situation of *Lettres portuguaises*, nor indeed the epistolary action in Haywood, where plots of amatory conflict are not just reported by, but take place through the agency of, the letters that make up the text. Only a few documents are exchanged between the maidservant Pamela and her master Mr B, who as a Member of Parliament, Justice of the Peace and aspiring peer – 'he is to be made a Lord. – I wish they may make him an honest man' (68) – seems to stand for the ruling elite in Sir Robert Walpole's England. This was an elite in which Richardson had been viewed with suspicion in early career, when he printed some politically dissident works, but with which he now enjoyed professionally lucrative ties. For her part, Pamela is not strictly plebeian, and her father is an impecunious former schoolmaster, invested at one point with the same aura of incorruptible plainness that Alexander Pope evokes in his *Epistle to Arburthnot* (1735) as a counterpoint to ministerial venality. Like the idealised parent of Pope's poem, who 'knew no schoolman's subtle art, | No language, but the language of the heart' (lines 398–9), Pamela's father is 'A Man who knows no Guile ... who would not deceive or oppress to gain a Kingdom' (*Pamela*, 219). The same political overtones are quietly at work in Richardson's novel, a tale of power and its abuse written at a time when the opposition campaign against Walpole was colouring the output of almost every major writer then active. That said, modern readers have been struck instead by the broad socio-economic aspects of the novel's main conflict, and this effect is reinforced on every page by Pamela's distinctive epistolary style. In early editions above all, her language suggests the rustic idiom, and sometimes also the Bunyanesque truculence, of a Bedfordshire peasant, amplifying the plot with implications nicely caught by Terry Eagleton's comment that 'Richardson's novels are among other things great allegories of class warfare, narratives of alliance and antagonism between a predatory nobility and a pious bourgeoisie'.[15] In the original text of 1740, moreover, Pamela is not even securely bourgeois, nor deferentially pious. 'And so, belike, their Clacks run for half an Hour in my Praises' (53), she spits with reference to the vacuous fine ladies of the neighbourhood; this was among the outbursts that Richardson removed from later editions in an apparent effort to soften his novel's socially controversial edge.

It is this sense of an authentic voice from below that lends energy to *Pamela*'s narrative, reinforcing its claim to embody a kind of disclosure that is spontaneous, artless, even reckless. The equation between private correspondence and the intimate self is further reinforced by her habit of thrusting letters into her bosom or sewing them into her underclothes, and by one conspicuously Haywoodian passage in which Mr B attempts to retrieve them with a gloating full-body search: 'Now, said he, it is my Opinion they are about you; and I never undrest a Girl in my Life; but I will now begin to strip my pretty *Pamela*' (235). Yet there is also another side to passages like this. If on one hand they associate epistolary discourse with the secret self, on the other they demonstrate the self-consciousness about narrative form that characterises all Richardson's fiction, where the letters that communicate the action also function importantly as material objects within it, and as objects in particular of interpretative dispute. It is not simply that so much attention is lavished in *Pamela* – still more in the claustrophobic *Clarissa* – on the devices employed by the heroine to procure the pens and ink she needs in order to narrate, and then on the further devices required to smuggle her narrative to its addressee (crevices in garden walls are a favourite hiding place). More important for our view of the novel as 'static' or otherwise in its handling of form is the way early phases of the narrative are so widely read and debated during later phases, so that the text comes to incorporate an explicit commentary on itself.

This commentary, moreover, is interestingly divided. By the end of the novel, Pamela's enemies are won over to recognise her virtue and her entitlement to elevation in marriage, and they reach this recognition not least by reading her letters. As Pamela explains the process herself in the case of Mr B's suspicious sister, the letters prove her to be not a manipulative social climber but a providentially rewarded innocent: 'And I hope, when she sees them all ... she will see it is all God Almighty's Doings, and that a Gentleman of his Parts and Knowledge was not to be drawn in by such a poor young Body as me' (472). Pamela's narrative, in other words, is very powerfully instrumental, not only on its initial addressees but also on the characters depicted within it who then become its second-tier readers: on Mr B, whom it persuades to abandon molestation for marriage, and on his family and friends, whom it reconciles to a spectacular breach of social hierarchy.

No suggestion is made at this point that the letters work so well on Pamela's behalf as a consequence of rhetorical performance as opposed to luminous truth-telling. But suggestions of this kind are frequently to be found at earlier points. For Mr B in his unreformed condition, the narrative is a cynical manifesto, a mask concealing the real Pamela and a weapon targeted against him, not least in the religious rhetoric it deploys to such telling effect: 'for I find she is a mighty Letter-writer ... in which she makes herself an Angel of Light, and me, her kind Master and Benefactor, a Devil Incarnate!' (36). And while Mr B is hardly a creditable source at this point, his objection to the overwrought hyperboles and spiritual polarities of Pamela's narrative (which Richardson has him repeat on several occasions) is an unsettling reminder that rhetorical pattern is as much a feature of her prose as artless disclosure. Her letters may not be written like those of a 'kinetic' epistolary novel to her primary antagonist in terms of plot, but they are readable as masks and weapons nonetheless, and as components of a narrative that makes the responses of its various fictional readers a primary subject of interest. By the end, even Pamela comes to doubt her own reliability as a narrator, and she looks back on her early demonisation of Mr B as a period of incipient love, albeit unacknowledged. It now seems that for much of the novel – while Pamela excoriates Mr B as satanic and forgoes opportunities to flee his house so that she can first embroider him a waistcoat – this was indeed a period when the heart was deceitful. In this context, perhaps the subtlest analysis we ever get of what is happening comes in the glimpses occasionally offered in the narrative of neutral viewpoints: the view of the housekeeper Mrs Jervis, for example, for whom Mr B is neither the black-hearted wretch of Pamela's letters nor the kind benefactor of his own protestations. Instead, he is a confused, insecure, weak-willed man, a rabbit frozen in the headlights of social convention: 'He has a noble Estate; and yet I believe he loves my good Maiden, tho' his Servant, better than all the Ladies in the Land; and he has try'd to overcome it, because he knows you are so much his Inferior; and 'tis my Opinion he finds he can't; and that vexes his proud Heart' (41).

Henry Fielding's parodic *Shamela* seized gleefully on hints and loose ends of this kind. Dashed off in a debtors' prison within months of *Pamela*'s publication, *Shamela* has multiple satirical targets beyond Richardson's novel, but all are linked in one way or another with the behavioural and rhetorical hypocrisy that Fielding wittily reads into the heroine. These range from the self-promoting poet laureate Colley Cibber and the sanctimonious celebrity preacher George Whitefield to the powerful but now teetering kleptocracy of Prime Minister Walpole, whose ruling passions of 'Avarice and Ambition'[16] are figured forth, in an exuberant reversal of Richardson's political hints, by Shamela's Machiavellian climb to wealth and power.

Alongside these scattershot elements of personal lampoon and political invective, *Shamela* may also be approached as a rather technical satire about narrative procedure, exposing not only the dubious conventions but also the uncontrollable meanings of Richardson's novel. When Mr B, now deftly reimagined as Squire Booby, blunders into the bedroom his maidservant shares with Mrs Jervis, Fielding mocks the precarious premise of writing to the moment and the associated colloquial style: 'Odsbobs! I hear him just coming in at the Door. You see I write in the present Tense, as Parson *Williams* says. Well, he is in Bed between us, we both shamming a Sleep, he steals his Hand into my Bosom' (318). More interestingly, Fielding also highlights the possibility, as soon as one starts to think of Pamela as shamming on the page as well as in life, of a radically alternative story underlying her text. Richardson had toyed uneasily with this alternative himself, from his early hint that the novel's action might cut two ways – 'I might draw him in, or be drawn in by him' (*Pamela*, 21) – to the final lingering suspicions of Lady Davers. But Fielding lets it loose – the evil twin, we might say, of her official story – to dominate the surface of his text. Now we must imagine the original narrative as falsehood and misrepresentation, or as the fraudulent concoction of a heroine who endeavours 'by perverting and misrepresenting Facts to be thought to deserve what she now enjoys' (*Joseph Andrews and Shamela*, 313). Crazily, *Shamela* itself, in which a scheming hypocrite ensnares her master in marriage and squanders his wealth, is the underlying truth.

Nor did this brilliantly perverse rereading of *Pamela* end there. It powerfully entered the culture at large, and shaped responses to Richardson's novel across Europe. As the Danish playwright Ludvig Holberg memorably put it, the text became an interpretative free-for-all wherever it went, polarising the world between 'Pamelists' who read the narrative at face value and 'Antipamelists' who read it as ironic. For the latter group, *Pamela* revealed not the virtue rewarded of its subtitle but instead 'the Behaviour of an hypocritical, crafty Girl, in her Courtship; who understands the Art of bringing a Man to her Lure'.[17]

Richardson was outraged by Fielding's burlesque, though it is intriguing to note that a few years later there was a short-lived rapprochement between the two, perhaps because Fielding, who instantly recognised *Clarissa* as a masterpiece, also hailed it as such in a public forum. Even here, however, Fielding's attention continued to focus on the instability of meaning generated by Richardson's technique, and he imagines a scene in which readers once more fail to agree about the heroine's moral identity. '*Clarissa* is undutiful; she is too dutiful', he writes in his periodical the *Jacobite's Journal* for 2 January 1748: 'She is too cold; she is too fond. She uses her Father, Mother, Uncles, Brother, Sister, Lover, Friend, too ill, too well.' The difference is that this time Richardson himself was obviously aware of the effect, and as his work on *Clarissa* began in the disruptive wake of the *Pamela* controversy, questions about the instability of epistolary meaning were right at the centre of his thinking. If first-person narration could be so irreducibly ambiguous, especially in a form that highlighted the address to, and variable responses of, particular readers, how might a novelist control the openness of interpretation that results, or turn it to creative advantage?

Richardson's sense of this dilemma does much to explain the protracted history of initial composition, manuscript circulation and pre-publication revision that distinguishes *Clarissa* from its hastily produced precursor. It remains unclear exactly when the work was first drafted, but some kind of full text seems to have existed at least three years before publication began, and for an extended period, an unknown number of manuscript copies, some interleaved with blank response sheets, moved within a quorum of at least a dozen readers, who included Cibber, Hill and Young as well as more exotic acquaintances such as the scientist and mystic John Freke and the scandalous Irish poet Laetitia Pilkington. The great exponent of the expansive print culture of the day had fallen back on the age-old practice of scribal publication within a defined coterie, albeit only as a tactical and temporary retreat. Throughout this period, he painstakingly revised the text in the light of – which is far from meaning in obedience to – the responses that reached him, and he then went to press forewarned and forearmed. He continued in the work of revision even as publication proceeded – *Clarissa* came out in three massive instalments between December 1747 and December 1748, closely tracking a plot that occupies a calendar year – and after the second instalment he resisted heavy pressure from readers who urged a rerun of *Pamela*'s euphoric ending, persisting instead in the relentless tragic logic of the new work.

Even then, Richardson's attentiveness to reception was not exhausted, and the complexity of the debates generated by his novel can still be gathered from correspondences he pursued with readers such as the fiery bluestocking Hester Mulso, who objected to the novel's authoritarian implications, and a Lancashire gentlewoman named Lady Bradshaigh, who wrote pseudonymously during publication to press for a happy ending, and whose correspondence with Richardson grew into what he called 'the best Commentary that cd. be written on the History of Clarissa' (*Selected Letters*, 336). The same dynamics of reciprocity and debate can also be observed in the novel's expanded third edition of 1751, which is annotated at points of interpretative openness or stress with the footnotes of an editorial voice, and from Lady Bradshaigh's surviving personal copy (now at Princeton), its margins crowded with her manuscript responses, some of which are then annotated in Richardson's hand with counter-responses of his own.

Half a century later, Richardson's first significant biographer Anna Laetitia Barbauld used the term 'female senate'[18] to describe the effect of enfranchisement, even a kind of devolution of authority, involved in these interactions with readers. Barbauld was referring in particular to the dialogues and consultations from which Richardson's experimental but uneventful last novel, *Sir Charles Grandison*, emerged in the 1750s, and by this time Richardson himself was speaking wryly of readers as his 'Sovereign Judges', or as 'Carvers' licensed by his way of writing to choose between alternative interpretations (*Selected Letters*, 280, 296). After seven volumes of *Grandison*, and long after he had run out of creative steam, the process reached its logical conclusion in a plan – which made mercifully little progress in practice – to have readers such as Mulso and Bradshaigh continue the text themselves, writing in the voice of a different narrator each, with himself merely coordinating their contributions.

*Clarissa* represents more than thirty different voices, but four carry the main narrative burden. In contrast to the monologic *Pamela*, the novel is constructed in what Richardson calls a 'double yet separate correspondence' (*Clarissa*, 35): a pair of epistolary dialogues between the two protagonists and their respective confidants that corresponds roughly to the Jost–Altman category of 'static polylogue'. The most obvious result of this structure is uncompromising length, which is why this profound, endlessly astonishing work – 'le chef-d'œuvre des romans', as the author of *Les Liaisons dangereuses* called it[19] – rarely features on student curricula below graduate level. In effect, Richardson is now known to most of his readers from the least of his achievements (as though we might know George Eliot from *Adam Bede* or James Joyce from *A Portrait of the Artist*), and from the most rudimentary instance of his characteristic form. It may well be, to judge from relative numbers of editions published in his lifetime, that this was always so.

Yet it remains important, even for readers who know only *Pamela* at first hand, to understand how much more arises from *Clarissa*'s 'double yet separate' structure than narrative prolixity alone. As well as undertaking a complex tragic reprise of the basic seduction plot of the earlier novel – as close to *Pamela* in its reach and impact as *King Lear* is to a cartoon – *Clarissa* also achieves a massive complication of its precursor's narrative form. It does so in ways that reveal, moreover, the limitations of the 'static'/ 'kinetic' binary, *Clarissa* being flexible enough to accommodate within its overarching structure of 'static' letters to detached observers elements of 'kinetic' correspondence between antagonists in the plot that dramatise the antagonism in themselves. These elements include correspondences between Clarissa and her new-money family who aim to marry her off for dynastic advancement (their surname, Harlowe, implies this intended exchange of flesh for cash),[20] and between Clarissa and her old-blood suitor Lovelace ('Loveless' was standard pronunciation; Fielding spells the name 'Lovelass')[21] who entangles her in a clandestine correspondence with the aim of fulfilling his libertine credo that all virtue can be corrupted. *Clarissa* is thus 'static' and 'kinetic' at once, the more so in that the static element of correspondence with uninvolved addressees takes on a primary narrative interest, with the letters functioning as agents, not mere reports, of shifting relations and understandings between the writers and readers involved. Both addressees, Anna Howe and John Belford, begin as passive recipients of the rival parallel narratives of Clarissa and Lovelace, but both become increasingly resistant to, or sceptical of, the explanations, interpretations and justifications of the letters they receive. 'A stander-by may see more of the game than one that plays' (407), Anna insists as her view develops of Clarissa's narrative, with its blind spots and tendentious rhetoric, as in crucial ways unreliable, and in need of supplementation or critique. In one of the novel's several submerged plots, Belford matures morally as he recoils from Lovelace's narration, and in a reference to forensic practice that becomes the novel's dominant analogy for narrative rhetoric, he comes to see Lovelace as writing like a devious courtroom plaintiff or defendant, a 'whitener of his *own* cause, or blackener of *another*'s ... throwing dust in the eyes of his judges' (1295). In the final phase of the novel, which maps on to the 'double yet separate' structure a sequence of different predominant voices across the three instalments, Richardson's masterstroke is to reverse the established epistolary flow and make Belford the primary narrator. Meanwhile, Clarissa (dominant in volumes I–II) and Lovelace (dominant in volumes III–IV) recede from view in spiritualised silence and incipient madness respectively.

After *Clarissa*, it may have seemed that there was nowhere left for the epistolary novel to go, and after decades of sentimental imitations of Richardson the form fell into abeyance for two centuries – with the odd virtuoso exception such as Dostoevsky's *Poor Folk* (1846) and John Barth's *LETTERS* (1979) – until its very recent reanimation in the age of emails and tweets. Yet for all its power and sophistication as a narrative exercise, *Clarissa* left open areas of unfulfilled potential that were brilliantly exploited in a few landmark works of the later eighteenth century. In *Humphry Clinker*, Smollett converted the tragic divergences of *Clarissa*'s multi-voiced structure into a bravura comedy of relative perceptions, with five narrators reporting their world in irreconcilable ways. As befits a work that celebrates the philosophy of the Scottish Enlightenment, Smollett's novel systematically implies the discontinuity of identity, the unreliability of perception and the inaccessibility of objective reality outside the subject-ive conduits of sense and feeling. Thereafter, only *Les Liaisons dangereuses* eclipses *Humphry Clinker* as a demonstration of what the novel in letters could do, and the epistolary duels, sieges and wars in which Laclos pits his protagonists – the most celebrated letter in this novel reads simply 'Hé bien! la guerre' (*Œuvres complètes*, 351) – achieve a uniquely concen-trated interfusion of form and action. Here the dangerous liaisons, in an important sense, are those of correspondence itself. Yet even in *Les Liaisons dangereuses* the shadow of *Clarissa* looms, and with it a distinctively Richardsonian sense of alternative meanings and effects. When the virtuous Mme de Tourvel elopes with the libertine Valmont, she has just been reading, we learn, 'le premier [volume] d'un Livre, qui a pour titre *Clarisse*' (248).

But does she fall because she has been reading Richardson's novel, or because she has read only a corrupt translation, or because she has read only the start? Laclos leaves open these teasing questions, and comments merely in a later essay that *Clarissa* depends for its effect on one's way of seeing, one's 'manière de voir' (440), and that the meaning of Clarissa's departure from her father's house – an event Richardson surrounds with limitless connotation, psychosexual, ethical, political, theological – is up to the reader to decide.

## Note on editions

*Pamela*, ed. Albert J. Rivero (Cambridge University Press, 2011), and *Early Works*, ed. Alexander Petit (2012), are the inaugural volumes of The Cambridge Edition of the Works and Correspondence of Samuel Richardson. Editions of *Pamela in Her Exalted Condition*, *Clarissa* and *Sir Charles Grandison* are in preparation. Good textbook editions of *Clarissa* are published by Penguin (ed. Angus Ross, 1985) and Broadview (ed. and abridged Toni Bowers and John Richetti, 2010). For *Sir Charles Grandison* see Jocelyn Harris's pioneering edition (Oxford University Press, 1972).

## Notes

1 *Selected Letters of Samuel Richardson*, ed. John Carroll (Oxford: Clarendon Press, 1964), p. 234; see also p. 230. Subsequent page references are included in parenthesis in the text.

2 Wolfgang Zach, 'Mrs. Aubin and Richardson's Earliest Literary Manifesto (1739)', *English Studies*, 62 (1981), 282. For Richardson's letter of 6 December 1750 to Sarah Chapone, see *Selected Letters*, p. 173 n.

3 Robert Adams Day, *Told in Letters: Epistolary Fiction before Richardson* (Ann Arbor: University of Michigan Press, 1966), p. 5.

4 Eliza Haywood, *Secret Histories, Novels, and Poems*, 3rd edn (1732), II.64. Subsequent references are given in parenthesis in the text.

5 *The Works of Alexander Pope*, ed. William Warburton, 9 vols. (1751), IV.169, quoted by T. C. Duncan Eaves and Ben D. Kimpel, *Samuel Richardson: A Biography* (Oxford: Clarendon Press, 1971), p. 195.

6 Samuel Richardson, *Sir Charles Grandison*, ed. Jocelyn Harris, 3 vols. (London: Oxford University Press, 1972), p. 4; 14 February 1754, in *Selected Letters*, 289.

7 *Gentleman's Magazine*, 19 (June 1748); *Bibliothèque raisonnée*, 42 (April–June 1749). On the *Pamela* review in the *Göttingische Zeitungen von Gelehrten Sachen* (February 1741), see A. D. McKillop, *Samuel Richardson: Printer and Novelist* (Chapel Hill, NC: University of North Carolina Press, 1936), p. 36.

8 Marquis de Sade, 'Reflections on the Novel' (1800), in *The One Hundred and Twenty Days of Sodom and Other Writings*, trans. Austryn Wainhouse and Richard Seaver (London: Arrow, 1990), p. 106.

9 Samuel Richardson, ed., *Aesop's Fables* (1739), pp. vii–viii.

10 Comte de Guilleragues, trans. Roger L'Estrange, *Five Love-Letters from a Nun to a Cavalier*, in Charles C. Mish, ed., *Restoration Prose Fiction, 1666–1700* (Lincoln, NE: University of Nebraska Press, 1969), pp. 44, 51. Further page references to this edition are in parenthesis in the text.

11 See Samuel Richardson, *Pamela*, ed. Thomas Keymer and Alice Wakely, intr. Thomas Keymer (Oxford: Oxford World's Classics, 2001), pp. xi–xii. Further page references to this edition are in parenthesis in the text.

12 Ian Watt, *The Rise of the Novel: Studies in Defoe, Richardson and Fielding* (London: Chatto and Windus, 1957), p. 173. For *Pamela Censured* and Richardson's rumoured involvement, see Thomas Keymer and Peter Sabor, *Pamela in the Marketplace: Literary Controversy and Print Culture in Eighteenth-Century Britain and Ireland* (Cambridge University Press, 2005), pp. 34–6.

13 Samuel Richardson, *Clarissa*, ed. Angus Ross (London: Penguin, 1985), p. 400. Further page references to this edition are in parenthesis in the text.

14 Janet Gurkin Altman, *Epistolarity: Approaches to a Form* (Columbus, OH: Ohio State University Press, 1982), p. 194; see also p. 8.

15 Terry Eagleton, *The Rape of Clarissa: Writing, Sexuality and Class Struggle in Samuel Richardson* (Oxford: Blackwell, 1982), p. 4.

16 *Joseph Andrews and Shamela*, ed. Douglas Brooks-Davies, rev. and intr. Thomas Keymer (Oxford: Oxford World's Classics, 1999), p. 312. Further page references to this edition are in parenthesis in the text.

17 Peter Shaw, *The Reflector* (1750), p. 14; this is the earliest version in English of Holberg's 1744 essay, translated without acknowledgement.

18 *The Correspondence of Samuel Richardson*, ed. Anna Laetitia Barbauld, 6 vols. (1804), I.cxxiii.

19 Choderlos de Laclos, 'Des femmes et de leur éducation' (1783), in *Œuvres complètes*, ed. Laurent Versini (Paris: Gallimard, 1979), p. 440.

20 One need only remember Margot Asquith's reported put-down when Jean Harlow mispronounced her name: 'The *t* is silent, as in *Harlow*' (*Oxford Dictionary of Quotations*, ed. Elizabeth M. Knowles (Oxford University Press, 1999), p. 31).

21 *The Correspondence of Henry and Sarah Fielding*, ed. Martin C. Battestin and Clive T. Probyn (Oxford: Clarendon Press, 1993), p. 70.

*Further reading*

Altman, Janet Gurkin, *Epistolarity: Approaches to a Form* (Columbus, OH: Ohio State University Press, 1982)

Beebee, Thomas O., *Epistolary Fiction in Europe, 1500–1850* (Cambridge University Press, 1999)

Blewett, David, ed., *Passion and Virtue: Essays on the Novels of Samuel Richardson* (University of Toronto Press, 2001)

Bray, Joe, *The Epistolary Novel: Representations of Consciousness* (London: Routledge, 2003)

Castle, Terry, *Clarissa's Ciphers: Meaning and Disruption in Richardson's Clarissa* (Ithaca, NY: Cornell University Press, 1982)

Day, Robert Adams, *Told in Letters: Epistolary Fiction before Richardson* (Ann Arbor: University of Michigan Press, 1966)

Doody, Margaret Anne, *A Natural Passion: A Study of the Novels of Samuel Richardson* (Oxford University Press, 1974)
    and Peter Sabor, eds., *Samuel Richardson: Tercentenary Essays* (Cambridge University Press, 2005)
Eaves, T. C. Duncan and Ben D. Kimpel, *Samuel Richardson: A Biography* (Oxford: Clarendon Press, 1971)
Keymer, Thomas, *Richardson's Clarissa and the Eighteenth-Century Reader* (Cambridge University Press, 1992)
    and Peter Sabor, *Pamela in the Marketplace: Literary Controversy and Print Culture in Eighteenth-Century Britain and Ireland* (Cambridge University Press, 2005)
Maslen, Keith, *Samuel Richardson of London, Printer* (Dunedin: University of Otago, 2001)
Rivero, Albert J., ed., *New Essays on Samuel Richardson*, (New York: St Martin's Press, 1996)
Zunshine, Lisa and Jocelyn Harris, eds., *Approaches to Teaching the Novels of Samuel Richardson* (New York: Modern Language Association, 2006)

# 4

THOMAS LOCKWOOD

# Henry Fielding (1707–1754):
# The comic epic in prose

Fielding was long admired for his representation of a certain classic Englishness to be found nowhere else in such perfection outside the borders of his novels. His own contemporaries were not so much given to this view as the readers and writers of the next century and after, when Parson Adams and Tom Jones and Squire Western had begun to seem the inhabitants of a more distant and dreamlike England: 'when the days were longer', as George Eliot says in a famous tribute to Fielding's digressive genius, 'when summer afternoons were spacious, and the clock ticked slowly in the winter evenings'.[1] Or George Gordon Byron: 'There now are no Squire Westerns as of old.'[2] William Makepeace Thackeray called him 'Harry' Fielding,[3] like some friendly compatriot, and for all who wrote about the novelists of the eighteenth century it was Fielding who stood as the truest historian of that England. You have to be English to relish his writings fully, said Walter Scott – even if you are Scottish or Irish they may be slightly out of reach. 'Parson Adams, Towwouse, Partridge, above all Squire Western, are personages as peculiar to England as they are unknown to other countries ... and scarce an incident occurs, without its being marked by something which could not well have happened in any other country.'[4] Maybe so. But Fielding also belongs to Europe and European traditions more closely than that durable image of an Anglo-Saxon chauvinist Harry Fielding would suggest.

Fielding wrote the immensely popular song 'The Roast Beef of Old England', with its taunting lines about the dainty foods that 'effeminate' Italy, France and Spain. It was first heard in a play about the cross-cultural exposure of an old European hero to parochial Englishness – *Don Quixote in England* (1734) – where Fielding tried rather touchingly to transplant the Quixote and Sancho he so loved and make them come to life in his own soil. But the attempt was a mistake, as Fielding himself said in his Preface, because he could not figure out how to vary his hero 'sufficiently to distinguish a *Quixote* in *England* from a *Quixote* in *Spain*'. From a classic Spanish template Fielding thus made a play that ironically rises to brighter quality only where it is most local and insular, as in its Squire Western prototype Squire Badger, who brings his pack of dogs along with him when he goes courting.

Fielding's great modern European stimulus was Molière. There he found a more successful purchase, brilliantly 'transplanting' *Le Médecin malgré lui* and *L'Avare* as *The Mock Doctor* (1732) and *The Miser* (1733), with their original design and characters much more convincingly naturalised than the stubborn Quixote. Voltaire admired his version of *The Miser*, notably for what he called its 'several beauties of dialogue peculiar to his nation'.[5] And within a decade Fielding by a vibrant creative stroke had imagined how to transplant Quixote likewise, as Parson Adams in *Joseph Andrews*. In both cases, the Continental European influence intensified the self-conscious Englishness of the result. Those national peculiarities Voltaire cited are brought to life by Fielding with the sympathetic fluency of a native speaker. But in his critical outlook he is nevertheless far closer to the internationalist Voltaire than to Thackeray's Harry Fielding.

## Life and career

Fielding was born in and spent his childhood near the village of East Stour in Dorset, amid small farms and pastureland broken up by the 'sweetly winding' river Stour, as he recalled it in *Tom Jones* (IV.viii). As a novelist, he evoked this West Country world and its people with an observant ease matched or bettered only by Thomas Hardy. Like Hardy too, he went to London to follow a career but unlike Hardy never reinhabited that childhood country, except in his books. Fielding went to Eton when he was twelve, where he fed happily on the totalitarian classical diet there with schoolfellows of his time like William Pitt, and by the age of twenty was in London writing verses and a first play, *Love in Several Masques* (1728). By his own admission he was an indifferent poet,[6] to put it mildly, but after two broken terms of more classical Latin studies at the University of Leyden in the faculty of letters, he found a creative home in the London theatre. There, in an uneven but vivid outpouring of comedies and ballad operas from 1728 to 1737, he made himself the most important playwright and theatrical entrepreneur since the days of Dryden.

Fielding evidently travelled elsewhere in Holland while at Leyden in 1729, and may have done further European touring at that time. But he spent the rest of his life within London, or on a narrow track of country travel westward towards Bath and Bristol. In his novels and other writings, he can be found trading on the most shop-worn English clichés about Dutch greed, Jesuit priestcraft, overpaid Italian singers or French dancing-masters.

He was mildly obsessed by dandified *petits maîtres* like Beau Didapper in *Joseph Andrews*, and would drag them onto his stage or page to engineer a comic shudder at their epicene manner and un-English affectation. That too is an old routine of English identity affirmation against a courtly or Continental effete, like Hotspur's disgusted description of the mincing lord, 'perfumed like a milliner', who came to take delivery of his prisoners.[7] And yet in his most artful renditions of such clichés he stands outside his own Englishness, using his native knowledge of a national character like Squire Western to make him irresistibly believable while also realising in him the perfection of every violently xenophobic little Englander or Eurosceptic past or to come.

Fielding wrote and staged more than two dozen plays over the ten years he worked in theatre. It was a hit-or-miss but brilliant career, in experimental daring and sheer theatrical presence beyond anything else to be seen again in London before the twentieth century. He longed to write original stage comedy in the manner of Sir John Vanbrugh and William Wycherley but repeated outings in that form eventually drove home the truth that he had no hand at it. At 'irregular' and mixed forms of stage entertainment answering to commercial demand, on the other hand, like the parody *Tragedy of Tragedies* (1731) or his long-surviving ballad operas, there was no beating him. It was this unruly alternative drama, saturated with the topical foolishness and political noise-making of their moment, that saw Fielding off in flames at the end of his two seasons as author-manager at the Little Theatre in the Haymarket, with cheerfully audacious, tumultuously popular productions of *Pasquin* (1736) and *The Historical Register* (1737). A two-shilling ticket to the latter would buy you a graphically personalised scene of the prime minister Robert Walpole literally fiddling the money out of his political adversaries' pockets while they danced. An unamused Sir Robert pushed through the Licensing Act of 1737, putting an end to any more such unsanctioned productions. Fielding vacated his playhouse life and steered into law studies. He was only 30. No other major English novelist came to prose fiction from such a settled métier in writing for the stage. Miguel de Cervantes did, as also Alain-René Le Sage and Pierre Carlet de Chamblain de Marivaux. And Fielding, like Cervantes, seems to have found the ability to speak for himself in his novel-writing, without assigning the words to some other: a vital creative opening.

Fielding was called to the bar in 1740, making a very hurried three years to that goal. He also started his first newspaper *The Champion* during his final year of attendance at the Middle Temple. Richardson's novel *Pamela* was published in 1740, and that weirdly compelling work, with all its publicity and cultural to-do, brought Fielding onto the field of prose fictional narrative, first with the inspired mimicry of *Shamela* (1741), followed quickly thereafter by his dazzlingly original 'comic epic poem in prose' *Joseph Andrews* (1742). The year after came his mordantly ironic exaltation of a thuggish criminal hero in the mock-heroic fiction *Jonathan Wild*, exposing the shibboleths of respectability as much as the villainy of the criminal, in a vein of black comedy whose descent has been traced to the work of modern European kindred like Alfred Jarry.[8]

Around 1745, Fielding began work on the history of a foundling, as he called it, whose good-hearted, pleasure-loving character Fielding set forth as a touchstone for the England he inhabits. This was *Tom Jones*, published in 1749, a comic masterpiece of romantic idealism but with an unromantically savage eye for the false and self-serving. It is a story of travels and mishaps through a crowded universe of local English places and characters, famously intricate in its plotting, and pitched on a scale of diversity and range, in both story and ever-talkative storyteller, that does really feel 'epic' in the reading experience. In justifying that idea of a comic epic in prose, or work of heroic pretensions wrought from everyday material, Fielding came close to matching the example of his beloved *Don Quixote*, and *Tom Jones* would eventually – after some cavilling – take its place on that same high historic shelf. The decade of the 1740s was one of the greatest such periods in the history of the English novel, with *Pamela* in 1740, answered two years later by *Joseph Andrews*, followed in 1747–8 by Samuel Richardson's great tragic novel of *Clarissa*, moving fiction deeply inward, and finally then the extroverted *Tom Jones*. *Clarissa* made possible a historic fictional shift towards the representation of interior life. *Tom Jones* drew from the older tradition of learned jest and story represented by François Rabelais or Cervantes to create for the developing English novel a form of worldly narrative screened through an authoritative comic intelligence, as in Jane Austen, Charles Dickens, Thackeray, Anthony Trollope or James Joyce.

Fielding had followed a significant career of journalism during all this time, from *The Champion* (1739–41) through two pro-government papers called forth by the Jacobite rising of 1745, *The True Patriot* (1745–6) and *The Jacobite's Journal* (1747–8). *The Champion* was modelled on Richard Steele's *Tatler*, much beloved of Fielding, who veered between bright miscellaneous essays on social and literary subjects, done to a turn worthy of his model, and the grimmer anti-ministerial party political papers which increasingly took over the proceedings. The two later papers have less purely literary interest, but his final outing as the author of a newspaper, in *The Covent-Garden Journal* (1752), saw him free of any partisan agenda and producing some of his very best essays in that form. And it is worth observing that while Fielding does not much matter to literary history as a journalist, nevertheless 'journalism', taken as a writing-up of the experience of the day, is a powerful constituent of the work of his that does matter to literary history. His plays have been plausibly described as a form of 'dramatic journalism',[9] and his novels likewise respond to the world they record in a fashion of intensely observant, albeit highly inflected, reportage.

Fielding's last novel, *Amelia* (1751), was an extraordinary experiment in domestic fiction of a kind never before quite seen, in telling the story of a loving married couple in a nevertheless troubled marriage. The tone is rather sombre and the slightly menacing urban setting, and atmosphere of cynical self-interest, leave us worlds away from the cheery milieu of *Tom Jones*. Fielding put immense effort and ambition into this work but nobody much liked it, with some indeed hooting it as vulgar and 'low'. His public were understandably looking for laughs, and there aren't many. Yet the work matters for its forward-looking conception of what sort of story a novel might allowably tell.

Fielding by now was principal justice of the peace for London and Middlesex, taking depositions and ruling on prison commitments and petty fines for an endless queue of street criminals and complainants in his Bow Street house, just across from Covent Garden Theatre. He was a 'reforming' magistrate who wrote vividly on social and legal subjects and was responsible for significant improvements in local law enforcement, including the beginnings of a professional constabulary. But his health was collapsing. He sailed to Lisbon in 1754, hoping for benefit from the warmer climate, but not long after arriving he died and was buried in the Protestant cemetery of that city – this most English of authors ironically thus stopping for good in of all places Portugal, as was to happen some years later in Italy for the furiously Scottish novelist Tobias Smollett, in a grave at Leghorn. Fielding was 47. He left a dark but grimly funny account of his experience of this sea passage in *The Journal of a Voyage to Lisbon*, published posthumously in 1755.

## European afterlife

*Joseph Andrews* and *Tom Jones* were translated into French as well as Dutch shortly after publication,[10] though with significant omissions or alterations. *Amelia* was in Dutch by 1758 and in two French versions in 1762.[11] *Jonathan Wild* was also translated into Dutch (1757) and French (1763), and the Lucianic *Journey from This World to the Next*, originally part of Fielding's *Miscellanies* (1743), appeared in German, French and Danish by 1769. In the 1760s and 1770s there were translations of *Joseph Andrews* and *Tom Jones* in Italian, German and Russian, in most cases made second hand from the French versions which mainly represented the novels in Continental Europe.

Fielding had a powerful presence in eighteenth-century European letters, and an avid following, from Desfontaines to the reviewer in *L'Année littéraire* who saw him as having been 'immortalised' by *Joseph Andrews* and *Tom Jones*.[12] Horace Walpole's great correspondent Madame du Deffand loved *Tom Jones*, more indeed than the fastidious Walpole; Voltaire said he found nothing passable there except the barber, but from La Place's translation of *Tom Jones* he may have borrowed a circumstance for *Candide*.[13] Fielding's European reputation went up and down, with the French especially at first showing the same inevitable aversion to the *grossièreté* as some English readers, but *Tom Jones* won through easily to classic status, with a wide reach of popularity extending to eighteenth-century Russia.[14] By 1838 Stendhal could say it was to other novels what the *Iliad* was among epics.[15] French critics particularly have made out an essential likeness of intellectual and artistic spirit between Fielding and Molière.[16] Apart from the comparatively short period of intense European engagement with Richardson's *Clarissa*, in the 1760s following the Abbé Prévost's translation and Denis Diderot's 'éloge', Fielding has been the most important and durable eighteenth-century English novelist in Europe. *Clarissa* eventually retreated to its original language form only, but *Tom Jones* is still in print in French, German, Italian, Spanish and other European languages.

## *Joseph Andrews* (1742)

It is hard to get an unobstructed view of *Joseph Andrews*, since we look back at it with some column or corner of *Tom Jones* inevitably blocking the line of sight. For two and a half centuries, it has been the predecessor of a more imposing successor, but there was a brief season of seven years when it stood alone as Fielding's greatest work, and on some counts, if not all, may still be. If *Tom Jones* interferes with our view of this novel on one side, *Pamela* sits distractingly on the other. Fielding began his novel from that prompt, and borrows from the Richardson story for an Andrews brother. But *Pamela* drew Fielding not because it could be parodied but because it was modern and real. What Fielding parodies or otherwise rebuts of the original has little importance next to that realistic modernity he recreates from Richardson in his own entirely different idiom.

In its essential creative character *Joseph Andrews* belongs purely to itself, but this self-possession is something the book grows into rather slowly, over the first ten chapters. Fielding was certainly aiming all along at an imaginative result wholly his own – for who could explain the result he did achieve as an accident? But for a long fictional narrative this was aiming where he had never gone before, and he does therefore linger doubtfully at first within the margin of Richardson's world until he finds a crossing to his own. Fielding also knew Marivaux's work well and rated him highly for his gifts of humour.[17] *La Vie de Marianne* (1731–42) and *Le Paysan parvenu* (1735–6) both had a probable if not certain influence on his conception of a virtuous young hero left to make his way through a hypocritical and self-interested social world. But in narrative method, not to mention *marivaudage*, Fielding takes nothing from that source.

The story material of *Joseph Andrews* was pure *rosbif* English. But the storyteller's thinking about its form was intellectualist European. In the Preface, Fielding maps out a family of classical and modern European literary genres, from Homer through François Fénelon and the French heroic romance, within which he makes a place for *Joseph Andrews* as comic romance or 'comic Epic-Poem in Prose'. And he continues these self-defining theoretical reflections elsewhere within the novel, particularly in the initial chapters of its first three books, following a discursive method he was to enlarge dramatically in *Tom Jones*. The chapter on the truthfulness of fictional biography which begins Book III of *Joseph Andrews* is a rich argumentative survey of Spanish, French and English examples and critical commentary. The analysis he offers there of the 'Samaritan' lawyer from the local, deeply English episode of Joseph's 'rescue' by the stagecoach (bk I, ch. 12) aspires to globally wider scope of place and time, dated from 'when the first mean selfish Creature appeared on the human Stage'.

Most critical readers have had nothing good to say about the plot of *Joseph Andrews*. 'The incidents are ill laid and without invention', wrote Thomas Gray (who preferred Marivaux and Prosper Jolyot de Crébillon) in a famous letter to Richard West,[18] and his opinion seems virtually endorsed by Fielding himself in *Tom Jones*, which so spectacularly redeems the weakness of this shaky first effort of plot artistry. *Joseph Andrews* became famous for one of its characters, whereas *Tom Jones* is celebrated as a great constructive whole. *Joseph Andrews* begins in a world of borrowed matter, leaning towards parody, but then enters an utterly different imaginative world of original scenery and people, drawn with arresting fidelity; and turns yet elsewhere again at the end, putting the principals, and the reader, through an unnatural denouement of gypsy stories and stage farce. These diverse forms can be argued into some kind of unity by remote fetches of criticism, but it is obvious that Fielding, though so powerfully imagining his characters and scenes, had little power to imagine any whole they might form. The best invention of his plot is the passion of Lady Booby, which drives Joseph back to Somerset, and then again drives some of the events in the final book. But she is a limited influence, and after Joseph has left her, the history assumes the form simply of an adventure narrative, little different in that respect from the old picaresque. And yet this too is the very part of the work where its genius shines, as if plot design and that 'spirit' so often admired in this novel were working in inverse relation. Fielding's imagination comes into its own only where there is little or no matter to be invented – where he can be the imaginative observer of what he has seen, not the pretended observer of what he has imagined. 'I have writ little more than I have seen' (bk III, ch. 1).

Fielding is not the maker of his material – not a poet. The characters of *Joseph Andrews* come ready made from what he has seen – literally in the case of Parson Adams, taken from his friend William Young – but Fielding in this novel comes closer to the poet in his realisation of character than he would ever again. Not only is this the book of his one greatest character, but the whole of the character ensemble has a living force, and seeming independence of the page, that the cast even of *Tom Jones* does not quite possess. They are the same people, justices and squires and servants and parsons, but the handling is different – or the handler, who takes a more unassuming place on the stage of this story than he does in *Tom Jones*, where he is his own greatest character, with the result that in *Joseph Andrews* he seems able to reproduce a vital otherness of character more freely than he could, or would, in the more elaborately self-conscious mood of *Tom Jones*. The characters of *Joseph Andrews* are not so much summoned imaginarily into our presence as are we into theirs. And no character summons us more completely than Parson Adams, one of the few genuinely Shakespearean creations of that age and its literature, without Falstaff's advantage of lovable wickedness either, and Cervantean too, though without the Quixotic melancholy: 'not so much copied from life into literature', as George Saintsbury said, 'as passing direct from literature into life'.[19] But Adams was a miraculous exception for Fielding, who is almost always at his heroic best, artistically, with *l'homme moyen sensuel* and all the unheroic characters of averagely sensual and selfish mankind.

Take the 'interview' (as Fielding calls it) between Parson Adams and Parson Trulliber (bk II, ch. 14), one of the scenes every reader would class as among the greatest of the story. It gets some of its vitality and humour from Adams of course, as when he cries out from the depths of the pigsty, 'Nihil habeo cum porcis'. But the scene in all its explosive contrasts and dark subtext belongs to the hog-farming Trulliber, who is brought to horrific life at his breakfast table, 'caaling vurst' for the ale he snatches from Adams and silencing his wife in words vibrating with remembered blows. This is no caricature of a parson as a pig; instead a pig has turned into a parson and Fielding seems merely to be describing the perfectly convincing result. Trulliber is appalling, but funny too, and in this scene, like so many in *Joseph Andrews*, Fielding creates an imaginative environment that breathes freely, so to speak, and its breath is humour. I will not attempt the impossible, or undesirable, in analysing the humour, but it is the prime spiritual constituent of this novel, and Fielding's great achievement is to open up this breathing space, where the humour is not 'produced' but instead discovers itself, or seems to. Against the example of a *Tom Jones* yet to come, his personal narrative presence in such scenes is restrained and discontinuous (though against his own professed example of Cervantes it is considerably more abundant). He talks less, and when he does talk, he does so with less authority though more authenticity as to the platform of his talking, which sits close to the ground where his characters themselves walk and talk – as witness his derivative Cervantean trick of pretending to take the information of his story directly from the people of the story: 'Mr. *Adams*, from whom we had most of this Relation' (bk III, ch. 7). That pretence belongs to classical 'true history' and is mostly dropped for *Tom Jones*, where Fielding holds communication rather with his readers than with his characters.

*Joseph Andrews* was notoriously 'low' – George Cheyne told Richardson it was 'fit only for porters and watermen'[20] – and Fielding memorably unfolds a 'Dissertation concerning high People and low People' (bk II, ch. 13), between whom the only difference turns out to be what time you get up. As a matter of fact, there are no porters or watermen in the novel, but Fielding's preference for the socially indiscriminate setting of the road, and his indiscriminate tone of address, make it seem that such characters might be freely welcome, no less than their betters and maybe more. That authorial tone itself is not low but privileged-sounding, as in its perfect vicarious attunement to the high-bred horror of the contaminating low. Fielding himself, on the contrary, felt a horror of the empty high, and in *Joseph Andrews* he mostly passes over the whole powdered and laced part of creation as if they did not exist – they whose life is 'much the dullest', as he later drily observed in *Tom Jones*, and 'no very great Resource to a Writer whose Province is Comedy' (bk XIV, ch. 1). Yet they are present, in that he cannot write about chambermaids or postilions without bringing in their mistresses and masters. And it is mainly those betters, and their deficiencies of betterness, that preoccupy Fielding's social outlook. If he has only a condescending faith in the virtue of servants, in *Joseph Andrews* he has no faith whatever in the virtue of masters; and likewise as to poor and rich, little and great, governed and governor. There is something reck-lessly egalitarian about the spirit of this book: not from its system of levelling high down to low (*Pamela*, levelling low up to high, was potentially more reckless), but from the impatient freedom of tone it takes towards privilege, and what William Hazlitt called the 'farce of respectability'.[21] No other contemporary European novel even dreamt of such liberties.

*Tom Jones* has an authoritative tone, and behind the tone a spirit, of mastery. But *Joseph Andrews* remains marked by a characteristic spirit more of freedom than mastery. For Fielding, this novel was a liberating stroke of creative will, the moment and record of a great imaginative release. It gave him what he had been looking for since his earliest theatre days, namely, a means of writing freely about modern life, in a true history of his own times. *Tom Jones* was to be the apotheosis of this finding, the great working-out of his original discovery. But nothing else, not even *Tom Jones*, ever came up to the spiritual *élan* of the discovering original itself. Two centuries later the notably unenchantable Samuel Beckett was 'enchanted' by it – like *The Vicar of Wakefield* and *Jacques le fataliste* rolled into one, he said.[22]

## Tom Jones (1749)

From first publication, *Tom Jones* was almost immediately recognised as a work of international importance. Just as rapidly too, it became a case for debate about the moral purpose of fiction. Richardson thought it coarse and called the hero who allowed himself to be kept by Lady Bellaston 'the Lowest of all Fellows'.[23] Samuel Johnson wrote against it, though not by name, in *The Rambler* (31 March 1750), arguing powerfully against a realism he believed to be indiscriminate and falsely seductive – if art is merely to mirror nature, without shaping a moral meaning, why not simply turn our gaze directly upon nature? This was his criticism of William Shakespeare too, and set the terms of debate over this novel for more than a century to come. The early French response was admiring but squeamish about Tom's loose conduct. Thackeray found him to be an 'inadmissible' hero.[24] But for the modern history of the novel, *Tom Jones* was the great breakthrough on the very values which the early critical tradition accurately perceived to be decisive: range of material, especially downward to the 'low' of gamekeeper, servant or thief, and welcoming treatment of that material, on a declared principle of realistic over didactic purpose. In the days of Scott and Thackeray, *Tom Jones* was a book thought unfit for family libraries, and a light smoke of indecency trailed the novel well into the twentieth century.

It is ironic that a writer who asserted such ostentatious control over his narrative in the narrating of it should have been reckoned as one who mirrored the world directly, without moral mediation. But these have been the two characteristics of *Tom Jones* most often recognised: an intensely if companionably self-conscious narrator, holding discourse while telling a story he identifies in his first chapter as belonging to the 'prodigious variety' of human nature, and as such beyond his remit to alter or soften without departing from the rule of truth he lays down as sacred. His book is not romance but 'history', after all. Fielding's great achievement in *Tom Jones* was to create a form of realism which so openly acknowledges its artificiality. This he does by the very wall he seems to create between the matter of his story and his own commentary upon it. The so-called 'intrusive narrator' would eventually be criticised, by Henry James among others, as undermining a supposedly crucial illusion of reality. But for the future of the novel, especially in Britain but also in Continental Europe, Russia and America, Fielding created a heroic standard of artistic conviction and flexibility in the freely speaking omniscient narrator, reproduced and significantly developed in Laurence Sterne, Scott, Austen, Stendhal, Thackeray, Honoré de Balzac, Dickens, Nikolai Gogol, Eliot, Trollope, Mark Twain, Thomas Mann, André Gide and others. His interference in the narrative, not only by direct commentary but also by his fluently variable command of his characters' speech and dialogue, from more to less direct representation, was beyond anything seen in previous early modern fiction. Austen is said to have preferred Frances Burney to the less creditable author of *Tom Jones*, but for the little miracles of free indirect discourse she performs in realising character, the path goes back only to Fielding.

*Tom Jones* is a love story, built up around the simple action of thwarted romance Fielding had followed in his first play. The theme of the action is equally simple, that merit counts more than rank or money – or should. Fielding at 18 had tried to elope with a Lyme Regis heiress called Sarah Andrew and found merit and love no match for property and relations. That first play revisited this experience, which ends happily on the stage, as would *Tom Jones*, in each case not without some sacrifice of the worldly realism otherwise prevailing in the story. Within the medium of that realism, Fielding's happy endings are unbelievable but authenticated on a different scoring system of moral rather than worldly truth. The author who has faithfully exposed the mostly vicious reflexes of everyday self-interest and social power against the claims of undefended love or innocence, and whose picture of this world carries such conviction, grants an indulgence of wholly inconsistent escape from all that at the end and is indulged in turn perhaps by the reader. As in *Joseph Andrews*, the story matter taken by itself, without the principal characters and the leavening humour, is bleak: an ignorant squire given to ugly domestic outbursts and physical abuse, a corrupt magistracy, empty-headed nobility, debased and drunken soldiery, a resentful serving class, sycophantic clergy, all grasping for selfish advantage under ridiculous masks of polite form, in voices cold with respectable indifference or heated up in moral sloganeering. It's a good thing Fielding makes that material funny, because in itself it is anything but.

More even than in *Joseph Andrews*, Fielding works to the model of a comic epic prose narrative. *Tom Jones* is three times the length of its predecessor, and gives an even greater and more deliberately cultivated impression of comprehensive volume and reach, from country to city, low rank to high. Whereas, in *Joseph Andrews*, Fielding had argued somewhat defensively for a classical epic lineage, he is far more confident about that association in *Tom Jones*. He copies gestures of epic form into the work in the mock-heroic similes or embedded stories like those of the Man of the Hill and Mrs Fitzpatrick. The quality of ancient epic is reproduced more truly, however, in the sheer comprehensiveness and variety of the story matter, rendered in that highly distinctive centralised narrative voice which is supplied in poetical epic by the singing voice of the poetry itself. In its comic prosaic modernity, *Tom Jones* nevertheless recaptures the classic epic impression of a world revealed in literal totality rather than by any method of selection and exclusion, the sense that everything of significance from this world is being included in the work, directly along the path of the main story or indirectly through digressive interpolation.

Fielding in *Tom Jones* mastered a representation of character more fluent, complex and varied than that of *Joseph Andrews*. He knows how to let his characters talk freely, or seem to, in speech and dialogue nevertheless still coloured and intensified by his own narrative presence. He assembles scenes of multiple characters in directly and indirectly quoted speech with an adroit touch, balancing the purposes of plot against comic display and cutting off the dialogue when it threatens to drift. The scene in which Honour is hauled before Western 'in the character of a magistrate' (bk. VII, ch. 9), to be sacked and committed to Bridewell for her having called Mrs Western ugly (or as Mrs Western's own maid eagerly reports it, 'ugly old Cat'), is typical. Fielding deploys Western and his sister in a comic tangle fuelled by the rage of the plaintiff, keeping the two characters in view while also introducing the little back story of Mrs Western's 'forgiving Temper' towards the highwayman who called her a 'handsome bitch', and then Western's own history of shaky knowledge of the law, when his clerk has to remind him that he cannot commit anyone to jail 'only for Ill-breeding'. Western and his sister fall into what Fielding calls 'a very learned Dispute' over the law, 'which we would insert', he goes on, 'if we imagined many of our Readers could understand it'.

Beyond the comic turns of the scene, and the narrative irony, what distinguishes the result here, as throughout the novel, is the proportion, movement and timing of the various parts of the representation: the focus shifting fluidly from one character to the other, and from background to present time, in an unerringly controlled mix of direct and indirect speech, sometimes also falling into that peculiar middle zone between the two in which the apparatus of direct quotation has not quite transformed the third-person pronoun belonging to the relative clause of indirect speech into the first-person form pronoun logically required ('Mrs. *Western* said, "she knew the Law much better"'). Fielding's merciful omission of the learned dispute is worth noticing too, not only as another of his transparent pretences of authenticity in material of which he is the historian as opposed to inventor, but also for his more regular use of this conceit in *Tom Jones*, where it parades the very editorial freedom and power so crucial to his own part in the book. How little difference there is (would seem to be the arch suggestion) between the suppression of direct speech by indirect, for example, and the suppression of speech altogether, as of Western and his brother squire at the end of the hunt, saluting each other 'in all Squire-like Greeting': 'The Conversation was entertaining enough', says the deadpan Fielding, 'and what we may perhaps relate in an Appendix, or on some other Occasion' (bk XII, ch. 2). In an Appendix!

The intellectual heart of *Tom Jones* is a preoccupation with moral judgement, often taking the form of a rhetorical enactment of the process by which any true judgement of action and motive is to be managed. The deception and murkiness of that process are part of the enactment, as when we are led through the indirectly represented pre-matrimonial thinking of Bridget Allworthy and Captain Blifil, as they each determine upon the charms and satisfactions of the other, with Fielding adopting successively more revealing language to mimic the detective art of coming at the truth through layers of interested mystification. Finally, we are told 'plainly' that the captain from the beginning 'had been greatly enamoured' – a lingering last leaf of hypocrisy Fielding affords his utterly love-incapable character there in a semicolon pause – 'greatly enamoured; that is to say, of Mr Allworthy's House and Gardens, and of his Lands, Tenements, and Hereditaments' (bk I, ch. 11). The swerve upward from common to law language exposes the exact truth of character perfectly: you can be human and love a house and gardens, but not really legal tenements, and still less be 'so passionately fond' of anything for which the correct word could ever be hereditaments.

Truth of character in *Tom Jones*, as well as *Joseph Andrews*, is defined by likeness rather than difference: what links many under a 'species' matters more than any differences at the level of the individual. And while the typing of character remains the representational principle on which Fielding fills up the pages of *Tom Jones* with people, from pert servants and rustic squires to lazy parsons and idle lords, Fielding concentrates so on perfecting his discriminations within such types that the individual example can seem less exemplary than individualised. 'There are certain Characteristics', he says, 'in which most Individuals of every Profession and Occupation agree. To be able to preserve these Characteristics, and at the same Time to diversify their Operations, is one Talent of a good Writer' (bk x, ch. 1). It is this diversification that brings the characters of *Tom Jones* closer to a modern fictional ideal of realistic individualisation – the opposite end of the road from the artificial personages of Gaultier de Costes, Seigneur de La Calprenède, or allegorical figures like Helpful and Obstinate in John Bunyan's *The Pilgrim's Progress*. But while Sophia's maid Honour is beautifully distinguished from within her category of intriguing soubrette, this individualisation is a bit of a trick and whatever meaning her character might have is still controlled by that category; and likewise even with the ultimate such example in the book, if not also in the whole of the period literature, Squire Western, who despite his classic identification with the type of the Tory country squire, even to his allegorical name, nevertheless makes you think first only of himself, inimitable and unlike any other. This is ultimately perhaps an artful effect of theatrical or externalised diversification, rather than individuation based on inward personal identity, and as such may not mark a station on the road leading to canonical forms of characterisation in the developed modern novel. But it is an extraordinary achievement of art.

## Conclusion

What non-English readers have always admired about Fielding is not so much his Englishness as the realism of the Englishness he reproduces. Maxim Gorky called Fielding 'the creator of the realistic novel, a man of wonderful knowledge of his country's mode of life'.[25] Meanwhile, his novels show him contriving to find an equivalently realistic place for himself within his narratives. From ten years in theatre without any such place came a moment, first in *Joseph Andrews* and then consummately in *Tom Jones*, when he put himself into those books in such perfectly tuned relation to the world he wrote about, lighting it up with a comic imagination of such depth and rarity, that the result has seldom been approached again anywhere in the English or for that matter European novel. This moment did not last, because something happened in *Amelia* to drive the author off the page. In telling the story of Booth and Amelia he seems to have lost his own place and voice. Fielding believed in love, and love is what redeems a world he describes in all his novels as darkly seized otherwise by a grim rule of self. But the discursive comic imagination that inflected his portrayal of that world in *Joseph Andrews* and *Tom Jones* seems to have become impossible in *Amelia*.

The imagination and critical intelligence represented by the narrator of those two great novels, and especially *Tom Jones*, belong to a classical European tradition from Aristophanes and Lucian through Giovanni Boccaccio, Rabelais, Michel de Montaigne, Cervantes, Molière and Jonathan Swift. It is an intellectual as much as purely creative tradition, grounded in everyday experience imaginatively rethought rather than transcended. Fielding is a modern mind, with pagan roots. He has an Enlightenment contempt for ignorance and credulity, but no Enlightenment vision of a new social order. Byron thought that had Fielding been his own contemporary he would have been classed with the revolutionaries,[26] but that is unlikely. He has a bracing disdain for privilege that might seem revolutionary. But he also loves the order of society, including its privileged characters of every rank, for the creative best it brings out in him, which is not philosophy or moral teaching but laughter.

## Note on editions

The standard is the Wesleyan Edition of the Works of Henry Fielding, ed. William B. Coley and others (Oxford: Clarendon Press, 1967–2011). Useful other editions of the novels are *Joseph Andrews and Shamela*, ed. Douglas Brooks-Davies and revised by Thomas Keymer (Oxford World's Classics, 1999); *Tom Jones* (Norton Critical Edition), ed. Sheridan Baker, 2nd edn (1995), Penguin edition, ed. Thomas Keymer and Alice Wakeley (2005); *Jonathan Wild*, ed. Claude Rawson and Linda Bree (Oxford World's Classics, 2003); *Amelia*, ed. Linda Bree (Peterborough, ON: Broadview Press, 2010).

## Notes

1 George Eliot, *Middlemarch*, ch. 15.
2 George Gordon Byron, *Don Juan*, canto XIII, stanza 110.
3 Cf. e.g. William Makepeace Thackeray, the lecture on 'Hogarth, Smollett, and Fielding', published as part of *The English Humourists of the Eighteenth Century* (1853).
4 Walter Scott, 'Henry Fielding', in *Lives of the Novelists* (1821–4).
5 Voltaire, *Vie de Molière* (1739), in *Voltaire électronique*, ed. Ulla Kölving (Oxford: Voltaire Foundation, 1998), ¶ 122.

6 'This Branch of Writing is what I very little pretend to' (Henry Fielding, Preface to *Miscellanies*, 1743).

7 William Shakespeare, *Henry IV, Part 1*, I.iii.

8 See C. J. Rawson, *Henry Fielding and the Augustan Ideal Under Stress* (London: Routledge & Kegan Paul, 1972), pp. 171–227.

9 Charles B. Woods, 'Introduction', in Woods, ed., *The Author's Farce* (Lincoln, NB: University of Nebraska Press, 1966), p. xiv.

10 *Les avantures de Joseph Andrews, et du Ministre Abraham Adams* (1744), trans. Pierre François Guyot Desfontaines; *Histoire de Tom Jones, ou l'enfant trouvé* (1750), trans. Pierre Antoine de la Place; the Dutch versions appear in the same years.

11 The first being *Amélie*, trans. Marie Jeanne Riccoboni, with many cuts and changes, the other more faithfully by P. F. de Puisieux, who observes in his Preface that the reader can now choose between two Amelias, one French, the other English.

12 (Amsterdam, 1763), II.26–7 (review dated 23 February 1763): 'M. Fielding s'est rendu immortel par les Romans de *Joseph Andrews* et *Tom Jones*; on baise aujourd'hui toutes les traces de ses pas.'

13 Letter of 14 July 1773, *Correspondence of Horace Walpole*, ed. W. S. Lewis (New Haven: Yale University Press, 1937–83), v.383; Voltaire, letter to Mme du Deffand, 13 October 1759, no. 7806 in *Voltaire's Correspondence*, ed. Theodore Besterman (Geneva: Institut et Musée Voltaire, 1958), XXXVII.134; E. M. Langille, 'La Place's *Histoire de Tom Jones, ou l'enfant trouvé* and *Candide*', *Eighteenth-Century Fiction*, 19 (2007), 267–89.

14 See Iu. D. Levin, 'Translations of Henry Fielding's Works in Eighteenth-Century Russia', *The Slavonic and East European Review*, 68 (1990), 217–33.

15 Entry for Nivernais, 18 April 1837, in *Mémoires d'un Touriste* (Paris, 1838).

16 As e.g. Louis-Claude Chéron de la Bruyère, in the Preface of his translation of *Tom Jones* (Paris, 1804): 'Il est resté comme *Molière* seul de sa classe', or Aurélien Digeon, speaking of *Joseph Andrews* in *Les Romans de Fielding* (Paris: Librairie Hachette, 1923): 'L'esprit qui l'anime est bien celui qui animait Molière. Il a ses méthodes, il parle de ses personnages et de son art dans les mêmes termes que lui' (p. 115).

17 See Henry Fielding, *Tom Jones*, XIII.i.; cf. also Henry Fielding, *Joseph Andrews*, III.i.

18 [8] April [1742], in *Correspondence of Thomas Gray*, ed. Paget Toynbee and Leonard Whibley (Oxford: Clarendon Press, 1935), I.191.

19 George Saintsbury, *The Peace of the Augustans* (London: G. Bell and Sons, 1916), p. 122.

20 George Cheyne, Letter of 9 March 1741/2, in Alan D. McKillop, *Samuel Richardson* (Chapel Hill, NC: University of North Carolina Press, 1936), p. 77.

21 William Hazlitt, 'On Respectable People' (1818), in *The Plain Speaker* (1826).

22 i.e. Oliver Goldsmith's *Vicar of Wakefield* (1766) and Denis Diderot's *Jacques le fataliste* (posthumously publ. 1796). Letter to Thomas McGreevy, 8 October 1732, in *The Letters of Samuel Beckett*, vol. I, ed. Martha Dow Fehsenfeld and Lois More Overbeck (Cambridge University Press, 2009), p. 129.

23 Samuel Richardson, Letter to Astraea and Minerva Hill, 4 August 1749, in *Henry Fielding: The Critical Heritage*, ed. Ronald Paulson and Thomas Lockwood (London: Routledge & Kegan Paul, 1969), p. 174.

24 In the 'Hogarth, Smollett, and Fielding' lecture, cited above.
25 Quoted in Levin, 'Translations of Henry Fielding's Works', p. 233.
26 See entry 116 (1821), *Byron's Letters and Journals*, ed. Leslie A. Marchand (Cambridge, MA: Harvard University Press, 1973–82), IX.50.

## Further reading

### Biographical

Battestin, Martin C. with Ruthe R. Battestin, *Henry Fielding: A Life* (London/New York: Routledge, 1989). The standard modern biography

Rogers, Pat, *Henry Fielding: A Biography* (London: Paul Elek, 1979). The best short biography

### Critical studies

*(including those especially useful for Fielding in a European context)*

Alter, Robert, *Fielding and the Nature of the Novel* (Cambridge: Harvard University Press, 1968)

Hunter, J. Paul, *Occasional Form: Henry Fielding and the Chains of Circumstance* (Baltimore, MD: Johns Hopkins University Press, 1975)

Knight, Charles A., 'Fielding's Afterlife', in *The Cambridge Companion to Henry Fielding*, ed. Claude Rawson (Cambridge University Press, 2007), pp. 175–89

Mace, Nancy A., *Henry Fielding's Novels and the Classical Tradition* (Newark, DE: University of Delaware Press, 1987)

Paulson, Ronald, *Satire and the Novel in Eighteenth-Century England* (New Haven: Yale University Press, 1967)

and Thomas Lockwood, *Fielding: The Critical Heritage* (London: Routledge & Kegan Paul, 1969)

Rawson, Claude, *Henry Fielding and the Augustan Ideal Under Stress* (London: Routledge & Kegan Paul, 1972)

ed., *The Cambridge Companion to Henry Fielding* (Cambridge University Press, 2007)

ed., *Henry Fielding: A Critical Anthology* (Harmondsworth: Penguin, 1973)

# 5

TIMOTHY O'HAGAN

# Jean-Jacques Rousseau (1712–1778): The novel of sensibility

First published in 1761, *Julie, ou la nouvelle Héloïse* has been described as 'perhaps the biggest best-seller of the century ... At least seventy editions were published before 1800 – probably more than for any other novel in the previous history of publishing.'[1] In the huge corpus of Rousseau's work, it was his one full-length novel. Set in a remote location on the shore of Lake Geneva at the foot of the Swiss Alps, it takes the form of an exchange of letters between a young woman, Julie, and her tutor, St Preux, who would become her lover. The other principal characters engaged in the correspondence are her cousin and confidante Claire, Wolmar, who is destined to become Julie's husband, and an English nobleman, Lord Edward Bomston. The affair is brought to an abrupt halt by Julie's brutal father, the Baron d'Étange, who then marries his unhappy daughter off to his old friend Wolmar. The rest of the novel tells of their apparently harmonious marriage, the exile and return of St Preux, and culminates in a dramatic denouement at Julie's deathbed.

Countless readers recorded their ecstatic, tearful responses in letters to the author. Women and men, aristocrats and commoners, English clergymen, Calvinist pastors like Paul-Claude Moultou and Catholic priests like the Abbé Cahagne, even some sceptical *philosophes* were overwhelmed by this convoluted narrative of thwarted passion and fragile virtue. They identified intensely with the characters. Many, particularly women, were convinced that Rousseau had put himself into the persona of St Preux, Julie's lover. In his *Confessions*, Rousseau suggests that he did indeed identify himself with the lover: 'What made women so favourable to me was their persuasion that I had written my own story and that I myself was the Hero of this novel.'[2] One aristocratic lady wanted Rousseau to let her see Julie's portrait. According to Rousseau himself, female readers responded to his picture of close friendship between two women, and to his careful observation of their contrasting characters. And they responded to what they took to be a bitter-sweet lesson in morality, as passion gives way to duty. Rousseau found that many of his readers understood his epistolary fiction very differently from himself.

Among the *philosophes*, Jean le Rond d'Alembert was most generous in his praise. David Hume, before he and Rousseau acrimoniously fell out, judged that *Julie* was Rousseau's 'Master-piece'. Voltaire and Friedrich-Melchior Grimm, in contrast, sneered at a naive provincial writer trying to compete with the literary sophisticates of Paris. While Voltaire's *Lettres sur la nouvelle Héloïse ou Aloïsia* still entertains as a brutally witty deconstruction of Rousseau's over-the-top effusions, Grimm's review was simply offensive. However, in both there is a whiff of sour grapes, a sense that their polished, cynical world of good taste and wit was threatened by Rousseau's novel, and that the newly emancipated reading public was hungry for a new kind of popular literature, passionate yet edifying, which they found, or thought they had found, in *Julie*.

Rousseau probably had little time to respond to fan mail as he was preoccupied by lengthy altercations with publishers and booksellers. At the same time, he was negotiating with the French government censor Guillaume-Chrétien de Lamoignon de Malesherbes. In 1762 Rousseau brought out two further masterpieces, *Du contrat social* and *Émile*. Malesherbes promptly banned the former, while the Archbishop of Paris anathematised the latter and ordered it to be publicly burned. The same fate awaited it in Geneva. An edict expelling Rousseau from France soon followed. His exile, in Switzerland then in England, would last eight years.

Unlike other eighteenth-century best-sellers, *Julie* seems to have lost its appeal to the modern public. In 1932, Étienne Gilson lamented that so few shared his enjoyment of the novel,[3] and a few years ago Robert Darnton, an enthusiastic champion of much pre-Revolutionary French fiction, judged it to be 'unreadable today'. Now the modern reader might well be put off by the whimsical, mock-apologetic First Preface in which Rousseau anticipates the mockery of Parisian critics, and defends the gauche behaviour of his characters, in particular their unsophisticated language. He declares that this is a tale of 'provincials, outsiders, young people, almost children', pretending to be philosophers. Of course if Rousseau had written such a tale of innocent 'children' playing in an Arcadian landscape, it would be unlikely to attract a following today. But if you immerse yourself in their world, you will find a dark, realistic depiction of adults engaged in elaborate games of manipulation and moral blackmail. Choderlos de Laclos, author of the most brutal of epistolary novels, recognised this when he took Rousseau's words as the motto for *Les Liaisons dangereuses* (*Dangerous Liaisons*): 'I have seen the morals of our time and I have published these letters.' Rousseau hoped that *Julie* would be a novel of multiple reconciliations between generations, between social classes, between ideologies, between men and women. In what follows I shall show that such harmony is not finally achieved in this novel, but remains for ever in the 'realm of chimeras' (*Julie*, VI.8.693/569).

## Sense and sensibility

In the life sciences of the eighteenth century, sensibility played an important role. The *Encyclopédie* (vol. XV, 1765) contains a long entry on *sensibilité* written by a medical doctor named Henri Fouquet, who describes it as that property of the living body which allows it 'to perceive impressions of external objects and thereby to produce appropriate movements in proportion to the degree of intensity of the perception.' In his *Eléments de physiologie* (1773–4), Denis Diderot expresses the same idea more succinctly: 'Sensibility is a property of the animal which makes it aware of the relations existing between it and all that surrounds it.' He proceeds to outline a materialist account of sensibility in terms of the neurological science of his time.

Rousseau shared this Enlightenment conception of sensibility, though he distanced himself from the out-and-out materialism which was implicit in it. The first axiom of Rousseau's *Émile, ou De l'éducation* (*Emile, or on Education*, 1762) was: 'We are born endowed with sensibility (*nous naissons sensibles*) and are affected in different ways by the objects which surround us'; and he goes on to discern in sensibility the faculty which allows the individual to discover his own identity as the bearer of 'an active force'.[4] Thus in the scientific terminology of the early modern period which Rousseau made his own, 'sensibility' designates the capacity of all animals to experience sensations through their sense organs and to respond to them; human beings are distinguished from other animals by having sentiments, those particular feelings which lead them to reflect on and control immediate sensory stimuli, and so to engage in moral relations with others.[5]

Rousseau exploits that idea of sensibility to show how one's personality is formed through interaction with one's natural and social environment. He called this 'the wise man's materialism' (*le matérialisme du sage*, *Confessions*, IX.4.9/343–4). He considered it wiser than the deterministic mechanism espoused by many of the *philosophes* because it accorded a degree of autonomy to the individual which he found lacking in their systems. From this perspective, sense (understood as common sense) and sensibility are not polar opposites. Rather, they represent differences in temperament which stem from two interdependent factors: the strength of our passions and the environment surrounding us. Thus those endowed with an *âme sensible* (sensitive soul) are subject to more powerful passions than those ruled by sense. This does not mean that a person's character is fixed for life. In response to changing circumstances the balance between sense and sensibility within a person's character also changes. In Rousseau's novel, sensibility is dominant in the two main protagonists, Julie and St Preux, while each has a counterpart representing sense: for Julie it is her cousin Claire, while for St Preux it is his patron, counsellor and surrogate father, Lord Edward Bomston. Only at the end of the book does Claire reveal the depth of her own passion.

As a heroine of sensibility, Julie is buffeted by conflicting passions. Among them, pity plays a dominant role at crucial moments. The Abbé Cahagne was worried that she had sacrificed love for duty, and thereby betrayed herself. In his reply to the Abbé, Rousseau declared that the task of the novelist is to depict the lives of his characters truthfully, not to pass judgement on their behaviour:

> Whenever in a novel one depicts a particular action one is not concerned with the moral question but with the imitation of nature. It is not a question of knowing whether Julie acted rightly or wrongly in marrying, but whether, acting freely in the given situation and consistently with her character, the decision she had to take was either to obey her father or, having seen him on his knees in floods of tears, to hold out against his despair, never allowing herself to be deflected.[6]

Looking back at the moment of weakness when she first submitted to St Preux's advances, Julie claims that this too was caused by pity. Even on her deathbed she was still moved by pity. Her last coherent words are prompted by distress at learning that the household servants, excited by the false rumour that she is recovering, have agreed to contribute to a fund to pay the doctor's fees. As Wolmar reports: 'This agreement was reached with such excitement that Julie heard from her bed the sound of their acclamations. Imagine the effect in the heart of a woman who feels herself dying! She gestured to me and said in my ear: I have been made to drink to the dregs the bitter-sweet cup of sensibility.'[7]

St Preux equals or surpasses his mistress in sensibility. Here is a typical effusion before the affair has been consummated:

> How changed is my state in just a few days! What bitterness is mixed with the sweetness of coming closer to you! What sad reflections besiege me! What obstacles my fears make me foresee. O Julie, what a fatal present from heaven is an *âme sensible*! He who has received it must expect to know nothing but pain and suffering in the world. (1.26.89/73)

Meanwhile, on the side of sense, Claire and Lord Edward play secondary but important roles in the novel, highlighting with flashes of wit and irony the excesses of sensibility in their respective counterparts. In a letter to her prospective husband, M. d'Orbe, Claire expresses herself with cool assurance and self knowledge: 'as a woman I am a sort of monster, and by I know not what quirk of nature friendship for me takes precedence over love' (1.64.179/146). Yet even Claire, who displays sense in dealing with every other aspect of her life, reveals a deep level of sensibility in her relationship with her cousin, although this becomes clear only at the very end of the novel when she reacts with near hysteria to Julie's death. In the meantime we find Claire, after the death of her husband, caustically turning down Julie's suggestion that she should marry St Preux, as a kind of consolation prize for them both.

Lord Edward shows his good sense and good nature in taking the dejected St Preux under his wing, talking him out of committing suicide, presenting his case to Julie's deranged father and proposing an eminently rational plan to set the young couple up in one of his estates in Yorkshire. He in turn falls prey to passion in Italy, but by then the roles have been reversed, and it is St Preux who leads the older man back to the path of conventional virtue.

### *Patria potestas*: a father's power unleashed

Julie's father, the Baron d'Étange, is an offensive snob, given to outbursts of violent bad temper. He had served as a mercenary for the French. During his military career, he had killed a friend in a duel resulting from an affair of honour, and had his own life saved by another friend, Wolmar. Dogged by guilt, the Baron attributed the death of his own infant son to divine retribution. Indebted to Wolmar, he promised him his daughter in marriage. Julie refers caustically to this arrangement: 'This barbarous, unnatural father turns his daughter into a piece of merchandise' (1.28.94/77).

In 1.63 Julie describes her father's assault, which will turn out to be the cause of her miscarriage (III.18). During the assault, her mother intercedes, and is also struck. The Baron shows some remorse for striking his wife and tries to comfort her, but none for what he has done to his daughter, because 'the heart of a father feels it is made to grant forgiveness, and not to have need of forgiveness' (1.63.175/143). There follows a quasi-incestuous attempt at reconciliation: 'Catching me by my dress and pulling me toward him without a word, he sat me down on his lap' (1.63.175/144). The scene is charged with a sexual intensity that cannot be unintended, and the sado-masochistic note is even more marked the next morning, as Julie, the classic victim, condones and connives in her father's violence:

> This morning, weariness and the after-effects of my fall having kept me in bed
> a bit late, my father came into my room before I had risen; he sat down beside

my bed, inquiring tenderly after my health; he took one of my hands in his, he humbled himself so far as to kiss it several times, calling me his dear daughter, and expressing his regret for his rage. For my part, I told him, and I believe it, that I would be only too happy to be beaten every day at the same price, and that there is no treatment so rough that a single caress from him would not blot it from my heart. (I.63.176/144)

The Baron occupies a central place in the novel, yet Rousseau lets him speak in his own voice in only one letter (III.10). There he expresses his unshakeable snobbery and uncontrollable anger, complete with threats of violence if his will is thwarted. This short letter, of just one paragraph, occurs at a pivotal point in the novel. It marks a point of no return, as a paternal edict is issued, backed by force not reason, against which there can be no appeal. Enclosed with this letter is a formal six-line note from Julie to her lover, written under duress, in which she announces the end of their affair. St Preux responds to the Baron with reserved dignity, accepting the exercise of *force majeure*. Lord Edward had already intervened in vain on St Preux's behalf. In a letter to Claire (II.2) he denounces these 'senseless prejudices', this 'vanity of a barbarous father' acting like a 'tyrant' towards his daughter (II.2.193/158). It is evident from a footnote that Rousseau concurred with this judgement, referring to a notorious recent case of an imposed marriage in France – such a scandal that the French censors forbade mention of it.[8]

Yet only at III.18 does the full extent of the Baron's manipulation become clear. This long letter has been judged to be the most important of the whole novel, and it has generated a corpus of commentary. In it Julie shows herself to be as well versed as her father in the art of moral blackmail. It emerges that her plan had been to pressurise him into allowing her to marry her lover by showing signs of her pregnancy and then issuing a 'public declaration of it ... in the presence of the whole family' which would cause the pastor to authorise the marriage with St Preux (III.18.344–5/283). But the plan does not succeed because of her 'accident', the miscarriage resulting from her father's assault. The Baron, realising that he can't get his way by 'authority', falls to his knees and breaks down in tears. Julie can no longer resist. All that remains is to give in, marry Wolmar and continue an adulterous liaison with St Preux.

In this extraordinary game of bluff and double bluff, the Baron appears to have seen through this move too. If she continues her affair, he tells Julie that it will be at the cost of his life, and she realises that she can escape only by appealing to *honour* (the one principle her father recognises), so she tells him she is bound to St Preux by the promise she gave him. We now finally understand the note which her father forced her to write, dissolving that obligation. We seem to be left with a stand-off, unresolved until Julie experiences a 'sudden revolution', hearing 'the voice of God' during the marriage service. Henceforth, her life is transformed by religious devotion which, more or less precariously, sustains her fidelity to Wolmar until her death. God takes the place of her father as she struggles to maintain order in her life: this has all the appearances of a morally edifying story until the dramatic denouement. Even on her deathbed, Julie remains anxious about her father's unexplained absence: 'Could he have ceased to love me? What, my father! ... That father so tender ... abandoned me thus!' Perceptive as ever, her husband judges that 'she would more easily bear the thought of her father ill than of her father indifferent' (VI.11.720/591).[9]

## Class struggles and enlightened despotism

The Baron's hostility to St Preux, rooted in an acute awareness of class superiority, must have been anomalous in egalitarian Switzerland, and would provoke the merciless mockery of Voltaire. Julie's father was a provincial squire (*hobereau*), and the bearer of a hereditary title doomed to extinction with the death of his son. The two other characters endowed with wealth and privilege, the English *Milord* Edward Bomston and the mysterious Russian landowner M. de Wolmar, are more at ease with their social standing. Bomston plays the familiar role of super-rich critic of conventional snobbery. Wolmar is passionless and omniscient, exercising power over his inferiors with detachment.

St Preux, in contrast, is stripped of all social status. He does not even have a name of his own. The letters between the lovers are headed simply 'from Julie' and 'to Julie' (until Part IV, when 'Julie' is replaced by 'Mme de Wolmar'). In the table of contents, he is referred to as 'Julie's lover'. Julie calls him 'my friend', whereas he invokes her name repeatedly. Early in the novel (I.21.73/60), St Preux writes to Julie of the difference between their stations. He has no place in society, so for him love and its object make up his whole world, whereas Julie, enmeshed in a web of social obligations, has only the smallest part of herself left over for her lover. While this may not be wholly fair to Julie, it clearly expresses St Preux's own awareness of his marginalised and disempowered position (one that the author often felt he himself occupied in French high society).

Julie's lover is such a social outsider that it is not until over halfway through the book that he receives a name. Even then it is not his own, but a pseudonym given him by Claire to conceal his presence from her staff when he returns unexpectedly to her house in the night, seeking to visit Julie on her sickbed. This stratagem is described at III.14, but the pseudonym is not revealed until IV.5. At that point, the lover reappears after his round-the-world voyage, to find himself welcomed into the household at Clarens. Claire pointedly emphasises the favour that has been done to him, as she now openly bestows his name upon him. But it is still a pseudonym, and his real name will never be revealed. Claire's gracious act only serves to reinforce St Preux's status as an outsider whose social position still depends on the favour of others: 'Welcome! A hundred times welcome, dear St. Preux; for I mean for you to keep this name, at least amongst ourselves. This I think tells you sufficiently that we do not intend to exclude you, unless the exclusion should come from you' (IV.5.417/342). Even before the Baron's intervention, the relationship between the two lovers reflects the inequality of their respective social positions. From the outset, Julie is in command. Right up to her 'fall' it is she who determines where and when their meetings are to take place. She has the money to pay for his first departure from the watchful eyes of her family. In a rapid exchange of letters (I.15, 16, 17, 18) Julie bids him go and proposes to pay for the trip. His pride offended, St Preux refuses the money, but finally gives way and accepts the offer which Julie has meanwhile doubled. St Preux's acute awareness of his subordination pours out in letter I.24. It would be intolerable, he claims, to continue as a paid tutor, a mere 'valet' in the household, while continuing to make love to his pupil.

Returning from his four-year absence on Anson's fleet, St Preux waxes lyrical as he approaches his native land. Everything pleases him, the fresh climate, the beauty of the Alps and the Lake, but above all 'the sight of a happy and free people' (IV.6.419/344). How far the inhabitants of Clarens, under the supposedly benign rule of Monsieur and Madame de Wolmar, are 'happy and free' remains to be seen.

The 'Idyll of Clarens' occupies much of Part IV of the novel. Commentators have described the regime as totalitarian and self-contained, under the all-seeing eye of Wolmar and his equally watchful wife. St Preux, now redeemed and accepted into the household, begins his account of 'a domestic economy which proclaims the happiness of the masters of the house and allows it to be shared by its inhabitants' (IV.10.441/363). These fall into several distinct social classes, all of them subordinate to their masters. St Preux's account of the social stratification of the Clarens domain is striking in its detail and makes clear that the whole system is held together by ties of *dépendance personnelle* (personal dependence). At Clarens, the sexual relations of the domestics are as tightly controlled by their master and mistress as every other aspect of their lives. Care is taken 'to prevent dangerous familiarity' between the sexes. This is done not by rules and authority, but by social engineering, so that men and women are kept apart by the different tasks they are allotted. As a result they come to live quite separate lives with 'entirely different occupations, habits, pleasures [and] tastes' (IV.10.449–50/370). The purpose of this rigorous apartheid is to preserve the unruffled, deathlike calm of life at Clarens, a calm which would be shattered by the intrusion of sexual passion.

So, if St Preux hoped to find his vision of a 'free people' realised at Clarens, it seems he would have been disappointed. Central to Rousseau's political writings, as well as to *Émile*, is a critique of *dépendance personnelle*.[10] The 'Idyll of Clarens', therefore, embodies everything that Rousseau rejected in those texts. It might perhaps be maintained that Clarens is not a complete political entity, but a self-contained unit within such an entity. The Canton as a whole could be governed by free, equal citizens, while containing within it semi-feudal pockets like Clarens. The Cantons have always jealously guarded their autonomy (and have continued to do so since entering the Swiss Confederation). From that perspective, the visions of the novelist and the political theorist could be made consistent. The Canton as a self-governing unity is free of external control, while denying full autonomy to many of its inhabitants. If that was Rousseau's view, he does not choose to expound it in the novel.[11]

## Wars of religion

In the *Confessions*, Rousseau defends himself against the charge that he has written a 'scandalous' novel. On the contrary, he claims he has recounted how a young person, born with a tender but honourable heart, could 'allow herself to be overcome by love as a girl, and as a woman become virtuous again'. He continues:

> Aside from this object of morals and conjugal decency ... I made myself a more secret one of concord and public peace, which is perhaps a greater and more important object in itself ... The storm excited by the *Encyclopédie* was then at its greatest strength ... The two parties resembled rabid wolves, desperate to tear each other to pieces rather than Christians and *philosophes* who reciprocally wish to enlighten, convince and restore each other to the path of truth. (IX.435–6/466)

Rousseau would soon learn that the antagonists were irreconcilable, but for the moment, he writes, 'I drew the two characters [of Wolmar and Julie] in a rapture that made me hope to succeed in making both of them lovable and, what is more, the one by means of the other'. According to this original plan, the marriage between the 'virtuous atheist' (or more accurately 'virtuous unbeliever') and the equally virtuous *dévote* would symbolise the concordat. But as we read the novel, we discover that Julie could never live happily with her husband's unbelief, just as the Church could not coexist with the rampant secular order promised by the *philosophes*.

Writing to St Preux, Julie describes the 'sudden revolution' she undergoes in church during her marriage service to Wolmar (III.18.354/291–2). She hears 'the voice of God' and feels herself watched by 'the eternal eye'. As a result, with both 'voice and heart' she promises obedience and fidelity to her husband. Before the 'revolution', she continues, she was 'a *dévote* in church and a *philosophe* at home'. Henceforth, she tells us, she will live the life of simple piety rather than of the false reasoning of the *philosophes*. She proceeds to instruct her former lover (himself a self-taught *philosophe*) in the elements of Rousseau's minimal theology. 'Adore the eternal Being, my wise and worthy friend', she commands him, 'and with one breath you will destroy those phantoms of reason, which have but a vain appearance and flee like a shadow in the face of immutable truth. Nothing exists except through him who is.' As Julie pours out her heart, we hear Rousseau's own voice most clearly: 'It is he who gives a foundation to virtue and a price to this short life employed to please him. It is he who ceaselessly cries out to the guilty that their crimes have been seen and who tells the forgotten just person: "Your virtues have a witness"' (III.18.358/295). Rousseau held that belief in God gives consolation to the downtrodden, and that this in itself is good reason to believe in him: a view that earned him the contempt of sceptics from Voltaire to Bertrand Russell. Yet no less a philosopher than Immanuel Kant was to develop Rousseau's thought into a full-blown 'moral proof' of the existence of God.

Julie continues: God is an 'unalterable substance ... the true model of the perfections of which we all carry an image in ourselves ... It is in contemplating this divine model that the soul purifies and elevates itself'. This minimal theology has no place for revealed religion: 'Everything one cannot separate from the idea of that essence is God; all the rest is the work of men.' So important is this model for the devout heart that 'even if the immense being which is the focus of its concern did not exist, it would still be good for it to be thus focused' (III.18.359/295). This is the positive version of the cynical old saw: 'If God did not exist, we should need to invent him!'

At v.5 St Preux, now a member of the household, writes to Lord Edward describing the relationship between his hosts, which appears to be perfect in all respects apart from one flaw: Julie's *chagrin* at her husband's unbelief. For after six years of marriage, Julie and Wolmar remain unaltered in their convictions. While he is unconcerned by their differences, regarding them with his usual lofty indifference, she is constantly pained by them. Her distress is increased by her husband's moral perfection, since if he were a reprobate, there might be some chance of a deathbed conversion.

In explaining Wolmar's loss of faith (v.5.588–9/481–2), Rousseau had numerous digs at the Catholic Church, thereby incurring the wrath of the French government censor. As Julie describes Wolmar's life to St Preux, it all happened early in her husband's life, when, having been raised in the Orthodox Church, he found its doctrines and practices so absurd that the only alternative for the rational person was out-and-out atheism. He then went to live in Catholic countries, where he found the prevailing religious practices no more reasonable than the ones he had left behind. At that point he plunged into the shallow metaphysics of the *philosophes*, from which he emerged as a sceptic, one who does not commit himself to dogmatic atheism, but who, in rejecting all religious beliefs, is in the eyes of the believer an atheist in all but name. Perhaps the most intense moment in the letter is the following:

> What a torment it is to share a withdrawn existence with one who cannot share the hope that endears it to us ... Imagine Julie out walking with her husband; she admiring, in the rich and brilliant adornment which the earth displays, the work and gifts of the author of creation; he seeing nothing in all this but a fortuitous combination in which nothing is linked to anything else except by a blind force. (v.5.591/484)

The distance between believer and unbeliever lies in their contrasting interpretations of any natural phenomenon. When out for a walk, the sight of a beautiful landscape arouses different feelings in the two observers, admiration in Julie, clinical analysis in Wolmar. The world presents itself to Julie holistically, as an aesthetically unified whole, glowing with 'rich and brilliant adornment'. At the same time, it presents itself religiously as 'the work and gifts of the author of creation'. However, the world presents itself differently to her husband. For him, as for Diderot, there is no essential unity or rational pattern to be discerned in nature. It is 'a fortuitous combination' linked only 'by a blind force'. Husband and wife are divided by different ways of seeing the world, and between them there is thus no possibility of communication. A page later, Rousseau returns to his moral arguments against unbelief. We are familiar with these from many of his other writings, but they are made more poignant here by his heroine's sensibility. She feels horror at the thought of an unrepentant Wolmar either going to hell or simply ceasing to exist after death. Reflecting the author's own agnosticism on the subject, she does not commit herself on which it would be.

Alongside her personal anxiety about Wolmar's salvation, Julie adds the more general claim that atheism is always the ally of the wicked and powerful. Rousseau expressed this latter view in his own voice on several occasions elsewhere. Once fear of divine punishment is removed, the last vestiges of restraint also disappear. However, since Wolmar, the virtuous unbeliever, hypocritically attends church services to set a good example to others, it would seem that he at least is an exception to that rule! He alone, it seems, acts virtuously without fear of divine retribution.

Julie gives the final statement of her piety on her deathbed (VI.11). This long letter is a dramatic masterpiece. In it, Wolmar describes to St Preux the unfolding scene, moment by moment, as hopes rise and are dashed. The heroine's profession of faith emerges in two utterances, interrupted by her increasing weakness and the comings and goings of those around her. Even Wolmar shows signs of emotion, though these are moderate in comparison to Claire's frenzied despair. Throughout, Wolmar is considerate towards the feelings of others. His recurrent worry is that his own sceptical arguments may have finally succeeded in undermining his wife's faith, thereby depriving her of comfort in her dying hours. However, in the event his anxiety on this score proves groundless.

Julie declares her unshaken confidence in a creator deity, omnipotent, omniscient and beneficent, the minimum list of attributes accepted by deists, but she commits herself to no specifically Christian doctrines, such as the Fall or the divinity of Christ. In this, she is the authentic bearer of Rousseau's own position, as expressed in the 'Profession of Faith of the Savoyard Vicar' (in Book IV of *Émile*) and in the letter to Christophe de Beaumont. What marks Julie out from the deists is her practice of devotion, reflecting her deep personal trust in the deity. Despite her continued anxieties about her own father, it is God who has now taken his place: 'One who goes to sleep on her father's lap is not worried about waking up' (VI.11.716/588).

Julie's confidence is based on her untroubled conscience, her certainty that even when she has sinned, her intentions and feelings have been right. This explains her remarkable serenity in the face of death, and there is none of the melodrama associated with Catholic practices which are roundly condemned by Julie and her pastor alike, thus once again earning Rousseau the particular wrath of the French censors. In a separate statement, following a private conversation with the pastor, Julie pointedly denies the possibility of the resurrection of the body, even though this forms part of both Catholic and Protestant doctrine.

While Julie's belief remains unshaken, so too does Wolmar's unbelief. He is deeply moved by his wife's fortitude, even if it is founded on what he sees as an irrational belief. However much Rousseau longed to bring believers and unbelievers together, the denouement of letter VI.11 is at most a truce, rather than a reconciliation, between the parties. In refusing to provide a happy ending to this conflict, Rousseau realised that he was giving ammunition to his critics, Catholic and Protestant clerics on the one side and *philosophes* on the other. It might seem that he made an attempt to placate the religious camp in the very last letter of the novel, when Claire suggests to St Preux that Wolmar, in shock after Julie's death, 'cannot believe she is obliterated; his heart revolts against his vain reason ... I think I can already see her oft expressed wish being fulfilled and it is up to you to complete this great task [of converting Wolmar]' (VI.13.744/611). But as Bernard Guyon notes, this was probably a late addition, inserted by Rousseau in a vain attempt to pre-empt condemnation by church authorities.[12] The reference to 'Wolmar's conversion' in the Table of Contents (793/648) should be taken the same way. The Table, published only in the second edition of the novel and not penned by Rousseau himself, provides still less support for the view that *Julie* concludes with a confident declaration that faith and reason were about to be reconciled.

## The battle of the sexes

In *Julie*, Rousseau felt he had broken new ground in presenting an intense friendship between two women. It is Claire who announces the news of Julie's death to St Preux (VI.10), but she is too devastated to complete the letter. That is left to Wolmar, who devotes much of his subsequent letter to describing 'Claire's despair', and it is Claire who writes the very last letter of the novel (VI.13), in which she tells the bereaved husband of her grief and sorrow at the loss of Julie: 'By myself I can neither weep, nor speak, nor make myself understood' (VI.13.743/611).

An equally important theme of the novel is the power play between the sexes. In Julie's dealings with St Preux, it is impossible fully to disentangle questions of gender from those of social class. St Preux starts by using his position as tutor and his relative intellectual maturity, along with his mastery of moral blackmail, to seduce his pupil. As Julie recalls on her deathbed: 'At first all I knew of him was his language, and I was seduced' (VI.11.725/595). But it is not long before the balance of forces begins to tilt in Julie's direction, as she, often with Claire as intermediary, begins to dictate her lover's moves. In one of his many expressions of remorse for his sexual misconduct as a tutor, St Preux asserts that Abelard had deserved his punishment of castration for seducing his pupil Héloïse. In a footnote, Rousseau mocked this hyperbole (I.24.85/70), but it reflects the bitter truth that St Preux resembles his forerunner not only in his lowly social status, but also in that he emerges from the affair, if not physically emasculated, at least morally disempowered as a man.

Julie's power is firmly established once St Preux is installed in Clarens after his return from exile. He describes it as follows:

> [On entering Julie's 'Elysium'] I was struck by a pleasantly cool sensation which dark shade, bright and lively greenery, flowers scattered on every side, the bubbling of flowing water, and the songs of a thousand birds impressed on my imagination at least as much as my senses; but at the same time I thought I was looking at the wildest, most solitary place in nature, and it seemed to me I was the first mortal who had ever set foot in this wilderness ... It is true, she said, that nature did it all, but under my direction, and there is nothing here that I have not designed. (IV.II.471/387–8)

Julie's power now extends to the natural world as well as to the passions of her former lover, as she applies an imperceptible magic to transform what is natural into what is manageable. Yet even Julie remains under Wolmar's all-seeing eye and subject to his manipulative power. Thus he sets her and St Preux tests to determine whether they have been fully 'cured' of their former passion. In the first test he leads them into the very grove (*le bosquet*) where they had first made love. There he joins the hands of the former lovers and addresses them as children, vowing that all three will be united in a 'durable attachment' (IV.12.490/402). He then reveals the 'secret of his birth' (though Julie does not share the secret with the reader!). He explains that he had already tested St Preux's 'cure' by lodging him at Clarens, and is now doing the same to Julie with the visit to the *bosquet*. He judges the experiment successful: 'Julie, fear this sanctuary no more; it has just been profaned' (IV.12.496/407). It was previously sacred to Julie, because she thought it secret. She now realises that Wolmar knew about the love affair all along. Wolmar forces St Preux and Julie to embrace under his gaze, shattering the sanctity of the *bosquet*. Julie thus recognises that her heart is 'more changed than I had heretofore dared believe'.

At IV.17, the two former lovers play out a scenario devised by Wolmar as the final test of his wife's fidelity. Wolmar's ruse is to depart on business, leaving Julie and St Preux alone together. If the experiment is to proceed according to plan, St Preux should then discover that he is in love with the remembered young girl, Julie d'Étange, not the real adult wife and mother, Mme de Wolmar. In the letter, St Preux recounts to Lord Edward how he and Julie took a boat trip on the lake, were caught in a storm and were driven on to the shore at Meillerie. There, torn between passionate nostalgia and a desperate temptation to drown them both, he was finally calmed by Julie's display of self-control: 'Let us go from here, my friend, she said with trembling voice, the air in this place is not good for me' (IV.17.519–20/427).

Thus, until the final Part, Julie appears to have dominated every character in the novel with the exception of her husband. But already at Letter IV.12, the apparently superhuman Wolmar reveals how he first became aware of his own vulnerability:

> The loneliness that always afflicted me was becoming painfully acute, and I could no longer hope to ignore it for long. Though I had not lost my coldness I needed an attachment; the perspective of decline without someone to comfort me grieved me before my time, and for the first time in my life I knew anxiety and sadness. (IV.12.492/404)

In response, the Baron offered him his daughter's hand in marriage. Whereupon the ageing rationalist, having entered matrimony out of weakness, finds himself assailed by guilt at his own behaviour, while at the same time falling in love with his young wife, all of whose passion has already been exhausted, but who he hopes might come at least to like him. In the words of Guyon: 'He was both odious and admirable; he becomes pathetic. Beneath his coldness we find modesty, beneath his calm exterior we find something like passion. Exhausted by life, he finds new hope, he experiences real love.'[13]

Julie, in her turn, settles into her roles as mother of her children and as matriarch of the Clarens estate. Rousseau was renowned for creating – or recreating – the cult of motherhood in the eighteenth century. While his critics sneered and pointed at the negligent way he had disposed of his own children, many women readers were convinced, and readily followed his recommendations to take up breast-feeding and abandon swaddling clothes. At Clarens, Julie embodies all the womanly virtues subsequently expounded in the *Émile* and elsewhere. As the book reaches its dramatic climax, it is Julie, the mother, who throws herself into the Lake, attempting to save her son who has tripped and fallen in (VI.9). The child is successfully rescued by others, but Julie fails to recover from her immersion and is soon on her deathbed. There she delivers an extended commentary on her life, in part to the pastor, in part to her husband, who vainly presses her to utter some regret at the prospect of leaving him. But to this he receives a bleak response:

> Maternal affection increases ceaselessly, while the children's tender feelings towards their mother diminish as they live at a greater distance from her. As they grew older, my own would have become more separated from me. Everything would have been gradually removed from me and there would have been nothing to replace what I had lost. (VI.11.726/596)

Yet even that is not Julie's last word, which is revealed in her testament to St Preux (VI.12). Here she reveals that she has never been fully cured of her love for him, and that she has managed to lead her exemplary life at Clarens only by stifling her passion and, therewith, her very will to live. Thus in subjecting St Preux to her will, Julie won only a pyrrhic victory. His submission was total, but the cost was her own extinction as an *âme sensible*.

## Rousseau and the European novel

Rousseau's *Julie* cast a long shadow over the future of the novel in Europe. As a narrative of failed reconciliations, personal, political and religious, it is, despite its often effusive style, both realistic and pessimistic. Rousseau's mastery of the epistolary form allowed him to give authentic voice to each pole of the unresolved conflicts. As we have seen, Laclos recognised the unsentimental realism of Rousseau's novel, which he would develop with a brutal, shocking cynicism in *Dangerous Liaisons*. In his *Die Leiden des jungen Werthers* (*Sorrows of the Young Werther*, 1774), Goethe transposed the tragic heroine of sensibility into the idiom of German romanticism, replacing the heroine by a hero who is driven by unrequited love to suicide.

In the nineteenth century, two novels bear the striking imprint of Rousseau's *Julie*: Jane Austen's *Sense and Sensibility* (1811) and Leo Tolstoy's *War and Peace* (1869). *Sense and Sensibility* can be read as an ironic take-off of *Julie*, with Marianne and Elinor assuming the roles of Julie and Claire in Rousseau's story. Austen treats both sisters sympathetically, while engaging in gentle mockery of the absurdities of Marianne's inflamed sensibility. In her fall from grace and in her redemption, Tolstoy's Natasha is a quintessential heroine of sensibility. The powerful influence of *Julie* on *War and Peace* comes out most clearly in the first epilogue to Tolstoy's masterpiece. In it he describes the married lives of four of the surviving characters, Marya Bolkonskaya with Nikolay Rostov and Natasha Rostova with Pierre Bezukhov. In depicting these two ménages, Tolstoy clearly had in mind the 'Idyll of Clarens' in *Julie*. In the first case, the couple rules a large estate of serfs with all the enlightened despotism exercised by Julie and Wolmar at Clarens. In the second case, passionate Natasha, having lost her virtue early in the novel, finds redemption, as Julie did, in marriage and motherhood. But Tolstoy does not suggest that his heroine was destined to end her days as Julie did, feeling lonely and desolate once her children grew up. On the contrary, Natasha seems blissfully happy. But then she is married to the eccentric, delightful Pierre, rather than the melancholy Wolmar.

## Acknowledgement

I should like to thank Carolina Armesteros, Jeremy Goodenough and Mavis Reynolds for the valuable help they have given me in writing this essay.

## Note on editions/translations

The following scholarly editions have been used: Jean-Jacques Rousseau, *Œuvres complètes* (OC), ed. Bernard Gagnebin and Marcel Raymond (Paris: Gallimard, 'Pléiade', 1959ff.): *Confessions*, vol. I; *La Nouvelle Héloïse*, vol. II; *Du contrat social*, vol. III; *Émile*, vol. IV; and the English translations in Jean-Jacques Rousseau, *Collected Writings* (CW) (Hanover, NH: University Press of New England, 1990ff.): *Confessions*, vol. V; *Julie*, vol. VI; *Social Contract*, vol. IV; *Émile*, vol. XIII. The *Collected Writings* are now available in paperback. References to Rousseau's correspondence are to *Correspondance complète*, ed. R. A. Leigh (Geneva: Institut et Musée Voltaire, 1965–71; Banbury: The Voltaire Foundation, 1972–89).

### Notes

1 See Robert Darnton, *Forbidden Best-sellers of Pre-Revolutionary France* (London: HarperCollins, 1996), p. 242.

2 All quotations are from the editions recommended in the Note on editions/translations above. Subsequent references are given in parenthesis in the text with the book number followed by page references to the French and English versions in turn: XI.547/458.

3 Étienne Gilson, 'La Méthode de M. de Wolmar', in *Les Lettres et les idées* (Paris: Vrin, 1935).

4 The quotation is from the edition recommended in the Note on editions/translations above with the book number followed by page references to the French and English texts in turn: I.248/163.

5 For an excellent brief survey of the topic, see Sylvana Tomaselli, 'Sensibility', in John W. Yolton, ed., *The Blackwell Companion to the Enlightenment* (Oxford: Blackwell, 1991). A more substantial study is John Mullan, 'Sensibility and Literary Criticism', in H. B. Nisbet and Claude Rawson, eds., *The Cambridge History of Literary Criticism*, vol. IV, *The Eighteenth Century* (Cambridge University Press, 2005).

6 Letter to the Abbé Cahagne, 3/4 March 1761, *Correspondance complète*, vol. VIII, letter 1336, p. 203.

7 Quotations are from the editions recommended in the Note on editions/translations above. Subsequent references are given parenthetically in the text with the part number, the letter number and the page references to the French and English versions in turn: VI.11.733/601.

8 'It is impossible to say to what extent in this country which is so courtly women are tyrannized by the laws. Should one be astonished that they so grievously avenge themselves through their morals?' (II.11.194n/159n).

9 See Tony Tanner, 'Julie and "la maison paternelle": Another Look at Rousseau's *La Nouvelle Héloïse*' in *Daedalus*, 105 (winter 1976).

10 On personal dependence, see *Social Contract*, II.11.391/217 and *Émile*, II.311/216. At *Social Contract*, I.2, Rousseau rejects the view that political authority could be founded on the 'natural' authority of the father in the family. See T. O'Hagan, *Rousseau* (London: Routledge, 2003), pp. 91–2, 118.

11  See Gilson, 'La Méthode', and Lester G. Crocker, 'Julie ou la nouvelle duplicité', in *Annales de la Société Jean-Jacques Roussseau*, 36 (1963–5).
12  Note by Bernard Guyon to VI.13 at *OC*, II.1813.
13  Guyon's note at *OC*, II.1618 provides a remarkable commentary on this passage in IV.12.

## Further reading

Badinter, Elisabeth, *L'Amour en plus: l'histoire de l'amour maternel, XVIIe au XXe siècles* (Paris: Flammarion, 1980)

Cranston, Maurice, *The Noble Savage: Jean-Jacques Rousseau, 1754–1762* (London: Allen Lane, The Penguin Press, 1991)

Gauthier, David, *Rousseau: The Sentiment of Existence* (Cambridge University Press, 2006)

Grimsley, Ronald, *Rousseau and the Religious Quest* (Oxford: Clarendon Press, 1963)

Hampson, Norman, *The Enlightenment: An Evaluation of its Assumptions, Attitudes and Values* (London: Penguin, 1980)

Kelly, Christopher, *Rousseau as Author: Dedicating One's Life to Truth* (University of Chicago Press, 2003)

Schiebinger, Londa, *The Mind Has no Sex?: Women in the Origins of Early Modern Science* (Cambridge, MA: Harvard University Press, 1989)

Schwartz, Joel, *The Sexual Politics of Jean-Jacques Rousseau* (University of Chicago Press, 1984)

Showalter, English, *The Evolution of the French Novel, 1641–1782* (Princeton University Press, 1972)

Starobinski, Jean, *Jean-Jacques Rousseau: la transparence et l'obstacle* (Paris: Gallimard, 1971)

Wokler, Robert, *Rousseau: A Very Short Introduction* (Oxford University Press, 2001)

# 6

MICHAEL BELL

# Laurence Sterne (1713–1768):
# The fiction of sentiment

Laurence Sterne was an eighteenth-century publishing sensation, who has continued to exercise a tangible yet elusive impact on novelists in Europe and beyond. As their full titles may suggest, his two important fictions, *The Life and Opinions of Tristram Shandy, Gent* (*TS*, 1759–67) and *A Sentimental Journey through France and Italy* (*SJ*, 1768), are classed as novels largely by default. Hence, as well as becoming iconic of a belief in the natural goodness of the heart, he has been an especially fruitful resource whenever the novel form has reflected upon its own limits or status, as was the case in the high theory of German romanticism, in European modernism and in late twentieth-century postmodernism.

In 1759, sparked partly by his satire on eccesiastical politics in York, *A Political Romance*, Sterne published the first two volumes of *Tristram Shandy*. In the light of their success he then produced seven further volumes at intervals. The book defies summary as the eponymous narrator, whose name means something like a 'sad and confused mixture', weaves together anecdotes concerning his eccentric family, consisting principally of his father, mother, Uncle Toby and Toby's manservant Corporal Trim, along with various servants and neighbours including Parson Yorick and the Papist Dr Slop. Although the narration is in the present of its publication dates, most of the action is set in the early decades of the century and extends to before Tristram's birth. The comedy of the anecdotes is inseparable from that of their narration as Tristram is carried into multiple digressions 'progressing' as much sideways or backwards as forwards. Most of the characters have, or are indeed defined by, personal obsessions or 'hobby horses'; Tristram's is the desire to tell his story in his own way. Uncle Toby, a wounded ex-soldier, has a military obsession as he enacts, with Trim, the progress of the Duke of Marlborough's Flanders campaigns in the miniaturised form of models built on the bowling green. But his hobby horse also has its root in an expressive need, for the military game relieves his otherwise nearly fatal incapacity to communicate the experience of his wounding at

Namur. Likewise, Corporal Trim loves to instruct, and the principal motor of the novel's action is the father, Walter Shandy's, desire to form his son. Walter wishes to write up the educational project in his *Tristra*-paedia; a coinage whose first use is in an appropriately mixed font (*TS*, v.16). Unfortunately, all his schemes miscarry: Tristram's impressive family nose, with its phallic overtones, is crushed at birth; the *Tristra*-paedia remains unfinished; and the father becomes Tristram's creation, in a mode of near caricature, rather than the reverse. Indeed, Jean-Jacques Rousseau's *Émile* (1762), with its optimistically confident envisaging of educational authority, was contemporary with the early volumes of *Tristram Shandy* and Sterne's novel stands already as an ironic reflection on the Enlightenment genre of the *Bildungsroman* which had its first great text in C. M. Wieland's *Geschichte des Agathon* (*History of Agathon*, 1766–7).

In so far as its themes of communication and education are focused by reference to the philosopher John Locke, *Tristram Shandy* is related to the eighteenth-century philosophical tale, a genre which could make intellectually penetrating use of caricature. Locke, known principally for *Two Treatises of Government* (1690) and *An Essay Concerning Human Understanding* (1690), was a foundational Enlightenment thinker whose insistence on sensory impressions and experience as underlying all human knowledge provided a philosophical framework for the contemporary cult of moral sensibility. But sensibility also helped to create the criteria by which Locke's thought was to appear increasingly limited and outdated by the end of the century. *Tristram Shandy* enacts the process of this change. Sterne is not disrespectful towards Locke: his satire, at least initially, is deeply traditional, aimed at human nature as such. But in so far as his conception of the human is formed within the Lockean model, the effect is increasingly to satirise the Lockean conception itself by criteria which already point to a different way of thinking about both feeling and thought. For Locke's model of the mind came to seem mechanistic, and was especially weak in dealing with feeling, creativity and humour, three themes crucial to Europe's imminent Romantic turn.

Locke argued that we have a stock of ideas derived from sensory impressions and designated by words. Thinking is the organisation of ideas according to various principles, such as cause and effect, and including the highly ambivalent 'association of ideas'. Locke's concern for perspicuity of thought meant that inappropriate associations were to be avoided. The hobby-horsical obsessions of the Shandy family are, therefore, Lockean disasters, but the text leads us to view them in a more complex light. Walter Shandy is Lockean man and, true to his master, he abhors a pun. Likewise, in the opening episode his habit of winding the clock on the same night as he performs his marital duties suggests a mechanical relation to both time and feeling. Yet Uncle Toby, who is perhaps the most 'Locked' within the vortex of his military associations, repeatedly evinces a genial emotional under- standing communicated precisely by means of the obsession. The hobby horse, which confounds the communication of ideas, expresses the individ- ual affective life of the character and gives it an externalised, shareable form. The mutual affection of Trim and Toby is realised in their joint activity on the bowling green. Tristram's hobby of writing is a yet more genial version of this as he recreates the characters, for his enjoyment and ours, by means of their hobby horses. And, of course, he enjoys puns, especially smutty ones, for these point to a crucial axis of the whole text.

*Tristram Shandy* begins quite explicitly in the mode of François Rabelais and Miguel de Cervantes with a traditional satire on human pretensions, not just personally but culturally, as in the forms of academic, philosophical and theological reason. In this tradition, the constant source of satiric corrective is the return of the repressed reality of the body. The word 'hobby' was a slang term for a prostitute and the hobby horse, as a childish wooden toy, points to a shadow of impotence, emotional rather than physical, that hangs over all the Shandy males. Hence, in Walter's case, as with D. H. Lawrence's war-wounded Clifford Chatterley, impotence has a symbolic force, but in Toby and Tristram it is increasingly modified by a new element that developed with Sterne's writing. Sterne was sensitive to the success of his sentimental episodes and the focus of the work began to shift from its pre-modern satiric mode towards working the fashionable vein of sensibility. So much so indeed, that he separately packaged the story of his Continental travels as *A Sentimental Journey* in which the body as a 'sensorium' undergoes a more positive, though internally ironised, valor- isation. Likewise Toby, as a man of feeling, is not so much impotent as endowed with female properties.

The shifting emphases in these works indicate how, although he is so rich in suggestion, Sterne was above all opportunistic and receptive. He developed a distinctive life attitude of humorous hedonism, while remaining elusive of systematic definition. He was the most flirtatious of writers, always leading the reader on, deferring or avoiding the expected climax, and his sponge-like receptivity to the tearful tastes of his world held its ambivalences in liquid fullness rather than in the squeezing grasp of the analytic intellect. That may be why so many later writers have claimed him for their own purposes, treating him at times as an honorary contemporary, and why critics have been tempted to create, for example, modernist or postmodernist Sternes who had already supposedly anticipated the devel- opments suggested by these generic labels. But to transpose Sterne into the terms of later literary conceptions is to lose his significant difference and historicity. Moreover, the two principal aspects of his work have had largely opposed impacts: he is at once the writer of delicate moral sensibility and of supreme fictive self-consciousness. During the romantic decades, he was mainly prized for his sensibility, whereas the twentieth century appreciated his formal self-consciousness. Although these rival aspects were principally associated with *Sentimental Journey* and *Tristram Shandy* respectively, they are not separated within the works themselves. Indeed, his enduring significance is to have shown the close relation between sensibility and the fictive, for Sterne leads us to recognise that the European novel was not merely a convenient vehicle for the exploration of the moral sensibility: there is an intrinsic, though usually unconscious, relation between fiction and the imaginative component in feeling. Hence, the key to understanding his long-term contribution is to understand him first in his own age, and this includes his created persona, mediated through the narrating personae of his fiction, for this is always a central feature of the work.

Sterne was the son of an army officer whose family had produced a succession of Anglican ecclesiatics. He studied at Jesus College, Cambridge, became minister for the parishes of Sutton and Stillingfleet in the diocese of York, where his uncle Jacques Sterne was Precentor, and then, after the success of *Tristram Shandy*, acquired the more desirable living of Coxwold. Early preferment may have been partly owing to his uncle, who was initially glad to have his young relative as an ally for his political ambitions in the world of York Minster, although uncle and nephew were quickly divided by the same political pressures. Sterne's ecclesiastical identity was multiply mingled with his fiction, as the character of Parson Yorick in *Tristram Shandy* was transposed into the narrating persona of *Sentimental Journey*, while Sterne's sermons, published as *The Sermons of Mr. Yorick* (1760, 1766), expressed the same quizzically realistic acceptance of human beings as did his fiction. If there was a scandalous tension between the moral intent, and decorum, of the sermons on the one hand and the Rabelaisian humour and innuendo of his fiction on the other, the scandal masked deeper connections, for the mutual porousness of Yorick the jester and Sterne the minister combined fictional play with the exploration of moral sensibility.

While satire on local ecclesiastical and other figures was a significant impetus to the writing of the first two volumes of *Tristram Shandy*, the novel's success derived from its chameleonic responsiveness to wider developments in the culture, which Sterne proceeded to exploit in the subsequent volumes. Presenting himself as a jester maintaining a Rabelaisian attack on all forms of false gravity, especially philosophical gravity, he was an entertainer with the lightest moral content, and it remains hard to judge his true awareness of the kind of interest his writing could generate. Although supremely self-aware at an immediate level of readerly manipulation, the fact that he was not a profound or systematic thinker enabled him to remain richly unaware of deeper crosscurrents beneath the foam. To appreciate this more fully, it is helpful to trace the contemporary development of his two important resources: the eighteenth-century cult of sensibility and the coming to consciousness of the novel as a distinct modern genre.

### Sentiment and sensibility

As the European Enlightenment sought to create a humane, post-religious social order, it faced the problem of the sources and authority of the moral life. In the inherited blend of classical and Christian traditions, morality had had its source in reason and its authority in God. The upright posture of man figured in microcosm the Great Chain of Being, whereby the seat of reason governed the passions of the animal nature. For man, in the words of the catechism, is 'prone to evil from his very childhood'. But even within this tradition, there was always a current of thought emphasising the desire of nature for the divine, and the fulfilment of the emotional self in the higher ethical life. The eighteenth century saw an increasing and programmatic emphasis on the human heart as the source of social benevolence. This was reflected in a movement among Anglican clergy around the turn of the eighteenth century known as Latitudinarianism. This was a shift from the seventeenth century's divisive emphasis on faith to the more inclusive virtue of charity and, in the early years of the century, Anthony Ashley Cooper, the Earl of Shaftesbury, without formally breaking with the authority of religion, argued that morality had a natural basis in human feeling. In so far as human feeling acted as a supplement to religious authority, Shaftesbury's natural benevolence could underwrite a deistical world-view without apparently threatening a theistical one. But the logic of the supplement was to prove double-edged. Any principle of authority that accepts a supplement attracts the suspicion that it needs one and, where absolute authority is in question, that can be fatal. Accordingly, the eighteenth-century cult of feeling had distinct phases focused particularly in the terms 'sentiment' and 'sensibility'.

Over the middle decades of the century, the word 'sentiment' underwent a significant change in meaning. The word was much more common at the time and if one were to substitute a modern word for its typical use by Samuel Richardson in the 1740s it would be something like moral 'principle'. When a man says 'these are my sentiments, Sir' he means these are the general principles by which he lives. Yet by the time of Sterne in the 1760s, the word 'sentiment' would usually mean the personal feelings.

The importance of this shift, however, is that there is no absolute change: it is a shift in the centre of semantic gravity whereby the one meaning always carries some implication of the other. For the discourse of sentiment was an attempt to accord to moral principle the immediate, spontaneous quality of a feeling, and to find in feeling the impersonal value of a principle. Unfortunately, much human experience enforces the traditional recognition that feelings and principles are too often opposed, and Immanuel Kant was to declare that only when duty conflicts with inclination can one be sure one is acting morally at all.

The eighteenth-century belief in moral sentiment, in other words, was a great Enlightenment myth. Nonetheless, the exploration of this unstable ambition, which required the dramatisation of concrete and individual cases rather than philosophical generalisation, was a pre-eminent task of the eighteenth-century novel, as it sought to discriminate the shades of sincerity and authenticity within the realm of feeling. The attempt to live up to this myth, or to attack it, whether by authors or by characters, gives a philo-sophical edge to Mme de Lafayette's *La Princesse de Clèves*, Samuel Richardson's *Clarissa*, Henry Fielding's *Amelia*, Rousseau's *Julie*, Johann Wolfgang von Goethe's *Werther*, Henry MacKenzie's *The Man of Feeling*, Choderlos de Laclos' *Les Liaisons dangereuses*, Mary Shelley's *Frankenstein* and the Marquis de Sade's *Justine* to name but a few. Moreover, despite its intrinsic instability, the cult of sentiment constituted an affective turn foun-dational to modernity. For although it was indeed absurd and impossible in its simplistic forms, which were naively expressed in the abundant literature of sentiment, the great novels of the period started the cultural work of discrimination now implicit in the later deprecatory use of the word 'sentimental'. For this word, in defining a mawkish self-indulgence, makes an all-important discrimination within the realm of feeling and thereby implies the importance of that realm as such.

As far as the novel is concerned, then, the cult of sentiment was not a theory or belief merely reflected in literature: it was a problematic to be explored. And this remains the case even where an author, such as arguably Richardson, may personally subscribe to a simpler view. As the problematic of sentiment unrolled, it yielded distinct phases. The gripping best-sellers of Richardson and Rousseau might be called novels of sentiment in that the drama hinges on their heroines' attempts under pressure to live up to a principled ideal of themselves. But these novels manifest the ambivalence of the sentimental myth in that, while the emotional intensity ostensibly arises from the heroines' commitment to their principles, one may sense that the moral situation is rather there to produce the intensity of feeling in the reader. For within the myth of sentiment, where emotion is a good in itself, there is a logical premium on its maximal intensity. One can see from this logic how the novel of sentiment modulated into the novel of sensibility. Increasingly, the interest would lie in the exemplary delicacy and intensity of moral sensibility, the readiness to feel, demonstrated by characters, authors and readers. The tragic moral situations of Clarissa or Julie are replaced by the capacity to show maximal sensibility at the most minimal external occasion. Not surprisingly, the excesses of sensibility generated a critical reaction, particularly in the 1770s. Goethe's *Werther* (1774) is an especially illuminating example, because its critical intent was so largely ignored by a sentimental readership while the novel had indeed to risk that response as part of its internal dramatic logic.[1] It was to this ambivalent and binarised moment in the evolution of sensibility that Sterne, as a latter-day Latitudinarian, responded with his characteristic lability, and he did so through the self-consciousness of the novel form.

## Fictional self-consciousness

It has been suggested in the Introduction that, in some of its most innovative and influential examples, the eighteenth-century novel went though a rapid evolution from the illusionistic memoir fiction of the early years to the high self-consciousness of Sterne. Such a growing self-consciousness was partly necessary to the creation of a new genre devoted to moral self-reflection in the conditions of modernity. But illusionistic fiction also continued throughout the century with a special importance to the cult of sentiment. If the primary purpose of a literature of moral sensibility was to produce the maximal intensity of emotional response in the reader, and the capacity for the emotion is believed to be a good in itself, as well as a cause of further goods, then the response to an apparently real-life situation was at a premium. For the response to a real person is significantly different from that occasioned by a fictional being, and the literature of sensibility was commonly accused of indulging emotion on fictive objects while neglecting real distress.

Richard Steele, an early promoter of moral sentiment, provided an illuminating Preface to one of his morally instructive *Spectator* papers:

> It is often said, after a Man has heard a Story with extraordinary Circumstances, it is a very good one if it be true: But as for the following Relation, I should be glad were I sure it were false. It is told with such Simplicity, and there are so many artless Touches of Distress in it, that I fear it comes too much from the Heart. (10 March 1712)[2]

He goes on to print a letter he has ostensibly received from a young woman from the country who has come to London, been seduced and abandoned.

The story is explicitly banal in itself, since its moral value lies in its being exemplary, its being a commonplace event, but Steele nudges the reader to respond to it emotionally as if it were true, for it might elicit a different response if it had truly occurred to a near relative or acquaintance. Whereas a fiction has normally to command attention by intrinsic interest and meaningfulness, the literature of sentiment typically exploited the literalistic illusionism of the memoir or epistolary forms. Of course, this does not entail a literal belief in the factual truth of the fiction. The readers who wrote to Richardson to 'save' Clarissa were clearly aware she was a fiction. Yet they were in the grip of a non-aesthetic response, a response as if to a real person rather than an element in a structure of narrative meanings. Steele's introductory remarks capitalise the key words in this complex of affective verisimilitude: the narrative terms, 'Story', 'Circumstance' and 'Relation' merge, through 'artless' 'Simplicity', with the language of sensibility, 'Distress' and 'Heart'. And he suggests an abrupt dualism of true and false, quietly eliding the middle zone of fiction which would most appropriately characterise the letter.

Whereas much of the now forgotten fiction of sensibility was set within such naively literalistic framing, the great novels variously exploited, resisted or transcended its limits. For example, a great deal of critical self-reflection about writing and representation creeps largely unnoticed into the major epistolary novels mentioned above, for it was the fiction of sentiment which created the greatest need to establish a critical and artistic distance. Indeed, it was from within the literature of sensibility, rather than from its avowed critics, that the most significant developments would occur. As Sterne caught the moment when the fashion for sensibility was coming to its height, while also anticipating the critical reaction which was about to set in against it, his self-conscious fictional play enabled him to ride both horses at once, and one of the most illuminating examples is the 'Story of Le Fever' from *Tristram Shandy* (VI. 6–13). The episode is so subtitled in Tristram's narrative; the subtitle quietly insinuating the importance of the narrative frame around the figure in distress.

In its own day, the episode was read, like *Werther*, in a sentimental spirit, and was even excerpted for separate publication, although readers were often bemused by its strange mixture of tone, the apparent undercutting of its indulgent sensibility. Tristram tells of Trim's discovery many years previously of Le Fever, an ensign of his and Toby's former regiment, dying in a nearby inn. Since Toby was confined at home by gout, Trim had to report to him so that his quaint narration and conversation with Toby compound the idiosyncrasy of Tristram's own narrative mediation. When Le Fever dies, Toby takes responsibility for his young son who has since grown up and been educated at Toby's expense.

The distancing of the sentimental occasion both in time and in its multiple narrative framings allows Sterne to create by non-analytic means, and therefore without disrupting its emotional impact, an implicit analysis of the sentimental response. At one level, we have simply the sentimental occasion enjoyed separately as such by many contemporary readers. At the same time, the quaintness of the narrative mediation indicates that Sterne had learned the lesson, to be so well understood later by Dickens, that humour, far from dispelling tender sentiment, may make it more subtle and palatable. A joke pays for a tear. But within this complex of humour and sentiment, Toby responds to Trim's tale differently from the reader who listens, as it were, over Toby's shoulder. Toby, who is in the same reality frame as Le Fever, does not enjoy the story. He is distressed, puts money in his pocket for the morning and upbraids Trim for not immediately offering Le Fever his purse. Unlike many sentimentalist heroes, Toby does not pay Le Fever with fine feelings instead of cash. His sentimentalism is morally active. But the reader is in a different relation to Le Fever. The reader enjoys a sentimental sympathy within the overall entertainment of Tristram's narrative, and is not called upon to respond with practical charity. Yet sharing Toby's response is central to enjoying the fiction, so that the episode effectively distinguishes between the moral and the aesthetic responses while superimposing them and insisting on their common root in moral feeling.[3]

Taken overall, the episode suggests why the internal instability of moral sentimentalism, when conceived as an immediate and literal moral efficacy, would lead to the late eighteenth-century invention of the aesthetic. More specifically, Friedrich Schiller's *Über die ästhetische Erziehung des Menschen* (*On the Aesthetic Education of Man*, 1795) developed a morally educative notion of the aesthetic as a non-practical condition in which the whole range of possible human values can be intensely and reflectively experienced because set free from the demand for immediate action. Schiller's aesthetic was morally enabling, in contrast to late nineteenth-century aesthetic*ism*, although hints of that can also be seen in Sterne. Schiller combined Rousseau's sensibility with Kant's rationalist critique of moral sentiment in such a way as to escape the limitations of each. For Schiller, Rousseau was too literalistic in his understanding of moral efficacy, and too hostile to aesthetic freedom, and was therefore rather the victim than the master of his own sensibility. Without possessing such a coherent and analytically discriminated account of the aesthetic, Sterne enacts the complex mutuality of moral sensibility and fictional framing which underlies Schiller's foundational thought. William Wordsworth's almost contemporary Preface to the *Lyrical Ballads* (1798), without invoking the category of the aesthetic, comparably argued a poetic transformation of sentiment, and the English nineteenth-century novel was to be characterised by its consciously fictional invocation of sentiment.

A broader link with the Schillerian aesthetic is that Sterne's humour is not satirically destructive so much as an intensification of self-consciousness, as can be seen in an episode that translates the layered complexity of the Le Fever story into a direct moral reflection. While *Sentimental Journey* celebrates Yorick's sensibility, there are constant indications of his egotism and displaced sexual motives. Indeed, a recurrent school of thought has seen the work as a satire on sensibility, but this is another modern over-interpretation which misses a crucial aspect of sentimentalism: its premium on self-consciousness as such.

Rousseau made explicit how the man of sensibility prized consciousness over action, sublimation over consummation. His most intense and prized relationships with women are so because they are unconsummated. But where Rousseau ennobles the sublimated emotion, Sterne typically exposes its bodily origins. In one episode, Yorick sits on a bed with a maidservant or *grisette*. Their intimacy arouses him but, instead of taking sexual advantage of her, he places a crown piece, rather suggestively, into her purse after which she excites him intensely by repairing a stitch in his clothing. He then goes on to reflect that, although his charitable behaviour towards her was driven by a predatory sexual desire, that does not make it inauthentic. He rather argues the realistic principle that

> If Nature has so wove her web of kindness, that some threads of love and desire are entangled with the piece—must the whole be rent in drawing them out?—— Whip me such stoics, great Governor of nature! Said I to myself—— Wherever thy providence shall place me for the trials of my virtue—whatever is my danger—whatever is my situation—let me feel the movements which rise out of it, and which belong to me as a man——and if I govern them as a good one, I will trust the issues to thy justice; for thou hast made us, and not we ourselves. (*SJ*, 'The Conquest')

This could be the Yorick of the sermons speaking. For Sterne, the lower, or bodily, sources of sensibility are not to be denied or suppressed, but gathered into consciousness. Indeed, Schiller used the word 'sentimental' to mean precisely 'self-conscious', and cited Sterne as a notable instance. For in the sentimental tradition, in which emotion was valued as such, there was a premium on making it as conscious as possible. It was good not only to have benevolent feelings, but to celebrate them, and celebrate oneself having them. Hence, like 'sentimental', the word 'complacent' had a positive meaning in the period, designating a legitimate awareness of this good state.

The now reversed implication of these words indicates the difficulty for a modern reader of judging the elements of satire and sentiment in Yorick's self-approval in *Sentimental Journey*. Instead of the indulgent self-consciousness of conventional sentimentalism, Sterne absorbed precisely the criticisms it had attracted and placed the resulting complex within a self-conscious, exploratory fictional frame. As in Schiller's aesthetic state, the darker motives are acknowledged but only to be held in mental suspension without being accorded immediate efficacy outside their fictional frame.

## Time and history

In the light of what has been said, it is not paradoxical that Sterne's proto-aestheticist play with fiction should largely exploit the literalism of his era. The jokes are typically about accurate transcription of experience rather than its literary representation, and yet this very literalism lends a special intimacy and power to its symbolic use. Over the course of producing *Tristram Shandy*, Sterne became ill of consumption, and both his novels play on the continuing narrative act as the continuance of life itself. His resistance to gravity becomes an almost literal flight from the grave, and *Tristram Shandy* is the first great novel, and perhaps the only one till the twentieth century, in which time, or rather the overcoming of time, is at once the major theme and the structuring principle of the narrative. The opening episode disrupts the internal psychological temporality of the sexual act with the absurd imposition of clock time. Similarly, although the narrative act is in the present, Tristram's emotional gaze is towards the past as a virtual infinity of narrative presents in which to dwell imaginatively. Most novels are narrated in the past tense to create a virtual present that constantly becomes past as we read. But the absence of linear order in *Tristram Shandy* allows its myriad pasts to be inhabited as eternally visitable presents. Epic time is constantly compressed into lyric feeling, as in this reminiscence of Tristram's youth:

> For I am at this moment walking across the market-place of *Auxerre* with my father and my Uncle Toby, in our way back to dinner——and I am at this moment also entering Lyons with my post-chaise broke into a thousand pieces——and I am moreover this moment in a handsome pavillion built by *Pringello*, upon the banks of the *Garonne*, which Mons. *Sligniac* has lent me, and where I now sit rhapsodizing all these affairs. (*TS*, VII.28)

Different narrative times are collapsed here, as the phrase 'this moment' refers to a temporality transposed into the eternal present of fiction. Although he uses quite different means, Sterne is an eighteenth-century Marcel Proust in his emotional overcoming of mortality through a fictive imagination and, again like Proust, he also had an eye to a larger contemporary history.

Sterne's philosophical suggestiveness stimulated generations of European novelists but he also contributed to a specifically English tradition and, indeed, a national consciousness as such. The second Jacobite rebellion against the Protestant Hanoverian dynasty had occurred as recently as 1745, and Sterne, strongly Anglican in his sympathies, introduced much anti-Papist humour into *Tristram Shandy* as in the figure of Dr Slop, and in Uncle Toby's whistling the Irish Protestant song *Lilliburlero*, although *Sentimental Journey* indicates that Sterne's attitude towards Catholic cultures was modified with closer knowledge. In this respect, the deeper contribution of Tristram and Toby to the formation of an idea of Englishness was in their capacity as lovable eccentrics. Tristram reflects that, whereas in Denmark he had found a uniformity of talents and characters, 'the case is quite different' in Britain, 'this unsettled island, where nature, in her gifts and dispositions of this kind, is more whimsical and capricious' (*TS*, I.11). William Shakespeare's Falstaff and Ben Jonson's Volpone were characters whose 'humour', in the old medieval sense of the word, denoted a dangerous excess in their disposition. Both had to be excluded from the social order. But over the following two centuries, the word 'humour' came to mean what is harmlessly amusing rather than dangerous and, as in the conscious construction of a tolerant society enacted in the *Spectator* papers, the eccentric came to be prized as a representative symbol of individual freedom, a principle which many English people associated with Protestantism and believed they had practically enshrined in the constitutional settlement of 1689, if not in the Magna Carta. Enlightened Continental thinkers, such as Voltaire, admired British political freedom and the eccentricities of Shandy Hall represented a national idea which would run through the English novel.

Yet, while *Tristram Shandy* reflects social history in such ways, its internal dynamic is also as resistant to public history as to the passage of personal time. Tristram's Lockean joke on the reader bears on a conscious disparity of scales in his own narrative:

> Pray, Sir, in all the reading which you have ever read, did you ever read such a book as *Locke's* Essay upon the Human Understanding——Don't answer me rashly,——because many, I know, quote the book, who have not read it,—— and many have read it who understand it not:——If either of these is your case, as I write to instruct, I will tell you in three words what the book is.—— It is a history.——A history! Of who? What? Where? When? Don't hurry yourself.——It is a history book, Sir, (which may possibly recommend it to the world) of what passes in a man's own mind. (*TS*, II.2)

Toby and Trim have participated in King William's wars at the end of the previous century and now follow on the bowling green the heroic progress of Marlborough's campaigns in Flanders. Once again, although it seems unlikely that one should read any single or sustained idea into this, the miniaturised military game is ambivalently suggestive. If, for the two old soldiers, it expresses patriotic and professional solidarity, the quaint and hobby-horsical miniaturisation has different implications for the reader. The bloody and destructive activity, well known as such to the two wounded veterans, has become an enjoyable game in which the positive emotions of the military life are at once given objective expression and rendered harmless. Once again, despite the disastrous associative vortex it occasions, it objectifies non-semantically the emotional lives of the participants and to that extent takes on an essentially aesthetic value. Their hobby-horsical conversations at times break into duets and arias. The games are not, then, a satire on the real battles; indeed, the peaceful enjoyment of the games depends on the battles being won, and yet the games themselves seem rather to celebrate an idiosyncratic private sphere. In Günter Grass's *Die Blechtrommel* (*The Tin Drum*, 1959), Oskar Matzerath describes a historical painting in which a distant village can be seen through the legs of a warhorse. In Sterne, we rather see the war from the distant standpoint of such a village, as Sterne helps to create the affectionate image of a private sphere. Yet even as public history is distanced, of course, it frames and conditions the private world. Unconsciously perhaps, he suggests how the foreground of the private space is premised on a larger national history or myth. Once again, he absorbs and suspends, rather than resolves, contemporary crosscurrents of feeling, form and ideas. It is hardly surprising that his subsequent use by European novelists has been so oblique and varied.

## Sterne and the European novel

Sterne's many translators and imitators across Europe are documented in the further reading.[4] I will, therefore, select some indicative moments of use or influence bearing in mind that his impact was most fruitful on the strong and original writers by whom it was most radically transformed.

On his visit to France he formed a friendship with Denis Diderot (1713–84) who, among his polymathic interests, wrote novels and tales, including *La Religieuse* (*The Nun*, 1760), a classic of affective verisimilitude, and promoted a new kind of sentimental bourgeois theatre. But Diderot also shared, in a more philosophical spirit, Sterne's humorous sense of the unstable ironies of both the human heart and the fictions in which it is reflected. In his overtly Sternean *Jacques le fataliste, et son maître* (1778,

1796) Jacques, the wayward manservant, exploits the conceit that his actions are not under his control because they are already 'written above'. Moral determinism is imaged as authorial control. Although Jacques' irreverence looks mainly backwards to a religious model, Diderot's joke on literary determinism casts a long shadow down the secular future of the novel. To what extent, for example, did late nineteenth-century naturalism represent a deterministic view of life through self-fulfilling narrative premises?

Sterne was valued in Germany principally as a 'free spirit'. British writing was a major resource for the extraordinary efflorescence of German culture in the latter half of the eighteenth century, and Christoph Martin Wieland (1733–1813) performed something of the function of Fielding by combining classical culture with contemporary sensibility in a sophisticated, ironic prose, but he also drew on Sterne and, in *Socrates Mainemenos, oder die Dialogen des Diogenes von Sinope (The Dialogues of Diogenes of Sinope,* 1770), he modulated the Sternean eccentric into the most radical and iconic of outsiders, the cynic philosopher Diogenes. Among writers of substance in the next generation, Jean Paul Richter (1763–1825) was known as 'the German Sterne', though increasingly perhaps as a challenge, rather than a simple compliment, to the original. His *Flegeljahre* (1804) was already more romantically softened and its humorous philosophical allusions are to the ego philosophy of the post-Kantian J. G. Fichte. E. T. A. Hoffmann (1766–1822), another Sterne enthusiast, created a distinctive imaginative world of his own with Gothic and proto-Freudian elements. In his very late novel *Wilhelm Meisters Wanderjahre (Wilhelm Meister's Years of Travel,* 1829), Goethe (1750–1832) summed up a guarded admiration for Sterne: 'A free spirit like his runs the risk of becoming impertinent unless ethical balance is restored by noble benevolence.' For by the turn of the century more innovative German writers were distancing themselves from Sterne both as English and as part of the Enlightenment generation.

Friedrich Schlegel developed a specific notion of the 'Romantic' novel for which Sterne was rather a precursor than a true example. The Romantic novel had Sterne's self-consciousness, subjectivity, playfulness and apparent disorder but was sustained by an inner artistic unity to create its own aesthetic world. In his view, Goethe's epoch-making *Wilhelm Meisters Lehrjahre (Wilhelm Meister's Apprenticeship,* 1796), despite its Enlightenment *gravitas* and its social mimesis, was infused with precisely such a humorous self-consciousness drawing together 'organically' the centripetal energies of its picaresque form. It may be because this notion of the Romantic novel existed largely as theory, and one resonant with contemporary post-Kantian philosophy, that Schlegel was so clear that Sterne approaches the threshold of his conception without the essential requirements for entry. Yet there remains a nagging feeling that he might just as easily have claimed Sterne as Romantic before his time, and he strikingly indicates Sterne's potential for enlistment into quite different, sometimes highly sophisticated, literary and philosophical conceptions.[5]

As well as the philosophical self-consciousness that characterised much of the German appreciation of Sterne, he remained also the iconic figure of delicate moral sensibility. This was the principal form of his reception in Russia, where the young Leo Tolstoy translated *Sentimental Journey* as a first step towards his mature examination of the subtle shades of truth and falsehood in the emotional life. At the same time, nineteenth-century realism had developed a more imaginative, even poetic, conception of representation than eighteenth-century literalism, and the workings of sentiment were likewise absorbed into a robustly fictional world. Hence, British fiction, which kept closest to the spirit of moral sentimentalism, had absorbed the Sternean impulse with little overt sense of him as a living resource. His smuttiness was famously disapproved of by William Makepeace Thackeray in *The English Humourists* (1853). But Sterne's spirit is alive in Charles Dickens's sentimentalism, his enjoyment of the eccentric and the grotesque and his focus on the inauthenticities of sentiment. This latter aspect passes strongly to Fyodor Dostoevsky in whom the vertiginous regress of sentimental inauthenticity in his characters indicates their ultimate descent from the eighteenth-century man of sentiment, of whom Sterne was a significant representative along with Rousseau.

The modernist generation appreciated above all the self-conscious formal play, and the subjective flow of the individual mind, in *Tristram Shandy*. In 1917, with an even stronger appropriation than Schlegel's, Viktor Shklovsky, the Russian formalist, claimed it as 'the most typical novel in world literature'.[6] He wished to privilege the self-consciousness of the literary work as such and, if this was an over-reading of Sterne, it nonetheless caught a vital aspect of the modernist turn. Once again, Sterne was not so much an influence on modernist writers as an object of appreciative appropriation. This already began with Friedrich Nietzsche, who articulated much of the modernist world-view, and was himself an admirer.

Most notably, Sterne's thematising of time and his representation of temporality touched on a central modernist concern. Sterne is part of the longer prehistory of the flow of individual association in James Joyce's *Ulysses* (1922), and Thomas Mann claimed that, when working on his tetralogy *Joseph und seine Brüder* (*Joseph and his Brothers*, 1934–43), he constantly reread Sterne to refresh his sense of the 'humour' with which his modern telling should infuse the biblical tale.[7] In the German tradition, as in

Schlegel, 'humour' here means formal self-consciousness. Even Lawrence loved *Tristram Shandy* and much of his longer fiction from *Mr Noon*, written in the late teens of the century although not published in his lifetime, engaged in Sternean parabasis, or direct address to the reader.[8] Proust is the most intriguing case among the modernists for, while there seems no record of his reading or commenting on Sterne, his great novel on temporality is extraordinarily Sternean in its themes and techniques.[9] *Ferdydurke* (1938), by the Polish novelist Witold Gombrowicz, was suppressed in turn by the Nazis, the Stalinists and the post-Stalinist Communist regime. Once again, the free spirit of Sterne's formal play is discernible within its Gogolian satiric world. Salman Rushdie's *Midnight's Children* (1981), the archetypal postcolonial novel, reverses Sterne's harmless miniaturising of great battles, as Saleem Sinai, the impotent, jesting, nasally challenged narrator, suffers the ignominies of history in his disintegrating body. Sterne's labile spirit continues to enrich novelists of the most varied kinds.[10]

## Note on editions

Scholarly editions of *Tristram Shandy*, *A Sentimental Journey* and the Sermons are available in the Florida Edition of the Works of Laurence Sterne (Gainesville, FL: University Presses of Florida, 1978–). Good paperback editions of *Tristram Shandy* are edited by Ian Campbell Ross (Oxford University Press, 1983); Melvyn New (Penguin, 2003); and Robert Folkenflik (Random House, 2004). For *A Sentimental Journey*, the Oxford World Classics, *A Sentimental Journey and Other Writings*, ed. Tim Parnell (Oxford University Press, 2003) and *A Sentimental Journey and Continuation of the Bramine's Journal, with Related Texts*, ed. Melvyn New and W. G. Day (Hackett, 2006), provide good texts along with other useful material.

### Notes

1 I discuss this in Michael Bell, *The Sentiment of Reality: Truth of Feeling in the European Novel* (London: Unwin, 1983), pp. 92–107.

2 *The Spectator*, ed. Donald F. Bond (London: Oxford University Press, 1965), vol. III, p. 178.

3 I discuss the episode in Michael Bell, *Sentimentalism, Ethics and the Culture of Feeling* (London: Palgrave, 2000), pp. 67–74.

4 P. de Voogd and J. Neubauer, eds., *The Reception of Laurence Sterne in Europe* (London: Thoemmes Continuum, 2004).

5 See Kathleen M. Wheeler, ed., *German Aesthetic and Literary Criticism: The Romantic Ironists and Goethe* (Cambridge University Press, 1984), pp. 5–80.

6 *Russian Formalist Criticism*, ed. Lemon T. Lee and Marion J. Reis (Lincoln, NE: University of Nebraska Press, 1965), p. 57.

7 On this, see Oskar Seidlin, 'Ironische Brüderschaft: Thomas Manns *Joseph der Ernährer* und Laurence Sternes *Tristram Shandy*', *Orbis Litterarum*, 13 (1958), 44–63.

8 D. H. Lawrence, Letter to Arthur MacLeod. 26 October 1913, in *The Letters of D. H. Lawrence*, vol. II, ed. James T. Boulton and George Zytaruk (Cambridge University Press, 1981), p. 90.

9 Cf. Michael Bell, 'Laurence Sterne and the Twentieth Century', in *Laurence Sterne in Modernism and Postmodernism*, ed. David Pierce and Peter de Voogd (Amsterdam/Atlanta, GA: Rodopi, 1996), pp. 39–54.

10 Cf. T. Keymer, ed., *The Cambridge Companion to Laurence Sterne* (Cambridge University Press, 2009) for further discussion of Sterne's relation to Rushdie and other modern writers.

*Further reading*

Cash, A. H., *Laurence Sterne: The Early and Middle Years* (London: Methuen, 1975)
   *Laurence Sterne: The Later Years* (London: Methuen, 1986)
Howes, A. B., ed., *Sterne: The Critical Heritage* (London: Routledge & Kegan Paul, 1974)
Keymer, T., *Laurence Sterne's 'Tristram Shandy': A Casebook* (Oxford University Press, 2006)
   *Sterne, the Moderns and the Novel* (Oxford University Press, 2002)
   ed., *The Cambridge Companion to Laurence Sterne* (Cambridge University Press, 2009)
Lanham, Richard A., *'Tristram Shandy': The Games of Pleasure* (Berkeley/London: University of Californa Press, 1973)
New, M., *Laurence Sterne as Satirist. A Reading of 'Tristram Shandy'* (Gainesville, FL: University of Florida Press, 1969)
   ed., *Critical Essays on Laurence Sterne* (New York: G. K. Hall, 1998)
   ed., *The Life and Opinions of Tristram Shandy, Gentleman, New Casebooks* (New York: St Martin's Press, 1992)
Voogd, P. de and J. Neubauer, eds., *The Reception of Laurence Sterne in Europe* (London: Thoemmes Continuum, 2004)

# 7

MARTIN SWALES

# Johann Wolfgang von Goethe (1749–1832): The German *Bildungsroman*

In 1774, a slim volume called *Die Leiden des jungen Werthers* (The Sorrows of Young Werther) appeared anonymously from the Leipzig publisher Weygand. It was the first work of German literature to achieve European best-seller status. Within Germany, it created an absolute furore – not least because the anonymous work did not remain so for long. The text was – and this was public knowledge at the time – embarrassingly close to real-life events.

Goethe, the charismatic angry young man of German letters in the early 1770s, worked for a time in Wetzlar, at the judicial centre of the Holy Roman Empire. There he fell in love with a young woman, Charlotte Buff, engaged to a man called Johann Christian Kestner. The 'eternal triangle' of the novel was uncomfortably close to the less-than-eternal triangle in Wetzlar. And while Goethe – who for the rest of his life could not escape being the author of that amazing best-seller – always resented being asked about the relationship between art and real life, he himself, in writing the work, exploited its umbilical linkage to extra-literary events. For the ferocious description of Werther's suicide at the end of the novel, he drew on a case of suicide at Wetzlar; a young man called Karl Wilhelm Jerusalem took his own life – and the event was much talked about both within and beyond Wetzlar. Goethe obtained a detailed account of the dire sequence of events from none other than Kestner and drew extensively on it for his novel.

The runaway success ensured a proliferation of editions. In 1775, a reprint appeared in an unauthorised edition of Goethe's works published by Himburg in Berlin, and was reprinted in 1777 and 1779. When Goethe agreed to rework the novel for an authorised edition of his collected works, by Göschen in Leipzig, he apparently had no copy of the original edition to hand and used Himburg's pirated edition as the basis for his significantly reworked second version of *Werther*, which appeared in Göschen's edition of *Goethes Schriften* (1787).

How are we to read *Werther*? Is it a superlative study of adolescent pathology, and therefore essentially a psychological document? Or is it an existential study of the unaccommodated human condition? Perhaps it is both – and more besides. One issue haunts us from the outset: that of specificity versus generality. The novel begins with a Preface from the editor figure which, in German (an effect not reproducible in English) moves from the more public *Ihr* (plural) to the intimate *du* (singular). Moreover, in the second paragraph of his prefatory statement, the editor modulates the plural of the novel's title 'The Sorrows' to the singular 'The Suffering':

> What I have been able to discover, by whatever means, of the story of poor Werther I have diligently put together, and I set it before you (plural) here, and I know that you (plural) will thank me for it. You (plural) cannot deny to his spirit and his character your (plural) admiration and love – nor to his fate your (plural) tears.
>
> And you (singular), good soul, you (singular) who feel the same promptings as he did, take comfort from his suffering (singular), and let this little book be your friend, if you (singular), whether from destiny's decree or your own fault, can find no closer friend.[1]

The salient point here is that Goethe, in this novel and throughout his novels, never tires of exploring the position of the bourgeois subject. He understands it as denoting both the particular inwardness of the individual self and the outward identity within the nexus of sociocultural relationships, as the (loyal or renegade) subject within prevailing social circumstances. The oscillation between singular and plural betokens a profound uncertainty within bourgeois culture: is the individual the supreme arbiter of values, or is the collective the locus of judgement? Goethe the novelist never tired of exploring these issues.

The extraordinary success of *Werther* has essentially to do with the contribution it makes to the novel's deployment, and exploration, of the rhetoric of subjectivity. Leaving aside the biographical details, it is important to note that Goethe's text engages with an all-important feature of contemporary literacy – the vogue for epistolary novels such as Samuel Richardson's *Pamela* and *Clarissa*, Jean-Jacques Rousseau's *Julie* and Choderlos de Laclos' *Les Liaisons dangereuses*. In comparison, *Werther* is striking on two counts. First, it is short. Second, it consists of only one set of letters, those of Werther addressed to his friend Wilhelm, and, as the novel unfolds and Werther's emotional distress deepens, addressed (we feel) increasingly to himself. In Goethe's hands, the epistolary novel becomes monologic and self-obsessed in a way that is not true of Richardson or Rousseau, whose protagonists write themselves into the public claims of reason and virtue. Goethe uses letters as the discursive form particularly attuned to the radically individualised self. The brevity of the text contributes to the powerful sense it conveys of emotional and cognitive claustrophobia.

*Werther* obeys the convention of the epistolary novel in having an editor figure who collects and orders the letters and commends them to our attentive and sympathetic reading. At one level, the editor serves to authenticate the fiction, to make it sound 'more real'. But as, over the last third of the text, he becomes more a narrator of the events, his account sustains a complex dialectic of detachment and complicity. At times we hear a resolutely documentary voice – and nowhere more so than in the two brutally laconic pages which close the novel with the description of Werther's ugly suicide. On other occasions, he brings us close to the inner processes of Werther's and Lotte's feelings. Having briefly noted the move from plural to singular forms of address in the editor's Preface, we also need to note the ambivalent and contradictory signals which it offers. The first paragraph impresses upon us the need to feel admiration and love for Werther, to shed tears at his sorry end. The second paragraph voices a kind of health warning, suggesting that whoever has no closer friend than this book is in danger. The reading experience provided by *Werther* is as destabilising as it is urgent.

How, then, are we to respond to this troublingly insistent text? Viewed in psychological terms, the novel brings us close to the sheer emotional intensity of a young man who will only live on all-or-nothing terms, who knows few compromises and accepts few conditions. He is impatient with anything less than total authenticity (in Lionel Trilling's sense of the term). The glory of his sensibility is inseparable from its catastrophe; Werther drives himself inexorably to self-obliteration. Within this interpretative framework, *Werther* has lost none of its power to capture – and/or to alienate – us. All the key themes that recur throughout Werther's letters – nature, love, religion, art – show us somebody who, in spite of his rhetoric of relatedness, of responding vibrantly to the world around him, withdraws ever more solipsistically into himself. The sequence of letters brings Werther's voice and person naggingly close to us.

Yet we do not respond only in psychological terms, for Werther's inwardness has a strongly historical signature: the signature of Rousseau. Schiller felt that *Werther* was Goethe's reckoning with the radical self-consciousness of modern culture, a self-consciousness (Schiller's term is *sentimentalisch*) that longs desperately to find the simplicity and integrity of 'naive' being in the world. The European eighteenth century is dominated by two seemingly opposed tendencies – Enlightenment and sentimentalism. The former esteemed the human self's capacity for rational reflection and critique; the latter valued intensity of feeling. Common to both these tendecies, however, for all their differences, is a radical individualism: all forms of received wisdom and institutionally promulgated dogma are set aside, truth can only be grounded in what, on his or her own terms, the individual thinks or feels. Moreover, we should recall that the German-speaking lands had a form of intensely inward Protestantism known as pietism. Many pietists saw self-scrutiny as the true path to godliness; hence, many of them produced autobiographical accounts of their introspection. Such writings conferred dignity and value on the inner struggles of ordinary men and women with their manifestly human psychological promptings. The language of pietism embodies a kind of two-way traffic: religious experience is made secular by being psychologised, while secular, psychological experience is theologised. The promptings of the human heart are endowed with religious significance, and religious fervour is equated with moral intensity. *Werther* supremely inhabits this middle ground: of the strength and fervour of the protagonist's feelings there can be no doubt; but what kind of value (if any) do they constitute?

I have been suggesting various ways in which we can react to Werther's inwardness. Three further possible reponses should be mentioned. One, particularly favoured by Marxist critics, is sociological. Werther belongs to a generation of gifted young people who, faced with the stagnation of the German-speaking lands in the 1770s, can find little or no outlet for their creative energies. On one occasion, Werther is rebuffed for having overstayed his welcome at a dinner table of aristocrats. The resentment and hurt he feels conspire to darken his mood. In addition to this sociological reading, two others take us into more existential ground. Time and again, Werther's letters express a profound mismatch between spirit and matter, between what the mind can conceive of and what the body can experience. In the following passage, for example, he produces a desolate parable, worthy of Franz Kafka, about the disenchantment that flows from the disjunction between expectation and actuality:

> A great, twilit wholeness rests before our soul, our feeling, like our eyes, swims and fades in it, and we long, ah, to surrender our whole being to it, to let ourselves be filled with the total bliss of one single, great, splendid feeling. – And alas, when we rush towards it, when the 'there' becomes a 'here', everything is as it was, and we stand in our poverty, in our constriction, and our soul longs for the refreshing draught that has slipped away. (bk 1, 21 June)

This magnificent passage throbs with Manichaean despair. Under this aspect, Werther inaugurates a line of novel heroes haunted by disgust with the material world. A second strand of this existential perspective derives from the analysis of romantic desire, forcefully expounded by Roland Barthes in his *Fragments d'un discours amoureux* (Fragments of a Loving Discourse), which sees Werther's letters as documents of the eternally desiring self.

Barthes argues that desire is grounded in the condition of lack or absence; that desire is less a temporary condition, which ends when the object of desire is either obtained or abandoned, than part of the ontology of the human subject. Hence, the one-way traffic of Werther's letters is the perfect correlative of the endlessly desiring self.

Any brief survey of possible responses to Goethe's *Werther*, such as I have given above, implies the complexity of the reader's or readers' (once again the issue of singular and plural comes back to haunt us) responses to the text. The text offers both validation and critique of Werther's sensibility. I have already drawn attention to the ambivalence of the editor's rhetoric. It is worth recalling that the 1775 printing had two prefatory poems – to Book I and Book II of the novel. They were subsequently removed. But they remind us of the hermeneutic volatility that pervades Goethe's text. The first poem registers the longing that men and women feel to love and to be loved, and describes that need as the 'holiest' of the imperatives known to the human species, and wonders why so often pain flows from this sublime craving. The second poem is more judgemental, and imagines the shade of Werther speaking to the 'dear soul' of the contemporary reader and urging: 'Be a man and do not follow after me.'

The interplay of these two poems suggests that *Werther* is a cautionary tale which is, like many cautionary tales, complicit in the experiences against which it warns. To which one might somewhat testily respond: where does this, then, leave the reader(s)? It may help to recall that Goethe's novel is a cult book about a society already well endowed with cult books. Literature is frequently invoked in the text for its input into men's and women's lived experience. When Werther and Lotte first meet, they witness a thunderstorm which reminds them irresistibly of a poem, 'The Festival of Spring', by a celebrated poet of the time, Friedrich Gottlieb Klopstock, which contained a magnificent description of a thunderstorm. Werther is an avid reader, initially of Homer, then (as his mood darkens and he becomes increasingly self-enclosed) of James McPherson's *Ossian*. This was a set of melancholy poems which the author presented as genuine survivals of ancient Scottish culture. In a crucial scene late in the novel, which arguably thematises the dangers of sentimental reading, Werther reads his translation of *Ossian* with Lotte, and they weep copiously. The German text of *Ossian* is incorporated at length into *Werther*. And finally, when Werther kills himself, he leaves open on his desk *Emilia Galotti*, a then famous tragedy of moral sensibility by Gotthald Ephraim Lessing, which contrasts the moral seriousness of bourgeois life with the appalling laxity of aristocratic life, and thereby perhaps reminds us of the social motivation of Werther's despair. In any event, it is important to note that one of Werther's last acts is a self-commentary and self-explication through literature.

What are we to make of Werther's presence as reader? One answer has to do with the culture from which *Werther* derives and to which it speaks. In an ever more secular world, works of literature (rather than the Bible) become bibles for the various communities of believers who define their common values through key texts. *Werther* thematises this process, and became its supreme exemplar (as is attested by its impassioned reception, even down to the wearing of the 'Werther costume'). The second reflection on the matter of readerliness in *Werther* raises an issue that pervades Goethe's novels. Time and again, he draws attention to the writing and reading of texts, time and again he interpolates texts within his own narrative; in short, he invites us to become self-conscious readers, to read and to reflect on our reading. I shall return to this issue at the end of this chapter.

The remainder of Goethe's novel production is dominated, in one form or another, by the Wilhelm Meister project which exists in four versions: *Wilhelm Meisters theatralische Sendung* (*Wilhelm Meister's Theatrical Mission*, 1777–85, but never published in Goethe's lifetime), *Wilhelm Meisters Lehrjahre* (*Wilhelm Meister's Apprenticeship Years*, 1795–6) and *Wilhelm Meisters Wanderjahre* (*Wilhelm Meister's Journeyman Years*, first version 1821, revised 1829). The *Journeyman Years* consists of a number of shorter tales held together by a loose narrative frame. One of these tales grew in scope until it became a novel in its own right – *Die Wahlverwandtschaften* (*The Elective Affinities*, 1809) – to which I shall return at the end of this chapter. It is important to keep the Meister novels together as a group – not least because they run in parallel to another lifelong project of Goethe's (which also exists in several versions), the great verse drama *Faust*. It is helpful to regard the two projects as two faces of the same coin. *Faust* explores the titanism of bourgeois enterprise and energy, whereas the Meister novels concern bourgeois adaptability and growth. Viewed in this light, one can perhaps understand the force of Friedrich Schlegel's seemingly eccentric observation in the 216th *Athenäumsfragment* to the effect that the French Revolution, Johann Gottlieb Fichte's epistemology and Goethe's Meister represented the three great tendencies of the age.

Schlegel's enthusiasm for German cultural products may seem excessive; but what his remark captures – at least as far as Goethe is concerned – is the sense in which the Meister narratives are central to the emergence of the novel as the paramount literary form of the modern bourgeois age in Europe. German culture provides both the theory and the practice of the novel. In 1774, in his essay on the theory of the novel, Friedrich von Blanckenburg registers that the novel comes of age when it invests the traditional episodic abundance of its plot line (depending on mistaken identities, long-lost relatives, wars, shipwrecks, etc.) with inward significance. Blanckenburg's argument refers principally to – but is by no means confined to – Christoph Martin Wieland's novel *Agathon* (1766–7). For Blanckenburg, Wieland's achievement consists of spiritualising the outwardness of the novel until it becomes the expression, in linear form, of the complexity of the human self. The novel becomes, then, as much interested in inner potentiality as outward actuality. Some time later, G. W. F. Hegel, in his *Vorlesungen über die Ästhetik* (*Aesthetics*), sees the modern novel as exploring the conflict between the inner poetry of the human heart and the outward prose of practical social circumstances. Schlegel praises the irony of the modern novel of which, for him, Goethe's Meister is the paradigmatic example. Moreover, the *Apprenticeship* was the subject of intense debate in the letters that passed between Goethe and Friedrich Schiller. No other literary work receives comparably detailed and scrupulous attention in their letters. I shall refer later to particular insights that emerge in this exchange; at this stage all I want to register is that Goethe's great novel project, at one all-important phase of its gestation, is accompanied by a theoretical debate of surpassing sophistication. In consequence, the Meister novels become a kind of narrative encyclopedia of modern culture; they put the novel on the map, once and for all.

*Wilhelm Meister's Theatrical Mission* is essentially a work of sociopsychological realism. Wilhelm turns away from the world of his bourgeois upbringing to pursue a career in the theatre, which holds a three-fold appeal for him. First, it is a place of exotic, bohemian colourfulness, one which immeasurably expands his social sympathies and his sexual responses (three all-important woman figures with whom he comes into contact, Marianne, Mignon and Natalie, have an androgynous fascination for him which extends from the physical to the spiritual). Second, the theatre challenges him intellectually as he discovers what is involved in putting on a play, especially *Hamlet*. Third, the theatre is a social institution dependent upon the vagaries of public taste and uncertain aristocratic patronage. Behind the colourful ups and downs of Wilhelm's time as a sort of actor-manager lies an issue that was particularly urgent in late eighteenth-century Germany – the project of founding a national theatre. In the fragmented condition of the German-speaking lands of the time, the creation of a national theatre might provide the representative forum which the nation itself lacked.

The *Theatrical Mission* is incomplete as it stands, but it provides the basis for approximately the first five books of the *Apprenticeship*. In that version, Wilhelm outgrows his enthusiasm for the theatre and becomes involved with the self-styled Society of the Tower, a secret society devoted to the spiritual and practical improvement of the social world. The *Apprenticeship* engages a number of features of the cultural life of the time. After five books devoted to theatre, the sixth book of the novel, entitled 'Confessions of a Beautiful Soul', is an interpolated manuscript written by Natalie's religious aunt. This chapter acknowledges the historico-cultural resonance of pietism with its concern for the narrative of the inner life already noted in discussing *Werther*. Moreover, the secret society was a phenomenon of late eighteenth-century Germany (one thinks especially of the Freemasons and the Illuminati) while the *Geheimbundroman*, secret society novel, was a vogue which, in perverted form, animates the fiction of the Marquis de Sade.

Many of the key members of the Society of the Tower are aristocrats. Wilhelm is not, and in a letter to his bourgeois friend Werner, he reflects on the differences between the aristocratic and the bourgeois way of life:

> If the nobleman through the deployment of his person says everything, the bourgeois says nothing through his personality – and is meant to say nothing. The former may, and should, be seen; but the latter is supposed only to be, and what he wants to be seen to be is risible and tasteless. The former should undertake certain activities and should achieve an effect. The latter should work hard and produce something. He should develop individual capacities in order to be a useful member of society, and it is not generally assumed that there is – nor should there be – any harmony in his being because he, in order to be useful in one particular way, has to neglect all the other possibilities. (bk v, ch. 3)

The bourgeois, according to Wilhelm, may – indeed should – work hard and be productive; but he lacks the social space in which his person can find representative expression; and the novel, we might add, is precisely the form that gives expression to that battle for social space. Whereas the aristocrat does not have to achieve anything; his being and way of life make effortless contributions to the public sphere. In these reflections, we can see a conciliatory answer to the French Revolution, one in which the energies of bourgeois and aristocrat can come together – as in the various activities of the Society of the Tower which reconcile hard work and aesthetic style, social responsibility and private property. The maxims of which the Socety is so fond frequently reflect on the interplay of individualism and collectivity. Goethe, like Schiller, sensed that modern culture was prone to restrict human activity to certain specialised choices. That ethos of a division of labour may release great energy, but it is an energy that needs to be enriched and humanised by being related to the experiential wholeness that may no longer be found in one person but rather in the social totality of which he or she is part.

That aspiration to reconcile particularity and totality, singular and plural, informs Wilhelm's quest which he defines as being 'mich selbst, ganz wie ich da bin, auszubilden' ('to develop myself, just [whole] as I am', bk v, ch. 3). He has a lively sense of the particularity of his own selfhood, and of the need to help that self to unfold and develop, just as it is and wholly as it is (the ambiguity of the little phrase 'ganz wie ich da bin' is untranslatable in English). This aspiration makes the *Apprenticeship* the paradigmatic instance of the *Bildungsroman*, a novel form which is often claimed to be the most significant German contribution to the European novel. It is, however, crucial to note that the story told is anything but a serene pilgrimage to harmonious self-fulfilment. A mere two pages from the end of the novel, Wilhelm laments that he has got everything wrong. He resents the sententiousness of the Society of the Tower. Moreover, when he is admitted to their number in a pretentiously grandiose ceremony, he is decidedly bad-tempered and bereft of any secure sense of his own achievement. Ultimately, the novel does have a happy ending and Wilhelm is united with Natalie – but it comes about more by luck than by judgement on Wilhelm's part. There is throughout the novel a tentativeness to the growing and learning process that is central to the irony of Goethe's narrative, for which it has been both praised and blamed. Wilhelm learns and forgets, he is both seeing and unseeing. In consequence, the *Apprenticeship* has an indeterminate and elusive feel. *Bildung* emerges as an ongoing process rather than a fixed goal.

That tentativeness figures constantly in the exchange of letters between Goethe and Schiller. At one point Goethe admits that 'precisely its incompleteness has caused me the most difficulty' (30 October 1797). The incompleteness of the novel, its lack of once-and-for-allness, made Schiller uncomfortable and he urged Goethe to give the novel greater conceptual clarity, a firmer articulation of its central idea. But Goethe resisted in the name of what he called his 'realistic tic' (9 July 1796); he knew that the novel had to have a kind of indirection at its heart. For all the differences that separated them, and for all their differences in temperament, Goethe and Schiller are both wonderfully perceptive about the unfolding Meister project. At one point Schiller reflects on the necessary indeterminacy of the central character:

> Wilhelm Meister is admittedly the most necessary but not the most important person; precisely that is utterly characteristic of your novel that it neither has nor needs such a most important person. Everything happens to him and around him – but not actually for his sake; because everything that surrounds him represents and expresses energies and educability, he necessarily has a different relationship to the other characters from that which applies to the hero of other novels. (28 November 1796)

In this brilliantly perceptive passage, Schiller recognises that Wilhelm is a knowable character with his whims and moods but that he is also, and more importantly, a cipher for the manifold potentiality of the human self.

He is the point of intersection on which so many of the human specificities of the novel converge. The novel's indeterminateness, its irony, is a form of complex knowingness; it is not nihilistic or disparaging. Ultimately, the *Apprenticeship* is affirmatory about the living process. Hence, two of the most appealing characters, Mignon and the Harper, who are moving precisely for the doom that they, in their pathological anguish, carry round with them, are written out of the novel. In the Hall of the Past, where Mignon's funeral takes place, there is an all-important motto: 'gedenke zu leben' – 'be mindful to live' (bk VIII, ch. 5). It inverts the expected memento mori, replacing the religious admonition by a secular commitment, one that urges us to keep faith with life. The *Apprenticeship* is so mindful, and it asks us, as readers, to be so mindful, to be alert to the shifting interplay of forces, values, persons, institutions, communities that make up the world of the novel. As we reflect on its kaleidoscopic interplay of chance and destiny, gifts and choices, impulse and discipline, spontaneity and repression, we continue the open-ended process of *Bildung* in our hermeneutic relationship to Goethe's extraordinary and necessarily elusive text.

That elusiveness becomes more dominant in the two versions of the *Journeyman Years* which continue the Meister project. The principle of movement and displacement is central to the plot, such as it is (Wilhelm must not stay three days under one roof, and, when he moves, he must put at least one mile between himself and his previous resting place). This principle of displacement is also central to both versions of the novel because they are essentially a loose grouping of stories. Characters appear both in the interpolated stories and in the outer frame. The second version draws on the first, taking up the first stories, reworking and repositioning them, and adding to their number. It also defines America as the goal for many of the members of the Society of Wanderers. It makes more of the Makarie figure, who becomes a fully worked-out character in the second version. Although old, frail and confined to a wheelchair, she is a source of wise counsel for many of the characters who are caught up in emotional turmoil. She is even a saintly figure, a transcendent spirit who lives most truly in the stars of the solar system. The second version ends with two collections of aphorisms – 'Contemplations in the Sense of the Wanderers' and 'From Makarie's Archive' – with two poems and finally the laconic words 'To be continued'. The *Journeyman Years*, already the continuation of an earlier novel, asks in its turn to be continued. The novel being an ongoing community of stories, the final version has an editor figure who draws on the material in the archives of Makarie and the Society of Wanderers. His presence serves less to authenticate the material than to provide the context for its telling, its refictionalisation.

The stories vary in quality and intensity. One of the most vivid comes not from the archives but from an account that Wilhelm sends Natalie of his first love, which was for a young boy who, tragically, drowned. The sense of fervent childhood emotion, of homosexual adoration is unforgettable. Yet much of the narrative comes nowhere near that energy. Perhaps we should recall the subtitle of both versions of the *Journeyman Years*: *The Renunciants*. Many of the stories explore passion with a sense that ultimately compromise and sublimation are the highest goals to be achieved in human affairs (the comparison with *Werther* could hardly be more striking). In a conversation with Kanzler von Müller (18 February 1830), Goethe referred to the *Journeyman Years* as a compendium of stories.[2] We know, too, that the decision to include the aphorisms and the two poems involved practical considerations: when it was decided that the novel would take up three, rather than two, volumes of the final authorised edition, extra material was needed for the additional pages. Clearly, Goethe felt that the aphorisms and poems made sense within the final phase of the Meister project; he would not indiscriminately include any material that came to hand. Yet equally, he clearly felt that the archival character of the work allowed for additions and subtractions to be made without endangering the coherence of the whole. If the novel is 'to be continued', it is perhaps in the process of our reading, which can be selective. We can open a page at random; we can pick out a story; we can riffle back and forth through the pages. That may truly be the measure of the creative freedom that Goethe's *Bildungsroman* allows us. In Barthes' terms, we are confronted with a text that is more writerly (*scriptible*) than readerly (*lisible*).

Such narrative elusiveness pervades a text that was originally destined for the *Journeyman Years*, but was expanded from a *Novelle* into a novel in its own right: *The Elective Affinities* (1809). Its theme, again reminiscent of *Werther*, is disastrous passion. Like *Werther*, it is both visceral and highly sophisticated. It is set on a small estate. Eduard and Charlotte, happily married and contented with their lot, decide to invite an old friend, the Captain, to visit them, and they also invite Ottilie, Charlotte's niece, a beautiful but withdrawn young woman, to join them. The well-laid plans go disastrously wrong. Eduard and Ottilie fall in love, as do Charlotte and the Captain. Charlotte gives birth to a child. She and Eduard are the genetic makers of that child; but during their love-making they imagine their absent partners (the Captain and Ottilie) to be present. The child's features show similarities to those of the two spiritually present but physically absent figures. In a catastrophic accident, the child, when entrusted to Ottilie's care, is drowned. Ottilie puts an end to the relationship with Eduard and refuses all food. She dies, and Eduard survives her only briefly.

It is helpful to consider *Elective Affinities* under three aspects. One can view it as a social novel. From a number of hints it is clear that the novel is set in the world contemporary with its publication, in the post-revolutionary, Napoleonic period. It was a troubled time; yet life on the estate continues in imperturbable, claustrophobic calm. It is the calm of the mausoleum. There is something barren about the life of these minor aristo-crats; many of their projects entail tinkerings with nature, fussy additions to their property. When new life is brought in, the whole house of cards collapses. Such a social reading implies, then, strenuous criticism of the petty aristocracy in the German-speaking lands. Yet this reading, however cogent, leaves a good deal of the text unexplored. The novel also offers a profound rumination on the existential freedom and/or entrapment of human beings. Once desire is unleashed, it takes a terrible toll; even the more mature and self-disciplined characters (Charlotte and the Captain) are no more proof against the inroads of passion than the more spontaneous and headlong figures of Eduard and Ottilie.

Eerily, three of the four main characters one evening discuss the processes of attraction, bonding, repulsion and separation in various chemical sub-stances and, as they do so, they make analogies with the human sphere. Charlotte is the first to protest, insisting on the difference between the human sphere on the one hand (where highly developed self-consciousness and mental maturity confer an all-important degree of choice) and, on the other, the behaviour of simple substances (oil, water, gypsum), where no such choice is given. Yet the 'chemical discussion' of these three characters, their ability to reflect, debate and differentiate, all these instances of human cognition and good sense, provide no protection against the force of primal desire. Time and again, the narrative invites us, explicitly and implicitly, to reflect on the issues involved in human knowing, 'knowing' understood both in the mental sense and in the older, biblical, carnal sense. Those two senses, and the interaction between them, come into scandalously vivid focus in the act of spiritual adultery (pt I, ch. 11), where the desire informing the act of love between Eduard and Charlotte is intensified by their fantasies about their longed-for partners.

One further aspect of the novel needs highlighting. *Elective Affinities* is little short of overwhelming in its self-consciousness. I have already stressed that self-consciousness is central to the book's thematic purpose. But it also informs its very narrative mode at every turn. In the chemical discussion of the laws of natural attraction, the phrase 'elective affinity' is strenuously debated. I can think of no other European novel that reflects so intensely on its own title. The title refers us to chemical experiments; and one could say that *Elective Affinities* is an experimental novel – in several senses of the term. It is a novel about a human experiment – of adding two people to an existing couple, and it asks what laws (if any) of physical or metaphysical attraction apply to human affairs. It also experiments with processes of human signification, and thereby reflects on its own over-determined condition. The four chief characters are supremely significatory spirits: prone to find meanings everywhere. And the narrative in which they figure capitalises on their significations, and adds its own. The upshot is a hall of mirrors. Time and again details proliferate which prefigure, replicate, reincarnate each other. Names are a case in point. The Captain's name is Otto. Eduard was originally named Otto. Charlotte and Ottilie are variations on Otto. The child who is born of the spiritual adultery is called Otto. Moreover, the name itself is a palindrome. When the four figures come together on the estate, their initial letters (Eduard, Charlotte, Captain (Hauptmann), Ottilie) spell ECHO. The goblet has engraved on it the letters E and O. The lakes that were one body of water have been brought into separate being for the purposes of elaborately stylised gardening (the novel thematises the difference between the English and the French garden), but, in a catastrophic event, they reconsitute themselves as one lake. At the very end of the novel, we are told that Eduard and Ottilie are buried side by side in the chapel on the estate, and that 'serene, related angelic images' look down upon them. The very last sentence of the novel invokes a key term from its title – 'related' (*verwandt*).

What are we to make of the echo? Perhaps there is a transcendental force to Eduard and Ottilie's unconditional love? But perhaps there is a more mundane explanation. The architect who designed the interior of the chapel was in love with Ottilie; hence, all the angels on the ceiling have her features. The 'angelic images' are truly related, then, by the complex indirections of human desire. At one point, *Elective Affinities* provides a *mise-en-abyme* of itself: it contains an interpolated *Novelle*, narrated by an English lord who visits the estate, which seems to provide a contrasting mirror image of events in the novel. Or does it? In other words, *Elective Affinities* generates an overkill of possible significations. The narrator is, to put it mildly, an oblique presence, now intruding with an interpretative or judgemental comment, now withdrawing his or her voice altogether. The upshot is a novel that teems with signfication but in meaning so many things it means no one thing and is fiendishly difficult to decipher. *Elective Affinities* is one of the most remarkable texts in European literature – a highly significant novel that reflects on its own processes and modes of signification at every turn.

How, ultimately, are we to assess Goethe's achievement as a novelist? Somehow he never seems a natural, a born novelist as Honoré de Balzac,

Charles Dickens, Marcel Proust or James Joyce – for all their differences – seem to be. Yet what Goethe does for and with the novel form is astonishing. His novel production is a remarkably precocious exploration of the possibilities inherent in the genre. He understands the post-feudal world as one in which traditional dogmas are gradually losing ground, in which the individual must find his or her way through the experiences that are available. Yet he also perceives the many constraints that are at work, above all those which indwell in the mentality of certain institutions – the family, the theatre, schools and religious communities, various classes (aristocrat, bourgeois), economic groupings (estate management, spinning and weaving, mining, bureaucracy). Referring to *Elective Affinities*, Goethe once said his aim as a novelist was 'to depict in symbolic concentration social relationships and the conflicts between them' (*Hamburger Ausgabe*, vol. VI, p. 638). That symbolic concentration allows him to focus less on day-to-day practicalities than on the cast of mind, the values and assumptions that inform a certain way of life. In his portrayal of human inwardness he explores the individual's need, within a secular, largely contingent world, for structures that confer value, purpose, meaning. Some of these structures are social and institutional, as we have already noted. Yet Goethe also understands that, even in a secular world, men and women can have immortal longings, and time and again, from Werther to Makarie, he delights in exploring characters who aspire to transcendental certainties.

Formally, Goethe is extraordinarily adventurous in his understanding of the flexibility of the novel form – and, above all, of its scope for self-referentiality. All his novels contain interpolated texts and by this token thematise the processes of reading and writing, of telling and hearing stories. Many of his novels exist in multiple versions; in this sense one has the impression that they are all intended 'to be continued' in the play of the reader's reflectivity. This is particularly true of the Meister project, the paradigmatic instance of the *Bildungsroman*. The term was first coined by Karl Morgenstern in a lecture of 1820, although it only entered general critical parlance some fifty years later, when Wilhelm Dilthey used it in his study of Schleiermacher. What Morgenstern and Dilthey seek to define is a novel text that is not narrowly about education, about growing up in the practical social world; territory that the realist novel explores superbly. Rather, the *Bildungsroman* is concerned with the gradual unfolding, forming, un-forming and re-forming of the self. In this sense it has a philosophical dimension: it is a questioning quest for the richness of human potentiality. Many German commentators see the genre as a paean in praise of harmonious wholeness. Yet many of the novels in the tradition – including Goethe's Meister novels, along with Gottfried Keller's *Green Henry* (first version 1855, second version 1880) and Thomas Mann's *Der Zauberberg* (*The Magic Mountain*, 1924) – are unstable, ironic, tentative rather than triumphant and sure of themselves. And they demand a condition of suspended judgement from the reader. This applies also to those of Goethe's novels which do not partake of the *Bildungsroman*'s preoccupation with the gradual growth of a young person. The self-consciousness of all of Goethe's novelistic writing is designed to keep the readers on their toes. The upshot is a corpus of fiction that, in the spirit of Schiller's aesthetics, engenders, through the experience of novel-reading, a complex mobilisation of all human faculties in thoughtful play. In that spirit, the novel becomes what Schlegel wanted it to be: an ironic encyclopedia of modern life.

For Goethe, the novel is essentially pluri-vocal. And it is so because the world which it knows and to which it speaks is in flux, is for ever in the making, is, as one might put it, democratic. Modern society, as Goethe understoood it, is a community of narratives. Modern society and the novel are made for each other because they are both conjectural rather than fixed, a set of experiments rather than a collection of dogmas. Goethe's influence on the European novel has been profound – even where he has been repudiated as an immoral writer (as happened throughout nineteenth-century English letters). Yet the accusation here is not that he advocates immoral behaviour but that he does not tell us where he stands, and, by extension, where we, as readers, should stand. There is some cogency to that charge. Goethe is difficult to pin down because he is so allusive and elusive. Thomas De Quincey thought *Wilhelm Meister* morally offensive and even Thomas Carlyle, as he worked on the translation, was troubled by the novel's lack of moral purpose. D. H. Lawrence is a splendid witness for the prosecution in his rejection of Goethe's Olympian superiority. Yet Goethe has not wanted for advocates such as Samuel Taylor Coleridge, Carlyle (in spite of his above-mentioned reservations), George Eliot, George Henry Lewes, Crabb Robinson, Matthew Arnold. In any event, any attempt to understand the poetics of the modern novel is somehow unthinkable without Goethe.

## Note on editions/translations

The most approachable and usefully annotated is still the Hamburg Edition (*Hamburger Ausgabe*), ed. Erich Trunz et al. in 14 volumes (rev. edn, Munich: Beck, 1981ff.). The novels and novellas are in volumes VI to VIII.

For a useful selection of Goethe's works in English, see *Goethe's Collected Works* ed. Victor Lange, Eric A. Blackall and Cyrus Hamlin, 12 vols. (New York: Suhrkamp, 1983–9). *Werther* and *Elective Affinities* tend to be the most retranslated novels as, for example, *Goethe, Selected Works*

(New York/London: Knopf, 'Everyman', 2000), which contains *Werther*, trans. Elizabeth Mayer and Louise Brogan, and *Elective Affinities* trans. David Constantine.

## Notes

1 All translations in this chapter are my own.
2 *Goethe Handbuch*, vol. III, ed. Bernd Witte and Peter Schmidt (Stuttgart/Weimar: Metzler, 1997) p. 195.

## Further reading

### On Goethe generally

Boyle, Nicholas, *Goethe, the Poet and the Age*, vol. I, *The Poetry of Desire, 1749–1790* (Oxford: Clarendon Press, 1991), vol. II, *Revolution and Renunciation, 1790–1803* (Oxford: Clarendon Press, 2000)
Reed, T. J., *Goethe* (Oxford University Press, 1998)
Williams, John R., *The Life of Goethe* (Oxford: Blackwell, 1998)

### On Goethe and the novel

Blackall, Eric, *Goethe and the Novel* (Ithaca, NY/New York: Cornell University Press, 1976)
Muenzer, Clark, *Figures of Identity: Goethe's Novels and the Enigmatic Self* (University Park, PA/London: Pennsylvania University Press, 1984)
Reiss, Hans, *Goethe's Novels* (London: Macmillan, 1969)

### On *Werther*

Barthes, Roland, *A Lover's Discourse: Fragments*, trans. Richard Howard (Harmondsworth: Penguin, 1990)
Swales, Martin, *Goethe:'The Sorrows of Young Werther'*, Landmarks of World Literature (Cambridge University Press, 1987)
Trilling, Lionel, *Sincerity and Authenticity* (London: Oxford University Press, 1972)

### On *Wilhelm Meister*

Bahr, Ehrhard, *The Novel as Archive: The Genesis, Reception, and Criticism of Goethe's Wilhelm Meisters Wanderjahre* (Columbia, SC: Camden House, 1998)
Blair, John, *Tracing Subversive Currents in Goethe's* Wilhelm Meister's Apprenticeship (Columbia, SC: Camden House, 1997)
Hardin, James, ed., *Reflection and Action: Essays in the* Bildungsroman (Columbia, SC: University of South Carolina Press, 1991)

### On *The Elective Affinities*

Barnes, H. G., *Goethe's Die Wahlverwandtschaften: A Literary Interpretation* (Oxford, Clarendon Press, 1976)

# 8

SUSAN MANNING

# Walter Scott (1771–1832): The historical novel

> [I]n the history of prose fiction there are but two epoch makers – Cervantes, who did the ancient and beloved art of pure story-telling to a cruel death, and Walter Scott, who brought it to a glorious resurrection.[1]

> Walter Scott raised to the dignity of the philosophy of History the literature which, from age to age, sets perennial gems in the poetic crown of every nation where letters are cultivated. He vivified it with the spirit of the past; he combined drama, dialogue, portrait, scenery, and description; he fused the marvelous with truth – the two elements of the times; and he brought poetry into close contact with the familiarity of the humblest speech.[2]

In the year of his death, Walter Scott envisaged a trip to Greece, returning through Germany to visit the poet Johann Wolfgang von Goethe. It was not to be; Scott's personal travel in Europe was limited to two visits to Paris, a trip to the battlefield of Waterloo and a cruise to the Mediterranean in sadly failing health. But his personal and literary lives were substantially European: in 1797 he married a Frenchwoman, Charlotte Charpentier, and his first literary foray in 1796 involved a translation of two German ballads, prompted by Henry Mackenzie's paper to the Royal Society of Edinburgh on German drama, which Scott remembered described 'scenes of wildest contrast, and all [the] boundless variety of character mingling, without hesitation, livelier with more serious incidents, and exchanging scenes of tragic distress as they occur in common life, with those of a comic tendency'.[3] Thus liberated from 'the rules so servilely adhered to by the French school', the young Scott set about learning German. Translating Goethe's historical play *Götz von Berlichingen* in 1799 consolidated his admiration for the German writer and led indirectly to their correspondence in the 1820s.

When Scott turned from poetry to novel-writing in 1814, the dramatic variety of the new German drama became a hallmark of his fiction. Scott was a 'European novelist' in the broadest of senses: his final work included a story set in Constantinople on the eve of the First Crusade, and a tale of the Knights of Malta, left unfinished at his death. Irrespective of setting, his novels were infused with encyclopedic knowledge of literature from Homer and Virgil through the medieval epics of Italy and the romances (and anti-romances) of Golden Age Spain, the tales of chivalry from Jean Froissart and the *Chanson de Roland*, and the great French drama of Molière and Pierre Corneille, the religious and historical writing of the Low Countries and the Gothic stories of Romantic Germany. Europe and European literature were not only the ground on which Scott's imagination played; they inhabit the texture of his prose. William Shakespeare apart, his favourite writer (judging by frequency and warmth of citation) was probably Miguel de Cervantes: one tag from *Don Quixote*, Durandarte's 'Patience, cousin, and shuffle the cards', appears in several novels. In Spain, he was known as 'el Cervantes escocés' (the Scottish Cervantes), and in 1815 the French periodical *Bibliothèque universelle* dubbed him 'the Ariosto of the North'. Like other literary figures of his time, Scott followed closely Napoleon's progress across Europe; after the deposed emperor's death, he wrote a biography in nine volumes that amounted to a history of modern Europe. His sources included the Russian patriot Denys Davidoff, who fought a guerrilla campaign against Napoleon's forces in 1812; the kind of larger-than-life character in whom Scott delighted, Davidoff is thought to be the historical model for Leo Tolstoy's Denisoff in *War and Peace*.

Well before this, the Waverley novels were established as European not only in scope but in their fundamental rationale. *Waverley, or 'Tis Sixty Years Since* appeared in 1814, as Napoleon's empire entered its final year. The French Revolution and its repercussions rocked Europe; for all but the most radical of Scott's contemporaries, fear of instability at home followed the Terror and the subsequent advance of Napoleon's ambitions. On the eve of Waterloo, the double time frame of *Waverley* juxtaposed current fears about invasion with the 1745 Jacobite attempt to reinstate a Stuart monarch. In Scott's most 'Scottish' fiction, local and national events bear the impress of a broader sphere; the twenty-six Waverley novels collectively offer an understanding of post-Napoleonic Europe. More surprisingly, perhaps, Europe is repeatedly shown to have been formed in historical encounters with the lands at its edges. As they had for Napoleon, whom Scott described half-admiringly in a letter of 1808 as 'possessing the genius and talents of an Eastern Conqueror', Africa and Asia helped to define the character as well as the extent of the continent.[4] Scott's refusal – notwithstanding obvious opportunities and the urging of friends and admirers – to write an 'American' novel is puzzling until one realises that it is the story of Europe that animates his historical imagination.

Europe soon claimed Scott as its own: Goethe pronounced *Waverley* 'without hesitation' fit to 'set beside the best works that have ever been written in this world'.[5] Franz Schubert wrote songs based on *Ivanhoe*, and Gaetano Donizetti's *Lucia di Lammermoor* is only the most celebrated of more than eighty operatic versions of Scott's stories; Alexandre Dumas pioneered European stage adaptations, and Eugène Delacroix produced striking paintings of scenes in the Waverley novels. The pan-European vogue for the novels, and through them all things Scottish, was sensational. Their success was helped by the context of their production: London and Edinburgh were centres of European publishing, and well-developed literary networks of publishers, booksellers and journals in Britain helped to advertise, review and circulate new works in a way that would, for example (as Goethe realised), have been simply impossible at the time in Germany.[6] But this is only a small part of the story. Scott was a formally inventive novelist of extraordinary imaginative range whose work expanded the possibilities for narrative fiction and revolutionised the status of the novel from a lightweight form disparaged even by its practitioners into the undisputed master-genre of nineteenth-century literature.

## The *Waverley* sequence: romance and modernity

The medieval genre of chivalric romance exploded by *Don Quixote* proved to have remarkable imaginative resilience; it took on surprising new life in the Enlightenment. Samuel Johnson's *Dictionary* defined romance as a 'military fable of the middle ages; a tale of wild adventure in war and love', but also as 'a lie; a fiction'. This double valency allowed eighteenth-century practitioners at once to elaborate and to disavow their fascination; Charlotte Lennox's *The Female Quixote, or The Adventures of Arabella* (1752), for example, gave a lively airing to romance's seduction of reason. The genre's reputation reached a critical nadir infused with political chauvinism: the morally bankrupt French *Ancien Régime* was identified as the natural source of these noxious emanations. They offered questionable pleasures without instructive guidance and they were deeply inimical to the masculinist picaresque of British novelists from Henry Fielding to Tobias Smollett.

*Waverley* begins in the mode of *The Female Quixote*: the hero's education has largely taken the form of romance-reading, and the works of Ludovico Ariosto and Torquato Tasso condition his expectations. Scott would repeat this marker of immaturity and unworldliness in *Rob Roy* (1817), whose protagonist Frank Osbaldistone aspires to translate Ariosto. *Waverley*'s copy of *Orlando Furioso*, lent in a romantic moment to Rose Bradwardine, ends up in the mud after the failure of the Jacobite aspirations. Waverley joins the army, but his failure of application to serious study becomes apparent in his inability to make proper sense of the events he observes. Playing at romance, his actions – or more precisely failures to act – bring about real consequences in a story precisely located in the historical events of 1745–6. The 'romantic' scenes of the Highlands and their Jacobite clans embody those romantic imaginings that he must learn to relinquish in order to become a loyal citizen of the Hanoverian settlement established by the 'Glorious Revolution' of 1689. Don Quixote is in the background as Waverley (like many of Scott's subsequent protagonists) embarks on a journey through hazardous country, in pursuit of a noble but lost cause, and a beautiful woman. But unlike Cervantes's hero, whose delusion is complete, Waverley's painful anagnorisis drives the resolution of the plot. In a dramatic moment of self-reflection, he renounces romance and embraces 'real history'.[7] To the extent that this is the narrative and ethical pivot of the novel and the turning point in the hero's education, *Waverley* is a classic *Bildungsroman*. But the taxonomy is insufficient. Against a Lockean version of character acquisition, whereby 'character' is inscribed on the blank personality by experience, must be set some acknowledgement of 'nature'; Waverley's propensity to dreaminess – a 'temper naturally retired and abstracted' (*W*, 34) – conditions his adventures and is implicated in the novel's denouement. *Bildungsroman* and romance imply different views of human nature, as well as of the relationship between character and environment. In terms of narrative, the novel still has some twelve chapters to run at the point when Waverley feels himself entitled to say with a sigh 'that the romance of his life was ended, and that its real history had begun', and 'he was soon called upon to justify his pretensions to reason and philosophy' (*W*, 301).

Further, Scott has a serious historical purpose: 'My plan requires that I should explain the motives on which its action proceeded; and these motives necessarily arose from the feelings, prejudices, and parties, of the times' (*W*, 26). Character, that is, must be seen as a compound product of 'nature', experience and context. This is a revolutionary insight in the history of the novel. But the innovation does not stop here, because *Waverley* is about much more than the character formation of its protagonist; its narrative method makes Scotland legible, and recent British history comprehensible. The adventures of Waverley and the heroine Rose Bradwardine sustain the romance plot, but he has additional functions as the reader's conduit to historical events, and as a marker of gentility that allows Scott to lead readers into varied scenes where 'character' of a broader kind may be exhibited.

Scott's fascination with the German drama's 'boundless variety of characters', and his delight in the stage dialogue of Shakespeare and Molière, encouraged him to expand the formal capacities of romance to evoke a densely populated fictional medium that would become the base for, for example, Charles Dickens's London. Through Waverley's experience, the reader learns about a public sphere of fanaticism, faction and murderous antagonisms. In this sense, he is more like the 'Banknote' of a popular type of eighteenth-century novel, undergoing vicissitudes and falling into the hands of various figures who manipulate him. By these vicarious means, readers gain access to Scottish manners and conditions, and grasp the motivations of the rebels. So *Waverley* is also an anti-*Bildungsroman*: the hero learns not to become a public player, but to stay at home and to go 'adventuring' (the Adventurer was one of Charles Edward Stuart's soubriquets) no more. This is a book about History, but also a book about the virtues of being a private, domestic person, not a figure of romantic interiority, nor of heroic or public stature. The modest, yet crucial, value of Waverley's experience lies in his increased capacity to accommodate individual aspirations to the political status quo, rather than in his attempt to intervene and manipulate public events.

Scott's Austrian admirer Adalbert Stifter described the Waverley novels as 'epic poetry in prose'; this catches their historical and geographical range but fails to register how they signal the end of the heroic and the triumph of ordinariness.[8] Starting with *Waverley*, Scott's conclusions typically move out of history as the hero settles into domesticity with a heroine from the opposing side. Domesticity is, pre-eminently, the quality of modernity that Karl Marx would later designate the bourgeois in civil society; Scott's interest in the relationship between aristocracy and the 'rising' middle classes – a powerful post-Revolutionary concern in Britain as in France – is responsible for some of the strongest characterisation and the most celebrated dialogues in the Waverley novels: aristocrats are proud and penniless; their bourgeois interlocutors are canny, self-interested, vain of their calling and (usually) right-headed. If romance was the realm of aristocratic representation, realism would become the literary medium of bourgeois modernity.

Scott's contemporaries recognised just how revolutionary this achievement was; the Russian novelist Alexander Pushkin declared in 1830 that 'the principal charm of [his] novels lies in the fact that we are introduced to the past not through the *enflure* of French tragedies, not through the primness of sentimental novels, but in a contemporary domestic manner'.[9] To post-Revolutionary Europe, Scott's novels showed the revolutionary moment as part of a social process in time: the violent horror of events did not imply that redemption was only possible in individual consciousness, what William Wordsworth called 'sovereignty within and peace at will'.[10] Drawing on traditional motifs of tribulation, the Waverley novels keep consciousness communal and celebrate the possibilities of continuity within inexorable processes of change. Their heroic action characteristically resolves in a romance of a very modern kind: the nuptials of hero and heroine from opposing sides promise a future perhaps compromised in its ideals but free from the repeated dialectic of conflict.

## History and antiquarianism

The Waverley novels collectively transformed what history meant, and fashioned historiography for the nineteenth century. Scott combined interest in the drivers of social change with a profound fascination for the unique character of a particular 'moment'. Two different models of historiography flourished in Britain and particularly in Scotland in the eighteenth century; broadly, these may be described as the 'philosophical' and the 'antiquarian'. Scott was committed to both: educated at the University of Edinburgh by students of William Robertson's celebrated histories of Scotland (1759), Europe (*Charles V*, 1769) and America (1777), and Adam Ferguson's *History of Civil Society* (1767), by temperament he was more in sympathy with the magpie dispositions of antiquarian collectors. 'Philosophical' history was universalist: it posited that all societies progress through a series of stages from savagery towards the civil or commercial state. History was dynamic and chartable; its processes were nowhere more evident than in Scotland. In his Postscript to *Waverley*, Scott wrote, 'There is no European nation which, within the course of half a century, or little more, has undergone so complete a change as this kingdom of Scotland' (*W*, 363).

The crucial insights of philosophical history for Scott's fiction were its link to geography, and the possibilities it offered for comparison: by gathering information about 'primitive' societies elsewhere (American Indians and Scottish Highlanders were paradigmatic examples of earlier states still available to view), Enlightened readers could learn about how their own culture had functioned in earlier ages, and by this means construct a continuous cultural inheritance at once distinctive and normative. Travel narratives became the key to a new historiography: beginning with *Waverley*, Scott's novels characteristically involve a kind of time travel as their protagonist ventures from home in civil society to a periphery where he encounters people whose lives display by analogy what life had been like for his forebears. The Waverley novels offered European readers a crucible for historical process as such; onto the heroes' journeys they could map their own intellectual development and that of their culture. They also provided the grounds for what G. W. F. Hegel would describe as the *Weltanschauung* or characteristic world-view of particular epochs and peoples, and – following from this – comparison between cultures.

Antiquarians, on the other hand, were the romantics of history, committed to preservation rather than progress. They *loved* the past, revelled in the particularity of unique and local 'finds' and sympathised with the people they imagined to have owned or made its artefacts. They contributed particularity to descriptions of cultural distinctiveness to support narratives of national uniqueness. Scott was himself a dedicated collector of old objects, romances, ballads and weaponry; from *Waverley* onwards, his novels feature antiquaries of recherché character. Waverley's uncle, Cosmo Comyne Bradwardine of Bradwardine and Tully Veolan, whom readers have found amusing and tiresome in equal measure, obviously tickled Scott; his second novel was *The Antiquary* (1815), in which two competing antiquarians of differing social status and political persuasions tussle on a battleground of antiquities over whose version of the past shall prevail. Its eponymous character, Jonathan Oldbuck, is the nearest Scott came to a fictional self-portrait. *The Antiquary*'s plot, based on a French invasion scare on the Fife coast in 1794 – a near-contemporary example of Scotland's closeness to the heart of Napoleonic Europe's affairs – melds character study with comic antiquarianism and melodrama. The antiquary's shady foil Hermann Dousterswivel is a German of a different stripe, whose machinations drive the plot's Gothic episodes and contribute to resolving the mysterious past of Lovel, the romance hero. The antiquary displaces his own literary ambitions onto a fantasy that Lovel is clandestinely writing, a Scottish national epic, the 'Caledoniad'.

The mystification was personal and systematic: Scott kept his authorship of the novels secret until financial ruin forced his hand in 1826. The Waverley novels are a complex tissue of recovered manuscripts, multiple narrators and multi-temporal juxtapositions that implicate the form of the novel with the patterns of history, and the act of narration with the fiction of authorship. So multifarious did these personae become that *The Betrothed* (1825) opens with the minute of a meeting of the fictional narrators to establish a Joint Stock Company for the 'production' of Waverley novels, at which Oldbuck as secretary objects to the inclusion of his charlatan double Dousterswivel. Scott was always ready to take a digression into writing about writing, after the manner of Laurence Sterne and Cervantes; his literary antiquarianism was a self-reflective hobby horse that held the immediacy and realism of the narrated events in tension with their irreducible fictionality. Readers who find these interventions tedious should understand them as reflections on that oxymoronic compound the 'historical novel'. The first series of 'Tales of My Landlord' (1816), 'Collected and

Arranged by Jedediah Cleishbotham', the pedantic Parish Clerk of the fictional hamlet of 'Gandercleuch', from manuscripts left by Peter Pattieson, opens with an epigraph from *Don Quixote* in which the innkeeper brings old books and manuscripts from a closet to verify a story. *Waverley* and its successors had such an impact as historical novels because they were also historiographical novels – stories that showed how history gets written, stories full of 'historians' who propound versions of the past that the action of the novels questions, confirms and supplements. At an individual level, history is shown to be a haphazard process of accident, misinterpretation, natural disaster and luck. Waverley blunders into the service of the Jacobites as a result of a misunderstanding; in *Old Mortality*, Henry Morton is similarly thrown into the arms of the Covenanters by a chance meeting with a man who remembers the hero's father as a noted performer in an earlier phase of the Cause. In a later chapter, 'a singular and instantaneous revolution' is effected in his character when he misunderstands an over-heard conversation.[11] But (true to Scott's Edinburgh education) the history into which the characters are inducted is the product of 'forces' – dynamic, but determined. The agent of change is time: a potent force in one era is powerless in another, and the action of Scott's novels characteristically takes place at the transition point between them.

In *The Historical Novel* (1937), the Hungarian Marxist philosopher and critic Georg Lukács, perhaps the most influential twentieth-century critic of Scott, described him as the first modern writer able to see society as a process of evolution, where any 'moment' in time is the product of all its constituent contexts. He praised as true historicism Scott's creation of characters whose traits derived from the particular conditions of their age. For Lukács, this made him the founder of the modern realist novel in Europe, with Honoré de Balzac his great successor. This European realist Scott was not that of contemporary British critics; though hugely important for Victorian novelists, Scott's novels were relegated to children's fiction after 1918. Their formal amplitude agreed ill with the emerging economy of literary modernism. Nurtured on the novels of Henry James, a generation of critics like E. M. Forster, in *Aspects of the Novel*, and Percy Lubbock, in *The Craft of Fiction*, sighed over storytelling and extolled psychological complexity. In fact, the disparagement came largely from critics; Virginia Woolf, for one, regarded 'Wandering Willie's Tale' in *Redgauntlet* as a masterpiece of compression which the 'superb genius' of Scott had rendered immortal in despite of fashion.[12] Establishing a genealogy of novelistic greatness markedly at odds with Lukács, F. R. Leavis infamously consigned Scott to a footnote in *The Great Tradition* as little more than an 'inspired folk-lorist'.[13] An egregious dismissal, certainly, yet it identified a crucial aspect of Scott's literary importance for Romantic nationalist movements in Europe. As Woolf recognised, Scott's historical intelligence comprehended an enquiry into the relation of history to legend which neither dismissed 'folklore' nor ultimately lent it credence. 'Reality' in the Waverley novels emerges as a composite construed from different perspectives of belief. Rational and supernatural explanations for historical events sit side by side in *Redgauntlet* or *The Bride of Lammermoor*; traditional wisdom, like romance, supplemented the experience of the past offered by narrative history. In the late eighteenth century, inspired by the Ossianic poems of James Macpherson, Johann Gottfried von Herder promulgated the *Volk*, or folk culture: an evidence-based, unique form of experience which expressed – and justified – German national self-consciousness; Scott's early excitement at the synthetic historical ballads of the *Volk* brought full circle back to Scotland a lifelong interest in melding folk experience into the rational literary forms of civil society. Across Europe, other writers would grasp their opportunity; Adam Mickiewicz's nationalistic Polish tale of Templar knights *Konrad Wallenrod* (1828), for example, drew heavily on Scott's use in *Ivanhoe* of national song and bardic minstrelsy.

## Realism and romance

Scott's realism, then, an amalgam of his Enlightenment education and his antiquarian enthusiasms, became the expressive form of bourgeois modernity. Waverley's rejection of romance for 'history' entailed a generic transformation as well as a personal one. His adventures in Scotland took place as that society moved into 'modernity': commerce, the marketplace and a different kind of contract between individuals. The Jacobites believed that feudal values might be re-asserted; events showed not only that history was not static, but that progress implied a different form of social narrative. In an essay on 'Romance' for the *Encyclopaedia Britannica*, Scott defined the novel as 'a fictitious narrative, differing from the romance, because accommodated to the ordinary train of human events, and to the modern state of society'.[14] A century before Lukács made an organic connection between Scott's historicism and his realism, William Hazlitt applauded his discovery that 'there is no romance like the romance of real life . . . [Scott] is like the man who having to imitate the squeaking of a pig upon the stage, brought the animal under his coat with him . . . He is only the amanuensis of truth and history'.[15] The 'venturousness' of 'the author of Waverley' is paradoxical and positively Quixotic: from the outset, his aim was to 'read a chapter to the public' 'from the great book of nature, the same through a thousand editions' (*W*, 6). If 'the real' is a text to be read, real*ism* was a writerly illusion that invited its reader to collude in 'naturalising' a fiction as 'history'.

Waverley's passivity and impotence in the face of public events is significant: the novels offer a window onto history rather than rewriting it, but it is the condition of modernity that the lives of ordinary people do nonetheless intersect with the largest public events. This is the claim, too, of *The Heart of Midlothian* (1818), in which Scott daringly replaced the genteel hero with a working-class heroine of homely aspect who came to be regarded as a foundational figure of modern European literary realism. Jeanie Deans was one of the nineteenth century's best-loved fictional characters and the model for – among others – Alexander Pushkin's *The Captain's Daughter* (1836), an account of Pugachev's rebellion in 1773–4 set 'sixty years since'. Jeanie walks to London to plead with the Queen for her sister's life, a prosaic pilgrimage that has its own romance. Like those of John Bunyan's Christian, her trials involve fortitude and strength of purpose; her reward is to return to domesticity (marriage, the keeping of cows) in a Scottish Arcadia preserved from the vicissitudes of time. This fairy tale, with its very unrealistic happy ending, begins with a mail coach rumbling through the countryside (a motif picked up by George Eliot in the novel in which she first explored the idea that 'there is no private life which has not been determined by a wider public life', *Felix Holt: The Radical*, set 'five-and-thirty' years in the past).[16] Travelling too fast, the herald of news and register of change overturns and ejects two fashionable young lawyers who, while waiting in Gandercleuch for alternative means of conveyance, regale the narrator with 'new pages of the human heart and turns of fortune far beyond what the boldest novelist ever attempted to produce from the coinage of his brain! . . . the true thing will triumph over the brightest inventions of the most ardent imagination'.[17] Pattieson, avid for new material for his chronicles, duly absorbs the anecdote which will become *The Heart of Midlothian*. Like *Waverley*'s 'book of nature' these 'pages of the human heart' alert us to the confected nature of the literary real. The 'true thing' is the story of the fictional smuggler Robertson alias Staunton, and his involvement in the historical (a different 'true') Porteous Affair, a notorious outbreak of popular antagonism to the exercise of English power in Scotland. Robertson/Staunton, it emerges, has been the seducer of Jeanie's sister Effie Deans, who is subsequently tried and condemned for the presumed murder of her illegitimate child. The tale of Jeanie Deans was actually based on the experience of a historical person, Helen Walker. The 'truth' of this multiply determined tale resides in the interwoven narratives of historical event, sentimental plot, personal quest and antiquarian information about Scottish life in the 1730s. When he derived Scott's realism from his grasp of the true nature of the historical dialectic, Lukács's high ideological purpose did not allow him to note the paradox that this realism is expressed by narrators who playfully recall the reader to the uncertain provenance of their tales. If Scott was indeed the father of modern European literary realism, he ensured that it should involve full recognition of the conditions of its own production.

## 'European' novels: history and nation

*Anne of Geierstein* (1829), set in Switzerland at the time of the English Wars of the Roses, explores the consequences of 'a land torn and bleeding with the strife of two desperate factions'.[18] Lukacs's dialectic pertains to the extent that contested ground is the locus of the historical novel; topographical historiography was an aspect of Scott's originality which would have enormous impact on the structure of European fiction. Border lands are the characteristic settings for his novels. Jeanie Deans undergoes trials like Bunyan's Pilgrim; Quentin Durward, finding a route through the forest to the lair of the Boar of the Ardennes, is 'a hero of romance'.[19] These bleak traverses underlie the deterministic travails on Thomas Hardy's Egdon Heath. Masterpieces of realistic description, such perilous journeys are not totally subsumed in historical realism; they try the traveller's soul and reveal the moral strengths by which he will prevail. Scott transformed the perilous forests and wildernesses of romance into the terrain of history; in *Waverley*, for example, the rugged Scottish landscape explains not only the Highlanders' preferred form of warfare, but their way of life, and the features that sustain or threaten it. Alessandro Manzoni's *I promessi sposi* (*The Betrothed*, 1827) adopted Scott's method of dispersing the sensibility of the hero into the landscape; picturesque descriptions capture the emotions of the characters, and the larger causes of his lovers' separation are found in the feudal fragmentation of Italy, across whose dangerous terrain they flee. No European novelists learned this lesson better than Balzac and Tolstoy. Scott's battle scenes, in particular, were hugely influential in European fiction from Balzac to William Makepeace Thackeray and Tolstoy: despite Tolstoy's professed disdain for Scott, in *War and Peace* Pierre Bezukhov stumbling around the battlefield of Borodino is a recollection of Waverley's disoriented experience at Prestonpans; between them stands Fabrice, the Waverley-like hero of Stendhal's *La Chartreuse de Parme* (*The Charterhouse of Parma*, 1839), educated in epic and romance with aspirations to follow Napoleon, and whose ill-preparedness for life is realised on the battlefield of Waterloo.

Samuel Taylor Coleridge anticipated Lukács in describing Scott's subject as the elemental struggle 'between the two great moving principles of social humanity; religious adherence to the past and the ancient, the desire and the admiration of permanence, on the one hand; and the passion for the increase of knowledge, for truth, as the offspring of reason – in short, the mighty instinct of *progression* and *free agency*, on the other'.[20] This he saw as not specifically a Scottish, or even a European, but a human 'subject', a conflict that underlies all social life. The Waverley novels were praised, imitated and adopted by revolutionaries and Legitimists, Catholics and Protestants, imperialists and separatists, across Europe. Historical romance was apparently so potent that Austrian authorities banned republication of seventeen of the Waverley novels.[21] Scott's Legitimist and conservative fiction seems on the face of it an unlikely vehicle for nationalist revolution. One reason for this is explored in the following section. The irony becomes less piquant, however, when we disentangle the emotional power of the fiction from its ideology.

Scott was clear, and humane, about the cost of progress. The compromise that allows most (though not all) of the Waverley plots to end on a note of hope for the future also sustains nostalgic melancholy for a passing world, and quietist cultural nationalism preserved the customs of Scotland against the homogenising processes of history. Sympathetic treatment of representatives of old Scotch ways of life would be turned to powerful political protest in the hands of Scott's European imitators, as national freedom movements picked up the challenge to power in voices of the people like Mause Headrigg (*Old Mortality*), Meg Merrilees (*Guy Mannering*) and Caleb Balderstone (*The Bride of Lammermoor*). Hungarians, Swiss, Catalans might all be compared to Scott's Romantic Highlanders. Compelling evocation of history's victims – Vich Ian Vohr and Flora MacIvor in *Waverley*; Ulrica, Rebecca and Isaac in *Ivanhoe*; Rob Roy and Ravenswood – embedded tragedy within the progressive conclusions of history.

Almost ten years after *Waverley*, *Quentin Durward* (1823) became the most popular and influential of Scott's works in France. Set in the fifteenth-century reign of Louis XI (whose first wife had been Margaret of Scotland), the novel combines the *Bildungsroman* of its young Scots protagonist with an analysis of the decline of feudalism in France and the inception of a 'modern' polity. Louis, who first appears in disguise as a silk merchant, is an anachronistic proponent of Machiavellian political pragmatism. The historical perspective is further complicated when in the first chapter the narrator encounters Quentin's nineteenth-century descendant, the Marquis de Haut-lieu, an aristocrat in circumstances reduced by the French Revolution. Their acquaintance warmed by the 'auld alliance' between Scotland and France, the Marquis and the narrator rediscover its embodiment in the young soldier of fortune who travelled to France to seek a position with Louis' Royal Company of Archers. The Marquis' antiquarian interest in genealogy connects the France of the fifteenth to that of the nineteenth century; the narrator's repeated association of his own circumstances and those of the Marquis establishes a sense of the wide consequential reach of the Revolution across national boundaries. Several pasts and presents interlock: Europe's modernity is implicated in the conflict between Louis and Charles of Burgundy, and Quentin becomes involved in threatened revolution. Scotland is there too, as 'the most distracted kingdom in Europe' (*QD*, 254), which has made an orphan of Quentin and driven him to seek his fortune in Europe. But the 'Waverley formula' changed subtly when Scott moved away from the cultural context of Scotland, where his knowledge of landscape, architecture, custom and language were detailed and extensive. The antiquarianism of his English and European novels is avowedly bookish, and representations of custom tend to the exotic. These novels have a narrative spareness less prone to be overwhelmed by local detail and exuberant character portrayal. Louis is really the only character who commands imaginative attention in *Quentin Durward*.

French writers of the post-Napoleonic era found a recipe for recording the anxiety of upheaval and the possibility of continuity within change. Where *Quentin Durward* looked to Louis XI's move away from feudalism for the origins of modern Europe, Alfred de Vigny applied Scott's historicised *Bildungsroman* to discover the origins of the French Revolution in the reign of Louis XIII. The eponymous hero of *Cinq-Mars* (1826), a young page of noble extraction, enters the service of Cardinal Richelieu and attracts the attention of the king. The trajectory of the plot is strikingly similar to that of *Quentin Durward*, though the novel acquires quite a different timbre through Vigny's evocation of Cinq-Mars as introspective, melancholy and consumed by unrequited desire. He is a Romantic hero rather than – like the acquiescent, optimistic Quentin – a hero of romance.

Scott was the yardstick against which Balzac measured both his own literary progress and his commercial success. *Les Chouans, ou la Bretagne il y a trente ans* (1829, revised 1845) alludes directly to *Waverley*. *Les Chouans* dramatises a confrontation between the forces of change and of legitimacy generated by Napoleon's return from Egypt; its 'question' is that of *Waverley*: will the Revolution last, or might the nation be persuaded to reinstate the old monarchy? Lavish balls in both novels dramatise the rebels' attempt to resuscitate the splendour of a royalist age, revealing their failure to grasp the unidirectional trajectory of history. Balzac shares Scott's view that the past may be revisited but not recovered; history legitimates change. The revolutionaries of 1689 are now the 'settled' (in Scott's term) government of the country, and the once-legitimate Stuart monarchy finds its justification usurped by the passage of time. Local colour is simultaneously disparaged and ostentatiously deployed in *Les Chouans*, whose beginning adopts Scott's manner so overtly as to suggest pastiche if not parody. The semi-ruined château of La Vivetière recalls Hautlieu, equally a collateral victim of the Revolution; the insurrectionary Chouans, like *Waverley*'s Highlanders, wage guerrilla warfare in a terrain hostile to conventional warfare.

Balzac planned *La Comédie humaine*, the greatest European fictional sequence to issue from the success of the Waverley novels, to illustrate the principal phases of French history. His topographical canvas, like Scott's is extensive; the *Avant-propos* (Preface) to the series which he wrote in 1842 cited Cervantes and Scott as sources for this panoramic anthropological study of human nature and social structure. *Les Illusions perdues* (*Lost Illusions*, 1837–43) is set in the early 1820s, as *Ivanhoe*-mania gripped France; Scott becomes part of the history of the present as Balzac charts the impact of the Waverley novels on the Parisian literary marketplace and on the life of his young hero. Lucien Chardon – 'Thistle' – approaches publishers with *The Archer of Charles IX*, his novel 'in the manner of Walter Scott[,] which presents the conflict between Catholics and Protestants, as a combat between two systems of government'.[22] Chardon takes the name Lucien de Rubempré to further his literary and social ambitions. Though all publishers seek a French Scott who will write a lucrative series on the Waverley model, Lucien is cast down by their 'brutally material' (*LI*, 174) approach to literature. He is advised by his Parisian friend D'Arthez that 'if you don't want to ape Walter Scott you must invent a different manner for yourself, whereas you have imitated him . . . depict the passions and you will have at your command the immense resources which this great genius denied himself' (*LI*, 183–4). D'Arthez's suggestion was already being followed by Balzac himself: *Les Chouans* is energised by passion. 'Love, avarice, and ambition' (*LI*, 278) drive the political plot hither and thither as Marie de Verneuil and the Gars Montauran adore, betray and re-find each other. Passionate individuals may be the victims of history, but their emotions command the reader's attention in a way quite foreign to the more equable temperature of Scott's heroes and heroines, while antiquarian detail becomes inert under Balzac's hand. His ambitions were followed by the Spanish writer Benito Perez Galdos (1843–1920) whose 46-novel epic cycle of Spanish history *Episodios nacionales* opened with *Trafalgar* (1873), a work set 'sixty years since' that echoes Scott's sober assessment of the human costs of military victory. Its octogenarian narrator is transported like Frank Osbaldistone in *Rob Roy* back into history by a 'wonderful fraud of the imagination', to relive his own coming of age with that of his country.

Towards the end of his life, Scott himself appears to have lost faith in this 'fraud of the imagination', the universalist historical progress narrative. His doubts are dramatised in an extraordinary confrontation of Europe with its 'other', Asia. *Count Robert of Paris* (1831) reverses Enlightenment history's inexorable story of advance with its opening image of a grafted plant 'exhibit[ing] symptoms of premature decay from its very commencement'.[23] Where *Quentin Durward* brought an imprecise but evocative 'East' to Europe in the persons of Bohemians and a devious astrologer, this novel evokes a period when Europe 'seems loosened from its foundations and about to precipitate itself upon Asia' (*CR*, 65). This is an anti-romance of quite a different kind from *Waverley*. Bound together by varying degrees of chivalric and self-interested motives, a motley band of warrior pilgrims from across Europe gathers in Constantinople prior to embarking for Palestine. The court of the emperor Alexius Comnenus becomes a meeting place not only of nations but of races, where these Europeans encounter for the first time the 'wonderful appearance' (*CR*, 128) of people from Africa and Asia who cannot be assimilated to their own sense of cultural superiority. A tale of chivalry is used by the schemer Agelastes to engage the commitment of the gullible Count Robert of Paris and his wife Brenhilda, for whom the crusade is an opportunity for questing according to the old romances. The pugnacious Franks are readily bamboozled by wonders of the strange environment, and their valour is mocked by demonic heathen Scythians holding a parodic tournament. Agelastes himself meets his end at the hands of an enraged orang-utan. The necromancer, the charlatan and the savage are at home, in a historical novel that puts the *Weltanschauung* of modern Europe into question. Scott's last work continued to chart new fictional territory, both geographically and speculatively, as he pulled back from realism to depict not a pre- but an anti-Enlightenment world.

## Legacies: translations, forgeries, impersonations

In the absence of international copyright (not enacted until the end of the nineteenth century), Scott's novels were pirated and translated across Europe. The French translation of *Quentin Durward* inaugurated a new wave of European Waverley-mania; by 1828 there were five different editions of Scott's complete works (to date) in circulation in Paris, and one third of *all* novels published in France in 1830 were Scott's. The French translator Auguste-Jean-Baptiste Defauconpret was a powerful agent of dispersal; from 1822 his versions appeared almost simultaneously with the originals and were read and retranslated across Europe, influencing Russian, Italian, Danish and Portuguese readers' knowledge of the Waverley novels. Europe's Scott in the nineteenth century was largely a French Scott, as translators worked mainly from French language editions. Defauconpret assimilated Scott's plots to his own Catholic, Legitimist and anti-reformist views. His simplified and conservative-leaning translation of *Old Mortality* (*Les Puritains d'Écosse*, 1817) became one of the most popular of the Waverley series on the Continent.[24] Defauconpret's Scott was more readily readable as endorsing monarchism against revolution and rebellion. But whether he was read through a conservative or a revolutionary lens, Scott evoked an activist, politicised response throughout Europe

*Walladmor* (1824) was published in Berlin as a German translation of a new novel by Scott, and retranslated into French the following year by Dufauconpret. Critics still argue over whether it should be regarded as a forgery, a parody or a literary hoax; its young author, Willibald Alexis, had already translated *The Lay of the Last Minstrel* and *The Lady of the Lake*, and written shrewd periodical analyses of the Waverley novels to date. In the mid 1820s, even a loose translation of a hoaxing work commanded attention throughout Europe, if Scott's name was involved. *Walladmor* had an absurdly complex plot with Welsh history and legend substituting for Scottish local interest. It also had a character called 'Sir Walter Scott'. Scott took revenge a year later by appropriating it in his own Welsh novel, *The Betrothed*, and attributing it to the charlatan Dousterswivel.

Meanwhile, *Walladmor* successfully launched Alexis's own career as a historical novelist in Germany. The boundaries between translation, pastiche, imitation and creative misprision are highly permeable; in Spain pastiches such as *Allan Cameron* and loose translations like *La maga de la montaña* (*The Highland Sorceress*, 1844) were attributed to Scott; the Spanish ISBN site in 1972 listed six different editions of *Robin Hood* – by Walter Scott.[25]

Jules Verne's *Les Indes noires* (1877) was an oddly destructive topographical inversion of the author's fascination with Scott and the romance of Scottish history and scenery. The adventure takes place in a vast cavern system stretching right across Scotland; the utopian community of this lucrative 'Coal Town' is almost erased when Loch Katrine (the scene of Scott's celebrated poem *The Lady of the Lake*) is undermined by a vindictive cave dweller, and collapses into the mine beneath. The huge hollowed-out mine which sits unknown to the inhabitants of Scotland's surface is at once a source of prosperity to the country and a structural weakness of literally unfathomable extent. The episode recalls an episode in *Anne of Geierstein* where the hero Philipson is confined in a dungeon containing a 'ghastly cleft' that reaches down into the bowels of the earth, from which 'subterranean abyss' 'sunless waves appeared murmuring for their victim' (*AG*, 154). Fiction itself, as Scott was always ready to remind his readers, was an 'airy nothing' spun from the imagination. Those who were tempted to believe in its solidity – and many such surrogate readers appear in his novels – had far to fall in their disappointment.

But such were the seductions of Scott's stories that this warning was easy to overlook. Readers of Scott in nineteenth-century European novels usually come to grief. Like Balzac's Chardon, Frédéric Moreau, the protagonist of Gustave Flaubert's *L'Éducation sentimentale* (*Sentimental Education* 1869), fantasises hopelessly about becoming 'the Walter Scott of France'. Emma Bovary's teenage reading of Scott gives her 'a passion for things historical', and she dreams about 'coffers, guardrooms and minstrels'.[26] Condemned to a stifling existence with a dull husband, Emma attends a performance of *Lucia di Lammermoor* which revives early romantic fantasies. Shortly, she will die herself in a histrionic intensification of Lucy Ashton's shocking fate. Flaubert's realism was altogether more austere than Scott's, but they shared an apprehension of the ways imaginative activity would continue to escape the containment of bourgeois modernity within the realist novel form.

## Note on editions

The standard edition is the nearly completed Edinburgh Edition of the Waverley Novels, gen. ed. David Hewitt (Edinburgh University Press, 1993–), selected titles of which are reprinted by Penguin. This edition seeks to recover the originally published texts rather than Scott's revised versions for his complete works, the 'Magnum' edition (1832). Most popular editions till 1993 follow the Magnum versions.

### Notes

1 Donald Carswell, *Scott and His Circle* (Garden City, NY: Doubleday, Doran and Company, 1930), p. 167.

2 Honoré de Balzac, *Avant-propos* to *La Comédie humaine* (1842); translation quoted from www.gutenberg.org/files/1968/1968.txt

3 Walter Scott, 'Essay on Imitations of the Ancient Ballad', in *Minstrelsy of the Scottish Border*, ed. T. F. Henderson, vol. IV (Edinburgh/London: William Blackwood and Sons; New York: Charles Scribner, 1902), pp. 1–52 (26).

4 *Letters of Sir Walter Scott*, ed. H. J. C. Grierson (London: Constable and Co. Ltd, 1932), vol. III, p. 451.

5 *Conversations of Goethe with Eckermann and Soret*, trans. John Oxenford, 2 vols. (London: Smith, Elder and Co., 1850), vol. II, p. 83.

6 *The Reception of Sir Walter Scott in Europe*, ed. Murray Pittock (London/New York: Continuum, 2006) has charted the publishing history and critical reception of the author; in this chapter I draw extensively on the information amassed by its contributors.

7 Walter Scott, *Waverley, or 'Tis Sixty Years Since*, ed. P. D. Garside (Edinburgh University Press, 2007), p. 301. Subsequent page references are in the text.

8 Pittock, ed., *Reception*, p. 92.

9 Quoted in Donald Davie, *The Heyday of Sir Walter Scott* (New York: Barnes & Noble, 1961), pp. 22–38 (22).

10 William Wordsworth, 'The Prelude of 1805 in Thirteen Books', in *The Prelude 1799, 1805, 1850: Authoritative Texts, Context and Reception. Recent Critical Essays*, ed. Jonathan Wordsworth, M. H. Abrams and Stephen Gill (New York/London: W. W. Norton, 1979), pp. 458–82 (464, line 114).

11 Walter Scott, *The Tale of Old Mortality*, ed. Douglas S. Mack (Edinburgh University Press, 1993), p. 114.

12 Virginia Woolf, *Granite and Rainbow* (London: Hogarth Press, 1960), p. 62.

13 F. R. Leavis, *The Great Tradition: George Eliot, Henry James, Joseph Conrad* (London: Chatto and Windus, 1948, 1950), p. 5.

14 'An Essay on Romance' (1824), in *The Prose Works of Sir Walter Scott, Bart* (Edinburgh: Robert Cadell; London: Whittaker and Co., 1834), vol. VI, pp. 127–216 (129).

15 William Hazlitt, *The Spirit of the Age, or Contemporary Portraits* (1825), ed. Robert Woof (Grasmere: The Wordsworth Trust, 2004), p. 166.

16 George Eliot, *Felix Holt: The Radical* (1866), ch. 3 (London/New York: Penguin Classics, 2006), p. 129.

17 Walter Scott, *The Heart of Midlothian*, ed. David Hewitt and Alison Lumsden (Edinburgh University Press, 2004), pp. 15–16.

18 Walter Scott, *Anne of Geierstein*, ed. J. H. Alexander (Edinburgh University Press, 2000), p. 41. Subsequent page references are in the text.

19 Walter Scott, *Quentin Durward*, ed. J. H. Alexander and G. A. M. Wood (Edinburgh University Press, 2001), p. 227. Subsequent page references are in the text.

20 Letter to Thomas Alsop, 8 April 1820; *Scott: The Critical Heritage*, ed. John O. Hayden (London: Routledge and Kegan Paul, 1970), p. 180.

21 Pittock, ed., *Reception*, p. 81.

22 *Lost Illusions*, trans. Herbert J. Hunt (London: The Folio Society, 2009), p. 175. Subsequent page references are in the text.

23 Walter Scott, *Count Robert of Paris*, ed. J. H. Alexander (Edinburgh University Press, 2006), p. 4. Subsequent page references are in the text.

24 Paul Barnaby discusses Defauconpret's translations and their European impact in Pittock, ed., *Reception*, ch. 2.

25 Pittock, ed., *Reception*, p. 50.

26 *Madame Bovary: Provincial Lives*, trans. Geoffrey Wall (London: Penguin, 2003), p. 35.

### Further reading

Carswell, Donald, *Scott and His Circle* (Garden City, NY: Doubleday, Doran and Company, 1930)

Crawford, Robert, 'Walter Scott and European Union', *Studies in Romanticism*, 40 (2001), 137–52

D'Arcy, Julian Meldon, *Subversive Scott: The Waverley Novels and Scottish Nationalism* (Reykjavik: Iceland University Press, 2005)

Davie Donald, *The Heyday of Sir Walter Scott* (New York: Barnes & Noble, 1961)

Duncan, Ian, *Scott's Shadow: The Novel in Romantic Edinburgh* (Princeton University Press, 2007)

Ferris, Ina, *The Achievement of Literary Authority: Gender, History and the Waverley Novels* (Ithaca, NY/London: Cornell University Press, 1991)

Hayden, John O., ed., *Scott: The Critical Heritage* (London: Routledge and Kegan Paul, 1970)

Hook, Andrew, 'Scotland and Romanticism: The International Scene', in *The History of Scottish Literature*, ed. Andrew Hook (Aberdeen University Press, 1987), vol. II, pp. 307–21

Lukács, Georg, *The Historical Novel* (1937), trans. Hannah Mitchell and Stanley Mitchell (London: Merlin Press, 1962)

McGann, Jerome, 'Walter Scott's Romantic Postmodernity', in *Scotland and the Borders of Romanticism*, ed. Leith Davis, Ian Duncan and Janet Sorenson (Cambridge University Press, 2004), pp. 113–29

Manning, Susan, 'Scott and France', in *Scotland and France in the Enlightenment*, ed. Deidre Dawson and Pierre Morère (Lewisburg, PA: Bucknell University Press, 2004)

Muir, Edwin, *Scott and Scotland: The Predicament of the Scottish Writer* (London: Routledge, 1937)

Pittock, Murray, ed., *The Reception of Sir Walter Scott in Europe* (London/New York: Continuum, 2006)

# 9

ANN JEFFERSON

# Stendhal (1783–1842): Romantic irony

Stendhal was the founder of the French realist tradition, the first novelist to portray contemporary France in its social, cultural and economic reality, but his horizons reach well beyond France and the French, and were never anything less than decidedly European. He came to the novel relatively late in life when, at the age of 43, he wrote *Armance* (1827), which he describes as a 'portrait' of the Parisian salons of the day. It was followed three years later by *Le Rouge et le noir* (*The Red and the Black*), which is subtitled 'Chronicle of 1830' and famously defines the novel as 'a mirror taken along a road'. In 1835, he abandoned his unfinished *Lucien Leuwen*, which recounts the life of a well-to-do young Parisian whose army commission takes him to provincial Nancy before returning him to the capital. *La Chartreuse de Parme* (*The Charterhouse of Parma*, 1839) describes contemporary Italy for the benefit of a contemporary French readership; and Stendhal's career as a novelist ends with the unfinished and, for many years, unpublished *Lamiel*, which narrates the adventures of a plucky young French woman who sets out from her native Normandy for Paris and adventure.

If contemporary France was the novelist Stendhal's chief literary subject, the literary context and the literary genealogy of his writing extended much further afield in time, place and genre. He regularly invokes Torquato Tasso and Ludovico Ariosto as his models for narrative; his reading as a child included the editions of Dante Alighieri left by his mother after her death, and *Don Quixote*, whose discovery he describes in his autobiography as the greatest moment of his life.[1] The pamphlets he wrote in support of an emergent romanticism (*Racine et Shakespeare*, 1823, 1825) defended William Shakespeare against the indigenous classical tradition derived from Jean Racine; he regarded George Gordon Byron and Walter Scott as the chief representatives of literary modernity; and he claims in one of the articles he wrote for the English readers of the *New Monthly Magazine* (January 1826) that French literature could be reinvigorated only by taking its cue from Anglo-Saxon examples. Finally, the dedication of *The Red and the Black* and *The Charterhouse of Parma* to 'the happy few' (in English in the original) comes from Oliver Goldsmith's *The Vicar of Wakefield* and carries echoes of the St Crispin's Day speech in Shakespeare's *Henry V*.

Novels aside, the rest of Stendhal's writing was equally wide-ranging in its cultural and geographical compass. Even his language was inclined to the polyglot, especially in his diary, where one constantly finds sentences such as the following, randomly chosen, entry from 5 March 1812, containing a characteristic mix of English, French and Italian: '*The departure of his uncle* m'a empêché de voir une autre expérience. *Tears yesterday, a little serrement di bracchio.*' One of his first published works was an *Histoire de la peinture en Italie* (*History of Italian Painting*, 1817); he wrote lives of Joseph Haydn, Wolfgang Amadeus Mozart and Metastasio (published in 1815, though largely plagiarised from a range of French and Italian sources), as well as of Gioacchino Rossini (1823) and Napoleon (it remained unpublished). His *Rome, Naples et Florence* (1817 and 1827) and the subsequent *Promenades dans Rome* (1829) are a combination of travel diary and travel guide. And his *De l'amour* (*On Love*, 1822), while advancing a theory of love and a notion of what he called 'crystallisation', nevertheless makes much of the fact that love takes different forms in different cultures, and claims that the nature of passion is largely determined by the historical moment and the national culture in which it is experienced. Stendhal was in this sense one of the first cultural relativists, and the irony which characterises so much of his work is rooted in his conviction that even our most personal and intimate experiences are moulded by the place and time in which they occur.

This ironic stance consists principally in the twin desires to transcend the limitations of particular circumstances by *being* elsewhere (a desire felt especially strongly when in France) and by *seeing* them from elsewhere (particularly necessary when considering France). Born in Grenoble in 1783, Stendhal loathed the world he grew up in, and he sought to escape at the earliest opportunity, first from Grenoble and then from the country altogether. Escape was not, however, his only goal; for one of the features he disliked most about French society was not just its vanity, its prudishness, its pettiness and its preoccupation with money, but its blindness to its own characteristics, a blindness that could be overcome only by viewing that society from a position outside its own system of values. Put very simply, the realist ambition that Stendhal has for the contemporary French novel requires a vantage point that is neither contemporary, nor French. To know modern France, one needs to be somewhere other than France – in a different place, and preferably at a different time, whether past or future. If Stendhal sometimes imagined his ideal reader as Mme Roland, a supporter of the French Revolution who fell foul of the Terror and was guillotined in 1793, he also said on various occasions that his best chance of being understood lay in the future – in 1885, 1900, 1935 or even in 2000.

He lived most of his adult life abroad and planned at one stage to be buried in Milan under the Italianised appellation Arrigo Beyle. Named, more prosaically, Marie-Henri Beyle, the eldest surviving son of an undistinguished lawyer, whom he despised as much as he adored the mother who died when he was seven, he liked to believe that his mother's side of the family descended from an Italian miscreant who had fled across the border after committing a murder of the kind so casually executed in *The Charterhouse of Parma*. He was never a professional writer, but earned his living mainly as an administrator, where, in the army under the Napoleonic Empire, he served variously in Milan, Brunswick, Vienna and Linz, and took part in the retreat from Moscow (during which the original manuscript for the *History of Italian Painting* went missing). The pseudonym Stendhal was one of many he devised for himself, and is a mistranscription of Stendal, the birthplace of the great eighteenth-century German art historian, Johann Joachim Winckelmann. At the age of 52, sitting on a bench above Lake Albano just south of Rome, and musing on the autobiography he was about to begin, he recalls the names of the twelve women he had loved most in his life: one was German, and five Italian, including his great unrequited passion, Métilde Dembowski. He spent the last twelve years of his life as French consul in Civitavecchia, and he died in Paris in 1842 while on leave from this post.

The genealogy, both familial and literary, that Stendhal chose for himself – and even the name by which he is now known – are decidedly and very strategically cosmopolitan. Posterity has rewarded this ambition with equally cosmopolitan and transhistorical recognition. Honoré de Balzac was the first writer to hail Stendhal's talent in a long review of *The Charterhouse of Parma*, but although he describes the book as one in which 'the sublime blazes forth from chapter after chapter', he also takes the opportunity to suggest a number of revisions that would recast the novel to resemble one of his own. Émile Zola saw in Stendhal a great observer of human psychology, but he too bent his portrait of the novelist and presents him as a precursor of the naturalists' ambition to describe the human passions as if they were 'sugar or vitriol'. This view of Stendhal as the subtle analyst of human emotion was widely held in the latter part of the nineteenth century and Friedrich Nietzsche – who had no novelistic ambitions – described Stendhal as 'the last great psychologist'. Henry James was perhaps one of the first to appreciate Stendhal's credentials as a novelist on his own terms, and writing in 1874 in the US periodical, *The Nation*, he numbered *The Charterhouse of Parma* among 'the dozen finest novels we possess'. He praised its author for his 'method', by which he meant the manner in which the characters, who are all 'grossly immoral, and the heroine . . . a kind of monster', are presented by the novelist's 'cynicism' so as to make them appear amiable, thus allowing readers to enjoy his 'clear vision of the mechanism of character, unclouded by the mists of prejudice'. James noted in passing the role of the 'magnificently sustained pauses in the narrative' in producing this effect, and fifty years later André Gide singled out this aspect of Stendhal's narrative method when, writing his only novel, *Les Faux-monnayeurs* (*The Counterfeiters*, 1926), he sought to create a modern narrative mode by replicating the way that Stendhal constantly interrupts the flow of events and refuses narrative continuity. As a young man, Jean-Paul Sartre announced that he wished to be 'Spinoza and Stendhal',[2] a combination of philosopher and novelist that he undoubtedly achieved, and where the role of Stendhal – about whom Sartre never wrote at any length – in providing a model for the future author of *Les Chemins de la liberté* (*The Roads to Freedom*, 1947–9) can perhaps be seen in his focus on the lived historical moment and in the wholesale adoption for his narrative of the limited point of view of each of his characters. This ability to enter the minds of others led Simone de Beauvoir in *Le Deuxième Sexe* (*The Second Sex*) to single out Stendhal as the first male writer to portray women as authentic creatures of flesh and blood, limited only by the 'besotting education' that French society imposed upon them. Italo Calvino, writing in 1982 about *The Charterhouse of Parma*, finds it miraculously contemporary, perhaps because, as he acknowledges, he belonged to a generation that had experienced war at first hand. He too finds a very modern narrative mode in Stendhal's fiction and comments on the novel's fragmentary character, observing that, as one reads, Stendhal's novel becomes a different novel, 'in fact several novels, all different from one another' – a method that Calvino's own *Se una notte d'inverno un viaggiatore* (*If on a Winter's Night a Traveller*, 1979) exploits in a particularly radical form. Stendhal was never a stylist in the way that Gustave Flaubert, for instance, was, and indeed Balzac remarked that *The Charterhouse of Parma* was flawed in this regard, but in the last essay that Roland Barthes wrote before he died (the manuscript was found in his typewriter after his death), he discerns in Stendhal a very twentieth-century sense that language is encountered as a problem and cannot be used innocently. For Barthes it is this sense of language as problem that distinguishes the writer from the mere 'scriptor', and in the case of Stendhal, this awareness is demonstrated in the fact that 'One always fails in speaking of what one loves', to cite the essay's title. It is tempting to see a connection between Barthes' late interest in Stendhal and his own desire to write a novel which he explored towards the end of his life.

Other writers have seen in Stendhal a human presence more than a novelist, and there is certainly something in his work that lends itself to this reading, not least because the very disparateness of his writing invites compensation in the image of a single overarching authorial figure. The most recent example of this tendency comes from the pen of W. G. Sebald, the German writer who, like Stendhal, lived his adult life in self-imposed exile (England in Sebald's case). His *Schwindel. Gefühle* (*Vertigo*, 1990) opens with a biographical portrait of Stendhal, 'Beyle, or Love is a Madness Most Discreet', which stresses the idiosyncrasy of perception, the unreliability of memory, and the fragility of all physical existence. It is the man rather than the work that interests Sebald, who bases his account principally on Stendhal's diary and his autobiography – whence no doubt his choice of the name 'Beyle' rather than 'Stendhal', a distinction that will return us in a moment to the issue of irony. But for now it would seem that Stendhal's work figures in the genealogies that many later novelists, whether French or not, have constructed for their own fiction.

## Genre and the novel

If Stendhal came to the novel relatively late in life, this is because it was not a genre for which he initially had any inclination or ambition. As a young man his literary aspirations were focused on the theatre and his goal was to 'live in Paris and write comedies like Molière'.[3] After a few abortive attempts, however, he abandoned this path, and, as the list of works cited above suggests, he devoted himself to a very eclectic range of forms, from biography, to art history, to travel guide, to the generically unclassifiable *On Love*. None of these texts has high aesthetic aims – at least in formal and stylistic terms – and all combine a strong element of social and cultural analysis with personal critical comment, albeit very often in the guise of a fictional persona such as Monsieur L., 'a commercial traveller in iron' who fronts the *Mémoires d'un touriste* (1838). It was only gradually, during the course of the 1820s, that Stendhal's thoughts turned towards the novel.

It is customary in literary histories of France to say that the novel had been eclipsed by the French Revolution and that it took the years between Choderlos de Laclos' *Les Liaisons dangereuses* (*Dangerous Liaisons*, 1782) and Stendhal's *The Red and the Black* for French fiction to absorb its effects. Lyric poetry was the dominant literary genre from the late 1810s and throughout the 1820s, and theatre provided the stage on which the battle between classicism and romanticism was publicly fought – literally in the case of the famous battle of *Hernani* at the first performance of Victor Hugo's play in the Comédie française in February 1830, just as Stendhal was beginning work on *The Red and the Black*. Stendhal never spoke well of Mme de Staël's novels *Delphine* (1803) and *Corinne* (1807), perhaps because *Corinne*, set mainly in Italy, occupies some of the territory that Stendhal would in due course make his own. François-René de Chateaubriand's *René* (1802), which diagnosed the *mal du siècle* of the early years of the century, is dismissed as the model for the feeble lookalike suitors whom Mathilde scorns in *The Red and the Black*, while Benjamin Constant's *Adolphe* (1815) gets only grudging recognition from Stendhal when it was republished in the 1820s.

One of the factors that determined Stendhal to consider the novel for his own literary project was the example of Walter Scott, who enjoyed an unparalleled reputation in France, beginning in the mid 1810s and reaching its apogee in the late 1820s. What Stendhal saw in Scott was the ambition to describe an entire society, an ambition which, as he realised, could be transferred from the distant past to the contemporary world. Between 1822 and 1829, Stendhal contributed a series of articles about the current literary and political scene in France to two English periodicals, the *London Magazine* and the *New Monthly Magazine*, in which he keeps returning to the absence of any accurate and up-to-date picture of French society among French writers, and deplores the anachronism that he finds in the novels of his (now mostly forgotten) contemporaries. Writing in the May 1828 number of the *New Monthly Magazine*, Stendhal comments that 'to pourtray these peculiarities and delicate shades of manner is the task of the novelist', as he himself was beginning to do.

At the same time, he regarded the very existence of the novel as an index of all that was wrong with French society. The phenomenon whereby – thanks to the introduction of the new *cabinets de lecture* – provincial women now read five or six novels a month, was a sign that reading fiction had become the only recourse in a world where social exchange was reduced to the minimum: the men went out hunting every day, while their wives, policed by their prudish neighbours, sat at home with no visitors and no distraction other than what fiction could provide. Stendhal admires the Italians for having no need of the genre, since in Italy conversation and the opera between them make the novel otiose, as is demonstrated by the very fact that the narrator of *The Charterhouse of Parma* first hears the story of the Duchess Sanseverina in the course of an evening gathering in Padua before turning it into a novel for the benefit of a French readership.

Despite their increasing popularity, novels stood relatively low in the literary hierarchy of the day: M. de Rênal ensures that the tutor he hires for his children has none in his possession, and Julien panders to his prejudices by suggesting that novels might corrupt the morals of Mme de

Rênal's maids, while she herself is said to have read no novels at all, or only a very few. Stendhal seems to share this evaluation of the form as morally corrupting, and he suggests that novels are responsible for promoting some of the worst conformist tendencies among the French by providing them with models for behaviour that they simply ape: a young woman in love will immediately compare herself to Jean-Jacques Rousseau's heroine Julie from *La Nouvelle Héloïse* (1761), thus turning passion into a pretext for self-congratulation. If Julien and Mme de Rênal had been regular readers of fiction, writes Stendhal, they would have had a key for interpreting their relation that would quickly have reduced it to the status of a conventional adulterous affair by putting a label on their situation, outlining for them 'the part to be played' and providing them with 'the model to copy' (bk 1, ch. 7). Indeed, it is just such an affair that is described with horrible plausibility in the letter that Mme de Rênal sends to M. de la Mole, on the eve of Julien's marriage to Mathilde, about his supposed practice of ingratiating himself with the woman of the house as a means of furthering his own interests. When Julien shoots Mme de Rênal in the church at Verrières he could be said to be taking his revenge on the kind of fictional writing that made such an account seem credible.

The novel, in Stendhal's estimation, seems poised between the virtues of potential mimetic accuracy on the one hand, and the vices of mimicry and banality on the other. However, the condition of French society in the 1820s and 1830s was such that, of all literary genres, only the novel seemed to offer the formal possibilities for matching it. Stendhal had an acute sense that historical events since 1789 had produced not only a very unstable world, but also a very fragmented one. The Revolution had established a new social order where even the months of the year were given new names and the years renumbered from scratch. It spawned the Terror of 1793 under which the king and the royal family were guillotined along with thousands of others. This was followed first by the *Directoire* and then by the Consulate with Napoleon as First Consul, until he declared himself emperor in 1804. During the succeeding ten years (years in which Stendhal served as an administrator in the imperial army), Napoleon created many of the social, legal and educational institutions that have survived to this day. Forced to abdicate in 1814 in favour of Louis XVIII and the first Restoration, Napoleon returned from exile for 100 days before being defeated at the battle of Waterloo, described so vividly by Stendhal in *The Charterhouse of Parma*. The second Restoration was presided over first by Louis XVIII and then by Charles X in conjunction with a number of different governments until the July Revolution of 1830 which placed the so-called bourgeois monarch, Louis-Philippe, on the throne.

This half-century of incessant political change – going from absolute monarchy to republic to empire and back again to monarchy, though of the constitutional variety – was accompanied by localised factionalism on the one hand, and, on the other, despite the restoration of the monarchy and the return of the aristocracy from exile, by the increased bourgeoisification of France and a class structure based on money rather than birth. Writing about his own times for an English readership, Stendhal repeatedly refers to the sense of instability in French society, reporting that 'in this country nothing is established in a secure fashion' and that 'today everything is unsettled in France'.[4] In addition to this political precariousness, France had lost any sense of social cohesion as different social groups and different generations each saw the world in terms of its own mindset and experience. Fathers and sons, Parisian aristocrats, like the De la Mole family, and provincial industrialists, like M. de Rênal, Liberals and Ultras, men and women, all have a different outlook. As Stendhal writes in his preface to *Armance*:

> If one asked for news of the Tuileries Gardens from the doves who sigh at the top of the tall trees, they would say: It's a vast plain of greenery where one enjoys the clearest light. We strollers would reply: It's a delightful dark promenade where one is sheltered from the heat, and above all from the full light of day that is so dispiriting in summer.
>
> Thus it is that the same thing is judged by each individual according to their position; it is in equally opposed terms that *equally respectable* people speak of the current state of society, and each wishes to follow a different path in order to lead us to happiness. But each ridicules the opposite party.

In his unpublished review of his own *The Red and the Black*, Stendhal wrote that fiction had replaced theatre in modern France largely because, whereas theatre presumes a single, cohesive audience, the novel is able to accommodate multiple readerships and thus acknowledge the social and cultural diversity of the 'equally respectable' people of the day.

Although Stendhal made a number of comments about the novel, he was never in any sense a theorist of the genre, and it is in somewhat defensive tones that, in a draft reply to Balzac's review of *The Charterhouse of Parma*, he writes, 'I have never given any thought to the art of constructing a novel ... I had no suspicion that there were rules to be observed.'[5] His two most famous pronouncements about the genre define it in very different terms: in one instance, the novel is 'a mirror taken along a road' (stated twice in *The Red and the Black*), but in the other it is a bow that plays upon the violin of its reader's soul.[6] Both definitions are applicable to Stendhal's own fiction, and indeed everything about the way he wrote his novels seems to suggest that he had a profound awareness of the potential for multiplicity offered by the genre, and it is in this sense that his work is thoroughly, and multifariously, ironic.

## Stendhalian irony

The term 'Romantic irony' is not one that would have meant anything to Stendhal himself, but it refers to a phenomenon that is very much of his own time. It was the German Romantics, and Friedrich Schlegel (1772–1829) in particular, who outlined the concept of a new kind of irony that, unlike its classical form where meaning can be reliably decoded from statements which appear to assert its contrary, undermines the possibility of any confident interpretation of intent. One account of this modern, Romantic irony describes it in a formulation that could have been designed for Stendhal himself: 'An author ironic in Schlegel's sense does not simply mean the opposite of what he seems to say; he means rather a little more or a little less, or something a shade different from the superficial intent of his words. He may even mean just what he says; yet he is not in unremitting, dead earnest as to the manner in which he says it.'[7] I shall have more to say about Stendhal's authorial persona in a moment, but his fictional worlds are constructed out of alternatives, each with its own validity (as with the doves and the strollers in the Tuileries Gardens): red and black, army and church, pink and green (the title of an unfinished novel begun in 1837), love and politics, epic and romance, knowledge and emotion, the provinces and Paris, Italy and France, love of the head and love of the heart, energy and quietism, an older and a younger heroine, and so on. Stendhal himself suggested that there were two kinds of novel in France, the novel for chambermaids and the novel of the salons, and even his own *The Red and the Black* and *The Charterhouse of Parma* are sometimes similarly regarded as alternatives by readers, as if an admiration for Stendhal obliged them to prefer one over the other. But if Stendhal's novels seem sometimes to support such preferences – Mme de Rênal's love of the heart ultimately being chosen by Julien over Mathilde's love of the head, and love being the world that Fabrice chooses over the court and its politics – the narrative requires both, not least as the perspective from which the other may be viewed, albeit often with total incomprehension.

## Authors

Stendhal barely discusses Laclos' *Dangerous Liaisons* – though he claims in his autobiography to have met the model for Mme de Merteuil in his childhood – but it offers an example of a novel composed of just such multiple value systems that may well have encouraged Stendhal to exploit this aspect of the genre. Consisting entirely of the letters written by its protagonists, and prefaced with two mutually contradictory claims about the novel's veracity by an editor and a publisher respectively, Laclos' novel also brings two mutually incompatible ideologies into confrontation through the figures of its two heroines: Mme de Merteuil and the Présidente de Tourvel, one representing the merits of the mind, and the other the virtues of the heart. Valmont's pusillanimous inability to choose between them underscores the impossibility of reconciling these alternatives. On the face of it, Stendhal's novels, with their garrulous author, might seem to be rather differently conceived from Laclos' authorless letter novel, but his author-persona is an invention almost on a par with that of his heroes and heroines among the dramatis personae of his fiction. Even the 'real' author of Stendhal's novels – as distinct from the author-persona within the fiction – appears in the series of more or less flagrantly false identities that he regularly adopted in his works. The *History of Italian Painting* appeared in 1817 signed by 'M. de Stendhal, cavalry officer', the name that he subsequently used for all his major novels. The autobiography – even though it was never published during Stendhal's lifetime – is styled as the life of 'Henry Brulard', and the articles for the English press are attributed to 'Grimm's grandson'. In a more comical vein, the review of his own *The Red and the Black* is signed by one 'D. Gruffot Papera'; elsewhere he appears variously as William Crocodile, Louis-Alexandre-César Bombet (the supposed author of the lives of Haydn, Mozart and Metastasio), or with mock aristocratic pretensions as Baron de Cotonnet and (this with obscene overtones) Baron de Cutendre. There are some 200 of these aliases in which one may read Stendhal's wish not to be his father's son, or a desire to evade the strict censorship of the period and the ire of a readership whose vanity has been offended. But above all, they allow him to speak from a position other than his own, to construct a provisional viewpoint from which to pass comment in a less than entirely serious manner on the action or argument of his texts.

This principle is also that of the author-persona proper whose comments are woven into the fiction. It is here that we find the Schlegelian ironist who means 'a little more or a little less', or something 'a shade different' from the overt meaning of his words. The function of Stendhal's author-persona is first and foremost to orchestrate the different perspectives of which his novel is composed, but it is also to contribute a perspective of his own. He is presented as both a witness to, and a participant in, the world he portrays. He writes himself into the opening pages of *The Red and the Black*, locating his own present in the real time of the novel as he introduces the inhabitants of Verrières: 'Since 1815 [M. de Rênal] has blushed at his connection with industry'; he spells out the values that underpin life in the town: 'There you have the great phrase that governs everything at Verrières: YIELD A RETURN'; and he portrays himself as a Parisian tourist admiring the local scenery: 'How often, my thoughts straying back to the ball-rooms of Paris, which I had forsaken overnight, my elbows leaning upon those great blocks of stone of a fine grey with a shade of blue in it, have I swept with my gaze the vale of the Doubs!' (bk 1, ch. 2). This has the effect of underwriting the claim made by the novel's subtitle to be a chronicle of contemporary reality.

A similar effect is produced in *The Charterhouse of Parma* by the author's prefatory account of the evening in Padua where he claims originally to have heard the story of the Duchess Sanseverina, and by the occasional allusion to first-hand knowledge of the events narrated: 'as Lieutenant Robert told me', or 'as she has told me a hundred times since' (ch. 1). Elsewhere he conveys familiarity with the places described, as he confirms that the enchanting landscape around Lake Como has no equal in the world, or that the storms there are 'terrible and unexpected' (ch. 2). More often than not, however, when the author draws attention to his own presence in the text it is to introduce a countervailing position: in reporting that M. de Rênal had widened the main avenue in Verrières by six feet against the wishes of the town council, the author comments gratuitously that 'although he is an Ultra and I myself a Liberal, I give him credit for it' (bk 1, ch. 2). This political positioning on the part of the author is not designed to construct an ideological framework of interpretation for the novel, but simply introduces, almost as a matter of principle, a difference of outlook on, and within, the world described: the mayor at odds with his council, the Liberal author in agreement with the Ultra (right-wing) M. de Rênal.

This partiality extends to the author's comments on his characters, both positive and negative: he describes Gina as being 'guilty of an enormously rash action' (ch. 20), or 'admits' at one point of Fabrice that 'our hero was very little of a hero' (ch. 3). In *The Red and the Black* the author comments in a similarly ambiguous vein on Julien's silent outrage at M. Valenod's treatment of the inmates of the poorhouse: 'I admit that the weakness which Julien displays in this monologue gives me a poor opinion of him' (bk 1, ch. 22). It is impossible to know how seriously to take these judgements since they appear sometimes to be endorsing the view that might be held by the public opinion that Stendhal so deplored. Elsewhere, however, he goes out of his way to counter such received opinion, as when he says of Mme de Rênal that she 'was one of those women to be found in the provinces whom one may easily take to be fools until one has known them for a fortnight' (bk 1, ch. 7). He frequently uses his position to turn the tables on the judgement of his presumed readership as when, having reminded us that Julien is 'only a young peasant' and recounted his inability to order himself a coffee in the café in Besançon and his awkwardness as he responds to the alluring waitress behind the bar, the author ends up castigating the readers who will pity Julien's provincial ineptitude:

> What pity will not our provincial inspire in the young scholars of Paris, who at fifteen, have already learned to enter a café with so distinguished an air! But these children, so stylish at fifteen, at eighteen begin to turn *common*. The passionate shyness that one meets in the provinces now and then overcomes itself, and then teaches its victim to desire. (bk 1, ch. 24)

The Parisian perspective is brought to bear on the provincial, and briefly given its due before being condemned in a sort of double bind whereby the shortcomings of the provincial prove to be the source of a quality – here, desire – from which the Parisian is excluded by virtue of his supposed superiority. The point, however, is not to defend provincial values against those of the metropolis, but to bring the outlook of each of the two worlds up against each other.

This kind of confrontation becomes almost systematic in *The Charterhouse of Parma*, where, from the outset, the author repeatedly stresses the difference between the Italians in his narrative and the French who comprise his readership:

> the characters being Italian will perhaps interest [the reader] less, hearts in that country differing considerably from hearts in France: the Italians are sincere, honest folk and, not taking offence, say what is in their minds; it is only when the mood seizes them that they shew any vanity; which then becomes passion, and goes by the name of *puntiglio*. Lastly, poverty is not, with them, a subject of ridicule.

And he continues: 'I heap the most moral censure upon many of their actions. To what purpose should I give them the exalted morality and the other graces of French characters, who love money above all other things, and sin scarcely ever from motives of hatred or love? The Italians in this tale are almost the opposite' ('To the Reader'). The critique is overt; but the value system with which the author is clearly aligning himself against his French readership claims, most disconcertingly, to combine confident moral censure with a defence of the capacity to sin from motives of hatred or love.

Moral values aside, the reader is repeatedly reminded by the author of his own ignorance of the world being described in the novel, whether in the matter of ecclesiastical titles or the use of the *tu* form in social exchange. The author presents himself as a mediator between French and Italian cultures, asking to be forgiven for a phrase translated from the Italian (ch. 6), or for Fabrice's Italian heart (ch. 8). He anticipates the responses of his French reader, pretending to concede that an episode should have been omitted from the narrative (ch. 8), and acknowledging that readers may be wearied by the description of all the machinations undertaken by Gina and Mosca to have Fabrice acquitted of Giletti's murder. But the perspective shifts again at this point as the author, having suggested that the moral to be derived from the whole business is that 'the man who mingles with a court compromises his happiness, if he is happy, and, in any event, makes his future depend on the intrigues of a chamber-maid', then immediately undercuts the implication of this northern view of Mediterranean shenanigans by continuing: 'On the other hand in America, in the Republic, one has to spend the whole weary day paying serious court to the shop-keepers in the street, and must become as stupid as they are; and there, one has no Opera' (ch. 24).

The phrase 'On the other hand' nicely sums up the strategy of Stendhal's author-persona as he intervenes in his own narration or sabotages his own inferences. This is because there is almost always more than one way in which events and behaviour can be seen. This systematic invocation of alternatives is also evident in the author's habit of informing his readers that the events themselves could have fallen out differently. The narrative is regularly side-tracked by hypothetical accounts of other outcomes. One such episode occurs when Julien, incensed at Mathilde's assertion of her horror at having given herself 'to the first comer', seizes a medieval sword kept as a curiosity on the library wall and makes as if to kill her. First, the reactions of the two lovers are poles apart: where Mathilde, 'in an ecstasy, could think only of the felicity of having come within an inch of being killed' by the only man she knows capable of 'such an impulse of passion', Julien, 'locked and double-locked in his room, was a prey to the most violent despair' at the idea that he has lost his claim to Mathilde's heart (bk 11, ch. 18). It is here that the alternative scenario is briefly sketched for comparison: 'If, instead of remaining hidden in a remote corner, he had wandered through the house and into the garden so as to be within reach of any opportunity, he might perhaps in a single instant have converted his fearful misery into the keenest happiness.' However, the author goes on to spell out the double bind whereby 'the adroitness with the want of which we are reproaching him would have debarred the sublime impulse of seizing the sword which, at that moment, made him appear so handsome in the eyes of Mademoiselle de La Mole'. The alternative plot shows Julien's misery to be unnecessary, but by the same token demonstrates that its absence would belong in the story of someone who lacks Julien's distinctive qualities.

The author-persona frequently intrudes in this manner to draw attention to the limitations of the viewpoint of the characters. In doing so, he simultaneously validates those limited perspectives, but in ways that the reader is shown to be incapable of endorsing. Moved by the music at the opera one evening, Mathilde imagines that she has conquered her love for Julien after a night of what the author describes as 'madness'. But even if he is implicitly accusing Mathilde of self-deception, the author also presents himself as having damaged his image in the eyes of his readers by suggesting that the young women of the day might be susceptible to the kind of passion he has briefly ascribed to his heroine. Out of mock deference to the prejudices of those readers, he concedes that she is 'wholly imaginary', while the reader himself is figured as the defender of the cautious and self-serving behaviour of the young women who 'shine in the drawing-rooms of Paris', and none of whom can be accused of 'unduly despising a brilliant fortune, horses, fine properties, and everything that ensures an agreeable position in society' (bk II, ch. 19). It is here that the author directly addresses the reader as a member of that society ('Sir') and informs him that 'a novel is a mirror carried along a high road'. Author, character and reader are all drawn into the text, each with mutually incompatible views of the world, leaving Stendhal's ideal reader – or even his actual ones – to orientate themselves as best they can in relation to these various perspectives.

It is not just the fictional reader who is wrong-footed in this way, since the characters themselves regularly misinterpret each other's motives, and none more so than the lovers, as illustrated by the example of Julien and Mathilde in the episode discussed above. The most sustained instance of the limited viewpoint is that of Fabrice at the battle of Waterloo, where his experience of combat is so peculiar – imprisoned as a spy, rescued by a series of women, unhorsed by his own side, too drunk to recognise Napoleon as he gallops past – that he himself feels the need to read a newspaper account of the battle to find out whether he had actually taken part in it. Stendhal allows his characters monologues in which their views are expressed at length until another perspective cuts across them. This is facilitated by the narrative's focus on its own present, shaped very often by the characters' erroneous interpretation of circumstances: Fabrice hidden in the Abbé Blanès's clocktower, is woken by 'an alarming noise', imagines 'that the end of the world had come' and then thinks 'that he was in prison'. The reader realises no sooner than Fabrice that the alarming noise is in fact 'the big bell, which forty peasants were setting in motion' for the local saint's day (ch. 9); and neither author nor character ever comments on the unmistakeable parallels with Fabrice's prison-cell at the top of the Farnese Tower.

The author's irony extends to silence on a number of apparently key issues. Fabrice's true paternity remains a surmise, and his belief in astrology, which so many of the events that befall him seem to confirm, is nevertheless left as an open question. The most striking authorial silence comes when Julien shoots Mme de Rênal in the church at Verrières: the event is anticipated at the very start of the novel when Julien enters the church on the way to take up his post as tutor in the Rênal household. He sees a scrap of printed paper reporting the execution of a near namesake, thinks he sees blood by the holy water stoup – though it is only light from the red drapery reflected in the water spilt on the floor – and responds to his secret terror by calling himself *'To arms!'* (bk 1, ch. 5). No authorial comment explains Julien's later action – he himself offers no interpretation of it – and none connects the shooting either with the earlier scene in the church or with Julien's rash impulse in the library with Mathilde. It is left for readers to establish those connections and to make what they will of them.

If such a response presupposes an impossible and finally rather rebarbative degree of knowingness on the part of the reader, Stendhal's irony can be seen as providing its own exit strategy in the form of a completely different kind of response. He himself distinguishes between two forms of storytelling: the 'philosophical' (which fosters the irony he exploits) and the 'narrative' from which the author is absent.[8] It is this latter form that allows the reader to become simply and unreflectingly absorbed in events as they unfold, and to experience the pleasures that Stendhal recalls of his reading as child. Alongside its many ironies, Stendhal's fiction also allows an entirely unironic reading that makes it possible to say, as he does in his autobiography, that 'a novel is like a bow, and the violin that *produces the sound* is the reader's soul'.

## Note on editions/translations

The best edition of Stendhal's fiction is in the Bibliothèque de la Pléiade, *Œuvres romanesques complètes*, ed. Philippe Berthier and Yves Ansel, vols. I and II (Paris: Gallimard, 2005–7). Volume III, forthcoming, will include *La Chartreuse de Parme*. Gallimard's 'Folio Classique' series has useful prefaces and notes.

The following translations are recommended: *The Red and the Black*, trans. C. K. Scott Moncrieff (London: Everyman Paperbacks, 1997); *The Charterhouse of Parma*, trans. C. K. Scott Moncrieff (London: Everyman's Library, 1992); *Armance*, trans. C. K. Scott Moncrieff, (London: Soho Book

Company, 1986); *Lamiel*, trans. T. W. Earp (London: Turnstile Press, 1951); *Lucien Leuwen*, trans. H. L. R. Edwards, rev. with a new introduction and notes by Robin Buss (Harmondsworth: Penguin, 1991); *On Love*, trans. Vyvyan Holland (London: Chatto and Windus, 1928); *The Life of Henry Brulard*, trans. John Sturrock (London: Penguin, 1995); *To the Happy Few: Selected Letters*, trans. Norman Cameron, ed. E. Boudot-Lamotte (London: Soho Book Company, 1986).

## Notes

1 Stendhal, *Henry Brulard*, ch. 9. Written in 1835, the autobiography was not published in Stendhal's lifetime.
2 As Simone de Beauvoir recalls at several points in *Adieux: A Farewell to Sartre* (1981), trans. Patrick O'Brian (London: Penguin, 1985).
3 Stendhal, *Henry Brulard*, ch. 16. All translations from Stendhal's works are taken from the versions listed in the Note on editions/translations.
4 See Stendhal, 'Tableau politique de la France', in *Lettres de Paris par le petit-fils de Grimm: Chroniques 1825–1829*, ed. José-Luis Diaz (Paris: Le Sycomore, 1983), vol. I, p. 278; and *New Monthly Magazine*, May 1826.
5 Stendhal, Letter to Balzac, 16 October 1840.
6 Stendhal, *Henry Brulard*, ch. 16.
7 Raymond Immerwahr, 'The Subjectivity or Objectivity of Friedrich Schlegel's Poetic Irony', *The Germanic Review*, 26.3 (1951), 173–91 (p. 184).
8 In a note to himself on the manuscript of his unfinished novel, *Lamiel*, Stendhal writes: 'For every event ask yourself: should this be recounted philosophically or narratively, in accordance with the doctrine of Ariosto?'

## Further reading

Auerbach, Erich, 'In the Hôtel de la Mole', in *Mimesis: The Representation of Reality in Western Literature* (1946), trans. Willard R. Trask (New York: Doubleday Anchor Books, 1957), pp. 400–10
Barthes, Roland, 'One Always Fails in Speaking of What One Loves', in *The Rustle of Language* (1984), trans. Richard Howard, (Oxford: Basil Blackwell, 1986), pp. 296–305
Beauvoir, Simone de, 'Stendhal or the Romantic of Reality', in *The Second Sex* (1949), trans. H. M. Parshley (London: Picador, 1988), pp. 268–78
Bersani, Leo, 'Stendhalian Prisons and Salons', in *From Balzac to Beckett*, (New York: Oxford University Press, 1970), pp. 91–139
Brooks, Peter, 'The Novel and the Guillotine, or Fathers and Sons in *Le Rouge et le Noir*', in *Reading for the Plot: Design and Intention in Narrative* (Oxford: Clarendon Press, 1984), pp. 62–89
Calvino, Italo, 'Guide to *The Charterhouse of Parma* for the Use of New Readers' and 'Stendhal's Knowledge of the "Milky Way"', in *The Literature Machine* (1982), trans. William Weaver (London: Picador, 1989), pp. 256–83
Gide, André, *Journal of the Counterfeiters* (1927), trans. and ed. Justin O'Brien, in *The Counterfeiters* (New York: Knopf, 1951)

Girard, René, *Deceit, Desire and the Novel: The Self and Other in Literary Structure* (1961), trans. Yvonne Freccero (Baltimore: Johns Hopkins University Press, 1965)

Handwerk, Gary, 'Romantic Irony', in Marshall Brown, ed., *The Cambridge History of Literary Criticism* (Cambridge University Press, 2000), pp. 203–25

James, Henry, 'Stendhal (Marie-Henri Beyle)', in *Literary Criticism: French Writers, Other European Writers, the Prefaces to the New York Edition*, ed. Leon Edel and Mark Wilson (New York: The Library of America, 1984), pp. 812–18

Jefferson, Ann, *Reading Realism in Stendhal* (Cambridge University Press, 1988)
  *Stendhal: La Chartreuse de Parme* (London: Grant and Cutler, 2003)

Keates, Jonathan, *Stendhal* (London: Sinclair-Stevenson, 1994)

Pearson, Roger, *Stendhal's Violin: A Novelist and his Reader* (Oxford: Clarendon Press, 1988)
  ed., *Stendhal: 'The Red and the Black' and 'The Charterhouse of Parma'*, (London/New York: Longman, 1994). This anthology of criticism contains extracts from the comments of Balzac and Zola as well as from other seminal discussions of Stendhal's novels.

Sebald, W. G., 'Beyle, or Love is a Madness Most Discreet', *Vertigo* (1990), trans. Michael Hulse (London: Harvill Press, 1999), pp. 1–30.

Wheeler, Kathleen, ed., *German Aesthetic and Literary Criticism: The Romantic Ironists and Goethe* (Cambridge University Press, 1984)

# 10

DAVID PUNTER

# Mary Shelley (1797–1851):
# The Gothic novel

The presumed scenario around the writing of Mary Shelley's *Frankenstein* in 1818 is well known. In the Villa Diodati in Switzerland, the twenty-year-old Mary, her young husband Percy Shelley, George Gordon Byron and Byron's personal physician John Polidori challenged each other, it is said, to write ghost stories: Polidori's tale, 'The Vampyre', became the first vampire story in English, while Mary wrote *Frankenstein*, which has since become one of the best-known novels in Britain, Europe and possibly the world.

The truth is, as usual, more complex. Mary Shelley was engaged in writing *Frankenstein* from 1816 onwards, a period when she was much disturbed by various deaths, and the idea for the book apparently sprang from a nightmare she records from 16 June of that year, when she 'saw the hideous phantasm of a man stretched out, and then, on the working of some powerful engine, show signs of life, and stir with an uneasy, half vital motion'.[1] This, clearly, is the central image of the book, and the one which remains in the common cultural memory: the initial stirring of the monster, the suggestion that it may be possible to create life from dead matter.

The plot of the novel, as opposed to later filmic simplifications, is quite complex. Victor Frankenstein is an intellectual, a scientist and, perhaps most importantly, a youth who feels no ties of affection for his family or, at the beginning, for anybody else. Instead he is possessed by a desire for knowledge, but of a particular kind:

> I confess that neither the structure of languages, nor the code of governments, nor the politics of various states, possessed attractions for me. It was the secrets of heaven and earth that I desired to learn; and whether it was the outward substance of things, or the inner spirit of nature and the mysterious soul of man that occupied me, still my enquiries were directed to the metaphysical, or, in its highest sense, the physical secrets of the world. (*Frankenstein*, 45)

Victor has an early interest in magical lore as a means of discovering these secrets, but in a crucial move he abandons this to study the natural sciences.

176

He forms the idea of creating life from the dead body parts he seeks out in charnel houses, and the creature he makes does indeed come to life. However, what then ensues is a battle for control. Victor almost immediately repents of his actions:

> I had worked hard for nearly two years, for the sole purpose of infusing life into an inanimate body. For this I had deprived myself of rest and health. I had desired it with an ardour which far exceeded moderation; but now that I had finished, the beauty of the dream vanished, and breathless horror and disgust filled my heart. (*Frankenstein*, 60–1)

Since it took her two years to complete the novel, it is hard not to read this as Mary Shelley's own comment on the difficulties of the writing process; however, the immediate point is that it has always been unclear exactly why Victor experiences such violent feelings. Is it a need to reject a creature who is in effect his offspring? Is it to do with what Victor at least thinks to be the creature's repulsive appearance? Or is it the sheer fear of having brought into being something which may be, or become, more powerful than himself?

At any rate, the creature (he is rarely referred to as a 'monster') is deeply wounded by Victor's rejection, and wreaks a terrible vengeance on his maker's family. At one point, he beseeches Victor to make him a mate, but Victor refuses, apparently fearing the propagation of an entire race of monsters, the blame for which could be attached to him. The ending is strangely inconclusive: Victor and his creature are pursuing each other across the northern wastes, when the creature appears to vanish, possibly to drown, although this is not certain. Victor is rescued by one Walton, an explorer and adventurer, whose letters to his sister Margaret form a frame to the central narrative. The significance of this framing device has been the subject of much speculation. It seems most probable that Walton is like Joseph Conrad's Marlow: his healthful explorations, albeit tinged with melancholia, are a counter to Victor's obsessive, inward-looking explorations into forbidden secrets.

What, we might ask, is the substance of this story, and the reason for its cultural longevity? First, we might say that it concerns the relation between the human and the divine. Victor sets himself up, essentially, as a God-like figure who can create life; he accepts no limits on his intellect or practice, and is happy to attempt to perform what has never been successfully done before. Second, and in much the same vein, Victor thus usurps the rights not only of God but of women, in attempting to emulate the reproductive process without female participation; this point is hardly made explicit in the novel, but has rightly been dwelled upon by subsequent critics. In both these respects, Victor transgresses what it is reasonable for man to do, and it is fitting that the creature becomes the engine of his punishment.

But *Frankenstein* is also a story about science or, better perhaps, technology, and this is probably how it has been most consistently viewed over the last two hundred years. The period in which Mary Shelley wrote saw a burgeoning of scientific – and pseudo-scientific – approaches and methods; it was a time when it did indeed seem as though the secrets of nature were available for revelation – relevant figures here would be Erasmus Darwin, the vitalist and cataloguer of the natural world, and Humphry Davy, poet, scientist and friend of Samuel Taylor Coleridge and William Wordsworth as well as of William Godwin, Mary Shelley's father. The question, of course – then as now – was what dangers would attend on these new methods for achieving knowledge; how might the nature of humanity itself be altered if we were to take full advantage of the powers which science could unleash?

So we might argue that the peculiar power of *Frankenstein* lies in its yoking together of what one might call perennial concerns – relations between parents and children in the case of Victor and the creature; the social and reproductive roles of women; perhaps even a question, which emerges in some of the ways in which Victor talks to his creation, about how we are differentiated from the animals – with ones which are more specific to the historical circumstances. What is at stake here is the extraordinary continuity which the reception of *Frankenstein* suggests between the early nineteenth century and the present day. Questions about what we might call a 'machine age' have remained germane over the years: the role of science, of course, but what we might now call the question of ethical research, and above all the reception of new technologies. Yet, for all this, *Frankenstein* is very frequently referred to as a 'Gothic' novel, and the reasons why have perhaps not been very obvious in what we have said so far, and so it is necessary to consider what the label 'Gothic' might mean for *Frankenstein*.

We usually think of the Gothic, at least in a British context, as a novel form, but this is not how the discourse of the Gothic in Britain originated. Rather, it has its roots in a wholesale cultural re-evaluation which went on in the mid eighteenth century, effectively a rejection of, or at least a counter to, the dominant neoclassicism of the earlier part of the century. Where neoclassicism sought classical models, the Gothic arose as an attempt to remind Britain of its own vernacular heritage. Crucial moments in this revaluation include Samuel Johnson's approach to William Shakespeare, which suggested that there were alternative measures of dramatic excellence to an unthinking acceptance of the Aristotelian unities; the 'Gothic' poetry of the Scottish forger James Macpherson, which hinted at an ancient past even before the dominance of written forms; and Bishop Hurd's letters on chivalry and romance, which suggested that there were aspects of British history, even in the feudal period, which should be celebrated rather than regretted. The crucial point where this cultural shift metamorphosed into the novel is usually taken to be Horace Walpole's *The Castle of Otranto* (1762) but it is important to bear in mind that Walpole himself, albeit naturally a boastful man, was diffident about his effort, claiming that it fell midway between a novel and a 'romance',[2] a genre regarded at the time as fundamentally lacking in seriousness.

Whatever Walpole's own attitudes or motives, *Otranto* was rapidly followed by an enormous outpouring of Gothic romances or novels. The best-known today are Ann Radcliffe's *The Mysteries of Udolpho* (1794) and *The Italian* (1797), and Matthew Lewis's *The Monk* (1796), but there were literally thousands of Gothic novels published between the 1780s and the 1810s; many of these were written by authors who wrote only in the Gothic genre, but in other cases Gothic was simply one set of conventions used by authors with multiple talents. Many of these books relied on stock elements. First among these would be the overall geographical setting, overwhelmingly in Spain or Italy, or in a less than clearly identifiable part of southern Europe. Frequently there would be a theme of imprisonment, typically with an innocent maiden incarcerated by a powerful villain until she is bent to his evil will – or, more usually, rescued by a latter-day knight in shining armour who carries her off to a life of marital bliss, which in the novels themselves is never described. Other stock elements were a castle, monastery or convent well stocked with ghosts and reminders of death, and, in the better works, frequent recourse to descriptions of sublime landscapes, albeit usually infested with *banditti* or other frightening outlaws.

What, then, are these novels actually about? There have been many interpretations. One is that they are a melodramatic attempt to depict and explore the plight of women at the turn of the century; that, as social change proceeded under the impetus of industrialisation and changes in labour practices, the role of women did not keep pace with these changes and large numbers of women remained effectively incarcerated, not by wicked barons but by the market forces of cottage industry. Another is essentially to do with religion: the settings of the novels are almost always associated with Catholic countries, and dastardly barons are often at least matched by a plethora of corrupt abbots and abbesses, signifying both the power of the church and the supposed prevalence of 'mystery' – in other words, superstition – in the south of Europe. Gothic novels are also frequently concerned with, indeed some are obsessed by, death, or in other words by the limits of human life. Ghosts in Gothic fiction are frequently ambiguous, and many of the apparently supernatural manifestations end up by being explained away: nonetheless the preoccupation with mortality remains. Gothic has also been seen as reflecting political change, with a distorted version of a historical passing of power away from a feudal aristocracy and into the hands of the middle classes, for whom the past – and Gothic novels are usually set in the past – is a place of darkness and fear from which they wish to escape into the brave new world of enlightenment.

It will be immediately obvious that this typical scenario is not precisely the scenario of *Frankenstein*, and neither can we map Gothic's preoccupations onto Mary Shelley's. *Frankenstein* does, of course, revolve around what we have since come to refer to as a monster, whose humanity or otherwise is in doubt; in this sense it could be seen as contiguous with the non-human creatures who appear, if only briefly, in classic Gothic fiction. But it is not set in a remote past. Victor Frankenstein's dwelling place, however it has been made over in films, is not a Gothic castle. And although there are innocent maidens in the story, they are hardly central, and certainly do not hold our attention as do Emily and Ellena, who are at the heart of Radcliffe's *Udolpho* and *The Italian* respectively. Furthermore, any religious subtext to the novel seems to be the reverse of the Gothic truisms: Victor is hardly a victim of primitive superstition, rather his fate is determined by an over-reliance on scientific experimentation.

In what way or ways, then, is it correct or useful to think of *Frankenstein* as a Gothic novel – or, to put it another way, why has it so frequently been considered to be such? The most obvious answer is that it follows the Gothic in its colouring of melodrama. The rise of the novel in the eighteenth century, as for example in Daniel Defoe and Henry Fielding, is associated with a constant insistence on the realities of the everyday world – this indeed, according to the greatest early critic of the novel, Ian Watt, is precisely what distinguishes the novel from its 'romance' predecessors, which were set in worlds of fantasy or myth.[3] *Frankenstein* is clearly a long way away from this tradition. A passage like the following is typical of many moments in the novel:

> At these moments I wept bitterly, and wished that peace would revisit my mind only that I might afford [my family] consolation and happiness. But that could not be. Remorse extinguished every hope. I had been the author of unalterable evils; and I lived in daily fear, lest the monster whom I had created should perpetrate some new wickedness. I had an obscure feeling that all was not over, and that he would still commit some signal crime, which by its enormity should almost efface the recollection of the past. There was always scope for fear, so long as anything I loved remained behind. (*Frankenstein*, 87)

This is the language of the Gothic: it involves heightened emotion, intensity of fear, a vision of unutterable evil. It is a far cry from Defoe, whose Robinson Crusoe, even when alone on his desert island, draws up a list of the advantages and disadvantages of his plight.[4] It is rather reminiscent of the much later stories of Edgar Allan Poe in its introspection, its constant sense of being locked up in a mind and in a situation from which there is no escape.

Another Gothic feature of *Frankenstein* is the theme of forbidden knowledge. Victor, as we have said, is determined to go beyond the boundaries of knowledge by whatever means come to hand; he is determined to expand the realm of human knowledge, regardless of the risk, and thus while we as readers may think him blameworthy in a number of respects, there is nonetheless an element of heroism to his attempts, although whether Mary Shelley intended the reader to share this heroic perception remains a vexed point.

Not many Gothic heroes are concerned with exactly this struggle to expand the realm of human knowledge, but they are very often, like Victor Frankenstein, transgressors. Often their transgression is similarly born of hubris, the fruit of pride: in Gothic we have a wealth of hero/villains – and it is important to note that in Gothic the terms 'hero' and 'villain' are not easy to separate – who challenge the supremacy of God, risk the temptations of the Devil and are then punished for attempting to exceed the bounds of human power. The archetypal figure for this in classic Western myth is, of course, Prometheus, which is why *Frankenstein* is subtitled 'The Modern Prometheus'. It was Prometheus who tried to wrest forbidden knowledge from the realm of the gods in the form of fire, and who was subjected to eternal punishment for his efforts. The modern archetype is Faust, which concerned Johann Wolfgang von Goethe over the same period. We can see this theme pursued in a number of Gothic novels, for example in Lewis's *The Monk*, where the protagonist Ambrosio essentially enters into a pact with the Devil (although he does not know it at the time) and is eventually carried away to hell for his presumption.

Victor, then, is in many ways a transgressor. He transgresses in his attempt to manufacture a living being, thereby usurping the roles of both God and woman, and people die as a result of his actions. He himself becomes cursed as he remains locked in mortal combat with his creation, and this is reminiscent of other cursed heroes from the Romantic period such as Coleridge's ancient mariner or Melmoth in C. R. Maturin's Gothic masterpiece, *Melmoth the Wanderer*, published only a few years after *Frankenstein* in 1822, and interesting too for its particularly virulent take on superstition and priestcraft, this time in the context of Ireland rather than southern Europe.

One quite distinctive feature of Frankenstein, however, is that he incurs his fate not merely through a presumptuous exercise of power but also through a version of creativity; this is in many ways the central crux of the novel, and perhaps one of the reasons why it has remained so alive and fertile to this day. For Mary Shelley was writing during the heyday of, and many would say in direct response to, romantic ideas – including those, of course, articulated by her husband – about the role and creative power of the human poetic imagination.[5] For Coleridge in particular, this power was second only to the divine creative power, and indeed it was closely linked with it.[6] It could be argued that, although Victor is apparently a scientist, there is also a dialogue going on between Mary Shelley and the Romantics about whether the imagination is really as powerful as it seems; or, if it is, whether it might therefore bring in its wake dangers which ought not to be risked. Divine inspiration might indeed be a description of the poetic process – and after all, it was a description which went back to the ancient Greeks: but how can one know, perhaps the text asks, whether the 'inspiration' is truly divine? What if it is diabolic in origin?

Thus the power of *Frankenstein* may derive from a curious crossover, which could perhaps only happen at a highly specific historical moment. It is an attack on the overweening pretensions of science, and at the same time on the vaunting power of the imagination. Yet the word 'attack' simplifies Mary Shelley's dealings with these problems: what *Frankenstein* articulates is a set of fears which are not wholly clear to the author herself, but which hover in the background and are given force and shape by the creature and by his unending battle with his master. Victor is a scientist, but he is also a creator: the creature is the result, so the novel claims, of technological work, but Victor is also a man with a great, if flawed, imagination, one which takes him, and thus in a sense takes the reader, beyond the accepted boundaries of life and death.

I have mentioned the subtitle 'The Modern Prometheus'; equally significant is the dedication to Mary Shelley's father, William Godwin. Godwin was a political thinker who wrote, among many other works, *Political Justice* (1793) and *Caleb Williams* (1794). *Political Justice* is a significant antecedent for *Frankenstein*; and it made an enormous impact when first published, for two principal reasons. The first was that it was seen as taking the principle of rationalism to its furthest limits; the second, intertwined with the first, was that it declared that moral evil does not exist – instead, vice flows from mistakes of understanding.

These ideas reverberate multiply in *Frankenstein*. Principally, there is the question of whether the creature himself can be considered evil. The answer seems to be that, whatever Victor himself thinks, he is not. Instead he is 'born' – or rather brought to life – as any child is born, as a blank slate, a *tabula rasa*, upon which life will inscribe its own messages. Thus when he is treated, as so often by Victor, with anger, scorn and contempt, he responds in kind; the fault here lies not in him but in the way in which he is regarded. He learns the only lessons that life offers him – although here we have to say that the text does not read as simply as this might suggest and that the authorial attitude to the creature seems to change from time to time; sometimes we appear to be invited to share the purely physical revulsion which Victor feels when he observes the fruits of his labours.

The tradition in which Godwin was writing was not only a British one, and here we can see *Frankenstein* opening out onto a wider European field; indeed, his main influences were the Enlightenment *philosophes* and the complex events of the French Revolution of 1789. *Frankenstein* itself operates within a related European milieu. A key part of the narrative is the creature's 'education', which takes place through his reading of four books: the comte de Volney's *Les Ruines, ou Méditations sur les révolutions des empires* (*The Ruins, or Meditation on the Revolutions of Empires*, 1791); Goethe's *Die Leiden des jungen Werthers* (*The Sorrows of Young Werther*, 1774); Plutarch's *Lives*; and John Milton's *Paradise Lost*. All of these books were widely read and translated; each of them was important in a European context.

The significance of Volney centres on his virulent attacks on all religions as obscuring the true origins of man. Volney refers to mankind as an orphan, who has been abandoned by some unknown power which has produced him. This is an extreme version of the deist view of God as a clockmaker who, having made the universe and, as it were, wound it up, has now stepped back, or indeed in the figure of the *deus absconditus* has disappeared entirely, leaving mankind to get on by itself. It has, however, an obvious relation to the plight of the creature who, seen in this light, is not merely a creation of a demented scientist but is also an Everyman figure, standing for a kind of primal loneliness which is brought to a new peak by Victor's refusal to make him a mate.

Goethe's *Werther*, often read as a meditation on the injustice of life and on the possible advantages of suicide, was a Europe-wide success when first published; its relevance in the context of *Frankenstein* hinges on Werther's sense of exclusion from society and the domestic realm. In a way, we might see Werther as the first existentialist hero, a forerunner of the melancholic and obsessive protagonists of Jean-Paul Sartre, Albert Camus and perhaps even Samuel Beckett; more importantly from the viewpoint of the creature, *Werther* underlines the fear of being an outcast from society – as the creature particularly feels in the scenes where he spies on the hermit's cottage in the thwarted hope of being allowed to share in its domestic felicity.

There are many connections between the first volume of Plutarch's *Lives*, which is the particular volume the creature finds, and his own situation. There are references to the difficulty of establishing origins (which, seen in another light, is also a key issue for the Gothic, with its constant ellipses and evasions about the course of history); there are issues to do with paternity and orphanage; and there are references to the use of religious terror to achieve political ends. Above all, we may feel that the book reflects something of the difficulty the creature feels in trying to supply an account of his own life: not human, yet belonging to no other identifiable race or species, with no family or anybody to share his feelings and thoughts, inspiring horror and disgust in all who meet him, how will it ever be possible for him to collect himself together in such a way as to give an 'account' of his life?

The reference to *Paradise Lost* is perhaps the most obvious of these intertextual locations. If God is the final father figure, then *Paradise Lost* signals both rebellion and abandonment: rebellion by Satan and the abandonment (as it may be seen) of Adam and Eve for having transgressed divine law. Seen in one light, the creature shares Adam and Eve's innocence and his sense of injustice stems from his exile from a home which he has barely known, from a sense that his rejection is no fault of his own but represents a kind of terrible fate which, for reasons unknown to him, he has no choice but to endure. Seen in another light – and this is how Victor repeatedly sees him – the creature is satanic, a force of evil, who deserves his exile and indeed needs to be destroyed to prevent the havoc he might wreak; from this position, of course, there is no further to fall: the creature needs to put no rein on his need for vengeance, and rapidly becomes precisely what he has been accused of being.

At this point there are two other matters to be noted. The first is that, behind the references above, there is another figure whose presence in *Frankenstein* it is impossible to doubt, namely Jean-Jacques Rousseau, whose *Émile ou De l'éducation* (*Émile, or Education*, 1762) forms a kind of template for the creature's development. This is crucially important because Rousseau, through his adoration of the natural, was a pivotal influence on European romanticism. In regard to the second, it is instructive to recall the other of Godwin's major texts, *Caleb Williams*, for *Caleb Williams* is a tale of pursuit in many ways very like *Frankenstein*. Caleb is a servant who unwittingly learns a secret about his employer, who thereafter pursues him throughout his life. Caleb is thus doomed in a way very similar to the creature: he has done nothing knowingly wrong, and yet for reasons completely beyond his control he is despised, vilified and threatened with death by the very person who ought to have the most care for him.

These reflections on *Frankenstein*, on Godwin, and on the creature's own reading (which is, we may note, very similar to Mary Shelley's own at the time of writing) perhaps enable us to re-approach the Gothic in general. At the heart of the Gothic lies the achievement and anxiety of Prometheus: the fate of the character who tries to know – or in some cases unwittingly comes to know – too much. We can therefore see it as no accident that the Gothic arises when it does; it emerges at least partly as a response, not merely to the Enlightenment or to the French Revolution, but rather to the problematic connection between the two. How, it asks, could the worship of reason, the promise of the *philosophes* to roll back the dark days of tyranny and superstition, have resulted in the violence and bloodshed in France?

In Gothic writing, the argument is run and rerun: are the forces left over from the feudal past (and still present, at least in fantasy, in the rituals and archaisms of the Catholic Church) still with us? Can they ever be overcome? Or – and here the argument proceeds into necessary psychological speculation – are there forces of the dark buried so deep within us that we cannot escape them, forces which render all our attempts at enlightenment, political justice and freedom illusory and doomed?

Seen thus, we may see the Gothic as proffering no single 'take' on, or solution to, social or political issues, but rather as providing a Europe-wide arena of debate. If Victor Frankenstein has overstepped the limits, where *are* those limits? If feudal barons and corrupt abbots wield the wrong kind of power, what is the right kind of power? If women are constantly persecuted, what – and this, of course, is of particular importance to Mary Shelley as it was to her mother Mary Wollstonecraft – is the way forward from this situation, how might the relations between the genders be improved?

What distinguishes *Frankenstein* from many other Gothic novels of its period is that it is far clearer about these arguments than were, for example, Radcliffe, Lewis or Maturin, who cloaked such thoughts in distant times and places, clothed them in an exoticism which removes the problematic decisively from the domestic fireside. It is interesting, though, to note that in the same year as *Frankenstein* another story was published, in Germany, 'Der Sandmann' ('The Sand-Man') by E. T. A. Hoffmann, which has sometimes been referred to as Gothic. 'The Sand-Man' is probably now best known as the literary example treated at length by Sigmund Freud in his essay on 'Das Unheimliche' ('The "Uncanny"', 1919),[7] but it is also, like *Frankenstein*, a fable about science and how far it can be allowed to go.

It is also a story about vision and perception: the folkloric figure of the sandman throws sand in children's eyes to help them (bizarrely) to sleep, and much of the story revolves around eyes, spectacles, mistakes of vision, what can, and cannot, be seen. This theme appears in *Frankenstein* too: 'I compassionated him', Victor says at one point of the creature, 'and sometimes felt a wish to console him; but when I looked upon him, when

I saw the filthy mass that moved and talked, my heart sickened, and my feelings were altered to those of horror and hatred' (*Frankenstein*, 130). And towards the end of the novel Victor is constantly tormented by occasional glimpses of the creature, glimpses which never fully reveal his whereabouts but which tantalise – like all ghosts and phantoms – by being somewhere around the periphery of vision – that periphery, we may speculate, which is occupied by the orphan, the outlaw, all those who are exiled from the centre, from the human norm.

But vision and perception are also more generally inwoven into the Gothic. There are constant questions about whether we are really seeing what we think we see, this entire difficulty being summarised in the nature of the ghost. Emily in *The Mysteries of Udolpho* is constantly seeing things: Gothic heroines as a whole see vast numbers of spirits, skeletons, the risen dead. Mostly they turn out to be apparitions, but then the very word 'apparition' begs a number of questions. These are questions famously put, of course, by Jane Austen in *Northanger Abbey* (1818), where Catherine Morland, by virtue of her excessive reading of Gothic romances, proves able to transmute the most mundane of circumstances into scenes of terror of which, of course, she – like many a reader of Gothic romances – is the heart.

The references I have made to the reading at the heart of *Frankenstein* indicate that the Gothic was by no means wholly a British phenomenon. Although *The Castle of Otranto* may have provided one root for Gothic fiction, there are many other connections, particularly with what we might have to loosely call the Germanic. Two such connections are particularly important. The first is that the revival of the Gothic as a cultural force in the mid eighteenth century relied heavily on a purported difference between southern Europe (tyrannical, priest-ridden, addicted to luxury) and northern Europe (democratic, Protestant, hard-working). In the service of producing a national myth about Britain, great recourse was had to presumed Germanic models – and, after all, it was in the Germanic lands that the 'original' Goths, so it was supposed, had originated.

The second is that, in any case, German writers were producing Gothic works at the same time as the British. Early translations of German terror fiction in English included Benedikte Naubert's *Hermann von Unna* in 1794 and C. A. Vulpius's *Rinaldo Rinaldini* in 1800, but probably the most significant was Friedrich Schiller's *Die Räuber* (*The Robbers*), translated in 1792, because, as in Godwin's *Caleb Williams*, the terror content was indissolubly linked to a political and indeed philosophical message, a message which was essentially about personal and political freedom. Lewis translated a number of works from the German; and in general, when the culturally righteous wished to rail against the corruption to British manners caused by Gothic horror, it was – as in the emblematic case of Wordsworth – the influx of the Germans that they were wont to invoke.

In order to take an analysis of the Gothic further forward in time, however, we have to confront difficulties with the term itself. Is it better used to describe a particular historical moment, or can we continue to use it across the centuries? The term itself is, of course, deeply problematic, linking as it does the 'original Goths' of the Dark Ages; medieval cathedral architecture; an eighteenth-century vernacular revival; novels of ghosts and terrors; the nineteenth-century 'Gothic revival' whose most vivid representation is the Houses of Parliament, where Gothic serves to evidence the oldest home of a northern European democracy; various schools of cinema; and the 'Goth culture' of the present day, at least as evident in Spain and Greece as in Britain.

There is no space here to look at all of these manifestations, but the word 'Gothic', whatever precisely it covers, shows no sign of going away. Indeed, it has entered into the 'mainstream' of the novel. We can list some obvious titles: Charles Dickens's *A Christmas Carol* (1843); Emily Brontë's *Wuthering Heights* (1847); Edith Wharton's *Tales of Men and Ghosts* (1910); William Faulkner's *Sanctuary* (1931); Daphne du Maurier's *Rebecca* (1938); Elizabeth Bowen's 'The Demon Lover' (1945); Angela Carter's *The Bloody Chamber* (1979) – arguably none of these would have been written except for the long shadow cast by the Gothic. We can also say that Gothic seems to have a curious propensity for throwing up images which enter deep into the cultural mythology. Frankenstein's creature is obviously one such, but several others emerged, particularly towards the end of the nineteenth century, within the Gothic tradition. I shall briefly mention three of them.

The first is Dracula, from the 1897 novel of the same name by Bram Stoker. Here, as with *Frankenstein*, we have a figure which has vastly exceeded the novel in which he first appeared. Dracula can be seen in many ways, but for our purposes the most important is that he is a figure who, again, threatens to challenge the accepted limits of life and death: he is quasi-immortal, and at the same time is an emblem of an old aristocracy (as we see so often in the eighteenth-century Gothic) which appears never to have died. He is, like Frankenstein's creature, both seen and not seen: a thing of darkness and moonlight which threatens the security of the daylight world and suggests that 'enlightenment' may never be a complete project, that it may merely push the more disturbing aspects of human nature back into the dark where they may wait to strike out again.

The second image occurs in Robert Louis Stevenson's *Dr Jekyll and Mr Hyde* (1886), which bears more obvious comparison with *Frankenstein*. For it is possible – although this is not an interpretation which I have yet mentioned – to see *Frankenstein* as the story of a divided self: Victor as a frail, introverted intellectual, the creature as the immensely strong, violent superman he longs to be and yet hates himself for wishing to inhabit. If this is so, then *Dr Jekyll and Mr Hyde* follows the image further in its account of a doctor – and an experimenter, in the true sense of the word, a scientist like Victor – who discovers an elixir which will allow him to gratify his deepest desires, if at the expense of a change of shape which will prove increasingly impossible to reverse. The message here about the penalties for transgression could hardly be clearer.

The third image, Richard Marsh's *The Beetle* (1897), is less well known and is one of many late nineteenth-century novels which reflect – and reflect upon – the impact of Charles Darwin's discoveries about evolution upon previously accepted theories of human nature. Effectively, Marsh's novel is a story of degeneration, a common theme in the 1890s, which sets out to explore what would happen if evolution were to go into reverse, what the consequences would be if we were to be in some way returned to a pre-human existence. Here too, I think we can see the influence of *Frankenstein*, in the sense of the mutual rejection of the 'monstrous' and the 'normal': we could say that texts like these both patrol the boundaries beyond which monstrous things might creep but at the same time demonstrate our attraction to, indeed our fascination with, those forms, those 'apparitions' which may seem human but in fact are not, a fascination which science may appear to wish to banish but cannot.

However, I would like now to return to Mary Shelley, for there are many issues unresolved – and it is probably fair to say that they never will be resolved. One is how such an extraordinary and rich book could have been written by a young woman of Mary Shelley's experience. Gallons of critical ink have been expended on this problem, but it seems to me that the answer is ready at hand. *Frankenstein* is the remarkable result of a strenuous attempt to deal with a sudden explosion of birth and death. Mary's mother had, of course, died in childbirth. Her first daughter was born and died in 1815. Her son William had been born in 1816, an event which was immediately succeeded by the suicides of her half-sister Fanny Imlay and Percy Shelley's wife Harriet Westbrook. Her daughter Clara was born in 1817 (to die nine months after the publication of *Frankenstein*, followed the succeeding year by the death of William). Issues of life and death would surely have had a strange timbre for the young Mary Shelley. Moreover, this preoccupation makes itself felt again in one of Mary's other novels, *The Last Man*, which appears to question what the limits of time are, and who might be left after the natural processes of death and succession are, eventually, completed.

But these matters also open onto wider concerns than the events, however extraordinary, of Mary Shelley's life; and I shall conclude by suggesting that they open in two ways. The first has to do with the nature of the Gothic, which is deeply implicated in questions of origin, and here we might turn to Freud and, at least in general terms, recognise his perception that what concerns us all to some degree – and what can throw us off balance in the case of mental illness – is the issue of where we came from. Gothic refracts this preoccupation in any number of ways: in the strange provenances of some of the early novels, which claimed to have been in some way 'reproduced' from older texts now vanished; in the endless labyrinths through which victims wander in Gothic novels, in an attempt to find a way out (or a way in to the real world from which they have been banished); in the endless search for heritage or for the truth about one's own birth, which preoccupies so many Gothic heroines.

If we cannot find out the answers to these questions of origin, Gothic suggests, then we may run the risk of remaining in some kind of limbo; we may find ourselves inhabiting a ghost place (like Anne Catherick in Wilkie Collins's wonderful novel *The Woman in White* (1860)) from which we cannot escape – and thus we can see a further reticulation of the Gothic trope of incarceration. Insofar as Victor and the creature are incarcerated, then they are incarcerated inside each other; just as Jekyll and Hyde would later be, but also just as mother and child, before birth, are mutually incarcerated.

And this brings me to my final point. There was a time when it was customary to speak of 'female Gothic', as though it was virtually a separate genre from the male equivalent (albeit by far the larger in terms of authors), although critics tend now to be less directive about the gender orientation of texts. However, two facts remain: most Gothic novels from the late eighteenth and early nineteenth centuries were written by women (although very few since), and Mary Shelley was a woman.

This brings us up against one of the most vexed of all critical questions, and it is one which has focused around the figure of Mary Shelley for at least the last twenty years: namely, is there such a thing as women's writing? If there is, can it be identified at a more fundamental level than those of theme or preoccupation, at a level, for example, of style? How could we *know* from the text itself (if we did not know otherwise), that *Frankenstein* was written by a woman? I have no answer to that question in terms of style or of what is sometimes called 'women's writing', but I do feel sure of my answer in terms of what Mary Shelley was writing *about*; it appears to me that the depth of feeling for the creature; the sense of his perpetual exile; the specific criticisms of Victor's faulty reasoning and imagination; the depiction of domestic detail and in particular the creature's yearning to find again all that he thought he had lost, even though he had never experienced it – all of these matters point ineluctably towards a female author. Some of them, also, we might want to consider to be the marks of a female Gothic author, or indeed to point to Gothic – or some aspects of Gothic – as a specifically female form. However, in fiction there is a great deal of cross-dressing and impersonation, for that is partly what fiction is about, and so we must be ever cautious in our dealings with writing and biography: perhaps that is another of the many legacies we have received from Mary Shelley.

## Note on editions

A recent modern text is *Frankenstein*, ed. Johanna M. Smith (Boston: Bedford; New York: St Martins, 2000). Reliable editions, with introductions and notes, are also available from Penguin and Oxford University Press.

### Notes

1 Mary Shelley, *Frankenstein*, ed. Johanna M. Smith (Boston: Bedford; New York: St Martin's, 2000), p. 24. All subsequent page references in the text are from this edition.
2 See Horace Walpole, *The Castle of Otranto*, ed. W. S. Lewis, introd. Emma Clery (Oxford University Press, 1996), p. 9.
3 See Ian Watt, *The Rise of the Novel: Studies in Defoe, Richardson and Fielding* (London: Chatto and Windus, 1957), pp. 9–35.
4 See Daniel Defoe, *Robinson Crusoe*, ed. Angus Ross (Harmondsworth: Penguin, 1965), pp. 83–4.
5 See Percy Bysshe Shelley, *A Defence of Poetry* (1821), in, e.g., *The Four Ages of Poetry*, ed. H. F. B. Brett-Smith (Oxford, Basil Blackwell, 1972), pp. 21–59.
6 See S. T. Coleridge, *Biographia Literaria* (1817), ed. George Watson (London: J. M. Dent, 1956), p. 167.
7 Sigmund Freud, 'The "Uncanny"', in *The Standard Edition of the Complete Psychological Works of Sigmund Freud*, ed. James Strachey et al., 24 vols. (London: The Hogarth Press, 1953–74), vol. XVII, pp. 217–56.

### Further reading

Baldick, Chris, *In Frankenstein's Shadow: Myth, Monstrosity, and Nineteenth-Century Writing* (Oxford: Clarendon Press, 1987)
Botting Fred, ed., *The Gothic* (Cambridge: D. S. Brewer, 2001)
Hoeveler, Diane Long, *Gothic Feminism: The Professionalisation of Gender from Charlotte Smith to the Brontës* (University Park, PA: Pennsylvania State University Press, 1998)

Horner, Avril, ed., *European Gothic: A Spirited Exchange 1760–1960*, (Manchester University Press, 2002)

Horner, Avril and Sue Zlosnik, eds., *Le Gothic: Influences and Appropriations in Europe and America* (London: Palgrave Macmillan, 2008)

Moers, Ellen, *Literary Women: The Great Writers* (Garden City, NY: Anchor Books, 1977)

Punter, David, *The Literature of Terror*, rev. edn, 2 vols. (London: Longman, 1996)

Smith, Andrew, *Gothic Literature* (Edinburgh University Press, 2007)

# 11

MICHAEL TILBY

# Honoré de Balzac (1799–1850): 'Realism' and authority

Balzac's central position in the tradition of the European novel is incontrovertible. The author of the ninety-odd, linked novels and stories comprising *La Comédie humaine*, which sought principally, though not quite exclusively, to offer a panoramic depiction of public and private life in France since the Revolution of 1789, is the undisputed master of the 'realist' novel in France and has remained the inevitable point of reference for later French novelists, whether they be imitators or, as in the case of certain *nouveaux romanciers* of the 1950s and 1960s (though not Michel Butor or Claude Simon), committed detractors.[1] Much as popular images of nineteenth-century France appear often to have been shaped by a reading of his fictions, so the format of the novel he inaugurated has become synonymous with the genre itself. While subject to periodic denunciation on grounds of inauthenticity, the 'Balzacian' stereotype has proved remarkably resilient, to the extent of obscuring the fact that the author's own compositions were innovatory exercises in artifice, rather than an unmediated reflection of the social and physical world they were concerned to depict. Yet it is undeniable that the author–narrator in Balzac's fictions is characterised by a belief in his own authority as the unrivalled source of knowledge, control and judgement. Bolstered by a contract with the reader, according to which the latter, in return for significant gratification or illumination, is invited to submit to that authority, the Balzacian novel takes as axiomatic its capacity to expose the workings of bourgeois society. In so doing, it provided a depiction of individuals who, for all their extraordinariness, not only recalled counterparts in everyday life, but also constituted models for the author's contemporaries to emulate or, more frequently, to avoid. Balzac's fictions duly engage with the implied reader's own experience, while seeking to complement it through the traversing of many a closed door or partition. The assumption Balzac sought to impose was that not only were his novels lifelike, Life was, in essence, novelistic.

There can be no doubt that Balzac's fictions, most of which are set in post-Revolutionary France, offer myriad insights into French society of that period and its relationship to the individual citizen. The mere fact of conceiving society as a socio-economic entity not only brings within the compass of the novel a host of complex connections that previously had had no part to play within French fiction, but also identifies the defining matrix of the new bourgeois age.[2] Money permeates every activity, providing a stimulus for advancement and self-fulfilment, but also riding roughshod over the dictates of codes of honour or morality and perverting those forms of sentiment associated with the individual's humanity. Prostitution is omnipresent, both literally in the case of the Parisian novels and metaphorically throughout the *Comédie humaine*. Love, while not absent, is characterised by a disconcerting fragility and an inability to withstand destructive pressures from other quarters. It is frequently replaced by a more frenzied and disordered form of erotic activity, with Balzac's commitment to differential categories leading to a bold inclusion of homosexual desire, both male and female (see the novels that form the 'Vautrin cycle' and *La Fille aux yeux d'or*) and various cases of sexual repression, notably in the case of the eponymous heroines of *La Cousine Bette* and, in more comic vein, *La Vieille Fille*. The historian of early nineteenth-century France is, furthermore, offered a range of specialist depictions of banking, trade (represented by such different figures as the perfumer César Birotteau and the commercial traveller known as 'l'Illustre Gaudissart'), medicine, the law, the church, the theatre, music and the visual arts, as well as publishing and journalism. No French novelist before Balzac had attempted to make the novel a container for such an array of factual detail relating to professional life.

The effect of the Code Napoléon on marriage and family relationships, which the young Balzac had observed as a lawyer's clerk, provided him with numerous starting points, thereby enabling him to liberate the novel from the tyranny of conventional plots. The vexed question of inheritance in particular leads to unparalleled degrees of complexity, with, for example in *Ursule Mirouët*, intra-familial antagonism and attempts to circumvent it leaning equally heavily on manipulation of the law. The scandalous mistreatment of a child may be familiar from fairy stories, and that of an unmarried daughter from the comedies of Molière, but the vignettes of the eponymous Pierrette's lot at the hands of her aunt and of the repressive treatment of Eugénie Grandet constitute, with other depictions of family life in the *Comédie humaine*, examples of a perversion of the institution Balzac considered the linchpin of Society. The treatment of 'Père' Goriot by his daughters, together with his own somewhat suspect emotional attachment to them, exemplifies the use of a dysfunctional family to illustrate a disintegrating society, in which paternal authority, symbolically represented in the *Comédie humaine* by the unfortunate Louis XVI, was widely undermined, not least by the 'fathers' themselves. Families in his fiction, whether literally or metaphorically constituted, and incorporating surrogate figures as well as individuals related by birth or marriage, frequently present a complex and, in relation to the idealising norm, unnatural rewriting of the unit as traditionally conceived. A related concern with the unsatisfactory legal status of marriage, the subject of his early *Physiologie du mariage*, was regarded by Balzac as still more crucial to his view of society. In a domain dominated by the tired stereotypes of popular theatre, it additionally afforded not merely an informative array of case studies, but further innovation with regard to plot, the authority of which benefited greatly from being underpinned by structures that were, by definition, extra-fictional. It was as a result of this perspective, and of the educatory relationships that Balzac enjoyed with several older women, that he was viewed, not always admiringly, as 'le romancier de la femme' (the novelist of women), a figure endowed with a remarkable degree of empathy with the feminine psyche. Certainly, the range of female types encountered in the *Comédie humaine* is strikingly diverse. It included such new species as 'la femme de trente ans' (the woman of thirty).

The most memorable of Balzac's illuminations of the age are, however, achieved through those of his characters who, loosely in the manner of the *Bildungsroman*, are portrayed in terms of their attempts to achieve success amid the treacherous waters of the French capital. Young men, notably Eugène de Rastignac and Lucien de Rubempré, both of whom start from a more precarious social position than their noble patronyms might suggest, learn many important lessons about the codes that regulate 'polite' society, the location of influence and power, the unprecedented importance of wealth and the ruthless egocentricity that Balzac saw as the principal motivation behind human endeavour in the period in which he was writing. (The writer and journalist Louis Ulbach would later dedicate his satirical *Lettres de Ferragus* 'to the memory of Honoré de Balzac, the most profound and merciless liquidator of human turpitude since W. Shakespeare'.)[3] If Rastignac becomes a government minister and peer, Lucien de Rubempré (baptised Lucien Chardon) eventually commits suicide, thereby recalling the earliest of the young male protagonists of the *Comédie humaine*, Raphaël de Valentin, who, at the outset of the 'realist fantasy' *La Peau de chagrin* (Sigmund Freud's death-bed reading), is ready to throw himself into the Seine. As a result of the Faustian pact with the owner of the magic skin that shrinks in proportion to the size of the wish it grants, the 'paralysed' Raphaël finds himself condemned to a prolonged Death-in-Life.

The authority of Balzac's novels as historical representations is reinforced by the way the characters' trajectories are precisely situated in relation to the prevailing political regime at each stage of their lives. The Revolution, as both the theatre of regicide and the primary influence on social, political and economic life, is the inevitable backcloth against which the subsequent destinies of families and individuals are defined. Père Goriot's economic success, like that of Balzac's own father, is entirely due to the possibilities afforded by the Revolution and the needs of its armies. Such picturesque characters as M. de Valois in *La Vieille Fille* and the figures highlighted by the title of its sequel, *Le Cabinet des antiques*, are first and foremost anachronisms, representatives of the *Ancien Régime*. The spectre of Napoleon (a figure physically present in one of Balzac's early short stories, 'La Vendetta', as well as in the later novel *Une ténébreuse affaire*) is the subject of frequent allusion, albeit problematically: if he is the embodiment of energy and a model of supreme personal achievement, revered by such military men as Maréchal Hulot in *La Cousine Bette*, it is the pompous bourgeois figure Crevel who affects a Napoleonic pose. The pose is, in fact, a double imitation in that Crevel is following in the footsteps of his former employer César Birotteau, whose forename inevitably recalls the Emperor's cult of a Roman inheritance. Yet César, arguably the most ambiguous of Balzac's creations, was a monarchist proud to have been shot by General Bonaparte on the steps of Saint-Roch on 13 Vendémiaire, Year IV. The novel that charts his chequered life is pointedly entitled, in echo of the Baron de Montesquieu's study of Ancient Rome, *Grandeur et décadence de César Birotteau* (the full title is twenty-seven words long and ends with a satirical 'etc.'). Similarly, if the response to civilian life by such former veterans of the Imperial Army as Genestas in *Le Médecin de campagne* and M. de Troisgros in *La Vieille Fille* is a dignified inactivity, so elsewhere, and notably in the case of Philippe Bridau in *La Rabouilleuse*, the half-pay officer is liable to be a disruptive social presence. The extent to which Napoleonic values fail to establish themselves in contemporary French society is illustrated by such different characters as Colonel Chabert, whose very identity is liquidated, and Hector Hulot, who, having been raised to the peerage by the emperor, defiles the latter's memory through his behaviour as an erotomaniac.

For Balzac, who became a sympathiser of the Bourbon Legitimist party in the early 1830s, the Restoration had provided an inevitable testing ground for the aristocracy. But, as works such as *La Duchesse de Langeais* and *Le Cabinet des antiques* reveal, it was a test the inflexible aristocracy was held to have failed. (If the monarchist heroine of *Le Lys dans la vallée*, Henriette de Mortsauf, is an admirer of Napoleon, she, significantly, dies young, as if in prediction of the way the subsequent death of the emperor and the revolution of 1830 that brought an end to the Bourbon Restoration would together put paid to both Bonapartist and Legitimist causes.) The nobility was charged by Balzac with having allowed the politically hybrid July Monarchy, the regime for which he reserved his particular opprobrium as a result of its worship of 'the all-powerful hundred-*sou* piece' (*La Cousine Bette*). Yet, the picture is frequently complicated by the fact that the vast majority of his fictions were written during the July Monarchy and can be read as being, at some levels at least, a reflection on contemporary political reality as well as attempts at accurate portrayals of the period in which the events are set. His compositions often hint at the presence of a vein of political allegory even when the political context is not foregrounded, though teasingly withholding sanction of any interpretation the reader may be tempted to extrapolate. Within the history of the novel, however, what is important is less the (complex) question of Balzac's own political standpoint and more the fact that the *Comédie humaine* consist-ently shows individual lives to be interwoven with, and indelibly marked by, the historical and political contexts in which the characters are placed.

Such a sketch of the representational scope of the Balzacian novel none-theless leaves much of its specificity unconsidered. While it indicates the awe-inspiring dimension of Balzac's fictional universe, it leaves out of account the fact that rarely has a major novelist been subjected to such radical criticism and even derision. The tendency, on the part of admirers and detractors alike, has been to try to separate Balzac's undoubted achieve-ments from his apparent flaws, which are usually considered to belong to the realm of form. Yet the perceived achievements and flaws are largely interdependent. And this argument also tends to imply that Balzacian representation embodies single-mindedness, the one-dimensional and a contentment with the taxonomical, all of which are, in fact, at the antipodes of both the author's creative imagination and his attempts to accord the latter's products appropriate linguistic expression. More revealing of his originality, and of the distance separating his work from the stereotype honed by subsequent practitioners, is a readiness to respect the alleged flaws as integral to that originality, which requires an examination of the Balzacian composition outside the restrictive framework of a classical aesthetics of the novel.

The criticisms that have been directed at Balzac touch on almost every aspect of his writing, with Henry James (an admirer) conceding his 'faults of pedantry, ponderosity, pretentiousness, bad taste and charmless form'.[4] His novels, which manifestly fail to conform to any single compositional ideal, are easily lambasted for their lack of proportion and an apparent random-ness in the length of episodes or descriptions. If readers of *Le Père Goriot* claim to have enjoyed the novel, it is often in spite of what they regard as the excessive detail of the initial description of Mme Vauquer's boarding-house. The evocation of Paris that constitutes the long opening section of *La Fille aux yeux d'or*, while a poetic *tour de force* in establishing the city as a mythical entity, bears scant resemblance to a conventional exordium: not a single character is introduced or mentioned. It is not difficult to understand why readers faced with the lengthy discussion of papermaking embedded in *Illusions perdues* vote with a rapid flick of their index finger. More generally, readers have been disconcerted by the way the Balzacian novel appears to hesitate between fiction and non-fiction.

The very notion of the *Comédie humaine*, and its underpinning feature of reappearing characters, follows from what a hostile critic can easily present as a failure to bring the individual novel to a satisfactory close, a 'shortcoming' easily related to Balzac's apparent inability in many of his fictions (though not *La Cousine Bette*) to align his composition with the development of a master plot. The fact that the device of reappearing characters suggested itself only with the publication of *Le Père Goriot* in 1834–5 (that is, after the publication of a fair number of works later incorporated into the *Comédie humaine*) leads to chronological inconsistencies or worse, following the need to shoehorn existing characters into the overall design. It is only by a sleight of hand that the Rastignac of *Le Père Goriot* can be presented as the same character as the minor figure who bears that name in *La Peau de chagrin*.[5] (The master-title itself made no appearance before the publication of the *Avant-propos* (Preface) in 1842, though the concept of grouping works thematically as various kinds of *scène* or *étude* has much earlier origins in Balzac's writing career. The looseness of such categories, however, may be inferred from the way *Le Père Goriot* began life as a 'Scène de la vie parisienne', only to become in the *Comédie humaine* a 'Scène de la vie privée'.) Other characters have been found to display contradictions or inconsistencies that critics have attributed to uncertainty in their creator's mind. César Birotteau and his wife, Constance, might be adduced as examples.

The Goncourt brothers (Edmond and Jules), diarists of striking literary acuteness as well as sexual frankness, were also critical. Notwithstanding Edmond's conviction that Balzac was 'le grand des grands' and 'le père et le maître de nous tous' (Henry James would say the 'father of us all' and Paul Bourget 'notre père à tous'),[6] they lamented the fact that he was 'perhaps not so much a great physiological anatomist as a great painter of interiors. It sometimes seems that he observes furniture more closely than characters'.[7] Extravagant plots, encounters between over-emphatically contrasted characters encompassing extremes of innocence and evil, and a general heightened emotion are evidence of a derivation from stage melodrama and popular fictional stereotypes alike.[8] Balzac's earliest detractors were also quick to remind the reading public that the novelist had begun his career with the production of a batch of pseudonymous potboilers (which, in their use of irony, parody, satirical reference and self-conscious literary borrowing, in fact go beyond straightforward imitation) and that this was instantly detectable in the works of his 'maturity'. His pretensions to the rank of thinker or scientist, most obviously apparent in the analogy he draws, in his *Avant-propos*, between the *Comédie humaine* and the work of the zoologist Geoffroy Saint-Hilaire, are often derided as examples of 'pseudo-science', especially as regards his theory that human beings were endowed with a finite amount of 'vital fluid'. His attempts to chart the destructive effects of artistic and intellectual passion (not to say Romantic genius) in many of the stories comprising his *Études philosophiques* are easily charged with taking the investigation beyond the bounds of reason (though the young Gustave Flaubert would claim to have been devastated by the depiction of Louis Lambert's madness in the novel that bears his name). The plot of *Ursule Mirouët* hinges on a belief in mesmerism, allowing it to be consigned to the same category as the author's exercise in Swedenborgian mysticism, *Séraphita*. Still harder to swallow for other, if not the same, readers is the author's indefatigable dispensing of knowledge, his categorical explanations and his apparent readiness to sit in explicit judgement on his characters. Certainly when it comes to name-dropping (the range includes writers, playwrights, thinkers, inventors, politicians, soldiers, explorers, *restaurateurs*, artists and sculptors, composers, singers, actors and actresses, as well as figures from the Bible, legend, mythology and literature, in short a veritable who's who of European history and culture as well as of everyday Parisian life), Balzac has no rival among his fellow novelists. If he has counterparts with regard to this proliferation of proper names, they are Dante Alighieri and François Rabelais.

As far as his actual writing is concerned, readers are not infrequently disconcerted by the hotchpotch of different forms his novels take and by the impression that they grow in accordance with only the vaguest of plans, developing in unexpected ways in the process of composition (in clear contrast to the later, 'scientific' method of Émile Zola). Some lengthy novels, such as *Le Cousin Pons*, were at their conception intended as short stories. A number of Balzac's compositions could be held to occupy an ambiguous position somewhere between the novel and the short story without conforming to the rigorous norms governing such genres as the *Novelle*. His writing has often been held to display a disregard for the norms of 'good style'. Its loose, associative nature appears dictated by a desire to allow the container to expand to include a proliferation not merely of factual detail and compulsive comparison with other spheres, but also of synonyms or related terms that smack of the thesaurus. Not only can there be said to be indifference, on Balzac's part, to the 'mot juste', but his sentences may often seem to wobble as a result of the degree of approximation that follows from an excess of associations. As a result of this multiplicity of association, and of the fact that his writing is, in the broadest sense of the term, grounded in 'quotation', the translator is faced with singular difficulty. The inevitable loss of resonance, compounded by the lack of familiarity of many of the cultural, historical, literary or political references and the extent to which the original text weaves together a tissue of contemporary linguistic usage that is often oral or journalistic in nature (while relating to contemporary literary compositions that were self-consciously idiosyncratic), leaves the alleged shortcomings of composition and writing still more exposed. It is thus easy to understand why Balzac has never found the number of admirers in the English-speaking world that certain other European novelists have enjoyed. Yet the fact that, to his chagrin, he never acquired truly popular status in France (in contrast to his rival Eugène Sue, who had the knack of streamlining his fiction to meet the requirements of the new genre of serialised fiction), confirms that, for all the immediacy of certain of his characters and the memorable scenes in which some of them appear, his writing represented from the start a challenge to his French readers as well.

Significantly, Balzac's work has been found compelling above all by other creative artists – in France they include Gustave Doré (illustrator of Balzac's *Contes drolatiques*), Marcel Proust, Auguste Rodin and François Truffaut (in whose film *Les Quatre Cents Coups* the autobiographical schoolboy Antoine Doinel not only erects a physical altar to Balzac, but also, when faced with the requirement to produce in class a creative-writing assignment, writes out from memory a passage from *La Recherche de l'absolu*). It is eloquent that he was admired by poets such as Théophile Gautier, Charles Baudelaire and Victor Hugo, but consistently attacked by the critic Charles-Augustin Sainte-Beuve. In Russia, the egregious example of an admirer is Fyodor Dostoevsky (who, aged sixteen, published a translation of *Eugénie Grandet*); in German-speaking countries, Hugo von Hofmannsthal and Stefan Zweig; in Italy, Italo Calvino; in Mexico, Carlos Fuentes, in Australia, Marcus Clarke; and in the United States, Henry James, Theodore Dreiser and Henry Miller (whose admiration was nonetheless reserved for the mystical works *Séraphita* and *Louis Lambert*). In England, those inspired by Balzac have included the Brownings (Robert and Elizabeth Barrett), Algernon Swinburne, Oscar

Wilde and such *fin-de-siècle* figures as Aubrey Beardsley, Ernest Dowson (illustrator and translator of *La Fille aux yeux d'or* respectively) and Arthur Symons, but also, with different emphases, W. B. Yeats (in respect of Louis Lambert), Arnold Bennett, George Moore, D. H. Lawrence (at least at the time of his first novel *The White Peacock*), John Cowper Powys, Aleister Crowley and A. S. Byatt, while the critic F. R. Leavis was notably dismissive, as was Samuel Beckett.[9] The majority of the writers mentioned here are evidence that admiration for Balzac's creative genius rarely translates into an act of recognisable imitation. Instead, it is more likely to constitute recognition of a kindred spirit possessed of a highly individual creative imagination that seeks expression in the monumental and is to be regarded as being, in the words of Peter Brooks with reference to James, 'unclassifiable'.[10] (The *Comédie humaine* itself, with its frequent, enthusiastic reference to writers and artists of both the Renaissance and the contemporary Romantic era, may itself be read as, in part, a celebration of the creative imagination.) As Powys, who, like Crowley, shared Balzac's abiding passion for Rabelais, observed: 'Such primal force, capable of evoking a whole world of passionate living figures, comes only once or twice in the history of a race. There will be thousands of clever psychologists, thousands of more felicitous stylists, thousands of more exact copiers of reality. There will never be another Balzac.'[11]

There is no doubt that Balzac's mode of literary production plays into the hands of his critics. The expansionary nature of his writing invariably invites explanation in terms of the professional writer's payment by the word or number of volumes. The haphazard way in which his different works were produced, sometimes being set aside while other compositions were started (and, on occasion, completed), together with the ease with which they sometimes appear to respond to a particular publishing opportunity, suggest imperatives other than ones dictated by the artistic project itself. Where the inspiration for one of his texts is prompted by the work of a previous writer of prominence, as in the case, for example, of *Modeste Mignon* (Johann Wolfgang von Goethe) or *Melmoth réconcilié* (Charles Robert Maturin), the impression is still one of randomness. The variety of different types of starting point not only reinforces this impression of the random, but also draws attention to their inherent limitations and thus their inability to constitute a master pattern. Although Balzac's genius for inventing names for his characters has rarely been surpassed, his choices of title are not always inspired, with them often acquiring resonance retrospectively from the narrative itself. Many works are given new titles at a later date. Awareness of his habit of reusing material from his journalism with minimal alteration in his fictions may encourage the discovery of awkwardness, for example in the evocation of Paris in *La Fille aux yeux d'or*, though in the case of *Autre étude de femme* (surely an example of an uninspiring title), his skilful distribution of one such text among various speakers at an after-dinner gathering shows that this need not be so. The same composition incorporates several of his earlier short narratives, including *La Grande Bretèche*, which was much admired by Edith Wharton, who reworked its story in 'The Duchess of Prayer' and used it as a model for *Ethan Frome*. Each becomes the property of one of the fictional speakers. If this is not ineffective, the stories nonetheless add up to something less than a novel as conventionally conceived. A sense of the compositional imperfection that could result from the stitching together of existing texts, can, however, be gained from a reading of *La Femme de trente ans*, the genesis of which was exceptionally drawn out and complex. Moreover, few readers of Balzac will be unaware of his substantial rewriting of his texts at proof stage, which can easily, if unjustly, be taken as further evidence of a spontaneous and rapid approach to composition that was both unthinking and uncritical.

It is clear that for some readers, at least, Balzac's work will fail to survive such a multifaceted indictment. Yet it can be argued that the seemingly prejudicial lack of order and control displayed by his compositions (accompanied, paradoxically, by the impression of an author disporting himself as demiurge) is in fact a symptom of the way the Balzacian text develops in response to an ambition to present a complex and ongoing engagement with the contemporary world, rather than a set of preformed judgements or observations.

Walter Benjamin noted that 'The *Human Comedy* comprises a series of works which are not novels, in the ordinary sense of the term, but something like epic transcription of the tradition from the first decades of the Restoration'.[12] As one modern-day historian has put it, 'Balzac's true concern ... was not the individual fates of his unheroic heroes and heroines, but the collective fate of French society.'[13] As a result, the novel and its constituent elements are placed by the author under constant critical scrutiny. A striking feature of the *Comédie humaine* is the extent to which fictions are recounted by characters within the composition itself and responded to, often ironically, by others, in a manner that loosely recalls such works as the sixteenth-century *Heptaméron* of Marguerite de Navarre. In *La Muse du département*, the irreverent journalist Lousteau performs a brilliant hatchet job on some sheets from a fictitious novel conventionally entitled *Olympia, ou les vengeances romaines*. For a novelist so often assumed to seek the reader's suspension of disbelief, it is striking how often in Balzac's work the fictional as a category is subjected to critical judgement, not to say adverse criticism.

For all its continuing reliance on character and plot, the Balzacian novel grows out of the sense of a mismatch between story and the ambition (derived from Walter Scott but here radicalised beyond recognition) to serve as the historian of contemporary French society. In its most basic form, the mismatch stems from story's defining characteristic: the possession of a beginning, middle and end. That closure was inimical to Balzac's ambition for the novel is clearly seen from the 'conclusion' to *Le Père Goriot*: Rastignac's celebrated challenge to Paris, which serves as a transition to a new opening, as well as providing an illustration of the way the 'device' of reappearing characters was a logical necessity imposed by the nature of his project. Still more significantly, story, through its commitment to resolution of conflict or uncertainty, was indelibly linked to naive forms of idealism. Balzac's response was to take categories of story in which this was most evidently the case, only to allow the stereotype to be distorted by the realities of society. An obvious example is the genre of the fairy story, to which Balzac's fictions frequently allude, but which, in its Balzacian version, inevitably fails to achieve its expected resolution.

A still more extensive concern with the liberation of the novel from the straitjacket of its components as traditionally conceived is, arguably, the key to Balzac's achievement. The consciousness within the text of a potential multiplicity of stories (or versions of a story) prevents any one of them from expanding to fill the composition, to the advantage of its overall scope and power. Just as there is no clear-cut distinction between major and minor characters (with seemingly major figures reappearing in minor roles in subsequent novels and vice versa), the conventional hierarchy with regard to plots is rarely observed. The very notion of plot is, in fact, inapplicable in any rigorous sense to Balzac's practice. Often what is presented is little more than a representative activity or behaviour indicative of character, though with the inestimable consequence of enhancing the composition's mimetic dimension. While story retains an obvious importance in Balzac's short fictions, once the latter begin to expand in scope, for example in the three works that comprise (the incomplete) *Histoire des Treize*,[14] the exaggerated nature of the peripeteia, or plot reversals, leads not so much to the failure of any desire to be found convincing, but to works that downgrade the importance of plot and bring into play levels of meaning other than those attached to the literal events recorded. Elsewhere in the *Comédie humaine*, stories escape the limitations they are prone to impose by remaining closer than might have been expected to their embryonic state. Balzac's practice in this respect provides a valuable aid to an understanding of the fact that it was the 'self-conscious' tradition represented by Rabelais and Laurence Sterne's *Tristram Shandy* to which he was instinctively drawn. Paradoxically, Sterne's radical deferral of the story of the 'King of Bohemia and his seven castles' has a profound, if muted, echo throughout Balzac's work, contrary to the implications of the discussion by Robert Alter, whose questionable conclusion that Balzac the realist stands in opposition to the European masterworks of self-conscious narrative epitomised by *Don Quixote* is dependent on an unduly restrictive focus on the way the reflection on the business of 'making books' incorporated into *Illusions perdues* merely assumes the form of a technical account of 'printing and paper production'.[15]

Character in the *Comédie humaine*, however memorable as far as its dominant traits are concerned, reveals, on closer examination, a similar embryonic nature. To take a single example, the retired clerk Poiret, now resident in the Pension Vauquer and the accomplice of Mlle Michonneau in the betrayal of the Balzacian 'hero' par excellence, the escaped convict (and future Head of Police) Vautrin, while incontrovertibly presented in a negative light, is, in respect of his past employment and its assumed effect on his facial appearance, teasingly evoked with the aid of a number of unresolved hypotheses.[16]

This is in keeping with Balzac's habitual emphasis on enigma, which is an important device in his foregrounding of an interpretative activity, but also a feature that exists in a state of (productive) tension with the apparently reliable information, provided by the character himself, that he had been a defence witness in a high-profile court case involving a widow found guilty of fraud and attempted murder. It has, however, a further significance, one rooted precisely in the character's 'unfinished' nature. By truncating Poiret's 'knowability', Balzac emphasises his potential to contain within him a host of different, if related, versions. He thereby reinforces the sense that his underlying concern is with the representative rather than the unique. As a result, not only is the reader given the impression that the character has the potential to develop (or acquire a past) in a number of different ways, depending on the conjunction of circumstances in which he finds himself, but there is also the concomitant realisation that, when it comes to a description and discussion of the figure in question, the narrator has an infinite number of possible details from which to choose at will. The focus is thereby transferred from the character's essence, conceived as the determinant of his behaviour in relation to the plot, to the question of how he is perceived, and indeed might further be perceived, by the observer. An otherwise banal figure becomes thereby an object of infinite fascination by virtue of an emphasis on potentiality. It might be objected that Poiret is a caricature rather than a character, but this is to ignore the fact that an explicit reference to caricature in his description serves to blur the distinction: the narrator muses that he would have appeared 'unreal' ('hors du vrai') if drawn by a caricaturist, when it is in terms of a verbal equivalent of caricature that he has already been depicted ('une espèce de mécanique' (a kind of clockwork figure)). Caricature thus hesitates between being a pre-existent component of the external world and an artistically distorted treatment. Furthermore, in tune with Balzac's omnipresent obsession with onomastic significance (which he traces back to *Tristram Shandy*), the name Poiret inevitably evokes the contemporary political caricatures of Louis-Philippe as a pear. While there is no question of the cadaverous clerk blossoming into the central figure of a fully developed political allegory, the momentary and, as it were, parenthetical link to the 'Citizen King' provides a pointer to the way Balzac's expansive and allusive representation of character proliferates potential meanings by virtue of a wilful hesitation between the real and the allegorical.

A similar logic may be considered to determine the nature of the Balzacian narrative persona. While endowed with a host of characteristics suggestive of the colourful and idiosyncratic author himself, and primordial among them an indefatigable intellectual curiosity that extends to all things great and small, the narrative persona is not a 'finished' version of the author,[17] but an embodiment of potentiality, an exploitation of the way the creative endeavour permits an enhancement of self, and a form of unrestricted self-expression, inconceivable outside the act of writing. Unimpeded by a requirement to provide an accurate or considered representation of his beliefs or position, the narrative persona is, in the terms of Roland Barthes, written by the text. The latter's expansion through association thereby multiplies the ways of evoking the subject of its representation. The dominant formal feature is the list, which, by virtue of its often unexpected length, has the paradoxical effect of highlighting the possibility of infinite continuation and thus its essentially 'unfinished' state. Both the list and the Balzacian narrator's relentless recourse to comparison, which makes use of a heterogeneous collection of cultural and other references, are key determinants of a textual fabric that is characterised by a mixing of high and low, learned and commonplace, oral and written, general and specific (or technical). A. S. Byatt speaks pertinently of Balzac's display of 'a kind of manic inclusiveness of many levels and styles of discourse'.[18] It was an idiom with which Balzac had experimented in his contributions to the satirical press in the early 1830s. While obviously at odds with certain aesthetic ideals, the Balzacian text constantly transcends its already multidimensional perspective to suggest that the picture can be evoked, and its significance understood, in manifold ways, few of which can be more than hinted at. As such, the narrator's seemingly emphatic pronouncements invite re-assessment, as provocative elements in a debate.

In its provision of a constant renewal of ways of looking at things, and as an embodiment of creative energy, the text may also be held to silence its cacophonous tendency. Through its emphasis on its medium, which includes constant exploitation of the latter's auditory dimension, the text also invites appreciation as a spectacle of language. Yet if Balzac's is a ludic idiom (one that continues through its self-conscious use of language to recall the writings of Rabelais), the ludic was not for him an aim in itself, however much he revelled in linguistic play, but a further means of incorporating an unstable, yet suggestive, realm of multiple reference, an authentic representation of a world characterised by constant change and uncertainty, and thus by the most grotesque of contrasts, a world that stimulated ever more numerous competing, and essentially incompatible, ways of making sense of its tensions and contradictions.

In short, what Balzac's works of fiction may be said to provide, in contrast with the novels with which his earliest readers were familiar, is a sort of 'pre-text', in which an initial sketch leads to further, alternative sketches rather than commitment to any one through its completion. If such writing has a parallel, it is with the artistic concept of the 'non-fini', with which Balzac would have been familiar through his having frequented various artists' studios in the early 1830s, or with what Baudelaire, in *Le Salon de 1859*, would later term, with reference to Eugène Delacroix, 'l'infini dans le fini' (the infinite in the finite). This conception of the Balzacian novel is in obvious contrast with the widely held view that regards it as a complete and finished product, characterised by an insistence on the explicit and the conclusive. Such a view, encouraged by the episode in Jean-Paul Sartre's *La Nausée* in which the protagonist contrasts, unfavourably, his reading of *Eugénie Grandet* with the chatter in the cafe around him, might indeed be regarded as positing precisely the type of composition that Balzac's procedures were designed to avoid. Its formulation is dependent on a reading that cuts through the apparent verbiage to the most accessible elements of characterisation and plot, which are then allowed to harden into an image suggestive of definitive representation. From the present perspective, such a reading can only be regarded as ducking the challenge presented by the extraordinarily complex texture of Balzac's writing, in which the question of signification is constantly in play (for example, in buildings, dress, physiognomy and gait), but with each potential interpretation being held in check by the very plurality of which it is part, in a way that also thwarts all attempts to establish a hierarchy of meaning.

The consequence of Balzac's highly original approach to narrative fiction is that the overall significance of his work is to be sought less in the trajectories of his characters or the particular outcome of events (which, arguably, could just as easily have produced the opposite conclusion, success in the *Comédie humaine* being disturbingly close to failure), than in the immediate experience of the real in its form as textual surrogate. Not only does the latter offer the reader an education in the way the familiar backcloth of everyday urban reality is saturated with meanings, the essentially associative nature of Balzacian *écriture* maximises the play of connotations. It thus offers a constant demonstration of the way in which textual elements interrelate to form kaleidoscopic patterns of signification that are both alluring and ultimately evasive, as a result of an inevitable encounter with what deconstructionists call *aporia*, or blind spots. In this way, the reader's assumptions are both solicited and challenged. Notwithstanding his advertised commitment to legitimate Monarchy, the Church and the Family, Balzac's practice suggests a superior compulsion to raise questions and thwart easy answers, through an identification of the numerous factors and potential viewpoints in play. The reader is left with the sense that any situation or outcome is the product of complex, interlinked, and constantly evolving chains of disparate and contingent detail. Everything is related. Everything has a knock-on effect. Individuals are perennially caught up in a web of circumstances to which they contribute but which remain beyond their control. In a representation that is rooted in a concept of relativism, any act will appear different according to the perspective from which it is viewed.[19] The result is ambiguity with regard to likeability no less than to morality. Above all, the Balzacian text invites the reader to engage at every level with an interplay between ignorance and knowledge, or, in Paul de Man's admirable phrase, 'blindness and insight'.[20]

## Note on editions/translations

The canonical edition of *La Comédie humaine* is in the Bibliothèque de la Pléiade, 12 vols. (Paris: Gallimard, 1976–81). Many of the novels are in French paperback editions, notably by Garnier-Flammarion and Folio, with invaluable critical apparatus.

Despite the challenge of Balzac's idiosyncratic writing, good English versions of his best-known works are available in Penguin Classics and OUP's World Classics. There has been no recent attempt to translate the whole *Comédie humaine* into English although the late nineteenth century produced three more or less complete editions, some of which have been reprinted, with new introductions, notably by Everyman's Library in the 1990s. For the history of Balzac in English, see Michael Tilby, 'Honoré de Balzac,' in Olive Classe, ed., *Encyclopedia of Literary Translation into English*, 3 vols. (London/Chicago: Fitzroy-Dearborn, 2000).

*Notes*

1 More recently, his writing has re-emerged as a potent source of inspiration, as can be seen in the work of some of the most significant contemporary French writers of fiction, notably Pierre Michon, Richard Millet and Régis Jauffret. See Aline Mura-Brunel, *Silences du roman: Balzac et le romanesque contemporain* (Amsterdam/New York: Rodopi, 2004), ch. 12.

2 'In Scott there is always an uncomplicated and direct interrelationship between ideology and composition. In the other great realists this connection is generally more indirect and complicated.' Georg Lukács, *Writer and Critic and Other Essays* (London: Merlin Press, 1970), p. 141.

3 Articles published as a volume in 1869. The name Ferragus is taken from the title character of one of the three stories that make up Balzac's *Histoire des Treize*. All translations of quotations used in this chapter are my own.

4 Henry James, 'The Lesson of Balzac', in James, *Literary Criticism*, ed. by Leon Edel (New York: Library of America, 1984), vol. II, p. 130. In the words of another nineteenth-century American critic: 'He [Balzac] had great acuteness of observation and brilliant fancy, but his delineations are often unnatural and extravagant, and his writings are deficient in moral elevation.' Joseph Thomas, *Universal Pronouncing Dictionary of Biography and Mythology* (Philadelphia: Lippincott, 1870), p. 256.

5 On the other hand, the du Bousquier of *La Vieille Fille* becomes, without explanation, du Croisier in *Le Cabinet des antiques*; the failure to harmonise the names, rather than constituting an authorial oversight, may be held to reflect complex, and ultimately unanswerable, questions as to whether they are one and the same figure.

6 Respectively, 'the foremost among the great'; 'the father and master of us all'; and 'our universal father'. In his funeral address, Victor Hugo had contented himself with the formulation 'un des premiers parmi les plus grands, un des plus hauts parmi les meilleurs' (one of the first among the greatest, one of the highest among the best).

7 Edmond and Jules de Goncourt, *Journal*, 6 October 1861.

8 Naomi Schor has noted: 'Ever since Genette, we have learned to view with suspicion the strategies enlisted by Balzac to institute and ensure the (pseudo-) verisimilitude of his fiction.' *Reading in Detail: Aesthetics and the Feminine* (London: Methuen, 1987), pp. 143–4.

9 With regard to *La Cousine Bette*, Beckett declared in a letter of February 1935 to Thomas McGreevy: 'The bathos of style & thought is so enormous that I wonder is he writing seriously or in parody. And yet I go on reading it.' *The Letters of Samuel Beckett*, ed. Martha Dow Fehsenfeld and Lois More Overbeck, vol. I, *1929–1940* (Cambridge University Press, 2009), p. 245, while the narrator of Beckett's *Dream of Fair to Middling Women* (London/Paris: Calder, 1993), p. 119, opines: 'To read Balzac is to receive the impression of a chloroformed world.' As for Naguib Mahfouz, the 'Egyptian Balzac', he claimed he was unable to read Balzac, having already read Flaubert and Stendhal (see Rasheed El-Enany, *Naguib Mahfouz: The Pursuit of Meaning* (London/New York: Routledge, 1993), p. 17.

10 Peter Brooks, *Henry James Goes to Paris* (Princeton University Press, 2007), p. 78.

11 John Cowper Powys, *Essays on Rousseau, Balzac, Victor Hugo* (Girard, KS: Haldeman-Julius, 1923), pp. 43–4.

12 Walter Benjamin, *The Arcades Project* (Cambridge, MA/London: Belknap, 1999), p. 850.
13 Sharif Gemie, 'Balzac and the Moral Crisis of the July Monarchy', *European History Quarterly*, 19 (1989), [469]–94 (p. 469).
14 Namely *Ferragus*, *La Duchesse de Langeais* and *La Fille aux yeux d'or*.
15 See Robert Alter, *Partial Magic: The Novel as Self-Conscious Genre* (Berkeley/ London: University of California Press, 1975), p. 105.
16 See, in this connection, Helen Small, *The Long Life* (Oxford University Press, 2007), p. 166. Small, however, maintains that this pretence of ignorance is in contrast to 'the usually omniscient narrative voice'.
17 In his preface to *Le Lys dans la vallée*, Balzac complains of those readers who confuse the narrator with the author. The apparent proliferation of authorial opinions might duly be likened to the 'opinions' of Tristram Shandy.
18 In her chapter on Balzac in Franco Moretti, ed., *The Novel* (Princeton University Press, 2006), vol. II, p. 402.
19 James's later experiments with perspectivism may thus be seen as derived from the 'lesson of Balzac' rather than its rejection.
20 Paul de Man, *Blindness and Insight: Essays in the Rhetoric of Contemporary Criticism* (Oxford University Press, 1971).

*Further reading*

Beizer, J., *Family Plots: Balzac's Narrative Generations* (New Haven, CT: Yale University Press, 1986)
Bellos, D., *Balzac Criticism in France 1850–1900: The Making of a Reputation* (Oxford: Clarendon Press, 1976)
Bersani, L., *Balzac to Beckett: Center and Circumference in French Fiction* (New York: Oxford University Press, 1970)
Butor, M., *Improvisations sur Balzac*, 3 vols. (Paris: Éditions de la Différence, 1998)
Farrant, T., *Balzac's Shorter Fictions: Genesis and Genre* (Oxford University Press, 2002)
Hunt, H. J., *Balzac's 'Comédie humaine'*, new edn (London: Athlone, 1964)
Massol, C., *Une poétique de l'enigme: le récit herméneutique balzacien* (Geneva: Droz, 2006)
Mitterand, H., *L'Illusion réaliste: de Balzac à Aragon* (Paris: Presses Universitaires de France, 1994)
Mozet, N., *Balzac au pluriel* (Paris: Presses Universitaires de France, 1990)
Prendergast, C., *Balzac: Fiction and Melodrama* (London: Arnold, 1978)
Schor, N., *Breaking the Chain: Women, Theory and French Realist Fiction* (New York: Columbia University Press, 1985)
Tilby, M., ed., *Balzac* (London/New York: Longman, 1995)

# 12

JOHN BOWEN

# Charles Dickens (1812–1870): Englishman and European

Charles Dickens drew deeply on his European precursors. The debt was repaid in the admiration and imitation of many later authors including Ivan Turgenev, Gustave Flaubert, Fyodor Dostoevsky, Leo Tolstoy, Henry James (albeit more ambivalently), Franz Kafka, James Joyce, Jorge Luis Borges, V. S. Naipaul and Salman Rushdie. Yet Dickens is often seen as simply and quintessentially English. He was, it is true, saturated in English culture, and his work invited to the fictional table the people that genteel fiction had largely relegated to walk-on parts: servants, children, working men and women, poor clerks, a drunken nurse or street crossing sweeper, an unnamed but unforgettable Chancery prisoner. No comparable *œuvre* grants the dispossessed such fictional centrality. But critics have been wrong to see this inclusiveness as a peculiarly national quality. While, in Malcolm Andrews's words, 'it is hard to think of any other English writer whose … books yield such an abundance of particularised national life', the rich depiction of English – and particularly London – life is regularly tested against those of other nations and cultures in his fiction, journalism and travel books alike.[1] This may be by a passing allusion, as when in *Bleak House*, Dickens recalls from his boyhood the 'poor Spanish refugees, walking about in cloaks, smoking little paper cigars' (ch. 43) but it also includes extended cultural comparisons and soundings of national difference, as in *A Tale of Two Cities*, *Martin Chuzzlewit*, *Little Dorrit*, *Pictures from Italy* and *American Notes*.

It is lopsided, therefore, to see, like F. G. Kitton, 'The Dickens Country' as only English or to argue, with Peter Ackroyd, that Dickens in America 'discovered his essential Englishness; indeed his need for English life … his sojourn on alien shores made him realise how English in fact he was'.[2] Dickens, whose readership and correspondence stretched from Siberia to San Francisco, was an experimental writer who borrowed liberally. He learned from many strands of European fiction, fluently assimilating and reinvigorating the work of his precursors. *A Christmas Carol*, for example, draws on Gothic and ghost stories, allegory, parable and conversion narrative, short story and fable, but transforms them into something distinctively new. Hence, it is right for Georg Lukács to link the early work, *Barnaby Rudge*, to the historical novel created by Walter Scott.[3] Dickens admired Scott and there are clear parallels between Madge Wildfire from *The Heart of Mid-Lothian* and Barnaby himself; and between the burning of the Tollbooth and the destruction of Newgate prison in these same works. But the book also owes much to the traditions of Gothic and the uncanny story. *Barnaby Rudge* shares with the work of E. T. A. Hoffmann (translated by Dickens's friend Thomas Carlyle) a fascination with uncanny effects and the permeable boundaries between animate and inanimate things. As in Hoffmann, the human is never definitively distinguished from the mechanical, the inanimate, the ghostly, the animal or the dead.

We see, then, a strange *crossing* of very different kinds of writing in Dickens. *David Copperfield*, for example – a story about the struggles and growth to emotional maturity of a sensitive young man – invokes the tradition of the European *Bildungsroman*. Yet, as Franco Moretti has shown, its valuing of the childlike and its fascinated intimacy with the monstrous and grotesque in characters such as Murdstone or Uriah Heep often cut across the guiding assumptions of that genre. For Moretti, the English novel, as encapsulated by *David Copperfield* or *Great Expectations*, devalues the developmental aspect of youthful opportunity in favour of a regressive attachment to childhood values and insight. Whereas Stendhal's *Le Rouge et le noir* (*The Red and the Black*) or Honoré de Balzac's *Illusions perdues* (*Lost Illusions*) show a society open to the life-changing adventure of adolescence, English fiction is the product of a 'culture of stability and conformity'.[4] But Moretti underestimates Dickens's conception of character, which is less a matter of psychological inwardness and depth, and more akin to a performance, a matter of repeated actions and behaviour rather than an intrinsic quality. Dickens is thus able to show more acutely than most of his contemporaries the force both of 'unconscious' motives and social determinism: the ways that characters act that are decided either above or below the level of the stable subject. *Great Expectations*, Dickens's later novel of development, brings the *Bildungsroman* radically into crisis. Pip discovers too late that his gentility, self-understanding and, indeed, entire social being, are predicated on a fundamental misrecognition: his wealth comes not from Miss Havisham but from the transported convict Magwitch. His life has been entangled in a plot determined long beforehand in a complex backstory of crime, violence and erotic betrayal. Pip's story is hardly one of emotional choice, development or fulfilment: knowledge comes too late and his sentimental education, like Flaubert's, is disillusion. The self is emptied out, not fulfilled.

Dickens left several accounts of his childhood reading, and a famous passage of *David Copperfield* seems closely autobiographical:

> My father had left a small collection of books in a little room upstairs, to which
> I had access (for it adjoined my own) and which nobody else in our house ever
> troubled. From that blessed little room, Roderick Random, Peregrine Pickle,
> Humphrey Clinker, Tom Jones, the Vicar of Wakefield, Don Quixote, Gil Blas,
> and Robinson Crusoe, came out, a glorious host, to keep me company. They
> kept alive my fancy, and my hope of something beyond that place and time, –
> they, and the Arabian Nights, and the Tales of the Genii. (ch. 4)

This is a long and varied list for such a small boy: a 'host' of different heroes, writers and kinds of writing, all of which matter. It is also an exclusively male tradition: male heroes and male authors. No Jane Austen, Mary Shelley, Maria Edgeworth or Fanny Burney here, although his early reading did include Elizabeth Inchbald's farces. He was later to admire the work of George Eliot and Elizabeth Gaskell, while *Great Expectations* contains a brilliantly complex allusion to Mary Shelley's *Frankenstein* in which Pip imagines himself not, like Frankenstein, a creator pursued by his monstrous creation but as the creation of a monster:

> The imaginary student pursued by the misshapen creature he had impiously
> made, was not more wretched than I, pursued by the creature who had made
> me, and recoiling from him with a stronger repulsion, the more he admired me
> and the fonder he was of me. (vol. iii, ch. 1)

But his early reading is in an overwhelmingly masculine and comic tradition, both mock-epic like Miguel de Cervantes's *Don Quixote* and Henry Fielding's *Tom Jones*, and picaresque where pride of place goes to Tobias Smollett, who wrote *Roderick Random*, *Peregrine Pickle* and *Humphrey Clinker* and translated *Gil Blas* (1715–35) by Alain-René Lesage. This lineage gives Dickens's earlier works, particularly *Nicholas Nickleby*, *The Pickwick Papers* and *The Old Curiosity Shop*, their characteristic freewheeling and open structures. The mention of Oliver Goldsmith's *The Vicar of Wakefield* (1766) and Dickens's affection for the work of Laurence Sterne signal another major affiliation: to the novel of sentiment and to the affective power of literature, its ability to move its readers to laughter, tears or righteous indignation. Finally, *Robinson Crusoe*'s presence registers Dickens's complex relationship to fictional realism. *Oliver Twist*, for example, is a pioneering text of social realism, yet its realist impulses are matched by an equally strong commitment to the power of language, fiction or 'Fancy' to transform the world.

The contemporary novelist whom Dickens most resembles is Balzac (1799–1850). They never met but share a heroic social range and energy of achievement, a love of theatrical and melodramatic plotting and an unquenchable appetite for fictional creation and investigation. Both are characteristically post-Revolutionary novelists, in that much of the potentially tragic energies of their plotting motivate not tragedy but the 'strong emotionalism; moral polarization and schematization; extreme states of being, situations, actions; overt villainy, persecution of the good, and final reward of virtue; inflated and extravagant expression; dark plottings, suspense, breathtaking peripety' that are the characteristic marks of melodrama.[5] Henry James saw an essential resemblance in their 'intensity of imaginative power, the power of evoking invisible objects and figures, seeing them with the force of hallucination and making others see them all but just as vividly', which he believed was only surpassed by William Shakespeare.[6] The evidence of what Dickens thought of Balzac's work is second-hand but shows a decidedly mixed set of feelings, both attraction and repulsion. One contemporary claimed that 'Dickens had an anxious, even frightened, admiration of Balzac. What he held against him was his frenzied exhibition of self'.[7] His close friend Wilkie Collins also reports Dickens's ambivalence, not because of Balzac's egotism but because of the complexity of his plotting: 'I ... firmly believe he never read one of Balzac's novels. There again the [plot] developments were too much for him!'[8] We do not usually think of Dickens as being impatient with complex plot developments.

Along with the many strands of European influence already identified, David Copperfield's love of *The Arabian Nights* (first translated into English in 1706) and *The Tales of the Genii* (a collection of pseudo-Oriental tales by James Ridley, 1764) were Dickens's also, and they show how his work exceeds a merely European and novelistic inheritance. *The Thousand and One* (or *Arabian*) *Nights* are a constant emotional resource for his work, often explicitly invoked at moments of emotional urgency. When the young David Copperfield bites his wicked stepfather Edward Murdstone, for example, he is sent away to school, where every night he tells stories to his new friend James Steerforth, comparing himself as he does so to 'the Sultana Scheherazade' (ch. 7). This is the first moment of storytelling in Dickens's most autobiographical work, a moment that will eventually lead David to a successful career as a writer, echoing that of his creator. It is also a scene of seduction, of two boys in bed together, one of whom, Steerforth, will betray the other. Fictional and novelistic energies in Dickens's work are never far from erotic and seductive ones.

Dickens shows an equally strong attraction to what the Russian critic and theorist Mikhail Bakhtin called 'the carnivalesque', in the thousands of plays, shows, entertainments, circuses and pantomimes that he delighted in seeing throughout his life, the consciousness of which saturates his fiction, from the description of Astley's Circus in *Sketches by Boz* to the plottings of Silas Wegg, the grotesque ballad seller of his last complete novel, *Our Mutual Friend*. Dickens draws deeply on theatrical modes of plotting and characterisation, and his writing is studded with allusions to Shakespeare and other dramatists. But his eye is as often drawn to Punch and Judy shows, circuses and fairs – entertainments that, through their bodily dexterity and expressivity, migrate easily across cultural and national boundaries. This appears most extensively in the circus worlds of *The Old Curiosity Shop* and *Hard Times* but occurs throughout his work. We see it in his fascination with grotesque bodies, their appetites and desires, and those strange prosthetic additions, such as wooden legs, 'false curls . . . false eyebrows . . . false teeth . . . false complexion' (*Dombey and Son*, ch. 21) and with the many machines, animals and birds, corpses, dolls and puppets that imitate, parody or act as simulacra of human beings. When Bella Wilfer marries John Rokesmith in *Our Mutual Friend*, they are accompanied to the wedding, for no apparent reason, by a character only known as 'old Gruff and Glum' who has not one but two wooden legs (bk II, ch. 4). When Fanny Dorrit is negotiating her romance with Mrs Merdle in *Little Dorrit*, a parrot joins in, who first of all completes Mrs Merdle's sentence 'so expressively that Mrs Merdle was under no necessity' to do so, then adds a 'most piercing shriek, as if its name were Society' before eventually breaking into 'a violent fit of laughter' (bk I, ch. 20). A highlight of Dickens's travel book *Pictures from Italy* is its description of an 'unspeakably ludicrous' puppet show in Genoa of Napoleon's last years on St Helena, which shows him guarded by its English governor, Sir Hudson Lowe, or, as the puppets call him '"Sir Yew ud se on Low" (the ow, as in cow).' The puppet Sir Hudson 'was a perfect mammoth of a man . . . hideously ugly, with a monstrously disproportionate face, and a great clump for the lower- jaw, to express his tyrannical and obdurate nature', whereas Napoleon is mainly characterised by his boots, which 'were so wonderfully beyond control, and did such marvellous things of their own accord: doubling themselves up, and getting under tables, and dangling in the air, and sometimes skating away with him, out of all human knowledge, when he was in full speech' (ch. 4). There was 'no plot at all'; great historical actors become grotesque puppets; their boots take charge of their lives. Through comic inversion, as with the military games of Sterne's Uncle Toby, the bitter European conflicts of a generation earlier transmogrify into farce.

So Dickens as a European novelist is flanked by his allegiances to other cultural forms, such as oriental tales, popular entertainments and uncanny stories, traditions which refresh and question what he learns from his novelist predecessors and contemporaries. Dickens transforms everything that he touches and, in characteristically Victorian fashion, loses a good deal of the harshness, sexual frankness and violence that often featured in the novels of Cervantes and Smollett. Sexually, he is a good deal less bold than, say, Fielding or Balzac and although he satirised in *Our Mutual Friend* the ghastly Mr Podsnap, who asks about everything whether 'it would bring a blush into the cheek of the young person?', he nevertheless wrote his novels intending that they should be family reading (ch. 11). This is not entirely a loss: the sexual energy of the works is not so much repressed as redistributed in ways that defy or estrange the norms of heterosexual romance. His works are full of 'queer' families, of same-sex and perverse desires, and show the compulsive oddity of eroticism, unconscious mental processes and emotional affect (Sigmund Freud was a great admirer of Dickens's work). This sometimes appears in the form of a sexuality that is disavowed or allied to death and transcendence but, even in those cases, it shows its affinity to sexual aggression and transgression. Quilp, for example, the grotesquely hand-rubbing villain of *Old Curiosity Shop*, asks the thirteen-year-old Little Nell if she would like to '"be Mrs Quilp the second, when Mrs Quilp the first is dead, sweet Nell," ... wrinkling up his eyes and luring her towards him with his bent forefinger, "to be my wife, my little cherry-cheeked, red-lipped wife"'(ch. 6). When he later takes over Nell's home, we find him 'coiled ... in the child's little bed' (ch. 11).

There is ambivalence about the representation of sexuality. In one of the most important statements that Dickens made about his art, he envied the relative freedom of Continental European novelists:

> I have always a fine feeling of the honest state into which we have got, when some smooth gentleman says to me or to some one else when I am by, how odd it is that the hero of an English book is always uninteresting – too good – too natural, &c. I am continually hearing this of Scott from English people here, who pass their lives with Balzac and Sand. But O my smooth friend, what a shining impostor you must think yourself and what an ass you must think me, when you suppose that by putting a brazen face upon it you can blot out of my knowledge the fact that this same unnatural young gentleman (if to be decent is to be necessarily unnatural), whom you meet in those other books and in mine, must be presented to you in that unnatural aspect by reason of your morality, and is not to have, I will not say any of the indecencies you like, but not even any of the experiences, trials, perplexities, and confusions insepar-able from the making or unmaking of all men! (*Letters*, VII.203)

Yet Dickens could say of Wilkie Collins, who was much more willing than he to challenge the pieties and prejudices of the Victorian reading public: 'He occasionally expounds a code of morals, taken from modern French Novels, which I instantly and with becoming gravity Smash' (*Letters*, IV.155).

## Dickens and Europe

Dickens's life coincided with an almost unbroken period of European peace. There were political upheavals, particularly in the revolutionary years of 1830 and 1848, but the single major military conflict between states was the Crimean War of 1853–6. Long years of peace enabled him to travel widely: he went to Belgium in 1836, probably to see the field of Waterloo as a possible subject for his fiction; he spent a year in Italy travelling via France in 1843, a trip commemorated in *Pictures from Italy*; he holidayed in Switzerland in 1846, and took many family holidays in northern France. In the last decade of his life he owned a secret getaway at Condette, near Boulogne. It is likely that his mistress, Ellen Ternan, lived in France for some years; they may have even had a child together there. Travel always excited him: on arriving in Marseilles, he wrote to his friend John Forster that 'Surrounded by strange and perfectly novel circumstances, I feel as if I had a new head on side by side with my old one' (*Letters*, IV.155). He read widely in European literature: one summer, for example, he 'took in all the minor tales as well as the plays of Voltaire, several of the novels (old favourites with him) of Paul de Kock'.[9] The inventory of his library in 1844 shows collected editions of Rabelais, as well as multi-volume anthologies of German and Italian novels (*Letters*, IV.712–25). A catalogue compiled after his death shows five volumes of Turgenev translated into French and nineteen volumes of Thomas Roscoe's translations of Italian, German and Spanish novels: 'the most interesting and valuable translations from the best authors, both ancient and modern, accompanied by critical and biographical notices'.[10] Likewise Michel de Montaigne, Alphonse de Lamartine and Friedrich Schiller, as well as fifty-six volumes of *Parnaso italiano* and a French translation of Nikolai Gogol, to say nothing of German, Dutch, Italian, Polish, Russian and French translations of his own work.

His son, Henry Fielding Dickens, reported that this archetypally 'English' writer 'used to say, laughingly, that his sympathies were so much with the French that he ought to have been born a Frenchman'.[11] He spoke French and Italian well and gave several of his novels, most notably *Little Dorrit* and *A Tale of Two Cities*, significant European dimensions, both in settings and characters. Paris was a particular love; Parisians he called 'the first people in the Universe' (*Letters*, v.42). George Orwell remarked that 'One very striking thing about Dickens, especially considering the time he lived in, is his lack of vulgar nationalism'.[12] Although *Little Dorrit* has a caricature French villain, Rigaud alias Blandois, whose 'moustache went up under his nose, and his nose came down over his moustache, in a very sinister and cruel manner', Dickens was notably unchauvinistic, in both his journalism and fiction (bk 1, ch. 1). A piece entitled 'A Monument of French Folly', for example, is actually an attack on English parochialism.[13] He admired the French legal code, asking his subeditor on the journal *Household Words* if it would 'be possible to … write popularly about the monstrous absurdity of our laws, and to compare them with the Code Napoleon?' (*Letters*, VIII.21). In his fiction we see a consistent debunking of English chauvinism and self-regard. The water-rate collector Mr Lillyvick, for example, interrogates Nicholas Nickleby about the French language:

> 'What sort of language do you consider French, sir?' …
> 'A pretty language, certainly,' replied Nicholas; 'and as it has a name for everything, and admits of elegant conversation about everything, I presume it is a sensible one.' …
> 'What's the water in French, sir?'
> 'L'EAU,' replied Nicholas.
> 'Ah!' said Mr Lillyvick, shaking his head mournfully, 'I thought as much. Lo, eh? I don't think anything of that language – nothing at all.'
> (ch. 16)

The same energy animates the pronouncements of Sapsea, the asinine Mayor of Cloisterham in the unfinished *The Mystery of Edwin Drood* (1870), who, when he 'has once declared anything to be Un-English, he considers that thing everlastingly sunk in the bottomless pit' (ch. 14). But Mr Podsnap in *Our Mutual Friend* is Dickens's most devastating presentation of British chauvinism:

> Mr Podsnap's world was not a very large world, morally; no, nor even geographically: seeing that although his business was sustained upon commerce with other countries, he considered other countries, with that important reservation, a mistake, and of their manners and customs would conclusively observe, 'Not English!' when, PRESTO! with a flourish of the arm, and a flush of the face, they were swept away. (bk 1, ch. 11)

Podsnap was probably based on Dickens's friend (and later biographer) John Forster. The contrast between Podsnappery and Dickens's own attitude is shown in the closing salutation of one of his letters to Forster:

Vive le Roi des Français! Roi de la nation la plus grande, et la plus noble, et la
plus extraordinairement merveilleuse, du monde! A bas des Anglais!
CHARLES DICKENS,
Français naturalisé, et Citoyen de Paris. (*Letters*, v. 5)

Some of the complex play of Dickens's inheritance from European fiction
and the European scale of his writing can be gathered from a seemingly
marginal text, *No Thoroughfare* (1867), which he co-authored with Wilkie
Collins as a Christmas story for his magazine *All the Year Round*. It uses the
classic material of Dickens's fiction and childhood memory in the story of
an impoverished, illegitimate child in London in the early 1820s who,
having been recovered by his supposed mother, goes on to become a successful merchant and wine importer. But Walter Wilding, whom we assume
to be the hero of the story, dies young, and a complex story about substituted identities emerges. That complexity is played out on a European stage,
climaxing not on the banks of the Thames where it begins but in the Swiss
Alps, where the true Walter Wilding – known as George Vendale – is
rescued from near death by his Swiss lover, Marguerite. She is of Swiss
peasant stock and that rare thing, a Victorian female action hero. Vendale
first meets her in Soho Square in London where she lives among:

> A curious colony of mountaineers ... Swiss watchmakers, Swiss silver-chasers,
> Swiss jewellers, Swiss importers of Swiss musical boxes and Swiss toys of
> various kinds, draw close together there. Swiss professors of music, painting,
> and languages; Swiss artificers in steady work; Swiss couriers, and other Swiss
> servants chronically out of place; industrious Swiss laundresses and clear-
> starchers; mysteriously existing Swiss of both sexes; Swiss creditable and Swiss
> discreditable; Swiss to be trusted by all means, and Swiss to be trusted by
> no means; these diverse Swiss particles are attracted to a centre in the district
> of Soho.[14]

It is a characteristic Dickens effect: national identity is not where you expect
to find it and is constitutively diverse. The Swiss are 'mysteriously existing ...
diverse particles', the products of perhaps the most resistant of all European
nations to a single national, cultural or linguistic identity. Personal identity is
equally vulnerable in this story: all three of the main male characters – Walter
Wilding, Obenreizer and George Vendale – are possible heirs to the wine
business; all may be illegitimate; none is sure of his parenthood. The most
Swiss location is in the middle of London. The villain of the story, Obenreizer,
is Swiss, but so too is Marguerite, whose rescue of her future husband
Dickens described to Collins as:

> A wintry flight and pursuit across the Alps, under lonely circumstances, and
> against warnings ... There we can get Ghostly interest, picturesque interest,

breathless interest of time and circumstance, and force the design up to any powerful climax we please ... we shall get a very Avalanche of power out of it, and thunder it down on the readers' heads. (*Letters*, XI.413)

A warehouse on the banks of the Thames, like the one that Dickens worked in as a child, is plugged through international trade and fictional melodrama into a sublimely different European landscape, where the mysteries it raises of birth, death and inheritance are finally resolved. This points to his understanding and use of European settings in his fiction; a feature seen most overtly and melodramatically in *A Tale of Two Cities*.

Before this, however, came *Little Dorrit*, Dickens's most European novel and the one most concerned with foreignness and exile, with cultural difference and the possibility and price of crossing borders. The novel is divided into two books – 'Poverty' and 'Riches' – both of which begin in liminal places: Marseilles 'burning in the heat' and the Great St Bernard Pass between Italy and France, respectively. The boundaries here are simultaneously textual, geographical, national, physical, psychological and cultural. Marseilles is where 'Hindoos, Russians, Chinese, Spaniards, Portuguese, Englishmen, Frenchmen, Genoese, Neapolitans, Venetians, Greeks, Turks, descendants from all the builders of Babel, come to trade' (bk I, ch. I). Venice and Martigny, other important locations of the book, are similarly international in their populations. The novel itself is one of confusion and translation, of people caught within and between the bonds of different languages and cultures. The most important of these is the villain Rigaud, of whom it is remarked, with evident authorial approval: 'there are people who must be dealt with as enemies of the human race. That there are people who have no human heart, and who must be crushed like savage beasts and cleared out of the way' (bk I, ch.11). But Rigaud is countered by a very different foreigner, John Baptist Cavalletto. A 'sunburned, quick, lithe man', Cavalletto is a smuggler and economic migrant, an 'officious refugee' (bk II, ch. 30) or 'contraband beast' (bk II, ch. 28) who is caught between three languages (Italian, French, English) and is never seen in his Genoese home, but lives first in prison in France and then in London in the slum of Bleeding Heart Yard. Cavalletto is the only character in the novel to be named in the same way as Amy Dorrit, the novel's heroine – he is 'Little Cavalletto', she 'Little Dorrit' – and although they never meet, they have a deep affinity in their unassertive moral goodness. Despised by others for their lack of gentility, both suffer and do good deeds without reward in prison and elsewhere.

Yet it would be wrong to idealise the relations between Cavalletto and those living beside him in the London slums who believe that 'every foreigner had a knife about him … that he ought to go back to his own country … that foreigners were always immoral' (bk 1, ch. 25). Even when they lose their suspicions, they struggle to accord him full humanity: 'treating him like a baby' or 'admiring him as if he were a mechanical toy' (bk 1, ch. 25). But gradually a more complex cultural exchange begins to take place, as Bleeding Hearters start to speak to him

> in very loud voices as if he were stone deaf. They constructed sentences, by way of teaching him the language in its purity, such as were addressed by the savages to Captain Cook, or by Friday to Robinson Crusoe. Mrs Plornish was particularly ingenious in this art; and attained so much celebrity for saying 'Me ope you leg well soon,' that it was considered in the Yard but a very short remove indeed from speaking Italian. Even Mrs Plornish herself began to think that she had a natural call towards that language. As he became more popular, household objects were brought into requisition for his instruction in a copious vocabulary; and whenever he appeared in the Yard ladies would fly out at their doors crying 'Mr Baptist – tea-pot!' 'Mr Baptist – dust-pan!' 'Mr Baptist – flour-dredger!' 'Mr Baptist – coffee-biggin!' At the same time exhibiting those articles, and penetrating him with a sense of the appalling difficulties of the Anglo-Saxon tongue. (bk 1, ch. 25)

These exchanges lead to some of the funniest moments of the novel, which culminate in two very different kinds of linguistic exchange. Mrs Plornish's self-invented Italian culminates in her magnificently interlingual, wonderfully Joycean expression of astonishment, 'Mooshattonisha padrona' (bk II, ch. 27), that 'Tuscan sentence … turned … with peculiar elegance'. Cavalletto, by contrast, contributes a single Italian word – 'altro' – to the vocabulary of the Bleeding Hearters, a privileged, polysemic fragment of his language and culture, which comes from the Latin 'alter', meaning other, different, opposite, another, the other: everything, indeed, that he represents. It is a word he uses on all possible occasions and which acts as 'a confirmation, a contradiction, an assertion, a denial, a taunt, a compliment, a joke and fifty other things' (bk 1, ch. 1). It comes from the mouth of a foreign prisoner whom we last see in another prison in another foreign land, England, exercising his characteristic care and kindness, bearing with them an irreducible linguistic plurality and otherness, an alterity whose usage cannot be predicted or known in advance.

*A Tale of Two Cities* (1859) returns to a European setting and pioneers a new kind of hero – or anti-hero – in Sydney Carton, lawyer and wastrel. The novel consistently undercuts any simple contrasts between the two cities, Paris and London, binding them together in multi-dimensional analogies and parallelisms. The virtuous are constitutively dual in their linguistic and national identities: the novel's heroine Lucie Manette is born in France but taken as a babe in arms to England; her husband Charles Darnay is also the heir to the Marquis de St Evrémonde (the name itself contains a bilingual pun); Carton studied in France and speaks good French. The similarities, which are never identities, are there from the very first page:

> There were a king with a large jaw and a queen with a plain face, on the throne of England; there were a king with a large jaw and a queen with a fair face, on the throne of France. In both countries it was clearer than crystal to the lords of the State preserves of loaves and fishes, that things in general were settled for ever. (bk i, ch. 1)

Later, the injustice of the French Revolutionary tribunal is matched by the unjust State trial of Darnay in England. There are mobs in both countries and the spy John Barsad works in turn for the British government and the French Revolution. France may have the guillotine but England is 'but newly released from the horror of being ogled ... by the heads exposed on Temple Bar with an insensate brutality and ferocity' (bk ii, ch. 1).

## Dickens and politics

Like his contemporary and admirer Karl Marx, Dickens was both repelled and fascinated by the violent and hierarchical forms that class difference in the nineteenth century took. But, unlike Marx, he opposed class conflict. For Dickens characteristically sees class not as a matter of *identity* determined by economic position, but as a complex, opportunistic form of *performance*, compulsory but also often brilliantly creative. Class is never free or undetermined, and few major novelists have known as directly as Dickens what it was to be poor, hungry and alone. Yet even very poor people in Dickens can be symbolically rich. The worst moments of Wilkins Micawber's life give rise to the most creative speech, as in the letter that he writes to David Copperfield when entangled in Uriah Heep's snares:

> Without more directly referring to any latent ability that may possibly exist on my part, of wielding the thunderbolt, or directing the devouring and avenging flame in any quarter, I may be permitted to observe, in passing, that my brightest visions are for ever dispelled – that my peace is shattered and my power of enjoyment destroyed – that my heart is no longer in the right place – and that I no more walk erect before my fellow man. The canker is in the flower. The cup is bitter to the brim. The worm is at his work, and will soon dispose of his victim. The sooner the better. But I will not digress. (ch. 49)

The worse things are, the more fertile and assured Micawber's language becomes: the promise not to digress merely begins yet another digression, powered by a simultaneously self-delighting and self-lacerating momentum, seemingly unstoppable in its force. At his most desperate, Micawber is linguistically and figuratively most fluent, raiding the stances and tropes of melodrama and the Romantic sublime, recharging them with an affective force as touching as it is absurd. This contrasts with the later novels of Émile Zola or Thomas Hardy, whose concern with the poor and dispossessed takes a more deterministic and miserable form.

It was this quality above all that led Marx to praise '[t]he present splendid brotherhood of fiction-writers in England, whose graphic and eloquent pages have issued to the world more political and social truths than have been uttered by all the professional politicians, publicists, and moralists put together'.[15] Dickens's own class origins (an active shaping force, both hidden and revealed throughout his work) were complexly marginal: a lower-middle-class family genteel in its aspirations but always in debt. John Dickens, the novelist's father, was the child of a butler and housekeeper, upper servants who were obliged to perform the daily rituals of service and deference and who could also observe, close up, how it was that the rich and powerful made themselves so, how class was acted out in what Dickens's friend Wilkie Collins called 'the secret theatre of home'.[16] Theatricality and marginality are thus the keynotes of Dickens's understanding of class. He is a particularly acute observer of those on the edges of class affiliation, the worlds of the shabby-genteel, the aspirant and falling in a market economy, where the precipice of poverty or bankruptcy, of radical loss and dispossession, is ever-present. When Pip in *Great Expectations* goes back, wealthy and well dressed, to the village where he had been apprenticed to the local blacksmith, he is followed down the road by the boy from Trabb the tailor's shop, who makes the triumphal return an excruciating, hilarious rout:

> Words cannot state the amount of aggravation and injury wreaked upon me by Trabb's boy, when passing abreast of me, he pulled up his shirt-collar, twined his side-hair, stuck an arm akimbo, and smirked extravagantly by, wriggling his elbows and body, and drawling to his attendants, 'Don't know yah, don't know yah, pon my soul don't know yah!' (vol. II, ch. II)

Trabb's boy, like Dickens himself, is a devastating imitator and parodist, hollowing out the gestures and rituals of class power. In a novel full of cross-class violence, it is a temporary triumph of the dispossessed against an oppressor who, only shortly before, had been one of themselves.

In his treatment of class, Dickens draws on two main threads from his European precursors. The first is the pairing of foolish master and wise servant, as in Cervantes's Don Quixote and Sancho Panza. In the shape of Sam Weller, full of streetwise charm and ready chaff, *Pickwick Papers* provides simultaneously the last major example of the figure of the witty servant within the Victorian novel and its apotheosis. His contemporaries immediately recognised in Mr Pickwick a 'Cockney Quixote of the nineteenth century'.[17] Even more important for his development as a novelist is a borrowing that he makes from Alain-René Lesage's *Le Diable boiteux* (1707; *The Devil upon Two Sticks*). Asmodeus, Lesage's Devil, is a mischievous and malevolent figure who removes the rooftops of the houses in Madrid to show Don Cleofas all the wickedness and vice that are taking place. In a passage that has often been taken as central to understanding Dickens's work, he transforms the satirical devil into the possibility and hope of a more benevolent and transforming urban knowledge:

> Oh for a good spirit who would take the house-tops off, with a more potent and benignant hand than the lame demon in the tale, and show a Christian people what dark shapes issue from amidst their homes, to swell the retinue of the Destroying Angel as he moves forth among them! ... Bright and blest the morning that should rise on such a night: for men, delayed no more by stumbling-blocks of their own making, which are but specks of dust upon the path between them and eternity, would then apply themselves, like creatures of one common origin, owning one duty to the Father of one family, and tending to one common end, to make the world a better place! (ch. 47)

The figure of the benevolent hand that can reveal suffering and injustice is, as Raymond Williams points out, also 'the hand of the novelist', a potent self-image.[18] The much freer range of rhetorical modes that his fiction can encompass – including direct address, typification and satire – enables a form of writing that both reaches back to the familiar intimacy of Henry Fielding and forward to the work of a writer such as Bertolt Brecht in its ability to break the conventions of realism to depict deep economic and social forces and needs. Later socialist and working-class novelists have often admired and borrowed from him, as did Robert Tressall in *The Ragged Trousered Philanthropists* (1914).

Particularly in his middle-period fiction, Dickens draws working-class characters as both emotionally and morally the equals, and often superiors, of their class 'betters'. This can lead to a willed idealisation in, for example, the figure of the oppressed millworker Stephen Blackpool in *Hard Times*, but in *Dombey and Son*, the Toodle family and Susan Nipper have a vigour, complexity and warmth that Dombey himself cannot begin to imagine. In that novel, emotional and moral value bubbles upwards from the working class, as in the tellingly understated exchange between the grand merchant Dombey and the railway stoker Mr Toodle:

'You have a son, I believe?' said Mr Dombey.
'Four on 'em, Sir. Four hims and a her. All alive!'
'Why, it's as much as you can afford to keep them!' said Mr Dombey.
'I couldn't hardly afford but one thing in the world less, Sir.'
'What is that?'
'To lose 'em, Sir.' (ch. 2)

In every novel, the actions of the main, usually middle-class (if only just) characters, are interwoven, counterpointed and contrasted with characters from the working poor to an extent that has rarely been rivalled by his contemporaries and successors.

Dickens also stands at the beginning of a significant transformation in the development of the novel as a global cultural form, driven by a decisive internationalisation of the literary market and the first conceptualisation by Goethe of the possibility of 'world literature'. Goethe's greatest advocate in Britain was Thomas Carlyle, a close friend of Dickens, who had assisted him with his research for *A Tale of Two Cities* and was the dedicatee of *Hard Times*.[19] Carlyle was the most important conduit of German romanticism into English culture and his *Sartor Resartus* (1833–4) married a Sternean self-consciousness with a fascinated exposition of German idealism. Professor Teufelsdröckh famously advises his readers to 'Close thy Byron; open thy Goethe'. Goethe and Carlyle corresponded about world literature and in 1830 the former's introduction to Carlyle's *Life of Schiller* describes the possibility of a 'general world literature' as 'the intellect gradually acquired the desire to be equally admitted to relatively free trade relations'.[20] These free trade relations were of great importance to Dickens, who spent a great deal of time and considerable business acumen in pressing for copyright reform and 'working' his own copyrights.

Hence, although critics have claimed Dickens for an exclusively 'English' tradition, as when F. R. Leavis offered to 'surrender the whole oeuvre of Flaubert for *Dombey and Son* or *Little Dorrit*', the traditions are deeply entwined.[21] His works were translated early and often, and he had excellent relations with Baron Tauchnitz, whose celebrated reprint series of British and American Authors took Dickens's works (and those of many of his contemporaries) to all corners of Europe. He wrote in friendly terms to Alexandre Dumas and George Sand, and met Turgenev (who admired him greatly) at William Makepeace Thackeray's home (*Letters*, XII.375n). After his Russian translator, Irinarch Ivanovich Vvedensky, told Dickens that 'from the banks of the Neva to the remotest parts of Siberia you are read with avidity', he would periodically threaten to head off, as Forster tells us, for the more sympathising and congenial climate of 'the remotest parts of Siberia' (*Letters*, V.611n).

Of course, Dickens's relationship with Europe was complicated, and to gain a full sense of it, one would have to look not merely at his fiction but at his many pieces of journalism about Europe. Yet his influence touched novelists very different from himself. Flaubert praised *Pickwick Papers* and *Nicholas Nickleby* and reread *Pickwick* shortly before beginning *Bouvard et Pécuchet*, his own sardonic treatment of the failures and delusions of modern ambitions to knowledge and culture. Bouvard and Pécuchet, liberated from their humdrum clerking existence by a fortunate legacy, fail repeatedly at all the topics they attempt to master, from archaeology to literature, love to gymnastics, landscape gardening to theology, as foolish in their theorising as Mr Pickwick, who 'traced to their source the mighty ponds of Hampstead, and agitated the scientific world with his Theory of Tittlebats' (ch. 1). A very different novelist from Flaubert, Tolstoy considered Dickens the greatest novelist of the nineteenth century. Kafka said of 'The Stoker' (which became the germ of *America* or *The Man who was Lost*) that 'It was my intention ... to write a Dickens novel, but enhanced by the sharper lights I should have taken from the times and the duller ones I should have got from myself'.[22] Henry James, with characteristic reluctance, relayed Turgenev's praise: 'The English writer (of our day) of whom I remember to have heard him speak with most admiration was Dickens, of whose faults he was conscious, but whose power of presenting to the eye a vivid, salient figure he rated very high.'[23] But perhaps the final word is best left to Dostoevsky, who most engagingly captures Dickens's simultaneously national and international qualities: 'We understand Dickens in Russia, I am convinced, almost as well as the English, and maybe even all the subtleties; maybe even we love him no less than his own countrymen; and yet how typical, distinctive [*svoebrazen*], and national Dickens is.'[24]

## Note on editions

The most authoritative texts of Dickens's novels are the Clarendon editions published by Oxford University Press, although the series is not yet complete. The Oxford World's Classics paperback editions print the Clarendon texts where available with informative introductions and notes. Penguin and Norton also have excellent paperback editions.

### Notes

1 Malcolm Andrews, *Dickens on England and the English* (Hassocks: Harvester, 1979), xvi.
2 F. G. Kitton, *The Dickens Country* (London: Black, 1925); Peter Ackroyd, *Dickens* (London: Sinclair-Stevenson, 1990), p. 390.

3  Georg Lukács, *The Historical Novel*, trans. Hannah and Stanley Mitchell (Harmondsworth: Penguin, 1969), p. 292.

4  Franco Moretti, *The Way of the World: The* Bildungsroman *in European Culture*, trans. Albert J. Sbragia (London: Verso, 2000), p. 181.

5  Peter Brooks, *The Melodramatic Imagination: Balzac, Henry James, Melodrama and the Mode of Excess* (New Haven, CT: Yale University Press, 1995), pp. 11–12.

6  Henry James, *French Poets and Novelists* (London, 1919), p. 147.

7  *The Letters of Charles Dickens: 1820–1870*, ed. Madeline House, Graham Storey et al., 12 vols. (Oxford University Press, 1965–2002), XII.493n. Subsequent references to *Letters* are by volume.

8  Wilkie Collins, letter to Robert du Pontavice de Heussey, 14 August 1885, in *The Letters of Wilkie Collins, vol. II, 1866–1889*, ed. William Baker and William M. Clarke (Basingstoke: Macmillan, 1997), p. 483.

9  John Forster, *The Life of Charles Dickens* (London: Chapman and Hall, n.d.), vol. IV.

10  *Catalogue of the Library of Charles Dickens from Gadshill*, ed. J. H. Stonehouse (London: Piccadilly Fountain, 1935).

11  Henry Fielding Dickens, *Memories of My Father* (London: Duffield & Co., 1929), p. 28.

12  George Orwell, 'Charles Dickens', in *The Collected Essays, Journalism and Letters of George Orwell, vol. I, An Age Like This 1920–40* (Harmondsworth: Penguin, 1970), pp. 454–504 (473).

13  Charles Dickens, 'A Monument of French Folly', in *The Dent Uniform Edition of Dickens' Journalism, vol. II. The Amusements of the People and Other Papers: Reports, Essays and Reviews 1834–51*, ed. Michael Slater (London: Dent, 1996), pp. 327–38.

14  Charles Dickens and Wilkie Collins, *No Thoroughfare*, in Dickens, *The Christmas Stories*, ed. Ruth Glancy (London: Dent, 1996), pp. 699–700.

15  Karl Marx, *Dispatches for the New York Tribune: Selected Journalism of Karl Marx*, ed. James Ledbetter (New York: Penguin, 2007), p. 143.

16  Wilkie Collins, *Basil*, ed. Dorothy Goldman (Oxford: World's Classics, 1990), p. 76.

17  *The Monthly Magazine*, 18, 6 January 1837, in *Charles Dickens: The Critical Heritage*, ed. Philip Collins (London: Routledge, 1971), p. 27.

18  Raymond Williams, *The English Novel from Dickens to Lawrence* (London: Hogarth, 1984), p. 34.

19  F. G. Kitton, *The Life of Charles Dickens* (Edinburgh: T. C. and A. C. Jack, 1902), p. 283.

20  Stefan Hoesel-Uhlig, 'Changing Fields', in *Debating World Literature*, ed. Christopher Prendergast (London: Verso, 2004), p. 38.

21  F. R. Leavis, letter to the *Spectator*, 4 January 1963, in *Letters in Criticism*, ed. John Tasker (London: Chatto and Windus, 1974), p. 96.

22  Stephen Wall, ed., *Charles Dickens* (Harmondsworth: Penguin, 1970), p. 257.

23  Henry James, *The Art of Criticism: Henry James on the Theory and the Practice of Fiction*, ed. William R. Veeder and Susan M. Griffin (University of Chicago Press, 1986), pp. 136–7.

24  N. M. Lary, *Dostoevsky and Dickens: A Study of Literary Influence* (London: Routledge and Kegan Paul, 1973), p. 150.

## Further reading

Ackroyd, Peter, *Dickens* (London: Sinclair-Stevenson, 1990)

Bowen, John, *Other Dickens: Pickwick to Chuzzlewit* (Oxford University Press, 2000)

Carey, John, *The Violent Effigy: A Study of Dickens's Imagination* (London: Faber and Faber, 1973, 2nd edn 1991)

Chesterton, G. K., *Charles Dickens* (London: Methuen, 1906)

Furneaux, Holly, *Queer Dickens: Erotics, Families, Masculinities* (Oxford University Press, 2009)

Gillooly, Eileen and Deirdre David, eds., *Contemporary Dickens* (Ohio University Press, 2008)

Hillis Miller, J., *Charles Dickens: The World of His Novels* (Cambridge University Press, 1958)

Hollington, Michael, *Dickens and the Grotesque* (London: Croom Helm, 1984)

James, Henry, *The Art of Criticism: Henry James on the Theory and Practice of Fiction*, ed. William R. Veeder and Susan M. Griffin (University of Chicago Press, 1986)

Jones, Colin, Jo McDonagh and Jon Mee, eds., *Charles Dickens, A Tale of Two Cities and the French Revolution* (Basingstoke: Palgrave, 2009)

Jordan, J. O., ed., *The Cambridge Companion to Dickens* (Cambridge University Press, 2001)

Leavis, F. R. and Q. D., *Dickens the Novelist* (London: Chatto and Windus, 1970)

Orwell, George, 'Charles Dickens', in *The Collected Essays, Journalism and Letters of George Orwell*, vol. I, *An Age Like This: 1920–40* (Harmondsworth: Penguin, 1970), pp. 454–504

Schlicke, Paul, *Dickens and Popular Entertainment* (London: Unwin Hyman, 1985)
    ed., *The Oxford Reader's Companion to Dickens* (Oxford University Press, 1999)

Slater, Michael, *Dickens: A Life Defined by Writing* (New Haven, CT/London: Yale University Press, 2009)
    *Dickens and Women* (London: Dent, 1983)

Stone, Harry, *Dickens and the Invisible World: Fairy Tales, Fantasy, and Novel-Making* (London: Macmillan, 1980)

Wilson, Edmund, 'Dickens: The Two Scrooges', in *The Wound and the Bow* (London: Allen, 1941)

# 13

JOHN RIGNALL

# George Eliot (1819–1880):
# Reality and sympathy

A great novelist of English provincial life, George Eliot had at the same time the most profound knowledge of European literature and culture of any English writer of her day. Before she began to write the fiction that made her name as George Eliot, Marian Evans had acquired a good knowledge of five European languages, ancient and modern, besides her own, and had already made a significant contribution to Victorian intellectual life as a translator, an editor and a reviewer of works in French, German and Italian as well as English. She had translated David Strauss's *Das Leben Jesu* (*The Life of Jesus*, 1846) and Ludwig Feuerbach's *Das Wesen des Christenthums* (*The Essence of Christianity*, 1854), and also Baruch Spinoza's *Ethica* (*Ethics*), although that translation was not published in her lifetime. She had been the effective editor of the *Westminster Review* from late 1851 to April 1854 and had written substantial review articles over a wide field for that and other serious journals.

When her fiction began to appear, contemporary reviewers had no hesitation in relating it to the wider context of the European novel. Richard Simpson, reviewing her career as a novelist up to 1863, saw its guiding principles to be derived from Johann Wolfgang von Goethe (1749–1832); Edith Simcox in a review of *Middlemarch* described it as like 'a *Wilhelm Meister* written by Balzac',[1] and George Eliot's first biographer, Mathilde Blind, compared her to George Sand (1804–76), Honoré de Balzac (1799–1850) and Gustave Flaubert (1821–80). That understanding of how her work belonged to a European tradition of fiction seems to have faded with the decline of her reputation in the late nineteenth century, and although the non-literary European sources of her inspiration, such as the writings of Feuerbach and Spinoza, became a staple of twentieth-century scholarship, they were usually seen as contributing to a distinctively English fictional world and moral vision. Thus F. R. Leavis in *The Great Tradition* (1948) saw her fiction as central to that tradition of the English novel which he partly defined by contrast with the work of a French novelist, Flaubert.

In 1955, George Steiner drew a similar contrast but different conclusions. Arguing that her work, like most Victorian fiction, lacked a metaphysical dimension and the kind of structural unity and mastery of technique that define the novel as an art form, he declared that she was thus not a European novelist in the same class as Leo Tolstoy and Fyodor Dostoyevsky, Flaubert and Thomas Mann.[2] It is only in recent years that criticism has come to a fuller and more sympathetic understanding of George Eliot's place in a European tradition of fiction.

The daughter of an artisan who had risen by his considerable abilities to be a land agent managing the estate of the Newdigate family at Arbury Hall near Nuneaton, Marian Evans, or Mary Anne as she was known in childhood, was educated at boarding schools in Nuneaton and Coventry until the age of sixteen when she became her father's housekeeper on the death of her mother. He was happy to encourage her further development by paying, for instance, for a language teacher to instruct her in Italian and German, and the extraordinary erudition she achieved is a tribute to the vitality of intellectual life in nineteenth-century provincial England. When she moved with her father to Coventry in 1841 and entered the lively radical circle around the free-thinking manufacturer Charles Bray and his wife Cara, she came into contact with people interested in the most advanced currents of European thought, especially in relation to the religious faith she had already begun to question as she developed into an agnostic after a period of evangelical piety in her teenage years. It was through this Coventry circle that she received the commission to translate Strauss and met leading liberal intellectuals like Herbert Spencer, Harriet Martineau and Ralph Waldo Emerson, as well as the radical publisher John Chapman who published *The Life of Jesus* and for whom she worked when he became the owner of the *Westminster Review* in 1851.

After the death of her father in 1849, the Brays took her on a European tour, at the end of which she chose to stay on in Geneva on her own from August 1849 to March 1850, adapting to a French-speaking environment and writing letters to her friends which, in their vivid and often acerbic pen portraits of the people she encountered, showed signs of the novelist she was later to become. This first experience of European life was followed four years later by an even more important one when she left London in July with G. H. Lewes (1817–78) to spend seven months in Weimar and Berlin helping him with the preparation of his biography of Goethe.

The journey to Germany marked the beginning of her life with Lewes, a marriage in all but name since he was unable to obtain a divorce; and European travel continued to play a significant part both in their relationship and in her career as a writer, providing the opportunity for recuperation after the labour of finishing a novel, or material and inspiration for writing a new one. In March 1860, for instance, after the completion of *The Mill on the Floss* (1860), the couple set off for a holiday in Italy where, in Florence, they conceived the idea of a historical romance about Savonarola, which was eventually to become her historical novel *Romola* (1862–3); and in 1872 George Eliot was to write the Finale to *Middlemarch* (1871–2) in a German spa, Bad Homburg, where the sight of a young English woman gambling in the casino provided the germ of the opening scene of her next and last novel *Daniel Deronda* (1876). In their many and varied visits to Continental Europe, she and Lewes appear from their letters and journals not only as adventurous travellers and indefatigable sightseers, but also as true citizens of Europe as they take rooms in foreign cities, attend opera and theatre performances whatever the language, and feel more at home with local people than with other English travellers they encounter abroad.

The imagined community to which she belonged and which her writings served was, indeed, as much European as English or British. Although the subject of most of her fiction was the life of that provincial England she had known from childhood, she brought to it the wider horizons of European life and culture. In her first full-length novel, *Adam Bede* (1859), whose immediate success made her name and fortune, the celebrated exposition of her realist aesthetic in Chapter 17 ('In which the story pauses a little') draws on the Dutch paintings she had recently seen with Lewes in Munich in 1858, holding up these 'pictures of a monotonous homely existence' as models of the artistic truthfulness her fiction aspired to. Later in that work, Hetty Sorrel's inner agony at her advancing pregnancy is illuminated by an analogy that lies beyond the bounds of her provincial English world when the narrator relates it to a wayside crucifix encountered in a smiling Continental landscape (ch. 35).

The second novel, *The Mill on the Floss*, spells out the assumptions the novelist makes about the range of experience she shares with her readers but not with her rural characters when the narrator refers with mild irony to 'our instructed vagrancy, which has hardly time to linger by the hedgerows, but runs away early to the tropics, and is at home with palms and banyans' (bk III, ch. 9). The contrast drawn in that novel between the landscapes of the Rhône and the Rhine, and the different versions of history that they seem to imply, appears to assume that the reader is familiar with such an experience as 'journeying down the Rhone on a summer's day' (bk IV, ch. 1), while that assumption is made explicit in the description of Mrs Garth in *Middlemarch*: 'In her snowy-frilled cap she reminded one of that delightful Frenchwoman whom we have all seen marketing basket on arm' (ch. 24).

These may be no more than incidental gestures in the narration but they indicate the larger consciousness that informs the fiction.

It is a measure of the importance of European culture in the formation of George Eliot that, of the six major review articles she wrote for the *Westminster Review* in the two years that preceded her first work of fiction, three were inspired by French or German texts. The first, 'Woman in France: Madame de Sablé', focuses on the role of women in the literary culture of seventeenth-century France and finds there an exemplary model both of female achievement and of how men and women can meet on equal terms as writers and intellectuals. This was followed by 'German Wit: Heinrich Heine' which was instrumental in introducing the work of the German poet to a British audience, and shows the beginnings of her interest in the Jewish contribution to European culture, a subject to which she was to return in *Daniel Deronda*. The third article, 'The Natural History of German Life', reviews the work of the German social historian Heinrich von Riehl and sets out what were to become basic principles of her fiction: the importance of an unsentimentally realistic and unidealised artistic representation of working people; a view of the function of art as the extension of sympathy, as 'a mode of amplifying experience and extending our contact with our fellow-men beyond the bounds of our personal lot'; and an organic understanding of society as 'incarnate history' in which change is evolutionary rather than revolutionary.[3] In addition, Spinoza's *Ethics*, which she was translating during her first visit to Germany with Lewes, was congenial for its stress on the limitations of human understanding and on sympathy for others, while Feuerbach's *Essence of Christianity*, her translation of which was published before she left for Germany in 1854, was particularly important for its appeal to, and encouragement of, a sceptical and interrogative attitude to notions of absolute truth and for its conception of an active, principled moral life that was independent of all transcendental notions of goodness. But perhaps the most important European writer for her future creative life was Goethe, whose work she already knew from her years in Coventry but which she returned to and read intensively during the months with Lewes in Weimar and Berlin.

What made Goethe so central to her own writing was a deep affinity of outlook in relation to the complex, entangled nature of human experience and the need to avoid generalised moral judgements. When she started learning German in the early 1840s, her first enthusiasm for a German writer was for Friedrich Schiller (1759–1805), and his replacement by Goethe as she matured marked a move from a high-minded idealism towards a more differentiated and relativised understanding of moral questions, such as is expressed in *The Mill on the Floss* when the narrator refers to 'the truth, that moral judgements must remain false and hollow, unless they are checked and enlightened by a perpetual reference to the special circumstances that mark the individual lot' (bk VII, ch. 2).While she drew inspiration from other writers, like Jean-Jacques Rousseau and George Sand, but made a point of distancing herself from their opinions and behaviour, with Goethe there were no such reservations. *His* vision and understanding could be trusted, for he was 'the man who helps us to rise to a lofty point of observation, so that we may see things in their relative proportions' (*Essays*, 297). 'Relative' is significant here: the lofty vantage point offers not absolute understanding but a broad and spacious perspective in which things may be seen and understood in relation to one another. It is this kind of wide and undogmatic vision that she shares with Goethe as a novelist. As has often been remarked, when she defends him against the charge of immorality in a short article on 'The Morality of *Wilhelm Meister*', published in the *Leader* in July 1855 to prepare the ground for Lewes's forthcoming *Life of Goethe* (1855), she praises qualities in his novel that her own fiction will soon display, in particular a 'large tolerance'; a 'mode of treatment' that is unhurried and without exaggeration as it 'quietly follows the stream of fact and of life'; and the creation of characters who are 'mixed and erring, and self-deluding' but not without some redeeming feature (*Essays*, 146–7).

It is significant that this article, her only one on Goethe's work, is devoted to his archetypal *Bildungsroman*, *Wilhelm Meisters Lehrjahre* (*Wilhelm Meister's Apprenticeship*, 1795–6), for many of her own novels could be described as *Bildungsromane* without stretching the term to the point where it serves no useful purpose of definition. The debt to Goethe is made explicit in *Daniel Deronda*, where Daniel longs to have 'the sort of apprenticeship to life which would not shape him too definitely' (ch. 16) and is granted the freedom to develop under guidance from mentors like Mordecai and Kalonymos; but there is a more general affinity in the theme of growth through error to be found throughout George Eliot's fiction. Despite the pedagogical machinery of the Society of the Tower in *Wilhelm Meister*, Goethe shows how true learning can only come through lived experience and not from imparted wisdom. Wilhelm has to make his mistakes and suffer from them before being brought to the brink of a happy union by self-conscious deployment of the novelist's art; and a similar pattern can be seen, for instance, in Dorothea's experience in *Middlemarch*. Goethe's elusively ironic mode of narration and the abstract setting of his novel are very different from George Eliot's direct commentary and vividly realised circumstantial world, but there is an affinity in the denouement of the central figures' emotional lives. Where the obstacles to the union of Wilhelm and

Nathalie are swept away by the opportune intervention of the jester figure of Friedrich, it is a convenient thunderstorm that finally dispels the inhibitions and scruples which keep Dorothea and Will Ladislaw apart. The device of the storm brings them together in their instinctive recoil from a 'vivid flash of lightning', and as they stand with 'their hands clasped, like two children, looking out on the storm' (ch. 83), George Eliot matches Goethe in her benignly ironic handling of her characters and self-conscious use of a romantic motif that carries an unobtrusive weight of symbolic significance. The device of the storm has a particular Goethean resonance, with clear echoes of Werther's first meeting with Lotte in *Die Leiden des jungen Werthers* (*The Sorrows of Young Werther*, 1774), when the two figures respond to the thunder and lightning in the same way and are brought together by a spontaneous allusion to the poet Friedrich Gottlieb Klopstock. It is in scenes like these, where there is an unembarrassed use of a symbolic motif that reaches beyond a narrowly conceived realism, as well as in those where chapter epigraphs or titles make overt reference to Goethe, that the informing presence of his work can be sensed in George Eliot's.

She was also acquainted with the work of the contemporary German writers of prose fiction who were Goethe's successors, and in 1858 she assisted G. H. Lewes in the preparation of his article 'Realism in Art: Modern German Fiction' for the *Westminster Review*. Lewes is largely dismissive of the stories and novels he refers to on the grounds that, in comparison with Balzac's (and in implicit comparison with the work of his partner, then writing *Adam Bede*), they are insufficiently realistic, but he justifiably argues that German fiction is found at its best in the shorter form of the *Novelle* and singles out for praise one story by the Swiss German writer Gottfried Keller (1819–90), George Eliot's exact contemporary who, like her, was marked by his reading of Strauss and Feuerbach. His story, 'A Village Romeo and Juliet' (1856), which she read at this point and again in 1871, exploits the kind of conflict she had noted in 'The Natural History of German Life' as typical of peasant culture and had illustrated like Keller with reference to William Shakespeare's play (*Essays*, 277). Keller's Romeo and Juliet are the children of two peasants who fall out over an unused plot of land between their two properties and ruin themselves through litigation, creating a division between the two families so insuperable that the young lovers, after spending a night together on a hay barge drifting down the river, seek death in each other's arms and slip into the river at dawn to drown. When George Eliot starts writing her tragedy of rural life, *The Mill on the Floss* (1860), in the following year, she takes similar thematic material – a family feud, destructive litigation, death by drowning and the association of the river with the strong current of desire – and works them into a richly circumstantial and expansive novel rather than Keller's poetically elegiac and fable-like story.

*The Mill on the Floss* also has an affinity with Keller's slightly earlier novel *Der grüne Heinrich* (*Green Henry*, 1854–5) which draws similarly on personal experience in tracing an individual's development from childhood to early adult life. Both works share a debt to Goethe but show how the Goethean model of personal development is impossible to combine with realism's attention to the social and psychological pressures that constrict an individual life, particularly a woman's life, as Maggie Tulliver's experience spells out. In their extended representation of childhood and adolescence leading to a disconcertingly abrupt ending in which death strikes the protagonist on the very threshold of adult life, both novels could be described as aborted *Bildungsromane* in which realism's insistence on the inescapable consequences of all behaviour leads to an impasse in which lives are unable to break free from the past.

Edith Simcox's suggestion that *Middlemarch* has affinities with Balzac as well as Goethe points to the importance of another strand of European fiction: the rich vein of French realism. For George Eliot the literatures of France and Germany were the other two great literatures of the world apart from English, and the two cultures represented in her view two 'differing forms of civilization'[4] whose contrary attractions are registered in her life and writing. After her engagement with German Higher Criticism in the labour of translating Strauss, she turned for relief to reading Rousseau and George Sand, who wakened her to fresh perceptions (*Letters*, 1.277); and when she was defending Goethe against the charge of immorality in the article on *Wilhelm Meister*, it was Balzac who provided the contrast. Although acclaiming him as 'perhaps the most wonderful writer of fiction the world has ever seen', she sees him as often overstepping the moral limits of art and dragging 'us by his magic force through scene after scene of unmitigated vice' (*Essays*, 146). This combination of admiration and disapproval can be discerned in the way that her own fiction reacts dialogically and dialectically to his when she attempts 'the delineation of quiet provincial life' in which she found he and Jane Austen (1775–1817) had set so high a standard.[5]

The title she gave to her first work, *Scenes of Clerical Life*, directly echoes the titles Balzac gave to the subdivisions of his *Comédie humaine* (*Human Comedy*), such as *Scenes of Private Life* and *Scenes of Provincial Life*, and her first story, 'The Sad Fortunes of the Rev Amos Barton', gives her own distinctive inflection to the downfall of a provincial cleric that Balzac dramatises in his *Le Curé de Tours* (*The Curé of Tours*, 1832), a work she greatly admired. In each case the clerical protagonist is first seen crossing a churchyard, ominously ill-dressed for the inclement weather, but the ensuing drama brings out the contrast between the two novelists' moral vision and understanding of social life. Balzac's cleric is thwarted in his modest aspirations and evicted from his comfortable home by the malice and ambitions of others, and society is shown to be driven by a perpetual struggle between the individual and the social system which seeks to exploit him and which he seeks to exploit for his own profit. Amos Barton, by contrast, is principally the victim of his own thoughtless behaviour and the misfortune of his wife's untimely death, and the story seeks to generate sympathy for an ordinary and singularly unprepossessing individual rather than to illustrate the workings of a heartless world of competitive individualism in which ambitious schemers succeed at the expense of the modest and unsuspecting. It is as though there is both homage to Balzac in this first story and at the same time a need to counter the potential cynicism of his social vision by insistence on the sympathetic claims of ordinary humanity.

The presence of Balzac can also be discerned behind *Silas Marner: The Weaver of Raveloe* (1861) which, like his *Eugénie Grandet* (1833), focuses on the figure of the miser and on the relationship between father and daughter. Indeed, *Silas Marner* can be read as a reworking of the material of the French novel to wrest the tale of the miser and his daughter from Balzac's bleak universe into a world where love and sympathy are not powerless in the face of material self-interest and ambition, but capable of overcoming them. Grandet's miserliness is a monomaniacal obsession which nothing can shake, and his daughter Eugénie never escapes from its shadow, from the gloomy isolation in which she has been raised and in which she ends her days after being spurned by her feckless cousin, the one great love of her life. By contrast, *Silas Marner*, the most fable-like of George Eliot's fictions, shows how the crabbed life of a miser can be redeemed by love and sympathy when the child Eppie wanders into Silas's cottage and is raised by him as his daughter; and in distributing rewards and punishments according to the principles of poetic justice, it can be read as an implied riposte to Balzac. The tale of a golden-haired child who drives out a man's obsession with gold, of a father, Godfrey Cass, who forfeits the love of his child and of an adoptive father, Silas, who wins it, sets the consoling simplicity of the fable against Balzac's polarised scheme of monomaniacal materialism and suffering victim. There is a distinct difference in social understanding as well as moral vision. Quiet provincial life is, it seems, subjected to two opposing interpretations. The narrowness of provincial existence that for Balzac helps explain Grandet's grasping miserliness and Eugénie's restricted horizons, is for George Eliot the closeness of community that can anchor and protect an individual life, as it does when Silas breaks out of his miserly isolation and seeks the assistance of his fellow villagers.

Despite these differences, however, there is still a vein of unillusioned realism in *Silas Marner* that is not so distant from Balzac. The original injustice that Silas suffers when he is falsely accused of theft and driven into exile in Raveloe is never put right and his innocence remains unconfirmed; and there is a dark margin of the irredeemable and undeserved around the ending of the story in which the childless Nancy Cass is left silently suffering for the wrongdoing of her husband and stoically enduring, like Balzac's Eugénie, the narrowness of a provincial woman's lot. This unobtrusive affinity with Balzac becomes more marked in George Eliot's later work, particularly in her last novel *Daniel Deronda* which, with its metropolitan setting, central motif of gambling and moments of melodramatic intensity, recalls his novels of Parisian rather than provincial life.

She read Balzac throughout her life but there is a particularly concentrated engagement with his work in 1870 at the beginning of the decade in which she produced both *Daniel Deronda* and *Middlemarch* (1871–2), the novel that most clearly ranks as one of the great works of European realism alongside those of Balzac and Flaubert, Tolstoy and Dostoyevsky. A multi-plotted novel that follows the fortunes of different sets of characters in an English provincial town at a particular historical moment, the period of the first Reform Act of 1832, *Middlemarch* both looks outwards to Europe with scenes in Paris and Rome and affinities with similarly encompassing novels like Tolstoy's *Anna Karenina*, and backwards to the history of European fiction. Like Walter Scott, the favourite novelist of her early years, George Eliot sets the action of the novel back some forty years from the time of writing, and like Scott she makes use of chapter epigraphs which here seek to situate her fiction in relation to a wider literary context, both English and European. For instance, the chapter in which Dorothea begins to conceive of the desiccated clergyman scholar Mr Casaubon as a prospective husband is headed by an epigraph from *Don Quixote*: a passage from the episode in which Don Quixote mistakes a barber's basin for Mambrino's helmet. The allusion invites us to identify Dorothea's behaviour as quixotic, subject to a delusion derived not, in her case, from a reading of romance literature but from drawing extravagant romantic parallels between Casaubon and great literary and intellectual figures such as Blaise Pascal and John Locke.

The epigraph from Miguel de Cervantes resonates in more than one way, however. On the one hand, the process by which Dorothea is disabused of her misunderstanding of Casaubon's character and intellectual stature takes its place in the long line of realist fiction that descends from *Don Quixote*. On the other, the allusion to a great predecessor has an element of Cervantean self-consciousness about it that points to the knowing nature of George Eliot's realism and serves as a reminder, if one were needed, that

*Middlemarch* is anything but the classic realist text of post-structuralist caricature, blind to its own conventions and procedures. This is a novel alert to the slipperiness of language – 'we all of us, grave or light, get our thoughts entangled in metaphors and act fatally on the strength of them' (ch. 10) – and it is also aware that the knowing and authoritative narrator who makes such pronouncements is subject to the same partiality of vision that is famously spelt out in the parable of the candle on the pier-glass in relation to Rosamond Vincy (ch. 27). The comprehensiveness of *Middlemarch*, indeed, includes its sophisticated awareness of problems of language, epistemology and representation.

One of the narrative devices it explicitly reflects upon is the controlling voice of the authoritative narrator, which is the subject of a comparison with Henry Fielding at the beginning of Chapter 15 that locates *Middlemarch* in the history of the English novel. Where the narrator of *Tom Jones* 'glories in his copious remarks and digressions' which roam across 'that tempting range of relevancies called the universe' (ch. 15), the nineteenth-century fictional historian can be allowed no such freedom as he or she endeavours to lay bare the complex relationships that constitute social life. The mind that seeks, like the narrator of *Middlemarch*, to unravel certain human lots by 'concentrating all the light I can command ... on this particular web', is thus closer to the scientist's with his microscope than to that of a classically educated English gentleman like Fielding; and this chapter of the novel is expressly concerned with the education of a gentleman, Lydgate, who abandons the study of classics for medical science. His scientific education takes him to Paris, while the implied analogy here between the scientist and the novelist brings George Eliot herself onto the same ground as the great French realists of the nineteenth century: Balzac, who compared his work with that of the zoologist Georges Cuvier, and Flaubert, who believed it was time to endow art with the exactness of the physical sciences. In George Eliot's case, it is not the impersonal exactitude of science that she seems to emulate so much as its spirit of sceptical enquiry. Where Flaubert notoriously aspires to a mode of narration that achieves objectivity by excluding the personal, the narrative voice of *Middlemarch* is marked not by its impersonality but by the variety of its shifting tones and registers which present the fictional world in searchingly different ways. Ranging between the sympathetic and the ironic, the solemn and the sarcastic, the appealingly personal and the authoritatively general, it commands both the 'masculine' discourse of science and the 'feminine' language of feeling, and it cannot be adequately defined by the general term 'omniscience' nor clearly categorised in terms of gender. It remains richly and stimulatingly varied and elusively androgynous.

With its quixotic heroine, Dorothea, *Middlemarch* can stand alongside another great descendant of Cervantes's novel in the middle years of the nineteenth century, Flaubert's *Madame Bovary*. It is not certain that George Eliot ever read Flaubert's novel but it has intriguing affinities of theme and character with her own, beginning with its subtitle 'Moeurs de province', often translated as 'A Story of Provincial Life' which brings it close to *Middlemarch*'s 'A Study of Provincial Life'. Aspects of Emma Bovary's personality and predicament are echoed in the two principal female figures in *Middlemarch*. Although Dorothea's altruistic idealism has little in common with Emma's self-indulgent romantic fantasies, she does bear some resemblance to her as a victim of romantic illusions and marriage to an inadequate man; while Rosamond Vincy, who becomes like Emma a doctor's wife, matches her in aspirations to a higher class, in consumer desires and accumulation of debts, and in her apparent readiness for extra-marital affairs. Rosamond, of course, does not in the end commit adultery, and George Eliot is necessarily more circumspect than Flaubert in the handling of sexual relationships. The possibility of a form of romantic love that is passionate, violent and destructive is certainly acknowledged in Lydgate's experience as a student in Paris, where he becomes infatuated with an actress who murders her husband on stage, but it is explicitly bracketed off as foreign territory and dealt with only in a retrospective summary of his education.

Nevertheless, although the world of *Middlemarch* is subjected to a searching moral scrutiny as opposed to Flaubert's coolly aesthetic detachment, George Eliot can match him in the subtly suggestive representation of gesture and feeling, as can be seen in two closely comparable scenes of first encounter when the two doctors, Charles Bovary and Lydgate, meet the young women who are to become their romantically fanciful, domineering and materially extravagant wives. Both encounters end with an incident of reaching for a whip that brings the man and the woman into disturbing proximity and hints at their future relationship. Unable to find his whip, Charles ferrets around clumsily and comes into physical contact with Emma as she reaches down for the object that, significantly, she is the first to see and to seize (pt I, ch. 2). Flaubert discreetly conveys the erotic charge of the encounter and at the same time hints at its fateful consequences in the collision between his clumsiness and her neat control, and in the implications of the whip. She blushes as she hands him the whip of ox sinew ('nerf de boeuf') that is not so much an emblem of mastery as an ironic pointer to his bovine nature that she is to find so insupportable. The irony in the *Middlemarch* scene is less pointed and its erotic component more muted, conveyed not by unintended physical contact but by an involuntary meeting of glances as Lydgate anticipates Rosamond and reaches the whip before her: 'their eyes met with that peculiar meeting which is never arrived at by effort, but seems like a divine clearance of haze' (ch. 12). The moment foreshadows the later scene where he retrieves the chain she has dropped and finds himself proposing marriage to her in an involuntary compassionate response to her tears that well up in an unwonted 'moment of naturalness' (ch. 31). In their different ways – Flaubert's narration is impersonal, spare and staccato; George Eliot's more sympathetic and expansive – these two scenes show how the realist novel can take a commonplace object and a conventional social gesture and charge them with subtle intimations of character, erotic excitement and ironic prolepsis.

The story of how Lydgate, with his high hopes of doing 'good small work for Middlemarch, and great work for the world', comes to be 'shapen after the average' (ch. 15) by a combination of his own impulsive nature and the financial and political pressures of social life, belongs in the company of the great French realist novels of failed ambition like Balzac's *Illusions perdues* (*Lost Illusions*, 1837–43). Dorothea's happier progress, on the other hand, from the mistaken marriage to Casaubon to eventual modest domestic happiness with Ladislaw, is closer to Goethe, as suggested earlier. When, at the climax of her moral development, she acts on the resolution she has made at the end of her sleepless night of mental anguish and goes to help the Lydgates, the chapter epigraph consists of lines from a scene at the beginning of the second part of Goethe's *Faust*, in which Faust, on waking from his healing sleep, resolves henceforth to strive continually towards the highest form of existence (ch. 81). We are invited to see, clothed in the personal moral struggle of a young woman of the English provincial upper-middle class, a version of the grander Faustian quest, of the dynamic, thrusting individualism of European modernity.

The conjunction is arresting and yet subject to a distinctive and characteristic inflection. Dorothea's resolution to strive after the highest comes not after the convenient oblivion granted to Faust, but after a night of anguished wakefulness that is the mark of the fully developed moral consciousness in George Eliot's world, where the past is not allowed to be buried and the right deed may demand a painful struggle. Thus Dorothea may have an ambition directly reminiscent of Faust's 'to take a great deal of land, and drain it, and make it a little colony' (ch. 55), but it is an ambition purged of Faust's corrupting drive for power and lust for boundless experience. Faustian striving is reimagined from a feminine standpoint as a woman's ideal in an illustration of how George Eliot's fiction not only exploits but also interrogates its European connections.

Such interrogation can be seen as another aspect of the Cervantean legacy, as a contemporary European novelist, Milan Kundera, has defined it: 'The wisdom of the novel comes from having a question for everything. When Don Quixote went out into the world, that world turned into a mystery before his eyes. That is the legacy of the first European novel to the entire subsequent history of the novel. The novelist teaches the reader to comprehend the world as a question.'[6] The specific question that *Middlemarch* raises in its Finale is a version of the 'woman question' so central to George Eliot's work in general: as Dorothea's early idealism gives way to a muted role as wife and mother, exercising an 'incalculably diffusive' effect upon those around her, she joins the company of that half of humanity 'who lived faithfully a hidden life, and rest in unvisited tombs' (Finale), leaving the reader to ponder on women's actual, and potential, relation to history.

That question is raised earlier in the novel in the Casaubons' honeymoon visit to Rome when Dorothea, armed only with 'that toy-box history of the world' afforded by her limited education as a woman (ch. 10), finds herself overwhelmed by the fragmentariness of the 'city of visible history', with its 'ruins and basilicas, palaces and colossi, set in the midst of a sordid present' (ch. 20). The Roman episode disturbingly widens the horizons of *Middlemarch*'s study of English provincial life, and it is only a man and a Middlemarch outsider, Ladislaw, with his Polish blood and German university education, who can feel at ease there, finding the city's fragmentariness stimulating rather than oppressive. Just as Ladislaw puts Casaubon's scholarly work on mythology into critical perspective by pointing out to Dorothea his damaging ignorance of German, so foreign travel exposes some of the limitations of English provincial life. Barbara Hardy has argued persuasively that George Eliot's life and work shows a 'need for foreignness',[7] and that need can be understood as an intellectual appetite for the larger perspectives of European culture and the critical purchase on English life that they offer. When her characters travel abroad they may be seen in a new and not always flattering light. Rome marks a crisis for Dorothea in which her poise and her confidence in her married future are lost; and in *Daniel Deronda*, when Grandcourt and Gwendolen arrive in Genoa on their Mediterranean cruise, there is an arresting shift of perspective as they emerge from their hotel, presenting a scene that 'was as good as a theatrical representation for all beholders': 'This handsome, fair-skinned English couple manifesting the usual eccentricity of their nation, both of them proud, pale, and calm, without a smile on their faces, moving like creatures who were fulfilling a supernatural destiny – it was a thing to go out and see, a thing to paint' (ch. 54). By slipping into the perspective of ordinary Europeans, the narrator exposes the strangeness of what to English eyes might appear normal, the extraordinary arrogance of the upper-class English at the height of their imperial power, considering themselves to stand at the centre of civilised life. The foreign perspective becomes an instrument of irony.

George Eliot's express intention in *Daniel Deronda* was to 'widen the English vision a little' (*Letters*, VI.304) with respect to the Jews and Judaism, but the novel widens that vision in other ways, too: in the geographical reach of the action, in its probing of the dark areas of the psyche – 'the unmapped country within us' (ch. 24) – and in its narrative form. The novel begins in a German spa, moves back to provincial England and then on to London; important scenes follow in both Germany and Italy and it ends with Deronda and Mirah about to set out for Palestine to pursue their proto-Zionist mission. The centrality of travel is a symptom of the restless modernity of contemporary life which the novelist is exploring for the first time in a full-length novel, and in ways that invite comparison with Flaubert's similar project in his *L'Éducation sentimentale* (*Sentimental Education*, 1869), which she read, at least in part, after completing the first volume of her own work. Both novels engage with the problem of vocation in the modern world and carry echoes of the Goethean *Bildungsroman* in following the development of a socially privileged young man to starkly different conclusions. Where Daniel's existence is, in the end, given direction and meaning by a fulfilling love and a life's mission, that of Flaubert's Frédéric Moreau is denied the shape of constructive purpose and fulfilled ambition and is ultimately emptied of significance. But despite these opposite trajectories, and although George Eliot's social critique is never as witheringly ironic as Flaubert's, both novels have at their centre a troubled relationship with a woman – Daniel's with Gwendolen, and Frédéric's with Mme Arnoux – which is initiated in the first scene of the book and reaches its climax in the penultimate one without ever fulfilling the narrative expectations raised at its inception. This pattern of incompleteness and final openness anticipates the modernist novel, as does the arresting opening of *Daniel Deronda* which, in plunging directly into the thoughts of an unidentified mind – 'Was she beautiful or not beautiful?' – is as disconcertingly unanchored in place, time and specific character as the famous first paragraph of Marcel Proust's *À la recherche du temps perdu* (*In Search of Time Lost*, 1913–27). In this and other ways George Eliot's last novel begins to break new ground in the direction of modernism.

If the journey to Continental Europe proves disturbing for the characters of *Middlemarch* and *Daniel Deronda*, the European progress of these and George Eliot's other works was smoother. They were published on the Continent in English by Tauchnitz in Leipzig, except for *Middlemarch*, which went to his rival Asher in Berlin, and they were soon translated into French,

German and Dutch. George Eliot's impact on other novelists was less immediate. She was on friendly terms with Ivan Turgenev (1818–83) whom she
met for the first time in London in 1871 and who admired *The Mill on the
Floss* in particular as the most natural and artistic of her works. Tolstoy,
whose work, unlike Turgenev's, she did not know, included her in the list
of those writers who made a great impression on him between the ages of
35 and 50, the period in which he wrote his greatest novels *War and Peace*
(1863–9) and *Anna Karenina* (1873–7). Although he singles out *Scenes of
Clerical Life* (1857–8) and *Felix Holt, the Radical* (1866) for particular praise
in his letters, it is *Middlemarch* that has the closest affinity with his own
fiction, especially *Anna Karenina*, which works out the tragic potential in the
marriage of a vital young woman to a cold and pedantic older man. George
Eliot's narrator may be more prominent and the moral discriminations of her
novel more emphatic than Tolstoy's, but in 'unravelling certain lots, and
seeing how they were woven and interwoven' (ch. 15), *Middlemarch* creates
a narrative web of different lives rather as his own novel does, with its 'endless
labyrinth of linkings' in which he saw that 'the essence of art resides'.[8]

The great novelist of Prussian social life, Theodor Fontane (1819–98),
knew and admired her work though he had reservations about the accumulation of descriptive detail which he found oppressive. In Germany the
reputation she won in her lifetime, although it never matched that of Scott
or Charles Dickens (1812–70), did not experience the steep decline after her
death that occurred in Britain. In France she was only widely read after the
critic Ferdinand Brunetière began to champion her in 1881 in his campaign
against Émile Zola's naturalism, but it was there that she had perhaps her
greatest effect on the European novel in her importance for Proust (1871–
1922). Her novels were, he claimed, the cult of his adolescence and two
pages of the novel he loved most, *The Mill on the Floss*, could reduce him to
tears. In drawing on the deep springs of memory and dwelling on the
determining power of early experience, George Eliot's novel has a lasting
legacy in Proust's creation of Combray and his profound exploration of, in
the words of the Prelude to *Middlemarch*, 'the history of man, and how that
mysterious mixture behaves under the varying experiments of Time'.

## Note on editions

The standard edition is the Clarendon Edition of the Novels of George Eliot,
published by Oxford University Press, which now includes all her major
fiction except *Silas Marner*. Oxford World's Classics follows the Clarendon
texts, while Everyman and Penguin have useful editions with introductions
and notes.

JOHN RIGNALL

## Notes

1 David Carroll, ed., *George Eliot: The Critical Heritage* (London: Routledge and Kegan Paul, 1971), p. 323.
2 George Steiner, 'A Preface to *Middlemarch*', *Nineteenth-Century Fiction*, 9 (1954–5), 262–79.
3 Thomas Pinney, ed., *Essays of George Eliot* (London: Routledge and Kegan Paul, 1963), pp. 271, 287. Cited hereafter as *Essays*, with page references.
4 Gordon S. Haight, ed., *The Letters of George Eliot*, 9 vols. (New Haven, CT/London: Yale University Press, 1954–79), vol. v, p. 113. Cited hereafter as *Letters*.
5 'Belles Lettres', *Westminster Review*, 66 (July 1856), 262.
6 Milan Kundera, *The Book of Laughter and Forgetting*, trans. Michael Henry Heim (Harmondsworth: Penguin, 1983), p. 237.
7 Barbara Hardy, 'Rome in *Middlemarch*: A Need for Foreignness', *George Eliot – George Henry Lewes Studies*, 24–5 (1993), 1–16; and in *George Eliot: A Critic's Life* (London: Continuum, 2008).
8 From a letter of 1876 in Henry Gifford, ed., *Tolstoy: A Critical Anthology* (Harmondsworth: Penguin, 1971), p. 48.

## Further reading

Ashton, Rosemary, *The German Idea: Four English Writers and the Reception of German Thought, 1800–1860* (Cambridge University Press, 1980)
'Mixed and Erring Humanity: George Eliot, G. H. Lewes and Goethe', *George Eliot – George Henry Lewes Studies*, 24–5 (1993), 93–17
Couch, John Philip, *George Eliot in France: A French Appraisal of George Eliot's Writings 1858–1960* (Chapel Hill, NC: University of North Carolina Press, 1967)
David, Deirdre, 'Getting Out of the Eel Jar: George Eliot's Literary Appropriation of Abroad', in Michael Cotsell, ed., *1830–1876: Creditable Warriors*, English Literature and the Wider World, 3 (London: Ashfield Press, 1990), pp. 257–72
Fleishman, Avrom, *George Eliot's Intellectual Life* (Cambridge University Press, 2010)
'George Eliot's Reading: A Chronological List', *George Eliot – George Henry Lewes Studies*, 54–5 (2008), 1–106
Guth, Deborah, *George Eliot and Schiller: Intertextuality and Cross-Cultural Discourse* (Aldershot: Ashgate, 2003)
Kendrick, Walter, 'Balzac and British Realism: Mid-Victorian Theories of the Novel', *Victorian Studies*, 20 (1976), 5–24
McCobb, Anthony, *George Eliot's Knowledge of German Life and Letters* (Salzburg: Institut für Anglistik und Amerikanistik, Universität Salzburg, 1982)
Redfield, Marc, *Phantom Formations: Aesthetic Ideology and the* Bildungsroman (Ithaca, NY: Cornell University Press, 1996)
Rignall, John, *George Eliot, European Novelist*, Farnham/Burlington, VT: Ashgate, 2011)
ed., *George Eliot and Europe* (Aldershot: Ashgate, 1997)
ed., *Oxford Reader's Companion to George Eliot* (Oxford University Press, 2000)

Röder-Bolton, Gerlinde, *George Eliot and Goethe: An Elective Affinity*, Texas Studies in Comparative Literature, 13 (Amsterdam/Atlanta, GA: Rodopi, 1998)

Shaffer, E. S., 'George Eliot and Goethe: "Hearing the Grass Grow"', *Publications of the English Goethe Society*, n.s. 66 (1996), 3–22

*'Kubla Khan' and 'The Fall of Jerusalem'* (Cambridge University Press, 1975)

Thompson, Andrew, *George Eliot and Italy: Literary, Cultural and Political Influences from Dante to the 'Risorgimento'* (Basingstoke: Macmillan, 1998)

# 14

TIMOTHY UNWIN

# Gustave Flaubert (1821–1880): Realism and aestheticism

If it is the case, as Milan Kundera once stated, that 'every novelist's work contains an implicit vision of the history of the novel, an idea of what the novel is',[1] there can be no more exemplary illustration of that truth than the work of Gustave Flaubert. Supremely preoccupied with style and with the refinement of techniques handed down by previous generations, Flaubert heralds a new era of self-consciousness in the novel. As he hones his texts through many drafts in the solitude of the family home at Croisset, near Rouen, he pursues his reflection on literatures ancient and modern on a daily basis, wresting his own fictions from a truly vast programme of reading. At the same time, he scrutinises the complexities of narrative with a new intensity, and contemplates his own place within the literary tradition. Prose, he writes to his mistress Louise Colet on 24 April 1852, is the modern form of writing par excellence, replacing the ancient and established literary form, poetry: 'Prose was born yesterday ... All the combinations of poetry have been tried out, but as for prose, far from it.' Flaubert's sense of his own mission and modernity as a writer is manifest throughout his exceptionally readable correspondence. 'Before Flaubert', writes the Peruvian novelist Mario Vargas Llosa, 'novelists sensed intuitively that form played a key role in the success or failure of their stories ... But only after Flaubert does this spontaneous, diffuse and intuitive idea become rational knowledge, theory, artistic consciousness.'[2]

Like his first and most enduring literary model, *Don Quixote* – which he describes in a letter of 19 June 1852 as 'the book I knew by heart before I knew how to read' – Flaubert's work is at some level always an ironic rereading of the very conventions that have produced it. Writing is itself sometimes the raw material of his plots. Emma Bovary is misled by it, Frédéric Moreau turns to it for consolation, Bouvard and Pécuchet become overwhelmed by it. Even where there is no reading, there are imagined and retold narratives. In *Salammbô* (1862) the circulation of dogma, superstition and rumour are central to the unfolding of the plot; and in 'A Simple

Heart', the first of the *Trois Contes* (*Three Tales*, 1877), the illiterate Félicité attempts to reconstruct the story of her nephew's life at sea through vague second-hand information. But it is partly because Flaubert's characters are often readers too that he is able to establish both a close relationship and an ironic distance vis-à-vis his literary models. Throughout his work, there is a careful 'unwriting' of his predecessors (most obviously, but by no means uniquely, of Balzac), even as their themes are assimilated into his work. Thus, in *L'Éducation sentimentale* (*Sentimental Education*, 1869), Frédéric is advised by his friend Deslauriers to follow the example of Rastignac in Honoré de Balzac's *La Comédie humaine* (*The Human Comedy*), and much of the subsequent narrative is an unravelling of the Balzacian master plot.

Stylistic experiment is apparent from the outset with Flaubert. From the mid 1830s he produces tales of the fantastic, mysteries, philosophical and autobiographical works, historical and realist narratives, plays, physiologies and critical sketches. While some of the hallmarks of his later style are unmistakably present in these juvenilia – the ternary arrangement of sentences, the unusual manipulation of conjunctions and the use of what Marcel Proust was to term 'Flaubert's eternal imperfect'[3] – the roll call of his early themes is very much that of a young Romantic taking an apocalyptic stance on life. Yet there is early insistence, too, on the inability of language to express the range of human emotions, a theme that will return self-reflexively throughout the mature works. When Flaubert writes his early first-person novels, *Mémoires d'un fou* (*Memoirs of a Madman*, 1838) and *Novembre* (*November*, 1842), he inaugurates a lifelong experiment with point of view and the representation of subjectivity. However, it is with the first *Sentimental Education* (this 1845 novel bears its title and some themes in common with the work of 1869, but is otherwise a different text altogether) that Flaubert sets out his artistic manifesto for the first time. Written during the period when Flaubert suffered the first of a series of epileptic attacks that recurred throughout his life, the novel alternates its attention between two heroes. In the latter stages, it focuses on the character of Jules, a writer developing his vision of art. This becomes Flaubert's own portrait of the artist as a young man, as he formally lays down the ground rules of his approach, insisting on the need for an impersonal and detached style in which originality of vision is reached through sustained contemplation rather than through artificial inspiration. Above all, Jules decides, the world should not be seen restrictively in terms of his own feelings, but filtered through an understanding of points of view that may be radically opposed to his own. This precept will be repeated many times in Flaubert's correspondence, and is nowhere more vehemently expressed than in his exchanges with George Sand from the mid 1860s onwards: 'A novelist *does not have the right to express his opinion on anything,*' he writes on 5 December 1866 (Flaubert's emphasis). 'Has the good Lord ever given his opinion on anything? ... The first passer-by is more interesting than Mr G. Flaubert, because he is more *general*, and consequently more typical.'

While Flaubert may have established his lifelong principles of writing by the age of twenty-four, he remained unpublished – by choice – for another eleven years. During this period he wrote the first version of *La Tentation de Saint Antoine* (*The Temptation of Saint Anthony*), completed in 1849 and twice later reworked in the course of his lifetime. Despite Flaubert's recently formulated principles he was, however, too close to his subject, and the work, which is in a predominantly dramatic rather than narrative style, gave free rein to excessive lyrical tendencies. According to his friend Maxime Du Camp, Flaubert read his work aloud to him and to Louis Bouilhet over a four-day period in 1849 and was devastated when they advised him to throw it on the fire and start again with a more pedestrian subject. But Flaubert reflected productively on this disappointment and, in the course of the following eighteen months as he travelled to Egypt and the Middle East, considered a variety of new subjects, eventually choosing a story of provincial adultery. By the time he finally burst onto the literary scene with the serialisation of *Madame Bovary* in the closing months of 1856, he had created a radically different type of fiction, one which took the prevailing framework of realism and turned it inside out. With its intricate layers of meaning and its subtle yet endless shifts of narrative viewpoint, *Madame Bovary* is an extraordinary feat of writing that defies the banality and the dreary provinciality of its subject. Flaubert's contemporary Charles Baudelaire was the first to articulate this when, in a review of *Madame Bovary*, he claimed that the novelist had deliberately taken the tired realist genre that had fallen so far since its Balzacian heyday, and had out of this unlikely model crafted a work of sublime beauty. *Madame Bovary*, said Baudelaire, was, like all great works of art, a wager, and Flaubert had won it handsomely through his use of irony and the magnificence of his literary style.[4] Baudelaire's comments closely echo Flaubert's own view of what he was doing. 'I am considered to be infatuated with reality, whereas I despise it. It is out of hatred for realism that I undertook this novel', he writes to Mme Roger des Genettes on 30 October 1856. Throughout his correspondence, he will repeatedly emphasise this quest for beauty in and through the most unpromising, lacklustre and 'unheroic' material.

We might see one of the keys to Flaubert as being this shift from subject to style, with the expressive tension that results from it. Like Baudelaire, he believed that the worst subjects, properly treated, could be radically transformed. However, the act of aesthetic transformation needs the unpromising material to start with, for the alchemist has no reason to turn gold into gold. Just as Baudelaire takes ennui or the squalid realities of city life as his starting point for poetry, so too Flaubert takes the apparently undramatic qualities of ordinary existence as the platform for prose. As with Baudelaire, beauty is not an intrinsic property of things, but a function of context and perspective. It is created, artificial, requiring aesthetic prowess and subtle combinations. A successful work of art must be the product of patience and persistence rather than of inspiration (a notion from which both writers were at pains to distance themselves). 'There are neither beautiful nor ugly subjects', writes Flaubert on 16 January 1852, 'style being in itself an absolute way of seeing things.' So in most of his writings, Flaubert's material is that of humdrum mediocrity, the dullness of the everyday, the platitudes that seep through our language, the failure of heroism, the false ideals and the stupidity of modern life. *Salammbô*, the novel about ancient Carthage, may initially appear to be an exception with, for example, its shimmering and sumptuous descriptions of the heroine's attire or the Temple of Tanit. But one merely needs to scratch the surface to find, here as elsewhere, the familiar stock of human fecklessness and the same sense of the absurdity of the human condition. Art, for Flaubert, is also a stand against the bleak recognition that reality fails to live up to our dreams and aspirations. It is the ultimate refuge, but also the ultimate gamble. When writing his final novel, *Bouvard et Pécuchet* (*Bouvard and Pécuchet*, uncompleted when he dies of a cerebral haemorrhage in 1880), Flaubert feels that he himself is drowning in the sheer inanity of this story about two clerks who run the gamut of human knowledge and fail to master anything. 'Their stupidity is my own, and I am dying of it', he writes to Mme Roger des Genettes on 15 April 1875. *Bouvard and Pécuchet* is, though, like every one of Flaubert's texts in its different way, an exploration of limits, an attempt to subject the form of the novel to extreme conditions by way of finding its stress points.

It may seem odd that a novelist so widely revered – both by professional writers (in a famous article Henry James called Flaubert 'the novelist's novelist')[5] and by generations of enthusiastic readers – appears on the face of it to have so little to offer in terms of a positive vision of the world or of the finer nuances of human behaviour. Flaubert might seem to be at the opposite end of the spectrum from a writer like Jane Austen, whose delicate and subtle probing of human motives nonetheless influenced his own approach, and whose use of free indirect style was a clear forerunner of his own experiments with the same technique.[6] However, it is a crucial part of Flaubert's modernity that he finds his real subject-matter in drift, mediocrity, failure and stupidity, and in this respect his characters (most notably the caricatured copyists of his final novel) anticipate the faceless and incomplete figures that we later find in, say, Franz Kafka or Samuel Beckett. 'Flaubert discovered stupidity. I dare say that is the greatest discovery of a century so proud of its scientific thought', says Kundera, no more than a trifle provocatively.[7] The truth is that Flaubert's novels needed stupidity to function properly, just as they also needed self-delusion and weakness, precisely because they articulate on almost every page the richness and complexity that is to be found in those very states that may seem such unpromising literary material. One of his many achievements was to have found tragic grandeur in naivety, for example with a character like Félicité in 'A Simple Heart'. While his language as a novelist might be seen as uncompromisingly highbrow, he is in this crucial respect a champion of the ordinary. To argue, as Henry James did, that characters such as Emma Bovary and Frédéric Moreau were proof of a failure of imagination on the novelist's part, is to miss the point entirely. Flaubert's art operates knowingly in that space of dullness and mediocrity, prising it open to find its unsuspected resonances. The contemporary British novelist Nick Hornby once wrote that what he had always loved about fiction was 'its ability to be smart about people who aren't themselves smart, or at least don't necessarily have the resources to describe their own emotional states'.[8] This is exactly what Flaubert does with so many of his characters. Emma Bovary fascinates us because, while she may, in the narrator's words, be 'of a more sentimental than artistic temperament' (*Madame Bovary*, pt 1, ch. 6), her world of silly self-delusion is articulated with fine-tuned and delicate empathy. It is the ironic and self-satisfied judges – like her lover Rodolphe – who are ironically judged in their turn. As readers, we too are drawn into this trap of judgement, only to realise that the lowly world of Emma, nourished on the nineteenth century's equivalent of 'chick lit', is astonishingly rich and intense. When Rodolphe begins to tire of Emma, mistakenly seeing her as no different from any other mistress, the narrator intervenes (some would claim in defiance of Flaubert's precept of impersonality) with a reminder that human language is a blunt instrument when it comes to expressing the individuality of emotions, 'as if the fullness of the soul did not sometimes overflow in the emptiest of metaphors, since no one can ever give the exact measure of their needs, their ideas or their sorrows; and since human speech is like a cracked cauldron, on which we hammer out melodies to make bears dance when we long to move the stars' (*Madame Bovary*, pt II, ch. 12). And through the use of free indirect style, to which I shall return later in this essay, Flaubert is able not only to probe his heroine's feelings and impressions, but also to express them in a way that allows the reader to share and understand them. The Nobel prize-winning novelist

Orhan Pamuk highlights this aspect of Flaubert's work as one of its finest achievements: 'Here was a writer who could identify so thoroughly with his protagonists that he could feel in his own heart the misery and predicament of a struggling, married woman, Madame Bovary, and convey that dilemma to readers in a clear idiom.'[9] It is the same kind of sympathy and transforming vision that enables Flaubert, at the end of *Sentimental Education*, to create an extraordinarily intense and moving love scene out of the helpless platitudes uttered by Frédéric and Madame Arnoux, as they seek to fictionalise and legitimise their own story; and yet again, at the end of 'A Simple Heart' when the deluded Félicité achieves mystical fulfilment through her relationship with a stuffed parrot. There is always irony in such apotheoses, of course; but as Flaubert observed memorably on 9 October 1852, 'irony takes nothing away from pathos; on the contrary, it increases it'.

How does Flaubert's irony work? While there are, as in the case of Rodolphe's dismissive opinion of Emma's platitudes, some obvious direct interventions by a narrator who offers a judgement or undercuts a character's viewpoint, these may also be signposts that flatter to deceive. The point of view changes constantly, and in the course of its silky transitions, Flaubertian narrative brings together perspectives that might otherwise seem irreconcilable. The first and greatest of Flaubertian ironies is that we do not know precisely who is being ironic about whom, even when it may seem devastatingly (and treacherously) clear. The reader has no single perspective from which to assess characters or events, so wrestles with the complexities of their representation. Art, wrote Flaubert to Louise Colet on 8 October 1852, should be practised from the perspective of a 'cosmic joke', an affirmation that was to infuriate critics such as Jonathan Culler, whose provocative and lively discussion of Flaubert (see the Further reading) stresses the writer's misanthropic wish to unsettle his reader by giving the illusion of coherence while simultaneously undermining the realist precepts on which his work is based. In fact, Flaubert's point is an epistemological one: he starts from the belief that there can be no single vantage point on truth, which can be sought only by covering as many different positions as possible. The notorious 'undecidability' of the Flaubertian text is the logical result of this position, in which numerous possible readings must coexist.

So, while the Balzacian narrator appears to intervene directly, telling the reader what is needed for an understanding of the story (hence the hallmark 'Voici pourquoi' as Balzac shifts to analepsis), Flaubert operates in a covert manner. Ironic comment is implied rather than directly offered, and is usually a result of the way in which a phrase or a sentence functions in its context. Flaubert's novels are full of bland little sentences which, taken on their own, seem to convey something entirely trivial. However, in context, they assume a resonance and a power that can be out of all proportion with their lowly status. When in the first chapter of *Sentimental Education* we read 'Leurs yeux se rencontrèrent' ('Their eyes met') as Madame Arnoux meets Frédéric's gaze for the first time, these few words might strike us as of little consequence, and in any case they swiftly disappear in the ongoing narrative. After all, this is an encounter scene, and the words might seem entirely conventional for the purpose. But that, precisely, is the point. The story is a parody of that conventional moment of recognition when two strangers look into the window of each other's souls and fall in love. Ironically, that is precisely what does not happen here. Despite Frédéric's repeated attempts to construe this relationship as a romantic and passionate adventure, the love affair is a long-drawn-out, passionless business, beset by errors, misrecognitions, hesitations, uncertainties and betrayals. Flaubert's little sentence tells us everything we need to know – that this is an unwriting of the traditional love story – yet one of the additional ironies about it is that we can understand its function only when we know the full context and can return to reread Flaubert's subtle exploitation of the platitude. Flaubert often operates by shifting the meanings of his text out of the limelight and into these little side alleys, where the placing and the timing are all-important. For the Flaubert enthusiast, the magic of his style is here, and it heralds something new in literature.

Theodor Fontane's delicate and understated irony in novels like *Effi Briest* (1894) takes up directly where Flaubert left off, making the words mean much more than they appear to say. Literature will subsequently be brimful with creative adaptations of the Flaubertian model. Perhaps even the blandness of Kafka, for example in that opening line of *Die Verwandlung* (*The Metamorphosis*, 'When Gregor Samsa awoke one morning from uneasy dreams he found himself transformed in his bed into a gigantic insect') which delivers such impact with so little, would not have been possible without Flaubert. If Flaubert maintains the classic 'set pieces' of style of his predecessors, he also turns 'style' into something quite different. 'Sentences in a book', he asserts to Louise Colet on 7 April 1854, 'must tremble like the leaves in a forest, each of them different in its similarity.' The different elements of the mechanism are arranged to function together, sometimes in counterpoint as at the agricultural show in *Madame Bovary* (pt II, ch. 8), where two platitudinous discourses, that of the sub-prefect as he addresses the crowd and that of Rodolphe as he sweet-talks Emma, are interwoven to devastating ironic effect. Combinations, in Flaubert, give maximum impact to the tiniest sentence or word, or in the end even to the blanks between the sentences (it was Proust who, citing the gap between the two final chapters of *Sentimental Education*, hailed the blanks in Flaubert's prose as one of his great achievements). While Flaubert is often seen as the high priest of the *mot juste* – and it is true that the right choice of word was crucial to him – it is no less the case that the arrangement of the words themselves, as they set off those intricate and delicate ironic motifs that draw the story on, is massively important. Small wonder that Flaubert also exerted such a compelling influence on James Joyce who, in a very Flaubertian manner, affirmed: 'I have the words already. What I am seeking is the perfect order of words in the sentence.'[10]

Flaubert is also highly effective at the sentence that sums up or concludes either an entire narrative, or a section of a narrative. Sometimes, in the case of the story endings, this creates a hermeneutic puzzle. The ending of *Salammbô* invites a rereading and a reinterpretation of the story by offering what seems a bafflingly reductive explanation of the heroine's death: 'Thus died Hamilcar's daughter, for having touched the veil of Tanit.' At the end of *Sentimental Education*, Frédéric and Deslauriers evoke a pitiful scene in a brothel that had first been referred to analeptically in the second chapter of the story. They conclude that it was 'the best time we ever had' and thus apparently invite comparison between this remembered scene that has no bearing on the plot, and the life stories that have occurred in between. At the end of 'The Legend of Saint Julian the Hospitaller', the second of the *Three Tales*, the narrator offers a jaunty metacommentary on his story: 'And that is the story of Saint Julian the Hospitaller, roughly as it is found on a stained glass window in a church in my home region.' But, with Flaubert, the throwaway line is anything but that. It is a pointed reminder of the fictional process itself, indeed of the distorting effect that fictions have on the lives of the very protagonists of fiction. It is a reminder, too, that stories can be construed in many different ways, and that the real story is the open, multifaceted one that the concluding commentary reflects back on. But concluding one-liners can be found everywhere where a transition is necessary in Flaubert's work, and their impact is often in inverse proportion to their simplicity. When Emma Bovary dances with the Viscount at the Vaubyessard ball, the episode is narrated in a brief and breathless few lines. Then, suddenly, the dance is over and the Viscount escorts her back to her seat, where she covers her eyes for a moment. In the next, three-line paragraph, she looks up again to see a lady opposite being beckoned onto the dance floor by three men, and we read: 'She chose the Viscount, and the violin struck up once more' (*Madame Bovary*, pt I, ch. 8). With this quietly shattering sentence Flaubert signals a major transition in the narrative, yet if we blink we have missed it. As the violin heralds a new dance – another possible story with other participants – Emma is left on her own with only her dreams and regrets. That little sentence carries a fund of pathos, precisely because so little is said. At the same time, it also exhibits – yet ever so discreetly and quietly – its own narrative function as, performatively, it moves the story on in rhythm with the dances themselves. Flaubert's ability to invest the tiniest constituent parts of his prose with such wealth of meaning, indeed of pathos, might also be exemplified in another transitional line, the one that occurs after the last encounter between Frédéric and Madame Arnoux in the penultimate chapter of *Sentimental Education*. As Madame Arnoux steps out into the street and hails a passing cab, then disappears, we read simply: 'And that was all.' The metacommentary, in this instance, operates like a signal in a children's story that this is 'the end' – except that this is no fairy-tale end, and indeed is not quite the end anyway; rather it is the moment of unthinkable nothingness against which the whole narrative has struggled yet lived. This tiny one-line paragraph allows the love affair to fade gently out of sight, while also seeming to shriek in protest against its very own necessity.

Alongside Flaubert's ability to extract unexpected meanings from the simplest, sometimes even the most platitudinous of remarks, he develops a host of techniques that throw single words into sharp relief or highlight a particular quality of a scene. In his article on Flaubert's style, Proust claimed that Flaubert's highly idiosyncratic approach to grammar had renewed our way of looking at the world just as much as Kant's categories had. Any school pupil would, says Proust, be able to find errors and inconsistencies in Flaubert's style, but the point was that these were deliberate. Proust is, in January 1920, responding in the *Nouvelle Revue Française* to an article written in the same periodical the previous November by Albert Thibaudet, who had controversially claimed that Flaubert was not a naturally gifted writer, and that he had mastered his style only with great difficulty. While both commentators focus on the unusual rhythms of Flaubertian prose – its use of commas, the odd placing of prepositions and pronouns, the use of present participles, the switching of tenses and so on – for Proust these particularities of style, so highly recognisable, were methodically refined by Flaubert over many years as a means of expressing a particular vision of the world. And often, for readers of Flaubert, that vision is one that can, by syntactical means alone, freeze a moment in its strangeness or perhaps its unreality. In the second chapter of *Salammbô*, as the Barbarians are heading away from Carthage, they come across a row of crucified lions. They are first amused, then amazed. We read: 'Les Barbares, cessant de rire, tombèrent dans un long étonnement' ('The Barbarians, their laughter ceasing, fell into a state of lengthy astonishment'). The proximity of a present participle ('cessant') and of a past historic ('tombèrent') suggest a momentary hesitation then a swift transition of the mood. Yet the insertion of that adjective 'long'

(Flaubert could simply have written 'tombèrent dans l'étonnement', the definite article providing precision and familiarity) changes the entire aspect of the sentence. The moment is held up, and the Barbarians' 'astonishment' comes across as a continuous, strangely particular yet somewhat unreal state. A small syntactical adjustment has completely altered the way in which the image strikes us. This is the sort of effect that we find again and again in Flaubert as he quietly chips away at the mimetic foundations of narrative. It is often achieved by something as simple as the placing of an adverb at the end of a sentence, or even, with the short story 'Hérodias', the third of the *Three Tales*, at the end of the story itself. Defying all rules of *le bon usage*, Flaubert gives us this concluding image, as three men carry off the head of John the Baptist: 'Comme elle était très lourde, ils la portèrent alternativement.' English translations naturally avoid placing an adverb at the end, and give something like 'Since it was very heavy, they each took turns to carry it'. Yet the adverb, in French, is precisely the point, not only because it reinforces the sense of weight and effort, but also because it arrests the scene in mid flow after that final verb in the past historic, with this vision of a severed head being passed between three men. Just as James Joyce was later to do, Flaubert disrupts normal syntactical patterns and deliberately puts single words like this into sharp relief. Not for nothing have the similarities between the two novelists so often been evoked in critical literature. As Hugh Kenner wrote in his landmark study: 'If we want to see something in English that resembles [Flaubert's set pieces], we cannot do better than consult *Ulysses*.'[11]

There is one technique above all with which Flaubert's name is indelibly associated: free indirect style. While Johann Wolfgang von Goethe and Jane Austen, among others, had experimented with this form before him, Flaubert gives it new resonance by his blurring of the boundary between the discourse of the characters and that of the narrative itself. But what is free indirect style? In its simplest form, it is a version of reported speech in which the introductory or *inquit* verb – 'he said', 'she exclaimed', 'they replied' – and its pronoun are omitted, the reported statement being run on directly. With direct speech, we might read something like: 'She said: "The Marquise is leaving"'; in indirect speech this gives: 'She said that the Marquise was leaving'; and in free indirect style, simply: 'The Marquise was leaving.' In both the indirect and the free indirect forms, the tense is switched from the present to the imperfect. To take one simple example from *Madame Bovary*, when Léon goes to visit Emma in her hotel room in Rouen after the opera (*Madame Bovary*, pt II, ch. 1), a few remarks are exchanged in direct speech, and then, when Emma protests that Léon does not understand things from a woman's point of view, we read his reply (my italics show the free indirect style): '*Mais les hommes avaient aussi leurs chagrins*, et la conversation s'engagea par quelques réflexions philosophiques' ('*But men had their sorrows too*, and the conversation began with a few philosophical reflections'). The direct speech equivalent of Léon's rejoinder would be the utterance: 'But men have their sorrows too', perhaps even with an exclamation mark to signal mild protest. Now, when Flaubert is reporting utterances that obviously have a vocalised equivalent, as here, the process is straightforward. However, since he uses the technique extensively to report inner monologues and reflections, in addition to embedding it in the onward flow of the narrative where the staple tense of description is also the imperfect, the consequence is that it can be very hard to determine whether a sentence is free indirect style or part of a more general narrative discourse. In the first chapter of *Sentimental Education* we read, as Frédéric contemplates Madame Arnoux: 'He looked at her workbasket with astonishment, as if it were some extraordinary object. What were her name, her home, her life, her past? He wanted to know about the furniture in her room, all the dresses she wore, the people she was friendly with; and even physical desire disappeared into a deeper longing.' Here, the questioning of the second sentence reveals that at least part of the passage is in free indirect style, possibly a direct transposition of Frédéric's own questions about Madame Arnoux. But what about what follows? Are these statements of information by a privileged narrator, or an echo of what Frédéric is saying to himself? Or both? All that is certain is that the Flaubertian character's thoughts, when rendered in free indirect style, acquire a 'stream of consciousness' quality that blends them into the ongoing story. Flaubert thus obscures the limits of subjectivity, and the character's consciousness spills slowly out into the narrative itself. In the case of a character like Emma Bovary, this also broadens the focus and generalises her predicament. Emma's unhappiness is skilfully articulated for her by the novelist and given a kind of legitimacy, as when one day she passes in front of her old convent and is led to a despairing reflection on human life: 'nothing was worth the effort; everything was a lie. Every smile concealed a yawn of boredom, every joy a curse, every pleasure disgust, and the sweetest kisses left upon your lips only the impossible wish for some greater delight' (*Madame Bovary*, pt III, ch. 6).

With both Emma and Frédéric, it seems that the novelist is often lurking in the background, giving a prompt or indeed embellishing the language of his character and turning it into something more refined and more literary. While Proust maintained that the language of Flaubert's novels sometimes became so ordinary that it really could have been the language of the characters, one only has to compare Flaubert's use of free indirect style to Émile Zola's to see what the difference is. As Brian Nelson shows in his essay on Zola in this volume, in a novel such as *L'Assommoir* (1877), Zola's language is the popular idiom of the people, and almost the entire story is narrated as if through their speech. With Zola, there is deliberately no attempt to transpose the language of the street into the language of literature, but with Flaubert, it is another process altogether. When we read, early in Emma's marriage as she reflects that she might confide in someone, 'But how could she explain an indefinable unease that changes its form like the clouds and swirls around like the wind?' (*Madame Bovary*, pt 1, ch. 7), we are doubtless being confronted with Emma's own thoughts and her own pain, but they are expressed in a language which is self-consciously 'literary' (even though it may also be an ironic reflection of some of the things she reads). A simple view of the progress of free indirect style might conclude that Flaubert's experiments with it are as yet timid, as he clings to a classical notion of literary style that will be jettisoned by Zola, who pushes the experiment further. But Flaubert's aim is, precisely, to create a fusion of viewpoints, a style in which we never quite know whose discourse it is. This is what allows Flaubert to be both inside and outside the action of his stories. As he put it in his memorable dictum penned on 9 December 1852: 'The artist in his work must be like God in the universe, present everywhere, yet visible nowhere.' Free indirect style enables Flaubert to achieve just such a combination of presence and absence.

A further effect of Flaubert's use of free indirect style is to produce a fascinatingly expressive relationship between the imperfect tense (the tense of continuity, habit or state) and the past historic tense (the tense of action). In English, this distinction can be difficult to make, since the imperfect, or continuous past, and the preterite, or simple past, are often conveyed by the same form. So in English, 'she understood' could refer either to a single act of comprehension or a general cognitive state; but in French, there is a world of difference between 'elle comprit' and 'elle comprenait'. This being the case, when Flaubert does introduce the past historic tense amid or after a series of imperfects, one might think it is a very clear signal that we are back to the events of the narrative. What occurs, though, is a process of narrative contamination, since focalisation through the character, established by free indirect style, is maintained even when the tenses and the discourse have shifted. This is one more way in which the character's subjectivity spills out into the narrative. But let us look at the overall effect of these subtle processes in a passage from the early stages of *Madame Bovary* (pt 1, ch. 7), where Emma has become increasingly aware of her husband's limitations:

> Charles's conversation was as flat as a street pavement [*était* plate comme un trottoir de rue], and the whole world's ideas trooped through it [y *défilaient*] in

their everyday garb, producing neither emotion, nor laughter, nor thought. He had never had the curiosity, he said, while he lived in Rouen, to go to the theatre to see the actors from Paris. He could neither swim, nor fence, nor shoot [il ne *savait* ni nager, ni faire les armes, ni tirer le pistolet], and one day he was unable [il ne *put*] to explain a horse-riding term that she had come across in a novel.

The passage is continuously focalised through Emma, despite the inclusion of reported speech from Charles in the second sentence, and despite the shift to the past historic in the third. The first sentence appears to give Emma's own thoughts about Charles in free indirect style, for the tone is hers, and her exasperation is expressed both by the simile of the street pavement, and by the threefold enumeration of the emotions his conversation fails to produce. Yet the sentence is balanced, rhythmical, finely wrought and it seems that the language of the writer gives precision to the thoughts of the character, thus bringing legitimacy to her frustration. But her mood appears to sharpen into indignation in the second sentence, as we learn from Charles himself that he never went to the theatre in Rouen (the continuous 'disait-il' in French acquires an almost accusatory force, perhaps because it suggests a habitual response to Emma's insistent questions). And in the final sentence, while it seems that the reported speech is continued (Charles is telling Emma that he cannot swim, fence or shoot), the focalisation of the narrative remains with Emma herself, and this free indirect style could also be seen as a transposition of her own thoughts ('He can neither swim, fence nor shoot!'), with the 'neither ... nor' ('ni ... ni ... ni ... ' in French, making it even stronger) reinforcing her sense of outrage. And then, at the end of the passage comes the final, devastating 'il ne *put* ... lui expliquer un terme d'équitation' – the single event that damns and degrades Charles definitively in Emma's eyes. While it is the narrator who supplies the event and arranges its ironies (Rodolphe will certainly know all the horse-riding terminology required of him), we are made to feel the event from Emma's point of view. While viewing her romantic aspirations ironically, Flaubert also makes us empathise with Emma in her desperation. Free indirect style, carefully embedded in the narrative, allows this double focus; and the shifting of tenses, far from drawing a line between a character's perceptions and the events of the narrative, makes the one merge into the other.

'Without Flaubert', wrote Vladimir Nabokov, 'there would have been no Marcel Proust in France, no James Joyce in Ireland.'[12] It is tempting to seek a simple progress narrative here – though hard to imagine that Proust and Joyce would have been stumped for words had Flaubert not existed. However, there is no doubt that Flaubert's legacy has been massive. Almost every single practitioner of the genre has subsequently looked to him for inspiration and insight, and the admiration he provokes in modern and very different writers such as Julian Barnes or Orhan Pamuk is proof that his legacy is alive and well. This is not only because of his extraordinary and exemplary pursuit of precision and perfection as a writer, nor even because of his ability to make ordinary words sing such complex notes, nor even still because of his innovative exploration of the relationship between the subjectivity of characters and the language of the writer. It is also because his writing continues to raise questions both about *what* it means, and indeed about *whether* it means (in other words, whether there is a legitimate process of interpretation for the reader to engage in). In Flaubert, anything can be ironic, which also means, unsettlingly, that there may be no irony at all and that we have reached the limits of meaning. Sooner or later, every reader of Flaubert comes up against this problem, typically present in this, my final example taken from *Bouvard and Pécuchet* (ch. 5), where the characters are studying the Revolution: 'For some, the Revolution is a diabolical event. Others claim it is a sublime exception. The conquered on either side, naturally, are martyrs.' Three little sentences here resonate with the endless complexities of Flaubertian narrative, leaving us only with questions. Is the novelist knowingly reporting the platitudes of his characters, and being ironic at their expense? Is he himself pointing to the undecidability of all debate – historical, scientific, religious, literary or philosophical? Is he covertly admitting, perhaps, that the writing of anything and everything must eventually degenerate into bland nonsense such as this, that the novelist himself cannot avoid contamination by the very unliterariness of the world? And is writing itself no more than a futile wager against absurdity, a losing battle against the terminal sickness of language?

## Note on editions/translations

The best French edition is still *Œuvres complètes* (Paris: Seuil, 1964).

There are several modern translations of *Madame Bovary*, *Sentimental Education* and *Three Tales*. Good translations of *Madame Bovary* (2003), *Salammbô* (2005), *The Temptation of Saint Anthony* (1983), *Three Tales* (2005), *Bouvard and Pécuchet and Dictionary of Received Ideas* (1976) are available from Penguin and *A Sentimental Education* in Oxford World Classics (2008). The standard translation of the correspondence is the two-volume edition selected and translated by Francis Steegmuller (London: Faber, 1981, 1984). All translations in this chapter are my own.

## Notes

1 Milan Kundera, *The Art of the Novel* (London: Faber and Faber, 1986), p. 1.
2 Mario Vargas Llosa, 'Flaubert, our Contemporary', in Timothy Unwin, ed., *The Cambridge Companion to Flaubert* (Cambridge University Press, 2004), pp. 220–4 (220).
3 Marcel Proust, 'À propos du style de Flaubert', *La Nouvelle Revue française*, 1 January 1920, 72–90. Translated as 'On the Style of Flaubert', in John Sturrock, ed., *Against Sainte-Beuve and Other Essays* (London: Penguin, 1988), pp. 261–74.
4 Charles Baudelaire, '*Madame Bovary* par Gustave Flaubert', in *L'Artiste*, 18 October 1857, online at www.bmlisieux.com/litterature/baudelaire/bovary.htm Translated in Paul de Man, ed., *Madame Bovary* (New York: Norton, 1965), pp. 336–43.
5 Henry James, 'Gustave Flaubert' (1914), in *Literary Criticism: French Writers: Other European Writers* (Cambridge University Press, 1984), pp. 314–46 (329).
6 Helpful parallels with Jane Austen's *Emma* are drawn by Alison Finch, 'The Stylistic Achievements of Flaubert's Fiction', in *The Cambridge Companion to Flaubert*, ed. Unwin, pp. 145–64 (147–8).
7 Kundera, *The Art of the Novel*, p. 162.
8 Nick Hornby, *The Complete Polysyllabic Spree* (London: Penguin, 2006), pp. 161–2.
9 Orhan Pamuk, 'Monsieur Flaubert, c'est moi', lecture given at the University of Rouen, 17 March 2009, http://flaubert.univ-rouen.fr/etudes/pamuk_anglais.php
10 Frank Budgen, *James Joyce and the Making of 'Ulysses'* (Oxford University Press, 1972), p. 20.
11 Hugh Kenner, *Flaubert, Joyce and Beckett: The Stoic Comedians* (Normal, IL: Dalkey Archive Press, 2005), p. 30.
12 Vladmir Nabokov, *Lectures on Literature* (London: Weidenfeld & Nicolson, 1980), p. 147.

## Further reading

Barnes, Julian, 'The Cost of Conscientious Literature', in *Something to Declare* (London: Picador, 2002), pp. 251–67
Brombert, Victor, *The Novels of Flaubert* (Princeton University Press, 1966)
Culler, Jonathan, *Flaubert: The Uses of Uncertainty* (London: Elek; Ithaca, NY: Cornell University Press, 1974)
Finch, Alison, 'Reality and its Representation in the Nineteenth-Century Novel', in Timothy Unwin, ed., *The Cambridge Companion to the French Novel: From 1800 to the Present* (Cambridge University Press, 1997), pp. 36–53
Knight, Diana, *Flaubert's Characters: The Language of Illusion* (Cambridge University Press, 1985)
Porter, Laurence M., *A Gustave Flaubert Encyclopedia* (Westport, CT: Greenwood, 2001)
Unwin, Timothy, ed., *The Cambridge Companion to Flaubert* (Cambridge University Press, 2004)

# 15

SARAH J. YOUNG

# Fyodor Dostoevsky (1821–1881): 'Fantastic realism'

In Dostoevsky's final novel, *The Brothers Karamazov* (1880), the eldest brother, Dmitry, laments the 'broadness' of man and his simultaneous attraction to the 'ideal of the Madonna' and the 'ideal of Sodom' (bk III, ch. 3).[1] This conception of the coexistence of radical opposites within man forms the foundation for Dostoevsky's dramatisation of the 'accursed questions' of faith and doubt in a large *œuvre* of short stories and sprawling novels (as well as a significant body of journalistic writing), which eschews the 'normal' in favour of the extremes of human experience and behaviour, and develops an experimental style that contrasts sharply with the realism of his contemporaries Leo Tolstoy and Ivan Turgenev. His novels are populated by nihilists and holy fools, murderers, thieves and monks, saintly prostitutes and *femmes fatales*, consumptives and epileptics, Christ figures and devils, and would-be Napoleons, Rothschilds and de Sades. Great poverty and huge wealth exist side by side, as the socially disadvantaged – the 'insulted and injured', as Dostoevsky called them in his short novel of 1861 – rub shoulders with their exploiters in taverns and slums, monasteries and society salons. Scripture and philosophical debate alternate with violence, sensuality and corruption, in an atmosphere of scandal, melodrama and the grotesque, which owes much to the European Gothic novels the author devoured in his youth, but remains rooted in Dmitry Karamazov's question, 'How will [man] be righteous without God?' (bk XI, ch. 4). Considered by many to be a proto-existentialist, Dostoevsky is famous for the variety of readers he inspired and influenced, from Friedrich Nietzsche ('the only psychologist from whom I was able to learn anything') and Sigmund Freud, whose essay 'Dostoevsky and Parricide' analyses both the author and his works,[2] to writers as varied as André Gide, Virginia Woolf, Kurt Vonnegut and J. M. Coetzee. Denounced by the reactionary philosopher Konstantin Leontiev as a heretic,[3] but now viewed in Russia as a profoundly Orthodox novelist, Dostoevsky's works provided a point of departure not only for the religious philosophy of Vladimir Solovyov and

Nikolay Berdyaev, but also for Mikhail Bakhtin's theories of dialogism and polyphony. His significance for later generations of Russian writers, including poets such as Alexander Blok and Anna Akhmatova, and novelists from Evgeny Zamyatin and Mikhail Bulgakov to Victor Pelevin, not to mention Vladimir Nabokov, despite the latter's protestations to the contrary, cannot be overestimated.

Fyodor Mikhailovich Dostoevsky was born in Moscow to an impoverished family of serf-owning minor nobility, his father working as an army doctor at a hospital for the poor. Educated in St Petersburg, and firmly associated with that city for much of his career, Dostoevsky initially came to public attention in 1846 with the publication of the sentimental epistolary novella, *Poor Folk*, which depicts the relationship between a poor middle-aged government clerk and the vulnerable young girl he loves. Lavishly praised, the work led to the influential literary and social critic Vissarion Belinsky proclaiming Dostoevsky as the inheritor of the 'natural school' tradition of critical realism;[4] he was widely touted as Nikolai Gogol's successor. However, as the hero of *Poor Folk*, Makar Devushkin, contemplates his own failure and how other people view him, Dostoevsky already goes beyond Gogol, insofar as, Bakhtin states, 'everything that usually serves an author in creating a fixed and stable image of the hero, "who he is," becomes in Dostoevsky the object of the hero's own introspection, the subject of his self-consciousness'.[5] Subsequent early works, including *The Double* (1846), a story in the fantastic genre about a socially inept – and again agonisingly self-aware – middle-ranking bureaucrat whose oppressive life results in the appearance of his *Doppelgänger*, received far less enthusiastic reviews, and the author quickly fell from favour. Although Dostoevsky later admitted that the form of the story had been unsuccessful, the idea of doubling, the external manifestation of internal schisms caused by tension between incompatible beliefs or emotions, remained a constant throughout his career, and he described it as his most serious contribution to literature.[6]

During this period, under the repressive regime of Nicholas I, Dostoevsky, like many of his contemporaries, became involved in a philosophical discussion group, in his case the Petrashevsky circle. In 1849 he was arrested and sentenced to death along with other members for political offences. The sentence was commuted moments before the prisoners faced the firing squad, and Dostoevsky spent four years in penal servitude in Omsk, followed by exile in Semipalatinsk, returning to St Petersburg at the end of the 1850s. Unsurprisingly, the profound effect of the death sentence and imprisonment is evident in the development and preoccupations of all his subsequent work. The publication in 1861–2 of *Notes from the House of the Dead*, a fictionalised account of his incarceration in the hard labour camp, restored Dostoevsky's literary credentials. *Notes from Underground* (1864), in which the 'paradoxical', irrational, spiteful narrator polemicises in the name of freedom with the radical ideas of the day, in particular the 'rational egoism' and utopian utilitarianism of Nikolay Chernyshevsky's popular novel *What is to be Done?* (1863), marked a shift towards the philosophical fiction of his mature career. The four great 'murder' novels for which Dostoevsky is best known were written in the last fifteen years of his life: *Crime and Punishment* (1866) charts the consequences of the murder by a poverty-stricken student, Raskolnikov, of a vicious old moneylender and her gentle sister; *The Idiot* (1868) portrays the disastrous encounter of an outsider, the naive, epileptic Prince Myshkin, with St Petersburg society, culminating in the death of the heroine, Nastasya Filippovna; *Demons* (1871–2, also translated as *The Devils* and *The Possessed*), inspired by the murder of a student at the anarchist Sergey Nechaev's instigation in 1869, depicts the chaos and murder wreaked on a provincial town by a small group of revolutionaries, against a background of intergenerational conflict; and *The Brothers Karamazov* revolves around family relationships and rivalries, the murder of the father, and the responsibility of his sons.[7]

In these novels, the critique of rationalism begun in *Notes from Underground* is developed in the recurring image of the 'anthill', as the dystopian epitome of social reorganisation into harmonious, homogenised order. The unity represented by the anthill is specious, as it depends on crushing the individual and denying freedom. Raskolnikov's Napoleonic aspirations, as he attempts to prove that he belongs to the 'one tenth' of humanity to whom ordinary laws do not apply, are transformed into a nightmarish vision of 'unlimited despotism' and enforced equality in Shigalyov's revolutionary doctrine in *Demons* (pt ii, ch. 7). The theory receives its most powerful expression in Ivan Karamazov's 'poem', 'The Grand Inquisitor', in which Christ reappears in sixteenth-century Seville and is incarcerated and accused of misunderstanding humanity. Out of love, the Inquisitor explains, the Catholic Church has rejected the burden of freedom entailed by Christ's refusal to accept the devil's temptations, and replaced it with 'miracle, mystery and authority', turning mankind into contented slaves (bk v, ch. 5). The anthill theory is significant not only as a response to contemporary 'ideas in the air' (or, indeed, as has frequently been suggested, as a prophecy of the Russian Revolution), but also in terms of its psychological impact on the characters and the effect this has on the form of the texts. In *Crime and Punishment*, Raskolnikov's apparent attempt to construct and live by a rational world-view is undone by the forces of irrationality: the dreams, hallucinations, illness and, ultimately, love, which pervade the text. Meanwhile, the obsessive focus of the narrative on the mind of the murderer as he attempts to understand why he committed the crime, his position with regard to his own theories, and his relationship to the rest of the world, undermines his, and the reader's, reality. Almost everything is excluded except his 'doubles', the nihilistic sensualist Svidrigaylov and the Christian prostitute Sonya, an intrusion of the fantastic in that they are not only 'real' characters but also emanations of Raskolnikov's psyche and embodiments of the choice he faces, between suicide and confession.

The 'idiot' hero of Dostoevsky's next novel, Prince Myshkin, represents a stark contrast to Raskolnikov, although he was originally conceived as an amoral character and underwent a radical transformation in the planning stages of the novel, emerging as a positive figure.[8] The origins of both Myshkin's spiritual world-view, in the transcendent experience of the moment before his epileptic fits, and his character – compared in the novel to Don Quixote (pt II, ch. 6) and linked in Dostoevsky's notebooks and letters to Christ[9] – confirm his association with the irrational and the fantastic. At the same time, his meekness, humility and compassion provide an alternative to Raskolnikov's violent solipsism, and radically alter the form of the novel, as the claustrophobic and compulsive narration of *Crime and Punishment* is dissipated through Myshkin's concern for the other. Not only are we presented with a much larger cast of characters, but Myshkin's self-effacement cedes the narrative to their preoccupations, chief among them the largely absent heroine, Nastasya Filippovna, and her relationship with the prince himself. The result is a curiously plotless text constructed from the characters' inserted narratives, which attempt to tell a story that nobody – neither characters, the narrator, nor the reader – knows. Myshkin's attempts to imbue compassion in others, meanwhile, not only fail, but lead to an erosion of his own goodness.

While *The Idiot* radiates outwards from Prince Myshkin, a reversal of this movement is evident in *Demons*, as the elusive, empty character of Nikolay Stavrogin acts as the focal point for narrative, characters and readers. Like Nastasya Filippovna, he is present for only a fraction of the novel, but is the subject of obsessive attention. In particular, his actions and words before the story begins are a source of endless discussion and fascination. The contrast with his silence, inaction and shadowy nature – he almost always appears at night – in the present time of the novel suggests that he is barely more than a construct of rumour, the combined production of the consciousnesses of his lovers – Shatov's wife and sister, and the young aristocratic woman Lizaveta Nikolayevna, as well as the wife he married for a dare, the crippled holy fool Maria Lebyadkina – and those he has inspired ideologically: the cynical revolutionary Pyotr Verkhovensky, the would-be man-God bent on suicide, Kirillov, and Shatov, the champion of Russian Orthodox messianism who cannot yet believe in God. Reverting to the model of *Crime and Punishment*, Dostoevsky, who had been preoccupied in the late 1860s with plans for two ultimately unwritten works, *Atheism* and *The Life of a Great Sinner*, the titles of which amply indicate their subject matter, in *Demons* intensifies the conception of amorality resulting from nihilist ideas to the point of insanity, as indicated by the novel's epigraph from the story of Jesus casting out devils (Luke 8.32–6). Stavrogin's ultimate, if passive, role in the frenzy of violence which ensues is related not only to the revolutionary conspiracy in the town but, as is made clear in the chapter suppressed by Dostoevsky's publisher, Mikhail Katkov, in which Stavrogin confesses to the rape of a child, also to his sexual predation; the murders of Maria Lebyadkina and her buffoonish brother, and Lizaveta, are all the result of Stavrogin's affair with the latter. The implicit connection between Svidrigaylov's moral nihilism and Raskolnikov's experimentation with political nihilism in *Crime and Punishment* is here made explicit and moved into the foreground.

The fragmented nature of Stavrogin, expressed in the presence of multiple doubles, apart from whom he has a minimal separate existence, channels and unifies all attention, and all levels of meaning in the novel, through his character. In Dostoevsky's final novel, the three Karamazov brothers, plus their probable illegitimate half-brother, Smerdyakov, create a composite character which is distilled in the concept of the all-encompassing, life-affirming 'Karamazov' nature and Dmitry's characterisation of man's 'broadness', and is epitomised by their debauched father, Fyodor Pavlovich. With Dmitry belonging primarily to the sensual realm, Ivan to the rational and Alyosha, the youngest, to the spiritual – thereby restoring the religious dynamic with which Dostoevsky experimented in *The Idiot*, albeit now in a healthier and less ethereal form – the unity of the brothers' portrayal is confirmed by the slippage they experience between categories: Alyosha, for example, is susceptible to both Dmitry's 'insect of sensuality' (bk III, ch. 3) and Ivan's rational arguments against God. Equally, the women associated with the family embody the connections between and contradictions within the men. Grushenka, a local woman of apparently easy virtue – reputations in Dostoevsky's gossip-ridden world frequently cannot be taken at face value – is the cause of much of the novel's conflict, as Fyodor Pavlovich intends to marry her and Dmitry falls in love with her, but she is changed during the novel in part through her friendship with Alyosha. Katerina Ivanovna, Dmitry's proud fiancée, is all too ready to betray him for Ivan's sake, and although we witness Alyosha's relationship with the sickly misfit child Liza Khokhlakova, we are disturbed by references to another bond developing in the margins of the page, between Liza and Ivan.

In addition to the interconnected configuration of the characters, the tension between two opposing world-views, exemplified by the theories attributed to Ivan, 'if there is no immortality of the soul, then there is no virtue, and therefore everything is permitted' (bk II, ch. 7), and the Elder Zosima, 'each of us is guilty before everyone in everything' (bk VI, ch. 2), informs the whole novel, in a conception which integrates all the facets of Dostoevsky's mature *œuvre*. Ivan's impassioned rebellion against God's world as basing future harmony on the suffering of children (bk V, ch. 4) is intensified in 'The Grand Inquisitor', where the idea of the salvation of humanity through Christ is ridiculed, and the price of human freedom questioned. The power of Ivan's argument led many early commentators to see him as a mouthpiece for Dostoevsky's views,[10] but there is little doubt that Dostoevsky, as he stated in a letter to Konstantin Pobedonostsev, procurator of the Holy Synod, intended both the hagiographic 'Life and Homilies of the Elder Zosima' (bk VI), and the novel as a whole, as a refutation of Ivan's ideas.[11] Without offering a direct answer to Ivan's charges (which are chosen because of their unanswerability), Zosima posits an alternative conception of reality based on brotherhood, humility and active love as unifying all of nature and providing the seed of the novel's epigraph from John's Gospel (12.24) which, when it falls to the ground, brings forth new life. As the novel progresses, much of Zosima's doctrine is actualised. It becomes increasingly apparent that the responsibility for the death of the father does indeed lie within all the sons, whether their sins are of commission or omission; Dmitry's realisation of his own guilt, following his dream of a crying baby, demonstrates, as does Alyosha's vision of the marriage feast at Cana following the Elder's death, that the miracle lies in faith itself; Ivan, meanwhile, is stuck in the hell Zosima describes, that of not being able to love.

## Knowing the other

The critique of rationalism that shapes the ideological framework of Dostoevsky's novels grew out of the transformation of Russian intellectual life in the 1850s, of which the author became acutely aware upon his return to European Russia. While Dostoevsky had by this stage abandoned his youthful attachment to Fourierist utopian socialism and was moving towards a more conservative position, albeit maintaining a strong concern for social justice throughout his life, radical thought had shifted away from the Hegelian idealism of the 1840s to a more overtly revolutionary position.

In particular, the combination, within the doctrine of the nihilists, as they became called, of atheism, utilitarianism and the Feuerbachian materialist anthropologism espoused by Chernyshevsky in *The Anthropological Principle in Philosophy* (1860), which posited man's wholeness and rejected the dualism of body and soul,[12] elicited a significant response from Dostoevsky. Already in the appearance of the *Doppelgänger* in *The Double*, but also in the use of doubles in all his major works, the fragmentation of Stavrogin and the triadic presentation of the Karamazov brothers, Dostoevsky's dualistic conception of man is evident. It is fundamental, moreover, to the double-voiced discourse, directed towards another's speech, defined by Bakhtin as the most prevalent form of dialogue in Dostoevsky,[13] because so much of that dialogue is internalised and cut off from the other. This is apparent in *Notes from Underground*, where the unnamed narrator, living in isolation following the miserable encounters with the world he describes in Part II, polemicises in Part I with the anticipated responses of the audience that exists only within his own mind, betraying his hostility towards the other's consciousness, and his simultaneous dependence on it.[14] In *Crime and Punishment* as well, Raskolnikov argues primarily with himself, and even restricts his communications with others to internal polemics, as in the case of his argument with his mother's plan to marry his sister, Dunya, to Luzhin, a wealthy, unscrupulous businessman, which consists of his repetitions of phrases from her letter and his own retorts (pt 1, ch. 4). As Raskolnikov's crisis intensifies, his doubles, Sonya and Svidrigaylov, manifest the polarised content of his internalised voices.

The content of the underground man's argument, as well as its form, develops from the same preoccupation; the idea of 'act[ing] directly contrary to one's own best interests' to prove one's 'independent volition' (pt 1, ch. 7) points towards the primacy of the dualistic conception in the assertion of free will. It suggests that individuality is dependent on freedom, and has its core in the irrational side of human nature. The dreams and hallucinations encountered frequently in Dostoevsky's works, such as those originating in Raskolnikov's sickness (and his conscience) and Svidrigaylov's proximity to death in *Crime and Punishment*, evince the existence of an unconscious, which is not only irrational but also, crucially, inaccessible to the other. These factors indicate that the insistence on duality emphasises the presence of a soul or inner being denied by the Chernyshevskian construct, and suggests that mankind is not amenable to rational social reorganisation not only because of his irrationality, but also because the unknowability of his inner being renders it resistant to calculation, even to oneself, as Raskolnikov, and later Ivan Karamazov, discover. At the same time, excluding the inner being from calculation results either in murder – Raskolnikov's response – or the slavery of Shigalyov's vision in *Demons*, which reduces men to outer bodies, as the 'nine tenths ... will have to lose their individuality and be turned into something like a herd, and through unlimited obedience will attain, by a series of regenerations, a state of primeval innocence, something like the primeval paradise, although they will work' (pt ii, ch. 7).

By describing human existence without consideration of inner being, Shigalyov's theory confirms its necessity and inviolability, but in doing so also emphasises the problem inherent in all interaction: the essence of the other – what makes him or her human and individual, what he or she thinks and feels – remains hidden and incalculable. A tension is therefore engendered between the knowable external person and the inaccessible inner being, which has a profound effect on both Dostoevsky's thematics of interpersonal relations, and his narrational and structural principles. This disrupts the intensely internalised discourse we see in *Notes from Underground* and *Crime and Punishment*, and introduces a different model of narrative in the later novels. From *The Idiot* onwards, attention shifts from the workings of a single consciousness to the dynamics of the crowd and the external interplay between characters. Internalised dialogue becomes much less frequent, and instead the characters' self-presentation dominates, in the form of inserted narratives and speeches directed towards the external other. In *The Idiot*, as characters recount the stories of their worst deeds (which are patently nothing of the sort), read out newspaper articles slandering the hero and parodically compare him to Alexander Pushkin's version of Don Quixote, the 'poor knight', the role of Prince Myshkin's compassion, humility and truthfulness as the eye of the storm of lies, gossip and accusation revolving around him emphasises the impossibility of knowing the other and the ease with which society can break down in the face of this, and poses the question of how humans therefore can act as moral beings in order to avert such a disaster.

As the focus of Dostoevsky's novels becomes externalised, corresponding changes in the position of the narrator have profound implications for both the form of narrative, and the possibility of storytelling itself. The confessional first-person narrative of *Notes from Underground*, and the omniscience of *Crime and Punishment* (also planned as a first-person narrative, and retaining traces of that form in its insistent focalisation on Raskolnikov) are adequate to the solitary, internalised consciousness of those works, but Dostoevsky's awareness of the limitations of these forms, in particular the ambiguities regarding motivation and manipulation of the audience inherent in confessional narratives – apparent in his repeated use of intertextual allusions to Jean-Jacques Rousseau[15] – impelled him towards new styles of narration. As a result, we see the author gradually move towards an embodied narrator-chronicler who knows no more than the characters or the reader. It is at this point that Dostoevsky's novels achieve the full polyphony defined by Bakhtin; the logical conclusion of the creation of the self-conscious hero who is the subject of his own discourse, and the dialogue of independent voices, is the rejection of hierarchical principles, so that the author–narrator becomes merely one voice in that dialogue. The depriveleging of the narrational voice, moreover, raises further questions about knowability (and reliability) in narrative: which story is being told, by whom, for what reason, and to what extent is it (un)knowable? In *The Brothers Karamazov*, the trial of Dmitry dramatises these questions, as the prosecution and defence – as well as rumours circulating in the town – create different versions of events, none of which has full access to their subject's actions, and the jury's decision ultimately depends on who can tell the best story.

In *The Idiot* and *Demons* as well, the limited purview of the narrator creates texts dominated by gaps and silence, while uncertainty over what the story really is leads to its substitution by rumour, further decentring the narrator and emphasising the unreliability of the narrative as a whole. The presence in *The Idiot* of a six-month lacuna during which the main events of the plot, the love triangle between Prince Myshkin, Nastasya Filippovna and Rogozhin, are played out – in the narrative as given, we witness only the protagonists' initial encounters, and the denouement of their relationships – highlights everything we cannot know and stresses, in the absence of an omniscient overview, the similarity in the position of characters and readers. In *Demons* the disintegration of narrative derives explicitly from the breakdown of personality and interpersonal relations. The empty nature of Stavrogin, manifested in the image of the mask, which recurs throughout Dostoevsky's *œuvre*, epitomises the mystery of the other, and the impossibility of seeing beyond externals. The narrator-chronicler reports that, 'it was said that [Stavrogin's] face resembled a mask' (pt I, ch. 2), but his later attempt to reject this characterisation does not stand up to scrutiny; he proves as incapable of understanding Stavrogin as everybody else. The impenetrability of Stavrogin is further accentuated in the representation of scenes to which the ostensibly embodied narrator – an inhabitant of the town who is marginally involved in events – logically can have no access. Frequently concentrating on Stavrogin's external appearance at moments when he is alone or being spied upon ('his face was pale and severe, just like a statue, motionless; his brow was somewhat crooked and knitted; he looked decidedly like a lifeless wax figure'; pt II, ch. 1), the point of view of the onlooker (here, Stavrogin's mother) intensifies rather than reduces his absolute unknowability, which inspires fear and prevents communication. Meanwhile, the overt inclusion of such formally 'impossible' scenes – a strategy likened to the presence of an invisible stenographer, which Dostoevsky derived from Victor Hugo's *Le Dernier Jour d'un condamné* and defined as 'fantastic' (*WD*, 1.678) – undermines the reader's trust by bringing into focus the inherent falsity of omniscience as a narrative strategy in the realist tradition. The limited purview shared by characters, narrator and reader obscures and fragments the psychological and ethical drama Stavrogin embodies. As the external, more obviously eventful, and tellable, disruption caused by the revolutionaries he has inspired takes over, the deflection of the narration away from the main story locates social collapse and narrative breakdown equally in the problematising of relationships. If human interaction is jeopardised by the impossibility of fully understanding or communicating with the other, then the form of Dostoevsky's works, structured on doubts surrounding narrative's ability to communicate, suggests that the reader's dialogue with the text is similarly unstable.

## Criminality and compassion

The inward-looking dialogic form for which Dostoevsky is perhaps still best known has its earliest complete expression in *The Double*. Based on the isolation of the main characters, as in the case of Mr Golyadkin and the narrator of *Notes from Underground*, their inability to communicate with and apprehend the other must thus be considered the fundamental problem. Conversely, a focus on the external aspects of this process, a prelude to his mature polyphonic text, is also apparent in Dostoevsky's early works. The epistolary form of *Poor Folk* foregrounds the question of communication, including the perils of self-revelation before another of whose motives one can have only the vaguest idea, and the ever-present possibility of misreading and misinterpretation, either accidental or wilful. In the unfinished *Bildungsroman* of a poor young girl, *Netochka Nezvanova* (1849), the publication of which was interrupted by Dostoevsky's arrest, the recurring theme of the heroine's failure to understand the other marks both her own relationships with her parents and the young princess Katya, with whom she falls in love, and her observation of others' relationships, including that of her mother and stepfather, and those in the aristocratic households in which she lives following the death of her parents. Her blind meddling in the marriage of her third guardians, which causes her to reflect that 'we only mystify one another ... and it all comes from lack of experience, from our being unaccustomed to accept external impressions',[16] provokes the final crisis of the extant text, and indicates that, had Dostoevsky been able to complete the novel, this would likely have remained a central theme.

At this stage, the inability to apprehend the other appears to be a predicament which primarily afflicts the 'insulted and injured', and may thus be viewed in relation to the author's early preoccupation with social justice. The development of this conception in his later works, however, pivots on Dostoevsky's most direct encounter with Russia's poor, the peasant convicts alongside whom he lived during his years of hard labour, and the depiction of the relationship of the narrator, Alexander Petrovich Goryanchikov, with these peasants in *Notes from the House of the Dead*. Goryanchikov, a nobleman convicted for murdering his wife – a somewhat inconsistently applied fiction created by Dostoevsky at least in part to overcome the censorship, which was to lead to misconceptions about the nature of his crime for the rest of his life (*WD*, 1.353) – refers constantly to his inability to know his fellow convicts (and vice versa) and the unbridgeable gulf that exists between them.[17] However much Goryanchikov focuses on the other in his 'notes', and attempts to adopt the perspective of an anthropologist ('out of curiosity I became more closely acquainted with him and studied him for a whole week'; pt I, ch. 4), he is consistently unable to gain access beyond the faces and actions of other prisoners. As a result, he resorts to sweeping assertions pointedly unsupported by any evidence: 'Scarcely a single one of them inwardly admitted his own lawlessness' (pt I, ch. 1); and extrapolation from the state of his own inner being; we see no direct evidence of Goryanchikov's acknowledgement of his own guilt. Equally, the peasants cannot, or will not, look beyond externals ('curiosity was unfashionable'; pt I, ch. 1), and judge Goryanchikov solely on the basis of his identity as a nobleman with whom, even where ostensibly cordial relations exist, they can have nothing in common; they are mystified, for example, by his desire to join their protest about the quality of food (pt II, ch. 7). The frame narrative that introduces Goryanchikov's story reinforces the theme of unknowability. The fictional editor who encounters Goryanchikov in a Siberian town following his release, and discovers his manuscript after his death, proves equally incapable of seeing beyond the face. The image he presents of Goryanchikov as gloomy, fearful of human relations and lacking in intellectual curiosity, is totally at odds with the image Goryanchikov presents of himself, creating an impasse in the novel which is resistant to interpretation; the reader cannot know Goryanchikov, who is at once double-faced and overwhelmingly faceless, either. Thus the impossibility of knowing the other becomes the central question not only in maintaining interpersonal relations both during and after imprisonment, but also in telling – or reading – the story of those relations.

The enforced communal existence Goryanchikov endures in the labour camp, which he describes as 'one more torment, which is almost more powerful than all the others' (pt 1, ch. 2), adds a further dimension to the question of the inaccessibility of the inner being. Living in such close proximity to the most violent and depraved criminals, who have by definition denied the autonomy and significance of the other as a human being, the need to know what they are thinking may be more acute than under normal circumstances, while ignorance of the contents of their hearts and minds may at the same time seem preferable. The extreme situation Goryanchikov faces, which echoes the communal existence of the anthill in Dostoevsky's later novels, exemplifies the tension between the necessity and impossibility of knowing the other, leaving communication on a knife-edge, as rejecting it is both desirable and potentially fatal.

The shift towards an externalised mode of narration in the context of the problem of both knowing and representing the brutality and hostility of the peasantry relates Dostoevsky's development as a writer to what he later described as the 'rebirth of [his] convictions' (WD, 1.290) as a result of his experience of the labour camp. The autobiographical short story 'The Peasant Marei' (1876), in which the recollection, while in the camp, of a kind deed performed during his childhood by one of his father's serfs, reminds Dostoevsky of the difference between the peasant's coarse, violent exterior and the potential for humanity within, and leads to the realisation that 'I could not look into his heart' (WD, 1.355). The incident does not appear in Notes from the House of the Dead, and may be considered primarily as evidence of Dostoevsky's evolving understanding of the significance of the peasantry in the years after his imprisonment. When a fellow prisoner, a Polish aristocrat, shudders, 'Je hais ces brigands! [I hate these brigands!]', the author's response, 'The unfortunate man! He could have no memories of any Mareis', indicates that as the peasantry moves to the centre of Dostoevsky's conception of national identity as the 'God-bearing' people, as Shatov calls them in Demons (pt 11, ch. 1), their very separation from educated Russians becomes the basis for acknowledgement of the problem of the unknowability of the other, and ultimately offers the possibility of a solution to the tensions this creates in interpersonal relationships.

In Notes from the House of the Dead, Goryanchikov insists that the peasant convicts exhibited 'not a trace of shame or repentance' (pt 1, ch. 1), yet in the same chapter he has already observed a taboo around discussions of crimes, which suggests the workings of conscience: 'it was unpleasant to talk about that'. He later acknowledges the presence of some Christian feeling, which again implies consciousness of their sins, in the fervour with which they accept the sacrament on religious holidays. The goodness attributed to Marei, however, not only seems entirely absent in Dostoevsky's earlier portrayal of the peasantry, but even the later story emphasises the presence of both extremes in such figures; the fearsome, depraved, drunken peasant Gazin 'could also, perhaps, be that same Marei'. Brutality and alienation from the ruling classes are central to Dostoevsky's image of the peasantry, and the idea of their redemption, and redemptive role for Russian society, is embedded in their capacity for violence and sin. This is not simply because even the greatest sinner can be redeemed, although the idea has much currency in Dostoevsky's world, where only the 'lukewarm' of Revelation are truly damned,[18] but because their brutality both originates in the suffering they have already endured, and itself causes them further suffering (WD, 1.161–3). This engenders the possibility of compassion for each other and judgement from within, and inspires in others both compassion and recognition of the impossibility of judging the peasants from without. In an echo of 'The Peasant Marei', when Prince Myshkin in The Idiot tells the story of a drunken soldier who swindles him by claiming the tin cross he is selling to buy more drink is silver, he comments, 'God knows what these weak, drunken hearts contain' (pt II, ch. 4); we can know neither what suffering drives people to such actions, nor what they will suffer for the crimes they commit.

Dostoevsky's encounter with the peasant convicts ultimately sparked his attempt to construct a messianic Russian identity. Aggressively promoted in his journalistic forum, A Writer's Diary, in the 1870s, and representing the most controversial and, probably, the weakest part of his thinking,[19] the Russian national idea, based on the notion of the innate moral capacity of the peasantry, who have Christ in their hearts despite their lack of understanding of Scripture (WD, 1.164), receives much more subtle treatment in his novels. The unknowability of the peasant becomes emblematic of the tensions and dilemmas inherent in all interpersonal relationships, and the extremes of the Russian experience engendered by the inequalities of society are writ large in the violent plots which fuel the characters' ethical and metaphysical dramas.

While the inability to perceive beyond the outer body is the norm among Dostoevsky's characters, in particular the anti-heroes whose ideologies lead to violence, the transformative potential, for both parties, of compassion and the refusal to judge, is related to the capacity for seeing the inner being of the other, which arises from an understanding of suffering. Sonya's anguish at her sin of prostitution in Crime and Punishment enables her to respond to Raskolnikov's suffering, while the detective Porfiry Petrovich, who perceives Raskolnikov's guilt, does not arrest him, because he understands that the greater part of punishment for the crime lies in the inner torment it brings, and that Raskolnikov, already aware that he is not one of the world's 'extraordinary' people and has no right to commit crimes, needs to repent.

Raskolnikov's suspicion that Porfiry is winking at him (pt III, ch. 5; pt IV, ch. 5) is assumed by the murderer to indicate perception of his guilt, in a visual metaphor which is expanded in Dostoevsky's next novel. In *The Idiot*, Prince Myshkin's overwhelming sense of compassion is evident in his attempts to restore the dignity of the drunken buffoon General Ivolgin, to assuage the agony and anger of Ippolit, a teenager dying of tuberculosis, and in particular, to save the outraged beauty, Nastasya Filippovna. That his compassion is associated with an insight into the inner suffering of others is made clear in the opening chapters of the novel. Visiting his distant relatives, the Yepanchin family, for the first time, he immediately turns to the wildly inappropriate subject of capital punishment, concentrating on the torment of the knowledge of certain death, based on Dostoevsky's own experience of the commuted death penalty in 1849. Affirming – as in *Notes from the House of the Dead* and in Sonya's and Porfiry's concern for Raskolnikov – that sinners are those most in need of compassion, Myshkin suggests a connection between compassion and perception when he tells one of the Yepanchin sisters who does not know 'how to look' that she should simply 'look and paint' (pt I, ch. 5). He then proposes as the subject for a 'useful' painting a criminal on the scaffold awaiting execution, his separation from and objectification by the crowd of spectators adding to his suffering. The idea of the aesthetic as a vehicle for ethics is confirmed by the presence of Nastasya Filippovna's portrait, which inspires Myshkin's compassion and his decision to attempt to save her; on first seeing it, he comments, 'she's suffered terribly, hasn't she' (pt I, ch. 3). Later he admits, 'I can't bear Nastasya Filippovna's face ... Even that first morning, looking at the portrait, I couldn't bear it' (pt IV, ch. 9). The shift in emphasis from the person to the visual image in relation to Nastasya Filippovna, whose suffering at her own sin stands at the centre of the novel, confirms the necessity of seeing as the first stage of compassion, in a world in which both are compromised, as is apparent from the opening paragraph, as Myshkin travels by train into St Petersburg: 'the weather was so damp and misty that it was hardly getting light; a dozen yards to the left or right of the track scarcely anything could be made out from the carriage windows at all'.[20] When Mrs Yepanchin tells Myshkin, 'move nearer to the light so I can see you' (pt I, ch. 5), the hero's primary function of attempting to open the eyes of those around him is made explicit.

Prince Myshkin's compassion proves unsustainable, in large part owing to his ill health and unworldliness in the face of Mammon, but the image he projects remains powerful. When Dostoevsky returns to the question in *The Brothers Karamazov*, it is endowed with a far more robust form. The charismatic monk, the Elder Zosima, shares Myshkin's insight and responds with compassion; during the scandalous meeting of the Karamazov family at the monastery which initiates the plot, Zosima bows down before Dmitry, in acknowledgement of the suffering he will face (bk II, ch. 6). Myshkin's belief in the need for compassion and ability to perceive suffering originate mystically in the harmony of his epileptic aura, while the torment of the fit that follows gives him insight into the suffering of the condemned man's final moments. Through this he understands that the greatest crimes lead to the greatest suffering, and that compassion must exclude no one, but his own sinlessness leads him to equate this idea naively with the innocence of all. Zosima's doctrine of active love, in contrast, emerges concretely from the pain he witnessed and caused as a young man, with the result that the impossibility of judging the other is transformed into the conception of universal responsibility, which begins with understanding one's own guilt. As he learns from his dying brother, another child who suffers unnecessarily, 'each of us is guilty before everyone in everything, *and I most of all*' (bk VI, ch. 2, italics added). Dmitry Karamazov's response to the crying baby in his dream emphasises the connection between clarity of self-perception, acknowledgement that one cannot judge the other and active compassion, which takes the form of assuming the burden of sin to assuage the suffering of others:

> Why did I dream of a 'baby' at that moment? 'Why is the baby poor?' It was a prophecy to me at that moment! I'll go [to Siberia] for the 'baby'. Because everyone is guilty for everyone. For all the 'babies', because there are little babies and big babies. All people are 'babies', I'll go for them all, because there has to be someone who will go for them all. I didn't kill father, but I must go. I accept! (bk XI, ch. 4)

Dmitry's own hostility towards his father contributes to an atmosphere in which murder is the most probable outcome, and he understands that intentions, as much as actions, constitute guilt. The choice is between causing, or alleviating, the other's suffering, and in the face of the unknowability of the other, accepting that even – perhaps especially – violence is a sign of suffering, as with the peasant convicts, is the first step towards the compassion and self-transformation which offer the only possibility of overcoming the impasse in human relations.

While his preoccupation with suffering and guilt may be responsible for Dostoevsky's popular – and not entirely undeserved, despite a capacity for biting satire and black humour – reputation as the gloomiest of all the Russian novelists, it is also for these fundamental questions, and his refusal to settle on easy answers, that he is read, whether as a precursor of existentialism, a profound psychologist or the great Christian novelist. Dostoevsky's novels deal above all with the ethical dilemmas inherent in interpersonal relationships, spiritual crises and the possibility of regeneration, and few writers have matched the intensity of his depictions of moral and mental anguish, or interrogated so relentlessly the consequences of faith and doubt for human beings, in isolation or in their relation to others and the world. Affirming the reality of the spiritual life and inner being, his works constantly strive to represent the inaccessible while maintaining the sense of its essential unknowability, resulting in a unique structure which goes far beyond the realist tradition of Honoré de Balzac that he admired so much, and anticipates many of the developments of the modernist novel, James Joyce calling him 'the man more than any other who has created modern prose, and intensified it to its present-day pitch'.[21] Readily classified as a precursor of postmodernism as well,[22] it is Dostoevsky's emphasis on the intractability of the 'accursed questions' and insistent search for new forms in which to address – rather than answer – them which transforms him for different readerships and different generations, and makes him always a contemporary novelist.

### Note on editions/translations

The standard reference edition remains the thirty-volume, Academy of Sciences, Complete Works of Dostoevsky: F. M. Dostoevskii, *Polnoe sobranie sochinenii v tridtsati tomakh* (Moscow/Leningrad; Nauka, 1972–90). A new edition, restoring pre-Revolutionary spelling and punctuation, is in progress: F. M. Dostoevskii, *Polnoe sobranie sochinenii: Kanonicheskie teksty* (Petrozavodsk: Voskresenie, 1995–).

There are multiple recent translations of Dostoevsky's works. Reliable versions include David McDuff's *Poor Folk and Other Stories*, *Notes from the House of the Dead* and *Crime and Punishment* (Penguin; a new translation of *Crime and Punishment* is in preparation for Penguin by Oliver Ready), Michael Katz's *Notes from Underground* (Norton Critical Editions) and *The Devils*, Alan Myers's *The Idiot*, Ignat Avsey's *The Karamazov Brothers* (all Oxford World's Classics) and Richard Pevear and Larissa Volokhonsky's translations of many of Dostoevsky's novels (Vintage Books and Everyman's Library Classics).

### Notes

1 Quotations from Dostoevsky are taken from the Academy Edition of his complete works: *Polnoe sobranie sochinenii v tridtsati tomakh* (Moscow/Leningrad: Nauka,

1972–90); hereafter, *PSS*. For Dostoevsky's major works, references to part/book and chapter number, rather than to specific editions, are given throughout. Translations are by the present author, unless otherwise stated.

2 Friedrich Nietzsche, *Nietzsches Werke* (Leipzig: Naumann, 1901), VIII.158; Sigmund Freud, 'Dostoevsky and Parricide', trans. D. F. Tait, rev. James Strachey, in *The Standard Edition of the Collected Psychological Works of Sigmund Freud*, ed. James Strachey, 24 vols. (London: Hogarth Press, 1955–74), XXI.177–94.

3 'Introduction: Reading Dostoevsky Religiously', in George Pattison and Diane Oenning Thompson, eds., *Dostoevsky and the Christian Tradition* (Cambridge University Press, 2001), pp. 6–7.

4 Joseph Frank, *Dostoevsky: The Seeds of Revolt, 1821–1849* (Princeton University Press, 1977), p. 138.

5 M. M. Bakhtin, *Problems of Dostoevsky's Poetics*, ed. and trans. Caryl Emerson (Minneapolis: Minnesota University Press, 1984), p. 48.

6 Fyodor Dostoyevsky, *A Writer's Diary*, trans. Kenneth Lantz, 2 vols. (Evanston, IL: Northwestern University Press, 1997), II.1184. Hereafter, *WD*; further references are given in the text.

7 Pressures of space prevent consideration of the fifth novel of Dostoevsky's mature career, *The Adolescent* (1875, also translated as *A Raw Youth* and *An Accidental Family*), which is generally considered less successful.

8 Joseph Frank, *Dostoevsky: The Miraculous Years, 1865–1871* (Princeton University Press, 1995), pp. 257–61.

9 *PSS*, IX.246, 249; XXVIII.2 241, 251. See Robin Feuer Miller, *Dostoevsky and 'The Idiot': Author, Narrator, and Reader* (Cambridge, MA/London: Harvard University Press, 1981), pp. 75–84.

10 For example, D. H. Lawrence, 'Preface to Dostoevsky's *The Grand Inquisitor*', in *Dostoevsky: A Collection of Critical Essays*, ed. René Wellek (Englewood Cliffs, NJ: Prentice Hall, 1962), pp. 90–7.

11 Letter of 24 August (5 September new style) 1879; *PSS*, XXX.1.121–2.

12 Andrzej Walicki, *A History of Russian Thought from the Enlightenment to Marxism*, trans. Hilda Andrews-Rusiecka (Stanford University Press, 1979), pp. 194–8.

13 Bakhtin, *Problems of Dostoevsky's Poetics*, p. 203.

14 *Ibid.*, p. 230.

15 Malcolm V. Jones, *Dostoyevsky after Bakhtin: Readings in Dostoyevsky's Fantastic Realism* (Cambridge University Press, 1990), pp. 149–63.

16 *PSS*, II.248.

17 Nancy Ruttenburg, *Dostoevsky's Democracy* (Princeton University Press, 2008), pp. 22, 44, 50–1.

18 'So because you are lukewarm, and neither cold nor hot, I am about to spit you out of my mouth', Revelation 3.15–16. The words are cited by Bishop Tikhon in the suppressed chapter of *Demons*, 'At Tikhon's' (*PSS*, XI.5–30).

19 James Scanlan, *Dostoevsky the Thinker* (Ithaca, NY/London: Cornell University Press, 2002), pp. 198–9.

20 Robert Louis Jackson, *Dialogues with Dostoevsky: The Overwhelming Questions* (Stanford University Press, 1993), p. 309n.

21 Stanley Sultan, *Eliot, Joyce and Company* (Oxford University Press, 1990), p. 82.

22 Malcolm Jones, *Dostoevsky and the Dynamics of Religious Experience* (London: Anthem, 2005), pp. xii, 106.

## Further reading

Apollonio, Carol, *Dostoevsky's Secrets: Reading Against the Grain* (Evanston, IL: Northwestern University Press, 2009)

Cassedy, Steven, *Dostoevsky's Religion* (Stanford University Press, 2005)

Catteau, Jacques, *Dostoyevsky and the Process of Literary Creation*, trans. A. Littlewood (Cambridge University Press, 1989)

Frank, Joseph, *Dostoevsky: The Mantle of the Prophet, 1871–1881* (Princeton University Press, 2002)

  *Dostoevsky: The Stir of Liberation, 1860–1865* (Princeton University Press, 1986)

  *Dostoevsky: The Years of Ordeal, 1850–1859* (Princeton University Press, 1983)

Fusso, Susanne, *Discovering Sexuality in Dostoevsky* (Evanston, IL: Northwestern University Press, 2006)

Girard, René, *Resurrection from the Underground: Feodor Dostoevsky*, trans. James G. Williams (New York: Crossroad, 1997)

Jackson, Robert Louis, *Dostoevsky's Quest for Form: A Study of his Philosophy of Art* (New Haven: Yale University Press, 1966)

Miller, Robin Feuer, *Dostoevsky's Unfinished Journey* (New Haven, CT: Yale University Press, 2007)

Murav, Harriet, *Holy Foolishness: Dostoevsky's Novels and Poetics of Cultural Critique* (Stanford University Press, 1992)

Williams, Rowan, *Dostoevsky: Language, Faith, Fiction* (London: Continuum, 2008)

# 16

DONNA TUSSING ORWIN

# Leo Tolstoy (1828–1910): Art and truth

Leo Tolstoy, who wrote three novels, insisted that the first and most ambitious of them – *War and Peace* (*WP*) – was not a novel at all: he called it a 'book' instead.[1] The second – *Anna Karenina* (*AK*) – he subtitled 'a novel'. The fact that *roman*, the Russian word for 'novel', also means 'love affair' ties the genre more closely to romantic love than in English. The 'novel' in the title of *Anna Karenina* is associated specifically with Anna's story, and the continuation of the book after her death asserts that novels end, while life – and Tolstoy's book – go on. In the 1890s, writing *Resurrection (R)*, Tolstoy referred to it casually and multiple times as a novel, but he also remarked in his 1893 diary that 'the novel form is on its way out'.[2] Here and elsewhere during the 1890s, he complained that it was shameful to invent stories for the decadent leisured classes,[3] and, as we shall see, he conceptualised *Resurrection* as a novel that reproaches its fellows. So, having hardly acknowledged the existence of the novel in his *œuvre* early on, Tolstoy was ready to usher it out in his old age. Nonetheless, in his own time and today he has been recognised as one of the world's greatest novelists.

We might attribute Tolstoy's resistance to the novel form to contrarianism; he loved to expose false pretences and undercut convention. Russian formalist critic Viktor Shklovsky located his unique greatness in such truth-seeking. One of the main purposes of art, according to Shklovsky, is to shake up automatic perceptions. *Ostranenie* ('making strange'), as he dubbed it, is 'a method of seeing things out of their normal context', and he claimed that several hundred such passages appear in Tolstoy's work.[4] They range from Voltairean exposés of vainglory lurking in supposedly rational debate (generals jockeying for position in the war council at Fili in *War and Peace* (vol. III, pt III, ch. 4), or intellectuals doing the same as they discuss agricultural policy in *Anna Karenina* (pt VII, ch. 3)) to a stunningly effective revelation of Laska the dog's point of view in the hunt in *Anna Karenina* (pt VI, ch. 12). They include lampoons of artistic forms: perhaps most famous are the attack in *War and Peace* on opera and on *King Lear* in

277

'Shakespeare and the Drama' (1904). Although he was in fact a master of the manipulation of literary tropes and conventions, Tolstoy sought to make his own fiction seem more 'real' by denying its literary character.

National pride also played a role in Tolstoy's wariness towards the novel. The genre came to Russia from Europe in the eighteenth century in translations and a few derivative homegrown efforts, and soon acted as a vehicle for the modernisation of the country. With the emergence of nationalism in the Napoleonic period, and then a turn to prose evident from the late 1820s, writers began to experiment with particularly Russian forms of the novel. All great Russian novelists preceding Tolstoy responded to this imperative, and all, Tolstoy pointed out, wrote books of fiction that did not conform to contemporary European ideas of the novel.[5] These included Alexander Pushkin's *Eugene Onegin*, a novel in verse (1833) and *The Captain's Daughter* (1836); Mikhail Lermontov's *Hero of Our Time* (1841); Gogol's *Dead Souls* (1842) and Dostoevsky's *Notes from the House of the Dead* (1862). Of course, the novel is a synthetic and innovating form, and nineteenth-century Russian novels insisting on their own uniqueness were taking advantage of its dynamics.

Like other educated Russians of his time, Tolstoy devoured foreign novels, reading them in French, German and English, and in Russian translation. His wife reported that he read English novels by the bucket when he himself was getting ready to write. *Childhood* (1852), his first published work, was influenced by Charles Dickens (notably *David Copperfield*), but especially by Laurence Sterne, whose *Sentimental Journey through France and Italy* he had once set out to translate. Sterne's attention to psychological detail in this work and in *Tristram Shandy* appealed to him, and he was intrigued by how the attempt to track the inner life in real time dissolved the formal structure, and any plotline, of Sterne's masterpieces. Starting at university in the mid 1840s, Tolstoy had kept diaries on his own behaviour and motivations with an eye to self-improvement. This goal proved elusive (though he never abandoned it), but the diaries provided the material for his first surviving fiction (the so-called 'History of Yesterday'), in which he imitated Sterne's technique.

Tolstoy's disclaimer notwithstanding, all of his novels fit Ian Watt's classic definition of the genre as the most perfect artistic embodiment of modern individualism, which had been given its philosophic expression in the thought of French philosopher René Descartes (1596–1650). In keeping with this, the 'primary criterion' in Tolstoy's fiction in general is 'truth to individual experience'.[6] The experience of individuals and their reactions explain everything explicable in it, including the great political, military and social movements depicted in *WP*. Tolstoy debunks other explanations of mass phenomena centered around ideology, military strategy or the charisma of extraordinary leaders. All three novels, each in a different historical moment, imagine the whole of Russian society through characters who are both typical of different classes and situations and act as individuals.

At the same time, the novels explore the moral limits of egotism, or life lived exclusively for oneself, which Tolstoy like other Russians associated with Western ideas. Such characters as the Kuragins and Berg are amoral egotists in *War and Peace*, as are Betsy Trubetskoi and her circle in *Anna Karenina*, and the Korchagin family in *Resurrection*. The Russian people (*narod*) also strive for personal happiness, but they do so more as members of a community than as self-assertive individuals. In *War and Peace* and *Anna Karenina* – though less so in the latter – the people include right-thinking gentry; in *Resurrection*, gentry life is almost entirely excluded from it. The people participate in an epic life of humanity that is cyclical rather than linear in time. Tolstoy's three novels reflect his evolving politics in their relation to epic: *War and Peace* ends with the passing of one epic cycle in the life of the people and the beginning of another; *Anna Karenina* contrasts the epic of family and rural life with Anna's doomed 'novel'; while Prince Dmitri Nekhliudov, the hero in *Resurrection*, abandons his narrow class-based egotism and admires the epic world of the people.

From the beginning, Tolstoy was as much moralist as psychologist. At its most outspoken, his authorial voice thunders in tones reminiscent of the First and Second Discourses of Jean-Jacques Rousseau. It delivers the moral generalisations for which Tolstoy was so famous in his own time. We rarely read Tolstoy's non-fictional tracts today, and the fictional works that appeal more to us make him seem more focused on individual self-improvement or even aesthetics than he in fact was. Descended from ancient princes on his mother's side (Volkonskys) and from counts on his father's, he took his social obligations seriously. In his old age particularly, he was as famous around the world for his social conscience as for his fiction.

In a diary passage from 30 November 1852, he planned two long novels: an autobiographical one that 'as the novel of an intelligent, sensitive and erring person … will be instructive, though not dogmatic'; and 'the novel of a Russian landowner' which would be 'dogmatic' (*PSS*, xlvi.150–1). Note that even at this early stage he equated 'dogma' with social issues. In the event, his novels combine the autobiographical, or psychological, with the 'dogmatic'. Where he seeks to be purely mimetic, he draws on his own experiences and observations of himself and others to replicate the inner life without regard to dogma or even reason. On the rhetorical level, by appealing to our memories of experiences, sense perceptions and our reactions to these, he entices readers to conjure up a fictional world that seems (and is) as much a product of our minds as his.[7] This technique generates the unparalleled 'realism' of his fiction. Once we have collaborated with him in creating his fictional world, he sets about interpreting it for us in various ways: this becomes the 'dogmatic' level of his art.

Comparison is essential to his rhetorical strategy. If readers are encouraged to identify fully with a character or outlook in one episode, other passages may introduce different and opposing viewpoints that should make us think, and may distance us from any one perspective. Tolstoy strives for authenticity and irony at the same time. Without being unreliable, his narrator is freed from his fictional narrative as it, to a certain extent, is free from him.

Tolstoy's mentor in combining fictional narrative with reflection was Plato, who along with Rousseau was the other foundational philosopher of his youth. Like Plato, as he read him, Tolstoy constructed his fictional world from the bottom up, and he does not sacrifice psychological truth to moral arguments. Readers may choose to follow him as far up the ladder of his reasoning as they wish, and many reject the view from the top. Readers may also reject some parts of Tolstoy's world while accepting others. In *War and Peace*, for instance, Prince Kutuzov, Napoleon's nemesis, supposedly senses an invisible hand guiding events and favouring a Russian victory in 1812. This justifies his passivity during what many historians have judged a disastrous performance at Borodino, where he was saved by Napoleon's equally poor generalship and the courage of the Russian soldier.[8] Alexander Solzhenitsyn, a student of Tolstoy and particularly *War and Peace*, criticises this aspect of the novel in his *August, 1914* in the person of the excessively passive General Samsonov. In another example, this time from *Resurrection*, Prince Nekhliudov eventually embraces Tolstoyan Christian anarchism, but admiring readers of the novel as varied as Franz Kafka (in *The Castle*) or Vladimir Ilyich Lenin in his polemics have felt free to ignore or reject it. At the same time, Tolstoy's moral conclusions are rooted in his fictional narrative, and readers who simply ignore them miss the full power of his writing.[9]

The novels are woven from the complexity of the inner life, or what Russians call the soul. Through Sterne and Rousseau, Tolstoy is connected to the Lockean tradition of empiricist psychology, but he rejected John Locke's theory of the mind as a blank sheet upon which experience writes itself. The soul according to Tolstoy speaks with many, often competing, often contradictory and sometimes collaborating voices, or wills, which issue in actions that can only be understood and judged by untangling their underlying motives.[10]

One voice that speaks loud and often is that of the body. As scholars have long noted, the body is an essential part of Tolstoy's fictional world.

He often indicates its presence in the text through physical markers such as the short upper lip of Lise Bolkonsky (*War and Peace*), Anna's light gait or Katiusha Maslova's squint (*Resurrection*). At a French restaurant in *Anna Karenina*, a Tatar waiter with hips so broad that they slightly part the tails of his tuxedo insists on naming dishes, even Russian ones, in French: the disconnect between this solid physique and the Tatar's airy foreign speech is deliciously ironic (pt 1, ch. 10).[11] Sometimes the body sits incongruously in the driver's seat. In *War and Peace*, a 'faint smile' lingers inappropriately on Pierre Bezukhov's face amid 'terror and fear' as he waits to see whether the Byronic Dolokhov will plunge from a windowsill to the ground far below while downing a bottle of rum in a single swig (vol. 1, pt 1, ch. 6). Anna Karenina throws herself under the train despite last-minute doubts because her body, primed to act, will not stop. In extreme situations, such as occur in wartime (and therefore most often in *WP*), characters may act out of simple motives of physical self-preservation. Babies or old people like Madame Rostova in the epilogue to *WP* live mechanically in response to bodily and mental urges. More often, these are contributing factors among the intricate motivations for behaviour that a reader must draw, one detail at a time, from Tolstoy's text.

Human animals also have big brains that transform us. Because of our stronger reasoning powers, we can scheme in our own, often incorrectly perceived, self-interest. Reason allows simple animal impulses like self-preservation or sex to expand into passions that flourish in a past and a projected future that do not exist for other animals. Aware of our own mortality as other animals are not, we value ourselves as individuals and struggle in different ways to avoid death, in the process often harming ourselves and others: this is the source of glory- and power-seeking and acquisitiveness. Much of what we call civilisation develops out of goals generated by such futile striving.

But the big brain is not all bad, and in fact provides the only solutions to the problems that it creates. Reason allows reflection on our own motivations, and therefore a moral life impossible for other animals. Although we are easily swayed by various inner and external forces, as subjects we can resist these. The most direct influence on Tolstoy's psychology in this regard is the Savoyard Vicar (in Rousseau's *Émile*), who introduced him to the idea of the conscience as the moral guardian of a soul otherwise agitated chaotically by impressions, feelings, impulses, passions, thoughts and memories. The voice of conscience is persistent, but weak: bon vivants like Stiva Oblonsky (*Anna Karenina*) ignore its promptings with little more than temporary discomfort. The noblest characters do not get off so lightly; Anna Karenina ends up under a train that represents modernity both literally and, as a symbol of runaway passions and lust for power, figuratively as well. Anna does not kill herself because of a guilty conscience, however. She wants to end the pain of unhappy love, and to punish her lover for rejecting her. When she is about to leap, an inner voice urges her to reconsider. Her final unspoken words – 'Lord, forgive me for everything!' – indicate a belated judgement by conscience on her self-destructive path.

The soul is fluid according to Tolstoy: a famous passage in *R* compares it to an ever-changing river in which 'sometimes one quality manifests itself, sometimes another, and the man often becomes unlike himself, while still remaining the same man' (pt 1, ch. 59).[12] The last subordinate clause is crucial for understanding Tolstoyan psychology. For all their flexibility, Tolstoy's protagonists possess immutable personalities, and they do not so much change as they strive for pure self-expression.

What makes Tolstoy's psychology so rich is the interaction of forces both within the soul and between the soul and the external world of other people, society and events. The psychological vectors along which his characters move are formed from such varied material that only the most careful and rational readers, like Marcel Proust, detect laws behind the magic.[13] Sequences expressing these laws are the bricks from which he constructs his fiction. Literary historian D. S. Mirsky considered 'A History of Yesterday' – bricks just lined up one after another – the most radically innovative work Tolstoy ever wrote.[14] Twentieth-century authors like Proust who might abhor Tolstoy's moralism are indebted to this feature of his prose. Nonetheless, Tolstoy never completed 'History', and it was published only posthumously. Like it, his mature fiction does encompass myriad details of inner life, and this led inevitably to works 'de longue haleine', as he dubbed both *War and Peace* and *Resurrection* (*PSS*, LX.451; LI.90). Yet his novels required structure more complex than that of 'History', or, at the very least, in his words in relation to *Anna Karenina*, 'scaffolding' (*PSS*, LXII.209). As Boris Eikhenbaum put it, Tolstoy's emphasis on the details of life needed generalisations to order these.[15] In *The Young Tolstoy*, Eikhenbaum shows how he assembled materials detail by detail, milieu by milieu, and built them into works in the 1850s that all contribute to the vast edifice of *War and Peace* in the 1860s.

Reacting to earlier moralising or ideological approaches to Tolstoy's work, Eikhenbaum and other Formalist critics treated Tolstoy's generalisations, whether applicable to particular situations (as in the case of his extensive use of the maxim) or overarching, merely as literary devices. This is unfair. Divesting them of substantive intent in this way distorts Tolstoy's purpose and diminishes his genius; he was always in search of eternal verities to which he contrasted the foibles of the day. He believed that such truths could be found within himself if he remained totally honest, and this led to radical and relentless self-analysis. Eikhenbaum is right that Tolstoy constantly questioned and often rejected his own motives and positive ideals.[16] But his 'cynicism', his breakdown of the psyche into a 'chemical process', was, *pace* Eikhenbaum, in the service of an extreme idealism typical of the Russian intelligentsia. In an 1870 notebook, Tolstoy wrote that 'Poetry is a flame burning in a person's soul. The flame burns, it warms and gives light … A real poet suffers involuntarily as he himself burns and he burns others. And that is the crux of the matter' (*PSS*, XLVIII.129). This need for complete authenticity of soul as required by his Cartesian individualism caused Tolstoy great pain, and, in his own mind, was the source of his greatness as a writer.

*War and Peace* (1865–9), the first and most ambitious of the three novels, is a meditation on the meaning of history, with Russia's participation in the later Napoleonic wars as the test case. Its influence on all subsequent war writing is enormous. Tolstoy researched in depth the period it covered – 1805–20 – and it is informed by his deep grasp. The opening scene at Anna Pavlovna Sherer's salon in St Petersburg in July 1805 is a *tour de force* in which characters not only dress and speak in a historically accurate manner, but have opinions rooted in the moment that the narrator lets pass without comment. In but one example among many, Pierre Bezukhov, who like many young men at this time worships Napoleon, is expecting a successful French invasion of England to be led by Admiral de Villeneuve, and does not anticipate the disastrous rout of the French fleet at the Battle of Trafalgar in October of that year.

So wedded was Tolstoy to the collection of facts about his subject that, to depict the climactic Battle of Borodino, he spent two days at the battle site and produced a map with his own revision of the initial positions of the opposing armies. Having done his homework, however, Tolstoy rejected the premises by which historians analyse their data. What is 'real' (in his words) in each event is the will of each individual participant, and therefore history is decided by the interaction of all such wills, even if these run to the thousands or millions. Each individual acts in a way that cannot be predicted in advance, but is psychologically comprehensible. Fear, anger, vanity and revenge mix to create a dehumanising 'force' that stalks the battlefield; and in response to it men band together or attack one another. *War and Peace* interweaves two trajectories: the historical one, and the personal stories of five main characters and two families, the Rostovs and the Bolkonskys. Other families, historical figures and dozens of other characters of varying degrees of importance appear as well, along with groups that include armies, lynch mobs, church congregations, peasants and city-dwellers. In the later parts of the novel, Tolstoy's narrator begins to comment extensively on the relation of individuals to history, until, in the second part of the epilogue, commentary has replaced fictional narrative altogether.

In practice, one can never know all the 'personal experiences' that comprise a historical event; therefore Tolstoy's theory of history stands as the structuring principle of the novel in place of a comprehensive, psychologically grounded account of the war it describes. In the epilogue and in other digressions, the author–narrator does suggest the possibility of a mystical, transcendental cause behind history in addition to psychological and epic ones. Within the fictional narrative, this explanation is present in the characterisation of Kutuzov as somehow directly in touch with it, in Petya Rostov's dream the night before his death of a great chorus in which he participates, and in the wonder felt by characters and the narrator at the irrationality and inhumanity inherent in mass movements such as war.

Individuals get caught up in historical events either unwillingly, or from passion. Such passions may be bad, even illegitimate, especially in their consequences, but they are not unnatural. Napoleon's striving for power is also apparent in Prince Andrei, in his adolescent son Prince Nikolenka at the end of the novel, and even in Pierre Bezukhov. What distinguishes Napoleon from Andrei and Pierre is the former's failure to modify his behaviour despite the bad results for himself and others that he himself acknowledges, at least to some extent. The exemplary peasant soldier Platon Karataev recommends the restriction of desire to private self-fulfilment through the family and the avoidance of evil wherever possible. That said, at the end of the novel, even Pierre, having been moderated by hardship and the advice of Karataev, securely at home in the bosom of his family, is engaged in a new cycle of public life that will lead to the disastrous 1825 Decembrist Uprising. Although Tolstoy would not put it openly this way, human beings naturally will, and even must, seize the brass ring of their own happiness and desires when fortune dangles it. This applies to female as well as male characters, and to the saintly Princess Marya Bolkonskaya as well as the capricious Natasha Rostova. Epic life in *War and Peace* therefore naturally includes states of war as well as peace, as one leads to the other. Furthermore, the natural aggressiveness of the human personality as depicted in *War and Peace* sanctions the embedded existence in it of plotted novels, if by this term we understand love stories with happy or unhappy endings: an example of the former is the romance of Princess Marya and Nikolai Rostov. Prince Andrei is marked for death because he ultimately cannot accept these mixed and humiliating conditions of earthly life. Only as he lies dying does he feel an eternal (and strangely disinterested) love that firmly rejects natural egotism, and endows him with the consistency of purpose and freedom that he seeks.

*Anna Karenina* (1875–8) is a novel of individual fulfilment within an epic structure based on eternal verities of life, death and family. Rather like Napoleon, though on a less grand and calculating scale, the eponymous heroine sets out on a quest that is doomed because it depends on the sacrifice of others to her happiness. Still living in the family apartment, but carrying on an affair with Count Vronsky, in the middle of the novel she reconciles herself with her husband on what she thinks is her deathbed as she prepares to give birth to Vronsky's daughter. Anna is at her moral peak at this moment, but unfortunately for her and those who love the trope of the repentant fallen woman, the novel does not end here. She recovers, and then abandons her husband and son for Vronsky, eventually committing suicide when she suspects him of infidelity.

The novel's second protagonist, Konstantin Levin, first loses his beloved Kitty to Vronsky, then weds her. From the novel's first appearance, readers have complained that the Levin and Anna lines are only superficially linked. This is not true, and in fact Tolstoy was especially proud of the deep connections between the stories of the two main characters. Levin is a man of ideas whose crisis of belief parallels Anna's departure from grace. The death of his brother Nikolai (named after Tolstoy's own beloved older brother who had died of TB in 1860) awakens a sense of despair in him about the meaninglessness of existence that neither the faith of Kitty, nor the subsequent birth of their son, nor the writings of philosophers old and new can quell. In the final part of the book, even as his family life flourishes, Levin contemplates suicide. It seems that the eternity guaranteed to humanity within cyclical epic time is not sufficient compensation for a modern self-aware individual who fears annihilation through death. This attention to personal fulfilment aligns Levin with Anna, while his need for individual autonomy and meaning reminds us of Prince Andrei, who dies seeking it in *War and Peace*. Levin escapes the fate of both these characters through a redemptive ethic that is first suggested to him by a peasant sage named Platon, but then wells up in his own mind as the voice of conscience. Through it, he discovers the existence in himself of eternal moral principles that help define him even if he is not always capable of applying them in particular instances. To the extent that he identifies with these principles, he is not simply his body, and escapes his own mortality.

*Resurrection* (1899) combines a story of personal redemption with a denunciation of late Imperial Russia. It grew out of a *povest'*, a Russian genre awkwardly rendered in English as a 'long short story' that centres around one character or event. In the finished novel, the main protagonist,

Nekhliudov, seduces and (unbeknown to himself, because he immediately departs) impregnates Katiusha Maslova, a maidservant and ward of his elderly aunts. Dispatched to an orphanage, the newborn dies, and Maslova descends into prostitution. This story is told in an extensive flashback, while the novel opens with the meeting some years later of the two when Nekhliudov is a juror at Maslova's trial for the poisoning death of a rich merchant at the brothel where she works. (This situation, altered to inflate the crime from theft to murder, is based on an actual incident told to Tolstoy by a lawyer friend.) When Maslova is unjustly convicted of murder through judicial error, Nekhliudov, who recognises her, tries to rectify this. As he fails, and then accompanies her to Siberia, both of them undergo a moral regeneration to which the novel's title refers. By the end, Nekhliudov has risen to the level of the author's understanding of both himself and society. While this process unfolds, and the ending of the *povest'* is delayed, the novel expands to include vast parts of Russia, with its impoverished countryside, its corrupt, self-indulgent gentry and bureaucracy, its unjust judicial system with its trials, prisons, labour camps and the prisoners themselves, from criminals to revolutionaries. Nekhliudov learns from all this, and thereby becomes the ideal witness to it: thus the *povest'* and the satirical novel blend together in a unique and powerful way.

Each of the three novels responds to particular circumstances of Tolstoy's life and time. *War and Peace* (1865–9) draws on his experience as a soldier. Decorated for heroism in the Crimean War, 1853–6, he fought on the front lines at Sevastopol as an artillery officer. For many readers who did not know Tolstoy's earlier writings, his three Sevastopol sketches, the first two of which he wrote during the war, made his reputation. Present at the eventual humiliating evacuation of the city, like many Russian officers he blamed this on a corrupt and bloated army structure. *War and Peace* was intended, among other things, to immortalise a war that Russia did win, and in which, as Tolstoy tells it, his own class, the landed gentry, unites with common soldiers to play the leading role.

Lost wars create instability, and therefore opportunity. Nicholas I, who led Russia into the Crimean conflict, died during it, and his heir, Alexander II, initiated what are known as the Great Reforms. The most important of these was the abolition of serfdom on 19 February 1861. Emancipation meant the end of the old political system, and brought about a crisis that generated tremendous creative ferment, as Russians strove to reinvent themselves. After emancipation, Tolstoy served as an arbiter of the peace, negotiating between newly freed but landless peasants and landowners deprived of near slave labour. *War and Peace* should also be understood within this context, as Tolstoy's contribution to reform. Napoleon's invasion of Russia as he imagined it in the novel is a pivotal event in which all classes coalesce to defend their homeland and expel a foreign invader. For this reason, he underplayed, though he did not omit, class tensions in the novel.

In 1862 Tolstoy married the eighteen-year-old Sofya Andreevna Behrs. In the first decade of his marriage, he wrote *War and Peace*, which concludes with young family life based on his own at the time. The second produced *Anna Karenina*. By 1872, he had six children, and in 1873, the year he began *Anna Karenina* in earnest, his baby son Pyotr died, 'the first death in our family in eleven years' (*PSS*, LXIII.55). *Anna Karenina* was written in the shadow of mortality, as this death and others intensified Tolstoy's search for meaning that transcended it.

Written when the debilitating effects of the dismantling of serfdom on both peasants and gentry were ever more apparent, *Anna Karenina* is politically less hopeful than *War and Peace*. As Levin attempts with limited success to introduce agricultural reforms on his estate, Tolstoy's theories about leadership, developed in *War and Peace*, apply remarkably well. Public life, whether political, social or military, appears only in satirised form. If there is no Napoleon in *Anna Karenina*, neither is there a Kutuzov nor an Alexander I. The novel also lacks the dimension of heroic sacrifice that war, for all its horrors, generates.

*Anna Karenina* began with an idea, mentioned to Sofya Andreevna in February 1870, about a fallen woman who is 'pitiful but not guilty'. No sooner had this come to Tolstoy than 'all the other personages and male types that had occurred to him earlier found their places and grouped themselves around this woman'.[17] In 1872, he viewed the body of a woman, the mistress of a neighbouring landowner, who had thrown herself under a train when she learned of her lover's betrayal. Anna's development in the drafts of the novel is illustrative of Tolstoy's creative method. She was intended to die from the beginning. Within this fate, however, she grew into a complex character who defies typological pigeon-holing, and in some ways resembles the author in her striving for intimacy and personal happiness.

*Anna Karenina* was intended as a contemporary novel, so much so that Tolstoy incorporated events, like the Russo-Turkish war, that only began after it was well under way. While he framed *War and Peace* with reflections about the Napoleonic period that were only possible retroactively, he could have no such theoretical perspective on his own time. Therefore the issue of structuring the fictional reality that he was creating became very pressing. First, he built the novel around Levin's search for meaning. Second, as *War and Peace* is about war, *Anna Karenina* is saturated with the family idea, which binds it together even if no simple conclusion about the family can be derived from it. Marriage is the bedrock of human society, where, Tolstoy hoped, happiness and duty, nature and convention, could be reconciled. Before and while he was writing the novel, and indeed for much of his life, Tolstoy was involved in pedagogy, and he saw family as the place where we learn moral lessons used for our entire life. Here he is yet again the faithful student of Rousseau, in this case mostly *Émile*, but also *La Nouvelle Héloïse* (*The New Heloise*). True to the mandate of a Russian novel of ideas, the author of *Anna Karenina* does not reserve reflections on its unifying theme for himself alone. Characters in it think about and discuss love, marriage and women. Among many other things, *Anna Karenina* is Tolstoy's response to the 'woman question' as it was posed by contemporaries like Alexandre Dumas fils (1824–95), author of *La Dame aux camélias* (1848) and *L'Homme-femme* (1872).[18] Indeed, this question is central to the history of the novel in Europe, and Tolstoy is one of its classic representations.

Another decade later, launching *Resurrection*, Tolstoy could no longer take refuge in family. His own home life had soured irremediably, partly because of an ever-increasing estrangement of which his wife disapproved from the political regime, but also because he now rejected all upper-class life as parasitical. Communal peasant life, which he had seen as the possible salvation of the country earlier, now, after the terrible famines of 1891–2, and the intensification of industrialisation and urbanisation, was dying out (as Nekhliudov discovers when he visits his estates). In Part II of the novel (ch. 42), Nekhliudov encounters peasant artisanal groups travelling on the train he is taking to Siberia with the prisoners, but, although he hopes such groups will replace the decadent gentry, he does not join them. By the novel's end, Nekhliudov, his marriage proposal rejected by Maslova, has become a consummate outsider. If truth be told, his 'resurrection' to this status is the equivalent of the good death of Prince Andrei in *War and Peace*. Maslova will now join the revolutionaries whom she meets in prison, but Nekhliudov is left utterly alone. Reading and parsing Gospel passages in the final pages of the novel, he seems to have moved right out of the fictional narrative into its didactic frame, which includes epigraphs from the Gospels.

As he began *Resurrection* in 1891, Tolstoy wrote in his diary that, whereas his first two novels had been 'unconscious creation', after ten years of thought and analysis he now knew 'what was what, and I can mix everything up again and work with this mixture' (1 January 1891; *PSS*, LII.6). To emphasise this reshuffling of old material, he chose Nekhliudov, who had first appeared in *Adolescence* (1854) as a moralising foil to its hero, Nikolenka Irteniev, as the male protagonist of his new novel. Significantly, it turns out in *Resurrection* that Nikolenka, the more spontaneous friend of Nekhliudov's youth, has died.[19] *Resurrection* embodies in fiction a grand project, the many parts of which Tolstoy laid out over two decades in a series of tracts, including among them *Confession* (1880), a harmonised version of the Gospels (1880–1), *What Then Should We Do?* (1884), *What I Believe* (1884), *On Life* (1888), *The Kingdom of Heaven is within Us* (1895), *What is Art?* (1898), and *The Slavery of Our Time* (1900). This project, directed towards Russia in particular, but with universal implications, had two facets: a political, social and a psychological, individual one. The injustice of society depends upon an implicit resistance to change in obedience to which even the virtuous among the powerful protect their privileges, and the weak covet these. Furthermore, changes introduced by the same methods of intimidation that enforce the old unjust ways guarantee their continuation under new masters. What is needed is individual reform to create better human beings who would then agree to a social contract fair to all. *On Life*, written around the time *Resurrection* was conceived, provides a psychological, and to that extent a possible, philosophical justification of the reasonable consciousness that will guide the new men. *Resurrection*, as both the expression of the author's reasonable consciousness and the account of Nekhliudov's path to it, follows the teaching of *What is Art?* according to which high art introduces and advocates the progressive moral stance of the day.

The unconscious man strives for his own happiness, but if each man does only this, then life turns into a war of all against all (*On Life*, ch. 28; *PSS*, XXVI.369). In *The Slavery of Our Time*, Tolstoy declared that all governments, their armed forces and the so-called rule of law are without exception nothing but tools of the powerful in this struggle. *Resurrection*, published just before *Slavery*, illustrates this Hobbesian scenario as it plays out in the Russian justice system.

After the trial, Nekhliudov becomes the chief agent of *ostranenie* within the fictional narrative. Where he is necessarily absent (as in the women's section of the prison), or lacks the proper perspective (the blasphemous description of the Eucharist in the prison church (pt 1, ch. 39) for which Tolstoy was excommunicated), the narrator takes over. He expresses truths that no one character in his novel sees as clearly as he does, because not one, not even Nekhliudov, until the very end, can be as objective as he. At the same time, the narrator is a poet who flaunts the subjectivity of reasonable consciousness as the source of truth. *R* begins with his lyrical outpouring about spring in the city (anticipating resurrection before it commences in Maslova and Nekhliudov), and it ends with a final brief comment from him. Much more openly than in the previous two novels, it is the narrator's point of view and his direct appeal to readers that unifies *Resurrection*. Therefore, if *War and Peace* had represented unity based on the nation, and *AK* on the family, this last novel was conceived as a 'general [*sovokupnoe*] letter' from the author to his readers.[20] As both a writer and a guru, Tolstoy had now bypassed even traditional institutions for an anarchistic and Christian kingdom of God on earth in which he aspired to be a leader.

Reasonable consciousness, though centred in the individual, was conceived partly to transform Russia one person at a time. That way, so Tolstoy imagined, a just society would come into being without the social engineering he abhorred. But the author who had written in the first chapter of the epilogue of *War and Peace* that life governed by reason was impossible must have had his doubts about his own utopian scheme; hence the abrupt and even fairytale end of *R*, as Nekhliudov seems to stand on the brink of achieving a utopia as rational consciousness for himself. This ending is far less believable psychologically than the passionate love affair of Nekhliudov and Maslova that initiates the plot of the novel.

Tolstoy was dissatisfied with *Resurrection*, and may have published it only to fund the transport from the Caucasus to Canada of a persecuted religious sect, the Doukhobors (Spirit Wrestlers). Nonetheless, it is a powerful novel that continues his struggle with the genre. In *WP* he used history to demonstrate that grand projects do not achieve the aims they intend. Their architects launch them in search of power and glory, which they imagine, wrongly, will spare them from death or, in the case of incipient Decembrists like Pierre and Nikolenka Bolkonsky, will issue in social justice. In *Anna Karenina*, Anna dies in pursuit of power over her lover, while Levin discovers the divine voice of self-regulation that abides within him though he cannot always heed it. Later, Tolstoy believed that he had found the moral goal towards which men should strive in reasonable consciousness; the fundamental adaptability of human psychology would make this journey possible, though by no means easy. *Resurrection*, in which the two main characters consciously discard their self-centred quest for personal happiness and centre their lives on the happiness of others, was intended as a novel to end all novels.

Tolstoy's art is not the same as his social ideas, however. Because of his method of constructing his prose from the bottom up, novelists as varied as Boris Pasternak, Vassily Grossman, Stephan Crane, Ernest Hemingway, James Joyce, Thomas Mann, Vladimir Nabokov, Vikram Seth, and many, many others have been able to borrow parts of it without embracing the author's world-view *in toto*. Mention of Tolstoy or clear references to his works pop up in the most unexpected places. Like his mentor Rousseau, he seems to be one of those seminal authors whom generations of readers and subsequent writers unpack item by item.

The subject of all Tolstoy's novels is the relation of the individual and society. Like many Russians, he was ambiguous about individualism as practised in the West, but he does not reject it outright. On the contrary, he regarded self-love as natural, and this gave rise to an attendant 'self-satisfaction' (*samodovol'nost'*) that John Bayley correctly identifies in his characters.[21] But if Tolstoy's characters outdo their Victorian English fictional counterparts in their earthiness and *joie de vivre*, they live in a world that imposes strict limits on their passions and ambitions. The unique structures of *War and Peace*, *Anna Karenina* and *Resurrection*, shaped variously from epic, the novel as Tolstoy narrowly defined it and the essay, reflect Tolstoy's attempt to assimilate modern individualism to traditional Russian culture and its communal dynamics. Russians still see themselves in the characters and their struggles, as do readers on the ever-expanding borders of modernity. Readers from countries where the novel originated are fascinated by the great anti-novel novelist who knows them better than they know themselves.

## Note on editions/translations

Work on a new complete edition of Tolstoy's *œuvre* is under way in Russia. Meanwhile, the 90-volume 'Jubilee' Tolstoy (*L. N. Tolstoi. Polnoe sobranie sochinenii* (Khudozhestvennaia literatura, 1928–58)) is still the most important Russian edition of his works. The 22-volume *L. N. Tolstoi. Sobranie sochinenii* (Khudozhestvennaia literatura, 1978–85) contains updated versions of the novels discussed in this essay.

Good English translations include those of *War and Peace* by Richard Pevear and Larissa Volkhonsky (Vintage Classics) and A. D. P. Briggs (Penguin Classics); of *Anna Karenina* by Pevear and Volokhonsky (Penguin Classics) and Constance Garnett as revised by Leonard J. Kent and Nina Berberova (Modern Library Classics); and *Resurrection* by Rosemary Edmonds (Penguin Classics).

## Notes

1 In Leo Tolstoy, 'A Few Words on *War and Peace*', published in 1868 while the novel was still appearing. See *L. N. Tolstoi, Polnoe sobranie sochinenii* (*PSS*), 90 vols. (Moscow: Gosudarstvennoe izdatel'stvo 'Khudozhestvennaia literatura', 1928–58), LXI.7. Subsequent references are given parenthetically in the text as *PSS*.
2 LII.93. Unless otherwise stated, all translations in this essay are my own.
3 *PSS*, LXVI.366; *PSS*, LXVIII.230.
4 Viktor Shklovsky, 'Art as Technique', in Lee T. Lemon and Marion J. Reis, trans., *Russian Formalist Criticism: Four Essays* (Lincoln, NE: University of Nebraska Press, 1965), p. 17.

5 In Tolstoy, 'A Few Words about *War and Peace*', *PSS*, XVI.7. Tolstoy specifically mentions only the works by Nikolai Gogol and Fyodor Dostoevsky.

6 Ian Watt, *The Rise of the Novel: Studies in Defoe, Richardson and Fielding* (1957; Berkeley: University of California Press, 1971), p. 13.

7 See George R. Clay, *Tolstoy's Phoenix: From Method to Meaning in 'War and Peace'* (Evanston, IL: Northwestern University Press, 1998), pp. 7–10.

8 For a recent account of the campaign that is critical of Kutuzov at Borodino, see Adam Zamoyski, *Moscow 1812: Napoleon's Fatal March 1812* (New York: Harper Perennial, 2005).

9 The most powerful representative of critics who want to separate Tolstoy's fiction from his systematising ideas is Isaiah Berlin, in *The Hedgehog and the Fox: An Essay on Tolstoy's View of History* (New York: Simon and Schuster, 1970).

10 On this subject, see Lydia Ginzburg, *On Psychological Prose*, trans. Judson Rosengrant (Princeton University Press, 1991).

11 In Tolstoy's lexicon, a Tatar would be more natural, more down-to-earth, than a European.

12 Translation by Louise Maude.

13 *Marcel Proust on Art and Literature 1896–1916 (Contre Saint-Beuve)*, trans. Sylvia Townsend Warner (New York: Meridian, 1958), pp. 378–9.

14 D. S. Mirsky, *A History of Russian Literature* (New York: Alfred A. Knopf, 1969), p. 254.

15 Boris Eikhenbaum, *The Young Tolstoi*, trans. and ed. Gary Kern (Ann Arbor: Ardis, 1972), p. 31. Eikhenbaum borrowed this formulation from Tolstoy's diary of 4 June 1852 (*PSS*, XLVI.121).

16 Boris Eikhenbaum, *Lev Tolstoi*, 2 vols. (1928, 1931; Munich: Wilhelm Fink, 1968), I.35.

17 Quoted in N. N. Gusev, *Letopis' zhizni i tvorchestva L'va Nikolaevicha Tolstogo* (Moscow: Goslitizdat, 1958), p. 369.

18 See Boris Eikhenbaum, *Lev Tolstoi, Semidesiatye gody* (Leningrad: Khudozhest-vennaia literatura, 1974), pp. 117–20.

19 Pt II, ch. 31; see also ch. 8.

20 Letter to P. I. Birikov, 16 December 1898; *PSS*, LXXI.515.

21 John Bayley, *Tolstoy and the Novel* (New York: Viking, 1966), pp. 48, 50–3, 60.


*Further reading*

Biographies

Maude, Aylmer, *The Life of Tolstoy*, 2 vols. in 1 (Oxford University Press, 1987)
Simmons, E. J., *Leo Tolstoy* (New York: Vintage, 1960)
Wilson, A. N., *Tolstoy* (New York: Norton, 1988)

Bibliographies

Egan, David R. and Melinda A. Egan, eds., *Leo Tolstoy: An Annotated Bibliography of English Language Sources to 1978* (Netuchen, NJ/London: Scarecrow Press, 1979)
*Leo Tolstoy: An Annotated Bibliography of English Language Sources from 1978 to 2003* (Netuchen, NJ/London: Scarecrow Press, 2005)

## Criticism

Bayley, John, *Tolstoy and the Novel* (New York: Viking, 1966)

Christian, R. F., *Tolstoy: A Critical Introduction* (Cambridge University Press, 1969)

Gustafson, Richard F., *Leo Tolstoy: Resident and Stranger: A Study in Fiction and Theology* (Princeton University Press, 1986)

Morson, Gary Saul, *Hidden in Plain View: Narrative and Creative Potentials in 'War and Peace'* (Stanford University Press, 1986)

Orwin, Donna Tussing, *Consequences of Consciousness: Turgenev, Dostoevsky, and Tolstoy* (Palo Alto, CA: Stanford University Press, 2007)

*Tolstoy's Art and Thought, 1847–1880* (Princeton University Press, 1993)

ed., *The Cambridge Companion to Tolstoy* (Cambridge University Press, 2002)

Wasiolek, Edward, *Tolstoy's Major Fiction* (University of Chicago Press, 1978)

See also *Tolstoy Studies Journal* and www.tolstoystudies.com

# 17

BRIAN NELSON

# Émile Zola (1840–1902): Naturalism

'Naturalism' was the dominant mode of the French novel in the late nineteenth century. The writer who played the pre-eminent role in its development was Émile Zola. At the heart of Zola's naturalism is a concern with integrity of representation. For Zola, this meant a commitment to the idea that literature has a social function: to engage with the 'order of the day' through a representation of the sorts of things that concerned people on a daily basis in their social and individual lives. Industrialisation, the growth of the cities, the birth of consumer culture, the condition of the working class, crime, prostitution, the follies and misdeeds of government – these were the issues that concerned Zola. And he wrote about them not simply forensically, as a would-be scientist, but subversively, ironically, satirically. As a body of literature, naturalist fiction represents a major assault on bourgeois morality and institutions. It takes an unmitigated delight – while also seeing the process as a serious duty – in revealing the vice and corruption behind the respectable facade. The last line of his novel *Le Ventre de Paris* (*The Belly of Paris*) is: 'Respectable people ... What bastards!' The shock factor of naturalist texts can be measured by the vehemence of Establishment critics' attacks on Zola and his work. These attacks were usually made on moral and aesthetic grounds. Zola was accused of sensationalism, immorality and intellectual and stylistic crudity. But in reality, the accusations reveal a political dimension: Zola's work provoked a great deal of reactionary fear among his bourgeois readers and critics.

Zola's ambition was to emulate Honoré de Balzac by writing a comprehensive history of contemporary society. Through the fortunes of his Rougon-Macquart family, he examined methodically the social, sexual and moral landscape of the late nineteenth century along with its political, financial and artistic contexts. Zola is the quintessential novelist of modernity, understood in terms of a sense of tumultuous change. The motor of change was the rapid expansion of capitalism, with all that that entailed in terms of the altered shapes of the city, new forms of social practice and economic organisation, and heightened political pressures. Zola was fascinated by change, and specifically by the emergence of a new, mass society. His epic type of realism is reflected not only in the vast sweep of his work, but also in its variety and complexity. In addition to his thirty-one novels, he wrote five collections of short stories, a large body of art, drama and literary criticism, several plays and libretti, and numerous articles on political and social issues published in the French press at various stages of his career as a journalist. He was a major critic of literature and painting, and a significant political commentator long before the Dreyfus Affair. His main achievement, however, was his twenty-volume novel cycle, *Les Rougon-Macquart*, published between 1871 and 1893. In eight months, during 1868 and 1869, Zola outlined the series of novels he intended to write on the theme of heredity: a family, the Rougon-Macquarts, tainted with alcoholism and mental instability, were to intermarry, to proliferate and to pass on their inherited weaknesses to subsequent generations. Their fortunes would be followed over several decades. Zola began work on the series in 1870 and devoted himself to it for the next quarter of a century. The various family members spread through all levels of society. The Rougons represent the hunt for wealth and position, their members rising to occupy commanding positions in the worlds of government and finance; the Mourets are the bourgeois tradesmen and provincial bourgeoisie; and the Macquarts, with the exception of Lisa Macquart (*The Belly of Paris*), are the submerged proletariat.

Zola's voice is a challenging moral and political voice. But although he was in many ways subversive, he was not a socialist. His work contains many contradictory strains; indeed, part of his abiding significance lies in the ways in which he articulated the contradictions of his time. In the early days, he was attacked almost as much by the humanitarian left as by the conservative right, on the grounds that he painted too black a picture of the lower classes. The critical controversies surrounding his working-class texts reflect ambiguities in the texts themselves. For Zola, the power of mass working-class movements was a radically new element in human history, and it aroused in him an equivocal mixture of sympathy and unease. *L'Assommoir* and *Germinal* create a sense of humanitarian warmth and tragic pathos in their portrayal of the downtrodden, but Zola shows no solidarity with those who propound radical social and economic solutions. Similarly, in his treatment of sex and marriage, Zola broke the mould of Victorian moral cant; but on the other hand, he admired what he saw as the bourgeois family ideal. The *bête noire* of the bourgeoisie, he was also a moralist who believed deeply in the traditional bourgeois virtues of self-discipline, hard work and moderation. A vision of bourgeois paternalism is explicit in his last, highly didactic novels, particularly in *Travail* (*Work*, 1903), where a bourgeois Messiah creates a sentimental utopia in which all problems have been dissolved and all classes live in harmony.

## Scientific observation and poetic vision

Although Zola rejected the social and moral content of the bourgeois world-view, he retained the central epistemological tenet on which it was based: 'scientific' objectivity. Zola's writings on the role of the writer and the function of literature reflect his enthusiasm for science and his acceptance of scientific determinism, the prevailing philosophy of the second half of the nineteenth century. Converted from a youthful romantic idealism to realism in art and literature, he began promoting a scientific view of literature inspired by the aims and methods of experimental medicine.

He called this new form of realism 'naturalism'. The subtitle of the Rougon-Macquart cycle, 'A Natural and Social History of a Family under the Second Empire', suggests Zola's two interconnected aims: to use fiction to demonstrate a number of 'scientific' notions about the ways in which human behaviour is determined by heredity and environment; and to use the symbolic possibilities of a family whose heredity is tainted to represent a diseased society – the corrupt yet dynamic France of the Second Empire (1852–70). Zola set out, in the Rougon-Macquart cycle, to tear the mask from the Second Empire and to expose the frantic pursuit of appetites of every kind that it unleashed. He was influenced by Balzac; by the views on heredity and environment of the positivist philosopher and cultural histor-ian Hippolyte Taine, whose proclamation that 'virtue and vice are products like vitriol and sugar' he adopted as the epigraph of *Thérèse Raquin* (1867); by Prosper Lucas, a largely forgotten nineteenth-century scientist, author of a treatise on natural heredity; and by the Darwinian view of man as essentially an animal (a complete translation of Charles Darwin's *Origin of Species*, first published in 1859, appeared in French in 1865). Zola himself claimed to have based his method largely on the physiologist Claude Bernard's *Introduction à l'étude de la médecine expérimentale* (*Introduction to the Study of Experimental Medicine*), which he had read soon after its appearance in 1865. The 'truth' for which Zola aimed could only be attained, he argued, through meticulous documentation and research; the work of the novelist represented a form of practical sociology, complement-ing the work of the scientist, whose hope was to change the world not by judging it but by understanding it. When the laws determining the material conditions of human life were understood, man would have only to act on this understanding to improve society.

Zola was most truly a naturalist, in the sense of being a writer who based his fiction on scientific theory, in the early novels *Thérèse Raquin* and *Madeleine Férat* (1868). In his 1868 Preface to the second edition of *Thérèse Raquin*, a compelling tale of adultery and murder, he defended the 'scientific' purpose of the book in the face of accusations that he was the purveyor of 'putrid literature'. His purpose, he said, was to use a strictly experimental methodology to analyse the processes by which his characters (whom he calls 'temperaments') are completely dominated by their nerves and blood, are devoid of free will and are drawn into every act of their lives by the inexorable laws of their physical nature. Theory and practice had diverged considerably by the time, over a decade later, he wrote his lengthy polemical essay 'Le Roman expérimental' ('The Experimental Novel', 1880). But in any case Zola's naturalism was not as naive and uncritical as is sometimes assumed. His formulation of the naturalist aesthetic, while it advocates a respect for truth that makes no concessions to self-indulgence, shows his clear awareness that 'observation' is not an unproblematic process. He recognises the importance of the observer in the act of observation, and this recognition is repeated in his celebrated formula, used in 'The Experimental Novel', in which he describes the work of art as 'a corner of nature seen through a temperament'. Zola fully acknowledges the importance, indeed the artistic necessity, of the selecting, structuring role of the individual artist and of the aesthetic he adopts. It is thus not surprising to find him, in a series of newspaper articles in 1866, leaping to the defence of Édouard Manet and the Impressionists – defending Manet as an artist with the courage to express his own temperament in defiance of current conventions. Zola's brilliant critical 'campaign' made Manet famous. Not only did he understand what modern painters like Manet were doing, but he was able to articulate it before they could.

Zola's 'scientific' representation of society in *Les Rougon-Macquart* is informed by a vast amount of dedicated first-hand observation, note-taking and research – in Les Halles (*The Belly of Paris*), the Paris slums (*L'Assommoir*, 1877), the department stores (*Au bonheur des dames* (*The Ladies' Paradise*, 1883)), the theatre (*Nana*, 1880), the coal fields (*Germinal*, 1885), the railways (*La Bête humaine*, 1890), the French countryside (*La Terre* (*The Earth*, 1887)). Zola combines the approach of a reporter and sociologist with the vision of a painter in his observation of the modes of existence, the patterns and practices that characterise particular milieux. The texture of his novels is infused with an intense concern with concrete detail, and the detailed planning notes he assembled for each novel represent a remarkable stock of documentary information about French society in the 1870s and 1880s.

Zola's fiction acquires its power, however, not so much from its ethnographic richness as from its imaginative qualities. In his narrative practice, he combines brilliantly the particular and the general, the individual and the mass, the everyday and the fantastic. His various narrative worlds, with their specific atmospheres, are always presented through the eyes of individuals, and are never separate from human experience. The interaction between people and their environments is evoked in his celebrated physical descriptions. These descriptions are not, however, mechanical products of his aesthetic credo, parts of the text that can easily be skipped; rather, they express the very meaning, and ideological tendencies, of his narratives. Consider, for example, the lengthy descriptions of the luxurious physical decor of bourgeois existence – houses, interiors, social gatherings – in *La Curée* (*The Kill*, 1872). The main syntactic characteristic of these passages is the eclipse of human subjects by abstract nouns and things, suggesting the absence of any controlling human agency and expressing a vision of a society which, organised under the aegis of the commodity, turns people into objects. Similarly, the descriptions of the sales in *The Ladies' Paradise*, with their cascading images and rising pitch, suggest loss of control, the female shoppers' quasi-sexual abandonment to consumer dreams, at the same time mirroring the perpetual expansion that defines the economic principles of consumerism. Description of the physical realities of workers' lives in *L'Assommoir* and *Germinal* reinforces the radicalism of those novels by pointing insistently to conditions of labour that are monstrously unjust.

Zola's descriptive style reveals a genius for pictorial representation. The observed reality of the world is the foundation for a poetic vision. The originality of Zola's fiction lies in its remarkable symbolising effects. Emblematic features of contemporary life – the market, the machine, the tenement building, the laundry, the mine, the apartment house, the department store, the stock exchange, the theatre, the city itself – are used as giant symbols of the society of his day. Zola sees allegories of contemporary life everywhere. In *The Kill*, the new city under construction at the hands of Haussmann's workmen becomes a vast symbol of the corruption, as well as the dynamism, of Second Empire society. In *The Ladies' Paradise*, the department store is emblematic of the new dream world of consumer culture and of the changes in sexual attitudes and class relations taking place at the time. Through the play of imagery and metaphor, Zola magnifies the material world, giving it a hyperbolic, hallucinatory quality. We think of Saccard, the protagonist of *The Kill*, swimming in a sea of gold coins, an image that aptly evokes his activities as a speculator; the fantastic visions of food in *The Belly of Paris*; the still in *L'Assommoir*, oozing with poisonous alcohol; Nana's mansion, like a vast vagina, swallowing up men and their fortunes; the dream-like proliferation of clothing and lingerie in *The Ladies' Paradise*; the devouring pithead in *Germinal*, lit by strange fires, rising spectrally out of the darkness.

Realist representation is imbued with mythic resonance. The pithead in *Germinal* is a modern figuration of the Minotaur, a monstrous beast that breathes, devours, digests and regurgitates. Reality is transfigured into a theatre of archetypal forces; and it is the mythopoeic dimension of Zola's work that makes him one of the great figures of the European novel. Heredity not only serves as a structuring device, analogous to Balzac's use of recurring characters, but also has great dramatic force, allowing Zola to give a mythical dimension to his representation of the human condition. For Balzac, money and ambition were the mainsprings of human conduct; for Zola, human conduct was determined by heredity and environment, and they pursue his characters as relentlessly as the forces of fate in an ancient tragedy.

Zola's use of myth is inseparable from his vision of history, and is essentially Darwinian. His conception of society is shaped by a biological model informed by the struggle between the life instinct and the death instinct, the forces of creation and destruction. This vision is marked by an ambivalence characteristic of modernity itself – a pessimistic attitude towards the present, but optimism about the future. Progress, for Zola, cannot be imagined without a form of barely contained primitive regression, as witnessed by Jacques Lantier's feelings of both veneration and destructive hatred towards his locomotive in *La Bête humaine*. Despite his faith in science, Zola's vision is strongly marked by the anxiety that accompanied industrialisation and modernity. Technological progress brings alienation as well as liberation, and modern man feels trapped by forces he has created but cannot fully control. The demons of modernity are figured in images of catastrophe: the pithead in *Germinal*, the runaway train in *La Bête humaine*, the city in flames in *La Débâcle* (1892). Zola's naturalist world is an entropic world, in which nature inevitably reverts to a state of chaos, despite human efforts to create order and to dominate its course. But there is also emphasis on regeneration, on collapse being part of a larger cycle of integration and disintegration. Zola's work always turns towards hope, as the very title of *Germinal* implies.

## Social class

In 1876, Zola published in serial form his first novel of working-class life, *L'Assommoir*, which describes the social and moral degradation of that class in contemporary Paris. The novel focuses on the life and death of a washer-woman, Gervaise Macquart. It was hugely successful, and it was also scandalous: the serialisation of the novel was stopped by the government, and several bourgeois critics noisily accused Zola of pornography. These violently hostile reactions to *L'Assommoir*, together with the novel's immense commercial success (ironically, it made Zola rich), indicated that something significantly new had happened to the novel. In 1877, when the novel appeared in book form, Zola added a Preface in response to the storm of controversy the novel had provoked. He characterised *L'Assommoir* as 'a work of truth, the first novel about the common people which does not tell lies but has the authentic smell of the people'.[1]

To understand the reasons for the scandal that surrounded the publication of *L'Assommoir*, and its success, we need to consider how the novel undermined the expectations of its contemporary readership. The novel in France was essentially a bourgeois genre, having developed in tandem with the bourgeoisie's political and material rise. It depended on a largely bourgeois readership, and was shaped by a bourgeois ideology of literary propriety. Conservative critics clearly considered that Zola had transgressed the limits of what could be written about. To focus entirely on urban workers was itself new and disturbing, and to make a working-class washerwoman a tragic heroine even more so. If the workers could take over the novel, perhaps they could also take over the government; the trauma of the Commune of 1871, when the people of Paris had repudiated their national government and set up their own, was still fresh in people's minds. What also greatly disturbed bourgeois critics was Zola's unflinching realism, the sheer force and candour of his representation of slum life, and especially his graphic portrayal, unprecedented in French fiction, of the workers' physical being, their bodies. Bourgeois thought generally concealed both the bourgeoisie's physical nature and the workers' humanity; this meant that Zola's emphasis on the body, by forcing the reader to recognise that the human condition is a universal, had a powerful subversive effect on the ideological justification for the capitalist hierarchy.

What disoriented contemporary readers most, however, was not the subject matter of *L'Assommoir*, but its style: its use of working-class language and urban slang. The workers are intrusively present – they can be 'smelt' – in the very language of *L'Assommoir*. Language itself is – aggressively and provocatively – socialised. During the course of the narrative, popular speech is not simply sprinkled throughout the text but becomes the medium of narration. It is as if the characters themselves take on a narrative function, telling their own story. The language of the characters is absorbed by the (traditionally 'bourgeois') narrator without quotation marks, as if the novel were spoken via the collective voice of the Goutte-d'Or district, using the lexicon and syntax of the street.

Zola achieved this effect by use of a special form of the technique known as free indirect style. His brilliant ability to capture popular speech patterns, even when writing indirectly, reflects his powers of psychological empathy, a capacity for evoking the workers' own vision of the world; and it also has significant ideological implications. Not only are the expectations associated with conventional bourgeois narrative disrupted, but the reader is also brought into more direct and authentic contact with the characters and their culture, their attitudes and values, than would have been the case had these been relayed exclusively by means of direct speech and conventional dialogue. It was his bold experiment with style that, according to Zola, explained why his bourgeois readers had been so upset. As he wrote in his Preface: 'They have taken exception to the words. My crime is that I have had the literary curiosity to collect the language of the people and pour it into a carefully wrought mould. The form! The form is the great crime.' His 'great crime' was to have shown that the novel is not an intrinsically bourgeois genre, tied to bourgeois discourse.

The novel's central chapter (ch. 7) describes Gervaise's celebration of her saint's day with a Rabelaisian feast where food, drink and companionship are the focus. The doors and windows are opened and the whole neighbourhood is invited to join in the merrymaking. The feast is a pivotal episode, marking the high point of Gervaise's professional success, but also a turning point in her fortunes. The sheer extravagance of the feast suggests the lurking dangers of dissipation, and the occasion also marks the fateful return of Lantier, Gervaise's malevolent former lover. Gervaise decides to spend all of her hard-won savings on the meal, and even pawns her wedding ring in order to buy superior wine. Above all, the extravagance of the feast expresses defiance, through recklessness and prodigality, of the constrictions – the prudence and thrift – of a life always on the edge of starvation. The workers' plight is expressed through the very description of their pleasure: 'The whole shop was dying for a binge. They needed an absolute blow-out.' The meal becomes an orgy, and the mounting excitement of the characters is matched by that of the narrative voice, which appears to blend joyously with the voices of the assembled company:

> God, yes, they really stuffed themselves! If you're going to do it, you might as well do it properly, eh? And if you only have a real binge once in a blue moon, you'd be bloody mad not to fill yourself up to the eyeballs. You could actually see their bellies getting bigger by the minute! The women looked pregnant. Every one of them was fit to burst, the greedy pigs! Their mouths wide open,

grease all over their chins, their faces were just like arses, so red that you'd swear they were rich folk's arses, with money pouring out of them.

And the wine, my friends! The wine flowed round the table like the water in the Seine.

The past definite tense used in the first sentence ('they really stuffed themselves!' ('on s'en flanqua une bosse!')) clearly identifies the passage as a part of the narrative, but the register and syntax – direct, simple, robustly colloquial – reflect the language of the characters. The characters' colloquial language is woven into the fabric of the narrative, absorbing the written discourse of the narrator. The use of *on* in the original ('And if you . . .' ('et si l'on . . . ')) is ambiguous (they? we?), blurring further the distinction between narrator and characters. A single voice dominates. The jovial apostrophe 'my friends!', its author and addressees uncertain, draws the reader into sharing in the general euphoria. The narrator sits at table with his characters, participating stylistically in the revelry and implicitly inviting the reader-spectator to join in too, thus subverting the moralistic perspectives on the workers' intemperance that so strongly marked contemporary discourse on social issues and contemporary reactions to the novel. Is it because Gervaise is self-indulgent and given to excess that she undergoes the tragedy of working people? Or is it because she undergoes the tragedy of working people that she becomes self-indulgent and given to excess? Is the feast an act of reprehensible folly, or an understandable symptom of the circumstances in which Gervaise lives?

The novel's style has clear ideological implications. Zola showed his readers things they would prefer not to see in a style making it impossible to look the other way. The ventriloquised storyteller is almost too close for comfort. It is not only impossible to look the other way, but difficult to keep one's distance. The critical debate surrounding *L'Assommoir*, both at the time of the novel's appearance and since, involved what might be called a politics of representation. The fact that the urban proletariat were considered by the bourgeoisie to be beyond the limits of narrative, beneath the level of narrative representation, was held implicitly to justify their exclusion from political representation. The strident attacks on *L'Assommoir* for pornography were motivated as much by reactionary fear as by prudishness; and the attacks Zola sustained throughout his career for vulgarity, tastelessness, stylistic crudity and a purported obsession with the filthy underside of society were largely political in nature – attempts by the Establishment to discredit him.

Eight years after *L'Assommoir*, Zola published *Germinal*. Through his description of a miners' strike, he evokes the awakening of the workers'

political consciousness. He depicts how torpid resignation is slowly transformed into conscious awareness, and how the miners begin to see themselves
as active subjects capable of creating their own history. In *L'Assommoir*,
Zola had used narrative technique, and narrative voice in particular, to
make articulate the inarticulate, to make us see and hear the world through
the workers' eyes and voices. In *Germinal*, he does something similar;
but in the later novel he also depicts a moment in history when the workers
find a political voice.

## The body and sex

Zola's social and sexual themes intersect at many points. In his sexual
themes, he ironically subverts the notion that bourgeois supremacy over
the workers is a natural rather than a cultural phenomenon. His description
in *Germinal* of the secret adultery of Madame Hennebeau with her nephew,
the engineer Négrel, exposes as myth the reactionary bourgeois supposition
that they, unlike the workers, are above nature – that they are able to
control their natural instincts and that their social supremacy is therefore
justified. Hennebeau is at first enraged when he discovers that his wife
is sleeping with her nephew; but he quickly decides to turn a blind eye to
her infidelity, reflecting that it is better to be cuckolded by his bourgeois
nephew than by his proletarian coachman. Adultery among the bourgeoisie
was much more significant than among the working class because, as
transgressors of their own law, the bourgeoisie put at risk an order of
civilisation structured to sustain their own privileged position. The more
searchingly and explicitly Zola investigated the theme of adultery, the more
he risked uncovering the arbitrariness and fragility of the whole bourgeois
social order.

In *Pot-bouille* (*Pot Luck*, 1882), Zola lifted the lid on the realities
of bourgeois mores, exposing the hypocrisy of the dominant class, who
are no more able to control their natural instincts than the workers but
are simply more dissimulating. The bourgeois go to extreme lengths to
maintain the segregation between themselves and the lower classes, whom
they insistently portray as dirty, immoral, promiscuous, stupid – at best a
lesser type of human, at worst some kind of wild beast. But class difference
is shown to be merely a matter of money and power, tenuously holding
down the raging forces of sexuality and corruption beneath the surface.
What we are left with is a melting pot, a stew, an undifferentiated world
where no clear boundaries remain.

Zola's naturalism, with its emphasis on integrity of representation, entailed
a new explicitness in the depiction of sexuality. To say less than all would be

to abdicate, as Zola saw it, from the novelist's intellectual and social function. He broke with academic convention to a degree hitherto unseen in literature. *Nana*, for example, represented a drastic advance towards erotic verisimilitude. The novel's opening scene dramatises this stripping away of cultural shields as Nana appears with progressively less clothing on the stage of a variety theatre. The theatre functions in *Nana* as a symbiosis of the themes of capitalism and sexuality, in its dual role as theatre and figurative brothel. It is the place where different classes meet and where the actress-prostitute Nana can display her wares, her body, on stage in her role as Venus. The theatre manager, Bordenave, alerts us to this other use of the theatre when he insists that his institution should be called a brothel, not a theatre. This house of ill repute, which holds within its walls people from all walks of life and social stations, presents risqué parodies of classical myths as well as other bawdy comedies. Nana's first appearance as Venus prefigures her future as a 'man-eater', for after this performance she becomes the object of desire of every man in the audience. Her performance is a masterstroke of marketing technique, showing how she and her agent Bordenave are able to merchandise her main commodity, her body, on a mass scale. The theatre in *Nana* is truly a brothel, a centre of capitalist commerce of the flesh, symbolising the decadence and hypocrisy of Second Empire society. Theatre is the essence of the world Nana embodies. In her mansion, doors open and close, and men enter unexpectedly, having to be hidden by the maid. Nana's power reaches all levels of society, and by the end of her career this working-class girl will have reached beyond her class to devastate the lives of aristocrats, bankers, journalists and government officials. Sex provides a power that reverses class hierarchies, converting the oppressor into the oppressed.

## The public writer

Zola broke taboos. His work was deemed scandalous in both form and content. At every stage of his life he was involved in controversy. As a journalist he championed Manet and the Impressionists against the upholders of academic art; he was an outspoken critic of the Second Empire and he attacked the stuffy moral conservatism of the early years of the Third Republic. As a novelist, he founded the naturalist school in opposition to 'polite' literature: there was the scandal of *L'Assommoir*, the provocation of *Nana*, the political warning of *Germinal*, the uncompromising candour of *Earth*, and the sustained critique of organised religion in *Les Trois Villes* (*Three Cities*, 1894–8). Zola never stopped being a danger to the established order. In 1898 he crowned his literary career with a political act, the famous open letter ('J'accuse ... !') to the President of the Republic in defence of Alfred Dreyfus – a frontal attack on state power.

Zola's courageous stand in the Affair – squarely in the tradition of Voltaire and Victor Hugo, and anticipating the work of writers like Jean-Paul Sartre and Albert Camus in the twentieth century – showed the public writer at his best. In 1893, Dreyfus, a Jewish army officer, had been accused of spying for Germany. He had been court-martialled, found guilty of treason and sentenced to life imprisonment on Devil's Island, off the coast of French Guiana. Despite clear evidence that emerged in 1897 showing that Dreyfus had been the victim of a conspiracy, the original verdict was upheld, to the outrage of Zola and his fellow Dreyfusards. By the time of 'J'accuse', French public opinion was polarised, not simply on the question of Dreyfus's innocence or guilt but on the future of the Republic itself. The clash of republicanism and anti-republicanism, clericalism and anticlericalism, reaction and social reform, blind patriotism and rational criticism, was whipped up further by xenophobia and anti-Semitism.

Zola's article transformed what began as a purely legal battle into a much wider conflict about what sort of France people wanted. It opposed, on one side, the advocates of truth, justice and human rights, and on the other the standard-bearers of nationalism, militarism and reasons of state. It was during the Dreyfus Affair that the noun 'intellectuel' first appeared in the French language. In broad terms, the 'intellectuel', whether of the left or the right, was one who defended a position with reference to an ideology, a set of general principles. During the Dreyfus Affair, writers like Maurice Barrès specifically supported the institutions – the church and the army – that, for them, enshrined and protected national traditions; while Zola and his allies maintained a general belief in principles whose origins lay in the values underpinning the Revolution of 1789 – principles which, they believed, should transcend matters of national self-interest. Zola's key strategy in his address to the jury at the time of his trial for libel in connection with the publication of 'J'accuse' was to present the unjust condemnation of Dreyfus as an aberration from the true Republic of 1789 and its principles of liberty and justice: 'There is no Dreyfus Affair any longer. There is only one issue: is France still the France of the Revolution and the Declaration of the Rights of Man?' Condemned to imprisonment for one year, Zola went into exile in England. The day after his sentence, the League of the Rights of Man was founded. The Dreyfus Affair was of seminal importance in relation to the unique role French intellectuals were destined to play on the world stage in the twentieth century as a result of the historical legacy of the Revolution.

## Zola and the European novel

Zola's influence on European fiction was enormous. The liberating effect of his writing cannot be overestimated. He opened up the novel to entirely new areas of experience.

Critical reactions to him were quite varied from country to country. Usually enthusiastic intermediaries emerged to introduce his work to their compatriots, like Michael Georg Conrad in Germany, Emilia Pardo Bazán in Spain or George Moore in England. Except in Germany, enthusiasm and assimilation were matched by strong currents of resistance. In several countries any literature based on deterministic premises, or depicting the life of the lower classes, or unreserved in its use of the common language or in the representation of sexual behaviour, tended to be ascribed to Zola's corrupting influence. Hostility to Zola's novels was particularly marked in England. Henry Vizetelly's translation of *La Terre* in 1888 led to a heated debate in the House of Commons, and Vizetelly was eventually prosecuted (twice) and imprisoned for three months for publishing 'obscene libels' as a result of the successful campaigns of the National Vigilance Association against so-called pernicious literature. Thomas Hardy, like Zola, questioned Victorian double standards in matters of sexual morality, and probed the established institutions for weak spots. As David Baguley (see Further reading) has argued, there is a strong case for considering Hardy a naturalist writer. His works, after all, were greeted in England with the same kind of opprobrium that was reserved for Zola, a sure sign that they were challenging the conventions that the Victorian reading public assumed it should find in novels.

The reception of literary works is never, of course, simply a passive reaction but reflects and interacts with processes of institutional control and cultural authority. The controversial nature of naturalism's subject-matter raised fundamental issues regarding censorship and the right of the state to intervene in literary matters in order to protect public decency. The debates surrounding naturalism had, at bottom, an ideological dimension. They were really debates about the challenge posed to accepted political and religious assumptions by the new scientific and analytical temper of the age, and about the defensibility or otherwise of hierarchical models of social organisation. The controversies that marked the critical engagement with naturalism in England must be seen in their cultural and political contexts. Much more was at stake than simply a literary mode or style. The debate about naturalism's extension of the franchise of fiction so as to open up new areas of representation (sexuality, the lower orders, women) also became a debate about the changing social relations and shifts of cultural authority that accompanied this extension. At the heart of the debate was a contest about aesthetic representation in which the key questions – who or what may be represented in fiction, in what manner, by whom and for whom – were deeply enmeshed with debates about political representation and with anxieties about authority and control, which permeated the culture.

In Spain, where conservative Catholicism had deep roots, the debate about naturalism took on a peculiar intensity. In the context of earlier attempts in Spain to develop a poetics of the novel, the movement towards naturalism marked a decisive advance towards the notion that the novel can be a serious art form, offering an analytic study of society, rather than remaining a form of escapist entertainment. In a speech to the Spanish Academy entitled 'Contemporary Society as Novelistic Material' (1897), Benito Pérez Galdós observed that 'examining the conditions of the social milieu in which we live' forced the writer to come to terms with new realities, which, in spite of their turbulence and confusion, constitute the experience of modernity. The writings of Galdós and Emilia Pardo Bazán reflected a perceptible shift of interest towards topics considered to be characteristically naturalist: the organic nature of society, the interaction of different social levels, the extension of the subject-matter of the novel to include the lower classes and their harsh working conditions, and the ways in which human behaviour is affected by the depersonalising forces of industrialisation or of primitive nature. On the other hand, while strongly influenced by naturalism, Pardo Bazán and Galdós maintained a sceptical attitude towards the determinism that underpinned Zola's view of human behaviour.

Naturalistic discourse, and in particular the naturalist paradigm of the biological imagination is central to Leopoldo Alas's *La Regenta* (1884–5), the culminating achievement of Spanish literary realism. The horrors of nineteenth-century life – uncontrolled sexuality, crime, madness, disease, filth, working-class rebellion – are converted in Alas's masterpiece into threatening metaphors of underground forces that can erupt plaguelike, invading the well-being and order of bourgeois society. These repressed elements burst to the surface at critical moments, like the nightmare of the novel's heroine, Ana Ozores. A web of images and associations connects the dream with other parts of the text by projecting nineteenth-century fears and obsessions onto Ana's body, which becomes a naturalist text that gives birth to the repressed in its social and psychological expressions. *La Regenta* is a perfect example of the capacity of the naturalist text to penetrate into the most protected domains of bourgeois proprieties.

In Italy, as in Spain, the assimilation of Zola's naturalism informed the context in which *verismo* developed and in which Giovanni Verga assumed his status as the father of modern Italian fiction. In his stories, *Novelle rusticane* (*Little Novels of Sicily*, 1883), and in his novels *I malavoglia* (*The House by the Medlar Tree*, 1881) and *Mastro Don Gesualdo* (1888), set in rural Sicily, Verga depicted characters caught in a world governed by the inexorable laws of their harsh natural environment and their own instincts. Within the largely peasant world of Verga, where appetite and ambition reign, the individual has little control over his or her life.

Zola's theories were taken most seriously in Germany, where he enjoyed a massive popular response, inspiring poets and dramatists as well as novelists. It is generally felt, however, that naturalism in Germany was much more successful in the theatre than in the novel. Thomas Mann's *Buddenbrooks* (1901) was described by Mann himself as 'perhaps the first and only naturalist novel in Germany'. It is indeed the closest approximation to a native German naturalist novel, its basic design fulfilling perfectly the naturalistic ideology of human beings as shaped by heredity, environment and the pressure of circumstance; but at the same time, it enacts a subversion of naturalism by incorporating into its naturalist schema a symbolising countertext of introverted decadence.

## Naturalism reassessed

Modern criticism of Zola and naturalism has tended to see naturalism less as a simple continuation of realism than as a distinct body of literature. This is the approach of Yves Chevrel and David Baguley, the authors of the two most distinguished generic studies of naturalism (see Further reading). They stress the originality and modernity of naturalism, which Chevrel dates from the Preface to Edmond and Jules Goncourt's *Germinie Lacerteux* (1864) to the première of Anton Chekhov's *The Cherry Orchard* (1904). They identify as the essential features of naturalism: the rejection of myths of transcendence but the displacement of tragedy into man's experience of social existence and everyday life; the positivistic ambition to demystify reality, to classify, understand and explain; the consequent tendency to erode traditional generic hierarchies; the prominence in its narrative poetics of the ironic modes satire and parody; its fascination with the pathological and the deviant; and its thematics of disintegration and decomposition – an 'entropic vision' that reflects a real crisis of human values. Both Chevrel and Baguley, by breaking completely with traditional historical approaches to naturalism, have helped us to overcome the problems created by naturalist writers themselves through the disparities between their pseudo-scientific theories and their narrative practice, and their tendency to deny the 'literariness' of their work. Similarly, much of the most interesting modern criticism of Zola has adopted thematic and formalist approaches that have revealed in his work, and in naturalist fiction generally, textual creations that are infinitely richer and more complex than past critical orthodoxy would ever have allowed.

## Note on editions/translations

*Les Rougon-Macquart* is available in a superb scholarly edition in the 'Bibliothèque de la Pléiade', ed. Henri Mitterand, 5 vols. (Paris: Gallimard, 1960–7). The *Contes et nouvelles* are available in the same series, ed. Roger Ripoll (Paris: Gallimard, 1976). Zola's *Œuvres complètes*, presented chronologically, are available in twenty volumes, and a supplement, under the general editorship of Henri Mitterand (Paris: Nouveau Monde Éditions, 2003–10). Numerous paperback editions exist in popular collections such as Folio and Classiques de Poche.

Nearly all Zola's novels, including the twenty volumes of the Rougon-Macquart cycle, have been translated into English. Those published by Oxford University Press (Oxford World's Classics) and Penguin Books are especially recommended. Reprints of late nineteenth-century translations, often expurgated, are best avoided.

## Note

1  All translations in this essay are mine.

## Further reading

Baguley, David, *Naturalist Fiction: The Entropic Vision* (Cambridge University Press, 1990)

Chevrel, Yves, *Le Naturalisme* (Paris: Presses Universitaires de France, 1982)

Hemmings, F. W. J., *Emile Zola*, 2nd edn (Oxford: Clarendon Press, 1966)

Mitterand, Henri, *Emile Zola: Fiction and Modernity*, trans. M. Lebron and D. Baguley (London: The Emile Zola Society, 2001)

Nelson, Brian, ed., *The Cambridge Companion to Zola* (Cambridge University Press, 2007)

  ed., *Naturalism in the European Novel: New Critical Perspectives* (Oxford/New York: Berg, 1992)

Wilson, Angus, *Emile Zola: An Introductory Study of his Novels* (1953; London: Secker and Warburg, 1964)

# 18

ANGUS WRENN

# Henry James (1843–1916): Henry James's Europe

The inclusion in a survey of European novelists of Henry James, born in New York, and who did not take British nationality until 1915, just a few months before his death, requires some explanation. The fact that he spent only the first year of his forty-one-year permanent, self-imposed exile from the United States in Continental Europe (in Paris), retreating from there to England, would perhaps seem to qualify his grounds for inclusion still further. However, this mere analysis of dates conceals a literary career which James himself always, from the earliest years, conceived in terms arguably more European than that of any other major practitioner of the novel in English in his period.

James was brought to Europe in infancy by his parents, in the 1840s, and then more significantly, for a three-year period, 1855–8, at the beginning of his teens, residing variously in Paris, Boulogne and Geneva, while he returned in 1859 and attended the École Toepffer as well as studying German in Bonn. In the early 1870s (1869–73) he travelled on the Continent, chiefly in Italy rather than France, owing to the Franco-Prussian War waged in this period. In 1875, coming to Europe for the first time unaccompanied as an adult, he endeavoured to settle in Paris, spending a year there until 1876 when, suffering some setbacks in his project to establish himself as a writer of 'letters home' reporting for an American journal on the Parisian scene, he moved on to London, where his career was to become established for the remainder of his life.

The early residence in Geneva, Paris and Boulogne enabled James to gain a mastery of the French language which, while he never wrote any fiction in it, allowed him to read with as much ease in French as in English. Numerous letters written entirely in French survive, while the testimony of no less a figure than Alphonse Daudet, 's'il se tire de sa langue comme de la nôtre, c'est un rude lapin' ('if he speaks his own language as well as he speaks ours he is impressive indeed'),[1] confirms his mastery, and is backed up by later remarks of Maurice Maeterlinck. Besides a fluency in French (his novels are peppered with interjections in French both by the narrators and by characters in dialogue) James also had considerable facility in Italian. At least one letter written entirely in Italian survives, and Italian phrases, if with less frequency than French, are frequently found in his prose.[2] James clearly read extensively in Italian (if on a lesser scale than his reading in French) and wrote on both Gabriele D'Annunzio (an important essay was published in the *Critical Quarterly* in 1904) and the Neapolitan novelist Matilde Serao, knowing the latter personally – a major essay was published in *Notes on Novelists* in 1914, and James reveals that he had known her work since the mid 1880s.

James is known to have studied German for one year in his teens and records working away at translation of Friedrich Schiller. Nevertheless, German is not a language which James appears to have spoken,[3] and in general German culture is something with which James was far less in sympathy than either French or Italian (there is none of the cultivation of German seriousness to be found in his older contemporary George Eliot, or his father's contemporary and correspondent, Thomas Carlyle).

Unlike French, German and Italian, James had no knowledge of the Russian language but was well read in the fiction of Ivan Turgenev, whom he met in Paris in 1875–6 and revered both then and later. James was also a close personal friend of the Russian émigré Paul Joukovsky and his extended short story of 1887 'The Aspern Papers', although set in Venice and drawing upon the legacy of the English Romantic poets Percy Bysshe Shelley and George Gordon Byron, arguably owes its largest literary debt to Alexander Pushkin's *The Queen of Spades*.[4]

When, in the 1890s, James turned to writing for the stage, his inspiration was certainly not American and not really English (he disparaged the English stage), but came instead from Norway (the radical new realist work of Henrik Ibsen) or, in still greater measure, the French nineteenth-century drama of Victorien Sardou, Émile Augier, Alexandre Dumas *fils* and Eugène Scribe,[5] and it is Paris and the French classical theatre which feature prominently in James's 1890 novel *The Tragic Muse*.

In this light it seems by no means surprising that James should be considered a European novelist and this view is reinforced in two further respects: the milieu, genre and setting of his fiction; and his approach to the art of writing fiction. In terms of both, James emerges as quintessentially European.

All but the first two of James's published full-length novels, *Watch and Ward* (1870) and *Roderick Hudson* (1875), were written after James had taken up what was to prove to be permanent residence in Europe. Of eighteen novels, only *Watch and Ward*, *The Europeans* (1879), *Washington Square* (1880) and *The Bostonians* (1884) feature plots which unfold entirely in America itself. Of the remaining fourteen novels the majority concern Americans abroad in Europe (*Roderick Hudson, Confidence, The Portrait of a Lady, The Reverberator, The Ambassadors, The Wings of the Dove* and *The Golden Bowl*) and a number from James's 'middle' period, from the later 1880s to the turn of the twentieth century, are set entirely in Britain or France with no episodes taking place in America and few significant roles for American characters (*The Princess Casamassima, The Tragic Muse, What Maisie Knew, The Spoils of Poynton, The Awkward Age* and *The Sacred Fount*). The typical plot of many of his novels concerns a usually ill-prepared or 'innocent' American attempting to enter sophisticated upper-class European circles: Roderick Hudson in thrall to Christina Light, admittedly American by birth but married to the Italian Prince Casamassima, in *Roderick Hudson*; Christopher Newman, the Californian self-made millionaire of *The American*; Isabel Archer fatally attracted to the Europeanised Osmond in *The Portrait of a Lady* and later Lambert Strether encountering Madame de Vionnet in *The Ambassadors*, as well as Maggie Verver's marriage to the Italian Prince Amerigo in *The Golden Bowl*. But on an examination of James's Notebooks and other source materials, this proves often to be a transatlantic reworking and amplification of a scenario repeatedly found in purely French fiction of the mid nineteenth century (the Second Empire of Napoleon III, 1852–70). That is to say, what is termed the 'International Theme' in James, represented by *Roderick Hudson, The Portrait of a Lady, The Ambassadors* and *The Wings of the Dove* and *The Golden Bowl*, and seen as having been chiefly inherited from Nathaniel Hawthorne's precedent in *The Marble Faun* (1863), of wealthy, naive Americans abroad often being treated as 'an applied handled hung-up tool, as senseless and convenient as mere shaped wood and iron'[6] by either Europeans like the Bellegardes or Prince Amerigo or highly Europeanised American expatriates such as Madame Merle, Gilbert Osmond, Christina Light or Charlotte Stant, has its origins in the works of Honoré de Balzac as well as lesser-known novelists of the Second Empire period. James was introduced to the work of the latter especially in the pages of the *Revue des deux mondes*, a journal to which his family subscribed both during and after their years in Europe.[7]

Peter Brooks has attributed the social exclusion vented upon Christopher Newman, the American aspirant suitor for the aristocratic Claire de Cintré in *The American*, to the example of Balzac's *La Duchesse de Langeais*.[8] James's aristocratic Bellegardes display the same Legitimist disdain both for more recent, *nouveau riche* Napoleonic French aristocrats and of course for Newman himself as a 'classless' albeit rich American, as the Duchesse's Legitimist relatives show towards her would-be suitor in Balzac's novella.

James gives to the purely French situation of exclusion by one social rank of another, inherited from Balzac (the tension between Bonapartists and Legitimists), the extra dimension of making his aspirant to the hand of the aristocratic bride in *The American* (Claire de Cintré) an American (and not even an American from 'old' New England but a Californian, at the date of publication a concept barely a generation old). Thus it may be said that James is at once inscribing his novel within a thoroughly European cultural context and giving it an extra, international dimension (the Legitimist Bellegardes are disdainful of the implicitly classless, republican and Protestant Newman). Clearly, any resultant marriage would have been strained and, as so often elsewhere, James frustrates such expectations of a marriage as the reader may entertain. The Bellegardes, having with ill grace swallowed their aristocratic pride and hauteur for the sake of Newman's millions, in the final part of the novel renege on their promise of Claire de Cintré's hand in marriage when an alternative suitor, sufficiently wealthy and an aristocrat into the bargain (the Irish Lord Deepmere) appears on the scene. Rather than go along with this arranged marriage Mme de Cintré goes into a convent and Newman returns chastened to America.

That novel serves as a demonstration of the degree to which James took his bearings from the hierarchical distinctions of French upper-class society. In itself this is ample evidence of James's European cast of thought, but it has also been argued by Richard Poirier and Oscar Cargill that *The American* may be viewed as a 'dramatization' of James's own predicament in Paris during 1875–6.[9]

James had settled there in the autumn of 1875 with the express intention of establishing himself in French literary circles. While he did not venture to write fiction or criticism in French he was clearly completely at home in the language. However, James was to be frustrated in his attempt on two counts. First, the source of journalistic income on which he had hoped to depend, payments from *The Tribune* in return for a series of 'letters home' describing contemporary French social, political and cultural life, was to be curtailed within a matter of months. The editor, James says in correspondence (and in a later memoir), found his letters 'too literary' and insufficiently 'newsy'.[10] Simultaneously, after initially encouraging developments, James became frustrated by his failure to make meaningful inroads into Parisian literary salons.

James met Gustave Flaubert in 1876 through Ivan Turgenev, to whom he had been given an introduction, although James was less enthusiastic about Flaubert's work, despite finding his personality compelling. With the younger generation of Flaubert's followers, the realist and naturalist writers, Émile Zola, Alphonse Daudet, Edmond de Goncourt (surviving brother of

Jules) and the young Guy de Maupassant, James found himself distinctly at odds. James seems to have been dismayed by their scant regard for various French novelists of the 1860s whom, though today all but forgotten, he had read with enthusiasm via the *Revue des deux mondes*. This was an artistic-ally conservative (and politically pro-monarchist) journal very much to be contrasted with the radical *Revue de Paris* in which Flaubert's *Madame Bovary* had initially been serialised. That led to a trial for blasphemy and, although Flaubert was exonerated of the charge, the journal was closed down by the Napoleon III regime.

At this date, James reacted negatively to the Zola–Daudet–Goncourt circle's literary doctrine of naturalism. He wrote to his mother on 24 January 1876 complaining that these writers were blinkered in their vision:

> I also spent a Sunday afternoon again at Flaubert's with his *cénacle*: E de Goncourt, Alphonse Daudet etc. They are a queer lot, and intellectually remote from my own sympathies. They are extremely narrow and it makes me rather scorn them that not a mother's son of them can read English. But this hardly matters for they couldn't understand it if they did.[11]

Worse, the naturalist writers disparaged the work of one of his favoured Second Empire novelists, Gustave Droz, according to James in a letter to Thomas Perry, as '*merde à la vanille*' ('shit scented with vanilla') and James went on 'I send you Zola's own latest [*La Joie de vivre*] *merde au naturel* [unadorned shit]'.[12] James criticised the Zola circle for being 'bornés' (limited in their vision) and implicitly confining themselves to a strictly francophone literary context ('and not a mother's son of them can read a word of English'). James went beyond personal correspondence by ampli-fying this point in one of the 'letters home' he was engaged to write for the *Tribune*:

> You ask a writer whose productions you admire about any other writer, for whose works you have also a relish. 'Oh, he is of the School of This or That: he is of the *queue* [camp] of So and So,' he answers. 'We think nothing of him: you mustn't talk of him here; for us he doesn't exist.' And you turn away, meditative, and perhaps with a little private elation at being yourself an unconsolidated American and able to enjoy both Mr A and Mr X who enjoy each other so little.[13]

Besides the distaste for 'unclean' subject-matter (perhaps a legacy of grow-ing up in a New England relatively puritan milieu), James's rejection of the most progressive, contemporary schools of French literature in 1875–6 was in some degree also aesthetic. In May 1876, James wrote to William Dean Howells: 'I have seen almost nothing of the literary fraternity, and there are fifty reasons why I should not become intimate with them. I don't like their wares, and they don't like any others; and besides, they are not *accueillants* [welcoming].'[14] By the end of July 1876 James was writing to his brother William, rejecting what France had stood for in literary terms:

> Your remarks on my French tricks in my letters are doubtless most just, and shall be heeded. But it's an odd thing that such tricks should grow at a time when my last layer of resistance to a long encroaching weariness and satiety with the French mind and its utterance has fallen from me like a garment. I have done with 'em, forever, & am turning English all over. I desire only to feel English life and the contact of English minds.[15]

Within months, James had moved to London and established what was arguably the most successful part of his career as a novelist; he was invited to dine repeatedly in London society, and even lionised.

The novels with which James made his name typically involved wealthy expatriate Americans among the denizens of European high society, their plots frequently taking place in drawing rooms in stately homes and at society balls. Representative of the early fiction (up to the mid 1880s) is Chapter 43 of *The Portrait of a Lady*, which describes an aristocratic ball. Save for the setting in Italy this might in all other regards be the world of Jane Austen back at the turn of the nineteenth century, with match-making and marriage the principal themes.

James's negative attitude to contemporary French fiction in 1875–6 was to change by the time he returned to Paris for an extended visit in 1884. Introduced to them again, this time by the American expatriate Theodore Child, James was surprised to discover that the members of the Zola circle actually remembered him from eight years before and knew of his literary achievements and standing as, by this stage, the author of *The American*, *Washington Square*, *The Europeans* and, above all, *The Portrait of a Lady*. James clearly relished his encounter with a serious literary school and spoke of them with approbation in a letter to Howells of 21 February 1884. He still retained reservations about the naturalist movement's concentration upon 'unclean' subject-matter but he praised their seriousness specifically by contrast with the 'tepid' fiction currently being produced in English:

> I have been seeing something of Daudet, Goncourt, & Zola; & there is nothing more interesting to me now than the effort & experiment of this little group, with its truly infernal intelligence of art, form, manner – in its intense artistic life. They do the only kind of work, to-day, that I respect; & in spite of their ferocious pessimism & their handling of unclean things, they are at least serious and honest. The floods of tepid soap and water which under the name of novels are being vomited forth in England, seem to me, by contrast, to do little honour to our race. I say this to you, because I regard you as the great American naturalist.[16]

This encounter was to bear fruit in two regards. A few months later, responding to Walter Besant, James produced his essay 'The Art of Fiction' which became virtually a manifesto for James's idea of a much-needed aesthetic for the novel in English. It is interesting that, where in the eighteenth century, English writers such as Samuel Richardson and Laurence Sterne could exert significant influence upon the novel on the Continent (for instance, upon Choderlos de Laclos and Denis Diderot), James in the late nineteenth century regards French literature as, whatever its defects of emphasis and subject-matter, implicitly more serious from a theoretical point of view than the novel in England. James's very insistence upon erecting an ideal of form to be pursued in the field of narrative prose fiction is itself surely a nod in the direction of the Flaubert–Zola school. By this date, besides some of his most enduring novels, such as *Thérèse Raquin* (1867), *L'Assommoir* (1877) and *Nana* (1880), Zola had produced *Le Roman expérimental* (1881).

> Only a short time ago it might have been supposed that the English novel was not what the French call *discutable* [worthy of discussion]. It had no air of having a theory, a conviction, a consciousness of itself behind it – of being the expression of an artistic faith, the result of choice and comparison. I do not say it was necessarily the worse for that; it would take much more courage than I possess to intimate that the form of the novel, as Dickens and Thackeray (for instance) saw it had any taint of incompleteness. It was, however, *naïf* [simplistic] (if I may help myself out with another French word); and, evidently, if it is destined to suffer in any way for having lost its *naïveté* [simplicity] it has now an idea of making sure of the corresponding advantages ... The successful application of any art is a delightful spectacle, but the theory, too, is interesting.[17]

However, James (by implication) takes issue with the Zola school at the same time. The key concept in James's essay is that of the 'glimpse' which gives rise to the author's recreation of a scene. This idea of the glimpse (of necessity selective) is to be contrasted with the overly detailed, documentary realism of the naturalists, which in turn can weary the reader and distract from aesthetic unity and focus. James gives in 'The Art of Fiction' the example of a novelist friend who produced a convincing portrayal of a French Protestant family merely on the basis of a single passing glimpse of them at dinner through an open doorway.

French Protestants also feature in Daudet's novel of the year before, *L'Évangéliste*. Outwardly, *The Bostonians* appears to deviate from the idea of James as an increasingly assimilated European novelist. However, while it is admittedly set in its entirety in America, and deals with the North–South divide and post-bellum politics of contemporary American society, James's stylistic ideal in the writing of *The Bostonians* is profoundly influenced by the French naturalists. James says, 'Daudet's *L'Évangéliste* has given me the idea of this kind of thing.'[18] James was to persist in the naturalist vein in his 1886 novel *The Princess Casamassima*.

James had made major strides in the previous decade, producing such masterpieces as *Daisy Miller* and *Washington Square* as well as *The Portrait of A Lady*, the longest of his novels, a success on both sides of the Atlantic, and arguably his most widely read work. *Daisy Miller* may also be viewed in a European context. Telling of the way in which the American expatriate community in Switzerland and Rome ostracise a free-spirited young American girl who responds too freely to the influence of European society, this novel, at least for his contemporary readership, hinges upon an intertextual reference to a Swiss novel written in French by Victor Cherbuliez, *Paule Méré* (1865), where a similar, but purely European free-spirited young girl is ostracised by a local Swiss Calvinist community every bit as self-righteous as James's New Englanders in exile. From a strictly commercial point of view, *Daisy Miller* constitutes James's great lost opportunity, and here too Europe played a part. Although the work was an immediate success, perhaps because of his residence in Europe rather than the United States James failed to secure copyright properly in North America and lost out hugely in terms of royalties.

Nowhere is the influence of contemporary European literature more plainly seen than in the pivotal novel from the middle of his career, *The Princess Casamassima* (*PC*). In the months prior to its publication, writing to Thomas Perry in the USA, James describes himself taking notes at Millbank Prison in London – the location for the opening scene, and as such very far from the hitherto typical Jamesian milieu: 'I have been all the morning at Millbank Prison (horrible place) collecting notes for a fiction scene. You see I am quite the Naturalist.'[19] Moreover, the hero of the new novel, Hyacinth Robinson, meets a fellow worker and revolutionary Paul Muniment, whose family have moved down to London from the collieries of the north-east, and by Chapter 9 James presents an extended description of industrial misery which none of his previous 'society' novels could have prepared the reader for:

> I think you would say so if you had ever been in the mines. Yes, in the mines, where the filthy coal is dug out. That's where my father came from – he was working in the pit when he was a child of ten. He never had a day's schooling in his life; but he climbed up out of his black hole into daylight and air, and he invented a machine, and he married my mother, who came out of Durham, and (by her people) out of the pits and misery too. My father had no great future, but *she* was magnificent – the finest woman in the country, and the

bravest, and the best. She's in her grave now, and I couldn't go to look at it even if it were in the nearest churchyard. My father was as black as the coal he worked in: I know I'm just his pattern, barring that *he* did have his legs, when the liquor hadn't got into them. But between him and my mother, for grand, high intelligence there wasn't much to choose. But what's the use of brains if you haven't got a backbone? My poor father had even less of that than I, for with me it's only the body can't stand up, and with him it was the spirit. He discovered a kind of wheel, and he sold it, at Bradford, for fifteen pounds: I mean the whole right of it, and every hope and pride of his family. He was always straying, and my mother always bringing him back. She had plenty to do, with me a puny, ailing brat from the moment I opened my eyes. Well, one night he strayed so far that he never came back; or only came back a loose, bloody bundle of clothes. He had fallen into a gravel-pit; he didn't know where he was going. That's the reason my brother will never touch so much as you could wet your finger with, and that I only have a drop once a week or so, in the way of a strengthener. I take what her ladyship brings me, but I take no more. If she could have come to us before my mother went, that would have been a saving! I was only nine when my father died, and I'm three years older than Paul. My mother did for us with all her might; and she kept us decent – if such a useless little mess as me can be said to be decent. At any rate, she kept me alive, and that's a proof she was handy. She went to the wash-tub, and she might have been a queen, as she stood there with her bare arms in the foul linen and her long hair braided on her head. (*PC*, bk 1, ch. 9)

This description is the diametric opposite of James's earlier work, where aristocratic families express scruples about accepting marriage proposals from rich but untitled suitors, and the scenes are frequently the noble quartiers of Paris, Tuscan palazzos or English stately homes either belonging to hereditary landlords such as Lord Warburton or wealthy expatriate American bankers such as Daniel Touchett. Its key elements – coal-mining, alcoholism and mothers forced to become breadwinners as washerwomen – could have come straight from the pages of *L'Assommoir* (1877) or *Germinal* (serialised just months before in 1885).

In James's earlier novels the scene had predominantly been either elegant drawing rooms or sublime outdoor settings – the Colosseum in *Roderick Hudson* and *Daisy Miller*, the hills around Florence in *The Portrait of a Lady*. Suspiciously few of his heroes – the heirs to inherited fortunes, Rowland Mallet, Winterbourne and Ralph Touchett, Lord Warburton, even Christopher Newman, although a self-made millionaire already retired before *The American*'s plot opens – do anything akin to working for a living. As late as 1915, when he was proposed by Edmund Gosse for the Order of Merit, Lord Morley complained that James wrote only of the 'idle rich'.[20] However, back in the 1880s, under the direct influence of Zola,

Daudet and the Goncourts, James set this novel, at least in its opening scenes, among the London working class, and in what James calls a 'horrible place' – Millbank Prison. Perhaps the prison opening, recalling *Little Dorrit* or the death of Fagin in *Oliver Twist*, and the working-class London setting, has led critics often to liken this work to Charles Dickens, but the closer influence is surely that of Zola. In terms of the speed (if not the extent) with which he responded to Continental influence and Zola in particular, James may be compared with the most progressive novelists in English of the day, such as George Moore, though unlike Moore James never risked having his novels officially censored. James presents a working-class hero, the orphan Hyacinth Robinson, and singularly among James characters he undertakes paid employment in a factory workshop. James also includes a cast of other working-class figures, such as Paul Muniment, and revolutionary activists. It is almost as if James were self-consciously and deliberately setting out to contradict all the expectations which the readership he had cultivated hitherto would have entertained. In the event, not only is the novel to prove the story of a revolutionary whose nerve fails, but arguably James's own nerve in assuming the role of 'romancier naturaliste' also lets him down.

In a way the signs are, retrospectively, there from the start of the novel. Although of the working class, at least in terms of having to work for a living, Hyacinth Robinson is also something of an artist (although few of the men in James's novels do paid jobs, quite a few are that strange, liminal creature, the artist – Roderick Hudson, Felix in *The Europeans*, even (by a stretch) Gilbert Osmond in *The Portrait of a Lady*, and Nick Dormer in *The Tragic Muse*). Hyacinth is a book-binder and proves to have an innate, cultivated artistic sense, for all his lowly upbringing. As the novel progresses, the revolutionaries single Hyacinth out for an assassination attempt on a visiting archduke precisely because he does not sound or appear out of place in upper-class surroundings. Earlier the Princess Casamassima, Christina Light, now separated from the Italian prince she married in *Roderick Hudson*, and dabbling in revolutionary politics, has succeeded in passing Hyacinth off as upper class in a polite drawing room (*PC*, bk III, ch. 23).

And this success is revealed to be no accident but attributable to Hyacinth's status as illegitimate son of an aristocrat. The moment when Hyacinth has a change of heart about his commitment to violent struggle on behalf of the proletariat is telling, inspired first by his meeting with the Princess Casamassima. Encountering her in a stately home which she has rented for the summer, Hyacinth is particularly moved by her allusion to a fashionable French novelist of the Second Empire, Octave Feuillet.

> She (the Princess) left him for a short time, giving him the last number of the *Revue des Deux Mondes* to entertain himself withal, and calling his attention, in particular, to a story of M. Octave Feuillet (she should be so curious to know what he thought of it); and reappeared with her hat and parasol, drawing on her long gloves and presenting herself to our young man, at that moment, as a sudden incarnation of the heroine of M. Feuillet's novel, in which he had instantly become immersed. (*PC*, bk III, ch. 22)

For all the Princess's profession of revolutionary sympathies, Feuillet is a conservative writer, and sometime courtier of Napoleon III, serialised in the equally conservative *Revue des deux mondes* (in fact during its brief reign in 1871, the Paris Commune had suppressed this publication for its monarchist sympathies). Hyacinth subsequently inherits a legacy from his guardian and uses it to make a trip to the Continent. Here he comes under the spell of Haussmann's boulevards (a lasting legacy of the Second Empire) and begins to waver in his devotion to proletarian revolution. This is expressed quite specifically in terms of the Paris Commune (a recent event in 1871) and its legacy, which are contrasted with the monarchist regime of the Second Empire. And in a letter home written while he is visiting Venice and then Paris, Hyacinth reveals how his experience of the European heritage of high art has tempered his previous revolutionary fervour:

> You know how extraordinary I think our Hoffendahl (to speak only of him); but if there is one thing that is more clear about him than another it is that he wouldn't have the least feeling for this incomparable, abominable old Venice. He would cut up the ceilings of the Veronese into strips, so that every one might have a little piece. I don't want everyone to have a little piece of anything, and I have a great horror of that kind of invidious jealousy which is at the bottom of the idea of a redistribution. (*PC*, bk IV, ch. 30)

By the end of the novel Hyacinth prefers to turn his gun on himself rather than shoot a fellow aristocrat. The hero has abandoned his left-wing political cause and the novelist has, after the initial prison and workplace scenes, abandoned a commitment to the naturalist novel à la Zola.

In the longer term, the influence of the naturalists was to prove malign, certainly as regards James's commercial career as a novelist. The works of the middle period failed to sell – *The Bostonians, The Princess Casamassima* and *The Tragic Muse* – precisely because James had so emphatically appeared to renounce the safe territory of the upper-class drawing room where he had made his name. At the same time, as the above extract from Hyacinth's letter surely shows, he had little success in couching his novel in anything like the language of the working class itself, something Zola had done so pre-eminently in *Germinal* and other novels. Paul Bourget in 1929 (in *Cent ans de vie française à la revue des deux mondes*) recalls Zola saying (of *L'Assommoir*):

> I'm writing a novel set in the working-class suburbs, but, in reading over the first few chapters this morning I said to myself, the dialogue is good because it is true to life, but the narrative with which this dialogue is interspersed is that of a man of letters. The characters who have just been speaking would not see life in this way. Then, chewing this idea over, it occurred to me. What if I were to conduct the narrative in the language the characters themselves might use.

This is surely the very problem which James could not overcome in *The Princess Casamassima.*

James lost a good measure of his earlier 'refined' readership through this deviation from his usual setting and social background, and this prompted him to turn to the idea of writing for the stage, in a letter to Robert Louis Stevenson saying 'my tales don't sell and it looks as if my plays might'.[21] He had earlier made an extensive study of French theatre, as a playgoer during his time in Paris, writing to William James in the 1870s, 'I know the Théâtre Français by heart' (*CP*, 41). The theatre to which James in mid career turned for inspiration was not any American or English tradition, which he held in low esteem (*CP*, 35), but the French model of the well-made five-act play: 'The five-act drama – serious or humorous, poetic or prosaic – is like a box of fixed dimensions and inelastic material, into which a mass of precious things are to be packed away' (*CP*, 38–9); and, as Leon Edel has remarked, the ideal of the well-made play for James was implicitly French, its 'few grave, rigid laws' corresponding to those which had been formulated by the pre-eminent critic Francisque Sarcey (*CP*, 35).

The other influence upon James's assault upon the stage, although experienced by James in English translation rather than the original, was again Continental (this time from Norway) in the form of the work of Henrik Ibsen. While this may have augured well for James – Ibsen was at the height of his success in the 1880s and 1890s and his influence can be clearly seen in *The Other House* (1899), which has been widely viewed as a response to *Rosmersholm* (*CP*, 678) – the drama James produced combined a formality inherited from the French and a humourless high seriousness, inherited from Ibsen. That proved commercially disastrous in the London climate of the 1890s, the decade of Oscar Wilde and Arthur Pinero, and culminated in the very public debacle which attended the premiere in London of *Guy Domville* in 1895.

By the 1890s, James's novels were emphatically centred in Europe or Britain rather than the United States, and American characters who feature in them are increasingly rare. Moreover, the European context remains strong. In *The Awkward Age* (1899) an 'unmentionable' risqué contemporary French novel is taken as an index of the depravity to which the heroine Nanda has become privy, growing up in Mrs Brookenham's 'fast set' London household characterised by loose morals. The French novel in question is Zola's *Nana*, the story of a *femme fatale* – prostitute par excellence. And from a formal perspective the novel again betokens Continental influence. James, in his Preface for the New York edition, acknowledges the example of the work of Gyp, the French novelist who in the 1880s and 1890s pioneered the *roman dialogué*, or novel in the form of dialogue, where authorial narration is minimised and the conversations become central. Of James's novels this is the one with least narration and in which the chapters are conceived (as also in *The Spoils of Poynton*) as theatrical scenes.

The novels of James's late phase, *The Wings of the Dove*, *The Ambassadors* and *The Golden Bowl*, all see him returning to the 'International Theme' of 'Americans abroad' which had culminated in *The Portrait of a Lady* some twenty years before, very much again responding to Continental European influence. In the first Notebook entry for what was to become *The Wings of the Dove* (3 November 1894), James says:

> If I were writing for a French public the whole thing would be simple – the elder, the 'other,' woman would simply be the mistress of the young man, and it would be a question of his taking on the dying girl for a time – having a temporary liaison with her. But one can do so little with English adultery – it is so much less inevitable, and so much more ugly in all its hiding and lying side. It is so undermined by our immemorial tradition of original freedom of choice, and by our practically universal acceptance of divorce ... the little action *que j'entrevois* [which I glimpse] here suddenly seems to remind me of Ed. About's Germaine, read long years ago and but dimly remembered. But I don't care for that.[22]

The last three novels, at first glance, see James returning to the transatlantic aspect which had been abandoned in his novels from *The Bostonians* (entirely American) and then *The Princess Casamassima* (entirely European but for the central figure), through the 1880s and 1890s. But now, the emphasis is quite the reverse. Back in 1881, in his most celebrated novel, his heroine Isabel Archer had ended unhappily married to Osmond, who for all his American heritage has spent his life in Italy and stands emphatically for the Old World. In the final chapter, it seems that, with Ralph Touchett dead, Isabel rejects the chance of happiness with Caspar Goodwood in America for the sake of her duty as a wife by remaining in Europe, albeit contrary to her wishes. By 1900, James increasingly seemed to view the world from a European, Old World perspective, talking of 'the Americans looming up – dim, vast, portentous – in their millions – like gathering waves – the barbarians of the Roman Empire'.[23] Where Claire de Cintré in *The American* or Pansy in *The Portrait of a Lady* had ended up confined in, or threatened with, the convent as a sort of living death, the corresponding fate in the late works becomes repatriation to the United States. For Chad Newsome his duties to his family's firm in Woollett, Massachusetts, in *The Ambassadors*, mean that he must give up Mme de Vionnet, unable to leave (at least geographically, if not sexually) the aristocratic husband to whom she is unhappily married. Worse still, for Charlotte Stant in *The Golden Bowl* (*GB*), there is sexual and geographical separation from her illicit lover Prince Amerigo, when her husband Adam Verver decides to take her back to the newly built cultural backwater 'American City'. In *The Wings of the Dove*, it is the English characters rather than the Americans, Kate Croy and Merton Densher, who provide the eyes through which the bulk of the narrative is seen, and James originally conceived *The Golden Bowl* as taking place in France:

> The young husband may be made a Frenchman – 'il faut, [it is necessary] for a short tale, que cela se passe à Paris [that this should take place in Paris]. He is poor but has some high social position or name – and is, after all, personally only the pleasant Français moyen [typical Frenchman] – clever, various, inconstant, amiable, cynical, unscrupulous – charming always to 'the other woman.' The other woman and the father and daughter all intensely American.[24]

Both the flirtation with naturalism and the attempt at writing for the stage were major failures in James's career, but they nevertheless exerted an important influence upon his later work as novelist. There is often a strong sense that chapters have been conceived almost as staged theatrical scenes. Nowhere is this clearer than the smashing of the golden bowl in the novel of that name, immediately after which Prince Amerigo arrives as it were on cue in a well-made play, as the pieces lie on the floor between his wife and Fanny Assingham, who has covered up the Prince's adultery with Maggie's stepmother Charlotte Stant which the purchase of the bowl has brought to light (*GB*, bk IV, ch. 9). Elsewhere in the same novel, Maggie Verver tellingly imagines herself to be an actress on stage (*GB*, bk. V, ch. I). The lasting influence of naturalism is perhaps a still more subtle affair. In the final novels James's focus is far from being upon the working class, and he returns to the upper-class drawing rooms, stately homes and palazzos found in *The Portrait of a Lady*, *The American* and other novels of the 1870s and 1880s. Once again, marriage is the focus of attention as regards the plot, and politics are nowhere to be found. However, the sheer importance of intensity of analysis remains. But no longer is it a matter of attributing his characters' development exclusively to their economic conditions or their heredity, as in a Zola novel. In James's late work he may be said to transfer the intensity of analysis from the empirical world (Zola compared the novelist to a doctor making a diagnosis) to the inner workings of consciousness itself.

The crucial episode in *The Ambassadors* (A) in which Strether discovers the sexual nature of Chad's relationship with Mme de Vionnet is prompted in the first instance by purely aesthetic considerations. Strether stumbles upon them out in the country of the Seine valley because he has gone in search of the scene in nature which he had once venerated in a painting by Lambinet. Strether is thus accidentally brought into consciousness of the relationship between the pair, and they acknowledge him. Yet in the remaining four pages of the chapter after the encounter, although Strether, Chad and Mme de Vionnet meet, dine and return together to Paris, James gives only a single line of dialogue, appropriately in French rather than English, Mme de Vionnet's exclamation: 'Comme cela se trouve!'(A, bk xi, ch. 4). Otherwise, the remaining seven pages of the chapter are entirely given over to Strether's gradually growing awareness of the significance of what he has seen. The following is a representative example:

> Yet his theory, as we know, had bountifully been that the facts were specific-ally none of his business, and were, over and above, so far as one had to do with them, intrinsically beautiful; and this might have prepared him for anything, as well as rendered him proof against mystification. When he reached home that night, however, he knew he had been, at bottom, neither prepared nor proof; and since we have spoken of what he was, after his return, to recall and interpret, it may as well immediately be said that his real experi-ence of these few hours put on, in that belated vision – for he scarce went to bed till morning – the aspect that is most to our purpose.
>
> He then knew more or less how he had been affected – he but half knew at the time. (A, bk xi, ch. 4)

The novel is far from dealing with the gross physical contingencies of life, as would have been expected from Zola. Indeed, as E. M. Forster famously remarked, the Newsomes are 'sound commercial people, who have made money over manufacturing a small article of domestic utility ... but for James to indicate how his characters made their pile – it would not do. The article is somewhat ignoble and ludicrous – that is enough'.[25] Yet instead we find that the intensity of analysis which Zola had applied to empirical facts and to matters of heredity James now applies to the succes-sive phases of his characters' awareness of their own responses. In these final novels the *objets d'art*, the elegant drawing rooms and the refined, controlled dialogue therefore become as it were necessary preliminaries of minimal importance in their own right, the equivalent of props and scenery in a virtual theatre where James's drama of consciousness plays out.

## Note on editions

Henry James revised most of his novels for a definitive edition published by Scribners in New York, 1907–9, and known as the New York Edition. Most subsequent reprints use these texts, but the Library of America is reprinting the original versions and a complete scholarly edition is being prepared by Cambridge University Press. Reliable paperback editions of the major novels are available from various publishers including Oxford University Press (Oxford World's Classics) and Penguin.

### Notes

1 Alphonse Daudet, letter to Theodore Child, quoted in Leon Edel, *Henry James*, vol. IV, *The Treacherous Years: 1895–1901* (London: Hart-Davis, 1969), p. 123.

2 James's letter of 8 March 1875 to Elizabeth Boott, some 35 lines long, is entirely in Italian (*Henry James Letters*, ed. Leon Edel, vol. I *1843–1875* (London: Macmillan, 1974), pp. 473–4).

3 Henry James, *Notes of a Son and Brother* (London: Macmillan, 1914), p. 26. James declined Paul Joukovsky's offer of an introduction to Richard Wagner on the grounds that Wagner spoke no English and he himself virtually no German.

4 Neil Cornwell, 'Pushkin and Henry James: Secrets, Papers and Figures' (*The Queen Of Spades*, *The Aspern Papers* and *The Figure in the Carpet*), in *Two Hundred Years of Pushkin*, ed. R. Reid and J. Andrews (Amsterdam/New York: Rodopi, 2004), pp. 193–208.

5 Henry James, '*À moi*, Scribe; *à moi*, Sardou, *à moi*, Dennery!', in notebook entry 12 May 1889, *Complete Notebooks*, ed. Leon Edel and Lyall H. Powers (London/New York: Oxford University Press, 1986), p. 53.

6 Henry James, *The Portrait of a Lady*, vol. II, ch. 52.

7 See Angus Wrenn, *Henry James and the Second Empire* (Oxford: Legenda, 2009), where works by Edmond About, Victor Cherbuliez, Octave Feuillet, Gustave Droz and Alexandre Dumas *fils* are examined.

8 Peter Brooks, *Henry James Goes to Paris* (Princeton University Press, 2007), p. 73.

9 Oscar Cargill, *The Novels of Henry James* (New York: Macmillan, 1961), pp. 41–61.

10 Henry James, *Parisian Sketches: Letters to the New York Tribune, 1875–1876*, ed. with an introduction by Leon Edel and Ilse Dusoir Lind (New York University Press, 1957), pp. xi–xxxvii.

11 Henry James, letter to Henry James Sr, 20 December 1875, in Leon Edel, ed., *Henry James Letters*, 4 vols. (Cambridge, MA/London: Harvard University Press, 1974–84), vol. II, pp. 14–15.

12 Henry James, letter to Thomas S. Perry, 2 May 1876, cited in Philip Horne, *Henry James: A Life in Letters* (London: Penguin/Allen Lane, 1999), p. 71.

13 Reprinted in Leon Edel, *Henry James: The Conquest of London* (London: Hart-Davis, 1962), p. 220.

14 Henry James, letter to W. D. Howells, 28 May 1876, in Edel, ed., *Letters*, vol. II, p. 52.

15 Henry James, letter to William James, 29 July 1876, in Horne, *A Life in Letters*, p. 71, citing *The Correspondence of William James: William and Henry*, ed. Ignas Skrupselis and Elizabeth M. Berkeley, 3 vols. (Charlottesville, VA/London: University Press of Virginia, 1992–4), vol. I, p. 271.

16 Henry James, letter to W. D. Howells, 21 February 1884, in Horne, *A Life in Letters*, p. 153.

17 Henry James, 'The Art of Fiction', *Longman's Magazine*, September 1884.

18 Henry James, notebook entry, 8 April 1883, in Edel and Powers, eds., *Complete Notebooks*, pp. 18–19.

19 Edel, ed., *Letters*, vol. III, p. 61.

20 Leon Edel, *Henry James: A Life* (New York: Harper & Row, 1985; London: Collins, 1987), p. 712.

21 Henry James, letter to Robert Louis Stevenson, 1891, quoted in Leon Edel, *The Complete Plays of Henry James* (London: Hart-Davis, 1949), p. 45. Subsequent references are given parenthetically in the text as *CP*.

22 Edel and Powers, eds., *Complete Notebooks*, pp. 102–7.

23 Henry James, 15 July 1895, in Edel and Powers, eds., *Complete Notebooks*, p. 126.

24 Henry James, 28 November 1892, in Edel and Powers, eds., *Complete Notebooks*, pp. 74–5.

25 E. M. Forster, *Aspects of the Novel* (London: Edward Arnold, 1927), pp. 196–7.

## Further reading

Ascari, Maurizio, *In the Palatial Chambers of the Mind: Comparative Essays on Henry James* (Pescara: Edizioni Tracce, 1997)

Brooks, Peter, *Henry James Goes to Paris* (Princeton University Press, 2007)

Edel, Leon, *The Complete Plays of Henry James* (London: Hart-Davis, 1949)
   *Henry James*, vol. IV, *The Treacherous Years: 1895–1901* (London: Hart-Davis, 1969)

Fussell, Edwin S., *The French Side of Henry James* (Oxford/New York: Oxford University Press, 1990)

Hovanec, Evelyn A., *Henry James and Germany* (Amsterdam/New York: Rodopi, 1979)

James, Henry, *The Art of Criticism: Henry James on the Theory and Practice of Fiction*, ed. W. Veeder and S. Griffin (Chicago/London: University of Chicago Press, 1986)
   *Italian Hours*, ed. J. Achard (Harmondsworth: Penguin, 1992)
   *A Little Tour In France*, ed. Leon Edel (Harmondsworth: Penguin, 1985)

Tintner, Adeline R., *The Cosmopolitan World of Henry James: An Intertextual Study* (Baton Rouge, CA: Louisiana State University Press, 1991)

Wrenn, Angus, *Henry James and the Second Empire* (Oxford: Legenda, 2009)

# 19

MARION SCHMID

# Marcel Proust (1871–1922): A modernist novel of time

Alongside ground-breaking works by Virginia Woolf, James Joyce and Thomas Mann, Marcel Proust's seven-volume *À la recherche du temps perdu* (*In Search of Lost Time*), published between 1913 and 1927, is universally recognised as one of the masterpieces of European modernism, a milestone in the study of human consciousness and a revolution in the history of prose writing. Written over more than a decade and brought to a close only by the author's death (the last three volumes were published posthumously), it is a work of formidable complexity, not only in its meandering, sinuous style and digressive, often chronology-defying narrative, but, above all, in the radically new vision it proposes of individuals in time and its quasi encyclopedic engagement with the most diverse forms of human experience and knowledge. Characteristically 'in-between centuries' in terms of the culture and the literary imaginary that have shaped it, *À la recherche* serves as a bridge between the nascent forms of modernism found in the work of predecessors such as Gustave Flaubert and Charles Baudelaire and the high modernism that was to challenge traditional genre conventions in the period between the two world wars. Though anchored in the nineteenth century, Proust is also a contemporary of Albert Einstein, Sigmund Freud, Igor Stravinsky and Pablo Picasso, a writer whose thinking was indelibly shaped by the artistic and technological revolutions of modernity and who, in turn, contributed to the new understanding of the world and the self that emerged in the early decades of the twentieth century. Proust is the first of the great modernists to reflect in depth on the nature of time and perception, to shatter traditional notions of a unified, transcendental self and to attack the premises of documentary realism which still governed traditional writing up to this point. His meditations on time and memory and his experiments with narrative structure and point of view not only coincide with some of the most innovative thinking and writing of the period, they were to prove highly influential for generations to come.

## On the threshold of modernity

Stripped down to its most basic form, *À la recherche du temps perdu* is first and foremost the story of a vocation. Over seven volumes and some three thousand pages of narrative, the novel recounts the narrator's long gestation of an *œuvre* harboured since childhood, but which the multiple distractions of salon and amorous life had prevented him from creating, until, threatened by old age and death and finally in possession of the material for his work which is revealed to him through involuntary memory, he will eventually heed his calling. Through its theme of an artistic quest, its portrayal of a young man's development from the naivety of childhood to a deeper understanding of himself and the world he inhabits and its meditation on the nature and function of the art work, *À la recherche* aligns itself with a number of generic models and foundation texts that have shaped European narratives for almost a thousand years. These include Dante Alighieri's *Divina commedia* (*Divine Comedy*) with its quest for spiritual transcendence, the *Bildungsroman* – a favourite among European novelists ever since Johann Wolfgang von Goethe's genre-defining *Wilhelm Meister* – as well as its sub-genre the *Künstlerroman* (artist novel). Proust's use of a first-person narrative and talent for comic and burlesque scenes equally evoke the *Mémoires* (*Memoirs*) of the Duc de Saint-Simon, one of the major influences on *À la recherche*, his sharp analysis of human nature recalls the analytical novel in the tradition of Madame de Lafayette and Benjamin Constant and his rich portrait of French society and search for an overarching intellectual construction are reminiscent of such epic works as Leo Tolstoy's *War and Peace*.

Yet while Proust undoubtedly assimilates and plays with all of these generic models, prompting Jean-Yves Tadié to comment that *À la recherche* 'recapitulates the entire literary tradition, from the Bible to Flaubert and Tolstoy, and all literary genres',[1] it suffices to read the novel's opening pages to realise that the Proustian journey will mark a radical departure from the literature that came before. *À la recherche* begins with an extended reflection on the individual's permeable position with regard to time and space. The disembodied voice of an anonymous narrator, situated in an unspecified time and geographical location, meditates on the mind's ability to navigate freely between different periods and places and on the temporal and spatial confusions encountered on the threshold between sleep and wakefulness:

> When a man is asleep, he has in a circle round him the chain of the hours, the sequence of the years, the order of the heavenly bodies. Instinctively he consults them when he awakes, and in an instant reads off his own position

on the earth's surface and the time that has elapsed during his slumbers; but this ordered procession is apt to grow confused, and to break its ranks. (*SLT*, 1.3/*RTP*, 1.5)

The self that speaks is surrounded by darkness, 'more destitute than the cave-dweller' (*SLT*, 1.4/*RTP*, 1.5), reduced to an animal-like consciousness deprived of any stable notion of identity. Memory will eventually rescue the narrator from this state of dissolution, helping him to piece together the different strata of his self. Yet, while a wilful act of remembrance can bring order into the apparitions of the past that haunt the narrator, it is unable to recreate the full flavour and atmosphere of the places he once inhabited.

This overture, in its function as a microcosm of the macrocosm that is *À la recherche*, introduces the novel's ontological project and sets the paradigms for the literary revolution that will take place over the next three thousand pages. This is not, we understand, a conventional *Bildungsroman* that will merely follow a character's sentimental education and quest for self-discovery, it is a text fundamentally concerned with the nature of time and memory and with the individual's experience of temporality. Proustian time, as becomes immediately evident in the opening, which famously left the novel's first critics bewildered (one reviewer commented 'I fail to understand why a chap should require thirty pages to describe how he tosses and turns in bed before he falls asleep')[2] and played no little part in the fact that the author was at first unable to find a publisher, is no longer subjected to traditional laws of linearity and chronology. The narrator can navigate freely in time and space thanks to the powers of memory and the unconscious, yet, at this early stage of his journey, he cannot grasp time in its duration and essence. Temporal duration fractures into a confused series of moments that flicker in front of his eyes like the images projected by a kinetoscope, that is, a predecessor of cinema.

*À la recherche du temps perdu*, as is promised by its title, traces the narrator's search for lost time, to be understood not so much as time lost in dispersal and distraction (although this is equally implied), but, rather, on a more metaphysical level, as the time we believed forever lost in oblivion, the time that lies behind us, but is no longer accessible to us. In his unfinished novel *Jean Santeuil* (begun in 1895), Proust had merely juxtaposed fragments of the protagonist's life in more or less chronological order, but failed to identify an appropriate novelistic form to integrate the disparate narrative units. In *À la recherche* he finally found the structure, at once simple, but also highly sophisticated and flexible, that allowed him to write his great novel of remembrance. Thanks to a technique known as double internal focalisation, an older narrator recounts the experiences and development of his younger self from childhood to maturity. This splitting up of the first person into two distinct unities – a narrating and a narrated, or, to put it in a temporal perspective, a remembering and a remembered self – offers far greater scope for reflection and abstraction than would a single internal focalisation. The older, more mature narrator is in a position to comment on the experiences and often erroneous perception of the world (a fact exploited to considerable comic effect in À la recherche) of his younger alter ego. The distance that separates the narrator from the protagonist endows the novel with a strong temporal dimension – it does in itself imply the passing of time – while, at the same time, installing a tension between a prospective (the life of the protagonist) and a retrospective movement (the remembrance of the narrator) that informs the novel's overall temporal structure. Oriented towards the future, that is the protagonist's fulfilment of his vocation and discovery of the meaning of existence, the text, at the same time, looks back into the past in a constant interpolation of temporal frames and criss-crossing of perspectives. It is only at the end of the last volume, Le Temps retrouvé (Time Regained), that the two facets of the self that constitute the narrative converge: the remembered self (the protagonist) finally merges with the remembering self (the narrator), as the protagonist formulates the aesthetics of the œuvre he has begun to write.

From the outset, as is manifest in the novel's opening pages, À la recherche prioritises forms of consciousness and interiority over the description of external events. Flaubert, with his experiments with free indirect discourse, had opened up new ways for exploring a character's thoughts, but no one before Proust had gone as far in the depiction of complex mental and emotional states and few after him have been as consistent in stripping down a fictional character to a phenomenon of pure consciousness. The narrator of the Recherche has neither name nor face: his physical portrait is reduced to one or two inconclusive descriptions given of him by other characters; we do not know his surname; the first name 'Marcel' which is often (erroneously) attributed to him is no more than a playful hypothesis in one of the posthumously published volumes, La Prisonnière (The Captive), which Proust would be likely to have removed had he had the time to revise his manuscript. The self that speaks, unlike the protagonists of the realist or naturalist novel, whose physical appearance and social environment are depicted in utmost detail, is above all a filter of consciousness, a voice that investigates and dissects human nature with the X-ray of the radiologist and the telescope of the astronomer, two among many optical instruments in the Recherche that symbolise its new outlook on reality. The shift from the outside to the inside and the point of view to which the narrator subjects all aspects of reality have important consequences for major aspects of the novel from the perception and treatment of time to the conception of self and other.

## Inner and outer time

In a 1913 article for the *Figaro* entitled 'Vacances de Pâques' ('Easter Holidays'), Proust declares polemically, 'Novelists who count by days and years are silly. Days may be equal for a clock, but not for a human being.' Like many fellow modernist writers, and, indeed, like leading thinkers of the time, most importantly the philosopher Henri Bergson (a cousin of Proust's through marriage), he establishes an important distinction between the objective time measured by clocks and calendars and the subjective time of lived experience, in other words, between outer and inner time. In *Le Temps retrouvé* he thus explains the difference between the two: 'An hour is not merely an hour, it is a vase full of scents and sounds and projects and climates' (*SLT*, VI.245/*RTP*, IV.467–8). Whereas outer time is merely quantitative, inner time is qualitative. Heavily laden with sensation and affect, it is a category of our sensibility and, therefore, variable according to the emotional states we are in. To the child of Combray, a morning spent reading in the garden rushes past almost imperceptibly, while, to the adult, an hour spent in anguished uncertainty as to whether Albertine will call for a visit extends to an eternity. 'Solar years' are endowed 'with a sort of sentimental counterpart in which the hours were defined not by the sun's position, but by the time spent waiting for a rendez-vous' (*SLT*, V.557/*RTP*, IV.69). Days are measured no longer by hours and minutes, but in terms of the soaring of the narrator's hopes and the progress of the two lovers' intimacy.

The novel's unconventional narrative structure with its sudden jumps between blocks of narration and its abrupt accelerations and dilutions conveys this elasticity of inner time through its very narrative fabric: in 'Combray', some ten years of the narrator's childhood are compressed into just under two hundred pages while, at its antipodes, the social gathering in 'Matinée chez la Princesse de Guermantes' ('Reception at the Princesse de Guermantes'), which takes little more than a few hours, occupies approximately the same narrative space. These changes in tempo, to use a musical analogy of which Proust was fond, signal the varying rhythms and tonalities at which we experience different episodes in our life. In *À la recherche*, time, though omnipresent, has lost its role as an external frame of reference. Not only do some blatant inconsistencies between external (the historical framework) and internal chronology (the chronology of fictional events) signal the author's disinterest in 'absolute' time, but historical time as such is manifestly devalued in favour of personal time. Proust mentions key historical events of the period he depicts (from the late 1870s to the years following World War I), yet these events are no longer examined in their own right, but in their role as catalysts and mirrors of human behaviour. Thus, the Dreyfus Affair, one of the major political scandals of the French *fin de siècle*, scattered over three volumes, serves Proust to analyse the contradictory and often opportunistic attitudes of the fictional characters and to illustrate the volatile nature of political opinion and ideology. Similarly, World War I offers the author a backdrop against which he can develop his biting critique of civilian hypocrisy and a historical cause for the cataclysmic social changes described in the novel's last two chapters. The Russian Revolution, mentioned in a sideline, accomplishes the hegemonic struggle between aristocracy, bourgeoisie and the people that is traced throughout *À la recherche* and seals the end of the old social order described in the last volume.

This subordination of historical events as mere catalysts for social phenomena radicalises a tendency already manifest in some of Proust's nineteenth-century predecessors who reduced history to a mere spectacle (most famously, Stendhal's treatment of the battle of Waterloo in *La Chartreuse de Parme* (*The Charterhouse of Parma*) and Flaubert's depiction of the 1848 Revolution in *L'Éducation sentimentale* (*Sentimental Education*)) and converges with a foregrounding of the personal, indeed, the quotidian dimension of human existence in the modernist novel more widely. Although modernist works are infused with history which permeates many aspects of the narrative, its treatment has become more diffuse and its events are subordinated to the life of individuals. In *To the Lighthouse*, Virginia Woolf famously relegates the Great War to an element in a longer list of events that have shattered the lives of the Ramsay family. Robert Musil uses the build-up to World War I as the backdrop to his ironic portrait of Austrian life in *Der Mann ohne Eigenschaften* (*The Man without Qualities*). And Joyce, in *Ulysses*, compresses the richness of human experience into one single day in the life of Leopold Bloom.

### Plural selves and multiple perspectives

While the realist works of the nineteenth century still largely upheld the illusion of a temporal continuity in which fictional characters are embedded, Proust, on the contrary, in tune with the new concept of time that begins to emerge at the dawn of the twentieth century, insists on the essentially discontinuous and fragmentary nature of human experience. In *À la recherche* temporal duration is shattered into a myriad of discrete moments which, in their succession, obstruct the individual's understanding of time's relentless flow. Although human beings are ineluctably subjected to the destructive force of time, as the narrator will become painfully aware in the 'Bal de têtes' episode, where his former friends and acquaintances appear to him as allegories of old age and reminders of his own transience, they are as oblivious to time's flux as to the earth's rotation: 'In theory one is aware that the earth revolves, but in practice one does not perceive it, the ground upon which one treads seems not to move, and one can rest assured. So it is with Time in one's life' (*SLT*, II.63/*RTP*, I.473–4). This new conception of time as a series of heterogeneous, discrete moments coincides with a new vision of existence that will come to characterise modernist fiction more widely: the abandonment of a unified, transcendental self capable of learning, insight and evolution in favour of an exploration of the complex and often contradictory states of human consciousness. Proust replaces the more stable notion of a self that gradually evolves over time which, despite the erosion of the traditional figure of the hero in the preceding centuries, still dominates fiction in the pre-war period, with that of an atomised self that shatters into a series of discontinuous *moi* which succeed one another in time, but also, to a certain extent, cohabit inside us. As Joshua Landy puts it, just as 'time breaks down into a series of discrete instants, . . . the self, as a result, fractures into a plurality of segregated *moi*, united only by a fantasy of cohesion'.[3] Subjected to a process of constant deaths and rebirths, the Proustian self lives a lizard-like existence of perpetual change, shedding earlier selves not only at the crucial transitional moments in human existence that are often evoked in literature – coming of age, midlife or the dawning of old age – but at the rhythm of his rapidly changing affective life. The death of Albertine, the 'mighty goddess of time', makes the narrator acutely aware that he is not one, but a panoply of conflicting selves: 'I was not one man only, but as it were the march-past of a composite army in which there were passionate men, indifferent men, jealous men – jealous men not one of whom was jealous of the same woman' (*SLT*, v.559–60/ *RTP*, IV.71). The various selves are unable to dialogue with one another, yet it is precisely their multiplicity which eventually allows the protagonist to overcome his suffering, since successive selves replace one another without his becoming fully aware of the transformation he is undergoing.

Just like the protagonist, the novel's other characters are also subjected to the passing of time as well as to multiple points of view. As in a cubist painting, time and perspective refract characters into a wealth of (often contradictory) appearances, without, however, unveiling their true essence or penetrating their mystery. To Saint-Loup, the actress Rachel is a priceless woman 'worth more than a million, more than family affection, more than all the most coveted positions in life' (*SLT*, III.177/*RTP*, II.457); to the narrator, she is the prostitute whose favours were on sale for twenty francs in a bordello. Far from concluding that one was wrong or the other right, the narrator insists on their diverging perspective, 'No doubt it was the same thin and narrow face that we saw, Robert and I. But we had arrived at it by two opposite ways which would never converge, and we would never both see it from the same side' (*SLT*, II.458/*RTP*, III.178). The venerable painter Elstir turns out to be no other than the pretentious and silly 'Monsieur Biche', who once was a favourite of the Verdurin salon; Swann 'inverts' from a refined member of the upper classes to a boastful promoter of his wife's bourgeois salon; Odette is, in turn, the respectable 'lady in pink' of the narrator's childhood, the manipulative courtesan for whom Swann has wasted years of his life and a woman who was 'madly in love' with her husband. More than just tracing a character's evolution in time, this cohabitation of often incongruous selves sketches out a radically new vision of character and personality. Abandoning any stable characterisation as well as the idea of one 'true' authentic self, Proust underlines instead the irrationality, incoherence and inconsistency inherent in human nature. Unlike the realist novel which explains and rationalises human behaviour, Proust merely juxtaposes the different manifestations of a character in time without 'patching up' the cracks between them. Swann, at the end of 'Un amour de Swann', famously realises that he has wasted years of his life for a woman who was not his type, yet some twenty pages later, in 'Noms de pays: le nom' ('Place-names: the Name'), we find him married to exactly this woman and father of their child. A narrative 'blank', that is, a temporal as well as a semantic gap, separates these two incarnations of his self.

Proust's rejection of a transcendental order where characters are still defined by their gender, class, religion or heredity in favour of a pure succession of their different incarnations in time constitutes a radical shift in the conception of self and other in tune with the new forms of subjectivity that, as scholars like Stephen Kern have shown,[4] emerged in the early twentieth century as a result of rapid technological and social change: in Proust's novel, contingency and flux have superseded causality and chronology; life is understood as a mere succession of phenomena, and the exploration of consciousness and perception is prioritised over psychology.[5] This is however not to say that Proust dispenses with psychology altogether: on the contrary, *À la recherche* offers an unprecedented insight into the human psyche, especially in its numerous abstract reflections on human behaviour which, in characteristically Proustian fashion, extract the general from the particular. Rather, Proust seeks to replace conventional, 'plane' psychology with what he calls 'psychology in time', in other words, with an examination of human behaviour that acknowledges the temporal dimension of life. For, as the narrator realises after Albertine's death, psychology must take account of one crucial factor – oblivion – which gradually erodes our memories and, with them, the selves we used to be:

> As there is a geometry in space, so there is a psychology in time, in which the calculations of a plane psychology would no longer be accurate because we should not be taking account of Time and one of the forms that it assumes, forgetting – forgetting, the force of which I was beginning to feel and which is so powerful an instrument of adaptation to reality because it gradually destroys in us the surviving past which is in perpetual contradiction with it. (*SLT*, v.637/*RTP*, IV.137)

## The redemptive power of memory

Is the self perpetually condemned to the state of existential uncertainty, fragmentation and nomadism that are so powerfully evoked in the novel's opening pages? Is oblivion the fate that seals human existence? As we have already seen in the overture, memory eventually rescues the self from the threat of dissolution, but it is only a special type of memory that makes the full recovery of time in the last volume, *Le Temps retrouvé*, possible. Proust famously distinguishes between two forms of memory: 'voluntary memory', that is, the memory of the intellect, is unable to recreate the world of the past in its complexity, for, according to Proust, the past is not stored in the mind, but in material objects, or more precisely, in the sensations triggered by such objects: 'The past is hidden somewhere outside the realm, beyond the reach of intellect, in some material object (in the sensation which that material object will give us) of which we have no inkling' (*SLT*, I.51/*RTP*, I.44). 'Involuntary memory' on the contrary, the memory of the body, as the narrator realises when dipping a madeleine cake in his tea, offers access to the past in its totality, since it unlocks the sense impressions (perfumes, sounds, odours, colours) that accompanied the experience. Only this more instinctive form of memory, in its shortcutting of reason and habit, can capture the essence of a past moment.

The power of involuntary memory to recover the past is postulated very early on in the novel – indeed from 'Combray II' onwards, the narrative is presented as having been triggered by the madeleine experience – yet its deeper metaphysical meaning remains veiled until *Le Temps retrouvé*, which resolves the dialectics of time lost and found that constitutes the work's basic narrative structure. It is at the moment of his greatest despair that the protagonist, resigned that he will never be a writer, experiences the epiphanies that help him rediscover a past he believed lost forever and finally fulfil a vocation he had deferred since childhood. The memory triggered by simple sensual stimuli (the stumbling over an uneven paving stone, the touch of a starched napkin, the sound of a spoon against a tea cup) unearths earlier strata of the narrator's existence which, in the process of remembrance, come to cohabit with his present self in a fusion between past and present. What is at stake here, and there lies the truly metaphysical dimension of Proust's conception of memory, is more than just the recovery of a time that seemed lost; it is man's transience and, more generally, the contingency of time that can be overcome in the ecstatic moments of epiphany. For, through its merging of past and present in a flash of extra-temporality, involuntary memory allows individuals to step out of time's linear, destructive flow and, thus, to conquer, be it only for a brief moment, their anguish of death:

> A minute freed from the order of time has re-created in us, to feel it, the man freed from the order of time. And one can understand that this man should have confidence in his joy, even if the simple taste of a madeleine does not seem logically to contain within it the reasons for this joy, one can understand that the word 'death' should have no meaning for him; situated outside time, why should he fear the future? (*SLT*, VI.224–5/*RTP*, IV.451)

Paradoxically, perhaps, it is only in these extra-temporal moments, earlier on called 'a fragment of time in the pure state' (*SLT*, VI.224/*RTP*, IV.451), that the dispersed self is able to regain a momentary sense of unity and to understand its stratified nature. In Malcolm Bowie's words, the 'sudden ecstatic rediscovery of a past that had been thought forever lost reveals the temporal architecture of the self, the invariant substratum that until then had been present but unrecognised beneath its fluid and accidental surface forms'.[6] Yet, as the narrator soon realises, the powers of resuscitation operated by involuntary memory are precarious and evanescent. The true essence of things that is revealed to him through the memory of the senses needs to be immobilised in a work of art in order to be made durable and permanent. The discovery of time's destructive force in the 'Bal de têtes' and the sudden awareness that he also is threatened by death, together with his realisation that the task of the writer is above all that of a translator of his or her interiority and, thus, that, over a lifetime, he has accumulated the materials for his work, enable the narrator to formulate and to put into practice the aesthetic principles of the *œuvre* that he will finally commence to write: a novel which has itself the form of time and which describes humanity in its temporal dimension.

*À la recherche* ends on the famous metaphor of men 'perched upon living stilts', attached to them an ever growing past until, suddenly, they fall.

The spatialisation of time in this final image, while putting into particularly urgent terms the self's journey in time and the fragility of old age, also helps us measure the distance that separates Proust, a contemporary of Einstein, from his nineteenth-century predecessors whose thinking was still shaped by a Newtonian world-view. Where Newton conceived of time and space as separate entities, in the world of Einstein they have become inseparable, space being conceived as relative to a moving point of reference. Throughout À la recherche, but perhaps most strikingly here, past and present are apprehended spatially, as stratifications, juxtapositions or distances. The journey in time is of course of necessity also a journey in space, yet the place reserved for humankind in space, as the narrator realises at the end of his quest, is infinitely smaller than that which they occupy in time, for memory allows them to simultaneously 'touch the distant epochs through which they have lived' (SLT, VI.451/RTP, IV.625).

## The critique of documentary realism: towards an aesthetics of perception

In the forty or so theoretical pages of 'Matinée chez la princesse de Guermantes' that constitute Proust's aesthetic programme, the author formulates an astute critique of the principles of documentary realism and introduces his own aesthetics of perception. Positioning himself against the anti-aesthetic poetics of popular and patriotic literature as well as against the demands of realist art more widely, he resolutely questions the notion of reality as an absolute graspable by mimetic description. Reality, he argues, resides not, as is commonly held, in the object world, but, on the contrary, is constituted by the relation between an individual's memories and sensory impression. Consequently, so-called 'realist' literature, in satisfying itself with merely describing surfaces, far from offering a faithful representation of reality, does in fact move away from it, since it fails to account for the subjectivity of human perception. Art forms that are merely concerned with mimetic representation, he argues, using the cinema as a counter-model to define his own anti-realist aesthetics, at best reduce reality to a 'waste product of experience':

> But my train of thought led me yet further. If reality were indeed a sort of waste product of experience, more or less identical for each one of us, since when we speak of bad weather, a war, a taxi rank, a brightly lit restaurant, a garden full of flowers, everybody knows what we mean, if reality were no more than this, no doubt a sort of cinematograph film of these things would be sufficient and the 'style', the 'literature' that departed from the simple data that they provide would be superfluous and artificial. But was it true that reality was no more than this? (SLT, VI.246–7/RTP, IV.468–9)

Proust's attack on the cinema here should not be read as an opposition in principle to the new visual technologies that emerged in his lifetime; rather, it testifies to his limited exposure – a fact he deplores in his correspondence – to the seventh art whose experiments with rendering human subjectivity did in fact to a considerable extent coincide with his own. What this and other such reflections on the nature of the art work and the process of artistic creation in À la recherche reveal, however, is the author's deep distrust towards any allegedly 'objective' depiction of reality against which he posits the subjective vision of the true artist. For Proust, the duty of art is above all to express subjectivity, to 'translate' the impressions the outside world has inscribed in us. The process whereby experience can be transmuted into art, the narrator discovers early on in the novel, is one of metaphor, the joining together of two different objects with a view to extracting their common essence. In À l'ombre des jeunes filles en fleurs (Within a Budding Grove), Elstir's marine paintings, characterised by their effacement of the demarcation line that traditionally separates the sea from the land and, thus, their fusing of the two entities into a new vision, had revealed to the narrator metaphor's power to alter our habitual perception of the world. Liberated from the constraints of realism and the dictates of habit and intelligence, an artist like Elstir can reconnect with the innocence of pure perception. In Le Temps retrouvé, in a more extended reflection on the nature of metaphor, Proust insists on its temporal dimension: metaphor, in joining together two temporally separate sensations, frees them from the contingencies of time (SLT, VI.246/RTP, IV.468). Metaphor, then, shares the same characteristics as involuntary memory, for it is based on simultaneity, the fusion of past and present. This insight retrospectively allows us to grasp better the nature of the two types of memory and their difference in reach: voluntary (metonymic) memory remains of necessity fragmented, since it can only remember closely associated things; involuntary (metaphoric) memory, by contrast, in its capacity to bring together widely removed sensations, allows for a total vision.[7]

For Proust, metaphor is essential to the new style with which he experiments in À la recherche. Harking back to the romantic principles established by Novalis, F. W. J. von Schelling and Arthur Schopenhauer, but also developing further Flaubert's premise of the primacy of style over story, Proust posits style not as a matter of technique, but of vision.[8] In revealing the multiple ways in which individuals behold reality, style incessantly recreates and multiplies our world: 'Thanks to art, instead of seeing one world only, our own, we see that world multiply itself and we have at our disposal as many worlds as there are original artists, worlds more different one from the other than those which revolve in infinite space' (SLT, VI.254/RTP,

IV.474). In *À la recherche*, and the same is true for most modernist works, the world, then, is no longer conceived as one shared space with common characteristics, but, rather, as a multitude of spaces beheld by a multitude of consciousnesses.[9] With Proust, a Copernican revolution in the history of the novel is being accomplished: literature is no longer considered as a mirror of external realities, but, above all, as a means of expressing the radical subjectivities of human consciousness and perception and of revealing the multiple and highly divergent ways in which individuals inhabit and apprehend the world.

## Proust's legacy

Ironically, Proust's modernity, while acknowledged by his first readers and critics, was largely lost on the generation of French writers after him. The surrealist writers of the interwar period vehemently criticised Proust for privileging analysis over instinct. In a rating of his work in the journal *Littérature* of March 1921, the four leading surrealists Louis Aragon, André Breton, Paul Eluard and Philippe Soupault give him 0/20, 6/20, −8/20 and 2/20 on a scale from −25 to 20. Tristan Tzara's spiteful −25 reserved for 'the strongest dislike' brings the average down to exactly zero, that is, 'total indifference'. The generation of committed writers that dominated French literature between the 1930s and 1950s, accusing Proust of having missed out on the major social preoccupations of his time, showed a similar hostility. So low had Proust sunk in critical esteem that the left-wing journal *Vendredi* could proclaim in 1937, 'Proust is dead, well dead, as far from us as one could possibly be, and God knows when he will rise again, if he is to rise at all.' Jean-Paul Sartre, in an act of what, in his own terms, can only be qualified as 'bad faith', while amply borrowing from Proust in his novel *La Nausée* (*Nausea*), nonetheless accused the author of collusion with the bourgeoisie and of promoting a harmful intellectualist psychology. It was only in the course of the 1950s, with the rise of the literary movement called the *nouveau roman* around authors such as Alain Robbe-Grillet, Michel Butor and Claude Simon, more interested in questions of form, vision and style, and with the advent of structuralist and post-structuralist theory around leading figures like Roland Barthes, Gérard Genette and Paul de Man, who took a keen interest in Proust, that the author's star began to rise again, beginning the inexorable ascension to the pantheon of French letters his work enjoys today.

British authors, on the other hand, as, indeed, critics and the public in the United Kingdom more widely, almost instantly recognised Proust's genius and novelty. Virginia Woolf, so enchanted by *À la recherche* that she delayed finishing the novel, is filled by what critics have called a 'mixture of fascination and dread' and 'an anxiety of influence'. In a 1922 letter to Roger Fry, she writes, 'Proust so titillates my desire for expression that I can hardly set out the sentence. Oh if I could write like that! I cry … Scarcely anyone so stimulates the nerves of language in me; it becomes an obsession.'[10] She was worried that her *Mrs Dalloway* did not live up to *À la recherche* and let herself be inspired by *Du côté de chez Swann* (*Swann's Way*) while writing *To the Lighthouse*. Joyce, whose status as an expatriate in Paris brought him into more direct contact with Proust, similarly impressed, but also challenged by *À la recherche*, seems to have felt what Elisabeth Ladenson calls an 'uncomfortable identification and rivalry'.[11] Sharing with Proust a deep fascination with the nature of time, he jokingly claims co-authorship of *À la recherche* by presenting it as a joint production 'par Marcelle Proyce et James Joust'.[12] Samuel Beckett, aged only 25, is one of the first to dedicate an extended essay to Proust in 1931, in which he focuses in particular on the role of time, memory and habit, that is, on themes that were to become central to his own work.

In the German-speaking world also, thanks to, among others, critical essays by Ernst Robert Curtius and Walter Benjamin, Proust rapidly emerged as a major literary influence. Benjamin, who was responsible for the translation into German of *À l'ombre des jeunes filles en fleurs*, shows a strong Proustian affinity and sensibility in his autobiographical *Berliner Kindheit um 1900* (*Berlin Childhood around 1900*). The Austrian modernist Robert Musil shares with the author the combination between fictional and essayistic modes and the interest in societal decadence and decline in the years prior to World War I. More recently, the writings of W. G. Sebald, one of Germany's most distinguished contemporary writers, align themselves with Proust in their attempt to recapture a lost world and their attention to the everyday aspects of human existence.

A recent series of colloquia on Proust in a comparative perspective has thrown into relief the extraordinary prestige that Proust continues to enjoy worldwide and the multiple echoes that link *À la recherche* to authors as diverse as the Mexican Carlos Fuentes, the Polish Joseph Czapski and the Turkish Nobel prizewinner Orhan Pamuk.[13] Yet, far from limited to literature and critical theory only, Proust's legacy has extended to practitioners of other art forms, most importantly film, theatre and ballet, who, over the years, have not merely adapted his novel, but have profoundly engaged with his modernist style and aesthetic. Among the many adaptations, it will suffice to mention the film versions of *Un amour de Swann*, *Le Temps retrouvé* and *La Prisonnière* by Volker Schlöndorff, Raoul Ruiz and Chantal Akerman, the acclaimed 2000/2001 Royal National Theatre production based on Harold Pinter's film script of À la recherche and Roland Petit's remarkable ballet Les Intermittences du cœur. Proust's modernist legacy in film, far broader than the number of adaptations strictly speaking may suggest, is traceable across a long tradition of both mainstream and alternative film-making and includes works as different as Vertigo, Alfred Hitchcock's famous thriller on the themes of human subjectivity and obsession, Chris Marker's La Jetée, a powerful exploration of time and memory, Luchino Visconti's Death in Venice, with its portrayal of death, decadence and decline, and, more recently, Jean-Luc Godard's Éloge de l'amour whose representation of time, as its director explains, is directly influenced by Proust's project of intensifying the past.[14] Finally, and perhaps most surprisingly, Proust is being gradually assimilated into popular culture, as is evidenced, among many other examples, by Stéphane Heuet's comic book adaptation of À la recherche, the presence of Proust in Japanese mangas and the recurrent allusions to the novel in many popular films, most recently Jonathan Dayton and Valerie Faris's 2006 road movie Little Miss Sunshine. Almost a hundred years after the first publication of Du côté de chez Swann, then, the riches of Proust's work seem far from being exhausted. With his extraordinary actuality and adaptability, Proust increasingly reveals himself not only as a genuine classic, but also as one of the greatest authors of our time.

## Note on editions/translations

The best edition for research purposes is À la recherche du temps perdu, ed. Jean-Yves Tadié, 4 vols. (Paris: Gallimard, 'Pléiade', 1987–9). The best paperback editions are: ed. Jean-Yves Tadié, 7 vols. (Paris: Gallimard, 'Folio Classique', 1988–90) and ed. Jean Milly, rev. edn, 10 vols. (Paris: Flammarion, 'GF Flammarion', 2009).

The most up-to-date English translations (based on the 1987 Pléiade edition) are: In Search of Lost Time ed. Christopher Prendergast, 6 vols. (London: Penguin Classics, 2003); In Search of Lost Time, 6 vols. (London: Vintage 1992); In Search of Lost Time, 6 vols. (New York: The Modern Library, 1993). The text of the Vintage and Modern Library editions is identical, but the pagination varies.

### Notes

1 Jean-Yves Tadié, 'Introduction', in Marcel Proust, À la recherche du temps perdu, 4 vols. (Paris: Gallimard, 'Pléiade', 1987–9), vol. i, p. x. All citations from the novel are from In Search of Lost Time, trans. C. K. Scott Moncrieff and Terence Kilmartin, rev. D. J. Enright (London: Chatto and Windus, 1992). Subsequent references are

given parenthetically in the text by volume and page numbers. References to the translation (SLT) are followed by those to the Pléiade edition directed by Tadié (RTP). Unless otherwise noted, other translations are the author's own.

2 Cited in Jean-Yves Tadié, *Marcel Proust*, trans. Euan Cameron (London: Viking, 2000), pp. 579–80.

3 Joshua Landy, 'The Texture of Proust's Novel', in *The Cambridge Companion to Proust*, ed. Richard Bales (Cambridge University Press, 2001), pp. 117–34 (120).

4 Stephen Kern, *The Culture of Time and Space, 1880–1918* (Cambridge, MA/London: Harvard University Press, 2003).

5 Cf. H. R. Jauss, *Zeit und Erinnerung in Marcel Prousts 'À la recherche du temps perdu'* (Frankfurt: Suhrkamp, 1986), p. 32.

6 Malcolm Bowie, *Proust Among the Stars* (New York: Columbia University Press, 2000), pp. 4–5.

7 See Michael Wetherill, *Du côté de chez Swann* (Glasgow: Glasgow French and German Publications, 1992), pp. 90–1.

8 See Hugo Azérad, *L'Univers constellé de Proust, Joyce et Faulkner: le concept d'épiphanie dans l'esthétique du modernisme* (Oxford: Peter Lang, 2002), p. 419.

9 See Jauss, *Zeit und Erinnerung*, p. 56.

10 Nigel Nicolson, ed., *The Letters of Virginia Woolf*, vol. II (Orlando, FL: Harvest Books, 1976), p. 525.

11 Elisabeth Ladenson, 'A Talk Consisting Solely of the Word "No": Joyce Meets Proust', *James Joyce Quarterly*, 31.3 (1994), 147–58 (p. 157).

12 Richard Ellmann, *James Joyce* (New York: Oxford University Press, 1982), p. 508n.

13 'Proust et l'incertitude', 'Visages étrangers de Proust', 'Proust et les mondes lointains', 'Proust: dialogues critiques': series of colloquia organised by Karen Haddad-Wotling and Vincent Ferré, Universities Paris X and Paris XIII, 2007–9.

14 For screen adaptations of Proust and his modernist legacy in film, see Martine Beugnet and Marion Schmid, *Proust at the Movies* (London: Ashgate, 2005).

*Further reading*

Bales, Richard, ed., *The Cambridge Companion to Proust* (Cambridge University Press, 2001)

Beckett, Samuel, *Proust* (London: Cedar and Boyars, 1965)

Bowie, Malcolm, *Proust Among the Stars* (New York: Columbia University Press, 2000)

Compagnon, Antoine, *Proust entre deux siècles* (Paris: Seuil, 1989)

Deleuze, Gilles, *Proust et les signes* (Paris: Presses Universitaires de France, 1964, rev. edn 1970)

Kristeva, Julia, *Le Temps sensible: Proust et l'expérience littéraire* (Paris: Gallimard, 1994)

Tadié, Jean-Yves, *Proust et le roman* (Paris: Gallimard, 1971, rep. 1986)

# 20

RITCHIE ROBERTSON

# Thomas Mann (1875–1955): Modernism and ideas

To leading German writers in the 1920s – Thomas Mann, Hermann Broch and Robert Musil – it was clear that the modern novel must be in some sense philosophical. G. W. F. Hegel had asserted a century earlier that the novel was 'the modern bourgeois epic' ('der modernen *bürgerlichen* Epopöe').[1] The Hegelian Marxist Georg Lukács, elaborating this idea in his *Die Theorie des Romans* (*Theory of the Novel*, published in book form in 1920), argued that, while Homer's epics showed a closed, limited, objective world and portrayed it as a totality, the complexity of modern life eluded any such depiction; the novelist could grasp the world as totality only through philosophical reflection. Hence everything in the novel, including the consciousness of the characters, had to be subordinate to the superior, and hence ironic, consciousness of the reflective narrator. Novelists in the German tradition found an honourable precedent in Johann Wolfgang von Goethe's classic *Bildungsroman*, *Wilhelm Meisters Lehrjahre*, where the naive protagonist stumbles towards his destiny under the ironic gaze of the sovereign narrator.

Not only in its structure, but also in its content, the novel needed to engage with the intellectual debates of the modern world. Mere storytelling risked triviality. The novel had somehow to accommodate diverse intellectual material. But how was this material to be integrated into fiction? What balance could be struck between the requirement of intellectual sophistication and the atavistic desire to have a story told? In their great works written in the 1920s – Mann's *Der Zauberberg (The Magic Mountain*, 1924), Musil's *Der Mann ohne Eigenschaften* (*The Man Without Qualities*, 1930–3) and Broch's *Die Schlafwandler (The Sleepwalkers*, 1931–2) – the three novelists each found a different answer to these questions.

## Broch, *The Sleepwalkers*

The most radical approach was Broch's. His trilogy is a portrait of his age. Its parts are set respectively in 1888, 1903 and 1918, and named after the main characters who in turn represent tendencies of their epoch. The protagonist of *Pasenow oder die Uniform* is a young officer obsessed with order and disorder. Order is symbolised by his military uniform, a carapace which protects him against the disturbingly fluid external world. Pasenow projects his inner uncertainties outwards in the form of a divided sexuality, split on racial lines between his idealised German fiancée and his sexy Slav girlfriend. Fifteen years later, Pasenow's military fictions of order are of no use to August Esch, an accounts clerk who, dismissed from his job at the beginning of *Esch oder die Anarchie*, finds the world in a chaotic state and seeks vaguely for an impossible redemption. No such yearnings trouble the central figure of *Huguenau oder die Sachlichkeit*, who, amid the real disorder of the war's end, concentrates with absolute amorality on profiteering at the expense of others.

Here Broch reveals the philosophical thesis concerning the 'disintegration of values' which has governed the trilogy all along. Huguenau's '*Sachlichkeit*', the narrow means–end rationality which ignores all wider moral considerations, typifies, along with the functional style of modern architecture, an age which has lost contact with any deeper sense of values. In the unified culture of the Middle Ages, all could agree on God as the central source of value. In the intervening centuries, however, different areas of human activity have become autonomous and self-referential. The slogans 'business is business', 'war is war', 'art for art's sake' all emerge in the nineteenth century and license the single-minded pursuit of each goal to its most radical extreme. Broch was probably indebted to the account of modern atomisation given by Friedrich Nietzsche in 'Schopenhauer als Erzieher') ('Schopenhauer as Educator').[2]

To convey this thesis, Broch needed a new kind of novel. He announced to his editor: 'The age of the polyhistorical novel has dawned.'[3] Alluding to the German word *Polyhistor*, 'polymath', Broch meant that the new novel must include reflection and information far beyond the scope of traditional storytelling. That implies, first, the explicit dominance of the narrator. In *Pasenow* and still more in *Esch* the free indirect speech of the main character often shades into narratorial reflections, and the characters clearly serve to illustrate the theses implied in the titles. In *Huguenau* Broch goes further. The central narrative concerning Huguenau is broken into sections and interspersed with fragmentary narratives which suggest from various angles the religious or metaphysical needs denied by the epoch's overriding functionality or *Sachlichkeit*. Thus we have the 'Story of the Salvation Army Girl in Berlin' (partly in verse) and the story of the mason Gödicke who is buried alive and, on being unearthed, says that he has risen from the dead. We also have a number of essayistic reflections in which the narrator expounds aspects of his theory of the disintegration of values, with no attempt to integrate them into any of the stories. Broch told his editor that Mann, Musil, André Gide and Aldous Huxley, all precursors of the poly-historical novel, had tried to integrate philosophical reflection by putting it in the mouths of fictional characters. But such a pretence of integration was utterly unconvincing. These educated conversations sat in the text like blocks of crystal. Far better to follow where Joyce had pointed the way, to refuse any concessions to the reader, to separate intellectual discourse firmly from the portrayal of character and psychology, and to disrupt the flow of narrative by introducing a quite different mode of literary experience.[4]

Broch was certainly thoroughgoing. In *The Sleepwalkers*, the flow of narrative is replaced by the progressive demonstration of a thesis. Characters are little more than illustrations of the disintegration of values. Broch debunks the primitive illusion that fictional characters can have a life of their own. But by holding his characters so firmly in check, Broch prevents them from having any interaction with his philosophical thesis. The characters and their actions are not allowed to suggest any qualifications, nuances or further complexities to the view that Broch means them to illustrate. The resources peculiar to the novel genre – narrative and character – wither away under the supremacy of the philosophical narrator.

## Musil, *The Man Without Qualities*

In his huge, unfinished and perhaps interminable *The Man Without Qualities*, Musil approached the relation between ideas and fiction in a very different way. Trained in mathematics, engineering, psychology and philosophy, and the author of a doctoral thesis on the epistemology of Ernst Mach, Musil looks like the supreme intellectual novelist. Immersed in rigorous abstract disciplines, he was equipped, if anyone was, to link the humanities with the sciences and provide the nearest thing to a comprehensive, intellectually satisfying portrayal of modern life.

Musil was moreover convinced that the fulfilment of this ambition demanded a new kind of novel. From the outset of *The Man Without Qualities*, narrative, action and character are dislodged from the central place they occupied in traditional novels. Ulrich, the 'man without qual-ities', resolves in August 1913 to take a year's holiday from life and pas-sively observe the world around him. He is drawn into the preparations for a '*Parallelaktion*' which plans to celebrate in 1918 the seventieth anni-versary of the Emperor Franz Joseph's accession to the throne (parallel to the simultaneous thirtieth anniversary of the accession of Wilhelm II of Germany). Unlike the reader, the characters cannot know that their plans are futile, so the action of the novel and the progress of history are ironised from the outset.

Narrative too seems obsolescent. Ulrich reflects that sequential narrative – the telling of a story in which you say 'first this happened and then that happened' – is a primitive means of structuring experience. Most people tell themselves stories about their own experience. But narrative no longer serves as a means of organising wider, social experience. It is too drastic a simplification – 'the simple sequence of events in which the overwhelmingly manifold nature of things is represented, in a unidimensional order, as a mathematician would say, stringing all that has occurred in space and time on a single thread, which calms us; that celebrated "thread of the story," which is, it seems, the thread of life itself'.[5]

Ulrich has not only grown out of the primitive desire for narrative order, but also out of the stable conception of the self. He shares with Musil and with Ernst Mach the conviction that the old anthropocentric cosmos has been dissolved. Not only is humanity no longer the centre of the universe; the 'self' is no longer the centre that organises subjective experience:

> A world of qualities without a man has arisen, of experiences without the person who experiences them, and it almost looks as though ideally private experience is a thing of the past, and that the friendly burden of personal responsibility is to dissolve into a system of formulas of possible meanings. Probably the dissolution of the anthropocentric point of view, which for such a long time considered man to be at the centre of the universe, but which has been fading away for centuries, has finally arrived at the 'I' itself. (*MWQ*, I.158–9)

The surprising consequence is that Musil is less interested in ideas than in experiences. His concern is not so much with abstract theses as with what it feels like to entertain an idea. The particular calling of the literary writer, he argues, is to explore morality and emotion, using poetic imagery as a precise cognitive instrument.[6] So in *The Man Without Qualities* he investigates the consciousness of the sex-murderer Moosbrugger, the soulful society lady 'Diotima', the hysterical Nietzschean Clarisse. All are far more vividly realised than Broch's relatively pallid figures; Musil has a talent for social comedy. But it is their inwardness that matters; we rarely know, for example, what they look like, but we enter into their feelings, and into other characters' feelings about them.

It is through his characters' subjectivity that Musil examines the implications of ideas. Clarisse is only one example of Nietzsche's pervasive presence in the novel; another is Ulrich's sister Agathe, who after their father's death performs a criminal action by altering the dead man's will. Clarisse urges

346

her husband to murder his friend Ulrich in order to become a better composer. While this serves to satirise one strand in the contemporary reception of Nietzsche, Agathe's action puts into practice, in a more serious and more challenging way, Nietzsche's advice that free spirits should create their own morality. With both, Musil conveys the heady excitement of transgressing conventional boundaries. In exploring Nietzsche's ideas, he shows what it feels like to live them out.

The comparison between Clarisse and Agathe as Nietzscheans also illustrates how *The Man Without Qualities*, with its meandering progression and many essayistic reflections, works less through structure than through texture. The narrative voice moves easily from one consciousness to another. Similarities like that between Clarisse and Agathe provide different perspectives on the novel's themes. But this richness of texture was attained at a heavy price. As Musil worked on the novel, it ramified in innumerable directions and became impossible to complete. In the immense torso we have, the many brilliant scenes and reflections are not structured by any overarching architectonic form.

## Mann, *The Magic Mountain*

In *The Magic Mountain*, with its reputation as 'the most massively intellectual of all novels',[7] Thomas Mann combined an ironic narrative voice superior to the characters with the traditional novelistic pleasures of characterisation, narrative and architectural shape. But there is room for dispute about how far *The Magic Mountain* is a novel of ideas. Mann had neither the philosophical training that Musil and Broch had gained, nor their capacity for abstract reflection. He was, however, steeped in Arthur Schopenhauer's thought, and still more in Nietzsche's. In his *Betrachtungen eines Unpolitischen* (*Reflections of an Unpolitical Man*), written during the war to define a German identity in opposition to the democratic and Francophile values espoused by his brother Heinrich, Mann emphasised his indebtedness to the 'triad of eternally linked spirits' Schopenhauer, Nietzsche and Richard Wagner.[8] In thus contrasting German *Kultur* with French (and more generally Western) *Zivilisation*, Mann is particularly echoing a passage in Nietzsche's *Der Wille zur Macht* (*The Will to Power*, a compilation made posthumously by his sister from his unpublished notebooks) in which culture is described as compatible with moral corruption, civilisation as a regime of domesticated animals with 'intolerance for the most spiritual and daring natures' (*The Will to Power*, no. 121). This antagonism is embodied and dramatised in the clashing figures of Naphta and Settembrini.

Approaches to *The Magic Mountain* as a philosophical novel have often focused on its discussions of time. However, in evoking how time moves slowly in the monotony of the sanatorium, Mann is recreating an experience through poetic prose rather than offering philosophical reflections. Proust drew on Henri Bergson for the conception of memory which structures *À la recherche du temps perdu*; Mann draws more opportunistically on Schopenhauer to justify departures from normal cognition. Hans Castorp's sudden vivid recollection of his fellow schoolboy Pribislav Hippe, his famous vision when lost in the snow, and the sight of his dead cousin Joachim at a spiritualist seance most probably derive their rationale from Schopenhauer's essay 'Versuch über Geistersehn und was damit zusammenhängt' ('On Seeing Ghosts, and What This Entails'), which argues that in dreams time and space are suspended, and that prophetic dreams can therefore very occasionally afford insight into the past or the future.[9]

Mann is more innovatory in his treatment of science, the object of more recent scholarly attention.[10] Although he does not aim to be a polymath, like Musil or Broch, he incorporates a substantial amount of scientific information. Hans Castorp spends seven years at the Berghof sanatorium at Davos in Switzerland, supposedly diagnosed as tubercular. Illness brings him to a new understanding of the body, assisted by extensive reading in physiology, embryology and anatomy, which Mann conveys to the reader in a readable and digestible form. In contrast, however, to Broch's self-contained essays or Musil's essayistic excursuses, Mann integrates these passages by making them the expression of Castorp's fascination, not only with his own body, but with that of the alluring Russian fellow patient Clawdia Chauchat. Fascination with organic life is inevitably also fascination with death: in a crucial episode, Hans is shown the bone structure of his hand in an X-ray, and understands for the first time that he will die. Thus natural science is present in the novel, not as raw fact, but as the means of a change in consciousness. It defamiliarises our attitude to our bodies and to ourselves. It makes us freshly aware of our own mortality. Thus the novel powerfully suggests that a traditional humanism must be adjusted to take account of modern science.

While thus looking forward, *The Magic Mountain* also looks back, not wholly in a spirit of parody, to the *Bildungsroman* typified by Goethe's *Wilhelm Meister*. Mann was seeking to establish himself as modern Germany's successor to Goethe. His relation to Goethe has been called by Michael Minden one of oedipal rivalry in accordance with Harold Bloom's model of literary anxiety.[11] Mann, like Goethe, treats his hero with sovereign irony and uses his experiences to guide him and the reader towards a humanistic message. To reach that message, however, Castorp has to explore illness and death much more thoroughly than Meister did. As he tells Clawdia late in the novel: 'There are two ways to life: the one is the regular direct, and good way. The other is bad, it leads through death, and that is the way of genius.'[12]

Although *The Magic Mountain* is certainly a novel of ideas, it presents ideas, not in their raw state, but embodied in the main characters. It might be tempting to describe them – Hans Castorp, his cousin Joachim, his mentors Settembrini and Naphta, his lover Clawdia Chauchat, and her later companion Peeperkorn – as allegorical figures. But it would also be misleading. Granted, each represents a cluster of ideas, amounting to an outlook on life, emotional even more than intellectual. But these outlooks are not easy to label, define or summarise. As we get to know the characters better, the outlooks they embody become more nuanced, complex, even contradictory. And the characters themselves are far more than the representatives of ideas. Each is a three-dimensional, sharply visualised character with his or her distinctive gestures and way of speaking. All Joachim's words and actions reveal his soldierly self-discipline, his taciturn self-control, his transparent decency; Settembrini stands out by his self-regarding eloquence and his shabby checked trousers; Naphta by such rhetorical tricks as confuting an opponent with a cry of 'Wrong!' and introducing a conclusive argument with an emphatic '*For* …'; and Peeperkorn by his massive physique, his thinning white hair which surrounds his head like a flame, and his ponderously impressive inarticulacy. *The Magic Mountain* is certainly an intellectual novel, but the vivid fullness of its characterisation makes it almost Dickensian.

As ideas of the epoch swirl around Hans Castorp, he responds to them with a mixture of dimness and acuity. So it is important to establish just who he is. Up to a point, he is a representative north German. Sprung from a patrician family in the commercial port of Hamburg, he has an instinctive liking for order, tidiness and decency. He hates, for example, to hear a door slammed, and on arriving at the Berghof, he is offended to hear the Russian couple next door noisily making love. He inherits the conservative disposition of his grandfather Hans Lorenz Castorp, who, as a Hamburg senator, steadfastly opposed all industrial and social innovations brought by the modern age. Castorp the younger inclines to a reverence, resting partly on inertia, for all established institutions and conditions. Although he trains as an engineer and plans to work for a firm of shipbuilders, Castorp shows little of the Protestant work ethic. He is a dreamy, musical soul, who finds congenial the contemplative life imposed on him in the sanatorium. He is somewhat inarticulate, feeling that many things cannot be verbalised or analysed; his childhood perceptions are 'unspoken and therefore uncritical, though enthusiastic for all that' (*MM*, 27). His character has been shaped, below the level of consciousness, by an early acquaintance with death. Both his parents died before he was seven; his grandfather died a few years later, leaving Hans to be brought up by an uncle. The sight especially of his grandfather's corpse has left him with an ambivalent attitude to death which he does not try to reason out. Death is dignified, solemn, spiritual; but it is also, in some strange way, indecent and degrading.

Hans Castorp is a likeable, though somewhat stiff and conventional young man; but he is certainly not an intellectual. On his first morning at the Berghof, however, he meets a fully fledged intellectual in the person of Lodovico Settembrini, who introduces him to a largely new, coherent and astonishing set of values. An Italian literary scholar with a German grand-mother, Settembrini is the exact opposite of the inarticulate Castorp. He not only discourses with amazing fluency and frequent wit; he praises the art of rhetoric, calls himself a humanist, upholds the word as 'the bearer of the human intellect' (*MM*, 133), and, to Castorp's dismay, disapproves of music. Music is semi-articulate, dreamy and obscure. It is a dangerous opiate which lures its hearers into a passive trance and distracts them from political activity. For Settembrini – like Mann's brother Heinrich – is a deeply political being. He believes passionately in the ideals of the French Revolution, in liberty, fraternity and equality, and in the Enlightenment from which they derive. Entering Castorp's bedroom, he promptly and symbolically switches on the light. He is a Freemason, and belongs to several other international organisations: one for encouraging cremation, another for the abolition of capital punishment, and a third which is composing an encyclopedia of suffering as a first step towards the complete abolition of suffering. All these endeavours are to serve the progress of civilisation (*Zivilisation*), a word constantly on Settembrini's lips.

Germany is for Settembrini not the land of poets, philosophers and musicians, but the country to which the world owes the invention of the printing press, which disseminated progressive ideals, and of gunpowder, which enabled people to fight for them. The ongoing revolutionary struggle is embodied for him in two heroes. One is his grandfather, who belonged to a secret society dedicated to winning Italy's freedom from Austrian occupation. The other is the poet Giosuè Carducci (1835–1907), his teacher at the University of Bologna. Carducci, a famous poet who was awarded the Nobel Prize for Literature in 1906, was, at least in his younger days, a republican and anticlerical writer. In his 'Inno a Satana' ('Hymn to Satan'), from which Settembrini enthusiastically quotes, he represented Satan as the first rebel and the proponent of reason. Settembrini recruits not only Satan but also Prometheus and Jesus into his revolutionary pantheon, depicting the latter as the prophet of human equality and individualist democracy. The nationalism of the nineteenth century, to which his grandfather was devoted, is for Settembrini merely the prelude to the establishment of a world republic, where the official language will be Esperanto. The world republic will represent the ultimate victory of European values, those of the classical past, the Renaissance and the Enlightenment, over what Settembrini considers their antithesis – the spirit of the Orient, embodied in Russia as the gateway to Asia. Europe is active and progressive, but the 'Asiatic principle' (*MM*, 186) is conservative, immobile, autocratic and irrational. The crowd of Russian patients at the Berghof makes Settembrini shudder, feeling himself stranded amid 'Mongolian Muscovites' (*MM*, 289).

In this novel, the touchstone against which all philosophies are tried is the ineluctable fact of death. On this, too, Settembrini is eloquent. He strongly disapproves of Hans Castorp's inclination to revere death. Death should be seen as a necessary but subordinate part of life; it should never be set against life as a countervailing force. The ancients were right to adorn their sarcophagi with symbols, even obscene ones, of life and procreation. 'Death is to be honoured as the cradle of life, the womb of renewal. Once separated from life, it becomes grotesque, a wraith – or even worse' (*MM*, 238).

Settembrini, a born teacher, thinks it his mission to instruct Hans Castorp in his progressive values. He is motivated also by a homosexual attraction at which he discreetly hints by praising the great Florentine teacher Benedetto Latini, whom Dante Alighieri places in the circle of hell destined for sodomites. But Castorp is only superficially a receptive pupil. His early acquaintance with death, and his contemplative disposition, give him an affinity with the very values that Settembrini wants to warn him against. Russia, the land of autocracy and immobility, is also the home of Clawdia Chauchat, with whom Castorp rapidly falls in love. Her bad habits of slamming doors and chewing her fingers only make her more attractive. Moreover, Castorp's attraction to her was prefigured by a youthful infatuation with a fellow schoolboy of Slav origin, Pribislav Hippe, whose narrow eyes earned him the sobriquet 'the Kirghiz'. Clawdia's narrow 'Kirghiz eyes' associate her with the vast Asiatic expanses that loom up behind Russia, as does her husband's employment among the oil wells of Daghestan, beyond the Caucasus.

Not daring to speak to Clawdia, Castorp approaches her by roundabout ways. Hofrat Behrens, the director of the sanatorium, has painted her portrait. Pretending to admire the artistry of this clumsy daub, Castorp submits to a lecture on how anatomical knowledge can help the painter, and then embarks on a vast course of scientific reading, in search of the still unknown secret that underlies organic life. Although the textbooks cannot tell him what life is, they do convey the message that life and death are interdependent. The study of living organisms is inevitably also the study of their decay and death. Castorp develops a fascination with death which finds expression in a round of visits to the 'moribund', the hopeless cases who are confined to their beds in expectation of imminent death. These visits satisfy 'his own spiritual need to take suffering and death seriously' (*MM*, 352).

This exploration of organic life, with its inevitable component death, culminates at Carnival time, when the inmates hold a fancy-dress party. The chapter is entitled 'Walpurgisnacht', recalling the famous episode of Goethe's *Faust* set at the annual gathering of German witches, and Settembrini, who of course knows German literature better than most Germans, provides many ironically apt quotations. He warns Castorp against the alluring Frau Chauchat, equating her with Lilith, the she-devil whom Hebrew legend (adopted by Goethe) claims to have been Adam's first wife. Castorp, however, has escaped from control. Rejecting Settembrini's advice with disrespect, he speaks to Clawdia for the first time, making the same request that he made many years ago to Pribislav Hippe – namely, for the loan of a pencil. A conversation ensues, conducted largely in French, in which Castorp, using phrases that Mann borrowed from Walt Whitman's 'I Sing the Body Electric', celebrates 'le corps, l'amour, la mort' ('the body, love, death', *MM*, 407). Clawdia is reluctantly impressed, and the narrative discreetly intimates that they spend the night together. The following day Clawdia leaves the sanatorium, and (for several hundred pages) the story, to visit her husband in Daghestan.

If *The Magic Mountain* can properly be called a *Bildungsroman*, then Castorp's education seems to consist largely in defying his self-appointed teacher Settembrini. Was he right to do so? To answer this question, we must be clear about who Settembrini is and why he matters. He is not simply a rounded and fascinating fictional character, nor a mere caricatural expression of the standpoint Mann ascribed to his brother Heinrich. His importance extends far beyond a parochial fraternal dispute, and far beyond the temporal context of Mann's novel. Humorous exaggeration aside, Settembrini stands broadly for a set of liberal, humanist, peace-loving, internationalist values to which most of us would readily subscribe. For the conservative Castorp, who feels instinctive reverence for any established order, Settembrini's radical standpoint comes as a salutary shock. Introduced as 'Satana' (Carducci's name for the rebellious Devil), with much Mephistophelean irony disguising his essentially kindly nature, Settembrini is the devil who disrupts Castorp's conservative Eden. But of course he does not have all the answers. His confident liberalism depends on disregarding vast and ultimately unignorable areas of experience. Castorp explores some of them, drawn onwards by his infatuation with Clawdia. But another mentor, far more devilish than Settembrini, soon enters the novel.

This is Leo Naphta, a Galician Jew who converted to Catholicism in order to join the Society of Jesus, but whose illness has prevented him from taking his final vows and obliged him to teach Latin in the school at Davos. A fellow lodger and intellectual sparring partner of Settembrini, he reveals only gradually the full subversiveness of his outlook. The first dispute we witness turns on politics. Against the world republic which Settembrini thinks will emerge from nationalism, Naphta sets the ideal of a single, cosmopolitan state ruled by the church in the name of God. He mercilessly exposes the weaknesses in Settembrini's vision. Settembrini has avoided talking about economics; Naphta denounces free-market liberalism and maintains that Settembrini's peaceful republic will be the arena of bitter struggles for economic survival. In subsequent conversations he advocates the abolition of private property. Such a revolutionary step will restore the social order maintained by the medieval church, which condemned lending at interest, the basis of the modern economy, as a sin against humanity. Liberal individualism is already dying. It will be succeeded by an authoritarian state that offers, not the enjoyment of freedom, but the much deeper satisfaction of obedience. This state will centre on the proletariat; and the means by which it will be established is terror.

For Naphta to be both a reactionary medievalist and a revolutionary Communist is an ingenious intellectual juggling act, rather than a tenable position. Mann uses Naphta not only to expose the element of dishonesty that taints Settembrini's ideals, but also to reveal the most rebarbative consequences of a thoroughly other-worldly religious outlook. A dualist, Naphta sees a gulf between spirit and nature that can never be overcome. The human body, being part of nature, is not the beautiful object idealised by classical art, but a sickly, decaying and worthless envelope for the spirit. He quotes St Paul's words from Romans 7.24: 'Who shall deliver me from the body of this death?' He possesses a medieval *pietà* in which the Virgin holds the broken body of the crucified Christ; and he commends those saintly medieval princesses who kissed leprous ulcers and drank the water in which they had washed away their patients' pus. In such a picture and such acts of devotion, the wretched body is transfigured by the spirit. And it is the sick, the abject human being who is most truly human.

Naphta's view of life is dominated by death. While Settembrini advocates the abolition of capital punishment, Naphta upholds it because it compels the criminal to confront his guilt. But 'guilt' is a metaphysical concept. The murderer, who in Settembrini's eyes is a mere victim of society, is for Naphta a truly authentic human being who has chosen to perform the most deeply pleasurable of all actions. Behind this assertion we may suspect the influence of Fyodor Dostoevsky, especially if we recall how the whole of *The Idiot* builds up to Rogozhin's ecstatic murder of Nastasya Filippovna. And this part of Naphta's doctrine also recalls the philosophical discussions that Clawdia Chauchat, as she tells Castorp, used to conduct with her fellow Russians. They thought that morality was to be found, not in conventional good behaviour, but in self-abandonment to sin, danger and destruction. 'The great moralists have never been especially virtuous, but rather adventurers in evil, great sinners who teach us as Christians how to stoop to misery' (*MM*, 405). For Naphta, too, religion has nothing to do with morality, which he dismisses as bourgeois virtue, and the conventional distinction between good and evil is an irreligious error.

Naphta is hardly a convincing spokesman for religion. His world-view owes far more to Dostoevsky and Nietzsche than it does to the Gospels. His vision of a modern Communist theocracy is far from inviting. It serves in the novel, not as a self-contained view of life, but as a radical critique of Settembrini's liberal utopia. He is a Mephistophelean spirit of critique and denial. Naphta's criticisms reveal that Settembrini's world republic rests on the hegemony of the bourgeoisie, on inhumane economic doctrines which it carefully conceals, and, still more tellingly, on an ultimate absence of value. His assertion that 'progress [is] pure nihilism' (*MM*, 622) is simply a more drastic version of the challenge that can be put to any utopian vision of a final and perfected human life: what is it all *for*? If and when suffering is abolished, and human beings no longer have difficulties to overcome, what meaning or purpose will their lives have? Most of us will reply, however, that we can cross that bridge when we come it, which will hardly be soon, and that Naphta's conception of life as blind servitude to a God understood vacuously as 'the conservative, positive Absolute' (*MM*, 622) is a great deal worse.

In the narrative architecture of Mann's novel, however, Naphta's view of life is put to a test which is not argumentative, but experiential and visionary. If in the chapter 'Walpurgisnacht' Castorp defied his mentor Settembrini, cast off civilised restraint, and took advantage of carnivalesque anarchy to plunge into the encounter with Clawdia, so, in the chapter 'Snow', he escapes from both his teachers and, without meaning to, finds himself exploring dangerous and forbidden territory. Having learnt to ski, Castorp makes illicit excursions into the wintry mountains. On one excursion he gets hopelessly lost. He drinks port to keep the cold out. That provides a possible physiological explanation for the visions that follow. First, Castorp has a delightful vision of young people disporting themselves on the seashore, talking with civilised restraint, or showing a special reverence for a young mother nursing a child. This sunlit scene, however, is overshadowed by an ancient temple, in whose recesses Castorp discovers something horrible. Two old women are tearing apart a child and devouring the fragments. On seeing him, they curse him, but he suffers the paralysis often found in dreams, and escapes only by waking from his trance and finding himself once more in the snow.

What we are to make of this dream is explained by Castorp's subsequent reflections. He has had an insight, not into his personal unconscious, but into the unconscious life of humanity, the dreams of the collective soul. His vision appears to disclose something fundamental about human nature: 'The great soul, of which we are just a little piece, dreams through us so to speak, dreams in its many different ways its own eternal, secret dream – about its youth, its hope, its joy, its peace, and its bloody feast' (*MM*, 586). The collective unconscious of humanity, it would seem, contains a vision of happy and healthy, civilised and courteous humanity, but also the fantasy of hideous, cannibalistic rites; and in the long run you cannot have one without the other. This scene is generally recognised as the key to the novel. But it also resists having its meaning put into words. Much commentary on *The Magic Mountain* is devoted ostensibly to interpreting it, really to evading its implications. Many commentators relate the goings-on in the temple to the myth of Dionysus being torn to pieces and thus providing, according to Nietzsche in *Die Geburt der Tragödie* (*The Birth of Tragedy*), the central action of Greek tragic drama, which in turn formed the basis of the Greeks' sense of community. But Dionysus is a comfortably distant mythical being, whose sufferings we can hardly care about, whereas the child in the old women's clutches is a blond European, and the women themselves curse the intruder in the dialect of his native Hamburg. They suggest a whole range of horrific fantasies – witchcraft, human sacrifice, child murder, cannibalism and the place that some of these have occupied in the world's religions. Nietzsche maintains in *Der Antichrist* (*The Antichrist*) that Christianity originally gained acceptance by the incorporation of barbarous practices such as 'blood-drinking in Communion' (*The Antichrist*, no. 22).

The temple scene remains deeply upsetting. It exceeds any interpretation that can be put on it. We can perhaps hint at its significance by recalling a paragraph from Mann's essay 'Gedanken im Krieg' ('Thoughts in Wartime', 1915), in which he argues that culture (*Kultur*) is compatible with many activities that to the modern, Settembrini-like proponent of civilisation (*Zivilisation*) must appear barbaric:

> Culture is unity, style, form, attitude, taste, is some spiritual organisation of the world, however eccentric, grotesque, savage, bloody and frightful it may be. Culture can include oracles, magic, pederasty, Vitzliputzli, human sacrifice,

orgiastic cults, Inquisitions, autos-da-fé, St Vitus' dance, witch trials, poisoning, and the most colourful atrocities. Civilisation, however, is reason, enlightenment, mildness, morality, scepticism, dissolution – spirit.[13]

We can hardly say that the Aztecs, who sacrificed innumerable prisoners to the god 'Vitzliputzli', lacked culture; nor can we say that of their Spanish conquerors, who nevertheless allowed the Inquisition to hunt down heretics and burn them alive in autos-da-fé. What modern Europeans recognise as civilisation is only a small segment – perhaps an impoverished, emasculated one – of the possibilities available to humanity.[14]

As he returns to waking consciousness, Castorp reflects on his dream. It seems to embody the antitheses of life and death into which the verbose philosophies of Settembrini and Naphta can ultimately be resolved. But it also offers a path leading beyond futile antitheses to an understanding of life in which humanity is greater than such antitheses and has the power to choose life over death, love over cruelty. Castorp's conclusion is printed in italics: '*For the sake of goodness and love, man shall grant death no dominion over his thoughts*' (MM, 588).

This experience confirms that Castorp has outgrown his mentors. Henceforth he regards them with ironic detachment and answers them, especially Settembrini, not with the muddled garrulity he showed earlier, but in an articulate and self-confident manner. Their merely verbal philosophies, which rest on the pleasing illusion of having all phenomena under your control because you can talk about them and arrange them in a system, have to be measured against real experiences. The first is the death of Castorp's cousin Joachim. Unable to bear vegetating on the Berghof any longer, Joachim returns to his regiment, but after a few months his illness compels him to reascend to the Berghof, where he dies. The pages evoking how Joachim faces his inevitable death with dignity, silence and an increasing sense of inner peace, are among the most moving Mann ever wrote. They convey, without sermonising, that there is a humane and worthy approach to death, and that there is no need either to trivialise it, as in Settembrini's humanism, or to make it, as in Naphta's outlook, the object of a terrifying cult. The second such experience is the return of Clawdia Chauchat. Having awaited her in the hope of continuing their relationship, Castorp is disconcerted to discover that she is now the companion of an elderly Dutchman. However, they talk matters through in an edgy conversation, alternating uneasily between the familiar 'Du' and the formal 'Sie', and ending with a deeply ambiguous kiss. Here Mann has wonderfully conveyed the combination of prickliness, tension and increasing self-revelation that brings them gradually closer together.

Clawdia's companion, Mynheer Pieter Peeperkorn, a wealthy coffee planter from the Dutch East Indies, is an experience in himself, and one that serves to relativise further the lessons of Settembrini and Naphta. A huge man with a powerful physical presence, he is grandly inarticulate. His speeches are a jumble of unfinished sentences. But what he *says* does not matter, compared to what he *is*. To Castorp, he is a 'personality' on a gigantic scale. His vast consumption of wine, gin, coffee and all sorts of delicacies makes Castorp compare him to the god Bacchus; Peeperkorn, annoyed when his guests at a lavish dinner drop off to sleep, self-pityingly compares himself to Christ in Gethsemane deserted by the sleepy disciples. His capacity for enjoyment makes him seem an embodiment of life itself – a powerful force that does not need words to communicate. His excitement on spying a predatory eagle evokes also life's ruthless, amoral nature. He regards himself as essentially a tool for the enjoyment of life. But he is tormented by his inability to rise to the demands of life – that is, as Castorp suspects, by impotence – and one night he is found dead, having committed suicide. Humanity, it seems, cannot live by the life force alone.

After Peeperkorn's death and Clawdia's final departure, the narrative appears at first sight to dissolve into a series of episodes, spread over several years. But if we look more closely, we find that they are unified by the memory of Joachim, who fills the emotional space left by Clawdia. Castorp's implicitly homosocial companionship with his cousin becomes more pronounced after the latter's death. The Berghof's acquisition of a gramophone allows a chapter to be devoted to an evocation of Hans Castorp's favourite musical pieces. One of these is the passage from Gounod's *Faust* (1859) that centres on the death of Valentin, Gretchen's upright soldier brother. In Goethe's *Faust*, which Gounod is following, Valentin's dying words are: 'Ich gehe durch den Todesschlaf | Zu Gott ein als Soldat und brav' ('I'll meet my Maker presently | As the soldier I'm still proud to be').[15] A few chapters earlier, the phrase 'Als Soldat und brav' ('A Good Soldier') provided Mann with the title for the chapter in which Joachim dies. And a little later, we return to Joachim in an unexpected context. A young female patient at the Berghof reveals telepathic and telekinetic abilities. A seance is held, at which she apparently communicates with a departed spirit. This spirit promises to show the apparition of a dead person; Castorp asks to see his cousin Joachim, and after some two hours of straining by the medium, Joachim is seen in a corner of the room, emaciated as he was before his death, and wearing a peculiar helmet – the kind that a few years later would become a standard part of military uniform in the First World War. That is enough for Castorp. Like Settembrini several hundred pages earlier, he switches on the light, thus ending the seance and showing that he has at least learnt not to delve far into the murky underworld of death.

The ambiguous ending of the novel suggests that Castorp has learnt another lesson – from Joachim. His spellbound residence at the Berghof is ended by a thunderclap, the outbreak of the First World War, which breaks the enchantment. The patients disperse to their various countries; Settembrini, the self-styled internationalist, shows his true colours by devoting himself to Italian war propaganda; and Castorp joins the German army. We last glimpse him struggling through the mud of either the Western or the Eastern front with little chance of surviving the shellfire, but with Franz Schubert's *Lindenbaum* (*The Linden Tree*) on his lips. In the musical chapter, this seemingly innocent *Lied* (song) was revealed as containing a Romantic fascination with death; so perhaps Castorp has either yielded to the death wish or has learned from its aesthetic containment. But in fighting for his country (whether its cause is right or wrong) Castorp is showing more integrity than Settembrini, and a courage and sense of duty that link him with his dead cousin Joachim. The novel's conclusion balances life with death.

The ambiguous open conclusion, ending with a question, contrasts curiously with the strongly affirmative conclusion of *The Sleepwalkers*, which ends with St Paul's words to the jailer when his prison is opened by an earthquake – 'Do thyself no harm: for we are all here' (Acts 16.28) – and offers them as 'the voice of comfort, hope and immediate kindness'. Broch's intentions were as humane as Mann's. But while Broch's explicit message is one of human solidarity, the structure of his novel marks a concession to the severely functional *Sachlichkeit* of his era. Mann, by giving Castorp's story a beginning, a narrative shape and an end, acknowledges the value of form, which he sees as a product of humane kindliness and '*Kultur*'. If Castorp strays from his over-formal bourgeois upbringing into an exploration of formlessness, the novel encloses this experience in an aesthetically satisfying fictional form.

## Note on editions/translations

The recommended editions are: *Der Zauberberg*, ed. Michael Neumann (Frankfurt a.M: Fischer, 2002), as vol. v.1 of the grosse Kommentierte Frankfurter Ausgabe; Robert Musil, *Der Mann ohne Eigenschaften*, in *Gesammelte Werke*, ed. Adolf Frisé, 5 vols. (Reinbek: Rowolt, 1978); Hermann Broch, *Die Schlafwandler*, ed. Paul Michael Lützeler (Frankfurt a.M: Suhrkamp, 1996).

The following translations are recommended: Thomas Mann, *The Magic Mountain*, trans. John E. Woods (New York: Knopf, 1995); Robert Musil,

*The Man Without Qualities*, trans. Sophie Wilkins, 2 vols. (London: Picador, 1995); Hermann Broch, *The Sleepwalkers*, trans. Willa and Edwin Muir (London: Secker, 1932).

## Notes

1 G. W. F. Hegel, *Ästhetik*, ed. Friedrich Bassenge (Berlin: Aufbau-Verlag, 1955), p. 983 (Hegel's emphasis). T. M. Knox's translation, 'romance, the modern popular epic' (*Aesthetics*, 2 vols. (Oxford: Clarendon Press, 1975), II.1092), stumbles over the notorious ambiguity of 'Roman', which, like the French *roman*, can mean novel or romance. Unless otherwise indicated, translations are the author's own.

2 See Friedrich Nietzsche, *Untimely Meditations*, trans. R. J. Hollingdale (Cambridge University Press, 1997), pp. 127–94.

3 Hermann Broch, letter to Daniel Brody, 5 August 1931, in Broch, *Briefe I (1913–1938)*, ed. Paul Michael Lützeler (Frankfurt a.M.: Suhrkamp, 1981), p. 151.

4 *Ibid.*; cf. letter to Frank Thiess, 6 April 1930, in *ibid.*, p. 84 (with reference to Joyce).

5 Robert Musil, *The Man Without Qualities*, trans. Sophie Wilkins, 2 vols. (London: Picador, 1995), II.708–9. Further references to this translation are cited in the text as *MWQ*.

6 See especially Musil's essay 'Sketch of What the Writer Knows' (1918), in *Precision and Soul: Essays and Addresses*, trans. Burton Pike and David S. Luft (Chicago/London: University of Chicago Press, 1990), pp. 61–5.

7 T. J. Reed, *Thomas Mann: The Uses of Tradition*, 2nd edn (Oxford: Clarendon Press, 1996), p. 249.

8 Thomas Mann, *Betrachtungen eines Unpolitischen*, in his *Gesammelte Werke*, 13 vols. (Frankfurt a.M.: Fischer, 1974), XII.71.

9 Arthur Schopenhauer, *Sämtliche Werke*, ed. Arthur Hübscher, Parerga und Paralipomena, 2 vols. (Wiesbaden: Brockhaus, 1946), I.241–329.

10 See Malte Herwig, *Bildungsbürger auf Abwegen: Naturwissenschaft im Werk Thomas Manns* (Frankfurt a.M.: Klostermann, 2004).

11 Michael Minden, *The German 'Bildungsroman': Incest and Inheritance* (Cambridge University Press, 1997), pp. 231–2.

12 Thomas Mann, *The Magic Mountain*, trans. John E. Woods, Everyman's Library (London: Knopf, 2005), p. 709. Future references in text to *MM*.

13 Thomas Mann, 'Gedanken im Krieg', in *Gesammelte Werke*, XIII.528.

14 See the reflections on this passage in Terry Eagleton, *Reason, Faith and Revolution: Reflections on the God Debate* (New Haven/London: Yale University Press, 2009).

15 Johann Wolfgang von Goethe, *Faust Part One*, trans. David Luke (Oxford University Press, 1987), p. 119.

## Further reading

### Thomas Mann

Beddow, Michael, *The Fiction of Humanity* (Cambridge University Press, 1982), ch. 4: 'Reconstructions *Der Zauberberg*'

Reed, T. J., *Thomas Mann: The Uses of Tradition* (Oxford: Clarendon Press, 1974; new edn 1996)

Robertson, Ritchie, ed., *The Cambridge Companion to Thomas Mann* (Cambridge University Press, 2002)

Swales, Martin, *Mann, 'Der Zauberberg', Critical Guides to German Texts 19* (London: Grant and Cutler, 2000)

Vaget, Hans Rudolf, ed., *Thomas Mann, The Magic Mountain: A Casebook* (New York: Oxford University Press, 2008)


Robert Musil

Luft, David, *Robert Musil and the Crisis of European Culture, 1880–1942* (Berkeley/ Los Angeles: University of California Press, 1980)

Payne, Philip, *Robert Musil's 'The Man Without Qualities': A Critical Study* (Cambridge University Press, 1988)

Graham Bartram and Galin Tihanov, eds., *A Companion to the Works of Robert Musil* (Rochester, NY: Camden House, 2007)


Herman Broch

Lützeler, Paul Michael, ed., *Hermann Broch, Visionary in Exile: The Yale 2001 Broch Symposium* (Rochester, NY: Camden House, 2003)

Schlant, Ernestine, *Hermann Broch* (Boston: Twayne, 1978)

# 21

CHRISTOPHER BUTLER

# James Joyce (1882–1941): Modernism and language

James Joyce published four major prose works – *Dubliners* (1914), *A Portrait of the Artist as a Young Man* (1916 US, 1917 GB), of which a partial early draft, *Stephen Hero* (1904–7), was published in 1944, *Ulysses* (1922), *Finnegans Wake* (1939) – and a play, *Exiles* (1918). All represent Ireland with scrupulous attention to historical and local detail, and yet none stems directly, or exclusively, from the British literary canon. What Stephen Dedalus admires in *A Portrait* is European. He thinks, as he walks to the university, about Gerhart Hauptmann, John Henry Newman, Guido Cavalcanti, Henrik Ibsen, Ben Jonson, Aristotle and Thomas Aquinas. As Anthony Burgess remarks: 'Add Blake, Bruno, Vico, and you have very nearly the entire Joyce library.'[1] He is a young man deeply interested in ideas, particularly aesthetic ones, and by the end of the novel he is thinking thoughts that would not be approved of by the Catholic church of his time, or the benighted Irish under its influence. In a post-Wildean way, 'The young men in the college regarded art as a continental vice.'[2] Indeed, sex haunts the aesthete too, however idealistic he seems to be, and they were partly right about Stephen, for his most visionary experience in *Portrait* (of the girl he sees on the seashore) only narrowly transcends a sexual response.

Joyce, like Stephen, was primarily driven by new ideas: he revered the Danish critic, Georg Brandes, and was deeply influenced by Ibsen, Gustave Flaubert (though he preferred Gabriele d'Annunzio to him in 1900) and Ernest Renan. Between 1900 and 1902 he read Émile Zola, Gerhart Hauptmann, Paul Verlaine, J. K. Huysmans and Leo Tolstoy, and was guided through the symbolist movement by Arthur Symons. By the time of writing *Portrait* (from 1904 to 1914) he 'was aware of some movement already proceeding out of Europe'. He liked the way this last phrase seemed to him 'to unroll the measurable world before the feet of the islanders' (*SH*, 39). The 'islanders' certainly needed this new measure, because *Dubliners*, which is more like Anton Chekhov than Arnold Bennett, offers an elaborately interconnected study of a 'paralysed' Irish culture, marooned offshore from England and

Europe, and whose citizens, though they feel trapped, are apparently incapable of taking the first step eastwards. *Portrait* shows why Stephen has to take the road to Paris. As Richard Ellmann remarks, 'To go to the continent was to escape the illusory sins and virtues of Ireland and, for an Irishman at least, to go beyond good and evil.'[3] Joyce had also declared himself a Nietzschean in 1902 and, after publishing *Ulysses*, was saluted by Valery Larbaud for giving to 'Young Ireland, an artistic physiognomy, an intellectual identity': he had done for his country what August Strindberg, Ibsen and Friedrich Nietzsche had done for theirs.[4] The European movement was politically and morally radical, socialist and feminist, and the student Stephen is told that his paper on 'Art and Life' 'represents the sum of modern unrest and modern freethinking' (*SH*, 96). Ibsen above all provided Joyce with the model of the intellectual outsider artist as the constant critic of a conforming bourgeois society.

Joyce is a European modernist in two further, technical, respects: his extensive exploitation of the tradition of past literature, and his willingness to experiment with language. While *Portrait* is firmly in the European tradition of the *Bildungsroman*, its opening pages are unprecedented: they are written in an experimental, fragmentary and imagistic prose, adopting the viewpoint of a very young child. *Ulysses* is a compendium of various kinds of experimental prose which places the Dublin of 1904 within the larger universal context of Homeric myth, as an exemplary great city, and so as part of a great modernist sequence of city works, which includes Andrei Biely's *Petersburg*, Alfred Döblin's *Berlin Alexanderplatz*, John Dos Passos's *Manhattan Transfer*, Robert Musil's *Der Mann ohne Eigenschoften* (*The Man Without Qualties*), as well as great city poems, such as Guillaume Apollinaire's 'Zones', 'Cendrars' and 'Pâques à New York', and T. S. Eliot's *The Waste Land*. It is the classic experimental modernist literary achievement, along with *The Waste Land* and Ezra Pound's *The Cantos*, both of which were profoundly influenced by their authors' reading of the early episodes of *Ulysses* in typescript.[5] *Ulysses* must have influenced Eliot's 'Tradition and the Individual Talent', which asks authors to have 'the literature of Europe since Homer' in mind and, in his review of the book, Eliot said Joyce's 'mythical method' compares with 'the discoveries of Einstein' concerning relativity, and is 'a step towards making the modern world possible for art'.[6]

Like Eliot's poem, *Ulysses* had a huge influence on later writers including Virginia Woolf, William Faulkner, Dos Passos, Döblin, Hermann Broch and Vladimir Nabokov. Indeed, many modernists, especially these three closely interacting expatriates, Joyce, Eliot and Pound, thought of themselves primarily as multi-lingual Europeans, quoting freely from Latin, Greek, French,

Italian, German and other languages. Joyce spoke French and Italian with ease, and signs off *Ulysses* as written in 'Trieste, Zurich, Paris 1914–21'. He witnessed the greater European modernist movement in all the arts, was recognised as one of its leaders, and wrote, according to Marcel Brion in 1928, the 'most prodigious book of our times' which would 'give birth to a whole new literature'.[7] Edmund Wilson by 1931 put Joyce in the avant-garde of ideas as well, with his own version of relativity: 'Joyce is indeed really the great poet of a new phase of human consciousness. Like Proust's or Whitehead's or Einstein's world, Joyce's world is always changing as it is perceived by different observers and by them at different times.'[8]

As a typically modernist artist hero, Joyce draws attention to his mastery of technique. Stephen Dedalus may be ironised, but the real irony is that this young man will indeed go on to write *Ulysses* (in which he is still seen as a mildly comic and pretentious figure) and in which Joyce, by allusion and imitation, assimilates past styles to confront the masterpieces of the past with one of his own. So did other heroic modernists, such as Henri Matisse, Pablo Picasso, Eliot, Igor Stravinsky, and Alban Berg, in works that also displayed an amazing mastery and reorganisation of past styles and forms: such as Picasso's *Vollard Suite*, Berg's *Wozzeck*, Stravinsky's *Apollo* and Eliot's *The Waste Land*.

By the time Joyce wrote *Finnegans Wake*, in a dream Esperanto 'English' requiring a knowledge of some forty languages, he had advanced beyond the willingness to imitate the past, and become an ally of the radical avant-garde in the surrealist movement, and in particular of Eugène Jolas, who proclaimed that Joyce, as a 'new artist of the word', had 'recognised the autonomy of language' and was attempting in the *Wake*, to 'hammer out a verbal vision that destroys time and space'.[9] This is as avant-garde as you need to be.

Joyce shared the concern of other early twentieth-century thinkers and artists with language; a concern which had three main aspects. First, how does it fit on to the world? Is a stripped-down, logical, scientific language the only truth-telling one? Are literary expression and moral judgement, for example, the mere expression of emotions? These questions preoccupied Ludwig Wittgenstein in his *Tractatus* (1922) and later the logical positivist school of Vienna. Modernist writers in general do not seem to have paid a great deal of attention to this epistemological concern, with the exception of Musil, who wrote a thesis on Ernst Mach, but it is implied in the modernist preoccupation with sense perceptions as the basis of our apprehension of the world.[10]

The second great modernist concern was to find forms of language which would most closely reflect subjective mental processes, including those of dream. Hence the interest in 'stream of consciousness', including the expression of sensation, image and symbol, and a concern for the 'real syntax' of our thinking processes, which are not bound by the public grammar of the spoken word (as Joyce's Leopold Bloom perpetually shows). The third, and uniquely avant-gardist, preoccupation was with modifying the very structure of language. What kind of intelligible expression might remain were we to disrupt the grammar of language itself? Such modification and recombination of linguistic elements was a preoccupation of the Dada movement – whose very title is a form of nonsense language – and it runs right through to *Finnegans Wake*, in which Joyce suggests that such an accretion and synthesis of languages reflects the processes of the dreaming mind, and indeed the inherited underlying mental structures of all mankind.

Joyce belongs to a period in which the basic mimetic commitments or 'normal' conventions of the arts were radically questioned. As has been seen, for literature this includes the underlying forms of grammar or syntax. Perspective is recast in cubism, so that the Renaissance perception of objects is not so much destroyed (for it is always implied – these are portraits and landscapes and still lifes after all), as analysed and taken apart, so that we are made more aware of the artificial and fallible nature of their workings. Hence, too, the autonomous power of the artist, who now makes designs on canvas which deliberately defy natural perception. Likewise, tonality, which offered a familiar perspectival landscape, in which the tonic and dominant are firmly in charge, and the final return to the tonic is a well-established teleological feature, is disrupted into all the more complex implications and the distracting byways of the extension of the tonal system, sometimes right into a mad or disoriented state of atonality, as in Arnold Schoenberg's *Erwartung* (1909), in which all the usual orientation points seem to be lost. So in literature the syntax of 'natural' language is disrupted by successive sceptical enquirers in the twentieth century – from the expressive subordination of word to sound (in Gerard Manley Hopkins, Stéphane Mallarmé and Joyce), to the post-structuralist attack on all language as an anti-individualist ideologised prison. Avant-garde literature thus develops towards a disruptive means of communication which delights in sheer play with the elements of language, as in Dada and *Finnegans Wake*.

This tradition in the experimental novel extended, most notably in America, to writers like Walter Abish, Donald Barthelme, Robert Coover, Guy Davenport, Stanley Elkin and Raymond Federman. And there are many positions in between. Yet all these developments needed some anchoring or primary motivation – for cubists, an analysis of the world which, in the end, subordinated the appearances to the artist's design; for musicians, the liberation into the sheer complexity of implication in atonal music, which in works with text, like *Pierrot Lunaire* and *Wozzeck*, allowed for a new approach to the complexity and the internal contradictions of human psychology. Joyce's approach to language included using it to bring out the importance of particulars, which seem to defy the universalising and essentialising properties of language (hence the technique of epiphany) and as playful revelation of its underlying social structures and conventions, as in the pastiche of past literature in 'Oxen', or the nationalist rhetoric of 'Cyclops', and also the break-up, in 'Circe', of logically connected language into a montage of image, symbol and apparent inconsequence, showing the libido at play and the horrors of nightmare.

Stephen's reflections on language and aesthetics are central to *Stephen Hero* and the *Portrait*. There are two major concerns here: the way in which language presents itself to consciousness, and the way in which that consciousness, when expressing itself, even in the free indirect speech of implied inner monologue, will (knowingly to Joyce and to the alert reader, or more or less unknowingly to Stephen and others) adopt a particular *style* of linguistic expression. This acutely calibrated sense of stylistic variation is the core of Joyce's art and yet it is always at the service of realism. 'How could a woman be a tower of ivory?' asks Stephen.[11] Moreover, it reflects the reality of inner states by its rhythm and musicality, for words are 'so beautiful and sad, like music' (*P*, 20).

> He drew forth a phrase from his treasure and spoke it softly to himself:
> - A day of dappled seaborne clouds.
> The phrase and the day and the scene harmonised in a chord. Words. Was it their colours? ... No, it was not their colours: it was the poise and balance of the period itself. Did he then love the rhythmic rise and fall of words better than their associations of legend and colour? Or was it that, being as weak of sight as he was shy of mind, he drew less pleasure from the reflection of the glowing sensible world through the prism of language many-coloured and richly storied than from the contemplation of an inner world of individual emotions mirrored perfectly in a lucid supple periodic prose? (*P*, 140)

In *Portrait*, language constantly seeks to catch the image as an immediate sensory impact: the model for the relation of language to the world, poignantly enough for the about-to-be-blind Joyce, is intensely visual. 'Words which he did not understand he said over and over to himself till he had learnt them by heart: and through them he had glimpses of the real world about him' (*P*, 52). Stephen typically sees images corresponding to an emotional state, which is vaguely ascribed to his senses or his soul; thus he wishes 'to meet in the real world the unsubstantial image which his soul so constantly beheld', and thinks of this in erotic terms, for 'in that moment of supreme tenderness he would be transfigured' (*P*, 54). This indeed happens in the epiphanic ending of Chapter 4, when he has his 'vision' of a 'winged form' above the waves of the sea, that is, the Icarus symbol. 'His strange name seemed to him a prophecy', and his vision 'the call of life to his soul' and not 'the inhuman voice that had called him to the pale service of the altar'. At this point his 'soul had arisen from the grave of boyhood' and 'He would create proudly out of the freedom and power of his soul, as the great artificer whose name he bore'. It is at this point that he sees a girl on the shore, described as a bird, and 'her image had passed into his soul for ever'. 'Her eyes had called to him and his soul had leaped at the call. To live, to err, to fall, to triumph, to recreate life out of life!' (*P*, 142, 143, 144, 145). So his realisation of his creative vocation as a writer is irreparably connected to the 'sudden spiritual manifestation' of epiphany, in a vision of a Greek and Holy Ghost-like muse. Later he sleeps: 'His soul was swooning into some new world', but the symbolism here is very close to that used for the climactic 'kiss' with a prostitute which had ended Chapter 2:

> Glimmering and trembling, trembling and unfolding, a breaking light, an opening flower, it spread in endless succession to itself, breaking in full crimson and unfolding and fading to palest rose, leaf by leaf and wave of light by wave of light, flooding all the heavens with its soft flushes, every flush deeper than the other. (*P*, 145)

When he awakes, 'A rim of the young moon cleft the pale waste of sky like the rim of a silver hoop embedded in grey sand; and the tide was flowing in fast to the land with a low whisper of her waves, islanding a few last figures in distant pools' (*P*, 145). But realism, in the sense of the sordid and disagreeable, soon comes back, as it often does in Joyce, with a brilliant transmutation of the image of the pool, at the beginning of the next chapter, and next sentence: 'He drained his third cup of watery tea to the dregs ... staring into the dark pool of the jar. The yellow dripping had been scooped out like a boghole' (*P*, 146).

The *language* in which Stephen expresses this vision has a very marked late nineteenth-century accent, recalling John Ruskin, Walter Pater and Newman, while echoing incidents in d'Annunzio's *Il fuoco* and Ibsen's *Brand* as well as Dante Alighieri's Beatrice.[12] Quite unlike the radically experimental, clearly twentieth-century, fragmented opening pages of *Portrait*, the mental style of Stephen on the beach confines him within the limited perspective of the aesthete, mingling religion and sex in his vision of beauty. A similar mixture of popular fiction and Mariolatry will, with greater ironic effect, surround Leopold Bloom as he ogles Gerty Macdowell on the beach in the 'Nausicaa' episode of *Ulysses*. But the inner styles of consciousness in the *Portrait*, like the scholastic jargon with which he tries to define the experience of art to Lynch, only temporarily define Stephen, who grows through them and ends his book with the relatively matter-of-fact prose of his diary. The difference here is between the conventions of a spoken dialogue between two students, Stephen pretentious and Lynch sarcastically cutting him down, while the implied inner consciousness of Stephen discovers his great vocation as a writer. Joyce wants us to appreciate that the dialogue is just debate, and the discovery a drama within the subjective consciousness. Thus Stephen, despite his stylistic derivativeness, can assume that there is no problem with language as such when expressing the artist's inner self. Indeed, Joyce's art is meant to move us even when we see the limitations of style. Although Stephen is at an ironic distance, we can be deeply moved (rather as in listening to Giacomo Puccini, or reading sentimental moments in Charles Dickens, or experiencing the hellfire sermon of Chapter 3) even when we are aware of a historical rhetoric with manifest designs upon us.

In *Ulysses* this preoccupation with styles of consciousness is continued, and 'normal' language is constantly disrupted by Joyce's view of human psychology, yet this essentially naturalistic endeavour is accompanied by something much more complicated: the casting of this story of a day, devoted as it is to the scrupulously truthful actualities of Dublin in 1904, into episodes which, certainly from the tenth on, are in alarmingly discrete styles.[13] We must interpret the styles, as well as the characters, for they have quite divergent purposes, derived from newspaper headlines in 'Aeolus', cheap popular fiction in 'Nausicaa', the question and answer of an encyclopedia in 'Eumaeus', and so on. Each reflects a different aspect of reality. But this divergence of implication, after Joyce's sheer absorption into the style has been admired, is full of ambiguity in its mixture of affirmative comedy and satire. For example, does Gerty MacDowell's absorption within sentimental fiction, to the extent that her private thoughts use its most embarrassing phraseology, help us to understand her sympathetically, as a young girl, or does the Joycean narrative Arranger satirise her as a victim of popular culture? The critics are divided on this, and a similar question hangs over Molly Bloom's final monologue: is she buried under the stereotypes of her relentless eight-sentence flow of ungrammatical language, or is the joke on the male reader, who is obliged to come to terms with the real sexual thoughts of a woman in 1904?

The presiding god here is the god of relativism, and the Arranger of them all, Joyce, is *using* all these styles so as to be himself trapped in none of them. Where, then, is the artist? He sees our apprehension of the world as essentially relative to the discourses we use to describe it. He clearly believes in the truth of facts, and there are plenty of points at which critics have compared Joyce's text to the world and found it accurate; but as a creator in language he identifies himself with no particular style and 'like the God of creation, remains within or beyond or above his handiwork, invisible, refined out of existence, paring his fingernails' (*P*, 181).

This encyclopedic planning in Joyce's work reflects an extraordinary epistemological confidence in a scholastic ordering, from Aristotle to Aquinas – where 'everything fits'. This rather Catholic view of things provides a universal order into which the interiority of Protestantism (or the stream of consciousness) can fit. To that extent, the Joycean Arranger is always our secret and utterly engaging opponent in the stylistic game of art, but he is always there. Joyce is not really the Flaubertian indifferent god mentioned above. Stephen's earlier declaration is more to the point:

> The simplest epical form is seen emerging out of lyrical literature when the artist prolongs and broods upon himself as the centre of an epical event and this form progresses until the centre of emotional gravity is equidistant from the artist himself and from others. The narrative is no longer purely personal. The personality of the artist passes into the narration itself, flowing round and round the persons and actions like a vital sea. (*P*, 180)

*Ulysses* is that epic.

These modernist formal strategies make *Ulysses* an amazing compendium of language use – 'Aeolus' alone, in its encyclopedic way, uses all the devices to be found in the rhetoric books. It is peculiarly modernist, too, in its interest in the newspaper and its use of headlines while its apparent jump-cutting and discontinuity reflect the newspaper as a symptom of modern life; always offering collage, montage and juxtaposition, rather than a single narrative. In that respect it is, like the city, as F. T. Marinetti pointed out in the *First Futurist Manifesto* (originally entitled 'Le Futurisme', 1909), a site for new modern materials, which are juxtaposed with one another like 'the great newspaper (synthesis of a day in the world's life)'.[14] As Karen Lawrence points out, defamiliarisation and parataxis are typical of this kind of writing, 'it catalogues without synthesising them', and so we come to think of this apparent discontinuity in modernist art as a sign of experiment.[15] But in the case of Joyce, the encyclopedic pattern-maker, this can be very misleading, for the discontinuity is only apparent and juxtaposition leaves us with interpretative work to do. For example, two paragraphs in the 'Citizen' episode describe the same event in different styles:

> And lo, as they quaffed their cup of joy, a godlike messenger came swiftly in, radiant as the eye of heaven, a comely youth and behind him there passed an elder of noble gait and countenance, bearing the sacred scrolls of law and with him his lady wife a dame of peerless lineage, fairest of her race.

Little Alf Bergan popped in round the door and hid behind Barney's snug, squeezed up with the laughing. And who was sitting up there in the corner that I hadn't seen snoring drunk blind to the world only Bob Doran. I didn't know what was up and Alf kept making signs out of the door. And begob what was it only that bloody old pantaloon Dennis Breen in his bath slippers with two bloody big books under his oxter and the wife hotfoot after him, unfortunate wretched woman, trotting like a poodle. I thought Alf would split.[16]

Joyce once asked Frank Budgen if *Ulysses* was 'futurist' and Budgen replied that it was cubist because 'every event is a many-sided object. You first state one view of it and then you draw it from another angle to another scale, and both aspects lie side by side in the same picture'.[17] And so in the example above we are to make a rather simple mock heroic versus low ironic comparison in this example of style versus reality – an exercise developed to heroic lengths in 'Oxen of the Sun'. Here Joyce sets up another simple drinking scene, of medical students in the lying-in hospital, and then challenges us to see what selective aspects are revealed or disguised by depicting it in discrete styles derived from a conventional history of English prose. He reminds us that in the past people lived in specifiably different linguistic worlds. The evolution of style reveals some things and excludes others. This is always the best we can manage, because in *Ulysses*, no quasi-theological, omniscient, 'realist' master language is in control.

We have to read Joyce as a poet, because the hidden schematas of his prose, along with its resonance of symbol and metaphor, let alone its music and rhythm, are as enactive and suggestive as poetry. Yet in typically odd-beat, prosaic ways: the long 'scientific' answer to the question 'What in water did Bloom, waterlover, drawer of water, watercarrier, returning to the range, admire?' (*U*, XVII.183ff.) has an extraordinary beauty, while his thoughts in an earlier episode about water also have a symbolic and metaphorical function:

He foresaw his pale body reclined in it at full, naked, in a womb of warmth, oiled by scented melting soap, sofly laved. He saw his trunk and limbs riprippled over and sustained, buoyed lightly upward, lemonyellow: his navel, bud of flesh: and saw the dark tangled curls of his bush floating, floating hair of the stream around the limp father of thousands, a languid floating flower. (*U*, v.567–72)

The schematic figure or leading symbol for this episode is 'genitals' and its Homeric parallel is the Lotos-Eaters. These associations control

much of its random detail: the warmth, the directionless walk, the gelded horses munching in their nosebags, the communicants in the church Bloom passes through, the chemists' chloroform and poppy syrup, the lemony smell of the soap, the anticipated warm bath. At this remove, questions of purpose fade away and we contemplate a pure array of narcotic elements, the narrative structure nearly unnoticeable, deeds and doers turned into a drift of symbols. (Kenner, *Ulysses*, p. 22)

But the baseline for these poetic variations lies in various forms of stream of consciousness such as Joyce knew from Eduard Dujardin's *Les Lauriers sont coupés* (1889) and Artur Schnitzler's 'Leutnant Gustl' ('Lieutenant Gustl'), both of which he had in his library. Character is always at issue, and it is not the case, as some critics claim, that all that we really experience here is language, because the *unifying* factors in processing language still rely upon 'uptake', that is to say, a plausible series of inferences about a speaker's psychology, its historical probability and its relevance to context. The disconcerting and radically innovatory element is the absence of a characterised voice in the storyteller.

The Arranger is certainly in charge: he remembers the exact form of words hundreds of pages earlier, and we infer that he expects us to think of the text backwards and forwards. It is only in the latter part of the book, for example, that we might realise that 'Bloom's dental windows' didn't belong to Leopold Bloom, but a dentist of the same surname, one Marcus Bloom, living at 2 Clare St in 1904. Likewise, in 'Sirens' details 'find their way on to the page without regard for the consciousness of anyone present, thoroughly subverting the premise of the initial style' (Kenner, *Ulysses*, p. 64). What is more, Joyce 'plays havoc with the rules of lexical formation, syntax, and discourse on which any continued use of language depends'.[18] This is because at this point he wants language to mimic operatic and instrumental music, since, as Gilbert reports, the technique in this episode is 'fuga per canonem'. This is prepared in the thematic fragmentariness of the 'overture' in the first two pages which ends with '*Done*' and starts with 'Begin'. I call it an overture, as it sets out the themes, and the leitmotif phrases, to be encountered later in more detail. These include all sorts of sounds, even natural ones, like the snap of a garter, or the concluding fart transcribed as 'Pprrpffrrppfff'.

Stream of consciousness is demanding in itself – even in *Portrait* Joyce had caused problems for readers: the reviewer in the *Manchester Guardian* (March 1917) thought that 'there are ellipses ... that go beyond the pardonable ... [and] obscure allusions. One has to be of the family, so to speak, to "catch on"' (Deming, *Critical Heritage*, 1.93). This psychological associativeness links Joyce to modernist writing in Europe and poses the same problems as does poetry of psychological association by Apollinaire, Blaise Cendrars, Eliot and Pound. Moreover, to achieve psychological plausibility, it demands some linguistic ingenuity from the reader, as Katie Wales demonstrates. Molly's monologue is essentially unpunctuated, and has many abrupt topic shifts, so that we have to intuit its phrasing. Likewise, Bloom expresses his mental associations with short, disjunct phrases, and in *Ulysses* such ellipses often involve high and low cultural references. Add to this the possibility – notably in 'Circe' – that these mental processes are disguised symptoms of something being repressed, and our difficulties of interpretation multiply. Moreover, there are particular problems, triumphantly solved, in getting language to suggest non-verbal experience: in our raw sensations, thinking in images, and a good deal of our simple recognitional looking at the world. Woolf develops this aspect of Joyce with an extraordinary poetic intensity, in *Mrs Dalloway* (1925), which also describes twenty-four hours in the lives of a few individuals moving around London.

Stephen, Bloom and Molly, as the prime centres of consciousness in *Ulysses*, extend a tradition which ran through Joseph Conrad, Thomas Mann, Marcel Proust and André Gide. As Ricardo Quinones points out, Bloom is, like Marcel in *À la recherche du temps perdu*, Hans Castorp in *Der Zauberberg* (*The Magic Mountain*), Tiresias in *The Waste Land*, Birkin in *Women in Love*, Jacob in *Jacob's Room* and Clarissa Dalloway in *Mrs Dalloway*, a 'reflective, passive, selfless and tolerant witness'. Quinones rightly concludes that 'the creation of these complex central consciousnesses constitutes one of the major achievements of modernism'.[19] Yet Bloom is also Ulysses, a modern man shadowed by the classical heroic in an ironic mode. When Ulysses returns to Penelope, he proves his identity by the strength he has to flex his bow. When Leopold returns to 7 Eccles Street in the 'Ithaca' episode, the unremarkable drooping trajectory of Bloom's urination reminds the implacable catechist how when a schoolboy Bloom 'had been capable of attaining the point of greatest altitude against the whole concurrent strength of the institution, 210 scholars' (*U*, XVII.1195–6). And when Bloom finally lies in bed with Molly, he sleeps as Everyman and the universal hero: 'Sinbad the Sailor and Tinbad the Tailor'. This sense of universal recurrence, the repetition of literary myth in contemporary life, strikingly exemplifies the neoclassical revival within modernism.

In the 'Circe' episode, Bloom and Stephen are in a brothel – a scene of metamorphosis echoing Circe's transformation of Odysseus' men into animals. The technique is hallucination. Because it's a brothel we wonder whether it is fantasy, or the 'real' acting out of a fantasy, for example by cross-dressing, or the uncensored expression in dreams of a libidinal desire. Joyce knew of Sigmund Freud and his modernist techniques present unconscious sexual repression. Freud once remarked that the elements of a dream often stem from the experience of the previous twenty-four hours, and Joyce's disguised allusions to earlier parts of *Ulysses* reinforce the internal unity of the work, yet the climax, and emotional 'truth', of the episode is the ghostly apparition to Stephen of an accusatory dying mother and to Bloom of an Eton-suited dead son.

The metamorphosis of objects and the metaphorical extension of language affront our habits at a deeply emotional and anxiety-provoking level, as was the intention of the surrealists. The exploration of consciousness forced many literary modernists into a 'crisis of language' which goes back to the work of Friedrich Hölderlin and Mallarmé, and Arthur Rimbaud's *Lettres du voyant*: 'Trouver une langue; du reste, toute parole étant idée, le temps d'un langage universel reviendra!' ('Find a language; besides, all words being ideas, the time of a universal language will return.') In *Finnegans Wake* Joyce simply bypasses Dada and surrealism in rising to Rimbaud's challenge. He presents us with a universal accretion of more than forty languages, and he adds to them, in a rather Jungian manner, the underlying myths which he believes to be inherent in their metaphorical structures. Here I think Joyce is mistaken in seeking a universalism beyond the European. Maybe the dream state is not as 'universal' as Jungians believed. We don't really drop out of our own culture into the whole past history of the world's cultures and languages when we sleep: 'Are we speachin d'anglas landadge or are you sprakin sea Djoytsch?'[20]

Joyce's 'night book', founded in the philosophy of Giambattista Vico, unsurprisingly met with resolute opposition from its early readers, and most hurtfully from his brother Stanislaus, who called it 'drivelling rigmarole', 'unspeakably wearisome' and 'the witless wandering of literature before its final extinction'; and Pound thought that 'nothing short of divine vision or a new cure for the clapp can possibly be worth all the circumambient peripheralisation'.[21] Indeed, 'This is nat language at any sinse of the world' (*FW*, 16), once Joyce superimposes the languages and stories of many races, under which are supposed to lie the simplest of (Viconian) mythical narratives. For rather as pitches freed from traditional tonal relationships manage to enter into hitherto prohibited relationships with one another, so Joyce brilliantly invents a vocabulary which allows the words of different languages to interact, within his own (primarily) portmanteau words (cf. Attridge, *Peculiar Language*, pp. 195ff.). For example, 'one eyegonblack' is a 'moment', from the German 'Augenblick': 'One eyegonblack. Bisons is bisons. Let me fore all your hasitency cross yourpalm witha trink gilt. Here have sylvan coyne, a piece of oak. Ghinees hies good for you' (*FW*, 16).

Joyce himself exploited the analogy with music, and Robert McAlmon tells us, 'he wishes to believe that anybody reading his work gets a sensation of understanding, which is the understanding which music is allowed without too much explanation' (Beckett, *Our Exagmination*, pp. 110f.). Even Beckett says that it is 'not only to be read. It is to be looked at and listened to' (*ibid.*, p. 14). This parallel is invoked with relief by nearly all the early commentators on the *Wake*, who are not so much concerned to situate it in the context of modernist culture, as to defend its language and attempt exegesis. But Joyce's 'aesthetic of the dream' results in a kind of total relativism, with no guide from belief, moral argument, plot, chronology or emotional coherence. Did HCE indecently expose himself in Dublin's Phoenix Park? Has he an incestuous attraction to his daughter Issy? Every critic has tried to make an interpretative selection from the text, and the hope that, if we were to be even better Freudians, it *would become* significant when the right interpreter comes along, has been perpetually defeated by this kind of surrealist prose, from Joyce to William Burroughs and beyond. Nonetheless, parts of the *Wake* such as 'Anna Livia Plurabelle' are wonderfully poetic and emotionally expressive, irrespective of their possible place in larger narrative structures.

Ellmann points out that:

> the larger implications of *Ulysses* follow from the accord of Bloom and Stephen about love. Both men are against the tyranny of Church and State, and the tyranny of jingoism – tyrannies that make history a nightmare from which Bloom like Stephen is trying to awake. What they are for is also explicit. If we consider the book as a whole, the theme of love will be seen to pervade it.[22]

Joyce was influenced by Richard Wagner and Ibsen to believe that love and art were inherently revolutionary: much art of the past may have reflected the beliefs of the community, but by the late nineteenth century, art can be revolutionary because it is opposed to the ruling spirit of the community. *Portrait* makes abundantly clear Joyce's desire to escape the commitments of nationalism and religion, and the great temptation in *Portrait* is priesthood, using the ritualistic, binding language of the Mass and the sacraments. Joyce wrote books of emancipation and, if anything, he committed himself to a mildly anarchist version of European socialism. As his brother Stanislaus put it: 'Jim boasts . . . of being modern. He calls himself a socialist but attaches himself to no school of socialism.'[23] For Joyce, governments use force, and artists use persuasion. 'My mind rejects the whole present social order and Christianity,' he told Nora, and his weapon against them is sceptical modernist irony, including his appropriation of religious language for aesthetic purposes, as in his use of epiphany.[24]

Most importantly, however, in seeking to reveal the function of fantasy in our everyday lives, he felt that he must rely on the absolute stability of truth, that is on an underlying realism. As he told Arthur Power:

> In realism you are down to facts on which the world is based: that sudden reality which smashes romanticism into a pulp. What makes most people's lives unhappy is some disappointed romanticism, some unrealizable or mis-conceived ideal. In fact you may say that idealism is the ruin of man, and if we lived down to fact, as primitive man had to do, we would be better off. That is what we were made for. Nature is quite unromantic. It is we who put romance into her, which is false attitude, an egotism, absurd like all egotisms. In Ulysses I tried to keep close to fact.[25]

Joyce's facts included a good deal of the political history of Ireland, as much recent criticism by Andrew Gibson and others, and the 'Cyclops' episode of *Ulysses*, show. But he presented this through the lens of neoclassical and universalist European commitments, which oddly reinforced his realism. He had noted, in a letter from Paris to Stanislaus of 15 July 1920, that the 'Odyssey is very much in the air here', referring to Anatole France, to Gabriel Fauré's *Penelope*, to Jean Giraudoux and to Apollinaire's *Les Mamelles de Tiresias* (Ellmann, *Letters*, 11.10). For Joyce the classicist, the basics never changed:

> A classical style is the syllogism of art, the only legitimate process from one world to another. Classicism is not the manner of any fixed age or of any fixed country: it is a constant state of the artistic mind. It is a temper of security and satisfaction and patience. The romantic temper, so often and so grievously misinterpreted and not more by others than by its own, is an insecure, unsat-isfied, impatient temper which sees no fit abode here for its ideals and chooses therefore to behold them under insensible figures. As a result of this choice it comes to disregard certain limitations. Its figures are blown to wild adven-tures, lacking the gravity of solid bodies, and the mind that has conceived them ends by disowning them. The classical temper on the other hand, ever mindful of limitations, chooses rather to bend upon these present things and so work on them and fashion them that the quick intelligence may go beyond them to their meaning which is still unuttered. In this method the sane and joyful spirit issues forth and achieves imperishable perfection, nature assisting with her good will and thanks. (*SH*, 85)

Despite its realist motive, the Homeric parallel echoes the invocation of myth in Eliot, Pound and W. B. Yeats by suggesting a post-Nietzschean and post-Jungian conception of history as repetition. But Joyce's neoclassicism is a high cultural matter, not a conservative political one. It has nothing to do with the desires of writers like Yeats, Pound, Eliot and Percy Wyndham Lewis for a more authoritarian political order. Of course, a socialist desire for revolution and reform has just as much potential for authoritarianism, but Joyce the anarchist never went along this route. It is wonderfully parodied in the 'new Bloomusalem' of 'Circe'.

The Homeric parallels are the signature of this high cultural neoclassicism and Pound was wrong to dismiss them as 'affaires de cuisine' more important to the chef than to the diner. On his return Odysseus kissed the soil of Ithaca; Bloom kisses his wife Molly's bottom. The four rivers of Homer's underworld meant that Joyce had to bring Paddy Dignam's funeral cortège across the Dodder to the Grand Canal, the Liffey and the Royal Canal; and had to place Dignam's house east of the Dodder, near the city's southern shore, where Thom's Dublin directory yielded a vacant house at 9 Newbridge Avenue, Sandymount. Joyce does this because he intends both continuity and ironic comparison between Greeks and Dubliners. It is crucial that tradition preserves virtues – of mourning, of respect, of consideration for the family of the dead. But there is a significant difference here, between the route beyond life to Hades, and that to the disgusting Catholic hell that frightened the young Stephen, which those in the carriage with Bloom may still fear. This sense of continuity and difference, from the opening parody of the Mass to Molly as earth mother at the end, provides a moral thread through the Daedalean labyrinth, and one which unites Europeans within a common heritage.

Joyce's work is a comedy of moral liberation. It wants sexual fulfilment, charitable love and simple kindness; it celebrates ordinariness, the family and human solidarity, and is opposed to the many rhetorics of politics, ideology and religion. He belongs in the tradition of Miguel de Cervantes, François Rabelais, Henry Fielding, Laurence Sterne, Dickens, Flaubert, Samuel Beckett and Milan Kundera.

## Note on editions

The standard edition of *Ulysses* for scholarly reference is Walter Gabler, ed. (London: Bodley Head, 1986). The 1922 text is edited with excellent annotations by Jeri Johnson as *Ulysses: The 1922 Text* (Oxford University Press, 1993). Johnson has also edited *A Portrait* and *Dubliners* (both Oxford University Press, 2000). *Poems and Exiles* is available as a Penguin Classic (1992). *Stephen Hero* is published by Jonathan Cape (1969). *Finnegans Wake* is available from Penguin Classics (2000).

### Notes

1 Anthony Burgess, *Here Comes Everybody* (London: Faber and Faber, 1969), p. 60.
2 James Joyce, *Stephen Hero* (London: Jonathan Cape, 1969), p. 60. Hereafter cited as *SH*.

3 Richard Ellmann, *The Consciousness of Joyce* (London: Faber and Faber, 1977).

4 Valery Larbaud, '*Ulysse* et James Joyce', *Nouvelle Revue Française*, 23, (January–June 1922), 388f., 4.

5 See Ronald Bush, *The Genesis of Ezra Pound's Cantos* (Princeton University Press, 1976), *passim*.

6 T. S. Eliot, '*Ulysses*, Order and Myth', *The Dial*, 70.5 (November 1923), 480–3 (p. 483).

7 Robert H. Deming, ed., *James Joyce: The Critical Heritage*, 2 vols. (London: Routledge, 1970), vol. II, p. 428.

8 Edmund Wilson, *Axel's Castle* (1931; London: Fontana, 1961), p. 221.

9 Samuel Beckett et al., *Our Exagmination Round His Factification for Incamination of Work in Progress* (1929; London: Faber and Faber, 1972), p. 79.

10 Sara Danius, *The Senses of Modernism* (Ithaca/London: Cornell University Press, 2002), pp. 147–88.

11 James Joyce, *A Portrait of the Artist as a Young Man*, ed. Jeri Johnson (Oxford/New York: Oxford University Press, 2000), p. 29. Hereafter cited as *P*.

12 Don Gifford, *Joyce Annotated*, 2nd edn (Berkeley: University of California Press, 1982), pp. 221–2.

13 See Hugh Kenner, *Ulysses* (London: Allen and Unwin, 1982), p. 61, and Karen Lawrence, *The Odyssey of Style in Ulysses* (Princeton University Press, 1981), pp. 49, 53.

14 Umbro Apollonio, ed., *Futurist Manifestos* (London: Thames and Hudson, 1973), p. 96.

15 Lawrence, *Odyssey of Style*, p. 83.

16 James Joyce, *Ulysses*, ed. Walter Gabler et al. (London: Bodley Head, 1986), XII. 244–56. Hereafter *U*. References are to episode number and line.

17 Frank Budgen, *James Joyce and the Making of 'Ulysses'* (Oxford University Press, 1972), pp. 156f.

18 Derek Attridge, *Peculiar Language: Literature as Difference from the Renaissance to James Joyce* (London: Methuen, 1988), p. 160.

19 Ricardo Quinones, *Mapping Literary Modernism* (Princeton University Press, 1985), p. 95.

20 James Joyce, *Finnegans Wake* (London: Faber and Faber, 1969), p. 485. Hereafter *FW*.

21 Richard Ellmann, *James Joyce* (Oxford University Press, 1982), p. 584.

22 Richard Ellmann, 'Introduction', in Joyce, *Ulysses*, ed. Gabler, p. xiii.

23 George Healy, ed., *The Complete Dublin Diary of Stanislaus Joyce* (Ithaca, NY: Cornell University Press, 1971), p. 54.

24 Richard Ellmann, ed., *Letters of James Joyce*, vol. II (New York: Viking, 1966), p. 48.

25 Arthur Power, *Conversations with James Joyce* (London: Lilliput Press, 1999), pp. 113–14.

*Further reading*

Beckett, Samuel, et al., *Our Exagmination Round His Factification for Incamination of Work in Progress* (1929; London: Faber and Faber, 1972)

Bishop, John, *Joyce's Book of the Dark: Finnegans Wake* (Madison: University of Wisconsin Press, 1986)

Budgen, Frank, *James Joyce and the Making of 'Ulysses'* (Oxford University Press 1972)

Cheng, Vincent J., *Joyce, Race and Empire* (Cambridge University Press 1995)

Deming, Robert H., ed., *James Joyce: The Critical Heritage*, 2 vols. (London: Routledge, 1970)

Ellmann, Richard, *The Consciousness of Joyce* (London: Faber and Faber, 1977)
  *James Joyce* (Oxford University Press, 1982)
  ed., *Letters of James Joyce*, vol. II (New York: Viking 1966)

Fairhall, James, *James Joyce and the Question of History* (Cambridge University Press 1993)

Gibson, Andrew, *Joyce's Revenge* (Oxford University Press, 2002)

Gifford, Don, *Joyce Annotated*, 2nd edn (Berkeley: University of California Press, 1982)

Kenner, Hugh, *Ulysses* (London: Allen and Unwin, 1982)

Kiberd, Declan, *Ulysses and Us: The Art of Everyday Living* (London: Faber and Faber, 2010)

Lawrence, Karen, *The Odyssey of Style in Ulysses* (Princeton University Press 1981)

Manganiello, Dominic, *Joyce's Politics* (London: Routledge & Kegan Paul, 1980)

Quinones, Ricardo, *Mapping Literary Modernism* (Princeton University Press, 1985)

Wales, Katie, *The Language of James Joyce* (London: Macmillan, 1992)

# 22

LAURA MARCUS

# Virginia Woolf (1882–1941): Re-forming the novel

In August 1908, as Virginia Woolf worked on what would become her first novel, *The Voyage Out* (1915), she wrote to her brother-in-law, the art critic Clive Bell: 'I think a great deal of my future, and settle what book I am going to write, how I shall re-form the novel and capture multitudes of things at present fugitive, enclose the whole, and shape infinite strange shapes' (*L*, 1.356). Two years later, she wrote: 'you will have to wait ... to see what has become of it ... I should say that my great change was in the way of courage, or conceit; and that I had given up adventuring after other people's forms' (*L*, 1.446). These letters show her ambition from the outset to reshape the novel as a genre and, a central tenet in her aesthetics, the desire to 'capture', in the whole and enduring work of art, the 'fugitive' and momentary. Marcel Proust became exemplary: 'The thing about Proust is his combination of the utmost sensibility with the utmost tenacity. He searches out these butterfly shades to the last grain. He is as tough as catgut & as evanescent as a butterfly's bloom' (*D*, III.7). Lily Briscoe, the artist heroine of *To the Lighthouse*, has similar aspirations for her painting: 'Beautiful and bright it should be on the surface, feathery and evanescent, one colour melting into another like the colours on a butterfly's wing; but beneath the fabric must be clamped together with bolts of iron' (*TL*, 186).

If *The Voyage Out* and *Night and Day* are female *Bildungsromane*, both novels question the very concept of 'formation'. The inner lives of these early heroines are radically at odds with the social worlds they inhabit, and the works struggle for expression. In *The Voyage Out* (whose sea voyage from London to South America reveals the influence of Joseph Conrad), Rachel – tentative and unformed – evades the difficulties of human inter-action in music and its 'impersonal expression ... from which rose a shape, a building' (*VO*, 54). In *Night and Day*, Katherine Hilbery turns away from literature (her mother is working on an interminable biography of her own father, a poet) to mathematics: 'She would not have cared to confess how infinitely she preferred the exactitude, the star-like impersonality, of figures to the confusion, agitation, and vagueness of the finest prose.' Woolf also sought to 'shape' the flow of her prose: to translate the terms of music and mathematics, as these novels envisaged them, into literary form.

'Impersonality', and its perceived connection with literary form, became central to Woolf's literary and gender aesthetics. As a tenet of modernist aesthetics, notably articulated by T. S. Eliot, it lay at the heart of modernist writers' complex and conflicted relationships to selfhood and subjectivity. For Woolf, questions of personality and impersonality seem connected to images of confinement in, or escape from, the domestic, private sphere, linked in turn to literary naturalism. 'We long', Woolf writes in 'Poetry, Fiction and the Future' (1927), discussing the future of women's writing, 'for some more impersonal relationship. We long for ideas, for dreams, for imaginations, for poetry' (*E*, IV.436). In *The Waves* (1931) such longings are manifest in the 'soliloquy in solitude' (*E*, IV.435) and in interludes devoted to the 'impersonal' elements of waves and water. In 'Women and Fiction', Woolf linked the 'turn towards the impersonal' which, she argued, women's fiction was beginning to attain, first to politics and then to poetics: 'The greater impersonality of women's lives will encourage the poetic spirit, and it is in poetry that women's fiction is still weakest ... They will look beyond the personal and political relationships to the wider questions which the poet tries to solve – of our destiny and the meaning of life' (*E*, V.34).

In *The Waves* and *To the Lighthouse*, Woolf transformed biography and autobiography through modes of impersonal narration. 'This shall be Childhood; but it must not be *my* childhood', she wrote of the opening section of *The Waves* (*D*, III.236). She would come to represent *Night and Day* as a text 'in the conventional style' (*L*, IV.231), and see her experimental stories of the late 1910s and early 1920s (especially 'The Mark on the Wall', 'Kew Gardens' and 'An Unwritten Novel') as her means of discovering a new method: 'how I could embody all my deposit of experience in a shape that fitted it' (*L*, IV.231). Some of her short fictions of this period experiment with digressive narrative voices and explore complexities of consciousness and subjectivity, including the possibility, or impossibility, of entry into other minds. Others, including the prose poem 'Blue and Green' and the short story 'Solid Objects', are in dialogue with theories of visual representation, and in particular of the 'aesthetic emotion' proposed by Clive Bell and the artist and art theorist Roger Fry: these writings became her arena for exploring the visual dimensions of prose, as well as connections between word and (mental) image.

In 'Solid Objects' the central protagonist collects pieces of glass and stone to the exclusion of all other occupations and ambitions: 'Looked at again and again half consciously by a mind thinking of something else, any object mixes itself so profoundly with the stuff of thought that it loses its actual form and recomposes itself a little differently in an ideal shape which haunts the brain when we least expect it' (*HH*, 98). Fry used the phrase 'solid objects' throughout 'An Essay in Aesthetics' and 'The Artist's Vision', an essay exploring the relationship between forms and colours as 'a whole field of vision'. Woolf used the phrase not only as a title, but as a definition of the short story as such. Reviewing Anton Chekhov stories in 1919, she claimed British readers were becoming attuned to Russian literature and 'alive to the fact that inconclusive stories are legitimate: ... though they leave us feeling melancholy and perhaps uncertain, yet somehow or other they provide a resting point for the mind – a solid object casting its shade of reflection and speculation' (*CE*, III.84). This suggests that, for Woolf, short fiction had qualities of the 'object' for the visual artist. The review shows her profound response to nineteenth-century Russian literature (especially Fyodor Dostoevsky, Leo Tolstoy, Ivan Turgenev and Chekhov), along with her appreciation of 'inconclusive stories'. Her novels often had 'open' endings, including the use of ellipses or question marks.

Woolf's diary records her plans for *Jacob's Room*, and how her short fiction had opened up a new way of writing: 'conceive mark on the wall, [K]ew [G]ardens, & unwritten novel taking hands and dancing in unity'. *Jacob's Room* was to be a book with 'no scaffolding; scarcely a brick to be seen' (*D*, II.13–14). The comment denotes not only her rejection of linear narrative and 'conventional' chapter divisions, which she had deployed in *Night and Day*, but her habitual critique (undoubtedly mixed with snobbery) of the naturalism of the 'Edwardian' novelists, exemplified by the 'materialists' H. G. Wells, Arnold Bennett and John Galsworthy. Bennett's 'house of fiction', in Henry James's phrase, was, Woolf implied, deeply suburban, and 'so well constructed and solid in its craftsmanship that it is difficult for the most exacting of critics to see through what chink or crevice decay can creep in ... And yet – if life should refuse to live there?' ('Modern Fiction', *E*, IV.158). The 'Time Passes' section of *To the Lighthouse* depicts an empty, crumbling house as Woolf evacuates her fictional world of characters and charts the processes of decay through chinks and crevices opened up by time and the elements. The 'eyeless' world, as she described it, of this section pushes 'impersonality' to the extreme.

An empty room is at the heart of *Jacob's Room*: 'Listless is the air in an empty room, just swelling the curtain; the flowers in the jar shift. One fibre in the wicker armchair creaks, though no one sits there.' As in *To the Lighthouse*, Woolf experimented with the question of who thinks and speaks the narrative in a third-person fiction. *Jacob's Room*, like *Orlando*, offers glimpses of a narrator figure who follows in the footsteps of his/her endlessly elusive subject. It has been called a *Bildungsroman*, yet (extending rather than fully departing from Woolf's first two novels) it also undoes the concept of 'formation'. The novel moves through the stages of Jacob's life in school, Cambridge, London and the Italy and Greece of 'the grand tour', but the loops and fragmentations of the narrative, with abrupt shifts in narrative perspective, make Jacob (who will die in World War I) a fugitive figure. Such 'characterisation' reflects Woolf's critique, at its height at the time of the novel's composition, of the character creations of 'the Edwardians', who, she argues, rendered their human figures as substantial and, paradoxically, as lifeless in their attempts at lifelikeness, as the material worlds of their novels.

On reading *Jacob's Room*, Woolf's friend, Lytton Strachey, the biographer and historian, wrote that the novel was 'more like poetry ... than anything else, and as such I prophecy immortal. The technique of the narrative is astonishing – how you manage to leave out everything that's dreary, and yet retain enough string for your pearls I can hardly understand'.[1] Woolf wrote back of 'the effort of breaking with complete representation ... Next time I mean to stick closer to facts' (*L*, 11.569). She expanded on this thought while working on her next novel:

> Mrs Dalloway has branched into a book; & I adumbrate here a study of insanity & suicide: the world seen by the sane & the insane side by side – something like that. Septimus Smith? – is that a good name? – & to be more close to the fact than Jacob: but I think Jacob was a necessary step, for me, in working free. (*D*, 11.207)

She also wrote of her 'tunnelling process, by which I tell my past in instalments as I need it. How I dig out beautiful caves behind my characters ... The idea is that the caves should connect and each comes to daylight at the present moment' (*D*, 11.272). The one-day structure of the novel (the day of Clarissa Dalloway's party) and its representation of the modern city make *Mrs Dalloway* a companion to James Joyce's *Ulysses*, sections of which Woolf had read in manuscript while composing her text. Discussing both texts as *Zeitromane* (time novels) in *Time and Narrative*, Paul Ricoeur noted *Mrs Dalloway*'s 'entanglement of the narrated present with the remembered past [which] confers a psychological depth on the characters without, however, giving them a stable identity, so discordant are the glimpses the characters have of one another and of themselves'.[2] Ricoeur noted 'the reverberation ... of one solitary experience in another solitary experience', a reverberation which connects, though they never meet, Clarissa Dalloway, the fifty-year-old hostess, and Septimus Smith, who carries with him the burden of his experience in the trenches, and who will kill himself before the day is out. *Mrs Dalloway* celebrates the energies of the city – 'I love London for writing it', Woolf wrote – but it also delineates a post-war world marked, like *Jacob's Room*, by mourning and memorialisation. Women mourners haunt the city in the imaginings of the novel's protagonists: 'Such are the visions … the figure of the mother whose sons have been killed in the battles of the world' (*MD*, 65). The ages of women are threaded through the text and, as in many of her feminist essays, which link the future of women and the future of fiction, Woolf glimpses, especially through the figure of the Dalloways' daughter, Elizabeth, a world of women's freedom.

In *To the Lighthouse* (1927), her most 'autobiographical' novel, Woolf pursued her experiment with the relations of time, consciousness and narrative. The 'shape' of the novel was to be 'two blocks joined by a corridor':[3] the novel's temporality comprises two days separated by the 'Time Passes' section, whose represented duration is ten years and, simultaneously, one night in the empty house, vacated after the death of the mother, Mrs Ramsay, during which time war breaks out and the world tosses and turns in the nightmare of history. The 'corridor' is also a time tunnel through which words and images travel from past to present. In the final section, 'The Lighthouse', the painter Lily Briscoe completes the picture of Mrs Ramsay on which she works in the first section, 'The Window', while the younger Ramsay children, Cam and James, make the trip to the lighthouse with their father, vetoed by him at the novel's opening. 'The Lighthouse' moves back and forth between these scenes – Lily painting on the shore and the boat journey to the lighthouse island – in ways surely influenced by the cinema, with its development of 'parallel editing' to represent simultaneity. Woolf had written an illuminating essay 'The Cinema' (1926) as she worked on the 'Time Passes' section.

In 'The Window', Woolf represented the ways in which her protagonists appear to each other and to themselves through the use of multiple consciousnesses, achieved through 'indirect speech' and 'indirect interior monologue', as well as shifts between characters as subjects and objects of perception. In his seminal work on European narrative representation, Erich Auerbach examined 'the brown stocking' episode that opens *To the Lighthouse*. He focused on the disappearance of 'the writer as narrator of objective facts'; the construction of character 'as it is reflected in and as it affects various figures in the novel'; the treatment of exterior and interior time; and the 'attempt to render the flow and the play of consciousness adrift in the current of changing impressions'.[4] The modern writer submits, Auerbach wrote, 'to the random contingency of real phenomena'. In Woolf,

Joyce and Proust, he argued, a shift of emphasis occurs expressing 'something we might call a transfer of confidence':

> The great exterior turning points and blows of fate are granted less importance; they are credited with less power of yielding decisive information concerning the subject; on the other hand there is confidence that in any random fragment plucked from the course of a life at any time the totality of its fate is contained and can be portrayed ... And in the process something new and elemental appeared: nothing less than the wealth of reality and depth of life in every moment to which we surrender ourselves without prejudice. (Auerbach, *Mimesis*, p. 547)

Auerbach's comments extend to Woolf's broader literary preoccupations and ambitions: most significantly, her fascination with the ephemeral, the contingent, and 'the moment'. He linked the focus on the momentary in modern fiction with the 'transfer of confidence', the shift from 'exterior turning points' to the 'random fragment'. His account of *To the Lighthouse* recalls Friedrich Nietzsche's 'transvaluation of values'. In 'Time Passes', birth, marriage and death are placed in parenthesis, while the body of the narrative describes the material processes occurring in the empty and unobserved house.

Although these aspects of Woolf's work were central to her own accounts of modern fiction, she appears not always fully persuaded by the altered emphases of the modern novelist. She criticised, in her essay 'Modern Fiction' (1925), the Edwardian 'materialists' who, writing of 'unimportant things', 'spend immense skill and immense industry making the trivial and the transitory appear the true and the enduring'. She contrasted 'the Edwardians' with 'the moderns', writing of Joyce in terms which seem to celebrate 'the trivial and the transitory':

> Let us record the atoms as they fall upon the mind in the order in which they fall, let us trace the pattern, however disconnected and incoherent in appearance, which each sight or incident scores upon the consciousness. Let us not take it for granted that life exists more fully in what is commonly thought big than in what is commonly thought small. (*CE*, iv.161)

Yet Joyce's emphasis on 'indecency', she suggested, also creates a world of imbalanced values, apparent if the reader were 'to open *Tristram Shandy* or even *Pendennis* and be by them convinced that there are not only other aspects of life, but more important ones into the bargain' (*E*, iv.162). It is Chekhov whom Woolf named in 'Modern Fiction' as the modern writer in whom 'the accent falls a little differently' and in whom she found the greatest significance:

> The emphasis [in his short story 'Gusev'] is laid upon such unexpected places that at first it seems as if there were no emphasis at all and then, as the eyes

accustom themselves to twilight and discern the shapes of things in a room we see how complete the story is, how profound, and how truly in obedience to his vision Tchekov has chosen this, that, and the other, and placed them together to compose something new. (*E*, IV.162–3)

Elsewhere Woolf defined the 'transfer' or 'reversal' as a 'difference in value' with an explicitly gendered dimension. In *A Room of One's Own*, she argued that:

> It is obvious that the values of women differ very often from the values which have been made by the other sex; naturally, this is so. Yet it is the masculine values that prevail. Speaking crudely, football and sport are 'important'; the worship of fashion, the buying of clothes 'trivial'. And these values are inevitably transferred from life to fiction. This is an important book, the critic assumes, because it deals with war. This is an insignificant book because it deals with the feelings of women in a drawing-room. A scene in a battle-field is more important than a scene in a shop – everywhere and much more subtly the difference of value persists. (*ROO*, 67)

Woolf envisaged a woman's novel recording the 'infinitely obscure lives' of women and the energies arising from 'the pressure of dumbness, the accumulation of unrecorded life', including those of 'drifting girls whose faces, like waves in sun and cloud, signal the coming of men and women and the flickering lights of shop windows'. You must say, she enjoined her imagined woman novelist, 'what is your relation to the ever-changing and turning world of gloves and shoes and stuffs swaying up and down among the faint scents that come through chemists' bottles down arcades of dress material over a floor of pseudo-marble' (*ROO*, 81–2). This 'scene in a shop' echoes Eliot's 'A Game of Chess' in *The Waste Land* (hand-printed by the Woolfs' Hogarth Press in 1923). Woolf's image of 'two in a taxi' (a girl and a young man) in *A Room of One's Own*, which introduces her discussion of creative 'androgyny', further recalls (though without Eliot's contempt for these 'ordinary lives') the androgynous or hermaphroditic figure of Eliot's poem observing a female typist and a clerk: 'when the human engine waits | Like a taxi throbbing waiting, | I Tiresias, though blind, throbbing between two lives, | Old man with wrinkled female breasts'. Woolf's allegory of the androgynous mind of the artist, 'manly-womanly' or 'womanly-manly', is couched in both speculative and curiously sexualised terms – 'Some marriage of opposites has to be consummated' – as if there were indeed no escape from the 'sex-consciousness' of the age, which she suggests is the very cause of the distorted nature of much modern literature, pushed as it is to the poles of a hyper-masculinity or of a femininity shaped (and deformed) by what it must react to and against.

*A Room of One's Own* brings together a tradition of women's writing – 'We think back through our mothers if we are women,' Woolf asserted – with a much more provisional exploration of 'books by the living' (*ROO*, 72). 'Thinking back' through the literary past is valuable for Woolf if it enables us, as she says in 'How it Strikes a Contemporary' (1923), to think forward, to 'see the past in relation to the future' (*E*, III.359). 'Is there no guidance nowadays', she asked in this essay, 'for a reader who yields to none in reverence for the dead, but is tormented by the suspicion that reverence for the dead is vitally connected with understanding of the living?' (*E*, III.354). In 'Poetry, Fiction and the Future' (1927), she envisaged a figure scanning the horizon of the future. The modern age and the 'modern mind' are characterised by contradiction and conflict, 'contrast and collision': 'Beauty is part ugliness; amusement part disgust; pleasure part pain. Emotions which used to enter the mind whole are now broken up on the threshold.' Prose rather than poetry can best express such complexities. Yet fiction must take on some of 'the attributes of poetry', which it can do once freed 'from the beast of burden work which so many novelists necessarily lay upon it of carrying loads of detail, bushels of fact'. The novel of the future

> will give the relations of man to Nature, to fate; his imagination, his dreams. But it will also give the sneer, the contrast, the question, the closeness and complexity of life. It will take the mould of that queer conglomeration of incongruous things – the modern mind. Therefore it will clasp to its breast the precious prerogatives of the democratic art of prose; its freedom, its fearlessness, its flexibility. (*E*, IV.436)

Novel criticism was a new and expanding field, and Woolf's reviewing in the late 1910s and 1920s encompassed Clayton Hamilton's *Materials and Methods of Fiction* and the study of the novel which she found most persuasive, Percy Lubbock's influential *The Craft of Fiction* (1921). Lubbock, much influenced by Henry James, argued the importance of 'form, design, composition'.[5] By distancing ourselves from the imaginative worlds of novels, Lubbock suggests, we can see them whole. The necessary duration of the reading process obscures the aesthetic unity of the novel as a whole. Moreover, we create our own visions from the 'series of glimpses and anecdotes' in the novel, those elements, such as 'an effective scene or a brilliant character' which strike us most powerfully as we read. 'These things', Lubbock writes,

> take shape in the mind of the reader; they are re-created and set up where the mind's eye can rest on them. They become works of art, no doubt, in their way, but they are not the book which the author offers us ... So far from

losing ourselves in the world of the novel, we must hold it away from us, see it in all its detachment, and use the whole of it to make the image we seek, the book itself. (Lubbock, *The Craft of Fiction*, p. 6)

In good Jamesian fashion, Lubbock substituted for the constructions of the reader's mind, and the outpourings of the author's mind, the concept of 'the story that is centred in somebody's consciousness, passed through a fashioned and constituted mind' (*ibid.*, p. 271).

Woolf questioned Lubbock's ideal of reading as a realisation of form, quoting his words: 'But with the book in the condition of a defined shape, firm of outline, its form shows for what it is indeed – not an attribute, one of many and possibly not the most important, but the book itself, as the form of the statue is the statue itself' (*ibid.*, p. 24). She disputed his idea of 'form' as appropriate to the visual arts but creating confusion in discussion of literature. Lubbock had closely analysed the techniques of Gustave Flaubert's *Madame Bovary*, exploring questions of represented consciousness, the use of irony and readerly identification with character. Woolf used Flaubert's *Un cœur simple* to construct a different model of 'attention' which, as we read the story, 'flickers this way and that' as 'the impressions accumulate'. It is 'moments of understanding', responses to particular words and sentences, which produce our ultimate relationship to the text: 'A sudden intensity of phrase, something which for good reasons or for bad, we feel to be emphatic startles us into a flash of understanding. We see now why the story was written':

> Therefore the 'book itself' is not form which you see, but emotion which you feel, and the more intense the writer's feeling the more exact without slip or chink its expression in words. And whenever Mr Lubbock talks of form it is as if something were interposed between us and the book as we know it. We feel the presence of an alien substance which requires to be visualized imposing itself upon emotions which we feel naturally, and name simply, and range in final order by feeling their right relations to each other. Thus we have reached our conception of *Un Cœur Simple* by working from the emotions outwards, and, the reading over, there is nothing to be seen; there is everything to be felt. (*CE*, II.126)

The terms 'feeling' and 'emotion' were, Woolf admitted, imprecise, and she was prepared to ask whether there was 'something beyond emotion, something which though it is inspired by emotion, tranquilizes it, orders it, composes it? – that which Mr Lubbock calls form, which, for simplicity's sake, we will call art?' (*CE*, II.127). This she saw as most fully realised in the process of rereading a novel. Despite Woolf's suggestion that aesthetic criteria drawn from the visual arts could not be readily applied to the verbal, her account of 'form' and 'emotion', and their interrelations, echoes Fry's and Bell's writings on art, in particular, Bell's theory of 'significant form'; the view that art produces 'aesthetic emotion' aroused by 'significant form', in its turn an expression of the artist's experience. Although she did not fully endorse Fry's and Bell's formalisms, finding their neo-Kantian models too remote from practical life, the paradox in Fry's definition of the artist's responses to 'any turn of the kaleidoscope of nature' as a 'detached and impassioned vision' was productive for Woolf. His account of the artistic process, how 'the particular field of vision, the (aesthetically) chaotic and accidental conjunction of forms and colours begins to crystallise into a harmony', setting up a 'rhythm' 'that obsesses the artist and crystallises his vision', underlies Lily Briscoe's art in *To the Lighthouse*:[6]

> And so pausing and so flickering, she attained a dancing rhythmical move-ment, as if the pauses were one part of the rhythm and the strokes another, and all were related; and so, lightly and swiftly pausing, striking, she scored her canvas with brown running nervous lines which had no sooner settled there than they enclosed (she felt it looming out at her) a space ... Here she was again, she thought, stepping back to look at it, drawn out of gossip, out of living, out of community with people into the presence of this formidable ancient enemy of hers – this other thing, this truth, this reality, which suddenly laid hands on her, emerged stark at the back of appearances and commanded her attention. (*TL*, 172–3)

Woolf's essays on fiction similarly explored the contradictory imperatives facing the writer. A necessary immersion in 'life' is combined with an equally essential withdrawal into solitude as 'life' becomes transmuted into 'art'. As she writes in 'Life and the Novelist', the writer's 'body is hardened into and fashioned into permanence by processes which, if they elude the critic, hold for him so profound a fascination' (*E*, IV.405).

Woolf tended to resist models of generic 'development': 'We do not come to write better; all that we can be said to do is to keep moving, now a little in this direction, now in that, but with a circular tendency should the whole course of the track be viewed from a sufficiently lofty pinnacle. It need scarcely be said that we make no claim to stand, even momentarily, upon that vantage ground' (*E*, IV.157). In a review essay on E. M. Forster's *Aspects of the Novel* (1927), she noted, with echoes of Eliot's 'Tradition and the Individual Talent', Forster's treatment of writers from different times as contemporaries: 'looking down on them, not from any great height, but, as he says, over their shoulders, he makes out, as he passes, that certain shapes and ideas tend to recur in their minds whatever their period' (*E*, IV.458). Like the passage from *To the Lighthouse*, this suggests

Woolf's engagement with Platonic thought, especially the concept of ideal 'forms' underlying surface 'appearances'.

When Woolf came to write her own study of the novel, 'Phases of Fiction', she also chose not to follow the linear path of 'development'. With examples from beyond English fiction, including Walter Scott, Robert Louis Stevenson (Scotland), Herman Melville, James (America), Tolstoy, Dostoevsky (Russia), Flaubert, Guy de Maupassant and Proust (France), Woolf divided the field into a number of categories – 'The Truth-tellers', 'The Romantics', 'The Character-mongers and Comedians', 'The Psychologists', 'The Satirists and Fantastics', 'The Poets' – traversing historical periods. Woolf envisaged a reader different from the critic or scholar. In *The Common Reader* (1925), she defined this as one 'guided by an instinct to create for himself, out of whatever odds and ends he can come by, some kind of whole – a portrait of a man, a sketch of an age, a theory of the art of writing' (*E*, IV.19) – and this image of the *bricoleur*, or *bricoleuse*, was linked to her writerly and readerly self-image as a literary 'outsider'.

'Phases of Fiction' was an

> attempt to record the impressions made upon the mind by reading a certain number of novels in succession ... It was allowed to read what it liked. It was not, that is to say, asked to read historically, nor was it asked to read critically ... It went its way, therefore, independent of time and reputation ... making itself a dwelling-place in accordance with its own appetites. (*E*, V.40–1)

The novel, 'the youngest and most vigorous of the arts', is understood as a genre in process, whose nature cannot be fixed: 'Prose perhaps is the instrument best fitted to the complexity and difficulty of modern life. And prose – we have to repeat it – is still so youthful that we scarcely know what powers it may not hold concealed within it.' The terms echo those which Woolf used, time and again, for the 'future' of women. 'What is a woman?' Woolf wrote in 'Professions for Women': 'I assure you, I do not know. I do not believe that you know. I do not believe that anybody can know until she has expressed herself in all the arts and professions open to human skill' (*CE*, II.286). The future of fiction (a genre habitually allegorised by Woolf as female) is intimately bound up for her with the future of women.

At the close of 'Modern Fiction', as elsewhere, Woolf celebrated the freedom and all-inclusiveness of the novel: 'everything is the proper stuff of fiction, every feeling, every thought ... no perception comes amiss.' Yet in her essay 'The Art of Fiction', pursuing the female personification of the novel, she criticised Forster for being too lax and vague about the rules of the genre. If the same demands were made of the English novel as of the French and Russian, then there would be 'an art of fiction' in England:

For possibly, if fiction is, as we suggest, in difficulties, it may be because nobody grasps her firmly and defines her severely. She has had no rules drawn up for her, very little thinking done on her behalf. And though rules may be wrong and must be broken, they have this advantage – they confer dignity and order upon their subject; they admit her to a place in civilized society; they prove that she is worthy of consideration. (*E*, IV.600)

Woolf's letters and diary entries between 1925 and 1928 reveal frustration in the composition of 'Phases of Fiction'. She wrote to Vita Sackville-West in October 1927:

Yesterday morning I was in despair: You know that bloody book which Dadie and Leonard extort, drop by drop from my breast? Fiction, or some title to that effect. I couldn't screw a word from me; and at last dropped my head in my hands: dipped my pen in the ink, and wrote these words, as if automatically, on a clean sheet: Orlando: A Biography. No sooner had I done this than my body was flooded with rapture and my brain with ideas. I wrote rapidly till 12. Then I did an hour to Romance. So every morning I am going to write fiction (my own fiction) till 12; and Romance till 1. But listen; suppose Orlando turns out to be Vita; and its all about you and the lusts of your flesh and the lure of your mind ... it sprung upon me how I could revolutionise biography in a night: and so if agreeable to you I would like to toss this up in the air and see what happens. (*L*, III.428–9)

Although Woolf contrasts the instantaneous conception of the fiction with the sterile planning of the critical work, they are partly continuous. *Orlando* is a literary history of a kind, and indeed a more linear one than 'Phases of Fiction', though historicism (in this instance the division of the historical continuum into discrete periods bounded by centuries) is itself one of the targets of her satire. It charts both changes and continuities in literature and in life as it moves through the 'styles' of the Elizabethans and Jacobeans, the Enlightenment, the Romantics and the Victorians, into the 'Present Day'. Some of the authors discussed in 'Phases of Fiction' – Daniel Defoe, Laurence Sterne, Emily Brontë – are central to *Orlando*, either in their own parodic modes or as objects of parody. Woolf wrote that, after completing *To the Lighthouse*, she felt drawn to write a different kind of fiction, 'an escapade after these serious poetic experimental books whose form is so closely considered' (*D*, III.13). She envisaged *Orlando* as 'a Defoe narrative ... Everything is to be tumbled in pall mall ... Satire is to be the main note – satire & wildness' (*D*, III.131). *Tristram Shandy* was also a powerful influence. As she commented in 'Phases of Fiction': 'So, finally, we get a book in which all the usual conventions are subsumed and yet no ruin or catastrophe comes to pass; the whole subsists complete by itself' (*E*, V.75).

Lytton Strachey had suggested, after she had completed *Mrs Dalloway*, that she write a Shandean narrative, and this emerges in Woolf's play with silences, digressions and parentheses which radically disrupt the narrative. Through all his/her other vocations – courtier, ambassador, society lady – Orlando (who lives through some four hundred years of history, and turns from man to woman in the eighteenth century) – remains a writer: life and literature are inextricably bound together.

*Orlando* appeared in October 1928, the month of Woolf's lectures on women and fiction, at Girton College Cambridge, which became *A Room of One's Own* (1929). Whereas 'Phases of Fiction' (*The Bookman*, April, May, June 1929) discussed women writers (including George Eliot and Jane Austen) with little explicit discussion of the vicissitudes of gender, *A Room of One's Own* places this issue at the heart of the argument, delineating a lineage of women's writing which would become of profound significance in the construction of feminist literary history in the later twentieth century. So, too, has her insistence that the creation of literature is not separable from material and social circumstances, but is powerfully shaped by them.

Towards the close, Woolf wrote of a fundamental 'reality' which might be 'something very erratic, very undependable – now to be found in a dusty road, now in a scrap of newspaper in the street, now in a daffodil in the sun ... whatever it touches, it fixes and makes permanent' (*ROO*, 99). This assertion (with its suggestion of photographic process) is a further example of the relationship Woolf habitually posited between the fleeting and the enduring. It echoes Charles Baudelaire's definition of modern painting (and modernity more broadly) as 'the ephemeral, the fugitive, the contingent, the half of art whose other half is the eternal and the immutable'.[7] It is the writer's fate or fortune, Woolf suggests, to 'live more than other people in the presence of this reality ... and communicate it to the rest of us. So at least I infer from reading *Lear* or *Emma* or *La Recherche du Temps Perdu*' (*ROO*, 99). She wrote of the intensity of this reality (always in contrast to literary 'realism') and of 'the moment' at the end of 1928 as she began to think about the work that would become *The Waves* (1931):

> The idea has come to me that what I want now to do is to saturate every atom. I mean to eliminate all waste, deadness, superfluity: to give the moment whole; whatever it includes. Say that the moment is a combination of thought; sensation; the voice of the sea. Waste, deadness, come from the inclusion of things that don't belong to the moment; this appalling narrative business of the realist: getting on from lunch to dinner: it is false, unreal, merely conventional. Why admit anything to literature that is not poetry – by which I mean saturated? Is that not my grudge against novel[ists]s – that they select nothing?

The poets succeed by simplifying: practically everything is left out. I want to put practically everything in; yet to saturate. (*D*, III.209–10)

Woolf conceived *The Waves* as 'prose yet poetry' (Wordsworth's *The Prelude*, which Woolf reread while writing the novel, was an important influence) and as 'a novel & a play'. The six selves of the narrative are represented by 'dramatic soliloquies' interspersed with 'poetic interludes', opening each section, which describe the diurnal passage of the sun across the sky and the rhythm of the waves. Woolf told the composer Ethel Smyth she was writing the novel 'to a rhythm and not to a plot' (*L*, IV.204), indicating the significance of musical composition to the piece. The association of 'rhythm' in prose with the natural rhythms of time and tide ('waxing and waning') indicates a different way of thinking about 'shape' and 'form' in fiction (frequently perceived, as we have seen, by Henry James and other contemporary 'theorists' of the novel in architectural terms).

It is further connected to the significance of the 1927 solar eclipse for Woolf: she wrote an essay on this event, 'The Sun and the Fish', and incorporated the spectacle into *The Waves*, granting her protagonist Bernard (the chronicler of the lives of the six friends) the perception of a world (and a selfhood) which dies and is reborn. On the final page Bernard perceives that 'Dawn is some sort of whitening of the sky; some sort of renewal' (*W*, 228). The image of renewal also closed her penultimate novel *The Years*. Its final sentence reads: 'The sun had risen, and the sky above the houses wore an air of extraordinary beauty, simplicity and peace' (*Y*, 318). This 'impersonal' vision of the sky above the city echoes the opening passages of the novel's sections, as the narrative follows the Pargiter family from 1880 through to the 'present day': these describe the weather and the sky before moving into the world of the human actors. 'The sun was rising' are the opening words of the 1911 section of the novel: 'Slowly the world emerged from darkness' (*Y*, 141). These passages are connected to the 'interludes' in *The Waves*: Woolf saw them as 'spaces of silence and poetry and contrast' (*D*, IV.332) into which she contracted the factual-historical 'essays' (describing, in particular, the lives of women across the generations) which had been part of the original plan for the novel, and which became central to her feminist pamphlet *Three Guineas* (1938). The 'interludes' in *The Years* also reveal, as Roberta Rubenstein has suggested, the influence of Turgenev on Woolf in the 1930s. In her 'reading notes' on Turgenev, Woolf observed the ways in which 'the landscape is made part of the scene' in *On the Eve*: commenting on *A Nest of Gentlefolk*, she wrote of Turgenev's strengths in 'the country scenes where the story sings its song where nature & character merge'.[8]

*The Years* also extended Woolf's preoccupation with representations of time and duration in fiction, bringing together the diurnal structure of a number of her novels (*Mrs Dalloway, To the Lighthouse, Between the Acts*) with the extended historical time span which *Orlando* had taken to its limit. Woolf planned the temporality of *The Years* as 'a curious uneven time sequence – a series of great balloons, linked by straight narrow passages of narrative' (*D*, IV.142). It covers half a century in an irregular movement (the sections, most of which cover the time of a day or evening, are titled 1880, 1891, 1908, 1910, 1911, 1913, 1914, 1917, 1918, Present Day). This sequencing breaks up the smooth flow of passing time and generation and (written during the growing threat of a second World War) produces a temporal clustering around the years of World War I.

The novel's time sequence explores patterns and repetitions across the years, and poses the question, like *To the Lighthouse*, of what it is of us that endures. The issue had become urgent for her as she wrote her final, posthumously published novel *Between the Acts*, set on a June day a few months before the declaration of war, and which returns to the primeval and evolutionary images of Woolf's first novel, *The Voyage Out*, and to the historical pageantry of *Orlando*. As in *The Waves*, originally conceived as a play poem, theatre is central to *Between the Acts*. In dramatising a village pageant of English literature from the Elizabethans to the present day, its mode of representation is piecemeal and fragmentary yet reaches towards the forms of literary and historical continuity which Woolf was exploring in her final, unpublished essays: 'Only when we put two and two together, two pencil strokes, two written words, two bricks do we overcome dissolution and set up some stake against oblivion.'[9]

## Note on editions

Scholarly editions of the novels are available from Blackwell's Shakespeare Head Press and Cambridge University Press. Reliable editions of the major novels are also available in Penguin and other publishers, in particular Oxford University Press. For further information see 'Abbreviations' below.

### Abbreviations

CE    *Collected Essays of Virginia Woolf*, 4 vols. (London: Hogarth Press, 1966–7)
D     *The Diary of Virginia Woolf*, ed. Anne Oliver Bell with Andrew Macneillie, 5 vols. (London: Hogarth Press, 1977–84)
E     *The Essays of Virginia Woolf*, 6 vols. (London: Hogarth Press, 1986), vols. I–IV, ed. Andrew, Macneillie (1986–94); vols. V–VI, ed. Stuart Clarke, 2009–11

HH      *A Haunted House: The Complete Shorter Fiction*, ed. Susan Dick (London: Vintage, 2003)

L        *The Letters of Virginia Woolf*, ed. Nigel Nicolson and Joanne Trautmann, 6 vols. (London: Chatto and Windus, 1975–80)

MD      *Mrs Dalloway* (Harmondsworth: Penguin, 1976)

ND      *Night and Day* (Harmondsworth: Penguin, 1969)

ROO     *A Room of One's Own* (Harmondsworth: Penguin 1993)

TL      *To the Lighthouse* (Harmondsworth: Penguin, 1992)

VO      *The Voyage Out* (Harmondsworth: Penguin, 1970)

W       *The Waves* (Harmondsworth: Penguin, 1992)

Y        *The Years* (Harmondsworth: Penguin, 1968)

## Notes

1 *Letters of Lytton Strachey*, ed. Paul Levy assisted by Penelope Marcus (London: Viking 2005) p. 523.

2 Paul Ricoeur, *Time and Narrative*, trans. K. McLaughlin and D. Pellauer (University of Chicago Press, 1984), vol II, p. 104.

3 *To the Lighthouse; The Original Holograph Draft*, transcribed and ed. Susan Dick (London: Hogarth Press, 1983), A48.

4 Erich Auerbach, *Mimesis: The Representation of Reality in Western Literature* (1946), trans. William R. Trask (Princeton University Press, 1953), pp. 534–5.

5 Percy Lubbock, *The Craft of Fiction* (1921; London: Jonathon Cape, 1965), p. 10.

6 Roger Fry, *Vision and Design* (1920; London: Pelican, 1937), p. 49.

7 Charles Baudelaire, *The Painter of Modern Life and Other Essays*, transcribed and ed. Jonathan Mayne (London: Phaidon, 1964), p. 13.

8 Roberta Rubenstein, *Virginia Woolf and the Russian Point of View* (Basingstoke: Palgrave Macmillan, 2009), p. 214.

9 '"Anon" and "The Reader": Virginia Woolf's Last Essays', ed. Brenda Silver, *Twentieth-Century Literature*, 25 (1979), 356–441.

## Further reading

Beer, Gillian, *Virginia Woolf: The Common Ground* (Edinburgh University Press, 1996)

Bowlby, Rachel, *Feminist Destinations and Further Writings on Virginia Woolf* (Edinburgh University Press, 1997)

Briggs, Julia, ed., *Virginia Woolf: Introductions to the Major Works* (London: Virago, 1984)

Lee, Hermione, *Virginia Woolf* (London: Chatto and Windus, 1996)

Marcus, Laura, *Virginia Woolf: Writers and Their Work*, 2nd edn (Tavistock: Northcote House, 2004)

Naremore, James, *The World Without a Self: Virginia Woolf and the Novel* (New Haven, CT: Yale University Press, 1973)

Snaith, Anna, *Virginia Woolf: Public and Private Negotiations* (London: Palgrave, 2000)

Zwerdling, Alex, *Virginia Woolf and the Real World* (Berkeley/Los Angeles: University of California Press, 1986)

# 23

LESLIE HILL

# Samuel Beckett (1906–1989): Language, narrative, authority

Late in 1950, in a Paris café opposite the premises of a recently relaunched, once clandestine publishing house in the rue Bernard-Palissy, a forty-four-year-old expatriate Irishman, the author of a modest body of work published in English more than a decade earlier, sat together with his partner considering the typescript of the three novels he had completed in his adoptive French during the previous two-and-a-half years. This was not the first time that the pair had sought a publisher. There had been, it seems, dozens of fruitless attempts already. Spirits were accordingly at a low ebb, and money was tight. As the two discussed the dwindling prospects of success, the writer is said to have turned to his companion, partly in jest but more likely in desperation, to deliver the following glum verdict: 'If they publish it this time, I'll treat you to a pack of cigarettes. But promise me you won't try again.'[1]

Some nineteen years later, in the autumn of 1969, the scene was very different. To the same protagonists, Samuel Beckett and Suzanne Deschevaux-Dumesnil, now married, and on holiday in Tunisia at the time, came a telegram bearing unexpected, even perturbing news: Beckett had just been awarded the 1969 Nobel Prize for Literature. The change in fortune could not have been more dramatic. At the award ceremony later that year, the poet, critic and dramatist Karl Ragnar Gierow explained the Swedish Academy's decision. Beckett's work of the late 1940s, he argued, notably the trilogy of novels written in French that had proved so hard to place only twenty years before (*Molloy*, *Malone meurt* and *L'Innommable*), together with the play *En attendant Godot*, first performed amid controversy in 1953, was grounded in an experience of the Second World War. 'But these works', the critic went on, 'are not about the war itself ... but about what happened afterwards, when peace came and the curtain was rent from the unholiest of unholies to reveal the terrifying spectacle of the lengths to which man can go in inhuman degradation – whether ordered or driven by himself – and how much of such degradation man can survive.' 'In this sense', the citation concluded:

the degradation of humanity is a recurrent theme in Beckett's writing and to this extent, his philosophy, simply accentuated by elements of the grotesque and of tragic farce, can be described as a negativism that cannot desist from descending to the depths. To the depths it must go because it is only there that pessimistic thought and poetry can work their miracles. What does one get when a negative is printed? A positive, a clarification, with black proving to be the light of day, the parts in deepest shade those which reflect the light source. Its name is fellow-feeling, charity.[2]

Beckett's writing, then, according to the Nobel Prize committee, was testimony to the ravages of a historical epoch, to an age of destruction, nihilism and meaninglessness. But if Beckett's work was distinguished by its unrelenting pessimism, by what the writer and philosopher Georges Bataille, in an early review of *Molloy*, called its '*absence* of humanity',[3] it was only in so far as it was nevertheless endowed, as far as the Academy was concerned, with cathartic or redemptive powers. In other words, the bleakness of Beckett's portrayal of human indigence, his iconoclastic rejection of inherited literary forms, the linguistic scepticism everywhere apparent in his writing, rather than undermining literature's authority, were a kind of covert endorsement of its humanising mission. In time, this interpretation of Beckett would appear overly sentimental and uncomfortably nostalgic. But in the late 1960s, it reflected the critical consensus that by then had grown up around Beckett's work. As so often in literary history, suspicion had given way to approval, rejection to assimilation, and what at one stage seemed outlandish, abstruse, even indecent (such were the terms in which early publishers' rejection slips had been couched) was then found, surprisingly, to embody the most traditional of values. In Beckett's case the effects of this volte-face were spectacular. The question raised by such a reversal, however, as with other experimental or avant-garde writers, is the extent to which Beckett's recognition both by the Swedish Academy and by the wider literary critical academy was inseparable from an attempt at domestication or recuperation.

Beckett's own reaction to the consecration that came with the Nobel Prize was something less than enthusiastic. Already thirteen years before, faced with the publicity surrounding early productions of *Godot*, he had written to Alan Schneider, responsible for directing the play's 1956 American première, suggesting 'the success of *Godot* had been very largely the result of a misunderstanding, or of various misunderstandings'. In the English version of the play, it was not for nothing therefore that, in Estragon's slanging match with Vladimir, Beckett should resort to the following, ultimate insult: the word 'Crritic!', delivered, says a stage direction, 'with finality'. 'Success and failure on the public level', Beckett explained to Schneider, 'never mattered much to me, in fact I feel much more at home with the latter, having breathed deep of its vivifying air all my writing life up to the last couple of years.'⁴ In the autumn of 1969, Beckett's reaction to the Nobel Prize was much the same. He shunned the exposure it brought, politely but pointedly refusing to attend the prize-giving ceremony in Stockholm, and quickly gave away the money associated with the award. In autumn 1969 it perhaps fell best to Suzanne to voice the writer's feelings. As she is said to have exclaimed on hearing the news: 'Quelle catastrophe!' 'How dreadful!' (Knowlson, *Damned to Fame*, p. 570).

In less than two decades, then, Beckett's work passed from being virtually unpublishable to becoming a pillar of the modern or postmodern literary canon. How this came about still merits surprise. Once Suzanne had delivered *Molloy* in typescript to the Éditions de Minuit in 1950 as an unpromising last resort, what happened next is the stuff of legend. As the novel languished on a colleague's desk, the twenty-five-year-old director and proprietor of Minuit, Jérôme Lindon, picked up Beckett's loose-leaved pages, and began reading them while on his way home that lunchtime in the Paris Métro. He was suddenly overcome with hoots of uncontrollable laughter, finished reading *Molloy* that evening and resolved immediately to write to Suzanne offering Beckett a contract for both *Molloy* and the rest. The date was 15 November 1950. Over the next three years *Molloy* (1951), *Malone meurt* (1951) and *L'Innommable* (1953) duly appeared in close succession alongside *En attendant Godot* (1953) under the Minuit imprint. The novels enjoyed significant critical acclaim in the left-leaning literary press, with positive reviews by such influential critics as Bataille, Maurice Blanchot and Maurice Nadeau. Sales were however at first unimpressive. *Molloy*, commercially the most successful, sold 694 copies in its first year, with *Malone meurt* and *L'Innommable* reaching figures of 241 and 476 respectively.

Jérôme Lindon's pioneering receptiveness to Beckett marked the beginning of a personal association that would continue until the writer's death in 1989. The wider consequences were no less significant. In the short term, publishing Beckett helped establish Minuit's reputation as a prime outlet for avant-garde writing in French which, among others, would shortly make it the home of the *nouveau roman* of the 1950s and 1960s, including such authors as Michel Butor, Alain Robbe-Grillet (who joined Minuit as a result of reading Beckett), Claude Simon and Robert Pinget (who collaborated with Beckett on the French version of the 1957 radio play, *All That Fall*; three years later, Beckett repaid the compliment by translating one of Pinget's plays under the title *The Old Tune*). More generally, Minuit's promotion of Beckett was itself indicative of a far-reaching sea change affecting the way in which the responsibilities facing prose writers in the post-war years had come to be understood. By the mid 1950s, as the relationship between literature and politics became less easily reducible to questions of party affiliation, Jean-Paul Sartre's influential doctrine of committed literature (*littérature engagée*), which held that artistic success was inseparable from the sociopolitical values a prose work sought to promote, had lost much of its prestige and urgency. As it did so, it was the work of Beckett, alongside the fiction and criticism of Bataille and Blanchot and the later work of Marguerite Duras (all of whom at one stage were published by Minuit), that came to be identified with this new, more radical turn. For if literature was no longer seen as a vehicle for moral values, it was not because it was regressive, but because it was more subversive and contestatory still. For many contemporaries the realisation came as a shock. In an interview from 1983, the philosopher and historian Michel Foucault (born 1926), described it as follows:

> I belong to a generation of people who as students were trapped within a horizon marked by Marxism, phenomenology, existentialism, and so on. All extremely interesting, stimulating things, but which after a while become rather stifling and make you want to look elsewhere. I was the same as every other philosophy student at the time. For me, the break came with Beckett's *En attendant Godot*. When I saw it, it took my breath away.[5]

Minuit in turn, during the 1950s and 1960s, became an important outlet for political texts challenging the legitimacy of the French Republic (like Henri Alleg's *La Question*, denouncing the use of torture by the French military in Algeria, published in 1958, or the novel *Le Déserteur*, defending the rights of conscripts in the war, published under the pseudonym of Maurienne in 1960, both of which were banned by the authorities). During the 1960s and 1970s, the publishing house helped launch and sustain the philosophical work of some of France's most inventive thinkers, including Gilles Deleuze, Jacques Derrida and Jean-François Lyotard, each of whom came to express profound admiration for Beckett's fiction. All this was part of a wide-ranging shift in direction as a result of which the significance of literature no longer lay in its ability to defend humanist values, but rather to question all essentialist definitions of literature whatever. Against this backdrop, Beckett's career as a writer prospered. As he embarked on a demanding programme of self-translation, producing English versions of texts written in French, and subsequently French translations of texts done in English, the impact of his work in French was soon matched by corresponding success in English, not least as a result of the support of such influential independent figures in English-language publishing as John Calder (initially with Calder and Boyars, then John Calder Ltd) and Barney Rosset (at Grove Press), who, together with Lindon, quickly established Beckett as one of the most provocative and paradigmatic of artistic presences in contemporary writing.

In 1950 all this belonged to the future. At the time, Beckett's difficulties in finding a publisher for his French trilogy came as little surprise. True enough, Beckett had behind him a nascent if fitful literary career in English which, alongside book reviews and critical essays, the most substantial of which was a slim volume on Proust (1931), had seen the publication of *More Pricks Than Kicks* (1934), a collection of stories deriving in part from the unpublished (and unpublishable) novel, *Dream of Fair to Middling Women* (1933), the poetry collection, *Echo's Bones* (1935) and the novel *Murphy*, which appeared in 1938. But this earlier work too had struggled for recognition, with Beckett often resorting to translating, mainly from the French, if only to make a living, an activity that culminated in a French version of *Murphy*, completed in tandem with his friend Alfred Péron, and published in 1947 with Bordas, who retained an option on subsequent work. Sales of the French *Murphy* were meagre at best, and Bordas declined to pursue their interest.

These early works, even if at times only by dint of their resistance to reading, had nevertheless begun to mark out a territory Beckett would soon call his own. By way of the reclusive character of Belacqua Shuah (this would not be the last time the slothful figure of Belacqua from Dante Alighieri's *Purgatorio* would feature in Beckett's prose, nor the last time Beckett would embody his own given name in fictional form, on this occasion by the simple expedient of reversing his initials), *More Pricks Than Kicks* explored the various constitutive poles of worldly experience – beginning and ending, living and dying, laughing and weeping, pleasure and pain, going forth and coming back – only to discover that the one penetrated or inhabited the other, dividing it from itself and forfeiting its own stability in the process. Oscillating motion was what resulted: to and fro, hither and thither, backwards and forwards, coming and going. 'From the ingle to the window, from the nursery to the bedroom, even from one quarter of the town to another', writes the narrator, 'these little acts of motion did do him [Belacqua] some good as a rule. It was the old story of the salad days, torment in the terms and in the intervals a measure of ease.'[6] A similar logic, treated in more sustained yet always ironic fashion, underpins the actions (or inaction) of the eponymous Murphy as he ventures forth into the world with the aim of withdrawing from it, but, in attempting to do so ('a mote in the dark of absolute freedom', Beckett writes), becomes the unfortunate victim of a gas leak and ensuing explosion, his earthly remains a handful of ash recycled across a bar-room floor. Such Murphy, whose life began with a whimper, but ends with a bang. 'Yes or no?', Beckett has him ask, only for the narrator tartly to reply: 'The eternal tautology'.[7]

If Beckett's texts of the 1930s were characterised by a marked restlessness of tone, idiom and genre, it was no doubt because Beckett's own existence during those years was much the same. Born in 1906 to a middle-class Protestant family from Foxrock, just outside Dublin, he had excelled at Trinity College Dublin as a student of French and Italian, spending the period between 1928 and 1930 at the École Normale Supérieure in Paris, where, among others, he became acquainted with the intellectual diaspora around James Joyce. Beckett had been primed for an academic career, but shrank from the authority it implied. He therefore left his teaching position at Trinity College Dublin in 1931 and spent the rest of the decade leading a nomadic existence in Paris (which he visited frequently), in London (where he completed *Murphy* while undergoing psychoanalysis with W. R. Bion) and in Germany (where he explored museums and art collections). At the outbreak of war, as a (neutral) Irish passport holder, he was able to return to Paris, where he continued to eke out a living. From September 1941, he became involved with the Resistance, and, threatened with arrest, was forced to flee the city altogether. Escaping with Suzanne to the Vaucluse, he completed another novel in English, *Watt*, which, after being turned down by numerous London publishers, eventually appeared nine years later with the Olympia Press in Paris. Like Beckett's other work, *Watt* has been diversely described: as a metaphysical allegory, a parodic *Bildungsroman*, a *reductio ad absurdum* of logical analysis. It is no doubt all this and more, as Deleuze among others suggests: a kind of manic cartography, which, exhausting the possible, exhausts itself, resulting in a kind of infinite exposure to the finite which has the effect of emptying the novel of all thematic or other stability.

The end of France's occupation in 1944 ushered in a period of intense political and cultural debate. In the literary field, it was a time of significant renewal. Against this backdrop, Beckett again set to work. In mid March 1946, having completed in English some twenty-nine pages of the story later entitled 'La Fin' ('The End'), Beckett reached a surprising decision. Drawing a line across the page, he continued writing the story in the language in which he had been living for some considerable time: French (Knowlson, *Damned to Fame*, p. 358). In the following months and years, he went on to produce more stories in the language ('Premier Amour', 'L'Expulsé', 'Le Calmant') together with an exploratory short novel (*Mercier et Camier*) and, most ambitiously of all, the three texts published by Minuit in the early 1950s. Beckett was not, of course, the first author of fiction to adopt a non-native tongue. Novelists as different as Joseph Conrad, Vladimir Nabokov,

Elie Wiesel or Andréï Makine, among others, each did the same. Beckett's case was nevertheless unusual, not only because he chose to write in French, rather than being forced to do so by historical or political circumstances, but also because a decade later he repeated the move by returning to his native English, not only to translate his French work, but also to produce original English-language texts (including among others the plays *All That Fall*, *Krapp's Last Tape*, *Happy Days*, *Not I*, *Rockaby* and *Footfalls*, and the prose texts *Company* and *Worstward Ho*), even as he continued to the end writing original work in French.

There was another shift. As he turned to writing in French, Beckett also began writing in the first person. Though not absolute, the convergence is nevertheless remarkable. Just as literature for Franz Kafka may be said to have begun with what Blanchot calls the 'liberating passage from the first person to the third',[8] so it seems that for Beckett writing in the first person and in French provoked a similar, if converse metamorphosis. It was not simply that writing in this second language allowed Beckett greater distance from his familial origins; more importantly, it imposed on the writer's work an essential detour. It was both a renegotiation and a restaging of Beckett's experience of language, an experimental re-enactment of the body's birth into speech not from the perspective of a constituted self, but as a function of the prior alterity of language without which no self would be constituted at all. In a much-quoted, programmatic letter written to Axel Kaun in German in July 1937, Beckett spoke of his own – English – language as being 'like a veil which one has to tear apart in order to get to those things (or the nothingness) lying behind it'.[9] A decade later, Beckett came to realise, it seems, that to cast aside the veil it was necessary to assume another veil, or veil of otherness, that a language not his own alone could supply. The most direct route was also the most indirect, and it was the mask of the other that was more revealing than the face.

To write in French, then, for Beckett, was to discard the sometimes manic protective armoury characteristic of his early prose in order to dramatise more simply, but also more radically, the enigmatic singularity of that event of birth that conjoins both a flesh and a name in an encounter as necessary as it is contingent, as meaningful as it is meaningless. Such an encounter is, however, anything but uneventful. As Beckett's work shows, it is the source of an infinite number of stories, each of which is only provisional, none of which is final, for even as flesh and name are defined by their encounter, neither is reducible to the other, which it necessarily exceeds. Between body and language there is mutual dependency but also radical heterogeneity. As Derrida once put it, speaking of his own relationship as a non-metropolitan Algerian Jew to the French language, 'I have only one language, and (but) it is not mine.'[10] Admittedly, unlike Derrida, who only felt at ease writing in French, Beckett had several languages at his disposal: English, French, German and Italian. But in each case, as he signed the sentences that were his, the words he used were not his own.

To write, then, is always to write in the language of the other. It was to be exposed to what Derrida, in a sequence of essays on the poet Francis Ponge and the novelist and dramatist Jean Genet, describes as the paradoxical, double structure of 'ex-appropriation', by which any writer, in order to write at all, is required to appropriate the words of others if only to leave a trace of his or her passing, but by that very token is just as surely expropriated of those words by the fact that they belong to another. The structure is a general one, since without it no text could be written or read at all. It applies quite particularly, however, to Beckett as a writer of French (and writer *tout court*). On the one hand, Beckett was able to bend standard literary French to his own distinctive idiom by overlaying, knowingly, but with disruptive comic results, the formal, often self-conscious knowledge of the language acquired doing translation exercises in the classrooms of Trinity College with the sometimes vulgar colloquialisms picked up living, working and reading in Paris. But on the other, remaining manifestly reliant on the words (and sometimes the linguistic expertise) of others, he was only too aware that to express oneself in language was always to be dispossessed by it. Beckett was able to make French his own, but only in so far as the language was not his. And if it seemed that one (maternal) language for Beckett was not enough, this meant it was in any case impossible to be at home in any language, and that to be born into words, in C. G. Jung's prophetic phrase first heard by Beckett in London in 1935, and cited in both *Watt* and *All That Fall*, was tantamount to having 'never been properly born' at all (Knowlson, *Damned to Fame*, p. 176).[11]

In a 1929 essay on James Joyce's 'Work in Progress' (the later *Finnegans Wake*), Beckett famously wrote that Joyce's 'writing is not *about* something; *it is that something itself*'.[12] The remark may be applied with equal validity to Beckett's trilogy. For it is not hard to read those three novels as a sustained exploration of their own eccentric enactment. Already the title of the first novel, *Molloy*, advertising its non-French provenance, poses a problem of pronunciation for the francophone reader. Numerous other details, from geography to currency, emphasise the work's exteriority to the language to which it ostensibly belongs. How to make sense, a reader might ask, of this odd doubleness of affiliation? The question is one that the novel explores at length as it undertakes a series of investigations into the enigma of doubleness, as reflected in the first instance in the two equal–unequal parts of the novel itself. In the first, a narrator, going uncertainly under the name of Molloy, travels by bicycle in search of his mother, whom he however fails to find, and ends up alone and abandoned in a ditch that recalls (or effaces) the mother's room where his story began. In the second part, a second narrator, who confidently asserts his name is Moran, Jacques Moran, like that of his son, leaves in search of someone possibly called Molloy, only to turn into his quarry's double, eventually finding himself back home, though the place seems abandoned, at which point he embarks on writing an account of his journey, the account the reader is perhaps reading, though its relationship to truth seems at best problematic. Two stories, then, two lines of affiliation (maternal here, paternal there), two directions (homeward here, abroad there), two modes of reading (truthful here, fictitious there), all compete for attention.

Traditionally, in so far as it allows the mind to compare elements or contrast them, repetition is an essential condition for understanding and interpretation. In Beckett, however, it creates doubt and confusion. Take for instance the narrator's two testicles, these two witnesses, the reader is told, for prosecution and defence alike (Beckett's French contains an untranslatable, partly etymological, double *double entendre* on the legal phrase *témoin à décharge*, with the word *témoin*, from the Latin *testis*, simultaneously implying witness and testicle, and *décharge* both plea of innocence and discharge of bodily fluid). Though seemingly symmetrical ('dangling at mid-thigh at the end of a meagre cord'), the pair display an essential but bizarrely reversible or indifferent dissymmetry, in so far as the right hangs lower than the left, 'or inversely, I forget', says the narrator, who likens them to two 'decaying circus clowns', a Laurel and Hardy, or Didi and Gogo, so to speak, of sexual potency (or impotence). Yet it is not clear which of the two, in this testicular double act, was the comedian and which the straight man (or vice versa), leaving the reader to puzzle over what sense, if any, to attach to this undecidable doubling of the narrator's parts (and words): same but different, different but same, inadequate yet superfluous, necessary yet contingent.[13]

*Malone meurt* continues in similar vein. Its narrator, whose name may or may not be Malone, begins confidently enough. 'This time', he declares, 'I know where I am going, it is no longer the ancient night, the recent night. Now it is a game, I am going to play' (*Mm*, 9; *M, MD, U*, 180). This air of authority soon turns, however, into its opposite. The programme of telling four separate stories, one after the other ('One about a man, another about a woman, a third about a thing and finally one about an animal, a bird probably', *Mm*, 10–11; *M, MD, U*, 181), in order to sum up his situation and reach a conclusion, soon unravels, not only because the stories develop a momentum of their own, but, more importantly, because instead of neatly filling the time available before the end, they can but in fact postpone that end. The end, paradoxically but necessarily, is radically unspeakable. If *Malone meurt* shows a narrator endeavouring to embody his own name, that is, to become the person who dies (or is dying) in the book's title, then, what the novel shows is the very impossibility of doing so. There is no self-sufficient present in which death (or indeed writing) may be said properly to occur. The only completion is radical incompletion, the only movement forwards movement backwards, and the only kind of passage an aporetic absence of passage. If *Malone meurt* begins by announcing the deferred prospect of the narrator's dying to life ('I shall soon be quite dead at last in spite of all'), it ends by evoking the protracted imminence of his birth into death ('I am being given, if I may venture the expression, birth to into death, such is my impression'). But strictly speaking, as far as language is concerned, neither birth nor death is possible at all, in so far as neither can be appropriated by the narrator as they happen, only experienced, if at all, in silence, as unavoidable expropriation. Rather than properly finishing, the novel in the end simply interrupts itself, giving way to 'gurgles of outflow' that are no more a conclusion than the opening of the text was a beginning (*Mm*, 7, 208, 216; *M, MD, U*, 179, 285, 289).

The end of *Malone meurt*, in other words, could not be other than provisional. The very impossibility of its ending made its continuation somehow necessary. But however inevitable, for the very same reasons as *Malone meurt*, no sequel could reach a conclusion. On the horns of this dilemma Beckett's next novel, *L'Innommable*, was poised. The book's title was itself already a paradox. Many readers take 'L'Innommable' or 'The Unnamable' to be a covert name for the narrator, but nothing is less certain. In so far as it signals the absence of a name, it inscribes at the centre of Beckett's writing both a demand for a name yet an impossibility of naming. As such, it is a word that exceeds and erases itself and points to a kind of constitutive impossibility, in much the same way that for Blanchot what speaks in the book is not subjectivity or consciousness, but the neutrality, irreducible to subject and object alike, of 'an experience pursued under the threat of the impersonal, an approach to a neutral speaking that speaks to itself alone, traverses whoever is listening, is without intimacy, excludes all intimacy, and cannot be silenced because it is that which is unceasing, interminable'.[14] Surprising in this context is the widespread belief among early critics that *L'Innommable* portrayed some post-mortem state of consciousness, bereft of all bodily presence. Nothing could be further from the truth. What distinguishes Beckett's work in modern literature as a whole is rather its attention to the body: not however as an adjunct to consciousness, a receptacle in which identity is located, but as an opaque materiality resistant to representation, which makes itself felt only as a grotesque or uncanny demand. 'Matter, matter, pawed and pummelled endlessly in vain', the nameless narrator puts it: this, then, not disembodied consciousness, is what *L'Innommable* attempts, and fails, to name.[15] Not for nothing is the novel exercised by the figure of crucifixion, that emblematic Christian and, even more so, post-Christian confrontation between word and flesh in which body and language are conjoined in a experience of violent exposure, to which there is however no redemptive conclusion, merely the obligation to carry on, even in the impossibility of doing so. As *L'Innommable* famously has it *in fine*: 'you must go on, I can't go on, I'll go on' (*I*, 262; *M, MD, U*, 418).

After *L'Innommable*, Beckett did nevertheless go on. In the years following, much of his energy was devoted to the theatre, in both French and English. As far as new narrative prose was concerned, he published only *Textes pour rien* (*Texts for Nothing*, 1958) and the unfinished torso, 'From an Abandoned Work' (1958). 'At the end of my work', he told Israel Shenker in 1956, 'there's nothing but dust: the namable. In the last book, *L'Innommable*, there's complete disintegration. No "I", no "have", no "being". No nominative, no accusative, no verb. There's no way to go on.'[16] Even in the absence of subject, object, or verb, it remained imperative to continue, not in order to repeat what was already written, but to reaffirm, reaccentuate and underwrite again the fragile otherness at the heart of repetition. It was not until 1961, in French, that Beckett completed his next full-length narrative. The text bore the falsely down-to-earth title: *Comment c'est, How It Is*. How it was for Beckett was very different from how it had ever been before in the European novel. Across nearly two hundred unpunctuated pages, or, better, where punctuation was imprinted invisibly on Beckett's strophe-like text by dint of the spoken rhythms of his writing and by the yawning blanks that separated each access of language or breath from the next, an unidentified voice, arriving from the outside, spoke the same ceaseless story – the story of its own ceaseless speaking – which was that of a body (hands, face, legs, fingernails, buttock) crawling through vast tracts of mud or excrement in search of some other, dragging a sack containing provisions in the form of cans of tuna, prey to spasmodic memory-like images coming from above, until, encountering another, it plants between the other's buttocks a tin-opener in order to extract a cry, a word or other sign of life. The grim cruelty of the text is unremitting, matched only by the grotesque comedy of a writing become the abyssal staging of its own impossible progress.

If *Comment c'est* was Beckett's most challenging novel to date, it also marked a turning point in the writer's output. Alongside a substantial body of work for the stage, Beckett continued to publish prose works, in French and English, until the end. But few, if any, of these texts might properly be described as belonging to the novel. Densely written, at times extremely brief, at times more sustained, often overtly fragmentary, the prose texts published by Beckett after 1961, including, among others, such titles as *Imagination morte imaginez* (*Imagination Dead Imagine*, 1965), *Bing* (*Ping*, 1966), *Sans* (*Lessness*, 1969), *Le Dépeupleur* (*The Lost Ones*, 1970), *Pour finir encore* (*For To End Yet Again*, 1975), *Foirades* (*Fizzles*, 1975), *Company* (*Compagnie*, 1980), *Mal vu mal dit* (*Ill Seen Ill Said*, 1981), and *Worstward Ho* (1983), were notably and remarkably various. If some were readable as concentrated prose poems, others seemed to tend towards allegory; if some appeared attributable to a human voice, others were decidedly impersonal; if some followed a careful pattern of rise and fall, others had recourse to seemingly arbitrary methods of composition; if some contained an unusual amount of autobiographical material, others were abstract and anonymous in the extreme. All, however, had one essential trait in common, which also explains their sceptical distance from the novel genre, which was their status as singular performative events. Each sought a means to name the irreducible, recalcitrant singularity of a body and inscribe it within a fictional space, in the knowledge that what marked the body's singularity by definition resisted capture, and that, as a result, to have recourse to words, either as sound or meaning, was to run the unavoidable risk that the text, instead of naming the body's singularity, would efface it, in which case it then became necessary to sabotage the performance itself, and the alienation it implied, in order, in destroying or suspending representation, to testify, by word, sound or image nonetheless, to the evanescent singularity of the body that necessarily eluded both representation and performance alike. It was as if the writer, unable to name what was of course unnameable, was required instead, so to speak, to unname the nameable that remained, and, in so doing, gesture ironically in silence towards that which resisted naming. In affirming his writing, then, Beckett could not but seek to sign, impossibly, either in English or in French, that which escaped each and every signature.

From the mid 1960s onwards, the critical response to Beckett's writing turned from a trickle into a flood. Today, Beckett's work is among the most written about in modern times. It has been the object of every kind of critical investigation. Early commentators saw it as the expression of a pessimistic world-view, support for which was found in some of Beckett's early critical writings, notably the *Three Dialogues* on painting he penned with Georges Duthuit in 1948. In these often peremptory and iconoclastic exchanges, Beckett famously responded to the paintings of Tal Coat by envisioning an art turning aside from the merely feasible, and preferring 'the expression that there is nothing to express, nothing with which to express, nothing from which to express, no power to express, no desire to express, together with the obligation to express'.[17] Much has been made of the apparent negativity of such pronouncements. What they show, however, is not a writing despairing of language, but a writer affirming art's resistance to the world. Beckett's name may have become a convenient byword for nihilism. But a more measured response to his work would have to insist on its affirmative rigour, its unrelenting patience in maintaining itself in the impasse of its own impossibility.

When critics have sought positives in Beckett, they have usually turned to his use of comedy. That there are many comic moments in Beckett is well known, and is readily confirmed by the many set-piece comic routines in his prose, like the famous sucking stones episode in *Molloy* (which recalls Beckett's memories of playing cricket at university: it is quite common for umpires to count the balls in an over by transferring pebbles between pockets). Often comedy is seen as a mere aesthetic gloss, a way of sweetening the bitter pill of knowledge. Not so, however, in Beckett, where comedy is invariably an art of disruption and disjunction, that speaks less of pleasure than of the precarious fragility of all meaning, including that of comedy itself. Already in *Murphy*, the world was said to divide 'into jokes that had once been good jokes and jokes that had never been good jokes' (*Murphy*, 48). Beckettian laughter, in other words, enforces no norms and subscribes to no authority. It serves instead constantly to divide meaning from itself by irradi-ating it with that – a remainder or an excess – which it cannot enclose.

Beckett's texts remove, then, with the left hand what they offer with the right. Of this there is no better illustration than the use of philosophical references. On the evidence of *Murphy* and others, much has been made by some critics, for instance, of Beckett's fondness for the seventeenth-century Flemish occasionalist Arnold Geulincx (1624–69), a follower of René Descartes who held that interaction between mind and body was a conse-quence of divine intervention. What attracted Beckett in Geulincx, however, as *Murphy* shows, was less doctrinal content, more an ancillary frame, one that, here, offered an intellectual formula for dramatising the perplexing encounter not between Cartesian mind and body, but between name and flesh in Beckett's own writing. It is revealing that, in drawing on Geulincx's dictum that where one is worth nothing one should desire nothing (*ubi nihil vales, ibi nihil velis*), what Beckett privileges is the philosopher's recourse to paronomasia, so reminiscent of Beckett's own use of repetition and differ-ence, symmetry and dissymmetry, chiasmus and oxymoron, by which words are constantly found to play havoc with established binary polarities and the meanings they sustain. What this suggests is that the relationship between literature and philosophy in Beckett was anything but illustrative. What was more visibly at stake was the power of literature not to confirm or negate philosophy, but, by suspending or neutralising its truth claims, to put them into crisis. For this reason too, philosophers as different as T. W. Adorno, Deleuze, Derrida or Alain Badiou were drawn to attempt to harness, even at times appropriate, the critical force with which philosophy in Beckett's writing is put into question.

Beckett shares with the Marquis de Sade, Leopold von Sacher-Masoch, Marcel Proust and Joyce the unenviable fate of having become an adjective. But if Beckett is a paradigmatic figure, it is paradoxically only in so far as his writing resists all exemplification, and it is this commitment to his own writing, in the face of hostility and incomprehension, that best explains Beckett's significance for that whole generation of writers, in several different languages, who, from the 1950s onwards, sought to reinvent the forms and language of contemporary writing. In 1975, in the television play *Ghost Trio*, bookending his long career as a writer, Beckett returned to a motif used more than forty years before in *More Pricks Than Kicks*, where Belacqua Shuah, this reverse alter ego, is described as having 'lived a Beethoven pause' – 'whatever he meant by that', as the narrator hastens to add (*MPTK*, 40). The phrase, however, says much. For as far as Beckett was concerned, in respect of what may, or may not, still call itself the novel, it was no longer a case of grasping and describing the empirical world as such, but of practising and affirming what interrupted, preceded and exceeded that world. To have signed an interruption which necessarily implied the interruption of any signature, this, perhaps, is the measure without measure of Beckett's enduring but unrepeatable legacy.

### Note on editions/translations

Samuel Becket is unusual among modern prose writers in that, with some exceptions, his novels exist either in the original English (including *Murphy*, *Watt*) and in subsequent French translations done by Beckett himself (sometimes in collaboration with others), or in the original French (*Molloy*, *Malone meurt*, *L'Innommable*, *Comment c'est*) and in English translations mainly by Beckett himself (*Molloy*, *Malone Dies*, *The Unnamable*, *How It Is*). Of course, all his works, both source texts and his own translations, may be regarded as original writing.

### Notes

1 The account given here is based on the following: James Knowlson, *Damned to Fame: The Life of Samuel Beckett* (London: Bloomsbury, 1996), pp. 376–8, and

Anne Simonin, *Les Éditions de Minuit, 1942–1955: le devoir d'insoumission* (Paris: IMEC Editions, 1994), pp. 377, 380–5.

2 The full text of the citation may be found on the Nobel Prize website: http://nobelprize.org/nobel_prizes/literature/laureates/1969/press.html

3 Georges Bataille, *Œuvres complètes*, 12 vols. (Paris, Gallimard, 1970–88), vol. xii, p. 86; author's emphasis.

4 *No Author Better Served: The Correspondence of Samuel Beckett and Alan Schneider*, ed. Maurice Harmon (Cambridge, MA: Harvard University Press, 1998), p. 8; Samuel Beckett, *Waiting for Godot* (London: Faber and Faber, 1965), p. 75.

5 Michel Foucault, 'Archéologie d'une passion', interview by C. Ruas (15 September 1983), *Dits et écrits 1954–1988*, 4 vols. (Paris: Gallimard, 1994), iv, p. 598; translation mine.

6 Samuel Beckett, *More Pricks Than Kicks (MPTK)* (London: Calder and Boyars, 1970), p. 39.

7 Samuel Beckett, *Murphy* (London: Calder and Boyars, 1963), p. 32.

8 Maurice Blanchot, *L'Espace littéraire* (Paris: Gallimard, 1955), p. 70; *Maurice Blanchot, The Space of Literature*, trans. Ann Smock (Lincoln, NE: University of Nebraska Press, 1982), p. 73.

9 *The Letters of Samuel Beckett 1929–1940*, ed. Martha Dow Fehsenfeld and Lois More Overbeck (Cambridge University Press, 2009), pp. 513–14, 518.

10 Jacques Derrida, *Le Monolinguisme de l'autre* (Paris: Galilée, 1996), p. 15; Jacques Derrida, *Monolingualism of the Other*, trans. Patrick Mensah (Stanford University Press, 1998), p. 2.

11 See Samuel Beckett, *Watt* (London: Calder and Boyars, 1963), p. 248. Compare Samuel Beckett, *Collected Shorter Plays* (London: Faber and Faber, 1984), p. 36.

12 Samuel Beckett, 'Dante ... Bruno. Vico.. Joyce', in *Our Exagmination Round His Factification for Incamination of Work in Progress* (1929; London: Faber and Faber, 1972), p. 14; author's emphasis.

13 Samuel Beckett, *Molloy* (Paris: Minuit, 1951), p. 52; Samuel Beckett, *Molloy, Malone Dies, The Unnamable (M, MD, U)*, translated by the author (London: Calder and Boyars, 1959), pp. 35–6.

14 Maurice Blanchot, *Le Livre à venir* (Paris: Gallimard, 1959), p. 259; Maurice Blanchot, *The Book to Come*, trans. Charlotte Mandell (Stanford University Press, 2003), p. 213; translation modified.

15 Samuel Beckett, *L'Innommable (I)* (Paris: Minuit, 1953), p. 124; *M, MD, U*, 350.

16 *Samuel Beckett: The Critical Heritage*, ed. Lawrence Graver and Raymond Federman (London: Routledge and Kegan Paul, 1979), p. 148.

17 Samuel Beckett, *Proust and Three Dialogues* (London: Calder and Boyars, 1970), p. 103.

*Further reading*

Bryden, Mary, *Samuel Beckett and the Idea of God* (Basingstoke: Macmillan, 1998)
Connor, Steven, *Samuel Beckett: Repetition, Theory and Text* (Oxford: Basil Blackwell, 1988)
Hill, Leslie, *Beckett's Fiction: In Different Words* (1990; Cambridge University Press, 2009)
Knowlson, James, *Damned to Fame: The Life of Samuel Beckett* (London: Bloomsbury, 1996)

Oppenheim, Lois, ed., *Palgrave Advances in Samuel Beckett Studies* (New York: Palgrave Macmillan, 2004)

Pilling, John, *Beckett Before Godot* (Cambridge University Press, 1997)

*Samuel Beckett Today/Aujourd'hui*, ed. Sjef Houppermans and Angela Moorjani (Amsterdam: Rodopi, 1992–)

Trezise, Thomas, *Into the Breach: Samuel Beckett and the Ends of Literature* (Princeton University Press, 1990)

Uhlmann, Anthony, *Beckett and Poststructuralism* (Cambridge University Press, 1999)

# 24

RAJENDRA A. CHITNIS

# Milan Kundera (1929–):
# The idea of the novel

The Czech-born poet, dramatist, essayist and novelist Milan Kundera (b. 1929) is internationally best known for the two once hugely fashionable novels he published after emigrating from Czechoslovakia to France in 1975: *The Book of Laughter and Forgetting* (*BLF*, 1979) and *The Unbearable Lightness of Being* (*ULB*, 1984). Both are examples of what he calls 'thinking novels', in which the plot elements are interpolated with extended authorial reflections on themes often identified in the title of the novel. His novels both reflect and have helped him refine his understanding of the nature and history of the novel, which he expounds in a series of books written originally in French, beginning with *The Art of the Novel* (*AN*, 1986). His ideas resonate not so much because of their originality as because of the 'anti-theoretical' accessibility of their expression. Drawing above all on the writing of Friedrich Nietzsche (1844–1900) and twentieth-century thinkers influenced by him, including the Russian Formalists, José Ortega y Gasset (1883–1955), Martin Heidegger (1889–1976) and the French existentialists, Kundera sets out a retrospective 'manifesto' for the European novel, and attempts in both his fiction and non-fiction to describe and demonstrate an alternative to predictions of its imminent death.

## Two ways of being

Throughout his fiction and non-fiction, Kundera suggests that the modern human being responds to existence in two distinct ways. The first response is marked by sentimental egocentrism and is associated with youth, romanticism and the placing of the intellect in the service of the emotions. The human being is consumed by an exhibitionist desire to be acknowledged, but also to belong, to participate in shared experiences, to be one with the shared destiny of humanity, resulting in conformity, homogeneity, mediocrity, superficiality and the 'stupidity of received ideas'. This attitude culminates in ecstatic absorption in the present moment, epitomised for

Kundera by, for example, speed, mass hysteria, rock songs and sexual climax, during which the human being 'loses sight of himself', his past and future, and proves capable of anything. The second response, by contrast, is marked by the desire to maintain ironic distance, to 'keep sight of oneself', scepticism, relativism, non-conformism, resistance to association with any one particular ideological position, the unending pursuit of greater knowledge and understanding, privacy, the preserved heterogeneity of empathy rather than the crushing homogeneity of identification with other human beings. It is associated in his work with maturity, experience, classical world-views like Stoicism, Epicureanism and hedonism, the delaying of gratification and, above all, with the novel. Kundera implicitly presents himself as a teacher and defender of this second perspective, which he perceives as unfashionable and under constant threat of effacement by the first, whether in the form of lyric poetry, utopian idealism or the kitsch of totalitarian or popular culture.

## Kundera's idea of the novel

Kundera links the emergence of these contrasting, coexisting attitudes to the rise of science and the birth of the novel at the start of the 'Modern Era'. In his view, that 'Era' is marked by the utopian pursuit of mastery over nature and the course of history through scientific progress. Following Edmund Husserl's assertion that the European scientific method 'reduced the world to a mere object of technical and mechanical investigation', Kundera argues: 'the more [man] advanced in knowledge, the less clearly could he see either the world as a whole or his own self, and he plunged further into what Husserl's pupil Heidegger called … "the forgetting of being"'.[1] For Kundera, the novel emerged to investigate this forgotten being. In contrast to the absolutist, positivist seriousness and certainty of rational progress, the novel is playful, questioning, tolerant of ambiguity, able to see the world in terms of competing, coexisting relative truths, imbued with only the 'wisdom of uncertainty'.

Like Nietzsche and the Formalists, Kundera favours the novelists of the seventeenth and eighteenth centuries – Miguel de Cervantes, François Rabelais, Laurence Sterne, Denis Diderot, Choderlos de Laclos – in whose work he finds the qualities of the novel exemplified. In *Testaments Betrayed* (*TB*, 1993), Kundera proposes that histories of both the novel and music are divided into 'two halves', corresponding to the two contrasting approaches to existence described above. He compares the attitude to melody in each half, implicitly linking its fate to that of story in the novel. For Kundera, it seems 'as if a Bach fugue, by bringing us to contemplate a being that is outside the subjective, aimed to make us forget our moods, our passions and pains, ourselves; and as if on the other hand Romantic melody aimed to make us plunge into ourselves, feel the self with a terrible intensity, and forget everything outside'.[2]

According to Kundera, the 'second half' of the history of the novel begins with Walter Scott and Honoré de Balzac and is marked by romanticisation and sentimentalisation, a shift from intellectual distance to emotional involvement, from serious playfulness to deadly seriousness, which Kundera finds impoverishing. In his view, the novelist of the 'second half' unnecessarily constrains the novel by attempting to provide an 'illusion of reality', reducing the novel to the limits of chronology, causality and plausibility. Moreover, 'the second half not only eclipsed the first, it *repressed* it' (*TB*, 59), making it more difficult for the human being to regain sight of himself. He notes that contemporary readers and listeners seem unable to appreciate the novels and music of the first without adapting them (through cinema, through new arrangements) to the aesthetic criteria of the second.

Effectively, in the 'second half' of its existence, Kundera suggests, the novel lost its ironic distance from human activity and aspirations, becoming wedded to the notion of historical progress that it mirrored. After World War I, however, four Central European novelists – Jaroslav Hašek (1883–1923), Franz Kafka (1883–1924), Robert Musil (1880–1942) and Hermann Broch (1886–1951) – were, in Kundera's view, the first to show that this earlier idealism was in crisis and that the human being's utopian dreams had been realised, but as nightmares. Kundera labels this time of crisis as the 'period of terminal paradoxes'. In *AN*, he writes: 'In the course of the Modern Era, Cartesian rationality has corroded, one after the other, all the values inherited from the Middle Ages. But just when reason wins a total victory, pure irrationality (force willing only its will) seizes the world stage, because there is no longer any generally accepted value system to block its path' (*AN*, 10–11). Similarly, the human dream of a world united in everlasting peace is realised in the twentieth century as a world united in unending war.

In this context, as these novelists show, all hierarchies, categories, concepts and assumptions are rendered meaningless. Kundera writes:

> Having brought off miracles in science and technology, this 'master and proprietor [of nature, in Descartes' famous formulation]' is suddenly realizing that he owns nothing and is master neither of nature (it is vanishing, little by little, from the planet), nor of History (it has escaped him), nor of himself (he is led by the irrational forces of his soul). But if God is gone and man is no longer master, then who is master? The planet is moving through the void without any master. There it is: the unbearable lightness of being. (*AN*, 41)

Though commentators might associate this description with the existentialism of Heidegger and Jean-Paul Sartre, fashionable in 1960s Czechoslovakia, it is significant for Kundera that their 'discoveries' were, in his opinion, preceded by those of novelists. Both to communicate and respond to their discovery, Hašek, Kafka, Musil and Broch turn against the nineteenth-century understanding of the novel, 'rehabilitating' the novelistic principles of the 'first half' in an attempt to 'redefine and broaden' the possibilities open to the novelist and enable him better to investigate the contemporary experience of existence. Kundera places his own fiction firmly in their tradition, arguing that the 'period of terminal paradoxes' is far from over.

## From idealism to scepticism, from poetry to prose

Kundera's critical attitude towards the sentimental egocentrism of the 'second half' of the history of the novel has its roots in his rejection of lyricism. Like many young intellectuals, as a student Kundera had supported the 1948 Communist takeover, which led to the Stalinisation of Czechoslovakia. Kundera began his literary career in this period as a lyric poet and translator, conforming to the optimistic, utopian imagery, mood and message prescribed by Stalinist Party ideologues. In the late 1950s and 1960s, the regime – in fits and starts – gradually retreated from the extremes of this period, and Czech literature moved from forced collective optimism to expressions of disillusion, scepticism and despair. Kundera writes that suddenly, in the late 1950s, he no longer recognised himself in his verse, and turned to literary scholarship and drama before 'finding himself' in prose. Thereafter, little in his work is more scathingly satirised than the 'lyricism' of youth, the vanity, foolishness and awkwardness of those yet to grow up intellectually, their self-centredness and need to be admired, their hastiness, their love of sentimentality, melodrama and grand gesture and their devotion to illusions over reality.

Kundera views 'lyricism' as an agent of 'totalitarianism'. His second novel, *Life is Elsewhere* (1973), analyses this relationship across the history of European revolutions, but the central depiction of a nauseating young poet who sacrifices his artistic gifts and ambitions to Stalinist cultural norms and becomes a police informer must surely also be read as an expression of Kundera's self-disgust. In an ostensibly autobiographical passage in *BLF*, motivated by the French poet Paul Éluard's refusal to protest the hanging in 1950 of his friend, the Czech surrealist Záviš Kalandra, Kundera depicts the post-revolutionary euphoria in Czechoslovakia as a mass ring dance of ecstatic 'self-forgetting', whirling ever more frenetically as those excluded from the dance are executed. In *TB*, Kundera writes: 'More than the Terror, the lyricization of the Terror was a trauma for me. It immunized me for good against all lyrical temptations. The only thing I deeply, avidly, wanted was a lucid, unillusioned eye. I finally found it in the art of the novel' (*TB*, 155–6).

Kundera's early fiction dramatises the lesson he claims to have just learned, depicting human beings awakening – or failing to awaken – from their dream of universal mastery to an awareness of the 'period of terminal paradoxes'. In his first short story, 'I, the Mournful God' (omitted from the now definitive French edition of *Laughable Loves* (1970)), Kundera's narrator says: 'Life is paradoxical. Our actions acquire the opposite meaning from the one we ascribe to them in advance. Our actions live their own lives independent of us.'[3] This 'discovery' underpins Kundera's subsequent work, and for some critics seems designed to absolve Kundera of responsibility for his own past actions. In the three cycles of *Laughable Loves*, one can find in embryo or miniature all the themes, types and techniques that Kundera develops in his novels, and one might even argue that the plots of most of Kundera's novels are really further 'laughable loves', interrupted by and subordinated to authorial reflections.

Some characters in *Laughable Loves* are not ready to 'wake up', most notably the young man and the girl in the brilliant 'The Hitchhiking Game', whose confidence in the stability of identity is shattered, but who respond by trying to 'paper over' the situation and continue as before. Those who do learn the lesson respond to their defeat with melancholy, amused resignation. For example, in 'Symposium', a notorious seducer reflects that the time of Don Juans has passed in a world where 'no one refuses you, where everything is possible and everything is permitted'. Communicating with Kundera-like precision the diminished experience of human existence at a time when all hierarchies and values have lost their force, he asserts that the 'Great Conqueror' of women, who 'sinned gaily and laughed at God' has been replaced by the 'Great Collector': 'Don Juan bore on his shoulders a dramatic burden that the Great Collector has no idea of, because in his world every burden has lost its weight . . . In the conqueror's world, a single glance was as important as ten years of the most ardent love-making in the collector's realm.'[4] The characters in Kundera's later novels are engaged in private struggles to come to terms with this unbearably light burden.

## The Joke

In Kundera's first novel, *The Joke* (1967), the banal crushing of private illusions in *Laughable Loves* becomes a metaphor for the dystopian realisation of the Enlightenment's utopian delusions that Kundera would later describe in *AN*. In a 1967 interview, he offers an early version of the 'terminal paradox' model, arguing that Stalinism was founded on the ideals and virtues of humanism, but gradually transformed them into their opposite. This assertion is dramatised in *The Joke*, which is told by four narrators who, in the late 1940s, were drawn to the Communist movement as the means of realising their different utopian world-views, and now, in middle age, reflect on their pasts.

The central character, Ludvík, says of his attraction to Communism:

> we were bewitched by history; we were drunk with the thought of jumping on its back and feeling it beneath us; admittedly, in most cases the result was an ugly lust for power, but (as all human affairs are ambiguous) there was still (and especially, perhaps, in us, the young), an altogether idealist illusion that we were inaugurating a human era in which man (all men) would be neither outside history, nor under the heel of history, but would create and direct it.[5]

Ludvík's faith in the human being's capacity to dictate the future is reflected in his belief in the possibility of revenge. Indeed, Communism may initially have attracted him as a means of revenge on the bourgeois family who brought him up but never ceased reminding him of his debt to them. Helena, the most cruelly satirised narrator, associates Communism with her first love, the student activist, Zemánek, who became her husband; once an unpopular, sickly child, she is delighted to be invited to join hands in the 'ring-dance'. She is the embodiment of Kundera's jaundiced view of lyricism, her name recalling two beautiful causes of trouble, Helen of Troy and Helena Gloryová from Karel Čapek's play *R.U.R.*, whose emotionally motivated, apparently well-meaning interventions bring about the destruction of humanity. Kostka, an evangelical Christian, saw in Communism the expression of Christ's message to love one another. The conservative Moravian patriot, Jaroslav, believed Communism would revive collective rural life and restore the meaning of folklore, the art of the common people.

In middle age, each character is critical of the way Communism has turned out, but unconsciously continues to approach life in accordance with his or her particular 'ideology'. The novel follows Ludvík's attempt to take revenge on [Helena's] Zemánek, his own friend too, who, back in the late 1940s, had publicly supported the decision of the authorities to expel Ludvík from the Party and university after he sent a postcard mocking Party orthodoxy to a girl who preferred Marxist-Leninist summer school to spending the summer with him. Ludvík describes his planned revenge to Kostka as 'a beautiful destruction', yet the 'beautiful destruction', which takes place in the final part of the novel, is actually the destruction of illusions like Ludvík's, the destruction of humanity's dreams for itself.

Kundera presents this destruction not as noble tragedy, but as humiliating farce. Ludvík has arranged an assignation with Helena in his home town, where they have sexual intercourse. Only then, however, does he discover that her marriage has long been over and that Zemánek is delighted to give them his blessing. Helena's world-view, however, is similarly shattered when she realises that Ludvík has used sex not as an expression of love, but as a means of revenge. As a final lyrical gesture, she attempts suicide, but the pills turn out to be laxatives. Meanwhile, in a separate plot, Jaroslav, who believes he has persuaded his reluctant son to accept the lead role in a traditional folk pageant, the Ride of Kings, discovers that, with the complicity of his supposedly loyal wife, his son has gone off on a thoroughly modern motorcycle, leaving a girl to take his place. At the end of the novel, Ludvík joins Jaroslav to play folk music as they had as young men, an assertion of the companionship that, for Kundera, provides fleeting solace in life. Jaroslav then has a heart attack, a symbol of the necessary death of the lyrical sentimentality and idealism that has brought them to this point. Kostka alone is spared travesty, though not loss of faith. He is last seen at the end of the penultimate part of the novel, wretchedly calling out to his God, whom he can no longer hear, a symbol of the modern human being who, having unseated God, now wants him back.

The narrators of *The Joke* only begin to confront reality, if at all, at the end of the novel. To use the language of Heidegger and Sartre, Kundera sets the 'inauthentic' response of his narrators, constantly trying to recoup their visions of a better world against the 'authentic' response of another character, Lucie, who seems to go through life in a permanent state of quiet horror. Ludvík meets her while doing his military service with the regiment for the politically suspect, but abandons her when she refuses to sleep with him. Later, by coincidence, Kostka meets her and earns her trust enough to learn that she was gang-raped as a young girl, an experience of 'pure irrationality' symbolic of the 'period of terminal paradoxes'. Kostka teaches her about Christian forgiveness; she tells him that she loves him and they make love. Rather than recognise this episode as an experience of what in Kundera constitutes real love, an expression of friendship, a momentary refuge from the loneliness of existence, Kostka, guided by his ideas, is ashamed of himself for sullying a pure, spiritual bond by giving in to sexual desire and, like Ludvík, though for exactly opposite reasons, abandons her.

Lucie has no narration of her own and the reader receives only fragments of information about her, communicated by unreliable narrators. Indeed, she appears to the reader as she does to Ludvík and Kostka, as a blank space. Their relationship with her strongly recalls Musil's story 'Tonka' (1922), in which a fatally over-sensitive, over-educated young Austrian intellectual creates and amends an image of his sweetheart, a Czech peasant girl, based on his emotional state, lyrical dreams, his reading and contemporary class and ethnic stereotypes, failing ever actually to know her. Both Ludvík and Kostka imagine an identity for Lucie, only to reject her – rather than their own delusions – when those identities prove false. Lucie perhaps represents the total uncertainty which lies outside all utopian models of existence, beyond the reach of knowledge or ideology, and which remains after all these have failed. Kundera devotes much analysis and authorial affection in his later novels to characters descended from Lucie, notably Tamina in *BLF*, Tereza in *ULB* and Agnes in *Immortality*, who in turn shed retrospective light on their more enigmatic forebear.

## Towards the 'thinking novel'

Kundera emerges as a prose writer in the 1960s amid fashionable, though not new claims that the novel was dead. In terms not far from Kundera's notion of the 'period of terminal paradoxes', Patricia Waugh associates the developments in fiction at this time with a 'sense that reality or history are provisional: no longer a world of eternal verities but a series of constructions, artifices, impermanent structures. The materialist, positivist and empiricist worldview on which realistic fiction is premised no longer exists'.[6] Kundera, however, distances himself from the 'destructive' emotional reaction of writers who seek to undermine the novel, assert its exhaustion and assist in its disintegration.

In Kundera's view, at worst only the novel of the 'second half' is exhausted; in this respect he shares his contemporaries' rejection of the realist novel, but is careful not to perceive that as the only possible novel. He sees the 'death' of the realist novel first in the 'officially sanctioned' novels published in the Soviet Union and elsewhere, which conform to and serve state ideology. Kundera's assertion that 'a novel that does not discover a hitherto unknown segment of existence is immoral' (*AN*, 6) is clearly directed at those novels which 'only confirm what has already been said; furthermore: in confirming what everyone says (what everyone must say), they fulfil their purpose, their glory, their usefulness to that society' (*AN*, 14). Second, Kundera sees the 'death' of the novel of the 'second half' in contemporary popular fiction. In *TB*, he writes:

> most novels produced today stand outside the history of the novel: novelized confessions, novelized journalism, novelized score-settling, novelized autobiographies, novelized indiscretions, novelized denunciations, novelized political arguments, novelized deaths of husbands, novelized deaths of fathers, novelized deaths of mothers, novelized deflowerings, novelized childbirths – novels ad

infinitum, to the end of time, that say nothing new, have no aesthetic ambition, bring no change to our understanding of man or to novelistic form, are each one like the next, are completely consumable in the morning and completely discardable in the afternoon. (*TB*, 17)

In *AN*, Kundera argues that the history of the novel is a 'cemetery of missed opportunities' waiting to be resurrected. He identifies particularly the notion of the novel as a game, the 'fusion of dream and reality', the possibility of making the novel the 'supreme intellectual synthesis' and the problem of collective time, the shared history of Europe. Later, he lists three specific technical aspects of Broch's *Die Schlafwandler* (*The Sleepwalkers*) that in his view are not successfully realised there, but inform his own experiments with the novel form. These are 'radical divestment', 'novelistic counterpoint' and the 'specifically novelistic essay'. In *The Joke*, Kundera is still working towards the type of novel that fully reflects these aspirations, but his progress can usefully be traced by comparing *The Joke* to his later work.

### 'Radical divestment'

By 'radical divestment', Kundera means rigorously reassessing what he describes as the automatic conventions of (implicitly realist) novel-writing, excising everything that is unessential in the description and explanation of character, plot, setting and context. By cutting to the heart of the matter, the novelist may succeed in 'encompassing the complexity of existence in the modern world' without writing an impossibly enormous work. Many critics note that Kundera chooses his words very precisely. As a result of this approach, Kundera, appearing as an actant in *Immortality*, can say, though aware of the Sisyphean nature of his task: 'if a reader skips a single sentence of my novel, he won't be able to understand it, and yet where in the world will you find a reader who never skips a line?'[7]

As the Czech novelist Jiří Kratochvil (b. 1940) has noted, *The Joke* retains remnants of the conventions associated with realism. The narrators provide details of their own and others' pasts, locations are named, the political context is sketched in. In particular, the authentic quality of Ludvík's depiction of his time in the army in Part III is unlike anything found subsequently in Kundera. Kundera was later critical of the excessive period detail in the novel, perhaps above all because it encouraged the interpretation of the novel in the specific historical context and in terms of his own biography. The removal of unnecessary historical and geographical detail helps Kundera to transform a specific temporal experience into a universalised existential experience that he is investigating on behalf of humanity, rather than just his generation or nation at a particular time.

The inclusion of details particularly about Ludvík's past – the references to his Communist father, who died in Auschwitz, or to the bourgeois family that brought him up – also encourage determinist psychological interpretations typical of realist novels. In later novels, Kundera would either exclude such detail or devote space to their analysis in the context of the themes of the novel, as for example in the exploration of Tereza's relationship with her sexually uninhibited mother in *ULB*. Indeed, the problem for Ludvík of his father's unassailable, eternal reputation, undeveloped in *The Joke*, prefigures Kundera's later reflections on immortality and the present's relationship to the past. Kundera's later characters are denied any more of a 'real past' than is relevant to the novel's themes. Kundera metafictionally dispels the 'illusion of reality' by describing what inspired him to create them: Tomáš in *ULB* is born from a phrase the author hears, Tereza from the rumbling of the author's stomach, Agnes in *Immortality* from the gesture of an unknown old woman at a swimming pool.

## Polyphony

After *The Joke*, Kundera abandons narration by character, perhaps because this strategy inhibits the process of 'radical divestment' and perhaps because Kundera found it increasingly artificial. Beginning with his next novel, *Life is Elsewhere*, Kundera instead uses an ironic, distant omniscient narrator, who explicitly identifies himself as the creator of the characters, mediates their thoughts, analyses their actions and emotions and in extended reflections shows how they prompt or arise from the themes of the novel. This omniscient narrating voice above all facilitates the unity of Kundera's 'novelistic counterpoint'. Kundera's first artistic training was in music, not literature; his father was a teacher and composer and the theory and history of music play a fundamental role in Kundera's approach to writing and understanding novels, and apparently his view of life. In *ULB*, he writes: '[human lives] are composed like music. Guided by his sense of beauty, an individual transforms a fortuitous occurrence (Beethoven's music, death under a train) into a motif, which then assumes a permanent place in the composition of the individual's life'.[8] Compositionally, his novels lend themselves easily to comparison with pieces of music. Kundera describes in *AN* how contrasts in tempo feature early in his planning of a novel, and suggests that the parts of his novels could carry dynamics and tempo indications, reflecting their dominant mood, their length, the time they take to read and the length of time they depict. This approach culminates in *Slowness* (1995), a celebration of taking one's time that is also his quickest novel to read.

The structure of a 'classic' Kundera novel has often been compared to that of a 'theme and variations'. This description particularly suits *BLF*, the seven parts of which function as independent stories at the level of plot, but are linked thematically; on this basis, Kundera has even retrospectively presented *Laughable Loves* as a novel in its German and Spanish translations. Both stylistically and thematically, Kundera's fiction and non-fiction seem an exercise in constant refinement. Because he returns constantly to a similar set of preoccupations, repeating ideas with slight changes of nuance or emphasis, critics like Eva Le Grand and François Ricard have found it easy to approach his body of fiction as a whole as a set of 'themes and variations'.

The core element of Kundera's 'novelistic counterpoint', however, is 'polyphony'. The musical term is commonly associated in literary theory with the Russian Mikhail Bakhtin (1895–1975), who, in his hugely influential study *Problems of Dostoevsky's Poetics*, finds in Dostoevsky's novels 'a plurality of independent and unmerged voices and consciousnesses; a genuine polyphony of fully valid voices is in fact the chief characteristic of Dostoevsky's novels'.[9] Bakhtin presents contrasting models of the novel: the 'monologic', where the voices and ideas of the characters are subordinate to the 'word of the author', and the 'polyphonic' or 'dialogic', where the author allows his characters the 'final word'. 'Polyphony' is also a key concept for the French *nouveau romancier*, Michel Butor (b. 1926), who adopts a more radically experimental stance on many of the same topics as Kundera, in particular the relationship between literature and music. Butor describes narration as 'a surface on which we isolate a certain number of lines',[10] leading in his work to the notional effacement of the author in a complex or collage of competing, coexisting texts.

Given the four narrating voices, it is tempting to regard *The Joke* as a 'polyphonic novel' in Bakhtin's sense. Each voice represents a different 'idea', even 'ideology', which Kundera communicates through the different styles of each narrator: Helena emotional, gushing; Jaroslav pastoral, dream-like; Kostka confessional, self-abasing; Ludvík rational, analytical. However, the reader senses the author's 'final word' in the shared trajectory of these ideological positions towards defeat. The different narrators are not, from the reader's perspective, really engaged in ideological dialogue, though they do supply different details about and contrasting interpretations of episodes in Ludvík's life. Rather, Kundera seeks to show the similarity of both motivation and outcome that lies behind each world-view. Indeed, one might even argue that this authorial 'final word' here imitates the 'totalitarianism' depicted in the novel, consuming the apparent heterogeneity of human hope and spitting it out as the homogeneity of despair. The novel reveals its musicality more in the abundance of scenes, episodes and characters that either echo or diametrically oppose one another.

Kundera's understanding of polyphony in fact relates to neither the voices of characters, nor the effacement of the author, but to the mixture of genres used in a novel. He notes how Fyodor Dostoevsky uses three different types of novel form in *The Possessed*, and how the third book of Broch's *The Sleepwalkers* is made up of 'novelistic' and 'poetic' narratives, short story, reportage and 'philosophical essay'. Kundera aspires, consistently from *ULB* onwards, to imitate more closely the simultaneity and equality of these heterogeneous voices and the indivisibility of the polyphonic whole found in music. The reader should not notice the shifts of form and genre, not experience them as ruptures, not be in any doubt that everything belongs in this novel, depicting in effect the natural, harmonious movement of the intellect and imagination over and around the problems the author wishes to explore.

Following *BLF*, one can imagine *ULB* as another series of independent stories, about love, about emigration, about parents and children, about conformity and dissidence, about the foolishness of idealism, were the different stories not held together by the four characters that feature across them all. The novel also has a central thread: the love story of 'doubting' Tomáš, caught between the eternally, passionately faithful, saintly Tereza and the endless 'betrayer' or pursuer of new experiences, Sabina, whose name is an allusion to a famous Bohemian traitor, Karel Sabina, a nineteenth-century Czech patriot who became a Habsburg police informant after 1848. Kundera, however, prevents this story from wholly absorbing the reader's focus. First, he begins not with his characters, but with two key themes of the text: what it means only to be able to live one's life once and whether it is preferable to experience existence as heavy or light. Second, he reveals the 'ending' of Tomáš and Tereza's story early in the novel. The 'story' of the novel's themes as they develop in shorter narratorial reflections and longer 'novelistic essays' is thus shown to carry at least as much weight as the plot of the novel. Some of these reflections are, loosely speaking, 'philosophical', others are metafictional, examining in particular the relationship between the author and his characters. Part of the novel is in the form of a 'short dictionary of misunderstood words'.

## The 'novelistic essay'

Kundera expresses his understanding of the 'novelistic essay' most completely in *The Curtain*:

> [it] has nothing to do with the thinking of a scientist or a philosopher; I would even say it is purposely a-philosophic, even anti-philosophic, that is to say

fiercely independent of any system of preconceived ideas; it does not judge; it does not proclaim truths; it questions, it marvels, it plumbs; its form is highly diverse: metaphoric, ironic, hypothetic, hyperbolic, aphoristic, droll, provocative, fanciful; and mainly it never leaves the magic circle of its characters' lives; those lives feed it and justify it.[11]

Kundera's first attempt at incorporating an essay into his novel is Jaroslav's musicological disquisition on folk music in *The Joke*. Though one may find several motivations for its relevance, the reader experiences it as a frustrating interruption in the plot, and, to Kundera's horror, the first translator of the novel into English chose to omit it altogether. The essay disrupts rather than augments partly because it does not live up to the above description, being too theoretical, and partly because of the dominance of the plot in *The Joke*, which militates against the polyphony Kundera later espouses. With the exception of *The Farewell Waltz* (1974), Kundera's skills as a plotter of stories are subsequently subordinated to his skills as an essayist and plotter of novelistic 'architecture'. Finally, to a greater extent than any other narratorial reflection in the novel, this section appears artificial, placed in the mouth of Jaroslav by the author in the words that he would use.

Kundera suggests that his move to an omniscient narrator paradoxically allows him to speak more authentically for his characters. In *AN*, he argues: 'Even if I'm the one speaking, my reflections are connected to a character. I want to think his attitudes, his way of seeing things, in his stead and more deeply than he could do it himself' (*AN*, 79). In the English translation of *ULB* (though not in the author-approved 2006 Czech version), Kundera writes: 'The characters in my novels are my own unrealized possibilities. That is why I am equally fond of them all and equally horrified by them. Each one has crossed a border that I myself have circumvented' (*ULB*, 215). Unlike the human being in history, through his characters, the novelist may live his life more than once. In effect, in *ULB*, Bakhtin's notion of the polyphonic novel is realised as a conversation between alternative authorial selves. As with Helena in *The Joke*, it is hard to see Kundera's fondness for the fourth major character in *ULB*, Franz, a Swiss intellectual still nostalgic for and susceptible to left-wing utopianism, whose autonomy does not survive Kundera's satirisation. However, far more than in *The Joke*, the distinct ways of living of Tomáš, Tereza and Sabina retain the 'last word', perhaps only, however, because they remain 'living' possibilities with which the author can empathise.

In his development as a novelist, Kundera plainly rethinks and outgrows the approach used in *The Joke*, yet many critics still consider it his best novel. One reason may be its greater openness to reader interpretation. Paradoxically, the Kundera novel with the most obvious 'lesson' leaves the most room for uncertainty and reader reflection, because of the details that go unremarked and the urgency and tension of the specific political context, and because many themes explicitly identified and examined in later novels are left implicit, to be disentangled and pondered without authorial help. Never again does Kundera give the reader a space as blank as Lucie. By *ULB*, the strategies that Kundera follows transform his novels into pieces of soothing background music, in which the reader becomes a listener rather than a participant in the unfolding and deepening of meaning.

## How novels should be read

Perhaps because of his imposing, for some even intimidating authorial personality, Kundera has tended either to seduce or repel critics, attracting gushing admiration and fierce, sometimes highly personal criticism, neither of which has generally pleased him.

In his non-fiction, Kundera often encourages the reader to unlearn present-day ways of reading novels and adopt others, perhaps because he sees his work as belonging to the 'first' tradition of the novel, one less fashionable and less well understood by today's reader. However, though expressed in terms of universal, abstract principles, the approach he advocates seems conveniently designed to ensure a specific way of reading his own fiction, insulating it from what he considers inappropriate speculation, misinterpretation and judgement.

This strategy may be seen in the context of the exceptional control that Kundera has famously sought to exercise over his works. As Michelle Woods discusses in detail, he has asserted his right to define the limits of his body of work, from which he has excluded many texts, especially those written in the 1950s, and personally supervised the translation and often retranslation of his novels into those languages he knows. For many Czech critics, this controlling tendency is not, however, merely innocent artistic perfectionism, but constitutes part of his apparent efforts, after emigration, to 'rewrite' the less flattering aspects of his past for an audience anxious to perceive him as a persecuted writer, and reflects his endless ability to adapt to the expectations of his changing audience, from Stalinist Party ideologues to Western bourgeois semi-intellectuals in the Cold War. Though Kundera rejects precisely this biographical reading of literary texts, the desire to control and dominate is an inherent element of both his plots and narrative style, and manifests itself also in his constant repetition and refinement in his work of a limited set of preoccupations, themes and motifs. It has also led some critics to describe his portrayal of women as misogynist.

Kundera is most exercised about the contexts used in interpreting a novel. He rejects the common academic approach whereby a novel is studied in the national context from which it emerged. In his view, to read his novels, one does not need to know more about the specific history of Czechoslovakia than the novel itself tells. Knowledge of the history of Europe, understood as a 'single common experience', should be enough for the reader to make sense of any novel. He argues that, for a novel's contribution – its 'aesthetic value' – to be understood, it must be studied as part of 'world literature'. In *AN*, he writes: 'The novel is Europe's creation; its discoveries, though made in various languages belong to the whole of Europe. The *sequence of discoveries* (not the sum of what was written) is what constitutes the history of the European novel. It is only in such a supranational context that ... the import of its discovery can be fully seen and understood' (*AN*, 6). This notion implicitly informs the present volume. In *The Curtain*, Kundera points out how the major novelists of the canon worked consistently in a supranational context, reacting in their works to the works of predecessors whose languages they did not even speak.

Kundera thus hopes to rescue his work from the political context in which much of it first became known. *The Joke* was first published abroad when sympathy for Czechoslovakia among Western intellectuals was at its height, affording those Czech writers perceived as opponents and victims of the regime a brief chance to be heard. However, even given this context, Kundera claims to have been bitterly disappointed by the reaction of French reviewers, which focused almost exclusively on the politics. He later wrote:

> the historical situation is not the real subject of the novel; its meaning rests for me in the way it casts a new, exceptionally bright light on existential subjects that fascinate me: revenge, forgetting, seriousness and unseriousness, the relationship of history and the human being, the alienation of one's own action, the splitting of sex and love and so on.[12]

Kundera presents himself as a most reluctant beneficiary of Western readers' interest in the exotic perspective of 'banned' writers from behind the Iron Curtain, which for his publishers long remained the main selling point of his novels, and narrow political interpretations of them persisted long after his emigration to France. His protests at these readings are somewhat undermined by his exploitation of post-1968 Czechoslovakia in both *BLF* and *ULB* that some Czech critics have seen as pandering to Western stereotypes to ingratiate himself with his new audience. Kundera's comments in *The Curtain* about the 'provincialism of small nations' seem plainly directed at those Czech critics who attacked his decision to emigrate rather than join the domestic opposition, his failure to ensure the availability of all his work in Czech, his abandonment of Czech for French and so on. Kundera writes: 'The small nation inculcates in its writer the conviction that he belongs to that place alone. To set his gaze beyond the boundary of the homeland, to join his colleagues in the supranational territory of art, is considered pretentious, disdainful of his own people' (*Curtain*, 38).

Kundera predictably reasserts the Formalists' strict separation of texts from their biographical authors, decrying the attempt to associate what is written in a literary text with the views of the person who wrote it, and on this basis to reach a moral judgement of that person: 'I have always, deeply, violently, detested those who look for a *position* (political, philosophical, religious, whatever) in a work of art rather than searching it for an *effort to know*, to understand, to grasp this or that aspect of reality' (*TB*, 89). For Kundera:

> being a novelist was more than just working in one 'literary genre' rather than another; it was an outlook, a wisdom, a position; a position that would rule out identification with any politics, any religion, any ideology, any moral doctrine, any group; a considered, stubborn, furious non-identification, conceived not as evasion or passivity, but as resistance, defiance, rebellion. (*TB*, 156)

In his view, the reader may make moral judgements, but the novelist himself eschews them. Kundera writes: 'suspending moral judgement is not the immorality of the novel; it is its morality. The morality that stands against the ineradicable human habit of judging instantly, ceaselessly, and everyone; of judging before, and in the absence of, understanding' (*TB*, 7).

## The utopia of the novel

In effect, Kundera has not abandoned his utopian idealism, but transferred it from the realm of life to the realm of the novel, where, he argues, the novelist enjoys the freedom that is denied him in the world outside it. In *TB*, he asserts:

> the history of humanity and the history of the novel are two very different things. The former is not man's to determine, it takes over like an alien force he cannot control, whereas the history of the novel (or of painting, of music) is born of man's freedom, of his wholly personal creations, of his own choices ... Because of its personal nature, the history of an art is a revenge by man against the impersonality of the history of humanity. (*TB*, 15–16)

Kundera shows that in history the human being is imprisoned in an image of himself, an identity that he does not recognise, imposed by the unforeseen consequences of his actions and the judgements of others. In *AN*, Kundera writes: 'man hopes to reveal his own image through his act, but that image bears no resemblance to him' (*AN*, 24). In *The Joke*, Ludvík's mistake is to try repeatedly to erase this discrepancy with further acts, which only exacerbates it. This is what Kundera means when he defines the novel as 'an investigation of human life in the trap the world has become' (*ULB*, 215). While investigating this trap, however, the novelist temporarily becomes creator, free to explore endlessly all the possibilities and variations of himself, to create and recreate his identity, to lead and mislead. Kundera knows that this revenge on history is futile, illusory; that is why he styles himself a 'mournful God'. However, his implicit message to the reader is that, to live best in this world, one must live it as a novelist.

## Note on editions/translations

Since Kundera has always reserved the right to revise his works repeatedly, and some have appeared in Czech or in translation without his involvement, there are competing versions of his fiction in different languages. He has indicated that the definitive versions are the last revised editions published in French by Gallimard. In English, the authorially approved translations of three novels are from the French by Aaron Asher published by Faber and Faber (UK) and Harper Perennial (USA): *The Joke* (1992), *The Farewell Waltz* (1998) and *Life is Elsewhere* (2000). The English translations of *The Book of Laughter and Forgetting* (1982) and *The Unbearable Lightness of Being* (1984) differ significantly from the author-approved French versions. There is only one English book version of his non-fiction and his novels since *Immortality* (1991), all published by Faber and Faber and Harper Perennial.

### Notes

1 Milan Kundera, *The Art of the Novel*, trans. Linda Asher (London: Faber and Faber, 2005), p. 3. Hereafter, *AN*.
2 Milan Kundera, *Testaments Betrayed*, trans. Linda Asher (London: Faber and Faber, 1996), p. 72. Hereafter, *TB*.
3 Milan Kundera, *Směšné lásky* (Prague: Československy spisovatel, 1963), pp. 21–2 (my translation).
4 Milan Kundera, *Laughable Loves*, trans. Suzanne Rappaport (London: Faber and Faber, 1999), p. 133.
5 Milan Kundera, *The Joke*, trans. Aaron Asher et al. (London: Faber and Faber, 1992), p. 71.
6 Patricia Waugh, *Metafiction: The Theory and Practice of Self-Conscious Fiction* (London/New York: Methuen, 1984), p. 7.
7 Milan Kundera, *Immortality*, trans. Peter Kussi (London: Faber and Faber, 1992), p. 375.

8 Milan Kundera, *The Unbearable Lightness of Being*, trans. Michael Henry Heim (London: Faber and Faber, 1995), p. 49. Hereafter, *ULB*.
9 Mikhail Bakhtin, *Problems of Dostoevsky's Poetics*, trans. Caryl Emerson (Manchester University Press, 1984), p. 8.
10 Michel Butor, *Inventory*, trans. Richard Howard (London: Jonathan Cape, 1970), p. 19.
11 M. Kundera, *The Curtain: An Essay in Seven Parts*, trans. Linda Asher (London: Faber and Faber, 2007), p. 71. Hereafter, *Curtain*.
12 Milan Kundera, *Žert* (Brno: Atlantis, 2007), p. 364 (my translation).

## Further reading

Aji, Aron, ed., *Milan Kundera and the Art of Fiction: Critical Essays* (New York/London: Garland, 1992)

Le Grand, Eva, *Kundera, or the Memory of Desire*, trans. Lin Burman (Waterloo, ON: Wilfred Laurier University Press, 1999)

Němcová-Banerjee, Marie, *Terminal Paradox: The Novels of Milan Kundera* (New York: Grove Weidenfeld, 1990)

Ricard, François, *Agnes's Final Afternoon: An Essay on the Work of Milan Kundera*, trans. Aaron Asher (London: Faber and Faber, 2003)

Steiner, Peter, *The Deserts of Bohemia* (Ithaca, NY/London: Cornell University Press, 2000)

Woods, Michelle, *Translating Milan Kundera* (Clevedon: Multilingual Matters, 2006)

# Conclusion: The European novel after 1900

As the story of the novel moves into the modernist decades, it is especially necessary to guard against the progressive fallacy. For although writers constantly create new forms out of the perceived limitations of their predecessors, this does not necessarily imply, as it would in the natural sciences, that the new is an advance. Hence, while the present account focuses on major new directions in the idea and practice of fiction in the twentieth century, every variety of the novel that has been invented continues to be practised and, above all, the omniscient realist narrative, as developed over the two preceding centuries, remains a mainstay of the genre not just numerically but qualitatively.

At the same time, as indicated in the preceding essays, the novel has at all times reflected on the ambiguity of its narrative premises which can be understood both as literary conventions and as extra-literary truth claims. And as the sense of a social whole becomes more problematic, so it matters more to determine what sort of truth the novel tells: historical, moral, poetic? All of the above, no doubt, but which most essentially? Is failure in one of them more damaging than in others? Does poetic power give dangerous conviction to historical falsehood? As such questions especially pressed themselves on European writers at the end of the nineteenth century, the literary imagination was frequently polarised into two contrary possibilities. One was the naturalist impulse which faced the reader with the shameful underside of contemporary society and a bleak view of collective human motivation. Moreover, the assumption of historical progress, shared by Enlightenment tradition and contemporary bourgeois practice, was now shadowed by an anxiety of decline focused by Max Nordau's sweeping analysis of modern life in his *Degeneration* (1890). At the other pole was the aestheticist impulse most influentially represented in the novel by Gustave Flaubert. Aestheticism was perhaps a great myth of the nineteenth century, just as a morality of sentiment had been for the eighteenth. That is to say, a pure case of 'art for art's sake' might be hard to find, and is perhaps not fully coherent. Most commonly it was a slogan of revolt against excessive moralism and perceived bourgeois complacency, as in Théophile Gautier's preface to *Mademoiselle de Maupin* (1835). Nonetheless, aestheticism had a metaphysical underpinning in Arthur Schopenhauer's pessimistic philosophy of the Will in *The World as Will and Idea* (1818). Schopenhauer saw all human desire, thought and perception as illusions serving the blind 'will' of the life process. Accordingly, the aesthetic, in its Kantian definition as 'purposiveness without purpose', was for him a means of psychological withdrawal from the illusory purposes of life. Although Schopenhauer had little impact on academic philosophy, for which G. W. F. Hegel's idealism provided the European centre, he struck a resonant chord for socially pessimistic artists, such as Thomas Hardy. It was out of these mixed and polarised elements, ranging from naturalism to aestheticism, that the great modernist syntheses were to be created.

### The modernist novel

The paradigm case of high modernist fiction is James Joyce's *Ulysses* (1922) which, in its early reception, was variously understood as naturalism run to seed and as an aestheticist remove. Following Flaubert, Joyce constructed a major work of art out of the undignified materials of everyday contemporary life, including the clichés of modern culture. In *Ulysses*, however, Joyce abandoned Flaubert's romantic hunger for transcendence, which he had echoed in the 'scrupulous meanness' of *Dubliners*, for a comedic celebration of the everyday. The Flaubertian posture of narrative indifference, which was in truth a morally charged device, becomes a more real impersonality as Joyce seeks to remove entirely the narrating personality.

The ultimate effect of Joyce's narrative is to give us the everyday object shorn of authorial interpretation. But this is not, of course, literally possible and removal of the author is a misleading way of putting it. There can be no non-interpretative, non-attitudinal narration, for man lives, as Rainer Maria Rilke put it in the first of his *Duino Elegies*, in an 'interpreted' world, and so Joyce's method is to fill the narrative with a comic plethora of competing voices all with their different ways of constructing the world. Precisely by foregrounding and parodying this Cervantean play of interpretation, the text empties its authority and allows an intuition of the object in itself. In other words, many acute insights and passionate convictions are uttered without any one of them acquiring dominance, while the encountered objects, such as soap or fried kidneys, are at once allowed their human connection *within* the narrative and yet freed from human definition *by* the narrative. In the opening episode, for example, the military tower and the 'scrotum-tightening' sea are accorded sexually symbolic characteristics which we may initially take as coordinates for understanding and judging the action. But as the book goes on, we may wonder whether these are not themselves examples of the interpretative activity of the characters and their inherited culture to which the sea itself is gloriously indifferent. By fore-grounding, and over-loading, the interpretative and evaluative activity of language, the narrative achieves an elusive intuition: respect for the sheer being of the world.

Moreover, this spirit of objectivity also applies at the level of the charac-ter. In this book, the principle of subjectivity is on the face of it taken to an extreme: the popular, if perhaps misleading, phrase 'stream of conscious-ness' rightly points to the typical location of the narrative within a mind. Yet if the world cannot be experienced without a consciousness, neither is consciousness experienced without a world. And so the process of individ-ual consciousness in *Ulysses* is itself experienced unsentimentally as if part of the phenomenal world, and as part of the impersonal process of language into which the whole action is increasingly subsumed. For as the book goes on, language itself, in its various cultural registers, becomes the primary actor. In this way, Cartesian dualism dissolves as the extreme of subjectivity is transposed into the extreme of objectivity, and this reflects a wider feature of modernist fiction. At the very moment that the individual has become an apparently supreme value, the individual as a category, what D. H. Lawrence called 'the old stable ego', has begun to dissolve.[1] The influential modern streams of thought, Freudian, Marxian and Nietzschean, all converge on this recognition. Even as they variously prize the individual, they insist that the traditional conception of the unitary, autonomous ego is an illusion. Much of the technique of modernist fiction is devoted to embodying this double recognition. While the characters conduct their individual lives, the narrative embodies the larger processes in which they are unconsciously caught up. In *Ulysses* this is not so much a personal or Freudian unconscious as a literary and cultural unconscious signalled by the book's title. The characters are unwitting avatars of the Homeric epic.

Joyce's epic sign is an important clue to the nature of much modernist fiction for, like the notion of the individual, the novel itself undergoes a double fate in this generation. Even while the early-twentieth-century novel was witnessing some of the supreme achievements of the form, its tradi-tional bases were being dissolved. The novel was ultimately a descendant of the primary epic, and had defined itself largely in contradistinction to the epic even while maintaining the connection, as in Henry Fielding and Leo Tolstoy, but Joyce's modernist novel returns with a clear-eyed philosophical consciousness to its epic womb. It is philosophical because it rests on a metaphysic of conscious mythopoeia; a complex standpoint that can be found in several major writers of the time.

The turn to myth, both as a structural principle and as a philosophical standpoint, in early-twentieth-century writers is a familiar theme, though it is not always well understood because its actual variety is often subsumed under some single interpretation. In one aspect it may express a modern primitivism. Paul Gauguin's rejection of modern society to live, in his case, in Polynesia was reflected in writers like Pierre Loti and, in some measure, D. H. Lawrence. Meanwhile there were others, such as Joseph Conrad in *Heart of Darkness* (1902), for whom the primitive was a dangerous propensity that must be eternally restrained. Sigmund Freud was to articulate theoretically this conception whereby civilisation rests on the suppression and sublimation of instinct, although Conrad also saw his 'primitive' Africans as exercising an internal restraint in contrast to the barbarism of the Europeans. Indeed, the notion of the primitive was usually part of a more complex internal reading of modernity and in this respect the turn to archaic myth has two important aspects both of which were articulated in Friedrich Nietzsche's *The Birth of Tragedy* (1872).

Myth may represent a lost psychological wholeness which Nietzsche expressed through the combination of Dionysos and Apollo, or it may represent a conscious recognition of the humanly created world which he imaged as the willingness to dream on. The Nietzschean terms are palpable in writers such as Lawrence, Robert Musil, Thomas Mann and Marcel Proust who are centrally concerned with psychological wholeness. But myth also provides an ontological signature. Lawrence's *The Rainbow*, Proust's lost paradise, Joyce's *Ulysses*, all rest not just on pre-existing myths, but on a mythopoeic process that is newly defined for modernity within the book. Most notably, Mann's biblical tetralogy, *Joseph and his Brothers* (1934–43), inaugurates a consciously mythic last phase in his whole *œuvre*. In his own words: 'In the life of humanity the mythic is indeed an early and primitive stage, but in the life of the individual a late and mature one.'[2] In this conception of myth, the civilised individual does not regress to the archaic condition but finds an equivalent within a modern sensibility and knowledge.

This paradoxical state of a consciously lived mythopoeia is realised in a new understanding of the aesthetic. Whereas Schopenhauer had seen the aesthetic as an escape *from* life, Nietzsche turned it into the central image *of* life: a concentrated purposive affirmation within an otherwise purposeless existence. Nietzsche stands to this line of modernism as Schopenhauer stands to aestheticism while the aesthetic becomes the modern form of mythopoeia. At the same time, such a new anthropological appreciation of mythopoeic world construction also displaced the authority of natural science. Overtly in *Ulysses* and *The Magic Mountain*, less overtly in Proust, Lawrence and Musil, science becomes one of the modes of world understanding but no longer the paradigmatic form of truth. Among Joyce's intellectual heroes was Gianbattista Vico, whose argument in *The New Science* (rev. edn, 1744) that human being was a collective, historical self-creation now came fully into its own and gave a different rationale to the novel form. Rather than the novel seeking to represent and comment on a pre-existing world, the novel now enacts the processes of its creation. As it does so, it affirms the values at stake in the creation of the human world, and here again the mythic signature is crucial in allowing us to distinguish human aspiration from the experience of history. In the nineteenth-century novel, as in the wider culture of the time, history was a dominant mode of understanding. The formal genre of the historical novel was an explicit index of the sense of causality, of historical process, at work in the novel at large. But by the end of the century it was becoming apparent that history itself is hardly an authoritative source of explanation. History is always a matter of interpretation in the light of values and interests. Hence, in so far as the historian seeks an objective understanding, this may be a suppression of the evaluative premises or, if the objectivity *were* ideally achieved, the history would be shorn of human significance.

In this respect, modernist mythopoeia transformed the historical novel. Myth is a trans-historical narrative concerned with a complex of values through which history itself is to be judged. Of course, there may have been a stage in human culture when myth was taken for history, or when the distinction was not made, but as myth separates itself from historical consciousness its function as an examination of values per se becomes apparent. Hence, modernist myth becomes a way of identifying the values through which history itself is to be understood. *Ulysses* is steeped in history but its narrative, concentrated into a single day, re-enacts an ancient structure of human relationships in Homer's *Odyssey*. In an early essay criticising the blind spots of nineteenth-century historicism, Nietzsche had suggested that the true value of historical knowledge was the capacity to see through the provinciality of one's own time with what he called a 'super-historical' consciousness.[3] That is an excellent definition of the standpoint of *Ulysses* and it is the underlying philosophical significance of the modernist 'spatialising' of time noted long ago by Joseph Frank.[4]

Lawrence's *The Rainbow* is an illuminating comparison. Before going on to his modernist and spatialised *Women in Love*, with its geographical symbolism of Nordic and African, Lawrence provided a prequel giving the nineteenth-century prehistory of his major characters in the apparently historical form of a family saga. Yet it was already very different in being conceived under the mythic signature of the Genesis story and here it is useful to draw on the opening chapter of Erich Auerbach's *Mimesis* (1953) in which he distinguishes two foundational narratives of European culture: Homer and the Bible. He characterises the Homeric world as one in which everything has value through its human connection, the narrative lingers over objects and experiences treasured for their associations. By contrast, the Old Testament world is 'fraught with background'.[5] The human foreground is shadowy except when irradiated by the relation to the divine, the true locus of significance. Auerbach's distinction is remarkably apt for the difference between *Ulysses* and *The Rainbow*. Lawrence, of course, has transposed religious sensibility into a psychological quest just as Joyce transposed religious discourse into aesthetic understanding. Nonetheless, the two authors express the fundamental difference of Hellenism and Hebraism as defined by Matthew Arnold. Joyce seeks clarity and detachment while Lawrence creates a world imbued with feeling. In both cases, the mythic signature affirms the active assertion of a complex of values in their respective understandings of history.

## The novel and modern history

While Joyce, Mann and Proust were achieving their high modernist syntheses of historical realism and self-conscious mythopoeia, there were other kinds of fiction equally significant for an understanding of this phase of modernity. Some writers were, indeed, suspicious precisely of the artistic will which produced these magisterial achievements. Much of what has been said so far applies, for example, to Virginia Woolf but, while she brings the randomness of life to an aesthetic order in a modernist spirit, she does not typically draw on the stabilising power of myth. Rather the reverse, as she highlights the fragility of this order, and resists the seductions of authority which often had a masculinist inflection. Lawrence, who explicitly disapproved of the artistic willpower of Joyce and Mann, abandoned after *Women in Love* the summative social novel and wrote a series of highly personal quest fictions. Indeed, the very fact of a non-completed novel hovers between failure and being a significant statement in itself. Most strikingly, Franz Kafka, one of the most definitive writers of modernity, never actually completed the novels for which he is known, and the very incompletion now seems an intrinsic part of their enigmatic power. So too, Robert Musil's decades of work on his monumental *The Man Without Qualities* never brought it to a final form and, once again, the reader senses within the work itself a resistance to any falsely optimistic, or merely artistic, synthesis. It is not just the difficulty of blending its elements of intellectual satire, historical interpretation and spiritual quest, but the radically self-questioning scepticism from which the narrative itself is generated.

In short, the resistance to resolution is a significant reflection on the conditions of modernity and may arise from the most gifted and penetrating novelists. Henry James is an oblique instance of similar strains. He continued to make consummate use of the nineteenth-century realist form, and yet the sophistication and obliquity of his late phase made him seem marginal and etiolated for many readers including his admired friend, Ivan Turgenev, who thought his work too *tarabiscoté*, too overdone.[6] James died without knowing the high value that posterity would accord to his capacity to place the moral ego under specifically modern pressures. In sum, even at the time of the modernist achievements, the truth-telling capacity of the novel was variously under strain.

In this respect, Walter Benjamin's essay 'The Storyteller' (1936) reflects an important turning point for the idea of the novel.[7] On the face of it, the early decades of the twentieth century had seen some of the most extraordinary achievements of the novel and seemed to vindicate a high idea of the form. The Russian Formalist critics appreciated the mastery of the genre in a philosophical spirit while E. M. Forster's more homely reflections in *Aspects of the Novel* (1927) likewise extolled the sophistication of the novel in contrast to the primitive naivety of story.[8] Yet only a few years later, Benjamin privileged oral storytelling as a significant communication of moral counsel in the form of experience, over the novel, whose sophistication and artistic mastery were for him precisely the index of its moral vacuity, the hollowness of its pretensions to moral wisdom. Benjamin's argument is vulnerable in almost all its terms, including the sharp contrast he draws between story and novel, yet he expresses a prescient insight for the rest of the century in which the novel continued to engage in a radical self-questioning against the standard of truth to experience. The political history of Europe in the 1930s may partly account for a distrust of modernism. Against the rise of fascism around the Continent, observers from George Orwell to Georg Lukács were to see the modernist generation as indulging an aesthetic solipsism.[9] Subsequent decades saw a variety of radical questionings of the novel form as, for example, in the French post-war *nouveau roman*. Samuel Beckett, while admiring very inwardly the achievements of Joyce and Proust, re-inflected them to face the dark underside of modernism as encapsulated, once again, in the impossibility of the novel form.

The acuteness of Benjamin's political and cultural antennae doubtless arose in part from his situation as a German Jew and from traditions of Jewish culture including the transmission of a folk experience beneath the level of any official national culture. In this respect, it is striking that Mann's

*Joseph and His Brothers* (1933, 1934, 1936, 1943), composed over the fascist years, retold the book of Genesis as the representative human story and specifically invoked the mode of oral transmission. It began with *The Tales of Jacob* in which Mann's narrative is constantly devolved into the traditional tales which guide the lives of the principal characters. A few years later, Primo Levi, as a talented young Jew surviving in captivity, used to read what he called 'Mann's Joseph stories'.[10] Later again, following the war, Levi was to tell his own life stories, which now included the definitive twentieth-century experience of Auschwitz, in the form of finely honed anecdotes. He defines *The Periodic Table* (1975), his late-twentieth-century masterpiece made up of such anecdotes, as 'in some fashion a history' (Levi, *Periodic Table*, p. 224) while making occasional allusions to the historical novelist, Alessandro Manzoni. Levi's book plays throughout on the ambivalence of tale-telling as he turns experience into counsel. For the real lesson, or challenge, of Benjamin's essay was that written narrative must somehow convey the weight of experience he attributed to the oral storyteller, and Levi was one of many twentieth-century writers who found ingenious ways to achieve this.

Thomas Bernhard and W. G. Sebald, for example, also used artful forms of personal memoir but in an opposite spirit to Levi's impersonality, for which science provides the dominant metaphor. Bernhard's coruscating critique of Austria in his five-volume biographical sequence (1975–82), translated in one volume as *Collecting Evidence*, and Sebald's meditation on historical transience in *The Rings of Saturn* (1995) are open to the charge that their narrators are respectively jaundiced and depressed. But the emotional subjectivity is acknowledged within the work and as it progresses the reader begins to feel not so much that the experience has been skewed by the personal emotion as that the emotional condition is the appropriate response to the experience. Something similar could be said of the bleak view of life in Beckett which keeps the reader off balance as it hovers between a general truth and an artfully concentrated construction. Taken simply as either, it would collapse into banality.

All these latter writers communicated, with varying degrees of indirection, the horrors of mid-twentieth-century European history. The Marquis de Sade, writing his *Ideas on the Novel* in prison, remarked that the excesses of recent history had outstripped the fictional imagination.[11] Sade's remark actually suggests a certain commonality whereby the French Revolution was indeed a dramatic spectacle which lent itself to fictional use. By contrast, mid-twentieth-century European history rather stripped than outstripped the imagination. The near extermination of the European Jews, which could not have been achieved without collaboration across the whole Continent, produced at first a period in which the dual conditions of trauma and guilt contributed to a general silence. And then, as it came to articulation, it had the force of a turning point in the history of human culture, and one that posed a special challenge to the truth of fiction. For the Shoah revealed the abyssal potential of all human beings when put under pressure, or when released from restraint, and all citizens of modernity carry this dark knowledge with them. Some believe this event should not be made the material of fiction at all, admitting only the austere tribute of testimony. But not all contemporaries are citizens of modernity in the sense just suggested, nor can the event be relied upon to articulate its own meaning, and so there is a supreme need for the kind of psychological understanding that fiction may provide. Hence as the novel moved into the latter half of the twentieth century, it entered a different phase again in its relation to history.

The first half of the nineteenth century saw the classic phase of the historical novel in which national myths were created from historical, or supposedly historical, materials. By the latter half of the century, a growing discomfort with the divergent truth claims of fiction and history made the form increasingly unviable but then, for the modernist generation, the turn to myth in a philosophically and anthropologically attuned spirit allowed for a new and critical self-consciousness about the mythic element in history. On the one hand, it was inescapable as man is a mythopoeic animal, and on the other hand, the inherited myths, including national ones, could be seen for what they are. So in Joyce, Mann and Lawrence, who responded intensely to the 1914–18 war, there is an appeal beyond the national principle to a more universal humanity of Homer, the Bible or pre-modern cultures. In these writers, the bringing of a mythopoeic consciousness to history is a liberating motive. But in the second half of the twentieth century, the relation of fiction to history changes again. It is now characterised, above all, by a sense of responsibility *to* history.

A work that both captured this post-war moment and provided a fruitful example for the future was Günter Grass's *The Tin Drum* (1959). In Grass's view, as the German post-war economic miracle cleared the physical rubble of the war, it was in danger of leaving a more important rubble unnoticed, the psychic rubble of German culture. So he engages the form of the *Bildungsroman* which had embodied the national ideal of Enlightened humanity achieved through a rounded culture. In *The Tin Drum*, the historical creation of the form is unravelled. Where Johann Wolfgang von Goethe had internalised the picaresque into the cumulative wisdom of an individual inner life, Grass's parody of the *Bildungsroman* rather recalls Christoph von Grimmelshausen's *Simplicius Simplicissimus* (1669), a work of picaresque energy set in the chaos and violence of the Thirty Years War. Oskar Matzerath, Grass's principal narrator, is multiply suggestive: in one aspect, he explodes the moral category of the individual while embodying the incoherent individual of the fascist state. Refusing to grow physically beyond three years old, he is endowed from birth with adult consciousness. Hence, the amoral egoism of a pre-socialised child is linked to the functional capacities of adult consciousness. The state of mind in which collective acts of extreme cruelty and injustice are performed is almost impossible to penetrate. As Hannah Arendt argued in *Eichmann in Jerusalem* (1963), whereas the deeds imply some extraordinary capacity for evil, the true horror is the banality of the perpetrator. Part of Grass's achievement is to create an imaginary figure who embodies a collective psychological condition. Unlike the typical nineteenth-century hero, such as Julien Sorel, whose individual life represents the collective experience, Oskar represents it by not being a coherent individual at all.

At the same time, Oskar is the conscious artist who unreliably narrates the book and, as his name suggests, he has aestheticist leanings in the several other art forms he practises, including breaking glass with his voice. In all these ways, the book suggests a destructive end point of the whole German tradition of humane aesthetics: Friedrich Schiller's belief that 'man is only fully human when he plays'[12] and that art is the highest form of play, become Oskar's drumming, itself a parody of Nietzsche's Dionysian music. Oskar's function is to keep the reader on the back foot, as a monster with whom we are obliged to identify, because, Grass implies, there is no morally secure standpoint from which the story can be told, at least by a German of this generation. It is possible, of course, to express post-war remorse, but who is to know whether this is any more than the new fashion, no more genuine than the fashionable emotions of the Nazi time? Oskar is Grass's way of getting the story told without claiming a moral standpoint outside the condition it depicts. *The Tin Drum* also stands in contrast to Mann's *Doktor Faustus* (1948), which subjects the history of German culture to a more penetrating and philosophical critique in a mode of high tragedy. Grass's dwarf-sized narrator, his eyes fixed on what happens below the table or the waist, allows no back-handed comfort from high cultural flights.

In its destructive reflection on previous cultural tradition embodied in classic works of fiction, *The Tin Drum* is an early version of a characteristically late-twentieth-century sub-genre: the rewritten classic. Two fine examples of this are Jean Rhys's *Wide Sargasso Sea* (1966) and J. M. Coetzee's *Foe* (1986). It is not accidental that these works should have been written by writers from the Caribbean and South Africa respectively. Indeed, at this point it is appropriate to note that the notion of the European novel becomes impossibly porous by the latter half of the century. Both readers and writers absorb fiction from around the world and the relevant criterion for being

European is no longer the origins of the writer but the work's relation to the traditions of European fiction. In this respect, both Rhys and Coetzee are deeply European. At the same time, as the colonial era came to an end after the 1939–45 war, and with substantial immigration from former colonies, so new histories and viewpoints sought expression in metropolitan fiction. Precisely because the novel embodied the inner, and often unwitting, structures of feeling in earlier cultural moments, it now provided the occasion for an equally inward deconstruction of them.

The rewritten classic, however, may take various forms, and its effects are not merely critical. As Rhys retells the story of Charlotte Brontë's *Jane Eyre*, for example, from the standpoint of Antoinette Cosway, aka Bertha Mason, aka the first Mrs Rochester, she does more than debunk the original by reversing it. In this respect, it is indicative that she encloses her story entirely within Brontë's narrative since this knowledge in the reader creates a further dimension of enclosure to highlight a truly tragic understanding that encompasses all the characters. Rhys's young Rochester is most significantly entrapped by his own cultural formation which leads him to reject Antoinette for the very qualities he should most prize. Meanwhile Antoinette, in finally knowing what she must do as she burns down the house, not only turns the mad act into a meaningful defiance, but expresses the historical entrapment that she symbolises for the reader. Moreover, in her defiant strength of character, she is a sister of Jane herself, albeit a less fortunate one, and her story deepens as much as it deconstructs the original.

By contrast, Coetzee's *Foe* is less a rewriting of *Robinson Crusoe* than a reflection on the perennial responsibilities of authorship. Accordingly, it proposes a completely different 'true' version of Crusoe's story which the well-known professional author, Daniel Defoe, is asked to write up by Susan Barton, possibly the central character of another Defoe novel, *Roxana*. She wishes to tell the story of Friday, whose tongue has been cut out, perhaps by 'Cruso' himself. In turning her true narrative into a quite different fiction, Defoe, who was originally called Foe, has erased the voices of both the woman and the black slave. Yet when he is challenged, he makes a good case for the superior saleability of his version; a version, moreover, which became one of the most influential of European fictions and an archetypal myth of modern individualism. And so the novel in its final chapter modulates, even more explicitly than *Wide Sargasso Sea*, from apparent realism to explicit metafictional poetry, as it imagines the silenced voice of Friday as an underwater scream filling unheard the oceans of the world. If *Foe* suggests the cultural historical structures in which the writer is caught, and to which he contributes, in *The Master of Petersburg* (1994) Coetzee imagines how a major literary achievement, in this case Fyodor Dostoevsky's, comes from dark sources in the writer. Then, in contrast to these male authors, he went on to develop an anguished female alter ego in the fictional novelist, Elizabeth Costello. Coetzee's *œuvre* is a sustained reflection on fiction as an irreducible mode of truth-telling, one that cannot be directly translated into politics, history or ethics, but which nonetheless enters the public arena to engage the most sensitive, politically charged topics. Its responsibilility to history is enacted in its irreducibility as fiction.

The traits of the rewritten classic appear differently again in the archetypal postcolonial novel, and one with an evident debt to *The Tin Drum*: Salman Rushdie's *Midnight's Children* (1980). This novel, rather than invoking a particular precursor, incorporates a whole body of previous fiction but on its own terms. It is narrated in a *babu* voice, the comic stereotype of English as spoken on the Indian subcontinent, but deploys it, as in G. V. Desani's *All About H. Hatter* (1948), with a wit ranging from the cultured to the demotic. Saleem Sinai, whose narrative, like his nose, recalls Laurence Sterne's Tristram Shandy, is another magic child. His magic property, telepathic reception of minds from all over the subcontinent, is more passive than Oskar's as it reflects a different focus on the burdens of representation understood in its double sense of mimesis and political voice.

The opening chapters, centred on a Dr Aziz, recall E. M. Forster's *A Passage to India* (1924), and through that a whole colonial literature, including Rudyard Kipling's *Kim* (1901), that sought to understand and represent India under Western eyes. In Saleem, by contrast, the very project of representation is subjected to Sternean parody and miscarriage, partly by concentration on his hapless body. The problems of representation cut both ways: neither the individual nor the historical social context can be understood without the other, yet each can be adequately known only through the other. As Saleem says in the opening paragraphs, and repeats thereafter, to understand an individual life you have 'to swallow a world'. In a book largely structured on metaphors of bodily fluids and consumption, this suggests a necessary condition predicated on impossibility and gullibility. But Saleem's magic gift places the burden of representation upon him and, when he first becomes aware that he can enter at will the consciousness of individuals all over the subcontinent, he rejoices in a felt power he defines as the 'illusion of the artist'.[13] This is, in effect, the Balzacian artist and one might ask whether it is India that cannot be represented as Honoré de Balzac represented France, or whether the Balzacian project is itself an illusion. Of course, the distinction is inconsequential because, by its very parody of such representation, this novel performs the same function. Even as it mocks the classic project of the European novel, Saleem's narrative enters, and expands, its grand tradition.

In effect, then, this novel differs only in emphasis from the Balzacian model. As Michael Tilby points out, while privileging the air of reality it creates, Balzac's fiction has a lurking awareness of its creative status. Yet the difference in emphasis is significant and it places *Midnight's Children* within another late-twentieth-century sub-genre: what Linda Hutcheon has called 'historiographic metafiction'.[14] This is a worldwide phenomenon including, for example, Gabriel García Márquez's *One Hundred Years of Solitude* (1967) and Thomas Pynchon's *Gravity's Rainbow* (1973). Such works thematise the problems of historical truth and representation through the formal self-consciousness of the fiction itself. In a general way, they share the recognition underlying modernist mythopoeia that mythopoeia is an inescapable condition of the human. But whereas the modernists typically sought a trans-national, universally human value in myth, a later generation found these models both Eurocentric and imbued with a totalising *gravitas* even when conceived in the comedic mode of Joyce. In these late-twentieth-century works, by contrast, the handling of myth is characteristically play-ful and relativistic.

Indeed, a relativistic consciousness becomes increasingly significant for the latter half of the century. An important social function of the novel in this period has been to express the experience of ethnic, social and gender groupings. In this respect, it reflects, and promotes, a larger post-war shift from economic class analysis of the whole society to identity politics. The class order that pertained in European societies throughout the history of the novel was also a means of understanding those societies and its relative occlusion since the 1960s makes a whole and proportionate percep-tion less feasible. Although new establishments have formed in the worlds of politics, broadcasting, business and finance, these are themselves second-ary, interpretative activities which, while they lend themselves very well to novelistic treatment, especially satire, exacerbate the sense that, as Karl Marx put it, 'all that is solid melts into air'. It is hard to say whether fiction in this respect finds contemporary society elusive to representation, or represents very well how that society feels.

The sense of relativity is not just a collective effect of the novel but enters into its self-conception. In the 1960s to 1980s, the writings of the Russian scholar Mikhail Bakhtin became very influential. His thinking had been developed in the pre-war decades and his belated impact in the West was owing to political circumstances, but it also reflects a special readiness at the time for his conception of the novel. In the early 1920s, in what was to become *Problems of Dostoevsky's Poetics*, Bakhtin had reversed the common reading of this author.[15] The great international vogue for Dostoevsky at that time received him as a religious and philosophical thinker who expressed himself in works of fiction. Bakhtin argued that these fictions were not to be read doctrinally, but dramatically. A variety of views were being made to challenge each other in the work. And more tellingly again, even when the author meant to put his own beliefs into the work, his power as a novelist was such that these became dramatic elements subject to the same dramatic testing. Bakhtin then developed this into a general conception of the novel as the key philosophical and psychological testing ground for modern societies. He went on to reinforce this with a conception of medieval carnival as a licensed disorder through which repressed psychic energies could be manifest.[16] The novel in his view was the cultural avatar of carnival: a licensed space of anarchic freedom in the imagination. His conception became important for late-twentieth-century writers, since this was a period that saw catastrophic attempts to construct new social orders on ideological blueprints. Writers felt the need to keep an inner freedom in relation to their material, and perhaps the more so when they themselves were inspired by powerful convictions.

Hence, when Milan Kundera, in *The Art of the Novel* (1986), picks up Bakhtinian ideas, such as Rabelaisian humour or the novel's experimental freedom, he clarifies early misreading of his work. As a dissident émigré from the then Soviet-controlled Czechoslovakia, he found works like *The Book of Laughter and Forgetting* (1979) and *The Unbearable Lightness of Being* (1984) read as critiques of Soviet ideology. But for him this ideology was just the immediately local and historical form of a general human tendency to form consensual groupings whose function is more psychological than intellectual. And at very fundamental levels, joining is not a choice: all use of language is already a form of it. And so Kundera privileges this Cervantean problematic over the totalising momentum of a single realist narrative by exploring it relativistically in a variety of complementary sub-narratives.

In this latter aspect, he suggests another twentieth-century sub-genre, the philosophical tale, for which Jorge Luis Borges provides the classic instances along with Kafka and Italo Calvino. These differ from their eighteenth-century predecessors in that the metaphysical insights and conundrums are not at the level of content but of form. All these writers are in some immediate sense anti-realist while invoking a weight of historical experience. In Kundera's case, historical references have a philosophical point as he weighs the different ontological orders of personal and historical life. But his ironic de-realising of these grave realities also shows his cousinship with the off-beat survivor's humour of Jaroslav Hasek's *The Brave Soldier Schweyk* (1923) and Bohumil Hrabel's *I Served the King of England* (1983). An elderly Polish professor once remarked to me that if you inhabit the same patch of ground and find within your lifetime that it belongs to different nation states, you will have a special awareness of the unreality of these political entities. Kundera gives expression to such recognitions.

The conditions that helped to produce Bakhtin's thought are evident in Mikhail Bulgakov's *The Master and Margarita* (1966), a novel which also provides a concluding focus for the idea of the novel in Europe by the latter half of the twentieth century. The novel records the irruption into the atheistical materialism of Soviet Moscow of a group of demons who produce a grotesque but carnivalesque mayhem. It also tells of the Master, a novelist who has capitulated to the state by burning his manuscript. But the devils, who, as in Kundera, are forces not of evil so much as creative subversion, have magically preserved it. Meanwhile, within these supernatural narratives are interspersed sections of the Master's novel which, in a tradition including D. H. Lawrence, Nikos Kazantsakis and José Saramago, retells the story of Christ in a purely secular spirit. But the central figure for Bulgakov is Pontius Pilate whose lost opportunity with respect to Christ aligns him with the remorse of the Master and, even more poignantly, provides an archetype of all those who have been knowing or permissive bystanders to the horrors of modern history. Meanwhile, in more formal terms, the Gospel story, itself one of the great works of magical realism, becomes a secular narrative while atheistical Moscow becomes the site of supernatural intervention. If such an inversion were done from the standpoint of religious faith, it would have a more limited and two-dimensional meaning. But Bulgakov's supernaturalism is a literary device invoking the imaginative powers of the great Russian novelists: Alexander Pushkin, Nikolai Gogol, Dostoevsky and Tolstoy are not just alluded to, they inform its narrative energies. The late-twentieth-century vogue for magical realism is often attributed to Latin American origins and is said to reflect a premodern sensibility. But works like *The Tin Drum* and *The Master and Margarita*, which were composed long before the Latin American 'boom' of the 1960s, point to internal literary traditions which morever are thematically foregrounded in the work. In effect, magical realism is not a sign of ethnographic exceptionalism but a signature of literariness, a clear hint that the work is making truth claims of a psychological or mythic order which cannot be contained within a narrow conception of realism. At the same time, the phrase 'magical realism' suggests a form *of* realism as much as a departure *from* it and in that respect it indicates a further modern phase of the originary dialogue of realism and romance which gave birth to the novel.

This concluding essay, like the introductory one, has offered only a brief indication of some key turning points in the history of the idea of the novel in Europe. Neither these essays, nor the whole volume, could suggest the extraordinary wealth and variety of the form and doubtless every reader will have a charge list of scandalous exclusions. But the circle of inclusion faces outwards and the reader is invited to use these essays for useful bearings on Jane Austen, Emilia Pardo Bazán, Thomas Bernhard, Colette, Marguérite Duras, Penelope FitzGerald, Witold Gombrowicz, Juan Goytisolo, Knut Hamsun, Bohumil Hrabel, Ismail Kadare, Madame de Lafayette, Doris Lessing, Sandor Marai, Javier Marias, Iris Murdoch, Vladimir Nabokov, Georges Perec, Joseph Roth, George Sand, José Saramago, Antal Szerb, Miguel de Unamuno, Christa Wolf, Stefan Zweig ...

## Notes

1 *The Letters of D. H. Lawrence*, vol. I, ed. George J. Zytaruk and James T. Boulton (Cambridge University Press, 1981), p. 183.

2 Thomas Mann, *Essays of Three Decades*, trans. H. T. Lowe-Porter (London: Secker and Warburg, 1947), p. 422.

3 Friedrich Nietzsche, 'On the Uses and Advantages of History for Life', in *Untimely Meditations*, trans. R. J. Hollingdale (Cambridge University Press, 1997), pp. 65–6.

4 Joseph Frank, 'Spatial Form in Modern Literature', in *The Widening Gyre: Crisis and Mastery in Modern Literature* (Brunswick, NJ: Rutgers University Press, 1963), pp. 59–123.

5 Erich Auerbach, *Mimesis: The Representation of Reality in Western Literature*, trans. Willard R. Trask (Princeton University Press, 1953), pp. 12–18.

6 Leon Edel, *The Life of Henry James*, vol. I (London: Penguin, 1953), p. 442.

7 Walter Benjamin, 'The Storyteller', in *Illuminations*, ed. Hannah Arendt, trans. Harry Zohn (London: Fontana, 1973), pp. 83–109.

8 For the Formalists, see *Russian Formalist Criticism*, ed. and trans. Lee T. Lemon and Marion Reiss (Lincoln, NE: University of Nebraska Press, 1965).

9 Georg Lukács, *The Meaning of Contemporary Realism*, trans. John and Necke Mander (London: Merlin Press, 1963); George Orwell, 'Inside the Whale', in *The Collected Essays, Journalism and Letters of George Orwell*, vol. I, *An Age like This 1920–1940* (London: Secker and Warburg, 1968), pp. 493–527.

10 Primo Levi, *The Periodic Table*, trans. Raymond Rosenthal (London: Abacus, 1986), p. 73.

11 Marquis de Sade, *Idées sur les romans* (Bordeaux: Ducros, 1970).

12 Friedrich Schiller, *On the Aesthetic Education of Man in a Series of Letters*, trans. Elizabeth M. Wilkinson and L. A. Willoughby (Oxford: Clarendon Press, 1967), p. 107.

13 Salman Rushdie, *Midnight's Children* (London: Jonathan Cape, 1981), p. 174.

14 Linda Hutcheon, *A Poetics of Postmodernism: History, Theory, Fiction* (London: Routledge, 1988), pp. 105–23.

15 Mikhail Bakhtin, *Problems of Dostoevsky's Poetics*, trans. Caryl Emerson (Minneapolis: University of Minnesota Press, 1984).

16 Mikhail Bakhtin, *Rabelais and his World*, trans. Hélène Iswolski (Bloomington, IN: Indiana University Press, 1984).

Allott, Miriam, ed., *Novelists on the Novel* (London: Routledge and Kegan Paul, 1959)

Alter, Robert, *Imagined Cities: Urban Experience and the Language of the Novel* (Newhaven, CT: Yale University Press, 2005)

*Partial Magic: The Novel as Self-Conscious Genre* (Berkeley/London: University of California Press, 1975)

Anderson, Benedict, *Imagined Communities: Reflections on the Origins and Spread of Nationalism* (London: Verso, rev. edn 1991)

Armstrong, Nancy, *Desire and Domestic Fiction: A Political History of the Novel* (New York/Oxford: Oxford University Press, 1987)

Auerbach, Erich, *Mimesis: The Representation of Reality in Western Literature* (1946), trans. Willard R. Trask (Princeton University Press, 1953)

Bakhtin, Mikhail M., *The Dialogic Imagination*, trans. Caryl Emerson and Michael Holquist (Austin, TX: University of Texas Press, 1981)

*Problems of Dostoevsky's Poetics*, trans. Caryl Emerson (Minneapolis: University of Minnesota Press, 1984)

*Rabelais and His World*, trans. Hélène Iswolsky (Bloomington, IN: Indiana University Press, 1984)

Barker-Benfield, G. S., *The Culture of Sensibility: Sex and Society in Eighteenth-Century Britain* (University of Chicago Press, 1992)

Bartram, Graham, ed., *The Cambridge Companion to the Modern German Novel* (Cambridge University Press, 2004)

Becker, George J., ed., *Documents of Literary Realism* (Princeton University Press, 1963)

Bell, David F., *Real Time: Accelerating Narrative from Balzac to Zola* (Urbana, IL: University of Illinois, 2004)

Bell, Michael, *The Sentiment of Reality: Truth of Feeling in the European Novel* (London: Unwin, 1983)

Benjamin, Walter, 'The Storyteller', in *Illuminations*, ed. Hannah Arendt, trans. Harry Zohn (London: Fontana, 1973)

Berman, Russell A., *The Rise of the Modern German Novel: Crisis and Charisma* (Cambridge, MA: Harvard University Press, 1986)

Bersani, Leo, *A Future for Astyanax: Character and Desire in Literature* (Boston/Toronto, ON: Little Brown & Co., 1969)

Blanckenburg, Friedrich von, *Versuch über den Roman* (1774; facs. edn, Stuttgart: Metzler, 1965)

Bondanella, Peter and Andrea Ciccarelli, eds., *The Cambridge Companion to the Italian Novel* (Cambridge University Press, 2003)

Booth, Wayne, *The Rhetoric of Fiction* (University of Chicago Press, 1973)

Breon, Mitchell, *James Joyce and the German Novel 1922–1933* (Athens, OH: Ohio University Press, 1976)

Brink, André, *The Novel: Language and Narrative from Cervantes to Calvino* (London: Macmillan, 1998)

Brissenden, A. H., *Virtue in Distress: Studies in the Novel of Sentiment from Richardson to de Sade* (London: Macmillan, 1974)

Brooks, Peter, *Body Work: Objects of Desire in Modern Narrative* (Newhaven, CT/London: Harvard University Press, 1993)

*The Melodramatic Imagination: Balzac, Henry James, Melodrama, and the Mode of Excess* (New York: Columbia University Press, 1976)

*The Novel of Worldiness: Crebillon, Marivaux, Laclos, Stendhal* (Princeton University Press, 1969)

*Reading for the Plot: Design and Intention in Narrative* (Oxford: Clarendon Press, 1984)

Chapple, J. A. V., *Science and Literature in the Nineteenth Century* (London: Macmillan, 1986)

Cohn, Dorrit, *Transparent Minds: Narrative Modes for Presenting Consciousness in Fiction* (Princeton University Press, 1978)

Daiches, David, *The Novel and the Modern World* (Chicago/London: University of Chicago Press, 1960)

Damrosch, David, *What is World Literature?* (Princeton University Press, 2003)

David, Deirdre, ed., *The Cambridge Companion to the Victorian Novel* (Cambridge University Press, 2001)

Davie, Donald, ed., *Russian Literature and Modern English Fiction: A Collection of Critical Essays* (Chicago/London: University of Chicago Press, 1965)

Doody, Margaret Anne, *The True Story of the Novel* (Piscataway, NJ: Rutgers University Press, 1996)

Ermarth, Elizabeth Deeds, *Realism and Consensus in the English Novel* (Princeton University Press, 1983)

Forster, E. M., *Aspects of the Novel* (London: Edward Arnold, 1927)

Foster, John Wilson, *The Cambridge Companion to the Irish Novel* (Cambridge University Press, 2006)

Freeborn, Richard, *The Russian Revolutionary Novel: Turgenev to Pasternak* (Cambridge University Press, 1982)

Garrard, John, *The Russian Novel from Pushkin to Pasternak* (Newhaven/London: Yale University Press, 1983)

Garrett, Stewart, *Reading Voices: Literature and the Phonotext* (Berkeley: University of California Press, 1990)

Girard, René, *Deceit, Desire and the Novel: The Self and Other in Literary Structure* (1961), trans. Yvonne Freccero (Baltimore: Johns Hopkins University Press, 1965)

Hale, Dorothy J., ed., *The Novel: An Anthology of Criticism and Theory, 1900–2000* (Oxford: Blackwell, 2006)

Hegel, G. W. F., *Aesthetics: Lectures on Fine Art*, trans. T. M. Knox (Oxford: Clarendon Press, 1975)

Herman, David, ed., *The Cambridge Companion to Narrative* (Cambridge University Press, 2007)

Hillis Miller, J., *Topographies* (Stanford University Press, 2006)

Jameson, Fredric, *The Political Unconscious: Narrative as a Socially Symbolic Act* (Ithaca, NY: Cornell University Press, 1981)

Jones, Malcolm V. and Robin Feuer Miller, eds., *The Cambridge Companion to the Classic Russian Novel* (Cambridge University Press, 1998)

Kenner, Hugh, *Flaubert, Joyce and Beckett: The Stoic Comedians* (London: Allen, 1964)

Kermode, Frank, *The Genesis of Secrecy: On the Interpretation of Narrative* (Cambridge, MA: Harvard University Press, 1979)

   *The Sense of an Ending: Studies in the Theory of Fiction, with a New Epilogue* (Oxford University Press, 2000)

Kettle, Arnold, *The Nineteenth-Century Novel: Critical Essays and Documents* (London: Heinemann, 1972, 1985)

LaCapra, Dominick, *History, Politics and the Novel* (Ithaca, NY: Cornell University Press, 1987)

Lawrence, D. H., *Study of Thomas Hardy and Other Essays*, ed. Bruce Steele (Cambridge University Press, 1985)

Leavis, F. R., *The Great Tradition: George Eliot, Henry James, Joseph Conrad* (London: Chatto and Windus, 1948)

Levin, Harry, *The Gates of Horn: A Study of Five French Realists* (Oxford University Press, 1963)

Lukács, Georg, *The Historical Novel*, trans. Hannah Mitchell and Stanley Mitchell (London: Merlin Press, 1962)

   *Studies in European Realism*, trans. Edith Bone (London: Hillway, 1950)

   *The Theory of the Novel*, trans. Anna Bostock (London: Merlin Press, 1971)

MacIntyre, Alasdair, *After Virtue* (London: Duckworth, 1981)

McKeon, Michael, *Origins of the English Novel 1600–1700* (Baltimore: Johns Hopkins University Press, 1987)

   ed., *Theory of the English Novel: A Historical Approach* (Baltimore: Johns Hopkins University Press, 2000)

Mander, Jenny, ed., *Remapping the Rise of the European Novel* (Oxford: Voltaire Foundation, 2007)

Moretti, Franco, *An Atlas of the European Novel* (London: Verso, 1998)

   *The Way of the World: The Bildungsroman in European Culture* (London: Verso, 1987)

   ed., *The Novel*, 2 vols. (Princeton University Press, 2006)

Nabokov, Vladimir, *Lectures on Literature*, ed. Fredson Bowers (London: Weidenfeld and Nicolson, 1980)

   *Lectures on Russian Literature* (London: Weidenfeld and Nicolson, 1982)

Orwin, Donna Tussing, *Consequences of Consciouness: Turgenev, Dostoevsky, and Tolstoy* (Palo Alto, CA: Stanford University Press, 2007)

Parrinder, Patrick, *Nation and the Novel: The English Novel from its Origins to the Present Day* (Oxford University Press, 2006)

Pascal, Roy, *The Dual Voice: Free Indirect Speech and its Functioning in the Nineteenth-Century Novel* (Manchester University Press, 1977)

   *The German Novel: Studies* (Manchester University Press, 1956)

Pasco, Allan H., *Novel Configurations: A Study of French Fiction: Stendhal, Balzac, Zola, Gide, Huysmans, Proust, Robbe-Grillet, Saporta* (Birmingham, AL: Summa Publications, 1987)

Paulson, Ronald, *Satire and the Novel in Eighteenth-Century England* (Newhaven, CT/London: Yale University Press, 1967)

Petrey, Sandy, *Realism and Revolution: Balzac, Stendhal, Zola, and the Performances of History* (Ithaca, NY: Cornell University Press, 1988)

Prendergast, Christopher, *The Order of Mimesis: Balzac, Stendhal, Nerval, Flaubert* (Cambridge University Press, 1986)

ed., *Debating World Literature* (London: Verso, 2004)

Richetti, John, ed., *The Cambridge Companion to the Eighteenth-Century Novel* (Cambridge University Press, 1996)

Steiner, George, *Tolstoy or Dostoevsky: A Study in Contrast* (London: Faber and Faber, 1960)

Stern, J. P., *On Realism* (London: Routledge, 1973)

Swales, Martin, *The German Bildungsroman from Wieland to Hesse* (Princeton University Press, 1978)

Tanner, Tony, *Adultery and the Novel: Contract and Transgression* (Baltimore: Johns Hopkins University Press, 1979)

Trilling, Lionel, *Sincerity and Authenticity* (London/New York: Oxford University Press, 1972)

Turner, Harriet and Adelaida López de Martínez, eds., *The Cambridge Companion to the Spanish Novel: 1600 to the Present* (Cambridge University Press, 2003)

Unwin, Timothy, ed., *The Cambridge Companion to the French Novel: From 1800 to the Present* (Cambridge University Press, 1997)

Watt, Ian, *The Rise of the Novel: Studies in Defoe, Richardson and Fielding* (London: Chatto and Windus, 1957)

Whitmarsh, Tim, ed., *The Cambridge Companion to the Greek and Roman Novel* (Cambridge University Press, 2008)

Williams, Raymond, *The English Novel from Dickens to Lawrence* (London: Hogarth, 1984)

Woloch, Alex, *The One vs the Many: Minor Characters and the Space of the Protagonist in the Novel* (Princeton University Press, 2003)

# INDEX

Abelard, Peter, 101
Abish, Walter, 364
Adorno, Theodor, 407
Akerman, Chantal, 340
Akhmatova, Anna, 260
Alas, Leopoldo, 15, 307
Alemán, Mateo, 19
Alembert, Jean le Rond d', 90
Alexander II, 286
Alexis, Willibald, 155
Alleg, Henri, 397
*Amadis of Gaul*, 20
Apollinaire, Guillaume, 362, 370
Aquinas, Thomas, 361
Aragon, Louis, 339
Arendt, Hannah, 437
Ariosto, Ludovico, 21, 23, 141, 142, 159
Aristophanes, 86
Aristotle, 361
Arnold, Matthew, 138, 433
Auerbach, Erich, 382, 433
Augier, Émile, 311
Austen, Jane, 2, 3, 82, 186, 233, 247, 253
authority, 1, 10, 23, 24, 25, 26, 31, 32,
    80, 94, 96, 111, 192–208, 236, 395,
    399, 402, 429, 433

Badiou, Alain, 407
Bakhtin, Mikhail, 24, 213, 260, 265, 420, 440
Balzac, Honoré de, 1, 4, 11, 147, 150, 161,
    162, 166, 212, 214, 227, 232, 233–5,
    236, 249, 274, 294, 296, 312, 412, 439
    *Autre étude de femme*, 201
    *Comédie humaine*, 192–206, 233, 245
    *Eugénie Grandet*, 193, 205, 234
    *Grandeur et décadence de César
        Birotteau*, 195
    *Histoire des Treize*, 202

    *Illusions perdues*, 197, 203, 238
    *La Cousine Bette*, 193, 195, 196, 197
    *La Duchesse de Langeais*, 195
    *La Femme de trente ans*, 194, 201
    *La Fille aux yeux d'or*, 193, 197, 200
    *La Grande Bretéche*, 201
    *La Muse du département*, 201
    *La Peau de chagrin*, 194, 197
    *La Rabouilleuse*, 195
    *La Vieille Fille*, 193, 195
    *Le Cabinet des antiques*, 195
    *Le Cousin Pons*, 198
    *Le Curé de Tours*, 233
    *Le Lys dans la vallée*, 195
    *Le Médecin de campagne*, 195
    *Le Père Goriot*, 196, 202, 203
    *Louis Lambert*, 199
    *Physiologie du mariage*, 194
    *Recherche de l'absolu*, 199
    *Séraphita*, 198, 199
    *Une ténébreuse affaire*, 195
    *Ursule Mirouet*, 193, 198
Barbauld, Anna Laetitia, 66
Barnes, Julian, 257
Barthelme, Donald, 364
Barthes, Roland, 127, 162, 204
Bataille, Georges, 395, 396, 397
Baudelaire, Charles, 199, 205, 247, 327
Beauvoir, Simone de, 162
Beckett, Samuel, 81, 200, 248, 373, 375,
    394–407, 434, 435
    *All That Fall*, 396, 400, 401
    *Bing*, 405
    *Comment c'est*, 404
    *Company*, 400
    *Dream of Fair to Middling Women*, 398
    *Echo's Bones*, 398
    *En attendant Godot*, 394, 395, 396, 397

*Foirades*, 405
*Footfalls*, 400
'From an Abandoned Work', 404
*Ghost Trio*, 407
*Happy Days*, 400
*Imagination morte imaginez*, 405
*Krapp's Last Tape*, 400
'Le Calmant', 399
*Le Dépeupleur*, 405
'Le Fin', 399
'L'Expulsé', 399
*L'Innommable*, 394, 396, 403
*Mal vu mal dit*, 405
*Malone meurt*, 394, 396, 402
*Mercier et Camier*, 399
*Molloy*, 394, 395, 396, 401, 406
*More Kicks Than Pricks*, 398, 407
*Murphy*, 398, 399, 406
*Not I*, 400
*Pour finir encore*, 405
'Premier Amour', 399
*Rockaby*, 400
*Sans*, 405
*Textes pour rien*, 404
*Three Dialogues*, 405
*Watt*, 399, 401
*Worstward Ho*, 400, 405
Behn, Aphra, 55, 56, 59
Belinsky, Vissarion, 260
Bell, Clive, 379, 387
Benjamin, Walter, 201, 340, 434–5
Bennett, Arnold, 200, 361, 380
Berdyaev, Nikolay, 260
Bergson, Henri, 331, 348
Bermhard, Thomas, 435
Bernard, Claude, 296
Besant, Walter, 316
Biely, Alexander, 362
*Bildungsroman*, 6, 8, 108, 132, 134, 137,
    138, 143, 144, 151, 194, 210, 231,
    233, 240, 268, 329, 343, 348, 352,
    362, 378, 381, 399, 436
Blake, William, 361
Blanchot, Maurice, 396, 397, 400
Blanckenburg, Friedrich von, 5, 9, 129
Blok, Alexander, 260
Boccaccio, 86
Borges, Jorge Luis, 2, 209, 441
Bourget, Paul, 197, 320
Bowen, Elizabeth, 187
Bradshaigh, Lady, 66
Brandes, Georg, 361
Brecht, Bertholt, 222

Breton, André, 339
Bretonne, Rétif de la, 56
Broch, Hermann, 343–5, 348, 362, 412,
    418, 421
    *The Sleepwalkers*, 343–5, 358
Brontë, Charlotte, 4, 438
Brontë, Emily, 4, 187
Brunetière, Ferdinand, 241
Bruno, Giordano, 361
Budgen, Frank, 369
Bulgakov, Mikhail, 260, 442
Bunyan, John, 10, 41, 85, 149
Burgess, Anthony, 361
Burney, Fanny, 211
Burroughs, William, 373
Butor, Michel, 192, 396, 420
Byatt, A. S., 200, 204
Byron, George Gordon, Lord, 72, 86,
    176, 311

Cahagne, Abbé, 89, 92
Calvino, Italo, 162, 199, 441
Camus, Albert, 305
Čapek, Karel, 415
Carducci, Giosuè, 350
Carlyle, Thomas, 138, 210, 223, 311
Carter, Angela, 187
Castro, Americo, 15
Cavalcanti, Guido, 361
Cendrars, Blaise, 362, 370
Cervantes, Miguel de, 1, 2, 3, 9, 14, 15,
    17–35, 75, 80, 86, 109, 140, 141, 143,
    146, 159, 203, 211, 214, 221, 235,
    244, 375, 411, 429, 441
    *Don Quixote*, 17–33
    *Exemplary Novels*, 19, 26
Chapone, Sarah, 55
Charles V, 17, 18
Charles X, 165
Chaucer, Geoffrey, 2
Chekhov, Anton, 308, 361, 380, 383
Cherbuliez, Victor, 317
Chernyshevsky, Nikolay, 261, 265
Child, Theodore, 315
Chrétien de Troyes, 20, 22
Coetzee, J. M., 259, 437
Coleridge, Samuel Taylor, 48, 138, 151, 178,
    181, 182
Collins, Wilkie, 189, 212, 215, 217
Conrad, Joseph, 177, 371, 378, 399, 431
Conrad, Michael Georg, 306
Constant, Benjamin, 164, 328
Coover, Robert, 364

Corneille, Pierre, 141
Crowley, Aleister, 200
Culler, Jonathan, 249
Curtius, Ernst Robert, 340
Czapsi, Joseph, 340

D'Annunzio, Gabriele, 311, 366
Dante Alighieri, 198, 328, 351, 366, 398
Darwin, Charles, 296
Darwin, Erasmus, 178
Daudet, Alphonse, 310, 313, 316, 319
Davenport, Guy, 364
Davidoff, Denys, 141
Davy, Humphry, 178
Davys, Mary, 56
De Quincey, Thomas, 138
Defoe, Daniel, 9, 14, 50, 180, 211, 389, 438
    A Journal of the Plague Year, 37, 41–5
    Captain Singleton, 37
    Farther Adventures of Robinson Crusoe, 37
    Moll Flanders, 37
    Review, 41
    Robinson Crusoe, 36, 37, 47–50, 181
    Roxana, 37, 45–7
    The Storm, 38–9
Delacroix, Eugène, 205
Deleuze, Gilles, 397, 399, 407
Derrida, Jacques, 397, 400, 407
Desani, G. V., 439
Descartes, René, 278, 406, 412
    Cartesian, 5, 283, 412
Dickens, Charles, 3, 4, 9, 12, 14, 115, 121, 144,
    187, 209–24, 278, 316, 319, 367, 375
    A Christmas Carol, 209
    A Tale of Two Cities, 215, 218,
        219–20, 223
    American Notes, 209
    Barnaby Rudge, 210
    Bleak House, 209
    David Copperfield, 211, 212, 220–1
    Dombey and Son, 213, 222
    Great Expectations, 210, 221
    Hard Times, 213, 222
    Household Words, 216
    Little Dorrit, 209, 213, 215, 218–19
    Martin Chuzzlewit, 209
    The Mystery of Edwin Drood, 216
    Nicholas Nickleby, 211, 216
    No Thoroughfare, 218
    The Old Curiosity Shop, 211, 213, 214
    Oliver Twist, 211
    Our Mutual Friend, 213, 214, 216
    The Pickwick Papers, 211, 221

Pictures from Italy, 209, 213
Sketches by Boz, 213
Diderot, Denis, 5, 14, 77, 120, 316, 411
Dilthey, Wilhelm, 137
Döblin, Alfred, 362
Doré, Gustave, 199
Dos Passos, John, 362
Dostoevsky, Fyodor, 8, 14, 68, 121, 199, 209,
    224, 228, 259–74, 278, 354, 380, 388,
    420, 421, 439, 440, 442
    A Writer's Diary, 271
    Atheism, 263
    Brothers Karamazov, 259, 261, 263–4,
        267, 273
    Crime and Punishment, 261, 262, 263,
        265, 271
    Demons, 261, 262, 263, 266, 267–8
    The Double, 265, 268
    The Idiot, 261, 262, 263, 267, 271, 272–3
    The Insulted and the Injured, 259
    The Life of a Great Sinner, 263
    Netochka Nezvanova, 268
    Notes from the House of the Dead,
        261, 269–71, 272
    Notes from Underground, 261, 265, 268
    Poor Folk, 260, 268
Dreiser, Theodore, 199
Dujardin, Eduard, 370
Dumas, Alexandre, 223, 288, 311
Duras, Marguerite, 397

Edgeworth, Maria, 211
Eikhenbaum, Boris, 282
Einstein, Albert, 362
Eliot, George, 3, 11, 14, 72, 138, 149, 211,
    227–41, 311
    Adam Bede, 229, 232
    Daniel Deronda, 229, 230, 235, 239–40
    Felix Holt, the Radical, 241
    Middlemarch, 227, 229, 233, 235–9
    The Mill on the Floss, 229, 230, 233
    Romola, 229
    Scenes of Clerical Life, 233
    Silas Marner, 234
Eliot, T. S., 362, 363, 370, 374, 379,
    384, 387
Elkin, Stanley, 364
Eluard, Paul, 339, 413
Emerson, Ralph Waldo, 228
epic, 4, 7, 9, 83, 201, 284, 291, 295, 328,
    343, 368, 430
    comic epic, 78
epistolary novel, 54

*Fanny Hill*, 41
Faulkner, William, 187, 362
Federman, Raymond, 364
Fénelon, François de Salignac de la
    Mothe, 78
Ferguson, Adam, 145
Feuerbach, Ludwig, 227, 230, 265
Fichte, J. G., 120
Fielding, Henry, 2, 3, 5, 6, 10, 11, 13, 14, 41,
    57, 72–85, 86, 112, 180, 211, 214,
    222, 236, 375, 430
  *Amelia*, 76
  *The Champion*, 75
  *The Covent Garden Journal*, 75
  *Don Quixote in England*, 72
  *The Historical Register*, 74
  *Jonathon Wild*, 75
  *Joseph Andrews*, 81
  *The Journal of a Voyage to Lisbon*, 76
  *Love in Several Masques*, 73
  *Pasquin*, 74
  *Shamela*, 65, 75
  *Tom Jones*, 81–5
  *Tragedy of Tragedies*, 74
  *The True Patriot*, 75
Flaubert, Gustave, 3, 11, 209, 211, 224,
    227, 236, 237, 240, 244–58, 313–14,
    327, 332, 338, 361, 368, 375,
    386, 388, 429
  *Bouvard and Pecuchet*, 224, 247, 257
  *Madame Bovary*, 246, 250, 251, 253,
    254, 255–6
  *Memoirs of a Madman*, 245
  *November*, 245
  *Salammbô*, 244, 247, 251, 252
  *Sentimental Education*, 227–41, 245, 248,
    250, 252, 254
  *The Temptaion of Saint Anthony*, 246
  *Three Tales*, 245, 248, 251, 253
Fletcher, John, 17
Fontane, Theodor, 241, 250
Forster, E. M., 147, 324, 387, 388,
    434, 439
Foucault, Michel, 397
Frank, Joseph, 432
Franz Joseph, Emperor, 345
French Revolution, 6, 7, 8, 131, 141, 151,
    152, 161, 163, 165, 183, 185, 192,
    195, 212, 257, 350, 435
Freud, Sigmund, 29, 185, 194, 259,
    372, 430, 431
Fry, Roger, 379, 387
Fuentes, Carlos, 199, 340

Galdós, Benito Pérez, 15, 153, 307
Galsworthy, John, 380
Gaskell, Elizabeth, 211
Gauguin, Paul, 431
Gautier, Théophile, 199, 429
Genet, Jean, 401
Gide, André, 162, 259, 345, 371
Girard, René, 3
Gissing, George, 12
Godard, Jean-Luc, 341
Godwin, William, 178, 182, 184, 186
Goethe, Johann Wolfgang von, 5, 6, 7, 9, 61,
    90, 112, 114, 120, 124–39, 140, 183,
    200, 227, 228, 230–2, 238, 253, 328,
    343, 348, 352, 357
  *Elective Affinities*, 134–6
  *Faust*, 129
  *The Sorrows of Young Werther*, 124–9
  *Wilhelm Meister's Apprenticeship*, 130–3
  *Wilhelm Meister's Journeyman Years*, 133–4
  *Wilhelm Meister's Theatrical Mission*, 130
Gogol, Nikolai, 122, 215, 260, 278, 442
Goldsmith, Oliver, 160, 211
Gombrowicz, Witold, 122
Goncourt, Brothers, 308, 313, 319
Gorky, Maxim, 85
Gothic, 3, 176–90, 259
Gounod, Charles, 357
Grass, Günter, 119, 436
Grimm, Friedrich-Melchior, 90
Grimmelshausen, Christoph von, 436
Grossman, Vassily, 290
Gustavus Adolphus, 45

Haller, Albrecht von, 57
Hamilton, Clayton, 385
Hardy, Thomas, 73, 150, 221, 306, 429
Hašek, Jaroslav, 412, 441
Hauptmann, Gerhart, 361
Hawthorne, Nathaniel, 312
Haywood, Eliza, 41, 56, 59, 60
Hazlitt, William, 148
Hegel, G. W. F., 8, 130, 343, 429
Heidegger, Martin, 12, 410, 411, 413, 416
Herder, Johann Gottfried, 7, 148
Heuet, Stéphane, 341
history, 9, 21, 81, 119, 144, 148, 179, 229, 284,
    290, 332, 346, 374, 412, 417, 424, 425,
    432, 433–7, 438, 439, 442
  historical, 8, 195, 257, 283–5, 332, 361,
    389, 392, 418, 424, 428, 433, 434,
    435, 438, 440, 441
  historical novel, 146, 147, 210, 432, 435, 436

Hitchcock, Alfred, 341
Hoffmann, E. T. A., 120, 185, 210
Hofmannsthal, Hugo von, 199
Hölderlin, Friedrich, 372
Homer, 78, 140, 343, 362, 369, 374, 430, 433, 436
Hopkins, Gerard Manley, 364
Howells, William Dean, 314, 315
Hrabel, Bohumil, 441
Hugo, Victor, 199, 305
Humboldt, Wilhelm von, 7
Hume, David, 90
Husserl, Edmund, 411
Huxley, Aldous, 345
Huysmans, J.-K., 361

Ibsen, Henrik, 311, 321, 361, 366
Inchbald, Elizabeth, 211

James, Henry, 33, 82, 161, 196, 197, 199, 200, 209, 247, 248, 310–25, 380, 388, 391, 434
    The Ambassadors, 312, 322, 323, 324
    The American, 312–13, 318
    'The Aspern Papers', 311
    The Awkward Age, 312, 322
    The Bostonians, 311, 316, 320, 322
    Confidence, 312
    Daisy Miller, 317, 318
    The Europeans, 311, 319
    The Golden Bowl, 312, 322, 323–4
    Guy Domville, 321
    The Portrait of a Lady, 312, 315, 317, 318, 319, 323
    The Princess Casamassima, 312, 317–21, 322
    The Reverberator, 312
    Roderick Hudson, 311, 312, 318, 319
    The Sacred Fount, 312
    The Spoils of Poynton, 312, 322
    The Tragic Muse, 311, 312, 319, 320
    Washington Square, 311, 317
    Watch and Ward, 311
    What Maisie Knew, 312
    The Wings of the Dove, 312, 322, 323
James, William, 315, 321
Johnson, Samuel, 13, 81, 142, 178
Jolas, Eugene, 363
Jonson, Ben, 118
Joukovsky, Paul, 311
Joyce, James, 121, 209, 251, 253, 256, 274, 290, 327, 332, 345, 361–75, 381, 383, 399, 401, 407, 433, 434, 436, 440

A Portrait of the Artist as a Young Man, 365–7, 370, 373
    Dubliners, 361, 429
    Exiles, 361
    Finnegans Wake, 361, 363, 364, 373
    Stephen Hero, 361
    Ulysses, 361, 365, 366, 373, 375, 429–31, 432
Joyce, Stanislaus, 372, 373
Jung, Carl Gustav, 372, 374, 401

Kafka, Franz, 127, 209, 224, 248, 250, 280, 400, 412, 433, 441
Kant, Immanuel, 98, 112, 115, 387, 429
Kazantsakis, Nikos, 442
Keller, Gottfried, 137, 232–3
Keneally, Thomas, 7
Kipling, Rudyard, 439
Kock, Paul de, 215
Kratochvil, Jiří, 418
Kundera, Milan, 1, 22, 239, 244, 248, 375, 410–26, 441, 442
    The Art of the Novel, 410, 412, 417, 419, 422, 424, 425
    The Book of Laughter and Forgetting, 410, 413, 417, 420, 421, 424
    The Curtain, 421, 424
    The Farewell Waltz, 422
    'I, the Mournful God', 414
    Immortality, 417, 418, 419
    The Joke, 414–17, 418, 419, 420, 422, 424, 426
    Laughable Loves, 414, 420
    Life is Elsewhere, 413, 419
    Slowness, 419
    Testaments Betrayed, 411, 417, 425
    The Unbearable Lightness of Being, 410, 417, 419, 421, 422, 423, 424, 426

L'Estrange, Sir Roger, 58
Laclos, Choderlos de, 3, 10, 14, 61, 68, 90, 112, 125, 163, 167, 316, 411
Lafayette, Mme de, 3, 112, 328
Larbaud, Valery, 362
Lavergne, Gabriel Joseph de, 56
Lawrence, D. H., 13, 109, 122, 138, 200, 371, 430, 431, 432, 433, 436, 442
Lazarillo de Tormes, 19
Leavis, F. R., 147, 223
Lennox, Charlotte, 142
Lermontov, Mikhail, 278
Lesage, Alain-René, 74, 211, 222
Lessing, G. E., 128

*Lettres portuguaises*, 59
Levi, Primo, 435
Lewes, George Henry, 138, 228, 229, 230, 232
Lewis, C. S., 2
Lewis, Matthew, 179, 181, 185
*libros de caballerías*, 20, 22
Locke, John, 108–9, 118, 280
Loti, Pierre, 431
Louis XI, 151
Louis XIII, 152
Louis XVI, 194
Louis XVIII, 165
Louis-Philippe, 165, 204
Lubbock, Percy, 147, 386
Lucian, 86
Lukács, G., 147, 151, 210, 343, 434
Lyotard, Jean-François, 397

Mach, Ernst, 345, 346, 363
MacKenzie, Henry, 112, 140
McPherson, James, 128, 148, 178
Maeterlinck, Maurice, 310
Makine, Andrei, 400
Malesherbes, Guillaume-Chrétien de Lamoignon de, 90
Mallarmé, Stéphane, 364, 372
Man, Paul de, 206
Manet, Édouard, 297, 304
Manley, Delarivier, 55
Mann, Thomas, 121, 138, 228, 290, 308, 327, 345, 347–58, 371, 431, 433, 435, 436, 437
    *The Magic Mountain*, 347–58
    'Thoughts in Wartime', 355
Manzoni, Alessandro, 15, 150, 435
Marinetti, Filippo, 368
Marivaux, Pierre Carlet de Chamblain de, 57, 74, 78
Marker, Chris, 341
Márquez, Gabriel García, 440
Marsh, Richard, 188
Martineau, Harriet, 228
Marx, Karl, 49, 127, 144, 220, 221, 397, 430, 440
Matisse, Henri, 363
Maturin, C. R., 181, 185, 200
Maupassant, Guy de, 314
Maurier, Daphne du, 187
Melville, Herman, 388
Mickiewicz, Adam, 148
Miller, Henry, 199
Milton, John, 3, 183, 184

modernism, 339, 340, 368, 372, 428, 429, 430, 431, 432, 433, 434, 436, 440
Molière, 73, 77, 86, 141, 143
Montaigne, Michel de, 86, 215
Moore, George, 200, 306, 319
Morgenstern, Karl, 137
Moultou, Paul, 89
Musil, Robert, 332, 340, 343, 345–7, 348, 362, 363, 412, 416, 431, 433

Nabokov, Vladimir, 256, 260, 290, 362, 399
Nadeau, Maurice, 396
Naipaul, V. S., 209
naturalism, 12, 313, 315, 317–21, 323, 330, 380, 428, 429
Naubert, Benedikte, 186
Newman, John Henry, 361, 366
Nicholas I, 260, 286
Nietzsche, Friedrich, 121, 161, 259, 344, 346, 347, 354, 355, 362, 374, 383, 410, 411, 430, 431, 432, 437
Nordau, Max, 428
Novalis, 338

Ortega y Gasset, José, 410
Orwell, George, 216, 434
Ovid, 56, 58

Pamuk, Orhan, 249, 257, 340
Pardo Bazán, Emilia, 306, 307
Pasternak, Boris, 290
Pater, Walter, 366
Pelevin, Victor, 260
Philip II, 18
philosophical tale, 108
*picaro*, 19, 26
    picaresque, 5, 19, 79, 436
Picasso, Pablo, 363
Pinero, Arthur, 321
Pinget, Robert, 396
Pinter, Harold, 341
Plato, 280, 388
Plutarch, 183, 184
Ponge, Francis, 401
Potocki, Count, 16
Pound, Ezra, 362, 370, 372, 374
Powys, John Cowper, 200
Prévost, Abbé, 77
Proust, Marcel, 3, 199, 240, 241, 256, 327–41, 348, 363, 371, 378, 383, 391, 398, 407, 431, 434

Proust, Marcel (cont.)
  *In Search of Lost Time*, 327–41
  *Jean Santeuil*, 329
Puccini, Giacomo, 367
Pushkin, Alexander, 144, 149, 278, 311, 442
Pynchon, Thomas, 440

Rabelais, François, 75, 86, 109, 198, 200,
    202, 205, 215, 375, 411, 441
Radcliffe, Anne, 3, 179, 180, 185, 186
realism, 1, 2, 4, 11, 44, 81, 82, 85, 116, 121,
    130, 132, 147, 159, 192, 232, 235, 259,
    260, 274, 295, 296, 311, 327, 330, 332,
    337–8, 366, 374, 390, 417, 418, 419,
    428, 433, 434, 438, 441, 442
Renan, Ernest, 361
Rhys, Jean, 437
Richardson, Samuel, 9, 10, 41, 54–69,
    90, 95, 111, 112, 114, 125, 316
  *Clarissa*, 54, 57, 60, 65–9
  *Pamela*, ix, 2, 41, 60, 61–5, 67,
    74, 77, 81
  *Sir Charles Grandison*, 54, 66
Richter, Jean Paul, 120
Ridley, James, 212
Riehl, Heinrich von, 230
Rilke, Rainer Maria, 429
Rimbaud, Arthur, 372
Robbe-Grillet, Alain, 396
Robertson, William, 145
Robinson, Crabb, 138
romance, 2, 11, 21, 22, 24, 27, 28,
    78, 141, 146, 148–50, 179,
    180, 389
  romantic, 110, 200, 250, 277, 358, 374,
    389, 410, 412
  romantic irony, 3, 167, 173
  romantic novel, 121
Rougement, Denis de, 3
Rousseau, Jean-Jacques, 2, 3, 5, 6, 9, 10, 56,
    89–105, 108, 112, 115, 116, 121, 125,
    165, 184, 231, 267, 279, 280, 281,
    288, 290
  *The Confessions*, 89, 97, 102
  *Émile*, 97, 103
  *Julie*, 89–105
Ruiz, Raoul, 340
Rushdie, Salman, 122, 209, 439
Ruskin, John, 366
Russell, Bertrand, 98

Sacher-Masoch, Leopold von, 407
Sade, Marquis de, 57, 112, 131, 407, 435

Saint-Hilaire, Geoffroy, 198
Sand, George, 223, 227, 231, 246
Saramago, José, 442
Sardou, Victorien, 311
Sartre, Jean-Paul, 3, 162, 205, 305, 397,
    413, 416
Schelling, Friedrich W. J., 338
Schiller, Friedrich, 7, 10, 115, 126, 131,
    132–3, 138, 186, 215, 311, 437
Schlegel, Friedrich, 6, 120, 122, 129, 130,
    138, 167
Schlöndorff, Volker, 340
Schnitzler, Artur, 370
Schoenberg, Arnold, 364
Schopenhauer, Arthur, 338, 347, 348,
    429, 431
Schubert, Franz, 358
science, 12, 18, 176, 236, 248, 257, 297,
    348, 351, 363, 369, 411, 412,
    428, 432
Scott, Walter, 15, 72, 140–56, 202, 210,
    388, 412
  *Anne of Geierstein*, 150
  *The Antiquary*, 146
  *The Betrothed*, 146
  *Cinq-Mars*, 152
  *Count Robert of Paris*, 154
  *Guy Mannering*, 151
  *The Heart of Midlothian*, 149
  *Ivanhoe*, 148
  *Lammermoor*, 148
  *Old Mortality*, 147, 151, 155
  *Quentin Durward*, 152, 154
  *Redgauntlet*, 147, 148
  *Rob Roy*, 142
  *Waverley*, 141–2
Scribe, Eugene, 311
Sebald, W. G., 163, 340, 435
sensibility, 91–3, 104, 108, 109, 113, 114,
    115, 116, 331
sentiment, 9, 111–13, 116, 121, 193, 428
  sentimental, 109, 248, 329, 331, 367,
    410, 413, 416
  sentimentalism, 115, 116, 121, 126
Serao, Matilde, 311
Seth, Vikram, 290
Shaftesbury, Anthony Ashley Cooper,
    Earl of, 111
Shakespeare, William, 3, 9, 17, 49, 81, 118,
    141, 143, 160, 212, 232, 278
Shelley, Mary, 14, 176–90, 211
  *Frankenstein*, 176–90
  *The Last Man*, 188

Shelley, Percy Bysshe, 176, 311
Shklovsky, Victor, 121, 277
Simon, Claude, 192, 396
Smollett, Tobias, 61, 68, 211, 214
Solovyov, Vladimir, 259
Solzhenitsyn, Alexander, 280
Spencer, Herbert, 228
Spenser, Edmund, 2
Spinoza, Baruch, 227, 230
Staël, Mme de, 164
Steele, Richard, 75, 114
Steiner, George, 228
Stendhal, 3, 77, 150, 159–73, 332, 437
    *Armance*, 159, 166
    *The Charterhouse of Parma*, 159,
        161, 162, 164, 165, 167,
        169, 170–1
    *Lamiel*, 159
    *Lucien Leuwen*, 159
    *On Love*, 160, 163
    *Racine and Shakespeare*, 159
    *The Red and the Black*, 159, 164, 166,
        167, 168, 170, 171–3, 210
Sterne, Laurence, 10, 14, 107–22, 146, 202,
    204, 211, 278, 280, 316, 375, 383,
    389, 411, 439
    *A Political Romance*, 107
    *A Sentimental Journey*, 107
    *The Sermons of Mr Yorick*, 110
    *Tristram Shandy*, 107–22
Stevenson, Robert Louis, 187, 321, 388
Stifter, Adalbert, 144
Strachey, Lytton, 381
Strauss, David, 227
Stravinsky, Igor, 363
Strindberg, August, 362
Sue, Eugène, 199
Swift, Jonathon, 13, 86
Symons, Arthur, 361

Taine, Hippolyte, 296
Taylor, Jeremy, 10
Thackeray, William Makepeace, 4, 12, 81,
    121, 223, 316, 383
Tolstoy, Leo, 8, 14, 104, 150, 209, 224, 228,
    235, 241, 259, 277–91, 328, 361, 380,
    388, 430, 442
    *Adolescence*, 288
    *Anna Karenina*, 277, 279, 281, 285, 287,
        290, 291
    *Childhood*, 278
    *Confession*, 289
    *The Kingdom of Heaven within Us*, 289

    *On Life*, 289
    *Resurrection*, 277, 279, 280, 281, 286,
        288, 289, 290, 291
    *The Slavery of Our Time*, 289
    *War and Peace*, 277, 278, 280, 281, 282,
        283–5, 286, 287, 288, 290, 291
    *What I Believe*, 289
    *What is Art?*, 289
    *What Then Should We Do?*, 289
Tressall, Robert, 222
Trollope, Anthony, 4
Truffaut, François, 199
Turgenev, Ivan, 209, 223, 241, 259, 313,
    380, 391, 434

Vargas Llosa, Mario, 244
Verga, Giovanni, 307
Verlaine, Paul, 361
Vico, Gianbattista, 12, 361, 372, 432
Virgil, 141
Visconti, Luchino, 341
Volney, Comte de, 183
Voltaire, 73, 90, 95, 98, 118, 215, 305
Vonnegut, Kurt, 259
Vulpius, C. A., 186

Wagner, Richard, 3, 347
Walpole, Horace, 179, 186
Walpole, Robert, 74
Warburton, William, 55
Wharton, Edith, 187, 201
Whitehead, Alfred North, 363
Whitman, Walt, 352
Wieland, Christoph Martin, 108, 120, 130
Wiesel, Elie, 400
Wilde, Oscar, 321, 361
Wilhelm II, 345
William III, 37, 119
Wittgenstein, Ludwig, 363
Wollstonecraft, Mary, 185
Woolf, Virginia, 147, 259, 327, 332, 362,
    371, 378–92, 433
    'A Room of One's Own', 384, 390
    'An Unwritten Novel', 379
    'The Art of Fiction', 388, 391
    *Between the Acts*, 392
    'Blue and Green', 379
    *The Common Reader*, 388
    'How it Strikes a Contemporary', 385
    *Jacob's Room*, 380–1, 382
    'Kew Gardens', 379
    'Life and the Novelist', 387
    'The Mark on the Wall', 379

Woolf, Virginia (cont.)
'Modern Fiction', 380, 383, 388
*Mrs Dalloway*, 381–2, 390, 392
*Night and Day*, 378, 380
*Orlando*, 380, 390, 392
'Phases of Fiction', 388, 389
'Poetry, Fiction and the Future', 385
'Solid Objects', 379
'The Sun and the Fish', 391
*Three Guineas*, 391
*To the Lighthouse*, 378, 379, 380, 382–3, 387, 389, 392
*The Voyage Out*, 378
*The Waves*, 379, 390–1
*The Years*, 392
Wordsworth, William, 115, 144, 178, 187
Wyndham Lewis, Percy, 374

Yeats, William Butler, 200, 374
Young, Edward, 55

Zamyatin, Evgeny, 260
Zola, Émile, 11, 161, 255, 294–309, 313, 314, 316, 318, 320, 322, 324
*Germinal*, 295, 297, 298, 299, 302–3, 304
*L'Assommoir*, 295, 297, 298, 299–303, 304
*The Belly of Paris*, 294, 295, 297
*The Debacle*, 299
*The Earth*, 297, 304, 306
*The Experimental Novel*, 297
*The Human Animal*, 297, 299
*The Kill*, 298
*The Ladies' Paradise*, 297, 298
*Madeleine Ferat*, 297
*Nana*, 297, 303–4
*Pot Luck*, 303
*The Rougon-Maquart*, 295, 296, 297
*Thérèse Raquin*, 296
*Three Cities*, 304
*Work*, 296
Zweig, Stefan, 199

# Cambridge Companions To ...

## AUTHORS

*Edward Albee* edited by Stephen J. Bottoms

*Margaret Atwood* edited by Coral Ann Howells

*W. H. Auden* edited by Stan Smith

*Jane Austen* edited by Edward Copeland and Juliet McMaster (*second edition*)

*Beckett* edited by John Pilling

*Bede* edited by Scott DeGregorio

*Aphra Behn* edited by Derek Hughes and Janet Todd

*Walter Benjamin* edited by David S. Ferris

*William Blake* edited by Morris Eaves

*Brecht* edited by Peter Thomson and Glendyr Sacks (*second edition*)

*The Brontës* edited by Heather Glen

*Bunyan* edited by Anne Dunan-Page

*Frances Burney* edited by Peter Sabor

*Byron* edited by Drummond Bone

*Albert Camus* edited by Edward J. Hughes

*Willa Cather* edited by Marilee Lindemann

*Cervantes* edited by Anthony J. Cascardi

*Chaucer* edited by Piero Boitani and Jill Mann (*second edition*)

*Chekhov* edited by Vera Gottlieb and Paul Allain

*Kate Chopin* edited by Janet Beer

*Caryl Churchill* edited by Elaine Aston and Elin Diamond

*Coleridge* edited by Lucy Newlyn

*Wilkie Collins* edited by Jenny Bourne Taylor

*Joseph Conrad* edited by J. H. Stape

*H. D.* edited by Nephie J. Christodoulides and Polina Mackay

*Dante* edited by Rachel Jacoff (*second edition*)

*Daniel Defoe* edited by John Richetti

*Don DeLillo* edited by John N. Duvall

*Charles Dickens* edited by John O. Jordan

*Emily Dickinson* edited by Wendy Martin

*John Donne* edited by Achsah Guibbory

*Dostoevskii* edited by W. J. Leatherbarrow

*Theodore Dreiser* edited by Leonard Cassuto and Claire Virginia Eby

*John Dryden* edited by Steven N. Zwicker

*W. E. B. Du Bois* edited by Shamoon Zamir

*George Eliot* edited by George Levine

*T. S. Eliot* edited by A. David Moody

*Ralph Ellison* edited by Ross Posnock

*Ralph Waldo Emerson* edited by Joel Porte and Saundra Morris

*William Faulkner* edited by Philip M. Weinstein

*Henry Fielding* edited by Claude Rawson

*F. Scott Fitzgerald* edited by Ruth Prigozy

*Flaubert* edited by Timothy Unwin

*E. M. Forster* edited by David Bradshaw

*Benjamin Franklin* edited by Carla Mulford

*Brian Friel* edited by Anthony Roche

*Robert Frost* edited by Robert Faggen

*Gabriel García Márquez* edited by Philip Swanson

*Elizabeth Gaskell* edited by Jill L. Matus

*Goethe* edited by Lesley Sharpe

*Günter Grass* edited by Stuart Taberner

*Thomas Hardy* edited by Dale Kramer

*David Hare* edited by Richard Boon

*Nathaniel Hawthorne* edited by Richard Millington

*Seamus Heaney* edited by Bernard O'Donoghue

*Ernest Hemingway* edited by Scott Donaldson

*Homer* edited by Robert Fowler

*Horace* edited by Stephen Harrison

*Ted Hughes* edited by Terry Gifford

*Ibsen* edited by James McFarlane

*Henry James* edited by Jonathan Freedman

*Samuel Johnson* edited by Greg Clingham

*Ben Jonson* edited by Richard Harp and Stanley Stewart

*James Joyce* edited by Derek Attridge (*second edition*)

*Kafka* edited by Julian Preece

*Keats* edited by Susan J. Wolfson

*Rudyard Kipling* edited by Howard J. Booth

*Lacan* edited by Jean-Michel Rabaté

*D. H. Lawrence* edited by Anne Fernihough

*Primo Levi* edited by Robert Gordon

*Lucretius* edited by Stuart Gillespie and Philip Hardie

*Machiavelli* edited by John M. Najemy

*David Mamet* edited by Christopher Bigsby

*Thomas Mann* edited by Ritchie Robertson

*Christopher Marlowe* edited by Patrick Cheney

*Andrew Marvell* edited by Derek Hirst and Steven N. Zwicker

*Herman Melville* edited by Robert S. Levine

*Arthur Miller* edited by Christopher Bigsby
(*second edition*)

*Milton* edited by Dennis Danielson
(*second edition*)

*Molière* edited by David Bradby and
Andrew Calder

*Toni Morrison* edited by Justine Tally

*Nabokov* edited by Julian W. Connolly

*Eugene O'Neill* edited by Michael Manheim

*George Orwell* edited by John Rodden

*Ovid* edited by Philip Hardie

*Harold Pinter* edited by Peter Raby
(*second edition*)

*Sylvia Plath* edited by Jo Gill

*Edgar Allan Poe* edited by Kevin J. Hayes

*Alexander Pope* edited by Pat Rogers

*Ezra Pound* edited by Ira B. Nadel

*Proust* edited by Richard Bales

*Pushkin* edited by Andrew Kahn

*Rabelais* edited by John O'Brien

*Rilke* edited by Karen Leeder
and Robert Vilain

*Philip Roth* edited by Timothy Parrish

*Salman Rushdie* edited by
Abdulrazak Gurnah

*Shakespeare* edited by Margareta de Grazia and
Stanley Wells (*second edition*)

*Shakespearean Comedy* edited by
Alexander Leggatt

*Shakespeare and Popular Culture* edited by
Robert Shaughnessy

*Shakespearean Tragedy* edited by
Claire McEachern

*Shakespeare on Film* edited by Russell Jackson
(*second edition*)

*Shakespeare on Stage* edited by Stanley Wells
and Sarah Stanton

*Shakespeare's History Plays* edited by
Michael Hattaway

*Shakespeare's Last Plays* edited by
Catherine M. S. Alexander

*Shakespeare's Poetry* edited by
Patrick Cheney

*George Bernard Shaw* edited by
Christopher Innes

*Shelley* edited by Timothy Morton

*Mary Shelley* edited by Esther Schor

*Sam Shepard* edited by
Matthew C. Roudané

*Spenser* edited by Andrew Hadfield

*Laurence Sterne* edited by Thomas Keymer

*Wallace Stevens* edited by John N. Serio

*Tom Stoppard* edited by Katherine E. Kelly

*Harriet Beecher Stowe* edited by
Cindy Weinstein

*August Strindberg* edited by
Michael Robinson

*Jonathan Swift* edited by Christopher Fox

*J. M. Synge* edited by P. J. Mathews

*Tacitus* edited by A. J. Woodman

*Henry David Thoreau* edited by
Joel Myerson

*Tolstoy* edited by Donna Tussing Orwin

*Anthony Trollope* edited by Carolyn Dever
and Lisa Niles

*Mark Twain* edited by Forrest G. Robinson

*John Updike* edited by Stacey Olster

*Mario Vargas Llosa* edited by Efrain Kristal
and John King

*Virgil* edited by Charles Martindale

*Voltaire* edited by Nicholas Cronk

*Edith Wharton* edited by
Millicent Bell

*Walt Whitman* edited by Ezra Greenspan

*Oscar Wilde* edited by Peter Raby

*Tennessee Williams* edited by C. Roudané

*August Wilson* edited by Christopher Bigsby

*Mary Wollstonecraft* edited by
Claudia L. Johnson

*Virginia Woolf* edited by Susan Sellers
(*second edition*)

*Wordsworth* edited by Stephen Gill

*W. B. Yeats* edited by Marjorie Howes and
John Kelly

*Zola* edited by Brian Nelson

## TOPICS

*The Actress* edited by Maggie B. Gale
and John Stokes

*The African American Novel* edited by
Maryemma Graham

*The African American Slave Narrative* edited by
Audrey A. Fisch

*Allegory* edited by Rita Copeland and
Peter Struck

*American Crime Fiction* edited by
Catherine Ross Nickerson

*American Modernism* edited by Walter Kalaidjian

*American Realism and Naturalism* edited by
Donald Pizer

*American Travel Writing* edited by
Alfred Bendixen and Judith Hamera

*American Women Playwrights* edited by
Brenda Murphy

*Ancient Rhetoric* edited by Erik Gunderson

*Arthurian Legend* edited by Elizabeth Archibald
and Ad Putter

*Australian Literature* edited by Elizabeth Webby

*British Literature of the French Revolution*
edited by Pamela Clemit

*British Romanticism* edited by Stuart Curran
(*second edition*)

*British Romantic Poetry* edited by James
Chandler and Maureen N. McLane

*British Theatre, 1730–1830*, edited by
Jane Moody and Daniel O'Quinn

*Canadian Literature* edited by
Eva-Marie Kröller

*Children's Literature* edited by M. O. Grenby
and Andrea Immel

*The Classic Russian Novel* edited by Malcolm V.
Jones and Robin Feuer Miller

*Contemporary Irish Poetry* edited by
Matthew Campbell

*Creative Writing* edited by David Morley and
Philip Neilsen

*Crime Fiction* edited by Martin Priestman

*Early Modern Women's Writing* edited by
Laura Lunger Knoppers

*The Eighteenth-Century Novel* edited by
John Richetti

*Eighteenth-Century Poetry* edited by John Sitter

*English Literature, 1500–1600* edited by
Arthur F. Kinney

*English Literature, 1650–1740* edited by
Steven N. Zwicker

*English Literature, 1740–1830* edited by
Thomas Keymer and Jon Mee

*English Literature, 1830–1914* edited by
Joanne Shattock

*English Novelists* edited by Adrian Poole

*English Poetry, Donne to Marvell* edited by
Thomas N. Corns

*English Poets* edited by Claude Rawson

*English Renaissance Drama* edited by
A. R. Braunmuller and Michael Hattaway
(*second edition*)

*English Renaissance Tragedy* edited by
Emma Smith and Garrett A. Sullivan Jr.

*English Restoration Theatre* edited by
Deborah C. Payne Fisk

*The Epic* edited by Catherine Bates

*European Modernism* edited by Pericles Lewis

*European Novelists* edited by Michael Bell

*Fantasy Literature* edited by Edward James and
Farah Mendlesohn

*Feminist Literary Theory* edited by Ellen Rooney

*Fiction in the Romantic Period* edited by
Richard Maxwell and Katie Trumpener

*The Fin de Siècle* edited by Gail Marshall

*The French Novel: From 1800 to the Present*
edited by Timothy Unwin

*Gay and Lesbian Writing* edited by
Hugh Stevens

*German Romanticism* edited by Nicholas Saul

*Gothic Fiction* edited by Jerrold E. Hogle

*The Greek and Roman Novel* edited by
Tim Whitmarsh

*Greek and Roman Theatre* edited by Marianne
McDonald and J. Michael Walton

*Greek Lyric* edited by Felix Budelmann

*Greek Mythology* edited by Roger D. Woodard

*Greek Tragedy* edited by P. E. Easterling

*The Harlem Renaissance* edited by
George Hutchinson

*The Irish Novel* edited by John Wilson Foster

*The Italian Novel* edited by Peter Bondanella
and Andrea Ciccarelli

*Jewish American Literature* edited by
Hana Wirth-Nesher and Michael P. Kramer

*The Latin American Novel* edited by
Efraín Kristal

*The Literature of London* edited by
Lawrence Manley

*The Literature of Los Angeles* edited by
Kevin R. McNamara

*The Literature of New York* edited by
Cyrus Patell and Bryan Waterman

*The Literature of the First World War* edited by
Vincent Sherry

*The Literature of World War II* edited by
Marina MacKay

*Literature on Screen* edited by Deborah Cartmell
and Imelda Whelehan

*Medieval English Culture* edited by
Andrew Galloway

*Medieval English Literature* edited by
Larry Scanlon

*Medieval English Mysticism* edited by
Samuel Fanous and Vincent Gillespie

*Medieval English Theatre* edited by
Richard Beadle and Alan J. Fletcher
(*second edition*)

*Medieval French Literature* edited by
Simon Gaunt and Sarah Kay

*Medieval Romance* edited by
Roberta L. Krueger

*Medieval Women's Writing* edited by
Carolyn Dinshaw and David Wallace

*Modern American Culture* edited by
Christopher Bigsby

*Modern British Women Playwrights* edited by
Elaine Aston and Janelle Reinelt

*Modern French Culture* edited by
Nicholas Hewitt

*Modern German Culture* edited by Eva Kolinsky
and Wilfried van der Will

*The Modern German Novel* edited by
Graham Bartram

*Modern Irish Culture* edited by Joe Cleary
and Claire Connolly

*Modern Italian Culture* edited by Zygmunt
G. Baranski and Rebecca J. West

*Modern Latin American Culture* edited by
John King

*Modern Russian Culture* edited by
Nicholas Rzhevsky

*Modern Spanish Culture* edited by David T. Gies

*Modernism* edited by Michael Levenson
(*second edition*)

*The Modernist Novel* edited by
Morag Shiach

*Modernist Poetry* edited by Alex Davis and Lee
M. Jenkins

*Modernist Women Writers* edited by
Maren Tova Linett

*Narrative* edited by David Herman

*Native American Literature* edited by Joy Porter
and Kenneth M. Roemer

*Nineteenth-Century American Women's Writing*
edited by Dale M. Bauer and
Philip Gould

*Old English Literature* edited by
Malcolm Godden and Michael Lapidge

*Performance Studies* edited by
Tracy C. Davis

*Popular Fiction* edited by
David Glover and Scott McCracken

*Postcolonial Literary Studies* edited by
Neil Lazarus

*Postmodernism* edited by Steven Connor

*Renaissance Humanism* edited by
Jill Kraye

*The Roman Historians* edited by
Andrew Feldherr

*Roman Satire* edited by Kirk Freudenburg

*Science Fiction* edited by Edward James and
Farah Mendlesohn

*Scottish Literature* edited by Gerald Carruthers
and Liam McIlvanney

*The Sonnet* edited by A. D. Cousins and
Peter Howarth

*The Spanish Novel: From 1600 to the Present*
edited by Harriet Turner and Adelaida López de
Martínez

*Travel Writing* edited by Peter Hulme
and Tim Youngs

*Twentieth-Century British and Irish Women's
Poetry* edited by Jane Dowson

*The Twentieth-Century English Novel* edited by
Robert L. Caserio

*Twentieth-Century English Poetry* edited by
Neil Corcoran

*Twentieth-Century Irish Drama* edited by
Shaun Richards

*Twentieth-Century Russian Literature*
edited by Marina Balina and
Evgeny Dobrenko

*Utopian Literature* edited by
Gregory Claeys

*Victorian and Edwardian Theatre* edited by
Kerry Powell

*The Victorian Novel* edited by
Deirdre David

*Victorian Poetry* edited by
Joseph Bristow

*War Writing* edited by
Kate McLoughlin

*Writing of the English Revolution* edited by
N. H. Keeble